Discourse Theory and Practice

Discourse Theory and Practice

This Reader provides the set readings for a 16-week module (D843 *Discourse Analysis*) which is offered by The Open University Masters in Social Sciences Programme.

The Open University Masters in Social Sciences

The Masters Programme enables students to select from a range of modules to create a programme to suit their own professional or personal development. Students can choose from a range of social science modules to obtain an MA in Social Sciences, or may specialize in a particular subject area.

There are study lines leading to:

MA in Cultural and Media Studies

MA in Environment, Policy and Society

MSc in Psychological Research Methods

MSc in Psychology

MA in Social Policy

MA in Social Policy and Criminology.

OU Supported Learning

The Open University's unique, supported open ('distance') learning Masters Programme in Social Sciences is designed to introduce the concepts, approaches, theories and techniques associated with a number of academic areas of study. The MA in Social Sciences programme provides great flexibility. Students study in their own environments, in their own time, anywhere in the European Union. They receive specially prepared course materials, benefit from structured tutorial support throughout all the coursework and assessment assignments, and have the chance to work with other students.

How to apply

If you would like to register for this programme, or simply find out more information, please write for the Masters in Social Sciences prospectus to the Call Centre, PO Box 724, The Open University, Milton Keynes MK7 6ZS, United Kingdom: tel. +44 (0)1908 653231, e-mail ces-gen@open.ac.uk

Alternatively, you may visit the Open University website at http://www.open.ac.uk where you can learn more about the wide range of courses and packs offered at all levels by The Open University.

Discourse Theory and Practice

A Reader

MARGARET WETHERELL, STEPHANIE TAYLOR
AND SIMEON J. YATES

Sage Publications
London • Thousand Oaks • New Delhi

SAGE Publications Ltd
6 Bonhill Street
London EC2A 4PU

SAGE Publications Inc
2455 Teller Road
Thousand Oaks, California 91320

SAGE Publications India Pvt Ltd
32, M-Block Market
Greater Kailash – I
New Delhi 110 048

British Library Cataloguing in Publication data

A catalogue record for this book is available
from the British Library

ISBN 0-7619-7155-6
ISBN 0-7619-7156-4 (pbk)

Library of Congress catalog card number available

Typeset by Mayhew Typesetting, Rhayader, Powys
Printed in Great Britain by The Cromwell Press Ltd,
Trowbridge, Wiltshire

Contents

Acknowledgements

The authors and the publishers wish to thank the following for permission to use copyright material. Every effort has been made to trace all the copyright holders, but it any have been inadvertently overlooked, the publishers will be pleased to make the necessary arrangement at the first opportunity.

Reading 1   The BBC and Panorama for extracts from the BBC's 'Panorama – Interview with Diana, Princess of Wales' programme

Reading 8   Blackwell Publishers for Erving Goffman (1981) *Forms of Talk* (pp. 124–157)

Reading 9   Blackwell Publishers for Harvey Sacks (1992) *Lectures on Conversation: Volume 1* edited by Gail Jefferson (pp. 3–11)

Reading 10   Sage Publications Ltd for extracts from David Silverman (1997) *Discourses of Counselling: HIV Counselling as Social Interaction* Ch. 4

Reading 11   Cambridge University Press for John Gumperz 'Interethnic Communication', from *Discourse Strategies* (1982) (pp. 172–186)

Reading 12   'The Relativity of Linguistic Strategies' by Deborah Tannen, from *Gender and Converational Interaction*, edited by Deborah Tannen, copyright 1993 by Deborah Tannen. Used by permission of Oxford University Press, Inc

Reading 13   Sage Publications Ltd for extracts from Celia Kitzinger and Hannah Frith (1999) 'Just say no? the use of conversation analysis in developing a feminist perspective on sexual refusal' *Discourse and Society*, 10 (3) (pp. 293–317)

Reading 14   Sage Publications Ltd for extracts from Jonathan Potter and Margaret Wetherell (1987) *Discourse and Social Psychology: Beyond Attitudes and Behaviour* Ch.2

Reading 15   Blackwell Publishers for 'Discursive, rhetorical, and ideological messages' by Michael Billig from *The Message of Social Psychology: Perspectives on Mind and Society* edited by Craig McGarty and S. Alexander Haslam (1997) (pp. 36–53)

Reading 16   Reprinted by permission of the publisher from *Voices of the Mind: a socio-cultural approach to mediated action* by J.V.Wertsch, 67–92, Cambridge, Mass.: Harvard University Press, Copyright 1991 by J.V. Wertsch

Reading 17   Sage Publications Ltd for extracts from Derek Edwards (1997) *Discourse and Cognition* Ch.7

Reading 18   oReprinted by permission of the publisher from *Realities and*

Relationships: soundings in social construction by K.J. Gergen, Cambridge, Mass.: Harvard University Press, Copyright 1994 by the President and Fellows of Harvard College

Reading 19   Blackwell Publishers Ltd/Executive Management Committee of JTSB for Bronwyn Davies and Rom Harré (1990) 'Positioning: The Discursive Production', *Journal for the Theory of Social Behvaiour*, 20 (1): 43–65

Reading 20   Taylor and Francis Ltd for extracts from ch.5 'Gender and difference and the Power of Subjectivity' by Wendy Hollway from *Changing the Subject: Psychology, social regulation and subjectivity* edited by Julian Henriques, Wendy Hollway, Cathy Urwin, Couze Vebb & Valerie Walkerdine (originally published by Methuen, 1984)

Reading 21   Blackwell Publishers for Robert Hodge and Gunther Kress (1988) *Social Semiotics* by (pp. 5–8, 64–67, 276: notes)

Reading 22   Sage Publications Ltd for Teun van Dijk (1993) 'Principles of Critical Discourse Analysis', *Discourse and Society*, 4 (2) (pp. 249–285)

Reading 23   Lexington Books for 'Textualising global politics' by Michael J. Shapiro from *International/Intertextual Relations: Postmodern Readings of World Politics* edited by James Der Derian and Michael J. Shapiro (1989) (Ch. 2, pp. 11–17, 21–23)

Reading 24   Sage Publications Ltd for extracts from Stuart Hall (1997) 'The Spectacle of the "Other"' from *Representation: Cultural Representations and Signifying Practices*, edited by Stuart Hall

Reading 25   The University of Chicago Press for 'The Construction of an LD Student: A Case Study in the Politics of Representation' by Hugh Mehan from *Natural Histories of Discourse* edited by Michael Silverstein and Greg Urban (1996) (pp. 253–275)

Reading 26   Cambridge University Press for Peter Miller and Nikolas Rose (1988) 'The Tavistock Programme', *Sociology*, 22 (2): 177–192

Figure 24.1   Photo component of cover – Stewart Fraser/Copyright Colorsport

Figure 24.2   Copyright ALLSPORT

Introduction

This Reader is intended as a guide and introduction to discourse theory and research in the social sciences. It presents over 25 examples of studies in discourse analysis from leading practitioners. These studies indicate the range of data discourse analysts work with, the concepts which organize discourse investigations and the diversity of topics open to discourse research. There is a companion volume to this Reader (Wetherell, Yates and Taylor, 2001) which focuses much more firmly on method. If this is what discourse research looks like, then how do you actually do it? Six distinct styles of empirical research on discourse are illustrated in detail along with an overview of the entire process of conducting a discourse analytic project. The two books together constitute a compendium for any student or researcher who wants to find out why the term 'discourse' is everywhere in the academy these days, what it means and what discourse research contributes to social science.

Discourse analysis is increasingly important in the social sciences. Finding out about discourse is a crucial part of learning how to be a social researcher. Discourse analysis is concerned with the meanings that events and experiences hold for social actors. It offers new methods and techniques for the social researcher interested in meaning-making. More than this, however, discourse analysis is also a theory of language and communication, a perspective on social interaction and an approach to knowledge construction across history, societies and cultures.

Becoming knowledgeable about discourse allows one to join in a range of debates, discussions and dialogues which are increasingly pervasive in the lecture halls and seminar rooms of universities. Becoming knowledgeable provides a set of tools for studying the social world and it also allows one to see that world differently. This Reader and its companion volume are directed particularly at psychologists, sociologists, cultural studies researchers and social policy analysts but they will also be relevant and useful for other social scientists such as political scientists, researchers in business studies, economists and geographers. The main aim is to provide a good, functional, working map of the field and a core reference point, designed for active researchers, and with the social scientist rather than the linguist in mind.

Defining discourse research

A first obvious question is what do we mean by discourse and what counts as discourse research? Consider the following list of scenes. These are the kinds of sites and phenomena discourse researchers have investigated or might investigate as part of their research projects. Indeed most of these examples come from studies in this Reader.

- Telephone calls to the emergency line of a psychiatric hospital.
- Conversations between female British Asian food servers and white British male cargo handlers in the staff cafeteria of a large airport.
- The archives, records and files found in the office of a school psychologist.
- Negotiations over budgets in a business meeting in a local television station.
- Discussions with the Ifaluk people from Micronesia in the Western Pacific about the words they use to describe different emotions.
- Representations of black athletes in various media such as magazines and newspapers.
- The talk and events in the delivery room of a hospital as a mother gives birth to her baby.
- Interviews with sales managers in a large London store about their working lives.
- Counselling sessions with patients seeking HIV tests.
- The back-and-forth dialogue in an internet chat room.
- The policy documents guiding American security policy in the Cold War.

These kinds of materials have been studied as part of various substantive research projects. Some of the data described above, for example, derive from a project on the psychology of the emotions. Other data come from a large-scale study on the sociology of new managerial strategies in retailing. Yet other material was collected as part of a consultancy to improve race relations in a workplace. Social scientists might study discourse as an element in a project on the development of eating disorders, perhaps as part of a study of changes in British democratic participation over the last one hundred years or for a project on how facts and truth are constructed in legal and semi-legal settings in different cultures, and so on. Discourse analysis, then, is a way of finding out how consequential bits of social life are done and this knowledge is relevant to the process of building knowledge and theory in the social sciences.

Discourse researchers, however, need not have only substantive or topic-relevant aims in mind. Investigations of any of the discursive events listed above could just as easily have been part of studies of talk, representation and communication *per se*. Studies of these scenes might have been part, for example, of a research project on how turn-taking is managed in telephone calls; part of a project on the principles behind the formation of identity and self-presentation in social interaction; part of an investigation into the 'contextualization cues' which allow a listener to make complex inferences about the social groups to which a speaker belongs; perhaps part of a study of the meshing of talk and gesture; or part of a piece of research on the way representations and ideologies from previous historical periods are re-worked in modern discourse.

Discourse researchers typically work with 'texts'. Texts include, perhaps most commonly, transcripts of recorded conversations. Research on therapy sessions, for instance, might work with tape or video recordings of the actual session and with transcripts of the words spoken. Texts also include written documents such as policy statements, the documents found in historical archives, diaries and business memos. Discourse data, typically in the form of texts, are thus gathered from the kinds of sites listed above. The site is then studied through some record of what went on.

Some of the sites discourse analysts study are naturally occurring in the sense that the discursive event would have happened whether the researcher was there or not. It is possible that the presence of the researcher or the tape recorder changed what happened but that is another issue. Researcher involvement could theoretically at least be minimal. Discourse research is also conducted, however, on discursive events which are set up and organized by the researcher. The most common example being the interview with a sample of participants about some topic of interest. Chapter One in the companion volume to this Reader takes up in more detail the methodological issues involved in these different styles of data collection.

What is being studied, then? What is discourse? The simplest answer is to say that the study of discourse is the study of language in use. All the examples above fit this definition. They are all examples of people communicating and using language to do things. Another relatively straightforward response is to say that the study of discourse is the study of human meaning-making. Again every example above is an instance of the production of meaning in social life. Meaning-making is a much broader definition of discourse, however. It is not so clearly a matter of language use (talk and writing) *per se*. Thus the doctors and nurses attending a woman in labour are using the meaning-making frames and technologies of modern medicine to coordinate their activities although there might be very little talk or writing going on. It will become clear as the Reader progresses that although most discourse researchers would be reasonably happy with one or both of these broad brush definitions, more complex definitions also emerge as discourse theories concerning the nature of language and social life are elaborated.

Discourse research and the social sciences

Why should social scientists be interested in language in use and human meaning making? Why are these not just matters for specialist language researchers? One reason for the very evident 'turn to discourse' found across the social sciences is practical and simply concerns the changing nature of social life and some recent radical transitions in the flows of information across societies. Contemporary societies are mediated through discourse. It is not clear how strong the contrasts are with previous historical periods since what is also becoming obvious is that every society circulates around discourse but take, for instance, a typical week in your life and ask some questions about it.

- How much of your week involves face-to-face talk with another human being?

- How much talk do you do which is mediated by technology (say the telephone, the internet, the fax machine)?

- How much writing and reading do you do in a typical week?

- What kinds of jobs these days do not involve communication as a central aspect of working?

- Consider some typical daily social practices you might be involved in such as child rearing, business meetings, commuting, physical-exercise classes, shopping, cooking, and socializing. How do these involve language?

Possibly none of these queries seem relevant. You spend your days entirely alone with your own thoughts while gardening, for instance. Is this a life beyond discourse? Replace the notion of talk with the notion of human meaning-making and consider, first, the extent to which people alone might be still engaged in mental conversations with themselves in reference to the words of real and imagined others. Now take something like gardening. Human work on the land is a social practice with a long history. In an important sense, however, that social practice is discursive, it is organized by human values, by representations of human needs and by human aesthetics – by the history of human meaning-making, in other words. The first reason, then, why social scientists should be interested in the study of discourse is because, in very basic ways, to 'do' social life is to 'do' discourse.

A second reason why social scientists should be interested in discourse is methodological. Whether acknowledged or not, data in social science are typically discursive. Social science research uses a range of approaches. Common ones include, for instance, the survey such as an opinion-poll survey or a questionnaire, along with the sophisticated statistical techniques which produce at the end of the process, percentages, bar charts, tables, numbers and reliable and significant data. What are being transformed, however, are people's discursive actions – the ways in which they represent a question, and formulate a response, perhaps as a tick or a cross. The same point can be made about the conduct of controlled experiments in disciplines such as psychology while other research techniques, such as the interview, are even more clearly about operations on people's discourse.

We noted earlier that discourse analysis involves trying to develop a theory of language in use. This effort forces the social science researcher to acquire further reflexivity and self-consciousness around method. When an interview is being analysed, for example, what assumptions are being made about language and how far the talk represents events and mental states? Discourse is core to social science method and becoming knowledgeable about discourse theory enhances and transforms ways of being a social scientist and doing research.

A final reason why social scientists should be interested in language in use and meaning-making is epistemological and connects with the internal history of theory development in the social sciences and the history of ideas in Western societies. Indeed noticing the pervasiveness of discourse and increasing reflexivity about method are two consequences of that history. The predominant intellectual movements in recent years – poststructuralism and postmodernism – have focused attention on how knowledge is constituted. The study of discourse and the development of new theories of language have been central to sceptical questioning of the 'grand narratives' of the Enlightenment. Postmodernism posits contingency, uncertainty and ambiguity in opposition to modernist notions of truth, progress, certainty through science and the rational control of self and society. At the heart of this more turbulent and perspectival view is a rejection of the capacity of language to fix meaning and pin things down once and for all.

To enter into the study of discourse, therefore, is to enter into debates about the foundations on which knowledge is built, subjectivity is constructed and society is managed. These are debates about the nature of meaning. As the papers in this Reader demonstrate (beginning with Reading One), at the heart of discourse studies are some complex but potent and profound discussions on what it means to be human, what counts as 'real' and what the 'social' is.

Discourse domains

We noted earlier that this Reader is designed for social scientists. This emphasis organizes the contents. In selecting the readings we focused on three central social scientific domains or topic areas:

- The study of social interaction (Part Two).

- The study of minds, selves and sense-making (Part Three).

- The study of culture and social relations (Part Four).

Like all scientific investigations, the study of discourse is about the discovery and theorization of pattern and order. In the first domain, the study of social interaction, we are interested in a particular level or mode of order. This is interactional order. It concerns the organization of talk as joint activity and as communication. How do people coordinate their talk? How are intersubjectivity and mutual understanding accomplished? What are people doing with language? How do they work it and use it to present themselves and accomplish social life? What do discursive practices make possible? This study is exciting because it interrogates the nature of *social action* – the fundamental building block of social life and social science.

Order in the second domain particularly interests psychologists but also sociologists, policy researchers, and cultural studies researchers since the focus is now on the production of *social actors*. The study of minds, selves and sense-making is about the construction of psychological order in discourse: the construction of identity, the process of making sense, and the emergence of collective and individual mind. Once more, the interest is in the possibilities that discourse and its normative and conventional social organization make available, and what people do in discourse.

In the final domain, the study of culture and social relations, order and pattern concern the historical and institutional features of discourse. How has meaning-making been organized over time? How has it sedimented into certain formations and ways of making sense and why those and not some other forms? How can we describe and understand this sedimenting process? Speculations here on order and pattern are speculations on *power* and the organization of social relations, whether that is relatively locally in an institution like a school, for instance, or in a retailing company, or much more broadly, such as the construction of the discursive space which makes up modern international relations or when considering the ordering principles such as race which construct forms of 'otherness' and marginality across social relations.

Discourse traditions

We noted that the study of discourse is the study of order and pattern but, as the field develops, increasingly, this is not something which needs to begin fresh each time. Each new discourse researcher builds on, adds to, extends and transforms previous ways of identifying, classifying and theorizing order. The field of discourse studies is very recent and embryonic compared to other areas of social science. Nonetheless research traditions are emerging (and these are often tied to particular domains or topics). Part One of the Reader reviews some of the history of language research which leads up to these traditions. Part One also reviews the work of some of the main pioneers of discourse research who began inductively, establishing their own schemes for order and pattern which then became influential and the starting point for subsequent research.

This Reader contains readings which draw upon six, more or less distinct, discourse traditions:

- conversation analysis and ethnomethodology;

- interactional sociolinguistics and the ethnography of communication;

- discursive psychology;

- critical discourse analysis and critical linguistics;

- Bakhtinian research;

- Foucauldian research.

One aim for the Reader is that those new to discourse analysis will have gained by the end a good working knowledge of the main characteristics of these styles of discourse work.

Some of these traditions are easier to separate than others. The distinctions between critical work in sociolinguistics, interactional sociolinguistics and the ethnography of communication, are difficult to disentangle. In general, because our base is in social science, we have been less concerned with the precise boundaries of traditions emerging from linguistics. Some traditions such as discursive psychology are more topic oriented, although each of the perspectives we have identified tends to have its preferred research topics and sphere of operation.

Finally we should note here that any Reader is selective. We have not tried, for example, to cover the large amount of work found in linguistics and discourse studies on pragmatics. We have also included narrative analysis only in the loosest sense as it bears on the study of identity and life history. We have paid most attention to the approaches which are used most by social scientists and which, in our view, are most relevant to social science concerns.

The reader as a teaching text

This Reader is designed primarily as a teaching text for Masters level and other advanced students. It presumes a student reader with an undergraduate background in the social sciences including some familiarity with the notion of qualitative research but who may not have been exposed to concepts of discourse, theories of language and examples of discourse studies. With this audience in mind, the Reader was constructed as a mix of previously published papers in Parts Two, Three and Four and original commissioned writing in Part One, 'Foundations and Building Blocks', where most ground work needs to be done. Previously published readings from eminent early pioneers including Foucault, Wittgenstein and Bakhtin, are often unhelpful in the early stages as they are not designed for those new to the field. Most of the readings from previously published sources have been edited in a way which we hope maintains their coherence while reproducing the essential gist. Where a significant amount of material, such as more than a few sentences, has been omitted this has been indicated by the symbol: [. . .].

Unlike Readers in general, this Reader runs a 'teaching voice' through the material. The emphasis is on guided study. Each Part begins with an introduction which summarizes the main points in each reading and their relationships to each other in a way that we hope might be helpful for organizing note-taking, essay writing and later examination revision, even if it is a little repetitious for the reader without those concerns who may want to skip these summaries. These introductions also try to locate the wider context for these readings and for the domain of study. At the end of the Reader, the threads are brought together in a discussion of over-arching debates and themes in the Conclusion.

A further feature of the text is worth noting. To aid note-taking, and the building of the student's own personal glossary of terms and definitions, key concepts in Part One have been highlighted in **bold**. A useful check for the student at the end of Part One, before proceeding, is to make a list of the terms in bold and ensure that they could write a paragraph or so on each.

Finally, we want to acknowledge that the production of this Reader has been a team effort. We have learnt an enormous amount from our External Assessor, Professor David Silverman, and the shape of the Reader has benefited from his advice. Teams of critical readers, peer and student readers, gave us feedback on early drafts and compilations for this Reader. Among the peer readers, we want to thank most particularly Ann Phoenix, Janet Maybin, Gail Lewis, Troy Cooper and Sharon Gewirtz and among the student readers Janet Ames, Sarah Seymour-Smith, Jill Reynolds, Jayne Artis and Anna Garleff. We also owe a huge debt to our very able Course Manager, Jacqueline Eustace and Course Secretary, Elaine Castle. A number of other people also made a major contribution to the success of this project, well beyond the call of duty, including Jonathan Hunt (of the Open University Co-Production Department), our Open University Editor, and at

Sage, Seth Edwards and Vanessa Harwood. This Reader will go out to several generations of students on the Open University Masters course, D843. We hope you and other readers find it stimulating and thought-provoking as well as immediately useful for your study.

Reference

Wetherell, M., Taylor, S. and Yates, S.J. (eds) (2001) *Discourse as Data: A Guide for Analysis.* London, Sage in association with the Open University.

PART ONE
FOUNDATIONS AND BUILDING BLOCKS

Editor's Introduction

Margaret Wetherell

The main aim of this first part of the Reader is to introduce some core themes and orientations in discourse research. A further aim is to explore some of the historical developments in thinking about language which set the scene for the emergence of discourse research in the last decades of the twentieth century. In effect, in this part we want to both illustrate discourse research and locate it. The first reading provides the illustration. Some discursive data are presented as a test case. The material is used as a probe and as a way into typical discourse questions and problematics. The readings which follow then take up the history. If Reading One reveals some of the current concerns of discourse analysts then what is their context? What were the key developments in fields like linguistics, philosophy, anthropology and social theory which provided the frame? Who were the pioneers? What tapestry of ideas and speculations about language acts as the background for contemporary discourse research?

We asked six eminent scholars and active researchers representing different discourse traditions to write about the ideas which influenced them. These historical reviews are not intended to be exhaustive. They are very much personal accounts oriented to the immediate concerns of researchers. They pick out some of the ideas from the history of academic studies of language which excited these particular researchers and challenged them and which also challenged established thinking. These readings, however, also provide a map of many of the main landmarks in the study of language and social life.

At the completion of Part One, therefore, the following should be in place:

- an emerging understanding of key themes in discourse research;

- a sense of the main figures who prefigure contemporary discourse research, such as Saussure, Labov, Gumperz, Halliday, Wittgenstein, Austin, Sapir/Whorf, Hymes, Bakhtin/Volosinov[1], Goffman, Garfinkel, Sacks and Foucault;

- definitions of key concepts, such as discursive formation, interaction order, speech community, dialogical, genre, heteroglossia, language game, speech act, langue and parole, among others;

- a preliminary feel for the kind of research a critical sociolinguist, an ethnographer of speaking, a Foucauldian discourse analyst, a discursive psychologist, a conversation analyst and a Bakhtinian scholar might want to conduct;

- a sense of some of the complex debates at stake in discourse research
  including debates around the origins of meaning, the relationship between
  discourse and reality and the role of human agency in meaning-making.

The readings

As noted, the first reading in Part One takes some data to illustrate key themes in
discourse research. Indeed this piece of data is infamous: the interview
conducted with Princess Diana for the British television programme *Panorama*.
The *Panorama* interview with Diana set new standards in confessional royalty
and in global gossip and reached an audience of many hundreds of millions.
What can be said about this discourse, however? When discourse analysts look at
material of this kind what do they see? What can they say which might go
beyond the casual comments of the *Panorama* viewer? What theoretical and
epistemological issues come up as a consequence?

Reading One by **Margaret Wetherell** introduces the notion of discourse as
social action. This notion underpins all contemporary discourse research. It is
one of those ideas which inspire and appear to provide a solid base yet prove to
be provokingly enigmatic and complicated. As this Reader as a whole will
demonstrate, different traditions of discourse research understand 'social action'
in different ways. Each tradition also defines discourse variously along with the
relationship between language and social life. In the process of these acts of
defining, all manner of questions about the relationship between the world and
the word also arise. 'Discourse as social action' is thus a good organizing frame –
an open question to begin the systematic study of discourse theory.

By the end of this Reader one goal must be to understand what the phrase
'discourse as social action' means substantively (in terms of concrete research on
actual discourse), theoretically (in terms of the different approaches and
perspectives found in discourse studies) and epistemologically (in terms of broad
philosophical debates about language and how it works). Reading One also
introduces the notion of discursive practices – most simply, the study of the ways
in which language is patterned. Order and pattern appear in talk at different
levels and in different modes and dimensions and some of the kinds of regularity
addressed in the Reader as a whole are anticipated here.

Having set up some core themes in Reading One, the six readings that follow
in this part then go back to history. Reading Two from **Gunther Kress** offers a
perspective from linguistics. If you are a linguist interested in language and social
life, then what ideas from the history of linguistics proved helpful and what ideas
stood in the way of developing 'sociolinguistics'? Kress sketches out the history of
the turn to the social in linguistics. He argues that structuralism and Saussure's
work pushed linguistics into a view of language as an autonomous and
independent system which held back concrete explorations of the social uses of
language. He reviews and critiques the work of Gumperz, Labov, Halliday and
the critical linguistics school before outlining a possible basis for current
sociolinguistics.

The next reading from **Jonathan Potter** turns to philosophy and the work of
Wittgenstein and Austin highlighting those aspects of their analyses which have

been most relevant to psychologists. In Reading Two Kress argued that before something like discourse research could exist, language needed to be rescued from linguists and entirely re-worked. Potter makes exactly the same point about philosophy. He shows how Wittgenstein disrupted the philosophical notions of language of his period and introduced a new set, including the notion of the 'language game'. When Wittgenstein's ideas had been absorbed, these orientations made it possible for analysts to focus in on language in use. Reading One on Diana noted how one of the main concerns of discourse researchers is to explore the normative pattern and order in talk. Potter shows how Wittgenstein prefigured this interest in the shape and nature of discursive practices and the relation between the order in talk and its contexts of use. It was Wittgenstein also who focused attention on the ways in which discourse is constitutive – building worlds. Austin's later theorizing strengthened these emphases and created further momentum towards the empirical study of language in use.

Reading Four from **John Heritage** then gives a view from sociology. Heritage describes a body of connected work: Goffman's research on the interaction order, Garfinkel's ethnomethodology and the development of conversation analysis. This set of approaches offers one route for sociologists and other social scientists interested in the study of language in use and has been a major influence on discourse research. An alternative route for sociologists and social scientists can be found in the work of Foucault, which we will come to later.

As noted, one strong emerging theme in discourse research is that an utterance is a social action. But that immediately raises the question of what is meant by 'social action'? Clearly, discourse research requires some answer to this question and ethnomethodology and conversation analysis together supply one. These perspectives provide a detailed description of the ways in which people co-ordinate their activities together in talk and social life and produce intersubjectivity or shared knowledge. Garfinkel's interest was in people's procedural methods for 'doing' bits of social life such as doctor–patient interaction. Conversation analysis extends this into the empirical study of transcripts, resulting in a large amount of research on the organization of everyday and institutional talk, some of which can be found in Part Two of the Reader. In sociology and social science, therefore, some of the precursors to contemporary discourse research have involved not just re-theorizing the nature of language but re-thinking ideas about social structures, social actors and social practices.

Reading Five from **Kristine Fitch** evokes another crucial moment in the history of the turn to more social views of language. This is the moment when the study of language in use went cross-cultural. Here the disciplinary focus is not on philosophy, linguistics or sociology but on anthropology and ethnography and the detailed study of culture. The study of different speech communities demonstrates the social basis of communicative competence and the links between cultural practices and language forms. It led to a new discipline – the ethnography of speaking – which informs modern discourse research. As Fitch notes, the comparison of discourse styles across cultures and speech communities was only possible when notions of language as a closed and abstract system came to be questioned. Cross-cultural work also contributed to such questioning. When Edward Sapir and Benjamin Whorf, for instance, began

exploring the relationship between words and experiences then the radical
senses in which language might be 'reality making' gained substance. Fitch also
demonstrates how conversation analysis, which was introduced in Reading Four,
has been applied and extended from sociology into the study of culture in
anthropology.

Reading Six from **Janet Maybin** takes up some research that has an older
provenance than much of the work considered so far. Bakhtin and Volosinov
were writing in the early part of the twentieth century in Russia but this work has
only become widely available to scholars in Western countries since the 1970s
and 1980s. This *oeuvre* is harder to place in disciplinary terms. In part the
Bakhtin/Volosinov focus is on linguistics and understandings of language *per se*
– Saussure was a counterpoint in their writings. Bakhtin, however, was also a
literary theorist while Volosinov also wrote a manifesto for social psychology.

Their ideas continue themes already established such as the open and fluid
nature of language, its indistinguishability from social process and the ways in
which meanings depend on actual patterns of use. As Maybin demonstrates,
Bakhtin/Volosinov add important new perspectives which, as the Readings in
Part Three in particular will illustrate, are becoming taken for granted as givens
about the ways in which discourse functions. Those ideas include more clearly
than in the previous readings the concept of power and the ways in which
language is marked by the values of social groups. They include the crucial
concept of dialogicality – that every utterance is in relation to some other
utterance – and they work through the implications of this for identity. The
suggestion is that the personal individual voice is also communal and social –
that is, to speak is always to speak through, with, and in relation to the voices of
others.

Ethnomethodology and conversation analysis covered in Reading Four offer a
fine-grain account of social action. But is this the only sense of social action
which is relevant to the study of order in discourse and discursive practices?
Reading One argued that it is possible to see a politics of representation in
discourse about Diana. In other words one can find competing representations
which set up different truths about her and which are contested and in conflict.
Within conservative political discourses on the monarchy, for example, she
carries one kind of significance, to feminists another kind of significance, to
readers of *Hello*! magazine concerned with fashion and celebrity, she conveys a
further set of meanings. These broader discourses have a history, a presence and
a mode of organization which extends beyond any immediate conversation. It is
discourse as social action in this more global sense which is the subject of the
final reading in this part from **Stuart Hall** on the French theorist, Michel
Foucault.

Writing in the 1960s and 1970s, Foucault was concerned with the historical
origins of meanings and the organization of knowledge in relation to power
across societies, cultures and epochs. His ideas thus connect with Bakhtin/
Volosinov's interest in the ideological and the ways in which language carries
forward echoes of the past and can instantiate current powerful orthodoxies. Hall
demonstrates how Foucault's definition of discourse overcomes the traditional
distinction between language and action and the word and the world. He aligns
Foucault with a constructionist theory of meaning and, in general, this

perspective on meaning underpins most discourse research. Hall also returns to a question raised by Gunther Kress. Kress criticized Saussure and structuralism for not paying enough attention to agency and the role of the human social actor. Foucault's understanding of the contribution of the subject, the actor, has some features in common with Saussure's – there is little scope for individual control over 'big discourse'. Yet it is interesting to consider the differences also and the ways in which Foucault's conceptualization of discourse and discursive formation put together language and social life in a way which has been much more promising for empirical work on talk and texts. Certainly, as we come to the end of Part One, we have moved a long way from early interest in language as a system to history, the social and the nature of meaning-making in general.

Note

Please note that correct spelling of Volosinov's name is a matter of debate and in this Reader he is also referred to as Volosinov.

Themes in Discourse Research: The Case of Diana

Margaret Wetherell

In this Reading I focus on a piece of data to introduce some of the main themes and issues in discourse research. The material I have chosen to examine has historical interest. It is a public text of some import for British society and yet it also has a curiously private and confessional aspect. I am going to look at extracts from Princess Diana's interview with Martin Bashir which was screened in 1995 on *Panorama* – a British news-documentary television programme.

What was striking about the *Panorama* interview was that it broke the conventions for British Royal appearances. The interview was revelatory about Diana's private life. It reshaped the usual boundaries between public and private for the British Royal family and here was perhaps 'the most powerful image in world popular culture today' and 'a case study in the modern cult of celebrity' talking openly (Paglia, 1992: 23). Diana seemed to be giving the inside story. The programme was watched by many hundreds of millions across the globe and the intensity of this public fascination was confirmed by the extent of the mourning when she died in 1997.

Although I focus on Diana's words, I should stress that this Reading is not about the Diana phenomenon. Some of the points discourse analysts would want to make about the *Panorama* interview cast light on her complex public representation. But I will be mainly interested in what the interview tells us about talk in general, about the construction of identity, about language and how it works, and about the sources of the order and patterning in social interaction.

Discourse as social action

Consider this first transcribed extract from the interview. Note that the numbers in brackets refer to pauses and give the length of the pause in seconds, while (.) signifies a micro-pause too small to count and .hhh indicates an audible in-breath.

Extract 1

BASHIR at this early stage would you say that you were happily married

DIANA very much so (1) but (.) er the pressure on – on us both as a couple (.) with the media was phenomenal (1) and misunderstood by a great many people (1) we'd be going round Australia for instance .hhh (2) and (.) you – all you could hear was oh (.) she's on the other side (1) now if you're a man (1) like my husband a proud man (.) you mind about that if you hear it every day for four weeks (.) and you feel (.) low about it y-know instead of feeling happy and sharing it

BASHIR   when you say she's on the other side what do you mean

DIANA   well they weren't on the right side (.) to wave at me (.) or to touch me (1) ehm

BASHIR   so they were expressing a preference even then for you rather than your husband

DIANA   yes (.) which I felt very uncomfortable with and I felt it was unfair (.) because I wanted to (.) share

BASHIR   but were you flattered by the media attention particularly

DIANA   no not particularly because with the media attention (.) came a lot of jealousy (1) a great deal (.) of (2) hhh complicated situations arose because of that

(Transcribed extract taken from Abell and Stokoe, 1999: 312)

This extract contains quite a complex account of events. Diana describes herself as a sharing kind of person. She describes Prince Charles as a proud man who felt low about the attention his wife was getting. She talks about her marriage. It was happy initially but disrupted by media pressure. Her account seems to do some business in presenting herself and Prince Charles. Her words are more than just an account, however, they can also be seen as a form of social action. This notion of **discourse as social action** is a central one and I want to look at three facets of this in some detail.

Discourse is constitutive

First we'll focus on Diana's utterances as a form of description. She is describing some events in the world and people's reactions to those. Social scientists deal with descriptions of this kind all the time. They are basic data. But what do we do with them? One way to respond is to move to judgements about adequacy and accuracy. Is this objective data? Is Diana telling it how it was? Would we want other sources of information about what really happened? Social science is made up of these kinds of decisions about the reliability of people's talk. Before we go down this path, however, it is worth pausing and considering what this emphasis on true or false (accurate or inaccurate) descriptions assumes about the world and about language. What is it saying about discourse and the way it works?

I think it assumes two things. First, it assumes that language works rather like a picture (see Reading Three). It represents the world and people's thoughts and opinions. This representation can be faithful or, if people are malicious or lying, it can be unfaithful and misleading. Language's main function, however, is representational. The second related assumption is that the world, language and people are separate entities. Language in its picturing and representational modes mediates between the world and people. But language itself is removed from the world. It adds nothing but simply conveys from one person to another the nature of the world, people's impressions, their thoughts and opinions. Language in this sense is the neutral servant of the people.

Together these two assumptions suggest that language mostly works as a **transparent medium**. It assumes that language is a vehicle for getting to the real nature of events, people's real experiences, their views about what is going on as they report those to an audience. If this is the case then social scientists need not have much interest in language. Why should they? What is interesting is what is really going on and what people think about things and language is a means of studying those things.

The notion of discourse as social action questions all these assumptions. A central point discourse researchers make is that **language is constructive**. It is **constitutive** of social life. Discourse builds objects, worlds, minds and social relations. It doesn't just reflect them. What does this mean exactly?

Words are about the world but they also form the world as they represent it. What is the case for humans, what reality is, what the world is, only emerges through human meaning-making. As Diana and others speak, on this and many other occasions, a formulation of the world comes into being. The world as described comes into existence at that moment. In an important sense, the social reality constructed in the *Panorama* interview and in other places of Diana's happy marriage buckling under media pressure did not exist before its emergence as discourse. Just as, for instance, we could say that whereas odd, discrepant or deviant behaviour might have always been found in human societies, it takes a certain kind of discourse and pattern of meaning-making to turn this into, for instance, 'schizophrenia' or 'witchcraft' or 'adolescent delinquency'. These are classifications which may be entirely unfamiliar in other societies. Once we have the notion 'schizophrenia' and it continues to be widely current (in a way witchcraft is no longer) then it is difficult to construct events alternatively. Indeed the very term 'deviant' relies on the forms of knowledge from social science.

As accounts and discourses become available and widely shared, they become social realities to be reckoned with; they become efficacious in future events. The account enters the discursive economy to be circulated, exchanged, stifled, marginalized or, perhaps, comes to dominate over other possible accounts and is thus marked as the 'definitive truth'. In discourse research, decisions about the truth and falsity of descriptions are typically suspended. Discourse analysts are much more interested in studying the process of construction itself, how 'truths' emerge, how social realities and identities are built and the consequences of these, than working out what 'really happened'. Part of what is meant, then, by the 'turn to discourse' is this epistemological stance which reflects the broader cultural and intellectual shifts of postmodernism.

The first facet, then, of the claim that discourse is social action is a rejection of the view that language is a 'do-nothing domain' (Edwards, 1997). It is worth pondering that notion of a 'do-nothing domain' a little longer. When language is seen as simply mediating between people and the world, then it tends to be seen as 'doing nothing'. If our notions of how language works are dominated by the metaphor of language as a picture then, again, language is seen as a passive rather than an active principle in social life. The alternative view is that texts (such as a transcribed interview) are not part of some natural process like a chemical reaction or electrons moving around a circuit. They are complex cultural and psychological products, constructed in ways which make things happen and which bring social worlds into being.

Discourse involves work

If discourse is doing something rather than doing nothing, what kinds of things are being done? We can see that Diana's account in Extract 1, like all accounts, constructs a **version** of social reality. When we talk we have open to us multiple possibilities for characterizing ourselves and events. Indeed, there are many ways Diana could have answered Bashir's first question in the extract above. Any one description competes with a range of alternatives and indeed some of these alternatives emerge in this particular interview. An interesting question for discourse analysts, therefore, is why *this* version or *this* utterance? What does it do? What does it accomplish here and now? And what does it tell us about the wider discursive economy or the politics of representation which influence what is available to be said and what can be heard?

This property of language – that it allows for multiple versions – creates an **argumentative and rhetorical context** (Billig, 1991). The notion of rhetoric comes from ancient studies of political oratory but it has an important modern resonance. It suggests that discourse is often **functional** (Potter and Wetherell, 1987). It is designed to be persuasive, to win hearts and minds. The study of rhetoric is, in part, the study of the persuasive work and the organization of discourse to that end. This study demonstrates that what is said is often produced, heard and read in relation to the things which are not said. Discourse is a designed activity. It involves work.

Let us consider some of the discursive work involved in the extract above in more detail (see Abell and Stokoe, 1999; Bull, 1997; Kurzon, 1996). As Bull notes, very many of Diana's responses in the interview involve equivocation, criticism is predominantly done implicitly. Abell and Stokoe unpack this further. They note that the construction of Charles as proud and the unspecified reference to jealousy in Extract 1 are carefully managed. Criticism is often most effective rhetorically when it looks as though it is coming from an unbiased and neutral source who is merely describing what is the case, or from a source who is otherwise positive about the person criticized. Diana constructs herself as understanding of her husband: he possesses good qualities (he is proud) and is doing what any man might do. Yet, by contrast with 'sharing', these same qualities become questionable. Similarly, Diana's formulation in the last lines of the extract avoids explicitly claiming that Prince Charles was jealous, instead it is not specified who is jealous, yet the general context allows this to be heard as Prince Charles.

Discourse, then, involves labour; it is an active construction. This principle does not just apply to Diana carefully choosing her words in front of an audience of millions. Utterances in general are organized for a context, in response to or in dialogue with previous utterances, and oriented to other possible versions. Later we will need to consider just how intentional this process might be and the extent of the speaker's control.

The co-production of meaning

The third sense in which discourse is a social action refers to the origins of meanings. Meaning emerges from complex social and historical processes (see Reading Two). It is conventional and normative. We have some idea what it signifies to say Prince Charles is a proud man because we are members of a speaking community and culture which has agreed associations for 'proud man'. We draw on those to make sense. Meaning is also **relational**. Proud signifies as it does because of the existence of other terms, the contrast with meek, arrogant, humble and so on. Discourse continually adds to, instantiates, extends and transforms the cultural storehouse of meanings.

Meaning is social not just in the very grand global sense of storehouses and dictionaries but also in a very local sense. Utterances are **indexical**. Their sense depends on their contexts of use. Thus Diana describes Charles as a proud man in what for us as readers is the immediate context of the rest of Extract 1. And, at the end of the extract we have a quite specific evaluation and frame of reference for 'proud man' coloured by what precedes and what follows.

There is a further sense in which **meaning is a joint production**. It is a production of culture but also of the participants engaged in any particular interaction. With conversation this point is obvious but it is the case also for writing. Writing is addressed to someone and writing and reading (interpretation) together make a text for that moment, always open, of course, to other readings so a piece of writing can become other potential texts. In the production of discourse we see people cooperating to generate social events which make shared sense (Garfinkel, 1967 and see Reading Four). Social life depends on this very possibility of coordinated action. Consider, for example, Martin Bashir's role in Extract 1. Together, these two (interviewer and interviewee), and the hidden institution of television, create a context where this talk is appropriate and works as communication.

Discursive practices

Some of the thinking behind the claim that discourse is social action has now been unpacked. But what explains the order and pattern in this social action? One source of regularity is the **discursive practices** which people collectively draw on to organize their conduct. Take a look back again at Extract 1.1. Even this short piece of discourse reveals many complex layers of these practices. It reveals that there is such a thing as an **interaction order** to use a concept developed by Goffman (1983 and see Reading Four). In other words, there are regular ways of doing things in talk – practices – which guide people and order discourse.

One obvious feature of the extract, for example, is that it fits within a familiar **discursive genre** of the news or documentary interview – other genres might be gossip or conversation with a young child, or a lecture, or giving testimony in a court of law (see Reading Six). Sociolinguists who study interaction argue people draw on a range of **contextualization cues** in deciding what kind of language event something is and how they should behave (Gumperz, 1982). According to Gumperz, contextualization cues guide people's expectations about how conversational and other exchanges should develop, appropriate modes of speaking, the interpersonal relations involved, and the speaking rights of those involved.

Interviewers in news interviews have a particular set of devices they employ which constitute this type of speech event or discursive genre and which relate to their task in this speech event of being neutral and professional and posing questions not on their own behalf but for 'the people' as an over-hearing audience (Heritage and Greatbatch, 1991). Thus Bashir, for instance, does not evaluate or respond to Diana's comments as a friend might; he does not talk about his own relationships or problems. He controls the flow of topics and the talk proceeds turn-by-turn within the normative frame of the interview with Diana, too, responding in part.

The practices which make up a speech event or the interaction order can be quite fine grained. In documentary programmes such as *Panorama*, for instance, interviewers have to be particularly sensitive to the accusation that they are biased, that they are not sufficiently detached or impartial. As Clayman (1992) demonstrates, one way interviewers achieve this while still asking pertinent and provocative questions is through adjusting their **footing**. The term 'footing' again comes from Goffman (see Reading Eight), and is the notion that when people talk they can speak as either the **author** of what they say, as the **principal** (the one the words are about) or as the **animator** of someone else's words. Often those three positions coincide, as in this line where Diana responds to a comment about the media's preference for her:

Extract 2

DIANA   which I felt very uncomfortable with and I felt it was unfair (.) because I wanted to (.) share.

Here she is the animator (she is the one speaking) and she is the author because these are her beliefs and sentiments being expressed and she is the principal since the authored words are about herself as the subject described. Compare that with some of the ways in which Bashir set up his questions in other parts of the interview.

Extract 3

BASHIR   It has been suggested in some newspapers that you were left largely to cope with your new status on your own. Do you feel that was your experience?

Extract 4

BASHIR   According to press reports, it was suggested that it was around this time things became so difficult that you actually tried to injure yourself.

The footings in these cases are more complicated. Bashir is the animator but could he be described as the author or the principal? And, what is accomplished by splitting the footing in these cases so that authorship becomes attributed elsewhere to 'newspapers' and 'press reports'? Clayman's work on other news interviews suggests that what Bashir accomplishes, and what is standardly accomplished with this kind of format, is attributional distance. In other words,

Bashir gets to make a potentially sensitive, controversial or critical point but in a way which does not compromise his status as a non-evaluative and neutral interviewer.

You might want to consider this in more detail. The genre of the news or documentary interview also often includes the notion of the interviewer as 'interrogator', getting to the truth for the people, against a potentially hostile or devious witness. Bashir, however, is not using the possibilities of footing to put critical or difficult questions. Look again at how he frames the questions in Extracts 3 and 4 and consider the kinds of identities he offers Diana. I would argue that these are sympathetic or understandable identities: she only injured herself because things became so difficult, she was left to cope on her own. You could argue that the discursive evidence suggests that other genres apart from the news interview are becoming implicated here – perhaps the genre of confessional 'therapeutic' shows such as Oprah Winfrey.

In general terms, then, the interaction order is not a set of hard and fast rules which people follow like social dopes. Rather, discursive practices are flexible and creative resources. Genres may be mixed together and new genres can emerge. Part of the task of ethnographers of communication (see Reading Five) is to try to describe the diversity across social situations. In effect, they are charting what they call **communicative ecologies** (Gumperz, 1999): the variable and dynamic discursive practices found in a community or which distinguish particular speech events. As Gumperz argues, it is these ecologies and the cultural knowledges that go with them which make it possible, for instance, to hear just a few words on the radio, out of context, and be able to immediately identify the words as coming from a comedy show, constituting 'the news', as a politician's answer to a question or as a 'vox pop', the voice of 'the person in the street', and so on.

The range of phenomena which make up discursive practices within wider speech events is large and varied. It includes, for instance, **turn taking** – how do two or more speakers manage to divide the conversational floor between them? Turn taking has been studied by conversation analysts who are also interested in the regular ways in which people perform different kinds of discursive activities such as turning down invitations, making requests, repairing mistakes, and so on. These are the craft skills of interaction, routinely performed and highly pervasive. In the discipline of ethnomethodology (see Reading Four) these are understood as **people's methods** for *doing* everyday life.

It is worth considering for a minute what kind of knowledge or method this is that people possess. Is this knowledge that people can clearly articulate? How intentional is it? Is it automatic and unconscious knowledge? Is it like following a recipe? Is it a skill like riding a bike? No one easy answer can be given. Consider, for instance, some of the other phenomena which sociolinguists study. Some sociolinguists have argued that there is such a thing as a **genderlect**. In other words there are distinctive ways of speaking and forms of interacting which are gender linked. There is such a thing as 'speaking like a man'. As will become clear (in Part Two of the Reader) the existence of and explanation for such genderlects are hotly debated. But if it was established that women used more modal adverbs (e.g. so, very, much) than men, for instance, would this be best described as a strategic performance? Sociolinguists are also interested in phenomena such as accent shifts in the course of a conversation, intonation patterns, tonal qualities and the social messages these convey to different audiences. Diana, for instance, conveys a great deal of information to her audience concerning the social groups she belongs to through these features of her voice and delivery, and yet accent is not something which is usually self-consciously performed.

Some of the things people do in talk – their discursive practices – are remarkably subtle. Take a look at another extract from the *Panorama* interview.

Extract 5

BASHIR Did you (.) allow your friends, your close friends, to speak to Andrew Morton?

DIANA Yes I did. Yes I did

BASHIR Why

DIANA I was (.) at the end of my tether (.) I was (.) desperate (.) I think I was fed up with being (.) seen as someone who was a basket case (.) because I am a very strong person (.) and I know that (.) causes complications, (.) in the system (.) that I live in. (1.0) ((smiles and purses lips))

BASHIR How would a book change that.

DIANA I dunno. ((raises eyebrows, looks away)) Maybe people have a better understanding (.) maybe there's a lot of women out there who suffer (.) on the same level but in a different environment (.) who are unable to (.) stand up for themselves (.) because (.) their self-esteem is (.) cut into two. I dunno ((shakes head))

(Extract adapted from Potter, 1997: 151)

In his analysis of this extract, Potter focuses on the phrase 'I dunno', which appears at the beginning and at the end of Diana's last turn above. This phrase seems throwaway, just one fragment, yet perhaps it illustrates something about people's methods or discursive practices more widely. Why is that phrase there? What work does it do? Given the point made in the previous section that events can always be described differently, why this description of this kind of mental state at this point in the conversation?

Potter proceeds by looking through various corpora of discursive data for other examples of the use of 'I don't know' and he argues on the basis of this that 'I don't know' appearing at particular points in conversations can be a method for doing what he calls **stake innoculation**. Potter suggests that questions of stake are key concerns of participants in an interaction. People treat each other as having vested interests, desires, motives and allegiances (as having a stake in some position or other) and this is a problem if one wants one's version of events to be heard as authoritative and persuasive, factual, not interested or biased but the simple, plain, unvarnished truth. I noted earlier how Diana manages to do indirect criticisms attentive to the ways in which such criticism might be heard. People have developed ways, then, of managing stake, inoculating against the appearance of having some interest.

Potter suggests that Diana's use of 'I dunno' works in this way. He argues that the topic of the conversation in the extract above – Diana's participation in Morton's book – is a controversial issue for her where her motives (was she just trying to get back at Charles?) have been frequently discussed in the media. Further

> the placement of the 'I dunno's' in the Princess's talk is precisely where the issue of motive is most acute. For the Princess to accept that the book was part of a planned and strategic campaign to present a particular view of the royal marriage and her role in it would be potentially culpable. The 'I dunno's' present her as not sure of the role of the book, perhaps thinking it fully over for the first time . . . the vagueness here is rather neatly in tune with both the 'on the hoof' quality presented by the 'I dunno's'; and the non-verbal finessing of the phrase with a look into the distance as though searching for the answer (in the first instance), and then shaking her head as though it is a difficult question which she did not have a ready or clear answer for (in the second instance).
>
> (Potter, 1997: 157)

Such an analysis reinforces the notion of discourse as a form of work or labour. It also implies a strategic speaker. But, again, is this the case? Are speakers strategic in this way or just doing what comes naturally? It can suggest, too, a duplicity in Diana's actions. Potter is not implying this, however. Rather, as knowledgeable speakers and competent members of discursive communities, we are all, like Diana, skilled in a range of methods for accomplishing different activities such as stake inoculation.

To sum up, I have argued that discourse is constructive and a form of social action, further this is a form of action with regularity and pattern to it. One of the interests of social scientists engaged in discourse research is to clarify the orderly practices involved and the implications of these for the conduct of social life. As this Reader will demonstrate, such research raises a number of issues and debates about the nature of these practices, how best to study them and the implications for the way we understand social life and the human actor.

Voice and the speaking subject

Discursive practices, as we have seen, order the shape of written and spoken discourse; they order the features which appear and the selection of words and phrases. But these properties are only a small subset of those which govern meaning-making. In this and in the next section we will be more concerned with patterns in the *content* of discourse and the psychological and sociological implications of those patterns. This will help elaborate further on the notion that language is constructive – that it builds social worlds.

I want to look first at some of the patterns in Diana's own representation of herself in the *Panorama* interview and then move on in the next section to consider Diana as a popular icon – Diana as the subject of discourse – and the many millions of words which have been written about her.

In an analysis of the *Panorama* interview, Lisa Blackman (1999) argues that in telling her story, Diana draws on a type of therapeutic discourse of strong women suffering and coping which has become characteristic in recent years in women's magazines. By discourse, Blackman means here an organized system of statements. The suggestion is that as members of a culture we are rarely original. Rather, to communicate at all, we have to draw on accepted and conventional images, ideas and modes of talking about ourselves and others. These modes, of course, are constantly changing so that any study of the content of women's magazines in the 1950s is likely to find very different discourses and modes of representation compared to the 1990s.

One of the startling aspects of the *Panorama* interview was its confessional quality. Diana discussed, for example, her bulimia, her own and her husband's adultery and her attempts at self-injury. But how did she represent these things? What broader **narratives** did she draw upon to contextualize these? Discourse researchers often focus on the kinds of stories people tell. They look at the way these stories are formed, the genres of storytelling they draw upon (such as romance or the heroic epic) and the ways in which stories construct identities and events (Bruner, 1990; Mishler, 1995; Riessman, 1993; and see readings in Part Three).

Blackman argues that the narratives Diana chose exemplify a sea change in our culture's representations of what might previously have been called 'madness'. Aspects of self which might once have been described as symptomatic of insanity are presented instead as the opportunity for work on one's self and a stimulus for self-development. The focus is on coping and self-empowerment. Bulimia is thus a failed coping strategy to be replaced by more constructive coping styles. This is not a story, then, of tragedy but a narrative of winning out over adversity.

Extract 6

BASHIR And so you subjected yourself to this phase of bingeing and vomiting?
DIANA You could say the word 'subjected' but it was my escape mechanism and it worked for me at the time.

(adapted from transcript in Blackman, 1999: 114)

Blackman argues that the ideal in Diana's talk and in modern women's magazines is of 'the autonomous woman who does not lean on or need others and who above all can "believe in herself"' (1999: 115). The goal is presented as gaining enough self-confidence to become so empowered. Diana presents herself as a victim who nonetheless emerges as a strong woman who has sorted herself out.

In this analysis, then, Blackman is identifying a pattern in Diana's talk and relating it to other similar methods of self-representation found in our culture. It is worth thinking through this in more detail. One key claim of discourse researchers (see Reading Seven) is that language positions people – discourse creates **subject positions**. What does this mean? To speak at all is to speak from a position (remember the discussion of footing in the previous section). Further than this, the positions or slots in culturally recognized patterns of talk such as the 'autonomous woman', the 'mad woman', 'the fragile victim' and so on, construct us as characters and give us a psychology. In other words, they provide us with a way of making sense of ourselves, our motives, experiences and reactions.

This raises a profound question. Who speaks when we speak? We could argue that our culture speaks through Diana, that she is animating or giving voice to collective and cultural identities. As a result, it becomes difficult when any person speaks to say what is personal and what is collective and cultural. In talking or writing we take on the discourses of our culture – we rehearse, elaborate and instantiate cultural modes of representation as we communicate. In describing Diana's self-representation in this way I am not trying to undermine its power or the efficacy of this way of talking. The fact that there may be alternative discourses, or that these are cultural first and personal second, does not mean that any particular account might not be a 'useful truth' for the women who use it.

So far we have considered this question of 'who speaks?' at a relatively global level. Discourse researchers (see Reading Six) have also argued that all talk is **dialogical**, meaning that when we speak we combine together many different pieces of other conversations and texts and, significantly, other voices. We are often quoting. Sometimes this quoting is marked as when we say 'he said . . . then she said . . .' but often it is indirect and unmarked as people take over the voices of others. We carry into our talk and writing fragments from many different sources which carry some of their old connotations with them and acquire new ones as they are used in new contexts. Research on the discourse of children, for example, demonstrates how the process of education and socialization is partly a process of learning to manage the voices of others such as teachers and turn these into an internal mental dialogue carried over, too, into external conversation. Even at higher levels, the process of learning to be a discourse analyst, for instance, is in a real sense a matter of learning to *talk as* a discourse analyst.

Discursive psychologists and conversation analysts who have worked through the implications of these and other ideas for psychological theories (Sacks, 1992; Reading Two and see the Readings in Part Three) have argued that the study of discourse has radical implications for the study of psychological states such as memory and emotion. Diana, as we have seen, often talked in the interview about her emotional states. Are these utterances best seen as simple reports of what she felt? The notion that discourse is an activity – a form of work – undermines this simple notion. To report on an emotion or a feeling is also very commonly a rhetorical activity and the display of emotion does some interactional business. Think back, for instance, to what is accomplished by Diana's self-characterization in Extract 1: 'I wanted to share'.

One response to this might be to see these kinds of examples as anomalous and think of how to arrange communication situations without any 'rhetorical noise', where there is nothing at stake for the participants so that internal mental states can be faithfully pictured, represented and described. Therapy, for example, could be seen as an attempt to construct a situation of this type. Perhaps this is a situation where people can talk honestly and openly about their experiences without trying to do any extra discursive work than simply represent in the clearest words possible what they feel. Yet, does therapy escape discursive history? Are we not back to the points Blackman makes, for instance, about the representation of mental states at different periods in history? Most of us have been exposed to popular psychology in one form or other – we have those discursive framings available and yet forty years ago they were not widely available. We might ask, too, about the kind of speech event which therapy constitutes and the contextualization cues which might be relevant.

Similarly, memory might be thought to be a better example of a 'pure' psychological state than emotion. Surely we know what we remember uninfluenced by any discursive framing? Yet is it possible to have memories independently of collective social constructions of events? Consider, for example, the kind of memories people might have of the death of Diana and the ways in which these evoke the narratives of her life and death through which the public response was mediated. It makes sense in these cases to talk of 'collective memory'. Even a collection of people's dreams of Diana (Frances, 1998) demonstrates these marks of her cultural and collective significance. We only know what kind of thing an event is – even the most private and idiosyncratic events – through cultural and conventional codes.

The politics of representation

We turn now to consider Diana as an icon, as the subject of discourse. It could be said that Diana and the many words written about her form a **discursive space** (Gilbert *et al.*, 1999; Silverstone, 1998). She is the rather enigmatic centre of many competing representations of royalty, femininity, democracy, the family, morality, celebrity, fashion, private versus public life which jostle with each other. Such a discursive space is a place of argument. To use another metaphor, it is an argumentative texture or a discursive fabric that brings together many different threads which can be combined and woven differently (Laclau, 1993).

The metaphors of 'discursive space' and 'argumentative texture' bring a number of points to our attention. First, we can note the emphasis on **contestation**. There is usually in social life a struggle over how things are to be understood and for that reason it makes sense to talk of a **politics of representation**. Second, power is at issue here. Social scientists who study discourse have been interested in how people, groups and institutions mobilize meanings (see Reading Seven). How have some interpretations become dominant and whose interests do they serve? It has been recognized that control over discourse is a vital source of power and also there are limits to this control because meanings are fluid and escape their users and can be mobilized and re-worked to resist domination.

The relationship between discourse and power is a complex one. If we are arguing that discourse is constitutive and new identities emerge for people, for instance, as new modes of representation emerge, then it is difficult to say if discourse is the governor or the servant of social actors. Is Diana, presented as a strong autonomous woman through a discourse of self-help and coping, the powerful subject mobilizing these meanings for her own ends or is she being subjected to this discourse? Is she being 'disciplined' by it and having her self powerfully constructed for her as she takes on this mode of representation? Who is in control? We will return to this point about power a number of times in the course of this Reader.

Finally, the notion of discursive space draws attention to the broader social practices which construct such spaces. Thus social scientists and discourse researchers have been interested in the practices of production of newspapers and the media and in the ways in which economic and technological developments construct discursive spaces. E-mail, the internet and computer-mediated communication are good examples of how changing practices produce new spaces which construct new kinds of discursive communities. In relation to Diana, I noted earlier Camille Paglia's assessment made in 1992 that Diana may be the most powerful image in world popular culture today. Such celebrity is similarly a new kind of discursive space made possible by innovative globalized technologies of meaning-making.

To make some of these points about the politics of representation a little more concrete, I would like to briefly consider one facet of the contestation over the discursive space which is Diana. Look at the two statements which follow. The first comes from the journalist Peter Hitchens writing in the UK newspaper the *Daily Express* in response to the *Panorama* interview.

> Monarchy's rules were not decreed by chance, any more than our great cathedrals or castles were thrown up by planless amateurs. The wise men who drew up those rules knew from hard and bloody experience that remoteness, majesty and an iron law of succession were necessary for authority and stability. Like so many children of this silly century, Diana believes she knows better, and has acted accordingly.
>
> (cited in Craig, 1997: 15)

The second statement is only three words long. It is the British Prime Minister Tony Blair's description of Diana after her death as 'the people's princess'.

Hitchens' view is a conservative one. He is highly critical of Diana's confessional style in her interview counterposing it against the majesty and authority of monarchy derived from centuries of stiff-lipped reticent tradition. One of the interesting features of his discourse is his construction of 'imagined communities' (Anderson, 1983). He talks, for example, of 'our great cathedrals'. Who is the 'we' that he is constructing here and what properties and qualities might be associated with this community? Who might be excluded from this 'we'?

Blair, of course, is constructing a very different imagined community – the people who mourn Diana's death – but his phrase also evokes chains of association. 'The people' has socialist significations; it is a phrase with a particular discursive history. It implies demotic and ordinary, and claims Diana for an alternative constructed constituency. Indeed part of the argumentative texture which surrounds Diana since her death includes her effect and the effect of the remarkable public mourning for her death on British politics *per se*. Is this a sea change in British concepts of 'the nation' and British identity? Does this represent the 'feminization' of politics? Has Blair claimed Diana for his own New Labour political project or does she have more radical feminist and socialist implications? (see Kirby, 1998; Wilson, 1997 and Special Issues of *New Formations*, 1999 and *Screen*, 1998).

To sum up. In this and the previous section I have tried to expand our notion of discursive practices and meaning-making to include the content of discourse, the representational work it does, and the **interpretative resources** which belong to cultures and societies. These, like the practices noted in the previous section, are also a source of order in discourse. In addition, they raise profound debates about power, agency, the nature of subjectivity and contestation.

Conclusion

So far we have traversed three kinds of domain in which the study of discourse is relevant. Discourse is often (but not necessarily) interactional and researchers have studied the order and pattern in social interaction. The study of discourse also has important psychological implications for the study of minds, selves and sense-making. Finally, discourse is about social relations, culture, government and politics. The readings in Parts Two, Three and Four of this Reader are organized around those three domains and elaborate and expand on points sketched here.

No doubt as you have been reading some problematic and confusing areas of debate have emerged. We will return to the tensions between different styles of discourse work in the Conclusion to the Reader. Here I want to note two related points of debate for further consideration. First, what are the boundaries of discourse? We could take as a simple definition that discourse is talk, language in use and human meaning-making activities. This definition suggests a couple of contrasting possibilities. The term 'talk' proposes quite tight boundaries; language in use is broader – it includes texts such as novels and newspapers – while 'human meaning-making activities' is very broad. Meaning-making activities might include, for instance, the visual such as films and works of art. It might include objects, such as gas cookers, for instance, since such objects represent a long history of meaningful work and the significations we have inherited in our cultural practices of eating and cooking (Chouliaraki, 2001).

With Diana, much of our information is visual. We have very few of her words. As Geraghty argues, 'for much of her married life, Diana was literally speechless; it was clearly her person, her body, which was the news. Her *being there* was what was important' (1998: 71, emphasis in the original). Are bodies part of discourse, however? What are the boundaries? What is discursive and what is extra-discursive? Is anything extra-discursive? The circumstances of Diana's death were intensely physical: the car crash and the mangled pile of steel in the tunnel. That, surely, is real, beyond talk. Yet what knowledge do we have of these things beyond human meaning-making?

Such queries raise immensely difficult epistemological issues and raise problems, too, for what we might be trying to do as analysts studying a piece of discourse. What is the status of our own interpretations of a piece of talk, for instance; are these outside discourse? Such debates reverberate through the discourse research community and will recur also in the pages of this Reader. What is clear, however, is the pervasiveness of discourse. Increasingly, everywhere, talk, self and other representation are becoming more and more central to how we define what work is, for example. In studying discourse, then, we cannot help but study social life.

Acknowledgements

I would like to thank Liz Stokoe and Jackie Abell for giving me access to their transcript of the *Panorama* interview and along with Peter Bull generously sharing their unpublished work and knowledge of Diana literature.

References

Abell, J. and Stokoe, E. (1999) '"I take full responsibility, I take some responsibility, I'll take half of it but no more than that": Princess Diana and the negotiation of blame in the Panorama interview', *Discourse and Society*, vol. 10, pp. 297–319.

Anderson, B. (1983) *Imagined Communities*, London, Verso.

Billig, M. (1991) *Ideology and Opinions: Studies in Rhetorical Psychology*, London, Sage.

Blackman, L. (1999) 'An extraordinary life: the legacy of an ambivalence', *New Formations*, vol. 36, pp. 111–25.

Bruner, J. (1990) *Acts of Meaning*, Cambridge, MA, Harvard University Press.

Bull, P. (1997) 'Queen of hearts or queen of the arts of implication?', *Social Psychological Review*, vol. 1, pp. 27–36.

Chouliaraki, L. (2001) *Discourse and Culture*, London, Sage.

Clayman, S.E. (1992) 'Footing in the achievement of neutrality: the case of news-interview discourse', in P. Drew and J. Heritage (eds) *Talk at Work: Interaction in Institutional Settings*, Cambridge, Cambridge University Press.

Craig, G. (1997) 'Princess Diana, journalism and the construction of the public', *Continuum*, vol. 11, pp. 12–22.

Edwards, D. (1997) *Discourse and Cognition*, London, Sage.

Frances, R. (1998) *Dreaming of Diana*, London, Robson Books.

Garfinkel, H. (1967) *Studies in Ethnomethodology*, Englewood Cliffs, N.J., Prentice-Hall.

Geraghty, C. (1998) 'Story', *Screen*, vol. 39, pp. 70–3.

Gilbert, J., Gover, D., Kaplan, C., Bourne Taylor, J. and Wheeler, W. (1999) 'Editorial', *New Formations*, pp. 36, pp. 1–9.

Goffman, E. (1983) 'The interaction order', *American Sociological Review*, vol. 48, pp. 1–17.

Gumperz, J. (1982) *Language and Social Identity*, Cambridge, Cambridge University Press.

Gumperz, J. (1999) 'On interactional sociolinguistic method', in S. Sarangi and C. Roberts (eds) *Talk, Work and Institutional Order*, Berlin, Mouton de Gruyter.

Heritage, J.C. and Greatbatch, D.L. (1991) 'On the institutional character of institutional talk: the case of news interviews', in D. Boden and D.H. Zimmerman (eds) *Talk and Social Structure: Studies in Ethnomethodology and Conversation Analysis*, Oxford, Polity.

Kirby, M. (1998) 'Death of a Princess', *Capital and Class*, vol. 64, pp. 29–41.

Kurzon, D. (1996) 'The maxim of quantity, hyponymy and Princess Diana', *Pragmatics*, vol. 6, pp. 217–27.

Laclau, E. (1993) 'Politics and the limits of modernity', in T. Docherty (ed.) *Postmodernism: A Reader*, London, Harvester Wheatsheaf.

Mishler, E. (1995) 'Models of narrative analysis: a typology', *Journal of Narrative and Life History*, vol. 5, pp. 87–123.

Paglia, C. (1992) The Diana Cult, *New Republic*, vol. 207, pp. 23–6.

Potter, J. (1997) 'Discourse analysis as a way of analysing naturally occurring talk', in D. Silverman (ed.) *Qualitative Research: Theory, Method and Practice*, London, Sage.

Potter, J. and Wetherell, M. (1987) *Discourse and Social Psychology*, London, Sage.

Riessman, C.K. (1993) *Narrative Analysis*, Newbury Park, CA, Sage.

Sacks, H. (1992) *Lectures on Conversation*, Volumes 1 and 2, Oxford, Blackwell.

Silverstone, R. (1998) 'Space', *Screen*, vol. 39, pp. 81–4.

Wilson, E. (1997) 'The unbearable lightness of Diana', *New Left Review*, vol. 226, pp. 136–46.

From Saussure to Critical Sociolinguistics: The Turn Towards a Social View of Language

Gunther Kress

There are many plausible ways to read the history of linguistics over the last one hundred years or so. The viewpoint that one takes is, in the end, shaped by one's own personal history and experience, and by what I will call an 'ethical/political stance'. 'Evidence' will not carry the day, because someone else's theory, resting on a different stance, will produce different kinds of evidence; or else it can recast my own in the shape of the other theory. My own position is that social factors take central place, that the influence of culture is crucial, and linguistic practice is seen as one among very many socially and culturally significant practices.

To approach this issue of the 'turn' towards a more social view of language we need to know what the 'turn' has been away from. That provides my starting point. I then want to formulate some of the questions which might characterize the two positions. The overarching question clearly is: What is a **social view of language**? And what, therefore, is not a social view of language? The 'non-social view' puts into the foreground questions about **language-as-system**: What is a system like? It may have subsidiary questions, such as: 'Why is the system (or why is language) as it is?' The first, the 'social view', puts into the foreground questions such as: 'What is the role of the social in relation to language?' Both ask questions about origins and characteristics: 'How does language come to be as it is?' And both have subsidiary questions that focus on the role of the individual, explicitly or implicitly, and on their potentials for action, for agency. The answers are deeply different in each case.

The mainstream in linguistic thinking in the twentieth century

'Western' linguistic thinking in the twentieth century has to be seen in the context of its origins in the previous century. That had been the century devoted to the revolutionary discovery that (nearly all) European languages, and many of those in the Middle East and of the Indian subcontinent (Hittite, Farsi, Hindi, Urdu) were members of the one Indo-European 'family' of languages. That insight gave rise to a century's work in which connections were discovered, relationships traced and documented, and 'laws' – general principles – established, which could account for the diversity, the proliferation, and the fragmentation of this 'family'. It is a story of constant change stretching across all of Europe, the Middle East and the Indian subcontinent.

Against this picture of ceaseless change, Ferdinand de Saussure (who himself had participated in this enterprise and written a definitive work on the sound-system of Indo-European languages) posed the question: 'But what does a language look like, what is it like at a particular moment?'. We know languages change from one moment to another, but what are their characteristics, if we could hold them still, freeze them, at one moment in time? The question was posed in a series of lectures Saussure gave at the University of Geneva between 1903 and 1904. After his death several of his students produced, from lecture notes that they had made, the *Course in General Linguistics* (1916).

Of course, ideas of such significance do not occur in isolation even if we can identify one individual as the seeming originator of them – they are 'about' at the time, however subtly that may be. It is that 'aboutness' which ensured that out of the rich and complex set of questions in the *Course* (many of them social and historical) this one became focal for linguistics in the twentieth century. The strand of linguistics that it gave rise to is generally referred to as **structuralist**; it became the dominant mode of intellectual inquiry in that century not only in linguistics but throughout the humanities and beyond.

The fundamental question posed in structuralism is that of the characteristics of the system. What are the elements of a structure (whatever it may be), and what are the relations between the elements? Saussure himself gave a complex answer in which the focus was on the **sign**, and on the all-encompassing entity in which signs exist, *language as such* or **langue**. I will return to the latter in a moment.

He focused on the characteristics of the sign in two ways: first on its internal characteristics, and second on its relation to entities outside the sign. He also speculated on the principles sustaining these characteristics and relations.

He saw the sign as participating in two kinds of structures: one, its place in an organized inventory of signs, which he referred to as the *axis of association*; and the other, its place in an actual, outwardly visible form, which he called the *axis of combination*. (The Danish linguist Louis Hjelmslev (1961) later named these the **paradigmatic** and the **syntagmatic** planes respectively, the names by which they are now referred to commonly.)

To exemplify: in the cultural system of furniture and the subsystems of objects you can sit in or on, we might have a paradigmatic set such as: chair, stool, bench, easy chair, sofa, beanbag. In a system such as language we might have a paradigmatic set such as the vowel sounds of (Standard Southern) English: short and long i, u, o, a, e; a reduced vowel (as in the final vowel of butt*er*), the ae sound as in b*ad*, etc.

Elements of these systems are combined into *syntagmatic* structures. An easy chair can be combined with an element from the subsystem of objects that you place things on – a coffee table, say – and with another object from the subsystem of objects that we might lie on – a sofa, let's say – to make the *structure* of 'an easy chair and coffee table and sofa: a comfortable corner in our living room'. In language, a vowel might be combined with a consonant to form a *syllable*: it, bi; or two consonants with one vowel: bit, sin, etc.

Even from this tiny exemplification a large number of consequences follow. When I said, 'can be combined with', I didn't specify the agent who did this combining. You might say, reasonably, that the syllables of a language such as

English are simply 'there', so there is no combining for me to do. You might even say that the same is true of the comfortable corner in the living room; go into ten thousand middle-class homes in Europe and you'll find such an arrangement. Is there choice? For Saussure the answer was that individuals *make use* of the structures and elements that are there, but they do not change them. The arrangements and elements are pre-given by society. This question of agency has been one of the central issues in the turn to a social view of language.

A second consequence, perhaps the central one in structuralism generally and in structuralist linguistics particularly, is that of meaning. If, in arranging the comfortable corner, I only have the one easy chair, coffee table and sofa, I simply use what I have. Of course, I can arrange them in different ways, and that makes a difference in how the room feels in its 'meaning'. But as I had no choice in what to use, no meaning attaches to my use of the three items. However, if I do have a choice (a comfy old chair or a smart new one, a glass-topped table or a wooden one) then meaning does attach to my choice. 'Glass-topped table and smart new easy chair' produces a different meaning to 'wooden table and a comfy old chair'. Meaning of one kind arises from the possibilities of selection from a range of elements within one paradigm. A second kind of meaning arises from the fact that different types of chairs are, in fact, cultural encodings of different possible forms of behaviour: A stool asks me to sit differently to an easy chair. Setting up the room for a job interview with a stool for the interviewee and easy chairs for the interviewers – to make a ridiculous example – would set the tone decisively. The elements in systems of choice have meaning because they refer to elements (objects or practices) in other systems of choice.

For Saussure both kinds of meaning were important. On the one hand, to put it too simply, the sign is based on the relation of reference. The sign is a device for permitting form to express meaning because it is a means for allowing one element to be the form (**the signifier**) through which another element, the meaning (**the signified**) finds it realization, its expression. A rose can be the form for the expression of the meaning 'love'. A connection is made between an element in the system of language, and an element in the system of culturally salient values. The former 'refers' to the latter. On the other hand, if there is a system of elements (vowel sounds in language; furniture in the system of cultural objects; different flowers in that system), and I can select from a number (a rose rather than an orchid), I have choice, therefore meaning attaches to my selection. To select a straight-backed chair 'means' not to have chosen an easy chair or stool that could also have been chosen. The meaning of an element in the system arises by virtue of its *opposition* to the other elements. That meaning is its *value*. The greater the number of elements in a system, the greater the possibility of choice, the smaller the value of each element. So, for example, if there are words such as *party, bash, get together, celebration, rave, a small do, drinks and nibbles* or *supper* in my everyday vocabulary, then my choice of one is significant in two ways: 'celebration' refers to the particular kind of event I have in mind and, at the same time, 'celebration' means 'not party', 'not bash', 'not supper'. My meaning is in effect, both of these together.

Saussure reflected on the relation of form and meaning in the sign and stated that in language it was both *arbitrary* and *conventional* (save some exceptions such as onomatopoeia, for instance). The English word *tree* is, in French, *arbre*, and in German, *baum*, showing, so Saussure asserted, that the same meaning can be expressed in very different forms; hence, he concluded, any form can be used to express any meaning, just so long as the relation of form and meaning is sustained by the force of *convention*. Given the power of convention the individual is unable to exert any influence on this arbitrary relation: the sign is there to be used, but cannot be altered. In Saussure's schema, this is so, both for the individual sign and for the collection of signs, for language as a whole. Langue, the system of a particular language, is the expression of a social force, both by making the arbitrary connection and in sustaining it in convention. The individual may make *use* of the system, in **parole**, but the individual cannot change the system, the language.

As I will point out in the last section, in my view this is a fundamental misconception. The relation of form and meaning is *motivated*, not arbitrary, *and*, at the same time, it is sustained by convention in particular ways. However, the significant point here is that Saussure's views on the characteristics of systems, structure, signs, on langue and parole, shaped the development of mainstream and non-mainstream linguistics in the twentieth century. In the mainstream these views allowed emphasis to be placed on relations within the system rather than on reference; on structure rather than on function; on arbitrariness, thus eliminating the force of individual agency, whether from the individual sign or from the system of signs, the langue; and to treat langue as a phenomenon not directly connected to the social. After all, if individual action in and with the system has no effect, then how can there be connections to the minutiae of social life, or of its organization in larger systems?

This emphasis on the autonomy of langue, on relations of form rather than on relations of meaning, on the power of the system rather than the effects of the individual's action coincided with other political and intellectual strands, in psychology for instance, as in certain forms of sociology. For linguistics, one potent development was the conjunction of cognitivist psychology with structuralism, as best and most influentially exemplified in the work of Noam Chomsky (1965a and 1965b). Chomsky's question initially was precisely that of 'origins'; it arose out of certain intractable problems that structuralism had run into, questions concerned with the definition of (classes of) elements in a structure. This is not the place to discuss that issue, but it centred on the problem of establishing relations and regularities in seemingly irregular and unrelated phenomena. His solution was to draw a distinction between the level of **surface structure** at which the irregularities existed, which he called **performance** (again related to but not identical with Saussure's *parole*), and a level below that, the **deep structure**, at which there was regularity, which he called (the speaker's) **competence** (related to but not identical with Saussure's *langue*). The two were related by processes of transformation, which changed (abstract) deep structures into (concrete/specific) surface structures.

With this move the question of origins was solved: linguistic competence was a property of the mind, and therefore common to all human minds. Linguistic performance was a kind of distortion of the real structure, which lay beyond or behind it. But with this move the question of origins was also answered decisively in favour of 'the mind' (or even the brain) and decisively against the social. Stephen Pinker's (1994) more recent writings are contemporary revivals of

Chomsky's ideas (themselves stemming from the political/intellectual world of radical sections of American intelligentsia in the 1940s and 1950s). Chomsky's political radicalism with his espousals of ideals of social and political equality is directly related to his assumption of the equality of all humans (all human minds). That political force is absent in Pinker's re-warming, where it becomes an a-political physiological cognitivism.

The force of the social

Speaking against this theoretical development is the 'evidence' of language-in-use. If, like Chomsky, we treat what speakers actually do, their performance, as mere 'noise' (and in his more recent writings he treats actual languages – Japanese, English, Swahili – in that fashion), as 'distortions' of the real, an exceedingly sparse inner, mentalist organization, then there really is nothing to explain. If, like Saussure, we think that what speakers do – parole – has no effect on the system, then we have no serious reason for investigating it. If, however, we think that what people do needs to be understood, then we have a series of questions. These are, as I said earlier, questions around the role of the social, about the possibilities of real action by an individual acting in social environments. Here I will outline three relatively distinct approaches to such questions. I will characterize them as that of **correlation**, that of **choice**, and that of **critique**.

The first approach is the *correlational*. It points to the fact that certain forms of linguistic behaviour can be shown to correlate quite clearly with certain aspects of social organization. In sociolinguistic work on 'code-switching' (Gumperz, 1982), it can be shown that speakers change the forms of language they use in quite precisely describable social circumstances. Speakers might switch from a 'high' form of their language to a 'low' form as and when the social environment suggests that they should do so: they speak, let's say, a standard educated form of their language in formal situations, and use a dialect form (whether social or geographical or both) of their language in informal, casual situations. Speakers are seen to be aware of the 'correlations'; that one social situation demands the use of a particular form of the language and that another social situation demands another.

What is the case on the macro-level code was shown by Labov (1972) to be the case with the micro-level of pronunciation. He showed conclusively that the pronunciation of specific words not only varied between speakers from different strata in a social hierarchy, but also varied for the same speakers in environments where either the degree of formality or the degree of attention drawn to the pronunciation of a word had been changed. In informal, casual speech, middle-class speakers in New York might pronounce the word 'beard' with an 'r'/biːrd/ whereas a taxi driver might say /biːd/. However, when asked to read the word in isolation, the taxi driver might also say /biːrd/.

For Labov, as for Gumperz, speakers are aware of a code-like relation between linguistic features and features of the social environment. The role of the social is to establish the correlation; the role of the individual is to implement and instantiate it as appropriate sociolinguistic behaviour. Speakers demonstrate a competence that goes well beyond the grammatical/syntactic competence proposed by Chomsky. In an enormously influential article originally published in 1966 (as a counter to Chomsky's position) Dell Hymes (see Hymes and Gumperz, 1972) called this **communication competence**, listing features that might be included in that. Correlation establishes a close connection between language and the social, but does so by leaving each as quite separate entities, and leaving language as autonomous; language itself is not changed by the actions of individuals. (Labov revealingly used Chomskian grammar – in my view theoretically quite at odds with his avowed purposes – to describe distinctions between American middle-class (White) English, and Black English, treating them as identical at the level of deep structure, and differing at the level of surface structure alone.)

The second approach, in which I will focus on the work of Michael Halliday, rests on the notion of *choice*. It takes the idea of the Saussurean (and Hjelmslevian) paradigm, and makes it and its correlates into the centre of the theory. In Halliday's theory (1978, 1985), grammar is a resource for meaning organized as systems of choices. The speaker/writer makes complex sets of choices which lead to the realizations of the meaning in an actual structure. The systems are grouped into three broad functions which correspond to the tasks that any communicational system is asked to perform. These functions are: saying something about the state of events in the world, which Halliday calls the **ideational function**; saying something about the state of the social relations between those who are interacting by means of the communicational system, which he calls the **interpersonal function**; and saying something about the organization of the structure as a message, which he calls the **textual function**.

Speakers choose simultaneously from options in each of these functions. So for example, I might choose, within the ideational function, to have a clause-type which highlights agency [rioters burn ten cars]; within the interpersonal component of the grammar I might choose a statement, so that the speaker has the role of someone who gives information (rather than asks a question or gives a command) which would make a quite different social relation between the people interacting within the textual component; I might choose to highlight the agents of the action 'it was the rioters who burned ten cars'.

The role of the speaker here is very different to that in the correlational view. Here they are active in selecting from the range of options available to them in response to the social contingencies in which they find themselves. Each of the choices made in the brief example above can be shown to be made as a result of the speaker's assessment of the environment in which the speaker made the choice. Instead of 'rioters burn ten cars' we could have had 'ten cars burned in riots'; instead of a statement we could have had the questions: 'Was it ten cars that were burned?', 'Did the rioters burn ten cars?'; and instead of highlighting the agents we could have had 'some loss of property in demonstrations'.

The third approach, that of *critique*, derives from a theoretical position such as Halliday's. If the speakers' actions in choosing options are prompted by their assessment of the social situation in which they find themselves, then we can, in principle at least, track back from the texts which have been produced to uncover the choices that have been made, and why. Laying bare the choices revealed in the structures is to lay bare the structures of the environments in which the choice was made.

In this move, text opens the door to an understanding of the social, and the individual's action within it. Understanding the meanings of the choices made is to understand the meanings of the social environment in which they were made. Text opens the way to an understanding of the social which goes beyond its overt content, and thus can open the way to critique of the social.

In my own approach to this question of critique, developed with others at the University of East Anglia in the early to mid 1970s (Aers *et al.*, 1982; Fowler *et al.*, 1979; Hodge and Kress, 1988) the crucial question for me was: What is it that gives rise to difference in language use? For myself the answer was 'power'. Power is at play in all linguistic (inter)action, and much of the work of **critical linguistics** focused on the working of power in linguistic practices.

Of course, to focus on power as the motor for linguistic production, as the generative principle of the very forms of linguistic utterances, was to invert the relation between the linguistic and the social, and to make the social prior. For Gumperz, as for Labov, the social caused selections of different codes, but it did not reach into the organization of code: language remained a discreet, autonomous system. For Halliday, the social was responsible for the shape of the system – for him, language is as it is because of its social functions – and the individual chooses within the potential of the system. Yet the conditions prompting ('causing', 'determining', 'shaping') the choice of the individual were not foregrounded in the theory, and the social conditions of choice were not developed theoretically. In critical linguistics the social is seen as a field of power, and the linguistic action of socially formed and positioned individuals is seen as shaped first and foremost by differences in power. All linguistic (inter)action is shaped by power differences of varying kinds, and no part of linguistic action escapes its effects.

This was decisively not a structuralist move: it put (social) function first, a position taken from the work of Michael Halliday. It also moved decisively away from the building-blocks theory of language, in which small units are combined to form larger units, which are then combined to the largest units. For example, sounds combine to form syllables, syllables are available to make the phonetic shape of the word; words are combined to make phrases; phrases to make clauses; clauses to make sentences; and, for certain theorists, sentences to make text (Harris, 1995; van Dijk, 1977). In critical linguistics, linguistics action is social action of which texts are the outward manifestation. The text, not the sentence (or the word, or the sound) is the basic unit, the starting point. All linguistic action is textual action. Language is a means to instantiate, to realize and to give shape to (aspects of) the social. There is no linguistic action other than as part of the unfolding making of text in social/linguistic action.

In critical linguistics, action, as social action, is central, and with that the question of the agency of individuals also moved to centre stage.

Towards a social view of language

The question 'What gives rise to difference in language use?' could now, as a result of work of critical linguistics be recast as: 'What are the possibilities of choice, and how does power enter into the possibilities of choosing?' Clearly, in any answer to this question it will be the powerful who are privileged, and it will be the powerful whose choices prevail. 'Politeness' can be seen as a (superficial, devious) concession to the non-powerful; and ideology as representation based on the inversion of truth can be uncovered in any utterance. The reason and origins of this view lie in the way in which the work of Marx had been taken up in the 1960s and 1970s in France (Althusser, 1971) and had influenced critical linguistics.

Critical linguistics has been subjected to much criticism, and this has been, in my view, one of the telling critiques. Even though it had set itself the project of uncovering the workings of power via an analysis of its working in text (as well as a secondary goal of 'reforming' mainstream linguistics in the direction of responsiveness to the social), in the end it remained caught somewhat in view of the overwhelmingly powerful system.

So what, for me, are the characteristics of a social view of language? Let me begin to answer this by a brief recapitulation of my argument so far. For Saussure the system was all-powerful, individual action was confined to usage which had no effect on the system. For sociolinguists, such as Gumperz and Labov, the linguistic is linked with, yet autonomous from, the social. The individual has the knowledge of codes, including codes which link the social and the linguistic. For Halliday, the linguistic is a socially shaped resource, organized as a system of choices, in which the action of the individual in making choices produces meaning. In critical linguistics the social is prior; it is a field of power; and power (and power differences) is the generative principle producing linguistic form and difference. Individuals are located in these fields of power, but the powerful carry the day, and the forms which they produce are the forms which shape the system.

Text, as the manifestation of social action, is the central category in critical linguistics. This is the case both for its meaning-aspect and its form-aspect. The meaning of the text arises out of the meaning of the social, and the form which the text 'has' – whether in its material manifestation such as a talk of fifteen minutes or a story of three pages length; whether in its generic shape or in its intra-textual organization; in the very form of its sentences and the shape of its syntax and its words – all arise out of the social conditions and the (inter)action of the participants who shape the text in their social/linguistic action.

Let me give a very brief example. In Australia the issue of relations between the indigenous population and the British and others who arrived after 1788 has been enormously contentious. Notice that in the sentence I have just written, I avoided the term 'the British settlers' as that implies the innocuous act of 'settling' in a, presumably, vacant, empty bit of space. I also avoided the term 'the British invaders' because that assumes yet another view, entirely opposed to that of 'settler'. An Australian historian writing in the early 1970s spoke of a 'white invasion' of the continent (not an 'invasion by whites'), that is, making the act of invading into an abstract noun, which had a colour; and he spoke of the 'white invasion of the coast'. In my use of English, 'invasion' involves political entities, states, and the transgression of their boundaries (such as 'the invasion of Hungary in 1956'); 'Coast' is not a political but a geographical entity. So the semantic and syntactic force of 'invasion' is changed – there was, seemingly, no political entity – and the meaning of 'coast' is also changed – it is something that can be invaded. The reasons for this use (and reshaping) of language are that the historian – so I assume – wished to indicate his awareness of the political issues, yet did not wish to adopt the perspective entailed in the use of 'invasion'.

The social conditions of the making of this utterance are thus *in* utterance, in its very form, in its shape. In my view, the syntactic potential of 'invasion', 'invade', as well as that of 'coast', are changed: the grammar of the language itself has been altered in this use. In this view the social is *in* the linguistic sign: it is not around it, not correlated with it nor is it there as a resource to use. **The social is in the sign**; in its use the sign is transformed to assume the form that best, most plausibly realizes the interest of the maker of the sign at that moment.

The complex of signs made by this historian, and each of the signs in the complex '*invasion of the coast*', '*a white invasion*', '*invasion* of the coast', 'invasion of *the coast*', '*white invasion*' arises out of this sign-maker's interest. I use 'interest' to capture a range of factors: his own social/historical formation, his assessment of the political context in which he is writing, his assessment of his audience, and his interest – his stance, his commitment, and his personal and professional investment in this highly fraught issue – as someone who, in 1972, was regarded as a progressive historian. At the moment of making the sign, he attempts to find the form that will best represent his meanings, form (such as the words, 'invasion', 'coast', 'white') which have their histories and their compactions and condensations of meaning from their prior use when they expressed the interests of other sign-makers in other environments. The forms carry the histories of the social (as Raymond Williams shows with such persuasiveness in his *Keywords*, 1990), that is, the histories of the making of signs by others in their social, political and personal/affective environments. Each sign-maker (never merely a sign-user) is therefore a transformer of the historically shaped resources for representation available in their culture in the light of their interest.

In a plausible social view of language, sign-makers transform the cultural/ linguistic resources available to them in their social environment and always within fields of power. 'Interest' factors in the power of the sign-maker in relation to the power of those who are the imagined audience/recipients of the sign-as-message (or utterance). Yet emphasis on 'interest' ensures that there is real agency, transformative action, *work*: agency in relation to and working with historically shaped resources.

The sign, the linguistic utterance (and this is the case for signs in *all* modes, whether image, gesture, music or 3D object) is the carrier of the meaning of the environment in which it was made; the meaning which represents the interest (social and personal) of the sign-maker. Once we adopt this position we have a social view of language in its fullest sense: the meanings of signs and the sign-complex are open to view as a hypothesis about the environment in which a sign was made, the structurings of power which obtained, and the interest of the sign-maker.

'Critique' as it is usually implied in a phrase such as 'critical sociolinguistics' is now redundant. It is now the taken-for-granted stance towards meaning. Critical sociolinguistics can be seen to have been a response to an implausible theory of language, and of meaning, where form is central, meaning is marginal, and the linguistic is autonomous from the social. A plausibly social view of language replaces critique with 'design', foregrounding the interested action of sign-makers aware of the histories and potentials of the resources of language and of their actions in making signs. But at that point sociolinguistics has become a plausible view of language; it has become a plausible linguistic theory.

Acknowledgement

I wish to express my gratitude to the Department of English at the City University of Hong Kong, where this chapter was written during an appointment as Visiting Professor.

References

Aers, D., Hodge, R. and Kress, G.R. (1982) *Literature, Language and Society in England 1580–1680*, Dublin, Macmillan.

Althusser, L. (1971) *Lenin and Philosophy and Other Essays*, London, New Left Books.

Bakhtin, M. (1968) *Rabelais and His World*, Cambridge, MA, MIT Press.

Bakhtin, M. (1986) *Speech Genres and Other Late Essays*, Austin, University of Texas Press.

Bernstein, B. (1971) *Class, Codes and Control*, vol. 1, London, Routledge and Kegan Paul.

Chomsky, N.A. (1965a) *Syntactic Structures*, Mouton, The Hague.

Chomsky, N.A. (1965b) *Aspects of the Theory of Syntax*, Cambridge, MA, MIT Press.

Fairclough, N. (1981) *Language and Power*, London, Longman.

Fairclough, N. (1992) *Discourse and Social Change*, Cambridge, Polity Press.

Fowler, R., Hodge, R., Kress, G.R. and Trew, T. (1979) *Language and Control*, London, Routledge and Kegan Paul.

Gumperz, J. (ed.) (1982) *Language and Social Identity*, Harmondsworth, Penguin.

Halliday, M.A.K. (1978) *Language as Social Semiotic*, London, Edward Arnold.

Halliday M.A.K. (1985) *An Introduction to Functional Grammar*, London, Edward Arnold.

Halliday, M.A.K., Hodge, R. and Kress, G.R. (1979) *Language as Ideology*, London, Routledge and Kegan Paul (2nd edition, 1993).

Harris, R. (1995) *Signs of Writing*, London, Routledge.

Hodge, R. and Kress, G.R. (1988) *Social Semiotics*, Cambridge, Polity Press.

Hymes, D. (1974) *Foundations in Sociolinguistics: An Ethnographic Approach*, Philadelphia, University of Pennsylvania Press.

Hymes, D. (1972) 'On communicative competence', in D. Hymes and J. Gumperz (eds) *Directions in Sociolinguistics: the Ethnography of Communication*, New York, Holt, Rinehart and Winston.

Kress, G.R. (1984/1989) *Linguistic Processes in Sociocultural Practice*, Geelong/Oxford, Deakin University Press/Oxford University Press.

Kress, G.R. (1997) *Before Writing: Rethinking the Paths to Literacy*, London, Routledge.

Labov, W. (1972) *Language in the Inner City: Studies in the Black English Vernacular*, Oxford, Blackwell.

Pinker, S. (1994) *The Language Instinct: the New Science of Language and Mind*, London, Allen Lane.

Saussure, F. de (1974) *Course in General Linguistics*, London, Fontana (first published 1916).

Van Dijk, T. (1977) *Text and Context: Explorations in the Semantics and Pragmatics of Discourse*, London, Longman.

Williams, R. (1990) *Keywords: A Vocabulary of Culture and Society*, London, Fontana Press.

Wittgenstein and Austin

Jonathan Potter

Ludwig Wittgenstein

Soon after I started my undergraduate psychology degree I overheard one of the lecturers telling his colleague that if you spent a week reading Wittgenstein it would change not only your view of psychology but also your whole understanding of the world. The bookshop quickly provided his scarily titled *Tractatus Logico-Philosophicus* and I spent a week trying to persuade myself that my ideas and life were changing. What I had not realized at the time was that Ludwig Wittgenstein had written not one, but two of the great works of twentieth century philosophy. The *Tractatus* was a spare, technical, work starting with the claim that 'the world is all that is the case' and ending with the teasing 'what we cannot speak about we must pass over in silence'; in between lay 73 pages of arguments developed with extraordinary technicality in a range of logical symbols. When he handed it in as his PhD thesis, Wittgenstein was supposed to have told his supervisor, Bertrand Russell: 'Here it is, you will never understand it'. It was written during World War I while Wittgenstein was near, and sometimes on, the frontline fighting for the Austrian army, and, apparently, hoping to die. He volunteered for the most dangerous positions, such as night duty at an observation post; 'Only then,' he wrote, 'will the war really begin for me and – maybe – even life. Perhaps the nearness of death will bring me the light of life' (Monk, 1990). It may be relevant here to note that two of his brothers had already committed suicide, along with an influential teacher and much-admired author. He certainly craved austerity: he inherited one of the largest fortunes in Europe and then, to the horror of his relatives, gave it all away.

The work that is most relevant to discourse analysis comes from Wittgenstein's later philosophy, published in 1953 as the *Philosophical Investigations*, two years after his death in Cambridge at the age of 61. The *Investigations* is rich and elusive; it is written in short numbered paragraphs, but these often contain more questions than assertions, and sometimes seem to be having arguments with themselves. It is definitely a book to change views and lives. Wittgenstein writes in the preface to this book that he should not like his writing 'to spare other people the trouble of thinking' (1953: viii). If any other of his ambitions is in doubt, this one is richly fulfilled. There is an industry of Wittgenstein scholarship across philosophy, sociology, and psychology; and the allusive nature of his writing has meant that it is all too easy to reconstruct assorted contemporary concerns as if they had their origins in his philosophical work. As I make connections between themes in his work and themes in discourse analysis I do not want this to indicate a plain linear influence. It is just as much that our concerns and arguments within discourse analysis provide new ways of understanding Wittgenstein's work.

To try and simplify things, I will focus on a number of the most relevant concerns, and in particular on the following: his general picture of language; his notion of language games; his discussion of descriptions and reference; his ideas about mentalistic language and the nature of mind; and his discussion of the (lack of) foundations for understanding.

Language as a toolkit

Wittgenstein's claims about language have a range of rhetorical targets, but most often it is his own early philosophy and similar technical, logical treatments of language as an abstract system of concepts whose principal role was to refer to objects in the world. Language was treated as a medium for abstract reasoning; a bit like mathematics but without the precision. Part of the role of the philosopher was to improve on this vagueness and thereby to be better able to tackle major philosophical problems.

Wittgenstein's aim was to counterpoise this 'picture' of language as a set of names for objects with a picture that emphasized both its practicality and its heterogeneity. Language is not one unified system, but a whole set of different parts with different roles. He proposed an alternative picture of **language as a toolkit**:

> Think of the tools in a tool-box: there is a hammer, pliers, a saw, a screw-driver, a rule, a glue-pot, glue, nails and screws – the functions of words are as diverse as the functions of these objects [. . .]
>
> Of course, what confuses us is the uniform appearance of words when we hear them spoken or meet them in script and print. For their *application* is not presented to us so clearly. Especially when we are doing philosophy!
>
> (Wittgenstein, 1953, para.11)

From our present intellectual position it is perhaps hard for us to see how radical this view of language is. But when Wittgenstein was writing, philosophical approaches to language had overwhelmingly considered issues of reference and logical connections. For Wittgenstein this was not merely a failure to capture the complexity of language but, more importantly, a major source of confusion in philosophy.

Famously he saw philosophical problems arising 'when language *goes on holiday*' (1953: #38). That is, they are pseudoproblems that are a consequence of abstracting words like 'belief', 'certainty', 'knowledge' and so on from their natural contexts of use. Instead, philosophers should start with a consideration of meaning that comes from inspecting actual uses of language: 'For a *large* class of cases – though not for all – in which we employ the word 'meaning' it can be defined thus: the meaning of a word is its use in the language' (1953: #43).

Language games and discourses

One of the strongest metaphors that Wittgenstein develops to capture this fragmented view of language is that of the '**language game**'. The picture is of language being composed of multitudes of different 'games' each with their own aims and rules – some big, some small. The user of language is thereby playing a role in these different games. Wittgenstein lists things such as giving orders and obeying them; describing the appearance of an object; reporting an event;

speculating about an event; making up a story and guessing riddles (1953: #23). His list makes a deliberate rhetorical contrast to the kinds of language use that characterized philosophical discussion at that time. In particular, it mixes uses such as reporting on the nature of objects, which had occasioned much philosophical analysis, with uses such as giving orders that had occasioned almost none. He challenged traditional philosophers (who had tried to reconstruct language as a set of names) as to whether they would be inclined to see exclamations such as 'Help!' and 'No!' as the 'names of objects' (1953: #27).

This metaphor can be used to support the widespread discourse analytic assumption that people's practices are organized around the use of particular discourses or interpretative repertoires. It cautions against the goal of providing an overall coherent account of language as an abstract system and focuses instead on specific practices tied to occasions and settings. When ethnomethodologists, for example, have drawn on Wittgenstein, they have often drawn on this practical, local, specific approach to language (Lynch, 1993).

Reference and description

Wittgenstein did much work in the areas of reference and description, which have become important topics in discourse analytic work. In particular, he stressed two things. First, reference is always various or open-ended. He noted that when trying to give an 'ostensive definition' of a person by pointing, the recipient may take it as the definition 'of a colour, of a race, or even of a point of the compass. That is to say: an ostensive definition can be variously interpreted in *every* case' (1953: #28). Second, Wittgenstein stressed that descriptions are not repetitions of words abstracted from practice; rather, descriptions are themselves practices that are used to perform a range of activities. They are instruments with particular uses, just as a machine may use a machine drawing, a cross-section or an elevation with measurements in different ways:

> Thinking of a description as a word-picture of the facts has something misleading about it: one tends to think only of such pictures as hang on our walls: which seem simply to portray how a thing looks, what it is like.
>
> (These pictures are as it were idle.) (1953: #291)

These arguments about the practical and open-ended nature of descriptions are very much alive in current discourse analysis. For example, they are picked up in studies of the way descriptions in institutional and everyday settings are used to perform activities (Potter, 1996). They are also live in debates over the nature of context and its role in explaining talk which have been a fundamental issue in discourse analysis (e.g. see Schegloff, 1997; Wetherell, 1998).

Mental language and discursive psychology

The nature of psychology is a major theme in Wittgenstein's work. It has this pre-eminent position because so much philosophy had assumed various mentalistic terms (knowing, seeing, understanding, etc.) as parts of arguments in epistemology. So psychology had to be sorted out as a step toward sorting out philosophy. Using a metaphor from psychology, Wittgenstein saw his work as a kind of 'therapy' for philosophy, dissolving many of its central problems by showing them to be based on a mistaken appreciation of the role of language and particularly the role of mental terms. Although philosophy was the primary target, he was particularly unimpressed by the empirical psychology of his time, which he saw as combining 'experimental methods and *conceptual confusion*' (1953, Part 2: #xiv).

Wittgenstein was especially critical of what we would now call a cognitivist interpretation of mental words; that is, an interpretation that treats them as a description of inner phenomena such as meanings or feelings. His general emphasis on language as a set of language games which are bound up with particular activities led him to reject the idea that there are 'meanings' passing through the mind as a ghostly correlation to the stream of speech; instead 'language is itself the vehicle of thought' (1953: #329).

A centrepiece of Wittgenstein's discussion of mind was his attack on the possibility of a private language. He developed a number of lines of critique against meaning originating and residing in a private psychological space that has the name 'mind'. He compared this to someone's right hand giving their left hand money – they could place it in the hand, and even write a receipt for it, but no practical consequences would follow (1953: #268). He instead emphasized the public, conventional nature of language use. In one form or another, such a perspective is followed in a wide range of discourse analytic work, including discursive psychology, rhetoric, ethnomethodology, and much of conversation analysis (Edwards, 1997).

Knowledge and foundations

It would be misleading to tie Wittgenstein directly into contemporary debates in the discourse field over realism, relativism, and the status of knowledge. Notwithstanding this, social analysts have sometimes picked out an anti-foundationalism strand in his work. At various places in the *Investigations* he spends time pouring cold water on the possibility of philosophers getting beyond language games to some more fundamental truth:

> Philosophy may in no way interfere with the actual use of language; it can in the end only describe it.
>
>   For it cannot give it any foundation either. It leaves everything as it is.
>
> (1953: #124).

Social scientists have drawn on Wittgenstein's somewhat unexplicated notion of 'form of life' to suggest that he is offering some kind of cultural relativity. The idea is that knowledge is grounded in a set of cultural practices (the form of life) and there is no position outside these practices from which to judge them. Some critics take Wittgenstein to be thereby promoting cultural conservatism that offers no space for grand social critique.

It is no doubt misguided, if not downright cheeky, to speculate about what Wittgenstein would have done with a Minidisc[TM] recorder and access to the kind of corpus of conversation that contemporary discourse analysts work with. Of course, Wittgenstein's arguments were with philosophy as it was done in his lifetime. And he was famous for developing a form of conceptual analysis that involved imaginary scenarios, thought experiments, and exploring word usage to see what seemed to make sense and what seemed odd. Yet we can find intriguing hints to something that might go a bit beyond the office-bound rigour of conceptual analysis:

> One cannot guess how a word functions. One has to *look at* its use and learn from that. But the difficulty is to remove the prejudice which stands in the way of doing this. It is not a *stupid* prejudice.
>
> (1953: #340)

This incipient tension between abstract philosophical argument and the empirical study of discourse is something that also arises when we consider the work of Austin.

John Austin

While Wittgenstein was troubled to the point that his writing sometimes takes on an almost psychotic quality, with its weave of internal voices and obsessional self-questioning, Austin was urbane and ironic. He was not without auto-critique, but he was resolutely light and playful; he loved understatement and the promiscuous breeding of neologisms. As people, Wittgenstein and Austin could hardly have been more different. Wittgenstein's intensely serious and often pessimistic approach to both life and philosophy contrasted sharply with Austin's pervasive gaiety. Austin developed his ideas in Oxford, frequently over lively unstructured discussions with his students that took place each Saturday morning. They would often search the *Oxford English Dictionary* for interesting verbs and consider their uses. Like Wittgenstein, his most important work was published after his death; in Austin's case this was a lecture series delivered at Harvard in 1955 and later published as *How to Do Things With Words* (1962).

As with Wittgenstein, Austin was fundamentally concerned with the flaws in philosophical conceptions of language and in particular with its treatment of language as an abstract referential system. Both emphasized the practical, active uses of language, but the most striking difference between them is in their overall conception of language. Whereas Wittgenstein has language fragmented into a huge number of diverse language games that are likely to defy a precise overall characterization, Austin's aim was specifically to give an overall, systematic account of this active language. I do not believe they met.

Austin's students claim that his ideas were well established before they had access to Wittgenstein's work, although they discussed the *Investigations* intensively in some of the Saturday-morning sessions prior to the delivery of his Harvard lectures. George Pitcher describes an occasion where he suggested to Austin that words were tools. And he quotes Austin as saying, 'Let's see what Witters has to say about that.' On reading the list of suggestions in paragraph 23, such as giving orders, making up a story, guessing riddles, (quoted above) Austin wondered if these things could be lumped together and suggested that 'utensils' might be a better word than 'tools'. Characteristically, his approach was to look through the dictionary for lists of candidates such as 'appliance', 'implement' and even 'gewgaw' (Pitcher, 1973: 24). Austin does not explicitly refer to Wittgenstein (or anyone else) in *How to Do Things With Words*. However, at the end of the book he glosses his aim as 'sorting out a bit the way things have already begun to go and are going with increasing momentum in some parts of philosophy', so we might speculate that Austin viewed his work (in part) as both developing and sorting out Wittgenstein's work. Whatever its debt to Wittgenstein, if anything, Austin's direct influence on discourse analysis has been the greater of the two.

Descriptions and actions

Austin starts out in *How to Do Things With Words* by developing a distinction between two classes of utterance: descriptive statements and utterances that perform actions (characteristically he made up the labels **constatives** and **performatives** for them). Again, we have to put some effort into remembering just how subversive this move was within the philosophy of the time. Philosophers had struggled throughout the century with problems of sense and reference; how words mean things and how they refer to things. Descriptive statements had become so much the accepted currency of such discussion that other forms of language use were simply ignored. Austin's apparently simple starting point was to observe that in addition to utterances that state things about the world there are utterances that perform actions. For example, 'I name this ship the Queen Elizabeth' is not reporting on the truth or falsity of something, it is making something the case; it is an *act* of ship naming.

Austin put considerable effort into explicating the nature of performative utterances. He noted that they could often be paraphrased into a particular grammatical form (first person, present, indicative): 'I hereby name this ship . . .'. But more importantly he considered the way that performatives could *misfire*. Unlike descriptive statements they could not be straightforwardly true or false (the classical philosophical concern), but they could be *infelicitous* for some other reason. Indeed, he offers six rules (**felicity conditions**) that an utterance such as 'I name this ship the Queen Elizabeth' must satisfy:

> (A.i)   There must exist an accepted conventional procedure having a certain conventional effect, and further,
>
> (A.ii)   the particular persons and circumstances in a given case must be appropriate for the invocation of the particular procedure.
>
> (B)   The procedure must be executed by all participants both (i) correctly and (ii) completely.
>
> (C)   Often (i) the persons must have certain thoughts, intentions, etc. which are specified in the procedure, (ii) the procedure specifies certain conduct which must be adhered to.
>
> (slightly modified from Austin, 1962: 14–15)

The act of ship naming could misfire if the wrong person broke the champagne, say, or hit the wrong ship. A child cannot smash a bottle of fizzy drink against an ocean liner and thereby change its name in a consequential way for captain and passengers.

One of the striking things about felicity conditions from a discourse analytic point of view is that they lock utterances directly into psychological and sociological concerns. The utterances only work with the right beliefs, conventions and so on. This is not only quite different from much of the philosophy he was criticizing, it is markedly in contrast to the dominant views of language in linguistics and psychology. It both socializes and psychologizes language in a way that current discourse analytic work is still building on.

The general theory of speech acts

Having seemingly established the existence of a class of utterances that do things rather than state things, and provided some observations about how such utterances might misfire, Austin tightened his rhetorical noose by unravelling his own distinction. He noted that the sort of criteria that had initially marked performatives from constatives could in fact be applied to both. Thus, although performatives are not simply true or false, *some things* must be true or false for them to work; 'I name this ship the Queen Elizabeth' is a problematic speech act if there is no ship. Likewise, descriptive statements can go wrong in ways that do not just reflect their truth or falsity; 'That dog is called Beethoven, but I don't believe it' seems to be troublesome, not because of truth of the claim about the dog, but because it seems to violate the felicity condition that uttering a descriptive statement required an appropriate belief. Indeed, a descriptive statement can be easily re-phrased into a first person, present indicative form characteristic of performatives: 'I hereby state that this dog is called Beethoven.'

What had started out as an uncontroversial observation about some features of language that had been overlooked in traditional philosophy thus turned into a radical reconsideration of the nature of descriptive language. Most importantly from the point of view of discourse analysis, what Austin did was emphasize that statements should not be accorded a special status: 'Stating, describing, Ac., are just two names among a very great many others for [speech] acts; they have no unique position' (Austin, 1962: 148–9).

They are acts like any other, and are therefore parts of practices, locked into psychology and sociology by a matrix of felicity conditions.

From the carefully arranged ruins of the performative/constative distinction, Austin went on to build what he called (with a connotative nod to Einstein) his *general theory* of **speech acts**. The centrepiece of this general theory is the notion of *force* (or **illocutionary force** as he named it!). The point is that, when they are used in utterances, particular words can be used with different forces. For example, 'Can you phone Elaine' could be used with the force of a request, a question, or some other force according to the precise circumstances. Whatever the sense and reference of the words in the utterance, it is the force that makes it a particular act. Broadly speaking, the *force* of an utterance is dependent on *felicity conditions*, while the *truth* of an utterance is dependent on issues of *sense and reference*. Where traditional philosophers had almost exclusively emphasized the truth/sense and reference pair; Austin argued for the equal importance of the force/felicity conditions pair. By doing this he transformed the study of language from an abstract logical enterprise, to one that would have to engage with language in situations, bound up with psychology, and part of social institutions.

Speech acts and discourse analysis

Austin's work has been massively influential for discourse analysis, particularly via its further development and systematization in his PhD student John Searle's book *Speech Acts* (1969). One of the best overviews of this work, and some of its linguistic problems, is still Levinson (1983). He presses some troubling questions:

how far can force and sense be kept separate? How can indirect speech acts ('can you pass the salt') be understood? Does speech-act theory exaggerate the social homogeneity of language? The philosopher Jacques Derrida engaged with speech-act theory to argue that it over-emphasized the intentional, sincere, literal uses of language while systematically downplaying ironic, playful, inauthentic uses; his debate with Searle is one of the most extraordinarily rich and entertaining discussions of speech acts in the last 20 years (Derrida, 1977a, 1977b; Searle, 1977).

From a quite different perspective, speech act theory has been criticized by conversation analysts. Their focus is on the troubled role of the '*uptake*' of speech acts (which Austin called the *perlocutionary act*). Although Austin accepted that uptake is vitally important, it never received sustained attention. From a conversation analytic perspective, the distinction between the speech act and the uptake is at least partly an arbitrary cutting into a sequence of speaker turns (see Schegloff, 1988). And it is notable that speech-act theorists have had more success with made-up talk than in applying the ideas to actual speech. For this we should not blame Austin; he died at the age of 49, effectively in mid-career. And there is no doubt that the theory would have been further developed and refined. In *How to Do Things With Words* he was keen to emphasize that his ideas were preliminary and that full analysis would in the end involve elucidating 'the total speech act in the total speech situation' (1962: 148). His arguments have a powerful elegance when directed at philosophical views of language but I believe that he too would have thought that a full study of talk and text as social practices – that is, a full study of *discourse* – would have meant going beyond the Saturday morning sessions with the dictionary.

References

Austin, J.L. (1962) *How to Do Things With Words*, Oxford, Clarendon Press.
Derrida, J. (1977a) 'Signature event context', *Glyph*, vol. I, pp. 172–97.
Derrida, J. (1977b). 'Limited Inc. abc', *Glyph*, vol. II, pp. 62–254.
Edwards, D. (1997) *Discourse and Cognition*, London and Beverly Hills, CA, Sage.
Levinson, S.C. (1983) *Pragmatics*, Cambridge, Cambridge University Press.
Lynch, M. (1993) *Scientific Practice and Ordinary Action: Ethnomethodology and Social Studies of Science*, Cambridge, Cambridge University Press.
Monk, R. (1990) *Ludwig Wittgenstein: The Duty of Genius*, London, Jonathan Cape.
Pitcher, G. (1973) 'Austin: a personal memoir', in I. Berlin, L.W. Ferguson, D.F. Pears, G. Pitcher, J.R. Searle, P.F. Strawson, G.J. Warnock (eds) *Essays on J.L. Austin*, Oxford, Oxford University Press.
Potter, J. (1996) *Representing Reality: Discourse, Rhetoric and Social Construction*, London, Sage.
Schegloff, E.A. (1988) 'Presequences and indirection: applying speech act theory to ordinary conversation', *Journal of Pragmatics*, vol. 12, pp. 55–62.
Schegloff, E.A. (1997) 'Whose text? Whose context?', *Discourse and Society*, vol. 8, pp. 165–87.
Searle, J.R. (1969) *Speech Acts: An Essay in the Philosophy of Language*, Cambridge, Cambridge University Press.
Searle, J.R. (1977) 'Reiterating the differences', *Glyph*, vol. 1, pp. 198–208.
Wetherell, M. (1998) 'Positioning and interpretative repertoires: conversation analysis and post-structuralism in dialogue', *Discourse and Society*, vol. 9, pp. 387–412.
Wittgenstein, L. (1922/1961) *Tractatus Logico-Philosophicus*, Trans. D.F. Pears and B.F. McGuiness, London, Routledge & Kegan Paul.
Wittgenstein, L. (1953/1958) *Philosophical Investigations*, Trans. G.E.M., Anscombe, Oxford, Blackwell, 2nd Edition, 1958.

READING FOUR

Goffman, Garfinkel and Conversation Analysis

John Heritage

Talk-in-interaction, Schegloff (1992) remarks, is 'the primordial site of human sociality.' It is the fundamental resource through which the business of all societies is managed, their cultures are transmitted, the identities of their participants are affirmed, and their social structures are reproduced. In almost every imaginable particular, our ability to grasp the nature of the social world and to participate in it is dependent on our capacities, skill and resourcefulness as social interactants. In the past, social scientists have had little to say about how interaction works, treating it as an invisible or inscrutable 'black box'. The advent of conversation analysis, which investigates interaction as a social institution, has begun to end this state of affairs.

Consider the following segment of talk from a medical consultation. The patient is a divorced, middle-aged woman who lives alone and works a sixty-hour week in a restaurant she owns. At Line 4, the doctor asks a 'lifestyle' question. Though opaquely phrased, the question hearably inquires into the extent to which she drinks. She responds with an apparently *bona fide* effort to estimate it (Line 6) as 'moderate'. Pressed further, she specifies this description in a turn that conveys, without directly stating, that her drinking is social and infrequent (Lines 9 and 10). The doctor is not satisfied with this, and pursues a more 'objective' numerically specified estimate (Lines 11–12). After a brief struggle, a compromise 'quasi-numerical' estimate is reached (Lines 15–16) and accepted (Line 18):

Extract 1

```
1   DOC    tch D'you smoke?, h
2   PAT    Hm mm.
3          (5.0)
4   DOC    Alcohol use?
5          (1.0)
6   PAT    Hm:: moderate I'd say.
7          (0.2)
8   DOC    Can you define that, hhhehh ((laughing outbreath))
9   PAT    Uh huh hah .hh I don't get off my- (0.2) outa
10         thuh restaurant very much but [(awh:)
11. DOC                                  [Daily do you use
12         alcohol or:=h
13  PAT    Pardon?
14  DOC    Daily? or[::
15  PAT             [Oh: huh uh. .hh No: uhm (3.0) probably:
```

16   I usually go out like once uh week.
17   (1.0)
18 **DOC**   °Kay.°

If you had been presented with this segment in 1960, you would have found few systematic resources with which to analyse what is going on in this segment, and none which could offer any significant clues as to the details of the actions the participants are engaged in. In general, the social science of the period was highly abstract and unconcerned with the specifics of everyday conduct. In fact, it was believed that individual episodes like the doctor–patient exchange above are fundamentally disorderly and that attempts at their systematic analysis would only be a waste of time (Sacks, 1984). Today, the details of this segment can be specified with a high degree of resolution (see Boyd and Heritage, forthcoming, for an account of this segment and some of the many analyses that bear on its details). This is possible because we now recognize not only that there is a 'world' of everyday life that is available to systematic study, but also that its texture is orderly to a degree that was hitherto unimaginable. My aim here is to describe how two great American social scientists – Erving Goffman and Harold Garfinkel – dissented from the idea that the details of the everyday world are an inherently disorderly and unresearchable mess. They are central figures in the demolition of this idea, and their perspectives have been combined to create a major social science paradigm, conversation analysis, which is beginning to unlock fundamental structural and processual features of social interaction.

Goffman

Goffman's fundamental achievement, developed over a lifetime of writing (see Goffman, 1955, 1983), was to establish that social interaction is a form of social organization in its own right. Social interaction, he argued, embodies a distinct moral and institutional order that can be treated like other social institutions, such as the family, education, religion etc. Goffman came to term this the **interaction order** (Goffman, 1983) and, he argued, it comprises a complex set of interactional rights and obligations which are linked both to '**face**' (a person's immediate claims about 'who s/he is' in an interaction), more enduring features of personal identity, and also to large-scale macro social institutions. Goffman further argued that the institutional order of interaction has a particular social significance. It underlies the operations of all the other institutions in society, and it mediates the business that they transact. The work of political, economic, educational and legal and other social institutions is all unavoidably transacted by means of the practices that make up the institution of social interaction.

Goffman's central insight was that the institution of interaction has what he called a '**syntax**'. In the Introduction to *Interaction Ritual* he observes:

> I assume that the proper study of interaction is not the individual and his psychology, but rather the syntactical relations among the acts of different persons mutually present to one another.

(Goffman, 1967: 2)

The participants use this 'syntax' – a socio-logic of interaction that provides for the sequential ordering of actions (see Goffman, 1971: 171–202) – to analyse one another's conduct. By looking at the choices people make within this syntax, persons can arrive at judgements about personal motivations and identities. This syntax, Goffman argued, is a core part of the moral order. It is the place where face, self and identity are expressed, and where they are also ratified, undermined or destroyed by the conduct of others.

Thus, in contrast to his predecessors, Goffman viewed the normative organization of practices and processes that makes up the interaction order as a domain to be studied in its own right. He repeatedly rejected the view that interaction is a colourless, odourless, frictionless substrate through which, for example, personality variables, dominance hierarchies, or institutional or macro-sociological processes operate (Goffman, 1964; Kendon, 1988). What is excluded in this latter conception is the interactional order as an autonomous site of authentic social processes that inform social action and interaction. With this framework, Goffman carved out a new conceptual space, and with it a new territory for systematic analysis: the interaction order as a social institution in its own right.

In retrospect it is clear that, while his work has been enormously influential, Goffman's inspired recognition of interaction as an autonomous domain of study was insufficiently developed to become the basis for a distinct social science field of discourse analysis. In part, these difficulties had to do with Goffman's attitude to data. As Schegloff (1988) has noted, Goffman did not so much demonstrate his theoretical observations as exemplify them. His interest in the empirical realm was exhausted by its role in illustrating brilliantly conceived theoretical analyses. A second order of difficulty was conceptual. Goffman's interest in the 'syntax' of interaction was one that connected social identity with the institutions of society. He was interested in how face and identity are associated with action, and how the inferences about them that are triggered by actions can *motivate* interactional conduct. He was less interested in, and did not pursue, other equally fundamental issues concerning how the participants understand one another in interaction and, just as important, know that they share their understandings. Largely for these reasons, Goffman's approach – brilliant though it was – failed to stabilize as a systematic approach to the analysis of interaction. There is no 'Goffman School' of interaction analysis, and Goffman's seminal insights might have been stillborn but for their intersection with a quite separate emergence of interest in cognition and meaning in the social sciences during the 1960s.

Garfinkel

This emergence can be traced, above all, to the extraordinary researches of Harold Garfinkel (1967). Garfinkel argued that all human action and human institutions, including Goffman's interaction order, rest on the primordial fact that persons are able to **make shared sense** of their circumstances and act on the shared sense they make. Garfinkel wanted to know how this is possible, and he hit on the notion that persons use **shared methods of practical reasoning** ('ethno-methods') to build this shared sense of their common context of action, and of the social world more generally. Garfinkel argued that coordinated and meaningful actions, regardless of whether they involve cooperation or conflict, are impossible without these shared understandings. Thus any conception of social action is incomplete without an analysis of how social actors use shared common-sense knowledge and shared methods of reasoning in the conduct of their joint affairs. It is these shared methods, for example, that enable our doctor and patient to build and navigate their sequence of interaction, knowing that issues are not quite resolved until the doctor says 'Kay' at Line 18 in Extract 1. Thus Garfinkel insisted that shared sense making is a primordial feature of the social world. Nothing can happen in the social world without it. His project – **ethnomethodology** – was to study how socially shared methods of practical reasoning are used to analyse, understand, and act in the common-sense world of everyday life.

In developing these ideas, Garfinkel drew for inspiration on the writings of Alfred Schütz (1962), who argued that common-sense knowledge is patchy and incomplete, is held in a form that is typified, approximate and revisable, and that shared understandings between persons are contingent achievements based on this knowledge. Using a series of quasi-experimental procedures (known as '**breaching experiments**') to create basic departures from taken-for-granted social expectations, Garfinkel (1967) was able to demonstrate the significance of these ideas.

For example, using the game of 'noughts and crosses,' Garfinkel (1963) had experimenters invite the subjects to make the first move, whereupon the experimenters erased the subject's mark, moved it to a new cell, and then made their own mark while acting as if nothing out of the ordinary was happening. These experimental departures engendered deep confusion and moral indignation in their subjects but, Garfinkel found, the deepest anger and indignation was engendered in those who *could not make sense of the situation*. From this Garfinkel concluded that the rules of noughts and crosses are not only rules that define how one should act within the game, what counts as winning and losing etc., they are also resources for *making sense* of another's move, and of the 'state of play' more generally. It is the rules of noughts and crosses that allow the one playing as 'O' to see that the situation in Figure 1 is 'hopeless.'

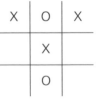

Figure 1   *Noughts and crosses – 'hopeless'*

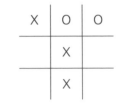

Figure 2   *Noughts and crosses – 'two in a row'*

Similarly, they can be used to see that in Figure 2 'X' has 'two in a row' and is threatening to beat 'O'. They can also be used to see that if you 'miss' noticing the 'two in a row' situation, you're being 'inattentive'. And other understandings can be laminated on to this one. If the 'O' player in Figure 2 is an adult, and the 'X' player is a child, missing 'two in a row' by putting the next 'O' in other than the bottom right square can leave the adult open to the accusation that 'it's no fun because you're letting me win'.

From quasi-experimental procedures like this, Garfinkel concluded that shared methods of practical reasoning inform both the *production* of action, and the *recognition* of action and its meanings. In fact, he argued, we produce action methodically to be recognized for what it is, and we recognize action because it is produced methodically in this way. As Garfinkel made the point in his own inimitable prose: 'The activities whereby members produce and manage the settings of organized everyday affairs are identical with members' procedures for making these settings account-able' (Garfinkel, 1967: 1).

Most of social life is a great deal more complicated than games. And Garfinkel used other 'breaching experiments' to demonstrate practical reasoning in these more complicated social situations. These experiments clearly indicated that social actions, shared understandings and, ultimately, social institutions are underpinned by a complex body of presuppositions, tacit assumptions and methods of inference – in short, a body of methods or methodology – that informs the production of culturally meaningful objects and actions, and that is equally profoundly involved in how we go about achieving understandings of them.

Methods of common-sense reasoning are fundamentally adapted to the recognition and understanding of events-in-context. In Garfinkel's analysis, ordinary understandings are the product of a circular process in which an event and its background are dynamically adjusted to one another to form a coherent 'gestalt'. Garfinkel described this process, following Mannheim, as '**the documentary method of interpretation**' and he argues that it is a ubiquitous feature of the recognition of all objects and events from the most mundane features of everyday existence to the most recondite of scientific or artistic achievements. In this process, linkages are assembled between an event and its physical and social background using a variegated array of presuppositions and inferential procedures. The documentary method embodies the property of **reflexivity**: changes in an understanding of an event's context will evoke some shift or elaboration of a person's grasp of the focal event and vice versa. When it is employed in a temporally dynamic context, which is a characteristic of all situations of social action and interaction, the documentary method forms the basis for temporally updated shared understandings of actions and events among the participants.

The upshot of Garfinkel's researches was that every aspect of shared understandings of the social world depends on a multiplicity of tacit methods of reasoning. These methods are socially shared and they are ceaselessly used during every waking moment to recognize ordinary social objects and events. These methods also function as a resource for the production of actions. Actors tacitly draw on them so as to produce actions that will be **accountable** – that is, recognizable and describable – in context. Thus, shared methods of reasoning are publicly available on the surface of social life because the results of their application are inscribed in social action and interaction.

Conversation analysis

Conversation analysis (CA), developed by Harvey Sacks in association with
Emanuel Schegloff and Gail Jefferson, emerged in the late 1960s at the intersection
of the perspectives developed by Goffman and Garfinkel. From Goffman, CA took
the notion that talk-in-interaction is a fundamental social domain that can be
studied as an institutional entity in its own right. From Garfinkel came the notion
that the practices and procedures with which parties produce and recognize talk
are talk's 'ethnomethods.' They form the resources which the parties unavoidably
must use and rely on to produce and recognize contributions to interaction which
are mutually intelligible in specific ways, and which advance the situation of
interaction in an incremental, step-by-step fashion.

In the early CA publications (e.g. Schegloff and Sacks, 1973) these two
perspectives were melded into a new methodology. Integral to the methodology
was a reversal of the old social science perspective that individual actions are
inherently disorderly, and that their patterns can only be approximated using
statistics. Instead CA insisted that social interaction is **orderly** on an individual,
action-by-action, case-by-case, level. Along with this came the insistence that this
order must be found in the **naturally occurring materials of interaction**,
rather than materials fabricated through experimental procedures or role plays.
And finally, since orderliness inheres in the details of interaction, there was an
insistence that these materials be recorded on audio or video tape rather than
being noted, coded, or, worse, simply recollected or imagined.

In keeping with the Goffmanian background of CA, this methodology was
directed at uncovering institutionalized practices, and the organization of them,
through which ordinary interaction is managed. These practices were conceived
as basically independent of the motivational, psychological or sociological
characteristics of individuals: the institution of interaction largely antedates the
characteristics of those who staff it. Just as important, Garfinkel's focus on the
importance of contextuality, reflexivity and intersubjectivity primarily emerged in
a focus on the sequential aspects of interaction.

Several fundamental ideas are condensed in this sequential focus. First, turns at
talk are overwhelmingly produced with an orientation to preceding talk, most
commonly the immediately preceding talk (Sacks 1987, 1992; Schegloff and Sacks,
1973). Speakers design their talk in ways that exploit this basic positioning,
thereby exposing the fundamental role of **sequential positioning** as a resource
for the production and understanding of their utterances (Schegloff, 1984).
Second, current actions ordinarily **project the relevance** of a particular (range
of) 'next' actions to be done by a subsequent speaker (Schegloff, 1972). Third, by
the production of next actions, speakers show an understanding of a prior action
and do so at a multiplicity of levels – for example, by an 'acceptance', an actor can
show an understanding that the prior turn was possibly complete, that it was
addressed to them, that it was an action of a particular type (e.g., an invitation)
and so on. CA methodology is premised on the notion that all three of these
features – the grasp of a 'next' action that a current projects, the production of that
next action, and its interpretation by the previous speaker – are methodically
achieved by means of a set of socially shared practices.

Consider the following sequence:

Extract 2

```
NANCY    a-> W'ts 'iz last name,
HYLA     b-> =Uh:: Freedla:nd. .hh[hh
NANCY    c->                     [Oh[:,
HYLA                                        [('r) Freedlind.=
NANCY    d-> =Nice Jewish bo:y?
              (.)
HYLA     e-> O:f cou:rse,=
NANCY    f-> ='v [cou:rse,]
HYLA          [hh-hh-hh]hnh .hhhhh=
NANCY         =Nice Jewish boy who doesn'like tih write letters?
```

In the first question-answer sequence (arrowed a-c), Nancy asks for the name of Hyla's current boyfriend, and subsequently acknowledges this information with 'Oh': (Line 3, arrowed c). With this response she shows, quite appropriately, that this information is 'news' for her, that she did not know it before, and thus that her question was a 'real' one that was informed by a desire to know the answer (Heritage, 1984a, 1984b, 1995). By contrast, in the second sequence (arrowed d-f), Nancy acknowledges Hyla's response with "v course', rather than 'oh'. By this means, she shows that the answer was not 'news' for her and, retroactively, that her 'question' at Line 5 (arrowed) was not a 'real' question so much as a solid inference (based on ethnographic knowledge of the last name), and that it was to be understood as a comment on the social desirability of the boyfriend. Here action, meaning, context, and intersubjectivity are bound together through simple practices of talking.

In summary, CA analyses of the use of conversational practices are simultaneously analyses of action, meaning, context management and intersubjectivity because all of these features are simultaneously, if tacitly, the objects of the actors' actions. The procedures that inform these activities are **normative** in that actors can be held morally accountable both for departures from their use and for the inferences which their use, or departures from their use, may engender. In these ideas, the perspective that Garfinkel had developed over a number of publications was crystallized into a clear set of empirical working practices which were applied, without exception, to tape recordings of naturally occurring interactions.

Operating in tandem with this methodology, was a commitment to the study of ordinary conversation as a domain which has substantive priority over other forms of interaction such as, for example, the rituals of public events or more specialized activities such as court hearings or business meetings. The initial body of CA research focused entirely on ordinary conversation, and even when drawing from data, such as group therapy or emergency telephone calls, its practitioners focused on what was 'ordinary' rather than what was 'institutional' or otherwise exceptional about them.

Based on this methodological framework, CA began the work of analysing conversation as a social institution. In the process, fundamental treatments of a range of basic dimensions of conversational practice were developed, including

turn-taking (Goodwin, 1981; Sacks *et al.*, 1974) sequence organization
(Pomerantz, 1978, 1984; Sacks, 1987 [1973]; Schegloff, 1972; Schegloff and Sacks,
1973); the overall structure of conversations (Schegloff 1968; Schegloff and Sacks
1973); the repair of difficulties in speaking, hearing and understanding talk
(Schegloff *et al.*, 1977); story telling (Sacks, 1974); word selection (Schegloff,
1972); and others. These studies carved out a range of sub-areas of conversational
organization which are of continuing relevance today.

Towards the end of this period, the field also began to diversify into domains of
interaction – such as legal proceedings, doctor–patient interaction, calls to the
emergency services, news interviews and classroom interaction – which are
socially and organizationally distinct from ordinary conversation. This
diversification into '**institutional talk**' has accelerated markedly in the past
decade. The distinct orientations of these two dimensions of CA research might be
summarized by suggesting that whereas CA studies of ordinary conversation
analyse the institution *of* talk as an entity in its own right, CA studies of
institutional talk effectively examine the management of social institutions *in* talk
(Drew and Heritage, 1992; Heritage, 1997). The assumptions underlying the study
of institutional talk are that ordinary conversation is more basic and primordial
than institutional talk. While the practices of ordinary conversation change
relatively slowly and appear to be very similar across many languages and
cultures, the practices involved in institutional talk can change quite quickly and
are subject to various kinds of social pressures. For example the 'consumer
movement' in medicine has evidently changed the ways in which doctors
normally deliver diagnoses (compare Byrne and Long, 1976, with Peräkylä, 1998).
Similarly, journalists have become notably more adversarial and less deferential in
their questioning of public figures during the past three decades (Clayman and
Heritage, 1999). There is no question that the study of talk in institutional settings
has become a major growth area in conversation analysis. But it has been made
possible by the remarkable range and stability of conversation analytic findings
that have been developed from ordinary conversation.

Conclusion

As its name implies, conversation analysis is a method for studying social
interaction. It is not designed for the analysis of texts, or of contexts where
activities are progressed by means other than social interaction. Instead, it is a
method designed to unpack the fundamental organization of social action and
interaction, and in its applied and institutional aspects, to link empirical findings
about the organization of action and interaction to other characteristics of social
actors and the settings they act in. Its strengths and limitations should be
appreciated in these terms.

References

Boyd, E. and Heritage, J. (forthcoming) 'Taking the patient's personal history: questioning during
    verbal examination', in Heritage, J. and Maynard, M. (eds) *Practising Medicine: Structure and
    Process in Primary Care Encounters*, Cambridge, Cambridge University Press.

Byrne, P.S. and Long, B.E.L. (1984 [1976]) *Doctors Talking to Patients: A Study of the Verbal Behaviours of Doctors in the Consultation*, Exeter, Royal College of General Practitioners.

Clayman, S. and Heritage, J. (1999) 'Questioning presidents: the evolution of questioning in presidential press conferences', Paper presented at the National Communication Association Meetings, Chicago IL.

Drew, P. and Heritage, J. (1992) 'Analyzing talk at work: an introduction', in P. Drew and J. Heritage (eds) *Talk at Work*, Cambridge, Cambridge University Press.

Garfinkel, H. (1963) 'A conception of, and experiments with, 'trust' as a condition of stable concerted actions', in O.J. Harvey (ed.) *Motivation and Social Interaction*, New York, Ronald Press.

Garfinkel, H. (1967) *Studies in Ethnomethodology*, Englewood Cliffs, N.J., Prentice-Hall.

Goffman, E. (1955) 'On face work', *Psychiatry*, no. 18, pp. 213–31.

Goffman, E. (1964) 'The neglected situation', *American Anthropologist*, vol. 66, pp. 133–6.

Goffman, E. (1967) *Interaction Ritual: Essays in Face to Face Behavior*, Garden City, New York, Doubleday.

Goffman, E. (1971) *Relations in Public: Microstudies of the Public Order*, Harmondsworth, Penguin.

Goffman, E. (1983) 'The interaction order', *American Sociological Review*, no. 48, pp. 1–17.

Goodwin, C. (1981) *Conversational Organization: Interaction Between Speakers and Hearers*, New York, Academic Press.

Heritage, J. (1984a) *Garfinkel and Ethnomethodology*, Cambridge, Polity Press.

Heritage, J. (1984b) 'A change-of-state token and aspects of its sequential placement', in J.M. Atkinson and J. Heritage (eds) *Structures of Social Action*, Cambridge, Cambridge University Press.

Heritage, J. (1995) 'Conversation analysis: methodological aspects', in U.M. Quasthoff (ed.) *Aspects of Oral Communication*, Berlin, De Gruyter.

Heritage, J. (1997) 'Conversation analysis and institutional talk: analyzing data', in D. Silverman (ed.) *Qualitative Analysis: Issues of Theory and Method*, London, Sage.

Kendon, A. (1988) 'Erving Goffman's contributions to the study of face-to-face interaction', in P. Drew and A. Wootton (eds) *Erving Goffman: Exploring in the Interaction Order*, Cambridge, Polity Press.

Kendon, A. (1990) 'Some context for context analysis: a view of the origins of structural studies of face-to-face interaction', in A. Kendon (ed.) *Conducting Interaction: Patterns of Behaviour in Focused Encounters*, Cambridge, Cambridge University Press.

Peräkylä, A. (1998) 'Authority and accountability: the delivery of diagnosis in primary health care', *Social Psychology Quarterly*, vol. 61, no. 4, pp. 301–20.

Pomerantz, A. (1978) 'Compliment responses: notes on the co-operation of multiple constraints', in J. Schenkein (ed.) *Studies in the Organization of Conversational Interaction*, New York, Academic Press.

Pomerantz, A. (1984) 'Agreeing and disagreeing with assessments: some features of preferred/ dispreferred turn shapes', in J.M. Atkinson and J. Heritage (eds) *Structures of Social Action: Studies in Conversation Analysis*, Cambridge, Cambridge University Press.

Sacks, H. (1974) 'An analysis of the course of a joke's telling in conversation', in R. Bauman and J. Sherzer (eds) *Explorations in the Ethnography of Speaking*, Cambridge, Cambridge University Press.

Sacks, H. (1984) 'Notes on methodology', in J.M. Atkinson and J. Heritage (eds) *Structures of Social Action*, Cambridge, Cambridge University Press. (Edited by Gail Jefferson from various lectures).

Sacks, H. (1987 [1973]) 'On the preferences for agreement and contiguity in sequences in conversation', in G. Button and J.R.E. Lee (eds) *Talk and Social Organisation*, Clevedon, England, Multilingual Matters.

Sacks, H. (1992 [1964–72]) *Lectures on Conversation* 2 vols., ed. E. Jefferson, Oxford, Blackwell.

Sacks, H., Schegloff, E.A. and Jefferson, G. (1974) 'A simplest systematics for the organization of turn-taking for conversation, *Language*, vol. 50, 696–735.

Schegloff, E.A. (1968) 'Sequencing in conversational openings', *American Anthropologist*, vol. 70, pp. 1075–95.

Schegloff, E.A. (1972) 'Notes on a conversational practice: formulating place', in D. Sudnow (ed.) *Studies in Social Interaction*, New York, Free Press.

Schegloff, E.A. and Sacks, H. (1973) 'Opening up closings', *Semiotica*, vol. 8, pp. 289–327.

Schegloff, E.A. (1984) 'On some questions and ambiguities in conversation', in J.M. Atkinson and J. Heritage (eds) *Structures of Social Action*, Cambridge, Cambridge University Press.

Schegloff, E.A. (1988) 'Goffman and the analysis of conversation', in P. Drew and A. Wootton (eds) *Erving Goffman: Exploring the Interaction Order*, Cambridge, Polity Press.

Schegloff, E.A. (1992) 'Repair after next turn: the last structurally provided for place for the defense of intersubjectivity in conversation', *American Journal of Sociology*, vol. 95, no. 5, pp. 1295–345.

Schegloff, E.A., Jefferson, G. and Sacks, H. (1977) 'The preference for self-correction in the organization of repair in conversation', *Language*, vol. 53, pp. 361–82.

Schütz, A. (1962) *Collected Papers, Volume 1: The Problem of Social Reality*, The Hague, Martinus Nijhoff.

The Ethnography of Speaking: Sapir/Whorf, Hymes and Moerman

Kristine Fitch

The ethnography of speaking is an approach to the study of discourse which focuses on particular ways of seeing and experiencing the world and how these are reflected in particular ways of speaking. Ethnographers observe patterns of communication, and the symbols and meanings, premises, and rules applied to speaking within specific groups of people. The groups studied by ethnographers may be quite large and diverse (e.g. Katriel and Philipsen's 1981 study of 'Americans'' symbolic uses of the term 'communication') or quite small and even temporary (e.g. Agar's 1973 study of heroin addicts in New York City). Prominent among the objects of study within this tradition are the following:

1 **ways of speaking**: patterns of talk distinctive of a particular group of people, and understood as symbolically meaningful within the broader spectrum of communicative behaviour generally;

2 **speech communities**: groups of people who share at least one valued way of speaking, and interpretive resources within which that way of speaking is located; and

3 **native terms for talk**: group-specific labels for communicative practices that index their symbolic importance and meaning.

By way of illustration, a study by Shoshana Blum-Kulka (1997) focused on family dinner-table conversations in three distinct speech communities: Israelis, US Americans, and American-immigrant families in Israel. She described perceptions of children's identities within the family in each of these communities as they were reflected in particular ways of speaking, including (among other communication phenomena) different styles of making requests and giving commands. Although parents in all three groups directed children's behaviour quite frequently and often in very direct ways, Israeli parents used nicknames and endearments to soften their directives whereas Americans used first names and conventional politeness forms, such as 'please.' Another contrast between the groups involved socializing children into correct and appropriate uses of language. Israeli parents explicitly taught rules of correct language use, reflecting a concern for the maintenance of Hebrew. By contrast, Americans were more concerned with everyone in the family having a fair share of turns at talk, reflecting cultural premises about the importance of expressing a unique, autonomous 'self' (a ritual included in the native term for such talk: 'real communication'; see also Katriel and Philipsen, 1981). This study showed similar forms of talk across cultures: the setting of the family dinner table as an important arena for family interaction and socialization of children, the use of direct speech when talking to children as opposed to adults, evaluation and correction of particular uses of language as part of socialization into a specific system of rules and meanings. It also showed culturally distinctive styles of language use that reflected cultural beliefs about personhood, relationships and communication itself and how those styles (and the system of symbols and meanings that make those styles distinctive) are conveyed from one generation to another within a particular speech community.

With the general theoretical orientation of ethnography of speaking and with a concrete illustration in mind of a piece of research conducted from that perspective, I will now briefly explore the historical roots of this intellectual tradition. The ethnography of speaking (or ethnography of communication; the terms are used interchangeably by many scholars) can be traced to anthropologists and linguists working in the early twentieth century, such as Bronislaw Malinowski, Franz Boaz, Edward Sapir and Benjamin Whorf. Of those central figures, a complex body of ideas that came to be known as the **Sapir/ Whorf Hypothesis** had perhaps the most noticeable impact on the evolution of the enterprise.

The fundamental observation of the Sapir/Whorf Hypothesis is that the structure of language shapes thought in profound and pervasive ways (those interested may find a thorough overview in Lucy, 1992; expansion and critique in Fishman, 1980, 1982; or explore the ideas from their origins in Sapir, 1921; and Whorf, 1956). It is a view that grew out of systematic comparison of languages structured very differently from one another, primarily North American Indian and African languages compared to what Whorf described as Standard Average European languages (though that term in itself would seem to encompass astonishing diversity, from Swedish to Portuguese to Greek).

> Language and our thought-grooves are inextricably interrelated, are, in a sense, one
> and the same . . . A society that has no knowledge of theosophy need have no name
> for it; aborigines that had never seen or heard of a horse were compelled to invent
> or borrow a word for the animal when they made his acquaintance.
>
> (Sapir, 1921: 217–19)

The reasoning that extended from this position (see Agar, 1994, among many others) was that, to the extent a word was specific to a single language, it must therefore reflect an experience unique to the members of that culture. This idea has been widely discussed and offered as evidence for the Sapir–Whorf Hypothesis (although the common claim along those lines that Eskimos have 20 or 40 words for snow has been decisively refuted by Pullum, 1991). In reality, although this 'hypothesis' has been explored empirically in a variety of ways, it is not the sort of claim that could be conclusively supported or disproved. One kind of experiment used to test the Sapir–Whorf Hypothesis, for example, examined whether people were more able to recognize and remember different shades of the same colour if their language has a name for the colour family those shades belong to, than if their language had no name for that colour family (see Brown and Lenneberg, 1954; Lenneberg and Roberts, 1956). Although some differences of this kind were found, there has been considerable debate about the nature and limits of the kinds of observations that can be supported from those findings.

A strong version of the Sapir/Whorf Hypothesis is that thought is determined – not merely shaped or influenced, but controlled in inescapable ways – by language structure. Among the important cases used to defend such a version are descriptions of Hopi, a North American Indian language that Whorf claimed had no linguistic means of distinguishing past from present, at least as those are understood by speakers of European languages. Critics argue that Whorf's grammatical generalizations were often faulty, and that patterns of language can in fact be quite flexible in contact with other languages (including grammatical categories as well as vocabulary). They also note the fact that translation across very different languages is generally possible, if laborious, as a further contradiction to strong versions of the hypothesis. Consider, for example, the Japanese word 'amae', roughly translatable into English as the bittersweet love between a mother and her child (see Suzuki, 1976 for a detailed discussion of amae). The fact that there is no direct translation into English would suggest, from the strong version of the Sapir/Whorf Hypothesis, that conceptions of relationships between mothers and their children are vastly different in Japan than in English-speaking countries. The fact that English speakers are able to understand, at least in rough terms, the kind of relationship captured in the term amae even if they have never experienced it in those linguistic terms, supports a weaker version of the Sapir/Whorf Hypothesis: Language shapes experience (e.g. the experience of love between mother and child) but does not inescapably determine it.

These debates aside, this conceptualization of the connections between language and thought reverberates pervasively in the ethnography of speaking. Consideration of connections between language and social context consistent with moderate versions of the Sapir/Whorf Hypothesis began to develop within a network of scholars from different disciplines at Berkeley and Stanford in the early 1960s. The work of Dell Hymes (1962, 1972) supplied one programmatic impetus for that group and subsequent generations of scholars in the area of language and society. Previously, established approaches to linguistic description took the phonology and grammar of a language as the principal frames of reference, an approach which privileged attention to linguistic signs as a closed, abstract linguistic system. Deviation from the formal system of a language was dismissed as free variation, as error, or as idiosyncrasy. Following Hymes, a goal of the ethnography of speaking has been to understand such 'deviations' as patterned, meaningful, and definitive of group boundaries. Consider, for example, using the term 'girl' to refer to an elderly female (as in a popular television show in the USA called 'The Golden Girls,' about several women in their fifties and sixties.) From a purely linguistic standpoint, calling adult females 'girls' is a mistaken use of the word. From the standpoint of the ethnography of speaking, referring to adult females as 'girls' is at least potentially meaningful, as long as it is a pattern of use understood in specific ways within a specific speech community. In other speech communities with different political commitments, using 'girl' in this way might be equally significant but far more negative: it might well be heard as condescending, even derisive, rather than affectionate. I chose this particular term, and its various and contradictory meanings, quite deliberately; I will return to the critical dimension of ethnography of speaking shortly.

Prior to the 1960s, patterns of speaking had been neglected in anthropological descriptions of cultures, as well as in linguistic descriptions of languages. Communicative activity was a taken-for-granted part of social life, an invisible (or at least transparent) tool used to reflect political, economic, agricultural, and kinship (and other) systems. The ethnography of speaking was intended to remedy the neglect of speaking, both in grammar and in ethnographic studies of culture, by providing a conceptual map for studying speaking in its own right. Towards that end, the initial formulation of the ethnography of speaking centred around frameworks for describing the specific ways of speaking, and their symbolic importance, in diverse speech communities.

A foundational premise of the ethnography of speaking is that diversity in the systems of language use is to be explored in all of its complexity. Societies differ as to what communicative resources are available to their members, in terms of languages, dialects, registers, routines, genres, artistic formulae, and so forth. They also differ in how these resources are patterned in use, in the work done (and doable) through speech and other communicative means, and in the evaluation of speaking as an instrument of social class.

The original framework for the ethnography of speaking was proposed as an **etic** (general or abstract) system of categories through which **emic** (specific) description could proceed (Pike, 1943). That is, Hymes suggested a contextual format for discovering, describing, and comparing cultural cases. The social units of analysis of Hymesian ethnography begin with the speech community, in which 'speech' is used as a referent for all forms of communicative activity, including written texts and nonverbal and nonvocal means of communication (singing, graffiti, sign language, and so forth). This positioning of speech as the heart of the defining unit of analysis centres ethnography of speaking around social, rather than linguistic, entities: one begins with a social group and considers the varieties of communication behaviour in it, rather than starting with any particular linguistic form (such as 'girl' for an adult female) and trying to establish who uses it and who does not.

Consonant with the notion of speech communities, Hymes proposed three other units of analysis for describing language in social life, arranged on decreasing levels of magnitude. **Speech situations** are occasions understood in terms of the appropriateness of speaking. A party at a pub, for example, a different kind of speech situation than a meditation session in a Buddhist temple, in terms of both the quantity and the kinds of talk that are considered appropriate. Within speech situations there are particular **speech events**: activities associated with norms and premises about the use of speech, in general, or particular forms of speech, such as ritual insults, 'sharing feelings' and rules for silence. Even more specific and localized are **speech acts**. Speech acts in the Hymesian sense are, similar to philosophical discussions of meaning, conceptualizations of the actions performed through communicative activity (see Reading Three). However, unlike the universalist approach taken by language philosophers (e.g. Austin, 1962; Searle, 1969), which proceeds on the basis of logical relationships between language and the world that are assumed to be independent of particular languages and cultures, the Hymesian conception of speech acts is that they implicate linguistic forms and social norms that are specific to particular speech communities. A philosophical investigation of the speech act of directives (requests and commands) would focus on, for example, characteristics of the act such as direction of fit between the words and the world (directives are attempts to change the world in the direction of the words uttered in the directive, such that 'it's cold in here' may be heard as a request to close the window (see Searle, 1979). An ethnographic examination of directives would, by contrast, focus on culture-specific ideas of the kinds of utterances that would count as directing behaviour, the symbolic weight of alternative linguistic forms for expressing directive intentions within a culture, and norms and patterns of directive use. Rushforth (1985), for example, describes how requests may be conveyed among the Bear Lake Athapaskans by way of utterances that seem completely non-directive, such as 'If I had a dog, I could go hunting'.

The ethnography of speaking has widened its sphere considerably from its origins in anthropological linguistics, and is now an influential perspective in many areas of the social sciences and humanities. Ethnographic studies of legal processes, health care, political and other public rhetorical forms, interpersonal communication and relationships, sociological aspects of group formation, organizational dynamics, and educational processes and settings have all been conducted under the rubric of ethnographic investigations centred around communication practices. Along with this expansion have arisen debates about whether Hymesian ethnography is theoretically suited to the task of cultural criticism (cf. Conquergood, 1991; Hammersley, 1992; Huspek, 1989/90). If one takes as a starting assumption the view that speech communities will vary in their patterns of premises, symbols, and evaluations of communication behaviour, a commitment arises to studying such systems on their own terms. Criticism becomes a more difficult task from this kind of relativist stance, i.e. a premise that every system of meanings has an internal coherence that may not be held accountable to evaluations based in other systems of meaning. One side of the argument thus holds ethnographers of speaking to be morally bankrupt, claiming that describing a cultural system that includes power imbalances – which is all of them, all the time – on its own terms reifies those power imbalances. The other side of the argument claims that a sensitive ethnographer is as equipped to describe power imbalances – and by rendering them visible, leaving them open to critique and transformation – as s/he is to describe any other feature of the social scene (see Huspek, 1989/90 for more discussion of this debate).

A quite different tack in the ethnography of speaking in recent years has been a proposal put forth by Michael Moerman (1988) to blend ethnographic questions of meaning with conversation analytic (CA) practices of data collection and analysis (see Reading Four). An anthropologist, Moerman became dissatisfied with traditional fieldwork practices such as asking questions of the natives (and taking their answers to be transparent representations of their norms, premises and world views) and relying upon such descriptions of talk as could be captured in, and retrieved from, fieldnotes written by the researcher. Under the influence of his colleague Harvey Sacks, Moerman introduced the idea of examining culture through careful attention to the sequential organization of talk, phenomena that could be retrieved only from close transcription of tape-recorded (or video-recorded) naturally occurring conversation. He argued that the utility of such methods to ethnography was that:

> traditional explainers of social action (such) as 'class,' 'ethnicity,' 'values,' etc., are not *things*, but processes – processes manipulated or, more radically, composed during the course of interaction . . . (Transcription) can hold the smoke of interaction still for study.
>
> (1988: 2–3)

At the same time, Moerman argued that conversation analysis conducted without regard to cultural context lost its power to capture speakers' understandings of social life. He pointed out that one could use CA methods of identifying principles and devices for structuring and coordinating talk to observe dynamics of interaction in close detail. From there, he claimed, variation in the particulars of those principles and devices could be selected for further analysis, and cultural explanations could be offered for them.

It would be a mistake to hear Moerman's proposal for incorporation of CA perspectives on language as merely a shift in research methods. His work created a need to, among other things, re-examine the idea of culture as a **context** within which people make sense of their own, and others', behaviour. Previous to Moerman's application of CA, ethnographers had generally (if implicitly) taken the view that culture was **extrinsic**, i.e. that it was a code of meaning, specific to a group of people, that transcended particular moments of interaction. Moerman proposed that context was to a significant degree **intrinsic** to the conversation itself: that people construct meaning from sequences, pauses, turn-taking, and other organizational features that are part of conversational practice everywhere. These ideas have encouraged ethnographers to rely more heavily on tape-recorded, transcribed conversations in order to ground cultural claims in data that readers can see for themselves, rather than from reports of talk as observed and reported by the researchers. They have also stimulated reworking notions of culture into a system of resources that is most importantly brought to bear on immediate conversational tasks faced by everyone, everywhere: construction of identity, managing misunderstanding, and generally making sense of lived experience.

References

Agar, M. (1973) *Ripping and Running: A Formal Ethnography of Urban Heroin Addicts*, New York, Seminar Press.

Agar, M. (1994) *Language Shock: Understanding the Cultural of Conversation*, New York, Morrow.

Austin, J.L. (1962) *How to Do Things With Words*, Cambridge, MA, Havard University Press.

Blum-Kulka, S. (1997) *Dinner Talk: Cultural Patterns of Sociability and Socialisation in Family Discourse*, Mahwah, NJ, Erlbaum.

Brown, R.W. and Lenneberg, E.H. (1954) 'A study in language and cognition', *Journal of American Social Policy*, vol. 49, pp. 454–62.

Conquergood, D. (1991) 'Rethinking ethnography: towards a critical cultural politics', *Communication Monographs*, vol. 58, pp. 179–94.

Fishman, J. (1980) 'The Whorfian hypothesis: varieties of valuation, confirmation and disconfirmation', *International Journal of the Sociology of Language*, vol. 26, pp. 25–40.

Fishman, J. (1982) 'Whorfianism of the third kind: ethnolinguistic diversity as a worldwide societal asset', *Language in Society*, vol. 4, pp. 1–14.

Hammersley, M. (1992) *What's Wrong with Ethnography?* London, Routledge.

Huspek, M. (1989/90) 'The idea of ethnography and its relation to cultural critique', *Research on Language and Social Interaction*, vol. 23, pp. 293–312.

Hymes, D. (1962) 'The ethnography of speaking' in T. Gladwin and W.C. Sturtevant (eds) *Anthropology and Human Behavior*, Washington DC, Anthropological Society of Washington.

Hymes, D. (1972) 'Models of the interaction of language and social life' in J. Gumperz and D. Hymes (eds) *Directions in Sociolinguistics: The Ethnography of Communication*, New York, Holt, Rinehart and Winston.

Katriel, T. and Philipsen, G. (1981) 'What we need is communication: 'communication' as a cultural term in some American speech', *Communication Monographs*, vol. 48, pp. 301–17.

Lenneberg, E.H. and Roberts, J.M. (1956) 'The language of experience: a case study', *Memoirs of the International Journal of American Linguistics*, no. 13, Bloomington, Indiana University.

Lucy, J. (1992) *Language, Diversity, and Thought: A Reformulation of the Linguistic Relativity Hypothesis*, Cambridge, Cambridge University Press.

Moerman, M. (1988) *Talking Culture: Ethnography and Conversation Analysis*, Philadelphia, University of Pennsylvania Press.

Pike, K.L. (1943) *Phonetics: A Critical Analysis of Phonetic Theory and a Technic for the Practical Description of Sounds*, London, Oxford University Press.

Pullum, G.K. (1991) *The Great Eskimo Vocabulary Hoax*, Chicago, University of Chicago Press.

Rushforth, S. (1985) 'Some directive illocutionary acts among the Bear Lake Athapaskans', *Anthropological Linguistics*, vol. 27 pp. 387–411.

Sapir, E. (1921) *Language: An Introduction to the Study of Speech*, New York, Harcourt Brace Jovanovich.

Searle, J. (1969) *Speech Acts*, New York, Cambridge University Press.

Searle, J. (1979) *Expression and Meaning*, New York, Cambridge University Press.

Suzuki, T. (1976) 'Language and behavior in Japan: the conceptualization of personal relations' in T. Lebra (ed.) *Japanese Patterns of Behavior*, Honolulu, University of Hawaii Press.

Whorf, B.L. (1956) *Language, Thought and Reality*, Cambridge, MA, MIT Press.

Language, Struggle and Voice: The Bakhtin/Volosinov Writings

Janet Maybin

Over the past twenty years, Bakhtinian ideas about language and literature have increasingly provoked, influenced and been appropriated by Western scholars. Born near Moscow in 1895, Bakhtin is a rather shadowy and controversial figure who spent most of his working life in provincial obscurity during the Stalinist era and only achieved recognition in the 1960s, after his retirement, when Soviet literary scholars began to take a serious interest in his work. During the 1970s and 1980s the books on language, literature and psychoanalysis which Bakhtin and close intellectual associates had written in the 1920s and 1930s became available in English translation, and the complex ideas they contained about voice, dialogue and the ideological nature of language were taken up in Western universities. Before going on to look at these ideas in more detail, it is important to note that there is continuing controversy over the precise authorship of a number of the writings from the Bakhtin circle, and also over how strongly Bakhtin's work should be identified with Marxism. The publications attributed to his colleague V.N. Volosinov are believed by some critics to have been authored by Bakhtin. There is no space here to examine this controversy, and since their ideas overlap in many areas I shall draw from both their writings in the discussion below. Two basic ideas underpinning the work of Bakhtin and Volosinov reflect their contemporary Marxist intellectual context: first, the view that language originates in social interactions and struggle and that these are always implicated in its use and meaning; secondly the replacement of the traditional linguistic transmission model of communication with a much more interactive and reciprocal notion of how language works. Bakhtinian ideas have been particularly appealing to scholars towards the end of the twentieth century who were interested in working with more poststructuralist ideas of language, communication and identity, and his work has been drawn on both as part of the 'social turn' in linguistics, and the 'language turn' in the social sciences.

Language as a site of social struggle

During most of the twentieth century, the dominant view of language was strongly shaped by Saussurean structuralist linguistics. Language was conceptualized as a decontextualized abstract system of signs, where the meaning of any element in the system is derived from its opposition to other elements. This model of language underpins the discipline of linguistics, and has strongly influenced sociolinguistics. Bakhtin and Volosinov position themselves in opposition to this traditional view, arguing that we should study language not as an abstract system, but in its concrete lived reality. They present a picture of language as essentially social and rooted in the struggle and ambiguities of everyday life. The meanings of words are derived not from fixed relationships between abstract signs, but from the accumulated dynamic social use of particular forms of language in different contexts and for different and sometimes conflicting purposes. The nuances and connotations of words reflect this social and often contested history. Volosinov expresses this in more explicitly Marxist terms: all social signs, including language, emerge from social interaction where language use is always motivated and therefore framed within the struggle between different social groups. Social conflict is evident both in the way language is used to put a particular interpretation on experience, and at the level of the sign itself in the struggle over the meaning and **evaluative accent** of particular words or phrases. By 'evaluative accent', Volosinov means the kind of judgement which words or phrases convey, about what they are referring to. To take a few contemporary examples, for instance, the term 'black' has been given a positive evaluative accent by anti-racist activists, against its strong negative connotations more generally within the English language. Conversely, recent changes in the dominant political influences within British education have changed the evaluative accent of the term 'progressive' from positive, to negative. In a different context, within Northern Ireland, the name 'King Billy' (William of Orange) has very strong positive connotations for one section of the community, and highly negative associations for another. Because of the way language inevitably passes judgement on the world, even as it describes it, Volosinov argues that rather than reflecting reality, language should be seen as 'refracting' it through the lens of social struggle. For Bakhtin and Volosinov, this ideological aspect of language does not only apply to its use within the grand social edifices of politics, education and religion, but is just as important in the apparently trivial, casual conversations of daily life. Comments about experience, other people, relationships or everyday activities are also at some level an evaluation of what is being talked about and will include assigning evaluative accenting to specific words and phrases.

This struggle within language is conceptualized more broadly by Bakhtin in terms of a conflict between the opposing forces of centralization and diversification. **Centripetal** forces produce the authoritative, fixed, inflexible discourses of religious dogma, scientific truth, and the political and moral status quo which are spoken by teachers, fathers and so on. This authoritative discourse is associated with political centralization and a unified cultural 'canon'. However, these centripetal forces are in constant tension with, and interpenetrated by, **centrifugal** forces, which result in language at any given moment being stratified and diversified into the language varieties associated with different genres, professions, age-groups and historical periods, each with their own associated views and evaluations of the social world around them. At their most extreme, centrifugal forces are associated with what Bakhtin terms 'inwardly persuasive discourse', which is expressed in everyday informal conversations and people's reflections on their experience, within inner dialogues. This discourse is open and provisional in the way it produces knowledge and is often swayed by other people's inwardly persuasive discourses and by the authoritative discourses which frame people's everyday actions. For instance, a strong government rhetoric about the increasing prosperity of a country may be contradicted by the experience of an individual and their close associates, who nevertheless may interpret this experience as exceptional, because of the dominant national discourse.

Bakhtin sees a dynamic tension between centripetal and centrifugal forces operating at every level of language use. For example, national drives to set up or maintain a standard language or a literature canon reflect centripetal forces, but working against this are the ways that language is used differently by different classes and different age groups, and the way in which usage varies across different contexts, and changes over time. For example, efforts to maintain Standard French have been undermined by the encroachment of English words and phrases into the language. Attempts to police a standard may have to be modified in the face of the natural diversity of language use and the canon may be contested by those whom it excludes, to the point at which it begins to lose authority. This tension between the opposing forces of centralization, standardization and codification on the one hand, and social, cultural and linguistic variation and diversity on the other, are evident even at the level of individual dialogues, as we negotiate our own personal goals in different contexts. At any point in time, one or other tendency may be dominant, but it will always be pulled back by the forces working in the opposite direction. It is this tension between the centre and the margins, between the standard and diversity and between dominant knowledge and everyday experience which keeps language alive, preventing it from ossifying and losing meaning potential in an over-rigid authoritative discourse at one extreme, or fragmenting to the point where meaning disintegrates and communication becomes impossible, at the other.

One of the diversifying elements within language, the notion of genre, is explored by Bakhtin at more length in his later work. In addition to the idea of there being different literary genres, Bakhtin argued that our everyday speech is patterned into **speech genres** by particular themes, constructions and linguistic style according to 'typical situations of speech communication'. These situations might include such commonplace events as a brief exchange with a neighbour passing on the street, a conversation with an old friend on the telephone, a business lunch, or a bedtime game with a child. Speech genres are associated with particular kinds of contextual features, and specific kinds of social purposes. Because for Bakhtin language use is intrinsically evaluative, the language which has been developed within these contexts will encode particular perspectives and judgements. Thus, the kind of things we say, the way we say them and the evaluations of experience that they carry will vary in the different speech genres we are engaged in over the course of a day. Some genres are more stable than others, but generally they are more plastic and flexible than the relatively fixed grammatical forms of language. However, speaking with others inevitably involves taking on socially acceptable ways of talking about particular topics associated with particular contexts, and using language entails buying in to some extent to conventional evaluations of themes and purposes. We learn genres as we learn the language, and communication would be impossible without them.

Bakhtin suggests that the primary genres of unmediated speech communication are absorbed and digested into the more culturally complex artistic, sociopolitical, and scientific 'secondary genres', which are primarily written. (Although Bakhtin does not discuss this, I would suggest that the oral genres of the theatre, church services and political speeches would count as more culturally complex, and, therefore, as 'secondary genres'.) Because people use and interpret language according to their knowledge of genres, and because generic style, structure and theme encode particular social expectations and evaluations, genres for Bakhtin are centrally important in articulating the relationship between language and culture. As he puts it, 'utterances and their types, that is, speech genres, are the drive belts from the history of society to the history of language' (Bakhtin, 1986: 65).

To summarize so far, language in the Bakhtin and Volosinov writings is characterized not as a decontextualized abstract system of signs, but as originating in social struggle, coloured by the history of its use, always evaluative and highly ideological. Language reflects and instantiates the omnipresent tension between centralizing centripetal forces, and the centrifugal forces of diversification, and its everyday use is shaped by conventions associated with different genres, social classes, professions and generations. These different social languages and genres 'cohabit', supplementing and contradicting each other, and intersecting or becoming hybridized in various ways. Bakhtin uses the term **heteroglossia** to refer to this dynamic multiplicity of voices, genres and social languages:

> . . . at any moment of its historical existence, language is heteroglot from top to bottom: it represents the coexistence of socio-ideological contradictions between the present and past, between differing epochs of the past, between different socio-ideological groups in the present, between tendencies, schools and so forth, all given a bodily form. These 'languages' of heteroglossia intersect each other in a variety of ways, forming new socially typifying 'languages'.
>
> (Bakhtin, 1981: 291)

Voice and communication

This view of language has quite profound implications for how we understand the nature of spoken and written texts, the ways in which people communicate and the concept of individual voice. Language for Bakhtin is not a neutral linguistic resource, but is already 'overpopulated' with other people's voices, and the social practices and contexts they invoke. When we use language, therefore, we struggle to produce our own meaning out of the myriad connotations and associations of the words we use.

> The word in language is always half someone else's. It becomes one's own only when the speaker populates it with their own intentions, their own accent, when they appropriate the word, adapting it to their own semantic and expressive intention. Prior to this moment of appropriation, the word does not exist in a neutral and impersonal language (it is not, after all, out of a dictionary, that the speaker gets their words!), but rather it exists in other people's mouths, in other people's concrete contexts, serving other people's intentions: it is from there that one must take the word, and make it one's own. There are no 'neutral' words and forms – words and forms that can belong to 'no-one'; language has been completely taken

over, shot through with intentions and accents. For any individual consciousness living in it, language is not an abstract system of normative forms but rather a concrete heteroglot conception of the world. All words have the 'taste' of a profession, a genre, a tendency, a party, a particular work, a particular person, a generation, an age group, the day and hour. Each word tastes of the context and contexts in which it has lived its socially charged life; all words and forms are populated by intentions.

(Bakhtin, 1981: 293–4)

As the dramatist Dennis Potter put it somewhat more flippantly: 'The trouble with words is that you don't know whose mouth they've been in.' Rather more seriously, Bakhtin's ideas would suggest that normative definitions of words are only a starting point in understanding how language creates meaning in particular contexts. Interestingly, his insistence on the 'taste' of words is substantiated by recent work in corpus linguistics where computer analysis of how words are used across thousands of texts throws up consistent patterns of evaluative meanings and connotations for particular phrases, which are not open to intuition, or recorded in dictionaries. For instance, the term 'undergo' has been shown to be persistently associated with negative and painful experiences, although this is not part of its official dictionary definition (Stubbs, 1998). We may not consciously choose the tastes of the words we use, but it seems that these are an important integral part of the meaning that is produced.

In this sense, every time we use language at all we are speaking with the voices of others. Sometimes, however, the voices we take on will be more readily identifiable. In everyday talk, people often repeat something they have read in the newspaper, heard on television, been told by a friend, or remember from childhood. We often reproduce the views of those who have been a strong influence on us, and we may invoke authoritative voices from law, the church or education to support a point we want to make. The voices of authoritative others are often particularly evident in children's speech. For Bakhtin and Volosinov, invoking a voice always also involves invoking an evaluative viewpoint, which may be used by the current speaker as a rhetorical resource to support their own speaking or writing purposes. In academic writing, for instance, arguments are often built up around quotations from the important theorists and researchers in a particular field. There are always in fact two layers of evaluation: the reported speech or writing conveys its own evaluative viewpoint, but the current speaker or writer also frames and evaluates this viewpoint in their turn (quite often in rather subtle ways), through the manner in which they reproduce and recontextualize the words they are quoting or reporting. Thus, for instance, people may complain that the meaning of their words was changed because a vital word was omitted, or that what they said was reported 'out of context'. Reporting the words of witnesses in law courts, political opponents in elections or a partner at a marriage guidance session may prove highly contentious, and crucial to the judgement of what counts as truth.

In more general terms, Volosinov suggests that we can identify two main directions in the way speech is reported. In the first **linear style** of reporting, the words are reproduced verbatim, and there is a clear and obvious boundary between the voice of the reporter, and the voice being reported. In the second or

pictorial style, however, the reported speech is infiltrated with the reporter's speech, and the boundaries become much more fuzzy. Volosinov suggests that the reporting mode is linked both to the nature of the voice being reported (authoritative voices tend to be reported in the linear style) and to prevailing ideological practices within a society (the linear style being associated with authoritarianism). In this section, for instance, I have included some linear reporting of quotations from Bakhtin's work so that his authoritative voice can speak directly, and in the more general discussion, his voice is still dominant in what is presented as knowledge. A more pictorial reporting might have interpreted or adapted these ideas and interwoven them more closely with my own research interests and data.

Texts often contain the various traces of voices that have been involved in their production, whether these are clearly reported voices, or voices that are taken on as if they were the author's own. Some texts are more clearly heteroglossic than others. A newspaper report, for instance, may have involved a journalist interviewing witnesses and spokespeople and incorporating their voices into his article. This report was then cut and edited by the newspaper sub-editor, and, finally, captioned and positioned in the paper in accordance with a senior editorial decision. The voices of witnesses and spokespeople (of varying degrees of authority), the journalist, sub-editor and editor all participate in constructing the message for the reader. Similarly, in a film text, the screenplay writer, director, camera operator, sound crew and set designer will all be involved in emphasizing the point of view of a particular protagonist to the audience.

In addition to the multiple voices which may be involved in the production of a text, its audience is also, in Bakhtin and Volosinov's view, centrally involved in creating the meaning of the texts they hear or read. Whereas the model of communication in Saussurean linguistics involved the speaker transmitting ideas via language to the listener, who then responded, Volosinov argues that meaning is not contained within the text or inside the heads of individuals, but is like an electric spark when the speaker and listener connect. In understanding the theme, or situated meaning, of another person's utterance (or a more extensive text), Volosinov suggests that the listener orientates themselves to it, locating it in relation to their own inner consciousness. 'For each word of the utterance that we are in the process of understanding, we, as it were, lay down a set of our own answering words. . . In essence, meaning belongs to a word in its position between speakers; that is, meaning is realized only in the process of active, responsive, understanding' (Volosinov, 1986: 102–3). Volosinov takes this view further, to argue that thought itself is dialogic, as we internally rerun the dialogues we have with others and their ideas and reflections feed into our own ongoing struggles with knowledge and meaning. The distinctions between speaker and listener, and between writer and reader become blurred as the purposes and understandings of each are anticipated by, and interpenetrate, the other. This **dialogic** quality of communication means that there is always at least one other respondent voice implicit in any utterance, and an implied dialogue with that voice shapes the form and meaning of the utterance. This is perhaps most obvious in utterances within a stretch of conversation, where one can see clearly how they both assume and anticipate future turns in the dialogue, as well as responding to past turns. But Bakhtin suggests that even the most apparently stand-alone writing, for example a philosophical or scientific treatise, is also a response to what has already been said about a particular topic or issue, and this responsivity will be evident in both the content and the structure of the text. Bakhtin's own work, as I suggested earlier, can be seen as a response to and a critique of structural linguistics. His own argument is shaped around a refutation of the Saussurean model of language and communication, and the examples he uses to illustrate it are drawn from texts and situations that were familiar to his contemporary audience. An utterance or text always, therefore, faces two ways: backwards towards previous utterances, and forwards towards its own addressees.

Conclusion

What implications do the Bakhtin/Volosinov ideas have for the analysis of a stretch of discourse? First, both spoken utterances and written texts need to be understood in terms of how they are responding to, and anticipating, other utterances or texts. The dialogical aspect of an utterance is crucial to its meaning. Second, a speaker may explicitly or implicitly report or appropriate other voices: from written texts, authoritative figures, or a comment earlier in the conversation. The content and evaluative viewpoint of a voice, and the way in which the speaker reproduces or frames it, is an important part of the speaker's construction of meaning. Thirdly, the words and phrases which speakers use bring with them their own social history and associations, and introduce a wealth of nuances and connotations into the current speech context, which speakers draw on and interpret in various ways. Finally, individual utterances and texts will reflect the heteroglossia of language itself, and the conflicts that permeate it, between centrifugal and centripetal forces and between authoritative and inwardly persuasive discourse.

If all utterances and their associated invoked voices respond to previous utterances and also anticipate future responses, and if the struggle between centrifugal and centripetal forces is present at every level of language, we can treat all discourse as essentially heteroglossic, dialogic, and the site of ideological struggle. The dialogic construction of meaning extends into inner thought, bringing dialogue with others, and the socio-historical and generic associations and evaluative perspectives inscribed within those dialogues, to the centre of individual consciousness. For Volosinov and Bakhtin, the heteroglossic and already bespoken nature of language ensures that our views and understanding of the world, our relations with others and our sense of our own identity are always evaluative and ideological. In this sense, 'the ideological becoming of a human being . . . is the process of selectively assimilating the words of others' (Bakhtin, 1981: 134).

References

Bakhtin, M. (1981) 'Discourse in the novel' in M. Holquist (ed.) *The Dialogic Imagination*, Austin, University of Texas Press.

Bakhtin, M. (1984) *Problems of Dostoevsky's Poetics* (edited and translated by C. Emerson), Manchester, Manchester University Press.

Bakhtin, M. (1986) *Speech genres and other Late Essays*, C. Emerson and M. Holquist (eds) Austin, University of Texas Press.

Stubbs, M. (1998) 'A note on the phraseological tendencies in the core vocabulary of English', *Studia Anglica Posnamiensia*, vol. XXXIII.

Volosinov, V.N. (1976) *Freudianism: a Marxist critique*, New York, Academic Press.

Volosinov, V.N. (1986) *Marxism and the Philosophy of Language* (translated by L. Matejka and I.R. Titunik), Cambridge, MA, Harvard University Press.

Foucault: Power, Knowledge and Discourse

Stuart Hall

In this reading Stuart Hall introduces the French philosopher, Michel Foucault's (b.1926; d.1984) discursive approach to language and representation. Hall outlines three of Foucault's major themes:

1 the concept of 'discourse';

2 power and knowledge;

3 the question of the 'subject'.

Source: Hall, S. (1997) 'The work of representation', in S. Hall (ed.) *Representation: cultural representations and signifying practices*. London: Sage, in association with the Open University.

From language to discourse

The first point to note is the shift of attention in Foucault from 'language' to 'discourse'. He studied not language, but **discourse as a system of representation**. Normally, the term 'discourse' is used as a linguistic concept. It simply means passages of connected writing or speech. Michel Foucault, however, gave it a different meaning. What interested him were the rules and practices that produced meaningful statements and regulated discourse in different historical periods. By 'discourse', Foucault meant 'a group of statements which provide a language for talking about – a way of representing the knowledge about – a particular topic at a particular historical moment . . . Discourse is about the production of knowledge through language. But . . . since all social practices entail *meaning*, and meanings shape and influence what we do – our conduct – all practices have a discursive aspect' (Hall, 1992: 291). It is important to note that the concept of *discourse* in this usage is not purely a 'linguistic' concept. It is about language *and* practice. It attempts to overcome the traditional distinction between what one *says* (language) and what one *does* (practice). Discourse, Foucault argues, constructs the topic. It defines and produces the objects of our knowledge. It governs the way that a topic can be meaningfully talked about and reasoned about. It also influences how ideas are put into practice and used to regulate the conduct of others. Just as a discourse 'rules in' certain ways of talking about a topic, defining an acceptable and intelligible way to talk, write, or conduct oneself, so also, by definition, it 'rules out', limits and restricts other ways of talking, of conducting ourselves in relation to the topic or constructing knowledge about it. Discourse. Foucault argued, never consists of one statement, one text, one action or one source. The same discourse, characteristic of the way of thinking or the state of knowledge at any one time (what Foucault called the **episteme**), will appear across a range of texts, and as forms of conduct, at a number of different institutional sites within society. However, whenever these discursive events 'refer to the same object, share the same style and . . . support a strategy . . . a common institutional, administrative or political drift and pattern' (Cousins and Hussain, 1984: 84–85), then they are said by Foucault to belong to the same **discursive formation**.

Meaning and meaningful practice is therefore constructed within discourse. Like the semioticians, Foucault was a 'constructionist'. However, unlike them, he was concerned with the production of knowledge and meaning, not through language but through discourse. There were therefore similarities, but also substantive differences between these two versions.

The idea that 'discourse produces the objects of knowledge' and that nothing which is meaningful exists outside discourse, is at first sight a disconcerting proposition, which seems to run right against the grain of common-sense thinking. It is worth spending a moment to explore this idea further. Is Foucault saying – as some of his critics have charged – that *nothing exists outside of discourse*? In fact, Foucault does *not* deny that things can have a real, material existence in the world. What he does argue is that 'nothing has any meaning outside of discourse' (Foucault: 1972). As Laclau and Mouffe put it, 'we use [the term discourse] to emphasize the fact that every social configuration is *meaningful*' (1990: 100). The concept of discourse is not about whether things exist but about where meaning comes from.

[. . .]

This idea that physical things and actions exist, but they only take on meaning and become objects of knowledge within discourse, is at the heart of the **constructionist theory of meaning and representation**. Foucault argues that since we can only have a knowledge of things if they have a meaning, it is discourse – not the things-in-themselves – which produces knowledge. Subjects like 'madness', 'punishment' and 'sexuality' only exist meaningfully *within* the discourses about them. Thus, the study of the discourses of madness, punishment or sexuality would have to include the following elements:

1 statements about 'madness', 'punishment' or 'sexuality' which give us a certain kind of knowledge about these things;

2 the rules which prescribe certain ways of talking about these topics and exclude other ways – which govern what is 'sayable' or 'thinkable' about insanity, punishment or sexuality, at a particular historical moment:

3 'subjects' who in some ways personify the discourse – the madman, the hysterical woman, the criminal, the deviant, the sexually perverse person; with the attributes we would expect these subjects to have, given the way knowledge about the topic was constructed at that time:

4 how this knowledge about the topic acquires authority, a sense of embodying the 'truth' about it; constituting the 'truth of the matter', at a historical moment;

5 the practices within institutions for dealing with the subjects – medical treatment for the insane, punishment regimes for the guilty, moral discipline

for the sexually deviant – whose conduct is being regulated and organized according to those ideas;

6 acknowledgement that a different discourse or *episteme* will arise at a later historical moment, supplanting the existing one, opening up a new *discursive formation*, and producing, in its turn, new conceptions of 'madness' or 'punishment' or 'sexuality', new discourses with the power and authority, the 'truth', to regulate social practices in new ways.

Historicizing discourse: discursive practices

The main point to get hold of here is the way discourse, representation, knowledge and 'truth' are radically *historicized* by Foucault, in contrast to the rather ahistorical tendency in semiotics. Things meant something and were 'true', he argued, only *within a specific historical context*. Foucault did not believe that the same phenomena would be found across different historical periods. He thought that, in each period, discourse produced forms of knowledge, objects, subjects and practices of knowledge, which differed radically from period to period, with no necessary continuity between them.

Thus, for Foucault, for example, mental illness was not an objective fact, which remained the same in all historical periods, and meant the same thing in all cultures. It was only *within* a definite discursive formation that the object, 'madness', could appear at all as a meaningful or intelligible construct. It was 'constituted by all that was said, in all the statements that named it, divided it up, described it, explained it, traced its development, indicated its various correlations, judged it, and possibly gave it speech by articulating, in its name, discourses that were to be taken as its own' (1972: 32). And it was only after a certain definition of 'madness' was put into practice, that the appropriate subject – 'the madman' as current medical and psychiatric knowledge defined 'him' – could appear.

Or, take some other examples of discursive practices from his work. There have always been sexual relations. But 'sexuality', as a specific way of talking about, studying and regulating sexual desire, its secrets and its fantasies, Foucault argued, only appeared in western societies at a particular historical moment (Foucault, 1978). There may always have been what we now call homosexual forms of behaviour. But 'the homosexual' as a specific kind of social subject, was *produced*, and could only make its appearance, within the moral, legal, medical and psychiatric discourses, practices and institutional apparatuses of the late nineteenth century, with their particular theories of sexual perversity (Weeks, 1981, 1985). Similarly, it makes nonsense to talk of the 'hysterical woman' outside of the nineteenth-century view of hysteria as a very widespread female malady. In *The Birth of the Clinic* (1973), Foucault charted how 'in less than half a century, the medical understanding of disease was transformed' from a classical notion that disease existed separate from the body, to the modern idea that disease arose within and could be mapped directly by its course through the human body (McNay, 1994). This discursive shift changed medical practice. It gave greater importance to the doctor's 'gaze' which could now 'read' the course of disease simply by a powerful look at what Foucault called 'the visible body' of the patient – following the 'routes . . . laid down in accordance with a now familiar geometry . . . the anatomical atlas' (Foucault, 1973: 3–4). This greater knowledge increased the doctor's power of surveillance vis-à-vis the patient.

Knowledge about and practices around *all* these subjects, Foucault argued, were historically and culturally specific. They did not and could not meaningfully exist outside specific discourses, i.e. outside the ways they were represented in discourse, produced in knowledge and regulated by the discursive practices and disciplinary techniques of a particular society and time. Far from accepting the trans-historical continuities of which historians are so fond, Foucault believed that more significant were the radical breaks, ruptures and discontinuities between one period and another, between one discursive formation and another.

From discourse to power/knowledge

In his later work Foucault became even more concerned with how knowledge was put to work through discursive practices in specific institutional settings to regulate the conduct of others. He focused on the relationship between knowledge and power, and how power operated within what he called an institutional **apparatus** and its **technologies** (techniques). Foucault's conception of the *apparatus* of punishment, for example, included a variety of diverse elements, linguistic and non-linguistic – 'discourses, institutions, architectural arrangements, regulations, laws, administrative measures, scientific statements, philosophic propositions, morality, philanthropy, etc. . . . The apparatus is thus always inscribed in a play of power, but it is also always linked to certain co-ordinates of knowledge . . . This is what the apparatus consists in: strategies of relations of forces supporting and supported by types of knowledge' (Foucault, 1980: 194, 196).

This approach took as one of its key subjects of investigation the relations between knowledge, power and the body in modern society. It saw knowledge as always inextricably enmeshed in relations of power because it was always being applied to the regulation of social conduct in practice (i.e. to particular 'bodies'). This foregrounding of the relation between discourse, knowledge and power marked a significant development in the *constructionist* approach to representation which we have been outlining. It rescued representation from the clutches of a purely formal theory and gave it a historical, practical and 'worldly' context of operation.

You may wonder to what extent this concern with discourse, knowledge and power brought Foucault's interests closer to those of the classical sociological theories of **ideology**, especially Marxism with its concern to identify the class positions and class interests concealed within particular forms of knowledge. Foucault, indeed, does come closer to addressing some of these questions about ideology. But Foucault had quite specific and cogent reasons why he rejected the classical Marxist problematic of 'ideology'. Marx had argued that, in every epoch, ideas reflect the economic basis of society, and thus the 'ruling ideas' are those of the ruling class which governs a capitalist economy, and correspond to its dominant interests. Foucault's main argument against the classical Marxist theory of ideology was that it tended to reduce all the relation between knowledge and power to a question of *class* power and *class* interests. Foucault did not deny the existence of classes, but he was strongly opposed to this powerful element of economic or class *reductionism* in the Marxist theory of ideology. Secondly, he argued that Marxism tended to contrast the 'distortions' of bourgeois knowledge, against its own claims to 'truth' – Marxist science. But Foucault did not believe that *any* form of thought could claim an absolute 'truth' of this kind, outside the play of discourse. *All* political and social forms of thought, he believed, were inevitably caught up in the interplay of knowledge and power. So, his work rejects the traditional Marxist question, 'in whose class interest does language, representation and power operate?'

[. . .]

What distinguished Foucault's position on discourse, knowledge and power from the Marxist theory of class interests and ideological 'distortion'? Foucault advanced at least two, radically novel, propositions.

1 Knowledge, power and truth

The first concerns the way Foucault conceived the linkage between knowledge and power. Hitherto, we have tended to think that power operates in a direct and brutally repressive fashion, dispensing with polite things like culture and knowledge. Foucault argued that not only is knowledge always a form of power, but power is implicated in the questions of whether and in what circumstances knowledge is to be applied or not. This question of the application and *effectiveness* of **power/knowledge** was more important, he thought, than the question of its 'truth'.

Knowledge linked to power, not only assumes the authority of 'the truth' but has the power to *make itself true*. All knowledge, once applied in the real world, has real effects, and in that sense at least, 'becomes true'. Knowledge, once used to regulate the conduct of others, entails constraint, regulation and the disciplining of practices. Thus, 'there is no power relation without the correlative constitution of a field of knowledge, nor any knowledge that does not presuppose and constitute at the same time, power relations' (Foucault, 1977: 27).

According to Foucault, what we think we 'know' in a particular period about, say, crime has a bearing on how we regulate, control and punish criminals. Knowledge does not operate in a void. It is put to work, through certain technologies and strategies of application, in specific situations, historical contexts and institutional regimes. To study punishment, you must study how the combination of discourse and power – power/knowledge – has produced a certain conception of crime and the criminal, has had certain real effects both for criminal and for the punisher, and how these have been set into practice in certain historically specific prison regimes.

This led Foucault to speak, not of the 'Truth' of knowledge in the absolute sense – a Truth which remained so, whatever the period, setting, context – but of a discursive formation sustaining a **regime of truth**. Thus, it may or may not be true that single parenting inevitably. leads to delinquency and crime. But if everyone believes it to be so, and punishes single parents accordingly, this will have real consequences for both parents and children and will become 'true' in terms of its real effects, even if in some absolute sense it has never been conclusively proven. In the human and social sciences, Foucault argued:

Truth isn't outside power . . . Truth is a thing of this world; it is produced only by virtue of multiple forms of constraint. And it induces regular effects of power. Each society has its regime of truth, its 'general politics' of truth; that is, the types of discourse which it accepts and makes function as true, the mechanisms and instances which enable one to distinguish true and false statements, the means by which each is sanctioned . . . the status of those who are charged with saying what counts as true.

(Foucault, 1980: 131)

2 New conceptions of power

Secondly, Foucault advanced an altogether novel conception of power. We tend to think of power as always radiating in a single direction – from top to bottom – and coming from a specific source – the sovereign, the state, the ruling class and so on. For Foucault, however, power does not 'function in the form of a chain' – it circulates. It is never monopolized by one centre. It is deployed and exercised through a net-like organization' (Foucault, 1980: 98). This suggests that we are all, to some degree, caught up in its circulation – oppressors and oppressed. It does not radiate downwards, either from one source or from one place. Power relations permeate all levels of social existence and are therefore to be found operating at every site of social life – in the private spheres of the family and sexuality as much as in the public spheres of politics, the economy and the law. What's more, power is not only negative, repressing what it seeks to control. It is also **productive**. It 'doesn't only weigh on us as a force that says no, but . . . it traverses and produces things, it induces pleasure, forms of knowledge, produces discourse. It needs to be thought of as a productive network which runs through the whole social body' (Foucault, 1980: 119).

The punishment system, for example, produces books, treatises, regulations, new strategies of control and resistance, debates in Parliament, conversations, confessions, legal briefs and appeals, training regimes for prison officers, and so on. The efforts to control sexuality produce a veritable explosion of discourse – talk about sex, television and radio programmes, sermons and legislation, novels, stories and magazine features, medical and counselling advice, essays and articles, learned theses and research programmes, as well as new sexual practices (e.g. 'safe' sex) and the pornography industry. Without denying that the state, the law, the sovereign or the dominant class may have positions of dominance, Foucault shifts our attention away from the grand, overall strategies of power, towards the many, localized circuits, tactics, mechanisms and effects through which power circulates – what Foucault calls the 'meticulous rituals' or the **'micro-physics' of power**. These power relations 'go right down to the depth of society' (Foucault, 1977: 27). They connect the way power is actually working on the ground to the great pyramids of power by what he calls a capillary movement (capillaries being the thin-walled vessels that aid the exchange of oxygen between the blood in our bodies and the surrounding tissues). Not because power at these lower levels merely reflects or 'reproduces, at the level of individuals, bodies, gestures and behaviour, the general form of the law or government' (Foucault, 1977: 27) but, on the contrary, because such an approach 'roots [power] in forms of behaviour, bodies and local relations of power which should not at all be seen as a simple projection of the central power' (Foucault, 1980: 201).

To what object are the micro-physics of power primarily applied, in Foucault's model? To the body. He places the body at the centre of the struggles between different formations of power/knowledge. The techniques of regulation are applied to the body. Different discursive formations and apparatuses divide, classify and inscribe the body differently in their respective regimes of power and 'truth'. In *Discipline and Punish*, for example, Foucault analyses the very different ways in which the body of the criminal is 'produced' and disciplined in different punishment regimes in France. In earlier periods, punishment was haphazard, prisons were places into which the public could wander and the ultimate punishment was inscribed violently on the body by means of instruments of torture and execution, etc. – a practice the essence of which is that it should be public, visible to everyone. The modern form of disciplinary regulation and power, by contrast, is private, individualized; prisoners are shut away from the public and often from one another, though continually under surveillance from the authorities; and punishment is individualized. Here, the body has become the site of a new kind of disciplinary regime.

Of course this 'body' is not simply the natural body which all human beings possess at all times. This body is *produced* within discourse, according to the different discursive formations – the state of knowledge about crime and the criminal, what counts as 'true' about how to change or deter criminal behaviour, the specific apparatus and technologies of punishment prevailing at the time. This is a radically historicized conception of the body – a sort of surface on which different regimes of power/knowledge write their meanings and effects. It thinks of the body as 'totally imprinted by history and the processes of history's deconstruction of the body' (Foucault, 1977: 63).

Summary: Foucault and representation

Foucault's approach to representation is not easy to summarize. He is concerned with the production of knowledge and meaning through discourse. Foucault does indeed analyse particular texts and representations, as the semioticians did. But he is more inclined to analyse the whole *discursive formation* to which a text or a practice belongs. His concern is with knowledge provided by the human and social sciences, which organizes conduct, understanding, practice and belief, the regulation of bodies as well as whole populations. Although his work is clearly done in the wake of, and profoundly influenced by, the 'turn to language' which marked the *constructionist* approach to representation, his definition of *discourse* is much broader than language, and includes many other elements of practice and institutional regulation which Saussure's approach, with its linguistic focus, excluded. Foucault is always much more historically specific, seeing forms of power/knowledge as always rooted in particular contexts and histories. Above all, for Foucault, the production of knowledge is always crossed with questions of power and the body; and this greatly expands the scope of what is involved in representation.

The major critique levelled against his work is that he tends to absorb too much into 'discourse', and this has the effect of encouraging his followers to neglect the influence of the material, economic and structural factors in the operation of power/knowledge. Some critics also find his rejection of any criterion of 'truth' in the human sciences in favour of the idea of a 'regime of truth' and the will-to-power (the will to make things 'true') vulnerable to the charge of relativism. Nevertheless, there is little doubt about the major impact which his work has had on contemporary theories of representation and meaning.

[. . .]

Where is 'the subject'?

We have traced the shift in Foucault's work from language to discourse and knowledge, and their relation to questions of power. But where in all this, you might ask, is the subject? Saussure tended to abolish the subject from the question of representation. Language, he argued, speaks us. The subject appears in Saussure's schema as the author of individual speech-acts (*paroles*). But, as we have seen, Saussure did not think that the level of the *paroles* was one at which a 'scientific' analysis of language could be conducted. In one sense, Foucault shares this position. For him, it is *discourse*, not the subject, which produces knowledge. Discourse is enmeshed with power, but it is not necessary to find 'a subject' – the king, the ruling class, the bourgeoisie, the state, etc. – for *power/knowledge* to operate.

On the other hand, Foucault *did* include the subject in his theorizing, though he did not restore the subject to its position as the centre and author of representation. Indeed, as his work developed, he became more and more concerned with questions about 'the subject', and in his very late and unfinished work, he even went so far as to give the subject a certain reflexive awareness of his or her own conduct, though this still stopped short of restoring the subject to his/her full sovereignty.

Foucault was certainly deeply critical of what we might call the traditional conception of the subject. The conventional notion thinks of 'the subject' as an individual who is fully endowed with consciousness; an autonomous and stable entity, the 'core' of the self, and the independent, authentic source of action and meaning. According to this conception, when we hear ourselves speak, we feel we are identical with what has been said. And this identity of the subject with what is said gives him or her a privileged position in relation to meaning. It suggests that, although other people may misunderstand us, *we* always understand ourselves because *we were the source of meaning in the first place*.

However, as we have seen, the shift towards a constructionist conception of language and representation did a great deal to displace the subject from a privileged position in relation to knowledge and meaning. The same is true of Foucault's discursive approach. It is discourse, not the subjects who speak it, which produces knowledge. Subjects may produce particular texts, but they are operating within the limits of the *episteme*, the *discursive formation*, the *regime of truth*, of a particular period and culture. Indeed, this is one of Foucault's most radical propositions: the 'subject' is *produced* within *discourse*. This subject *of* discourse cannot be outside discourse, because it must be **subjected to discourse**. It must submit to its rules and conventions, to its dispositions of power/knowledge. The subject can become the bearer of the kind of knowledge which discourse produces. It can become the object through which power is relayed. But it cannot stand outside power/knowledge as its source and author. In 'The subject and power' (1982), Foucault writes that 'my objective . . . has been to create a history of the different modes by which, in our culture, human beings are made subjects . . . It is a form of power which makes individuals subjects. There are two meanings of the word *subject*: subject to someone else's control and dependence, and tied to his (*sic*) own identity by a conscience and self-knowledge. Both meanings suggest a form of power which subjugates and makes subject to' (Foucault, 1982: 208, 212). Making discourse and representation more historical has therefore been matched, in Foucault, by an equally radical historicization of *the subject*. 'One has to dispense with the constituent subject, to get rid of the subject itself, that's to say, to arrive at an analysis which can account for the constitution of the subject within a historical framework' (Foucault, 1980: 115).

Where, then, is 'the subject' in this more discursive approach to meaning, representation and power?

Foucault's 'subject' seems to be produced through discourse in *two* different senses or places. First, the discourse itself produces 'subjects' – figures who personify the particular forms of knowledge which the discourse produces. These subjects have the attributes we would expect as these are defined by the discourse: the madman, the hysterical woman, the homosexual, the individualized criminal, and so on. These figures are specific to specific discursive regimes and historical periods. But the discourse also produces a place for the subject (i.e. the reader or viewer, who is also 'subjected to' discourse) from which its particular knowledge and meaning most makes sense. It is not inevitable that all individuals in a particular period will become the subjects of a particular discourse in this sense, and thus the bearers of its power/knowledge. But for them – us – to do so, they – we – must locate themselves/ourselves in the position from which the discourse makes most sense, and thus become its 'subjects' by 'subjecting' ourselves to its meanings, power and regulation. All discourses, then, construct **subject-positions**, from which alone they make sense.

This approach has radical implications for a theory of representation. For it suggests that discourses themselves construct the subject-positions from which they become meaningful and have effects. Individuals may differ as to their social class, gendered, 'racial' and ethnic characteristics (among other factors), but they will not be able to take meaning until they have identified with those positions which the discourse constructs, *subjected* themselves to its rules, and hence become the *subjects of its power/knowledge*. For example, pornography produced for men will only 'work' for women, according to this theory, if in some sense women put themselves in the position of the 'desiring male voyeur' – which is the ideal subject-position which the discourse of male pornography constructs – and look at the models from this 'masculine' discursive position. This may seem, and is, a highly contestable proposition.

[. . .]

References

Cousins, M. and Hussain, A. (1984) *Michel Foucault*, Basingstoke, Macmillan.
Foucault, M. (1972) *The Archaeology of Knowledge*, London, Tavistock.

Foucault, M. (1973) *The Birth of the Clinic*, London, Tavistock.

Foucault, M. (1977) *Discipline and Punish*. London, Tavistock.

Foucault, M. (1978) *The History of Sexuality*, Harmondsworth, Allen Lane/Penguin Books.

Foucault, M. (1980) *Power/Knowledge*, Brighton, Harvester.

Foucault, M. (1982) 'The subject and power' in H. Dreyfus and P. Rabinow (eds), *Beyond Structuralism and Hermeneutics*, Brighton, Harvester.

Hall, S. (1992) 'The west and the rest', in S. Hall and B. Gieben (eds) *Formations of Modernity*, Cambridge, Polity Press/The Open University.

Laclau, E. and Mouffe, C. (1990) 'Post-Marxism without apologies' in E. Laclau, (ed.) *New Reflections on the Revolutions of our Time*, London, Verso.

McNay, L. (1994) *Foucault: a critical introduction*, Cambridge, Polity Press.

Weeks, J. (1981) *Sex, Politics and Society*, London, Longman.

Weeks, J. (1985) *Sexuality and its Discontents*, London, Routledge.

PART TWO
SOCIAL INTERACTION

Editor's Introduction

Simeon J. Yates

The ideas presented in Part One clearly indicate that language use is part and parcel of *doing* and *being* social. How language use and the social are connected and how we use language to do and be social are questions explored in this Reader. Here in Part Two the readings focus on the use of language in social interaction. That is, how language use is central to and constitutive of the ways in which human beings conduct their interactions. This idea of 'social interaction' is essentially the 'common-sense' understanding of the term 'discourse'. 'Discourse' in this case is that thing, that linguistic output, which is produced by human beings when they meet, chat, work, and communicate in everyday life. Yet as both the readings in Part One and the readings to follow in Parts Two, Three and Four will note, discourse is much more than this 'stream of talk'. In this Part the readings bring to light some of the fascinating complexities that exist in our day-to-day interactions with others. Each of the readings looks at a specific aspect of social interaction though they all take slightly different analytic perspectives. The readings by Goffman and Sacks are concerned with the 'methods' we use to 'do things socially' in interactions. Silverman uses the ideas of Goffman and Sacks to explore specific interactions in specific institutional settings such as 'counselling'. Gumperz considers 'interethnic' interactions whilst Tannen, and Kitzinger and Frith consider gender and interaction.

What brings these readings together and how do they connect to the ideas presented in Part One? The anthropologist Malinowski (1923) argued that language use is embedded in a 'context of situation' and that utterances only become understandable within this 'context of situation'. Malinowski claimed that 'context' had to be viewed in a wider sociological and cultural framework. He also claimed that in any analysis of language use the context of use cannot be 'passed over as irrelevant' and therefore analysis must 'burst the bonds of mere linguistics' (Malinowski, 1923: 306; also see Duranti and Goodwin, 1992). Almost 80 years after Malinowski made these claims the notion that human acts of communication and interaction must be studied in relation to the context in which they took place is a taken-for-granted assumption. Yet the ideas presented by Malinowski, as well as those discussed in all of the readings in Part One, are what has brought us to this position today. What Malinowski has not provided a full answer to is this: *how* are context and language use connected? In many respects one can view the readings in Part Two as discussions of and solutions to, this 'how' question. Part Two presents two lines of work that carry forward the thinking of Malinowski and other pioneers of language research. The first line of work is essentially 'sociological' and focuses on the social behaviours and practices that make up language use in social context. The second line of work is 'linguistic' and explores the relationship between social context and the structure and function of language itself.

To take first the idea of a 'sociological' view of language use in social interaction. It would be wrong to argue that there is an overt intellectual development from writers such as Malinowski to all forms of contemporary sociological work on language use in context. Although one obvious line of development lies in the 'ethnography of speaking' tradition in anthropology and sociology, described by Kristine Fitch in Part One. This tradition has focused on the relationship between context, culture and language use. The 'ethnography of speaking' distinctly argues that any attempt to see these as separate is futile. Yet as Fitch notes the 'ethnography of speaking', following the work of Hymes (1974), has tended to focus on the 'sociological' aspects, such as culture, community, context in general, and less on the specifics of individual interactional situations. The question raised by Fitch at the end of her chapter is the 'how' question described above. She asks: is context linked to but outside of (extrinsic to) language use in a specific social interaction or is context part and parcel of (intrinsic to) language use? Fitch notes how later anthropologists, for example Moerman, have turned to conversation analysis in order to seek solutions to this question.

The readings by Goffman, Sacks, Silverman, and Kitzinger and Frith could all be described as falling into the 'sociological' approach to language use in context. This description stems from the fact that their work starts from a focus on social action within talk. This contrasts with linguistic positions which start from a view of language as some kind of a system in itself. Sacks and Silverman make use of conversation analysis. Conversation analysis has become the most dominant sociological approach to the study of discourse as social interaction. There are also readings in Part Three that are clearly influenced by conversation analysis. The reading by Goffman is a re-examination of context itself. It considers how we position ourselves in and are positioned by social interactions. Sacks, on the other hand, considers the complex and detailed methods we use to achieve social goals in interactions. This reading represents one of the first statements on conversation analysis. Silverman provides an example of contemporary conversation analysis in use as he analyses how 'delicate' topics – socially and culturally charged issues – are dealt with in counselling interviews. Kitzinger and Frith also start from conversation analysis in order to critique assumptions about 'confusion' in gender interactions.

In the case of the 'linguistic' approach to language use in social context one line of development links Malinowski to the work of Halliday (Duranti and Goodwin, 1992) which is described in Part One by Gunther Kress. Kress notes that for Halliday understanding linguistics required understanding the 'text' – not sentences, words or sounds but whole socially and contextually complete utterances produced by human beings in interaction. Halliday, in contrast to Chomsky, argued that the structure and function of language is a direct product of it being used to conduct social interaction in context. Halliday (1978) developed a specific model of the 'context of situation' proposed by Malinowski. In this model the analyst needs to consider three elements. First there are the socially defined topics or goals of an interaction – what Halliday calls the 'field/

ideational' elements. Second there are the roles in the interaction. These can be both social (e.g. doctor and patient) and also interactional (e.g. question asking). These roles are what Halliday calls the 'tenor/interpersonal' elements of the interaction. Third there is the specific channel of communication (e.g. speech, writing, e-mail etc.) – what Halliday calls the 'mode/textual' elements. Halliday argues that all of these elements link with the grammatical and lexical choices we make when we construct meaningful texts. For Halliday therefore language has to be understood as part and parcel of the social systems and contexts in which it is used. The development of such claims can be seen in several of the readings in this Part and also in Part Four. In this Part, Gumperz and Tannen are concerned with the relationship between specific linguistic forms and the 'tenor' elements of the 'context of situation'. Kitzinger and Frith take issue with some of the perceived implications of such linguistic work for communicative practice. Each of these readings explores ways in which social relationships and roles are constructed and interpreted through language use.

The readings

Erving Goffman's article begins with the description of an interaction between President Nixon and Helen Thomas, a newspaper reporter. This interaction clearly has sexist overtones but this is not Goffman's focus. Goffman uses this as an example of how we, or in this case the reporter, have to be constantly ready to change our orientation to the interaction. Why is this ability of interest? Goffman is trying to unpack many of the assumptions we have about interactions and the relationship between context and language use. Goffman states in the reading that he is providing an extended discussion of Dell Hymes' claim that: 'The common dyadic model of speaker-hearer specifies sometimes too many, sometimes too few, sometimes the wrong participants' (Hymes, 1974: 54).

So what is wrong with our 'common-sense' dyadic – two people talking – model of interaction? Goffman starts by examining the idea of a 'hearer' or audience. Goffman notes that there are intended and unintended hearers of conversations. Also when we talk in groups we can address ourselves to specific individuals whilst still taking account of the larger audience. 'Talk-in-interaction' then becomes, for speakers, a problem of 'managing' these various related and unrelated audiences. Conversely for the hearers it involves 'managing' being a member of the audience. These problems of management are not external to the interaction or to the context but intrinsic to it. One of the obvious ways this management is achieved is through the non-verbal and 'paralinguistic' activity that we use to indicate involvement in interaction. Goffman argues that these management skills are structured and ritualized – something we all become 'culturally competent' at. The members in an interaction have a 'participation status' in relation to each utterance. The whole set of members of the interaction form part of a 'participation framework'. Goffman does not see either of these as impositions on members of the interaction but as constructed by members of the interaction.

Goffman then turns his attention to the 'speaker' in an interaction. Goffman notes two important problems with the 'common-sense' idea of a speaker. First, in most interactions we do not simply stand and orate upon our own. Even when one person is clearly the 'speaker' in an interaction, others have the right to interject, to cooperatively talk, etc. Second, the idea of a speaker implies someone actively producing their own talk when in fact we often speak for others. We also do not always simply 'speak our own words' but rather draw upon and use the words of others. This idea links directly with the idea of 'voice' found in the work of Bakhtin discussed by Janet Maybin in Part One (see Reading Six).

When we make statements we also encode our relationship to the ideas within or to the purpose of the statement. For instance the phrases 'I think Goffman might be right' and 'I know Goffman is right' present two differing orientations of the speaker to Goffman's ideas. This difference, which linguists call modality, is an additional layer to Goffman's model. On top of this Goffman describes how we can further 'embed' relationships. For instance we can use the same words to describe something done in the past or to issue a command now (e.g. 'I said close the window'). Goffman finally notes that we can incorporate all of these layers. For example, the statement, 'to the best of my knowledge I think that I said I think Goffman might be right', contains three layers of embedded relationships between the speaker and the content of the utterance. They are marked by the phrases, 'I think', 'I said' and 'I think' again.

Goffman therefore argues that the combination of embedded relationships in our talk forms part of the 'production format' of speaker's talk. Our 'common-sense' model of two people interacting therefore obscures the complexities of the 'participation status', 'participation framework' and 'production format' of actual 'talk in interaction'. These three elements Goffman sees as being primarily sociologically analysable but with some key insights from linguistics. The arrangement of these elements forms for Goffman the 'footing' of the interaction. When the arrangement of these elements changes (e.g. from a press conference to a sexist exchange) then the footing of each member also changes. To understand an interaction we need to go beyond the 'bonds of linguistics' and explore the ways in which we choose and are required to shift 'footings' in interaction. 'Footing' is just one of a number of important concepts introduced by Goffman, others include 'framing' (Goffman, 1974), 'interaction rituals' (Goffman, 1972) and 'the presentation of self' (Goffman, 1959) as well as more general discussion of the structures of social interaction (Goffman, 1971, 1973, 1981).

In the discussion of Goffman above I used the phrase 'talk-in-interaction'. The same phrase used by John Heritage in Reading Four in Part One. 'Talk-in-interaction' is the central focus of conversation analytic work. As Heritage notes, this tradition of discourse research has its roots in the works of Goffman and Garfinkel and was pioneered by **Harvey Sacks** among others. The next reading is Lecture 1 of the collected transcribed lectures in which Sacks laid out his ideas. It begins with an insight by Sacks into the structure of telephone calls made to an emergency psychiatric hospital. Sacks found that when a phrase such as 'This is Mr Smith can I help you?' was used to answer the call – that is a phrase containing the speaker's name – most callers responded with an utterance that contained their own name. Any response from the caller that did not offer the caller's name caused 'trouble' for the conversation that was difficult to 'repair'. The caller's lack of a next turn containing their name made it conversationally difficult to then gain or request their name – something the hospital needed.

Sacks' insight was that the reasons for the patterns within the calls lie in the members' understanding and use of intricate 'rules of conversational sequence' which are akin to moves in a game. Sacks describes these moves as 'devices'. Even more insightfully Sacks notes that it is not the specific words 'I can't hear you' but the function they play in this situation that forms the device. For instance, saying 'hello' in a tone that indicates the listener is having trouble hearing could also work as the same device. For instance Sacks looks particularly at the phrase, 'May I help you'. Once again Sacks finds that this has several purposes and therefore several possible interpretations in an interaction. On the one hand it is a piece of etiquette that opens up the possibility for the respondents to describe the problems with which they need help. On another level it is a question about a possible role the speaker could take. In one case the response may be a long account; in the second 'I don't know' would be a viable answer. The same words acting and interpreted as different devices. Sacks goes on to note therefore that the turns in the interactions he studied were specific *social* devices. For example, 'This is Mr Smith', 'I can't hear you' and 'May I help you' were all used to achieve social goals. For Sacks these turns or moves are social objects used to construct activities. Exploring how we use such objects to construct activities is the focus of conversation analysis. Unfortunately Harvey Sacks died before publishing a great amount of work. The collected set of his lectures (Sacks, 1992) is the main source used by conversation analysis researchers. Sacks did publish some specific pieces including a discussion of using conversational data in sociology (Sacks, 1972a), and on specific types of interaction such as police interactions, 'jokes' and 'lies' (Sacks, 1972b, 1974, 1975). More general statements on conversation analysis from Sacks and his colleagues can be found in Sacks (1979, 1984a, 1984b), Sacks and Schegloff (1979) and Sacks *et al.* (1978). There have been a number of useful general outlines of conversation analysis theory and practice from other authors (Atkinson and Heritage, 1984; Hutchby and Wooffitt, 1998).

So what kinds of 'things' do we construct from the types of social object described by Sacks? In the next reading **David Silverman** explores a specific type of interaction and the construction of 'delicate' objects. The material examined by Silverman consists of interviews between counsellors and patients in an HIV-testing clinic. This context raises two socially and culturally 'delicate' issues: sex and death. Silverman states clearly at the start of the reading that he is not concerned about unpacking the possible social psychology of people talking about 'delicate' matters, rather he argues that delicate matters are 'locally produced and managed as participants themselves assemble some context for their talk'. You should note that Silverman sees participants as 'assembling' the context through interaction. Context is not something simply imposed from outside.

Silverman describes two concepts developed by Sacks to help with this task. The first is 'membership categorization devices' (MCDs). MCDs are 'collections' of categories that go together. When we employ an MCD in conversation we tend to allocate people to one specific category of the MCD. For instance the 'father' category of the MCD 'family'. Not only does this allocate a person to a category it excludes them from others and sets up possible 'standardized relational pairs' (SRPs) (e.g. father/mother, boyfriend/girlfriend, etc.). The second concept, proposed by Sacks, is 'category-bound activities' (CBAs). These are activities that are linked to allocated categories and vice versa. So, for instance, to say, 'she is reading Silverman's book' invokes possible categories such as student or academic – though there are other possibilities – into which 'she' is then assumed to sit.

In order to empirically examine how 'delicate' objects are constructed in talk Silverman looks for activities such as 'expressive caution'. In other words one way of indicating that a topic is 'delicate' is to express caution about the discussion of it. Silverman finds this in a number of features in the examples he provides. For instance, Silverman notes that talk prior to and around 'delicate' issues is 'turbulent' – it has many pauses and hesitations in turns and many 'repairs' of turns. Further evidence of 'expressive caution' comes in the pauses before the delivery of turns. Altogether Silverman finds five activities that indicate the setting up of 'delicate' objects. These activities range from 'expressive caution' through to attempts to put 'delicate' or 'dangerous' behaviours into 'normal' or 'positive' categories. For instance when discussing Extract 7 Silverman notes how both MCDs and SRPs are used to set up relationships, for example the use of 'girlfriend' to indicate a 'faithful partner'.

The important thing to note is that Silverman is not inferring that the account concerns a 'delicate' issue simply because it is about HIV. Rather Silverman is unpacking the sequential and ordered activities that take place in the interaction which provide both the members and the analyst with evidence that the members view this topic as 'delicate' in some way. We can therefore argue that there are two levels to Silverman's argument, and the approach of conversation analysis in general. First, by looking at pauses, repairs and hesitations Silverman is considering the methods used to organize and maintain the talk itself as interaction. Heritage, in his discussion of conversation analysis in Part One, notes how the initial focus of conversation analysis was upon the maintenance of 'ordered' and 'sequential' interaction itself (e.g. in the taking of turns). Second, the use of MCDs, SRPs and CBAs point to another level of organization that orientates to the context and the expectations about that context held by the members.

The reading from Silverman concerns very specific types of interaction in 'institutional settings'. The study of 'institutional discourse' is a major focus of both sociologically and linguistically focused research (Boden, 1994; Drew and Heritage, 1992). Conversation analysis has also been used to explore specific types of interaction (e.g. 'confrontations': Hutchby, 1996) as well as very specific contexts (e.g. 'psychic readings': Wooffitt, 1992; 2001).

The next reading from **John Gumperz** takes a different starting point. Here language is a system, if socially constructed, whose resources speakers draw upon. As with Goffman whose work helped to found, but was also contemporary with, various developments, so it is with the work of Gumperz. The work presented here falls into the category of the 'ethnography of speaking' (Gumperz and Hymes, 1972) and interactional sociolinguistics yet opens up a number of issues explored elsewhere in this Reader. It is worth noting that this work was published in the early 1980s. It therefore contains an orientation to issues of ethnicity that contrasts quite strikingly with those employed by more recent writers, especially those in Parts Three and Four of this volume. Most importantly it takes ethnicity to be a 'given' category (Indian, Pakistani, British) that can be employed in the explanation of language use. A questioning of the 'given' rather than 'socially constructed' nature of ethnicity is part of the questioning of the methods of the 'ethnography of speaking' discussed by Fitch – it is also central to the readings from Hall in Parts One and Four. It also contrasts with Silverman. In Silverman's work *how* delicate issues were constructed in talk-in-interaction was the focus. In this case the conceptualization of 'ethnicity' is outside the locally constructed meanings of those interacting. The analyst brings the categories of both 'ethnicity' and 'problematic communication' to the data. Having said this, Gumperz provides a detailed account of how different language practices at all levels of the interaction can lead to difficulties for the speakers in interethnic interactions (see also Gumperz, 1982b).

Gumperz begins by noting how differences in intonation lead to problems of interpretation in interactions between Indian, Pakistani and white British workers. Unlike the previous readings by Sacks and Silverman, which rely upon evidence elicited from speech actions indicated in transcripts, this example made use of a more interactive ethnographic methodology. This is an example of the kind of active research espoused by critical linguists and critical discourse analysts (See Kress in Part One and Van Dijk and also Hodge and Kress in Part Four) in which the results are used to raise 'critical language awareness' (Fairclough, 1992, 2001). The next example is a counselling interview. This example has many institutional features in common with those presented in the reading by Silverman. Once again a difficult problem has to be accounted for by the client. The interaction is presented as one in which the negotiation of the expected 'macro-structure' of the interaction – its expected phases – fails to take place. This then leads to problems in selecting the footings and orientations that the participants should take at any point in time. Gumperz notes that previous research has demonstrated that the maintenance of well-structured interactions and correct orientations required mutually understood systems of back-channel communication – the small social and linguistic behaviours that mark 'being in tune' with the interaction. Gumperz argues that the lack of well coordinated moves and turns is evidence that the members are not coordinating in their development of the interaction. Finally Gumperz notes how the overall interpretation of the social relations in the counselling interview differs for both parties. Gumperz accounts for these differences through noting their links to cultural differences in linguistic practices and expectations of interactions. Gumperz concludes much in the vein of Malinowski and Fitch that socio-cultural knowledge is not separate from language use. Following the criticisms raised by Kress in Part One against Chomsky and very much following Halliday as described above, Gumperz notes the grammatical and lexical options chosen by speakers are bound to the 'context-of-situation' and to wider cultural histories (Gumperz, 1982a).

The next reading from **Deborah Tannen** provides another example of work which takes an interactional sociolinguistic approach. This reading also begins by questioning the extent to which we can assume that all speakers and hearers – all members – of an interaction are interpreting things along the same lines. Tannen argues that the variety of cultural backgrounds from which members come directly influences their interpretations of interactions. Tannen discusses the 'ethnography of speaking' tradition as well as the work of Gumperz to make this assertion. Tannen notes that this claim also relates to gender differences as well as cultural differences. Tannen claims that sociolinguistic work on gender and interaction has tended to focus upon the means by which men dominate women both in general and in the specifics of an interaction (Coates, 1986). Tannen criticizes this work as it often focuses on certain behaviours (e.g. interruption) as simple evidence of male domination in conversation. Much like the claims of the conversation analysts, Tannen notes that it is not the words or the specific actions that form methods of dominance but rather the specific interpretation members make of those words and actions (Tannen, 1990, 1994). In fact Tannen argues that many of the methods used to dominate in interaction can also be used to foster solidarity – and therefore that such 'linguistic strategies' are 'ambiguous'.

The rest of the reading then explores the extent to which one can view any one 'linguistic strategy' as being tied directly to methods of dominance or solidarity in interaction. There are some important points to note about this reading. First, it is the first reading in Part Two to deal overtly with power and the exercise of power although issues of power have underlain previous readings, for example Goffman and Gumperz. Second, the reading makes use of a range of 'data' beyond the 'naturally occurring' talk used by conversation analysts. The 'data' or evidence presented include transcripts of boys interacting, sections of plays and novels and one of the earliest recorded epic stories (Gilgamesh). In each case the dynamic interplay between gender, power, solidarity and 'linguistic strategies' is examined. Third, the reading forms part of a wider debate in linguistics on the relationship between gender and language use. This debate has often been framed as the 'difference/dominance' debate (see Cameron, 1990). Put simply the question is this: to what extent is women's language use simply different from that of men or is it a product of the dominant position men have? Tannen is adding to this debate by questioning the extent to which one can simply read off from a 'linguistic strategy' that dominance or solidarity are being enacted (Coates and Cameron, 1989). There is also an ongoing debate in 'feminist linguistics' about the use of gender categories in relation to language use. Importantly, this debate questions the assertion made in the Tannen reading that gender can be treated as a 'cultural category'. For instance Cameron (1997) argues that the use of 'female' and 'male' as encompassing categories obscures the myriad of ideological functions that sex and gender are part of. Thus it also hides the complex links between ideologies and language practices.

The final reading brings together the various ideas in the previous readings. It is an attempt to demonstrate the usefulness of conversation analysis for feminist theory and practice. The reading critiques the arguments made for assertiveness 'just say no' training for young women designed to prevent 'date rape'. Importantly **Celia Kitzinger and Hannah Frith** overtly criticize what they see as the 'miscommunication' model of gender interactions. They see this model as based in the work of Tannen. On a general level the reading therefore discusses the links and differences between study of 'talk-in-interaction' and studies such as those of Tannen and Gumperz that connect language use and cultural groups. Their criticisms of Tannen and the training programmes are based on a countering of the claim that men and women 'miscommunicate' but rather that 'refusing' in general is a complex conversational activity which cannot be made simple by 'just saying no'.

Kitzinger and Frith begin their discussion with data from focus groups, a method linked to more ethnographic forms of research. They also make use of data from magazines and a 'handbook'. This type of data is similar to that employed by Tannen earlier and by various writers in Parts Three and Four of this Reader. The general 'qualitative' analysis of the focus group and printed data indicates that women find refusing unwanted sex complex and far from straightforward. These data also provide evidence that this difficulty and complexity is linked to issues around both identity and larger discourses about sexuality and sexual behaviours. Kitzinger and Frith go on to argue that 'saying no' is difficult in any context. The evidence from conversation analysis is that 'refusals' are often 'dispreferred responses' and as such require some account to be made by the person refusing. They are also likely to involve pauses, various prefaces and hedges, and palliatives or apologies and thus require much more conversational 'work' than the 'preferred' acceptance. Having made this claim Kitzinger and Frith return to their focus group data and demonstrate that the women interviewed have a complex understanding of refusals as dispreferred responses and the conversational work required to conduct them.

In the final part of the reading Kitzinger and Frith note that conversation analysis indicates there are problems with the claim that 'saying no' is key to 'date rape' prevention training. As we noted earlier what is heard and jointly developed is as important to a conversation as the overt 'meaning' of an utterance. Kitzinger and Frith provide a set of examples where a refusal is heard without the word 'no' or an overtly negative statement being made – in fact a silence can suffice to be heard as a refusal. Kitzinger and Frith conclude that the problem lies not in the articulation of refusals, or even in them being heard as refusals, but rather in the 'artful, complicit, and damning accomplishment' by which regularly interacting social groups (men and women in this case) 'attain' misunderstanding. The argument is therefore shifted to the 'disingenuous claims' of men not to understand or hear conventional conversational moves that indicate refusal. It also returns the debate to questions of male sexual violence rather than women's language use. Such an argument questions whether differences in genderlect (gender related language use) or sociolect (cultural group-related language use) alone explain problems of intercultural communication.

References

Atkinson, J.M. and Heritage, J. (eds) (1984) *Structures of Social Action: Studies in Conversation Analysis*, Cambridge, Cambridge University Press.

Boden, D. (1994) *The Business of Talk*, Cambridge, Polity Press.

Cameron D. (1997) 'Theoretical debates in feminist linguistics: questions of sex and gender' in R. Wodak (ed.) *Gender and Discourse*, London, Sage.

Cameron, D. (ed.) (1990) *The Feminist Critique of Language: A Reader*, London, Routledge.

Coates, J. (1986) *Women, Men and Language*, London, Longman.

Coates, J. and Cameron, D. (eds) (1989) *Women in Their Speech Communities*, London, Longman.

Drew, P. and Heritage, J. (eds) (1992) *Talk at Work: Interaction in Institutional Settings*, Cambridge, Cambridge University Press.

Duranti, A. and Goodwin, C. (eds) (1992) *Rethinking Context – Language as an Interactive Phenomenon*, Cambridge, Cambridge University Press.

Fairclough, N. (1992) *Critical Language Awareness*, Oxford, Polity.

Fairclough, N. (2001) 'The discourse of new labour: critical discourse analysis' in M. Wetherell, S. Taylor and S.J. Yates (eds) *Discourse as Data: A Guide For Analysis*, London, Sage in association with the Open University.

Goffman, E. (1959) *The Presentation of Self in Every-day Life*, New York, Doubleday.

Goffman, E. (1971) *Relations in Public: Micro Studies of the Public Order*, London, Allen Lane/ Penguin Press.

Goffman, E. (1972) *Interaction Ritual: Essays on Face-to-Face Behaviour*, London, Allen Lane.

Goffman, E. (1973) *Encounters*, London, Allen Lane/Penguin Press.

Goffman, E. (1974) 'Frame analysis: an essay on the organization of experience', Cambridge MA, Harvard University Press.

Goffman, E. (1981) *Forms of Talk*, Philadelphia PA, University of Pennsylvania Press.

Gumperz, J.J. (1982a) *Discourse Strategies*, Cambridge, Cambridge University Press.

Gumperz, J.J. (ed.) (1982b) *Language and Social Identity*, Cambridge, Cambridge University Press.

Gumperz, J.J. and Hymes, D. (eds) (1972) *Directions in Sociolinguistics; The Ethnography of Communication*, New York, Holt, Rinehart and Winston.

Halliday, M.A.K. (1978) *Language as Social Semiotic: The Social Interpretation of Language and Meaning*, London, Edward Arnold Ltd.

Hutchby, I. (1996) *Confrontation Talk: Arguments, Asymmetries and Power on Talk Radio*, Hillsdale, NJ, Erlbaum.

Hutchby, I. and Wooffitt, R. (1998) *Conversation Analysis: Principles, Practices and Applications*, Cambridge, Polity.

Hymes, D.H. (1974) *Foundations in Sociolinguistics*, Philadelphia, University of Pennsylvania Press.

Malinowski, B. (1923) 'The problem of meaning in primitive language' in C.K. Ogden and I.V. Richards (eds) *The Meaning of Meaning*, New York and London, Harcourt Brace, Kegan Paul Trench Trubner.

Sacks, H. (1972a) 'An initial investigation of the usability of conversational data for doing sociology' in D. Sudnow (ed.) *Studies in Social Interaction*, New York, The Free Press.

Sacks, H. (1972b) 'Notes on police assessment of moral character' in D. Sudnow (ed.) *Studies in Social Interaction*, New York, The Free Press.

Sacks, H. (1974) 'An analysis of the course of a joke's telling in conversation' in R. Bauman and J. Sherzer (eds) *Explorations in the Ethnography of Speaking*, New York, Cambridge University Press.

Sacks, H. (1975) 'Everyone has to lie' in M. Sanches and B. Blount (eds) *Sociocultural Dimensions of Language Use*, New York, Academic Press.

Sacks, H. (1979) 'Hotrodder: a revolutionary category' in G. Psathas (ed.) *Everyday Language: Studies in Ethnomethodology*, New York, Irvington Publishers.

Sacks, H. (1984a) 'Notes on methodology' in J.M. Atkinson and J. Heritage, *Structures of Social Action*, New York, Cambridge University Press.

Sacks, H. (1984b) 'On doing "being ordinary"' in J.M. Atkinson and J. Heritage, *Structures of Social Action*, New York, Cambridge University Press.

Sacks, H. (1992) 'Lectures on conversation', 2 vols, ed. G. Jefferson, Blackwell Publishers.

Sacks, H. and Schegloff, E. (1979) 'Two preferences in the organization of reference to persons in conversation and their interaction' in G. Psathas (ed.) *Everyday Language: Studies in Ethnomethodology*, New York, Irvington Publishers.

Sacks, H., Schegloff, E. and Jefferson, G. (1978) 'A simplest systematics for the organization of turn-taking for conversation' in J. Schenkein (ed.) *Studies in the Organization of Conversational Interaction*, New York, Academic Press.

Silverman, D. (1996) *Discourses of Counselling*, London, Sage.

Tannen, D. (1990) *You Just Don't Understand: Women and Men in Conversation*, New York, Ballantine.

Tannen, D. (1994) *Gender and Discourse*, New York, Oxford University.

Wooffitt, R. (1992) *Telling Tales of the Unexpected: Accounts of Paranormal Experiences*, Hemel Hempstead, Harvester.

Wooffitt, R. (2001) 'Researching psychic practitioners: conversation analysis' in M. Wetherell, S. Taylor and S.J. Yates (eds) *Discourse as Data: A Guide For Analysis*, London, Sage in association with the Open University.

Yates, S.J. (2001) 'Researching internet interaction: sociolinguistics and corpus analysis' in M. Wetherell, S. Taylor and S.J. Yates (eds) *Discourse as Data: A Guide For Analysis*, London, Sage in association with the Open University.

Footing

Erving Goffman

Source: Goffman, E. (1981) *Forms of Talk*, Oxford, Blackwell, Chapter 3.

Consider a journalistically reported strip of interaction, a news bureau release of 1973 on presidential doings.[1] The scene is the Oval Office, the participants an assemblage of government officers and newspaper reporters gathered in their professional capacities for a political ritual, the witnessing of the signing of a bill:

> WASHINGTON [UPI] – President Nixon, a gentleman of the old school, teased a newspaper woman yesterday about wearing slacks to the White House and made it clear that he prefers dresses on women.
>
> After a bill-signing ceremony in the Oval Office, the President stood up from his desk and in a teasing voice said to UPI's Helen Thomas: 'Helen, are you still wearing slacks? Do you prefer them actually? Every time I see girls in slacks it reminds me of China.'
>
> Miss Thomas, somewhat abashed, told the President that Chinese women were moving toward Western dress.
>
> 'This is not said in an uncomplimentary way, but slacks can do something for some people and some it can't.' He hastened to add, 'but I think you do very well. Turn around.'
>
> As Nixon, Attorney General Elliott L. Richardson, FBI Director Clarence Kelley and other high-ranking law enforcement officials smiling [*sic*], Miss Thomas did a pirouette for the President. She was wearing white pants, a navy blue jersey shirt, long white beads and navy blue patent leather shoes with red trim.
>
> Nixon asked Miss Thomas how her husband, Douglas Cornell, liked her wearing pants outfits.
>
> 'He doesn't mind,' she replied.
>
> 'Do they cost less than gowns?'
>
> 'No,' said Miss Thomas.
>
> 'Then change,' commanded the President with a wide grin as other reporters and cameramen roared with laughter.
>
> (*The Evening Bulletin* (Philadelphia), 1973)

This incident points to the power of the president to force an individual who is female from her occupational capacity into a sexual, domestic one during an occasion in which she (and the many women who could accord her the role of symbolic representative) might well be very concerned that she be given her full professional due, and that due only. And, of course, the incident points to a moment in gender politics when a president might unthinkingly exert such power. Behind this fact is something significant: the contemporary social definition that women must always be ready to receive comments on their 'appearance', the chief constraints being that the remarks should be favourable, delivered by someone with whom they are acquainted, and not interpretable as sarcasm. Implied, structurally, is that a woman must ever be ready to change ground, or, rather, have the ground changed for her, by virtue of being subject to becoming momentarily an object of approving attention, not – or not merely – a participant in it.

The Nixon sally can also remind us of some other things. In our society, whenever two acquainted individuals meet for business, professional, or service dealings, a period of 'small talk' may well initiate and terminate the transaction – a mini version of the 'preplay' and 'postplay' that bracket larger social affairs. [. . .] During the business proper of the encounter, the two interactants will presumably be in a more segmental relation, ordered by work requirements, functionally specific authority, and the like. Contrariwise, a planning session among the military may begin and end with a formal acknowledgment of rank, and in between shift into something closer to equalitarian decision making. In either case, in shifting in and out of the business at hand, a change of tone is involved, and an alteration in the social capacities in which the persons present claim to be active.

Finally, it might be observed that when such change of gears occurs among more than two persons, then a change commonly occurs regarding who is addressed. In the Nixon scene, Ms. Thomas is singled out as a specific recipient the moment that 'unserious' activity begins. (A change may also simultaneously occur in posture, here indeed very broadly with Mr. Nixon rising from his desk.)

The obvious candidate for illustrations of the Nixon shift comes from what linguists generally call 'code switching', code here referring to language or dialect. The work of John Gumperz and his colleagues provides a central source. A crude example may be cited:

> On one occasion, when we, as outsiders, stepped up to a group of locals engaged in conversation, our arrival caused a significant alteration in the casual posture of the group. Hands were removed from pockets and looks changed. Predictably, our remarks elicited a code switch marked simultaneously by a change in channel cues (i.e., sentence speed, rhythm, more hesitation pauses, etc.) and by a shift from (R) [a regional Norwegian dialect] to (B) [an official, standard form of Norwegian] grammar.
>
> (Blom & Gumperz, 1972: 424)

[. . .]

By 1976, in unpublished work on a community where Slovene and German are in active coexistence, matters are getting more delicate for Gumperz. Scraps of dialogue are collected between mothers and daughters, sisters and sisters, and code shifting is found to be present in almost every corner of conversational life. And Gumperz (1976) makes a stab at identifying what these shifts mark and how they function:

1 direct or reported speech;

2 selection of recipient;

3 interjections;

4 repetitions;

5 personal directness or involvement;

6 new and old information;

7 emphasis;

8 separation of topic and subject;

9 discourse type, e.g., lecture and discussion.

More important for our purposes here, Gumperz and his coworkers now also begin to look at code switching like behaviour that doesn't involve a code switch at all. Thus, from reconstituted notes on classroom observations, the Gumperzes provide three sequential statements by a teacher to a group of first-graders, the statements printed in listed form to mark the fact that three different stances were involved: the first a claim on the children's immediate behaviour, the second a review of experiences to come, and the third a side remark to a particular child (Cook-Gumperz and Gumperz, 1976: 8–9):

1 Now listen everybody.

2 At ten o'clock we'll have assembly. We'll all go out together and go to the auditorium and sit in the first two rows. Mr. Dock, the principal, is going to speak to us. When he comes in, sit quietly and listen carefully.

3 Don't wiggle your legs. Pay attention to what I'm saying.

The point being that, without access to bodily orientation and tone of voice, it would be easy to run the three segments into a continuous text and miss the fact that significant shifts in alignment of speaker to hearers were occurring.

I have illustrated through its changes what will be called 'footing'.[2] In rough summary:

1 Participant's alignment, or set, or stance, or posture, or projected self is somehow at issue.

2 The projection can be held across a strip of behaviour that is less long than a grammatical sentence, or longer, so sentence grammar won't help us all that much, although it seems clear that a cognitive unit of some kind is involved, minimally, perhaps, a 'phonemic clause'. Prosodic, not syntactic, segments are implied.

3 A continuum must be considered, from gross changes in stance to the most subtle shifts in tone that can be perceived.

4 For speakers, code switching is usually involved, and if not this then at least the sound markers that linguists study: pitch, volume, rhythm, stress, tonal quality.

5   The bracketing of a 'higher level' phase or episode of interaction is commonly involved, the new footing having a liminal role, serving as a buffer between two more substantially sustained episodes.

A change in footing implies a change in the alignment we take up to ourselves and the others present as expressed in the way we manage the production or reception of an utterance. A change in our footing is another way of talking about a change in our frame for events. This paper is largely concerned with pointing out that participants over the course of their speaking constantly change their footing, these changes being a persistent feature of natural talk.

[. . .] In this paper I want to make a pass at analysing the structural underpinnings of changes in footing. The task will be approached by re-examining the primitive notions of speaker and hearer, and some of our unstated presuppositions about spoken interaction.

Traditional analysis of saying and what gets said seems tacitly committed to the following paradigm: two and only two individuals are engaged together in it. During any moment in time, one will be speaking his own thoughts on a matter and expressing his own feelings, however circumspectly; the other listening. The full concern of the person speaking is given over to speaking and to its reception, the concern of the person listening to what is being said. The discourse, then, would be the main involvement of both of them. [. . .] Over the course of the interaction the roles of speaker and hearer will be interchanged in support of a statement–reply format, the acknowledged current-speaking right – the floor – passing back and forth. Finally, what is going on is said to be conversation or talk.

The two person arrangement here described seems in fact to be fairly common, and a good thing, too, being the one that informs the underlying imagery we have about face-to-face interaction. And it is an arrangement for which the terms 'speaker' and 'hearer' fully and neatly apply – lay terms here being perfectly adequate for all technical needs. Thus, it is felt that without requiring a basic change in the terms of the analysis, any modification of conditions can be handled: additional participants can be added, the ensemble can be situated in the immediate presence of nonparticipants, and so forth.

It is my belief that the language that students have drawn on for talking about speaking and hearing is not well adapted to its purpose. And I believe this is so both generally and for a consideration of something like footing. It is too gross to provide us with much of a beginning. It takes global folk categories (like speaker and hearer) for granted instead of decomposing them into smaller, analytically coherent elements.

For example, the terms 'speaker' and 'hearer' imply that sound alone is at issue, when, in fact, it is obvious that sight is organizationally very significant too, sometimes even touch. In the management of turn-taking, in the assessment of reception through visual back-channel cues, in the paralinguistic function of gesticulation, in the synchrony of gaze shift, in the provision of evidence of attention (as in the middle-distance look), in the assessment of engrossment through evidence of side-involvements and facial expression – in all of these ways it is apparent that sight is crucial, both for the speaker and for the hearer.

For the effective conduct of talk, speaker and hearer had best be in a position to *watch* each other. The fact that telephoning can be practicable without the visual channel, and that written transcriptions of talk also seem effective, is not to be taken as a sign that, indeed, conveying words is the only thing that is crucial, but that reconstruction and transformation are very powerful processes.

[. . .]

Turn first, then, to the notion of a hearer (or a recipient, or a listener). The process of auditing what a speaker says and following the gist of his remarks – hearing in the communication-system sense – is from the start to be distinguished from the social slot in which this activity usually occurs, namely, official status as a ratified participant in the encounter. For plainly, we might not be listening when indeed we have a ratified social place in the talk, and this in spite of normative expectations on the part of the speaker. Correspondingly, it is evident that when we are not an official participant in the encounter, we might still be following the talk closely, in one of two socially different ways: either we have purposely engineered this, resulting in 'eavesdropping', or the opportunity has unintentionally and inadvertently come about, as in 'overhearing'. In brief, a ratified participant may not be listening, and someone listening may not be a ratified participant.

Now consider that much of talk takes place in the visual and aural range of persons who are not ratified participants and whose access to the encounter, however minimal, is itself perceivable by the official participants. These adventitious participants are 'bystanders'. Their presence should be considered the rule, not the exception. [. . .] Ordinarily, however, we bystanders practice the situational ethic which obliges us to warn those who are, that they are, unknowingly accessible, obliging us also to enact a show of disinterest, and by disattending and withdrawing ecologically to minimize our actual access to the talk. [. . .] But however polite, bystanders will still be able to glean some information; for example, the language spoken, 'who' (whether in categorical or biographical terms) is in an encounter with whom, which of the participants is speaker and which are listeners, what the general mood of the conversational circle is, and so forth. Observe, too, that in managing the accessibility of an encounter both its participants and its bystanders will rely heavily on sight, not sound, providing another reason why our initial two-party paradigm is inadequate. [. . .]

The hearing sustained by our paradigmatic listener turns out to be an ambiguous act in an additional sense. The ratified hearer in two-person talk is necessarily also the 'addressed' one, that is, the one to whom the speaker addresses his visual attention and to whom, incidentally, he expects to turn over the speaking role. But obviously two-person encounters, however common, are not the only kind; three or more official participants are often found. In such cases it will often be feasible for the current speaker to address his remarks to the circle as a whole, encompassing all his hearers in his glance, according them something like equal status. But, more likely, the speaker will, at least during periods of his talk, address his remarks to one listener, so that among official hearers one must distinguish the addressed recipient from 'unaddressed' ones.

Observe again that this structurally important distinction between official recipients is often accomplished exclusively through visual cues, although vocatives are available for managing it through audible ones.

The relation(s) among speaker, addressed recipient, and unaddressed recipient(s) are complicated, significant, and not much explored. An ideal in friendly conversation is that no one participant serve more frequently, or for a longer summation of time, in any one of these three roles, than does any other participants. In practice, such an arrangement is hardly to be found, and every possible variation is met with. Even when a particular pair holds the floor for an extended period, the structural implication can vary; for example, their talk can move to private topics and increasingly chill the involvement of the remaining participants, or it can be played out as a display for the encircling hearers – a miniature version of the arrangement employed in TV talk shows, or a lawyer's examination of a witness before a jury.

Once the dyadic limits of talk are breached, and one admits bystanders and/or more than one ratified recipient to the scene, then 'subordinate communication' becomes a recognizable possibility: talk that is manned, timed, and pitched to constitute a perceivedly limited interference to what might be called the 'dominating communication' in its vicinity. Indeed, there are a great number of work settings where informal talk is subordinated to the task at hand, the accommodation being not to another conversation but to the exigencies of work in progress.

Those maintaining subordinate communication relative to a dominant state of talk may make no effort to conceal that they are communicating in this selective way, and apparently no pointed effort to conceal what it is they are communicating. Thus 'byplay': subordinated communication of a subset of ratified participants; 'crossplay': communication between ratified participants and bystanders across the boundaries of the dominant encounter; 'sideplay': respectfully hushed words exchanged entirely among bystanders. [. . .]

When an attempt *is* made to conceal subordinate communication, 'collusion' occurs, whether within the boundaries of an encounter (collusive byplay) or across these boundaries (collusive crossplay) or entirely outside the encounter, as when two bystanders surreptitiously editorialize on what they are overhearing (collusive sideplay). Collusion is accomplished variously: by concealing the subordinate communication, by affecting that the words the excolluded can't hear are innocuous, or by using allusive words ostensibly meant for all participants, but whose additional meaning will be caught by only some.
[. . .]

There remains to consider the dynamics of ratified participation. Plainly, a distinction must be drawn between opening or closing an encounter, and joining or leaving an ongoing one; conventional practices are to be found for distinguishably accomplishing both. And plainly, two differently manned encounters can occur under conditions of mutual accessibility, each bystanding the other. At point here, however, is another issue: the right to leave and to join, taken together, imply circumstances in which participants will shift from one encounter to another. At a 'higher' level, one must also consider the possibility of an encounter of four or more participants splitting, and of separate encounters merging. And it appears that in some microecological social circumstances these various changes are frequent. Thus, at table during convivial dinners of eight or so participants, marked instability of participation is often found. Here a speaker may feel it necessary to police his listenership, not so much to guard against eavesdroppers (for, indeed, at table overhearing hardly needs to be concealed), as to bring back strays and encourage incipient joiners. In such environments, interruption, pitch raising and trunk orientation seem to acquire a special function and significance. [. . .] Another example of structural instability is to be observed when couples meet. What had been two 'withs' provide the personnel for a momentarily inclusive encounter, which can then bifurcate so that each member of one of the entering withs can personally greet a member of the other with, after which greeting, partners are exchanged and another pair of greeting interchanges follows, and after *this*, a more sustained regrouping can occur.

Consider now that, in dealing with the notion of bystanders, a shift was tacitly made from the encounter as a point of reference to something somewhat wider, namely, the 'social situation', defining this as the full physical arena in which persons present are in sight and sound of one another. [. . .] For it turns out that routinely it is relative to a gathering, not merely to an encounter, that the interactional facts will have to be considered. Plainly, for example, speakers will modify how they speak, if not what they say, by virtue of conducting their talk in visual and aural range of nonparticipants. [. . .]

Perhaps the clearest evidence of the structural significance of the social situation for talk (and, incidentally, of the limitation of the conventional model of talk) is to be found in our verbal behavior when we are by ourselves yet in the immediate presence of passing strangers. Proscriptive rules of communication oblige us to desist in use of speech and wordlike, articulated sounds. But in fact there is a wide variety of circumstances in which we will audibly address statements to ourselves, blurt out imprecations, and utter 'response cries', such as *Oops!*, *Eek!*, and the like (Goffman, 1978). These vocalizations can be shown to have a self-management function, providing evidence to everyone who can hear that our observable plight is not something that should be taken to define us. To that end the volume of the sounding will be adjusted, so that those in the social situation who can perceive our plight will also hear our comment on it. No doubt, then, that we seek some response from those who can hear us, but not a specific reply. No doubt the intent is to provide information to everyone in range, but without taking the conversational floor to do so. What is sought is not hearers but overhearers, albeit intended ones. Plainly, the substantive natural unit of which self-directed remarks and response cries are a part need not be a conversation, whatever else it might be.

Finally, observe that if one starts with a particular individual in the act of speaking – a cross-sectional instantaneous view – one can describe the role or function of all the several members of the encompassing social gathering from this point of reference (whether they are ratified participants of the talk or not), couching the description in the concepts that have been reviewed. The relation of any one such member to this utterance can be called his 'participation status' relative to it, and that of all the persons in the gathering the 'participation framework' for that moment of speech. The same two terms can be employed when the point of reference is shifted from a given particular speaker to

something wider: all the activity in the situation itself. The point of all this, of
course, is that an utterance does not carve up the world beyond the speaker into
precisely two parts, recipients and non-recipients, but rather opens up an array
of structurally differentiated possibilities, establishing the participation
framework in which the speaker will be guiding his delivery.

I have argued that the notion of hearer or recipient is rather crude. In so doing,
however, I restricted myself to something akin to ordinary conversation. But
conversation is not the only context of talk. Obviously talk can (in modern
society) take the form of a platform monologue, as in the case of political
addresses, stand-up comedy routines, lectures, dramatic recitations, and poetry
readings. These entertainments involve long stretches of words coming from a
single speaker who has been given a relatively large set of listeners and exclusive
claim to the floor. Talk, after all, can occur at the town podium, as well as the
town pump.

And when talk comes from the podium, what does the hearing is an audience,
not a set of fellow conversationalists. Audiences hear in a way special to them.
Perhaps in conjunction with the fact that audience members are further removed
physically from the speaker than a co-conversationalist might be, they have the
right to examine the speaker directly, with an openness that might be offensive
in conversation. [. . .] Indeed, and fundamentally, the role of the audience is to
appreciate remarks made, not to reply in any direct way. They are to conjure up
what a reply might be, but not utter it; 'back-channel' response alone is what is
meant to be available to them. They give the floor but (except during the
question period) rarely get it.
    [. . .]
    Still further multiplicities of meaning must be addressed. Podiums are often
placed on a stage; this said, it becomes plain that podiums and their limpets are
not the only things one finds there. Stage actors are found there, too, performing
speeches to one another in character, all arranged so they can be listened in on
by those who are off the stage. We resolutely use one word, 'audience', to refer
to those who listen to a political speech and those who watch a play; but again
the many ways in which these two kinds of hearers are in the same position
shouldn't blind one to the very important ways in which their circumstances
differ. A town speaker's words are meant for his audience and are spoken to
them; were a reply to be made, it would have to come from these listeners, and
indeed, as suggested, signs of agreement and disagreement are often in order. It
is presumably because there are so many persons in an audience that direct
queries and replies must be omitted, or at least postponed to a time when the
speech itself can be considered over. Should a member of the audience assay to
reply in words to something that a speaker in midspeech says, the latter can elect
to answer and, if he knows what he's about, sustain the reality he is engaged in.
But the words addressed by one character in a play to another (at least in
modern Western dramaturgy) are eternally sealed off from the audience,
belonging entirely to a self-enclosed, make-believe realm – although the actors
who are performing these characters (and who in a way are also cut off from the
dramatic action) might well appreciate signs of audience attentiveness.
    [. . .]

And from here one can go on to still more difficult cases. There are, for example, church congregations of the revivalist type wherein an active interchange is sustained of calls and answers between minister and churchgoers. And there are lots of social arrangements in which a single speaking slot is organizationally central, and yet neither a stage event with its audience, nor a conversation with its participants, is taking place. Rather, something binding is: court trials, auctions, briefing sessions, and course lectures are examples. Although these podium occasions of binding talk can often support participants who are fully in the audience role, they also necessarily support another class of hearers, ones who are more committed by what is said and have more right to be heard than ordinarily occurs in platform entertainments.

Whether one deals with podium events of the recreational, congregational, or binding kind, a participation framework specific to it will be found, and the array of these will be different from, and additional to, the one generic to conversation. The participation framework paradigmatic of two-person talk doesn't tell us very much about participation frameworks as such.

It is claimed that to appreciate how many different kinds of hearers there are, first one must move from the notion of a conversational encounter to the social situation in which the encounter occurs; and then one must see that, instead of being part of a conversation, words can be part of a podium occasion where doings other than talk are often featured, words entering at the beginning and ending of phases of the programme, to announce, welcome, and thank. This might still incline one to hold that when words pass among a small number of persons, the prototypical unit to consider is nevertheless a conversation or a chat. However, this assumption must be questioned, too.

In canonical talk, the participants seem to share a focus of cognitive concern – a common subject matter – but less simply so a common focus of visual attention. The subject of attention is clear, the object of it less so. Listeners are obliged to avoid staring directly at the speaker too long lest they violate his territoriality, and yet they are encouraged to direct their visual attention so as to obtain gesticulatory cues to his meaning and provide him with evidence that he is being attended. It is as if they were to look into the speaker's words, which, after all, cannot be seen. It is as if they must look at the speaker, but not see him.

But, of course, it is possible for a speaker to direct the visual attention of his hearers to some passing object – say, a car or a view – in which case for a moment there will be a sharp difference between speaker and both cognitive and visual attention. And the same is true when this focus of both kinds of attention is a person, as when two individuals talking to each other remark on a person whom they see asleep or across the street. And so one must consider another possibility: when a patient shows a physician where something hurts, or a customer points to where a try-on shoe pinches, or a tailor demonstrates how the new jacket fits, the individual who is the object of attention is also a fully qualified participant. The rub is that in lots of these latter occasions a conversation is not really the context of the utterance; a physically elaborated, nonlinguistic undertaking is, one in which nonlinguistic events may have the floor. [. . .]

One standard nonlinguistic context for utterances is the perfunctory service contact, where a server and client come together momentarily in a coordinated transaction, often involving money on one side and goods or services on the other. Another involves those passing contacts between two strangers wherein the time is told, the salt is passed, or a narrow, crowded passageway is negotiated. Although a full-fledged ritual interchange is often found in these moments, physical transactions of some kind form the meaningful context and the relevant unit for analysis; the words spoken, whether by one participant or two, are an integral part of a mutually coordinated physical undertaking, not a talk. Ritual is so often truncated in these settings because it is nonconversational work that is being done. It is the execution of this work, not utterances, that will ordinarily be the chief concern of the participants. And it is when a hitch occurs in what would otherwise have been the routine interdigitation of their acts that a verbal interchange between them is most likely.

A similar picture can be seen in extended service transactions. Take, for example, mother–child pediatric consultations in Scottish public health clinics, as recently reported by Strong (1979; esp. chap. 6). Here a mother's business with a doctor (when she finally gets her turn) is apparently bracketed with little small talk, very little by way of preplay and postplay, although the child itself may be the recipient of a few ritual solicitudes. The mother sits before the doctor's desk and briefly answers such questions as he puts her, waiting patiently, quietly, and attentively between questions. She is on immediate call, poised to speak, but speaking only when spoken to, almost as well behaved as the machine that is of so much use to airline ticketers. The physician, for his part, intersperses his unceremoniously addressed queries with note-taking, note-reading, thoughtful musings, instruction to students, physical manipulation of the child, verbal exchanges with his nurse and colleagues, and movements away from his desk to get at such things as files and equipment – all of which actions appear warranted by his institutional role if not by the current examination. The mother's answers will sometimes lead the doctor to follow up with a next question, but often instead to some other sort of act on his part. For his social and professional status allows him to be very businesslike; he is running through the phases of an examination, or checklist, not a conversation, and only a scattering of items require a mother's verbal contribution. And indeed, the mother may not know with any specificity what any of the doctor's acts are leading up to or getting at, her being 'in on' the instrumentally meaningful sequence of events in no way being necessary for her contribution to it. So although she fits her turns at talk, and what she says, to the doctor's questionings (as in the organization of talk), what immediately precedes and what immediately follows these exchanges is not a speech environment. What is being sustained, then, is not a state of talk but a state of inquiry, and it is this latter to which utterances first must be referred if one is to get at their organization significance.

[. . .]

One clearly finds, then, that coordinated task activity – not conversation – is what lots of words are part of. A presumed common interest in effectively pursuing the activity at hand, in accordance with some sort of overall plan for doing so, is the contextual matrix which renders many utterances, especially brief ones, meaningful. And these are not unimportant words; it takes a linguist to overlook them.

It is apparent, then, that utterances can be an intimate, functionally integrated part of something that involves other words only in a peripheral and functionally optional way. A naturally bounded unit may be implied, but not one that could be called a speech event.

Beginning with the conversational paradigm, I have tried to decompose the global notion of hearer or recipient, and I have incidentally argued that the notion of a conversational encounter does not suffice in dealing with the context in which words are spoken; a social occasion involving a podium may be involved, or no speech event at all, and, in any case, the whole social situation, the whole surround, must always be considered. Provided, thus, has been a lengthy gloss on Hymes's admonition: 'The common dyadic model of speaker-hearer specifies sometimes too many, sometimes too few, sometimes the wrong participants' (1974: 54).

It is necessary now to look at the remaining element of the conversational paradigm, the notion of *speaker*.

In canonical talk, one of the two participants moves his lips up and down to the accompaniment of his own facial (and sometimes bodily) gesticulations, and words can be heard issuing from the locus of his mouth. [. . .] He is functioning as an 'animator'. Animator and recipient are part of the same level and mode of analysis, two terms cut from the same cloth, not social roles in the full sense so much as functional nodes in a communication system.

But, of course, when one uses the term 'speaker', one very often beclouds the issue, having additional things in mind, this being one reason why 'animator' cannot comfortably be termed a social role, merely an analytical one.

Sometimes one has in mind that there is an 'author' of the words that are heard, that is, someone who has selected the sentiments that are being expressed and the words in which they are encoded.

Sometimes one has in mind that a 'principal' (in the legalistic sense) is involved, that is, someone whose position is established by the words that are spoken, someone whose beliefs have been told, someone who is committed to what the words say. Note that one deals in this case not so much with a body or mind as with a person active in some particular social identity or role, some special capacity as a member of a group, office, category, relationship, association, or whatever, some socially based source of self-identification. Often this will mean that the individual speaks, explicitly or implicitly, in the name of 'we', not 'I' (but not for the reasons Queen Victoria or Nixon felt they had), the 'we' including more than the self (Moerman, 1968: 153–169; Spiegelberg, 1973: 129–156). And, of course, the same individual can rapidly alter the social role in which he is active, even though his capacity as animator and author remains constant – what in committee meetings is called 'changing hats'. (This, indeed, is what occurs during a considerable amount of code switching, as Gumperz has amply illustrated.) In thus introducing the name or capacity in which he speaks, the speaker goes some distance in establishing a corresponding reciprocal basis of identification for those to whom this stand-taking is addressed. To a degree, then, to select the capacity in which we are to be active is to select (or to attempt to select) the capacity in which the recipients of our action are present (Weinstein and Deutschberger, 1963: 454–466). All of this work is consolidated by naming practices and, in many languages, through choice among available second-person pronouns.

The notions of animator, author, and principal, taken together, can be said to tell us about the 'production format' of an utterance.

When one uses the term 'speaker', one often implies that the individual who animates is formulating his own text and staking out his own position through it: animator, author, and principal are one. What could be more natural? So natural indeed that I cannot avoid continuing to use the term 'speaker' in this sense, let alone the masculine pronoun as the unmarked singular form.

But, of course, the implied overlaying of roles has extensive institutionalized exceptions. Plainly, *reciting* a fully memorized text or *reading aloud* from a prepared script allows us to animate words we had no hand in formulating, and to express opinions, beliefs, and sentiments we do not hold. We can openly speak *for* someone else and *in* someone else's words, as we do, say, in reading a deposition or providing a simultaneous translation of a speech – the latter an interesting example because so often the original speaker's words, although ones that person commits himself to, are ones that someone else wrote for him. As will later be seen, the tricky problem is that often when we do engage in 'fresh talk', that is, the extemporaneous, ongoing formulation of a text under the exigency of immediate response to our current situation, it is not true to say that we always speak our own words and ourself take the position to which these words attest.

A final consideration. Just as we can listen to a conversation without being ratified hearers (or be ratified to listen but fail to do so), so as ratified listeners – participants who don't now have the floor – we can briefly interject our words and feelings into the temporal interstices within or between interchanges sustained by other participants (Goffman, 1976: 275–276). Moreover, once others tacitly have given us the promise of floor time to recount a tale or to develop an argument, we may tolerate or even invite kibitzing, knowing that there is a good chance that we can listen for a moment without ceasing to be the speaker, just as others can interrupt for a moment without ceasing to be listeners.

Given an utterance as a starting point of inquiry, I have recommended that our common-sense notions of hearer and speaker are crude, the first potentially concealing a complex differentiation of participation statuses, and the second, complex questions of production format.

The delineation of participation framework and production format provides a structural basis for analysing changes in footing. At least it does for the changes in footing described at the beginning of this paper. But the view that results systematically simplifies the bearing of participation frameworks and production formats on the structure of utterances. Sturdy, sober, sociological matters are engaged, but the freewheeling, self-referential character of speech receives no place. The essential fancifulness of talk is missed. And for these fluidities linguistics, not sociology, provides the lead. It is these matters that open up the possibility of finding some structural basis for even the subtlest shifts in footing.

A beginning can be made by examining the way statements are constructed, especially in regard to 'embedding', a tricky matter made more so by how easy it is to confuse it with an analytically quite different idea, the notion of multiple social roles already considered in connection with 'principal'.

You hear an individual grunt out an unadorned, naked utterance, hedged and parenthesized with no qualifier or pronoun, such as:

a directive: Shut the window.
an interrogative: Why here?
a declarative: The rain has started.
a commissive: The job will be done by three o'clock.

Commonly the words are heard as representing in some direct way the *current* desire, belief, perception, or intention of whoever animates the utterance. The current self of the person who animates seems inevitably involved in some way – what might be called the 'addressing self'. So, too, deixis in regard to time and place is commonly involved. One is close here to the expressive communication we think of as the kind an animal could manage through the small vocabulary of sound-gestures available to it. Observe that when such utterances are heard they are still heard as coming from an individual who not only animates the words but is active in a *particular* social capacity, the words taking their authority from this capacity.

Many, if not most, utterances, however, are not constructed in this fashion. Rather, as speaker, we represent ourselves through the offices of a personal pronoun, typically 'I', and it is thus a *figure* – a figure in a statement – that serves as the agent, a protagonist in a *described* scene, a 'character' in an anecdote, someone, after all, who belongs to the world that is spoken about, not the world in which the speaking occurs. And once this format is employed, an astonishing flexibility is created.

For one thing, hedges and qualifiers introduced in the form of performative modal verbs (I 'wish', 'think', 'could', 'hope', etc.) become possible, introducing some distance between the figure and its avowal. Indeed, a double distance is produced, for presumably some part of us unconditionally stands behind our conditional utterance, else we would have to say something like 'I think that I think . . .' Thus, when we slip on a word and elect to further interrupt the flow by interjecting a remedial statement such as, 'Whoops! I got that wrong . . .' or 'I meant to say . . .' we are projecting ourselves as animators into the talk. But this is a figure, nonetheless, and not the actual animator; it is merely a figure that comes closer than most to the individual who animates its presentation. And, of course, a point about these apologies for breaks in fluency is that they themselves can be animated fluently, exhibiting a property markedly different from the one they refer to, reminding one that howsoever we feel obliged to describe ourselves, we need not include in this description the capacity and propensity to project such descriptions. [. . .]

Second, as Hockett (1963: 11) recommends, unrestricted displacement in time and place becomes possible, such that our reference can be to what we did, wanted, thought, etc., at some distant time and place, when, incidentally, we were active in a social capacity we may currently no longer enjoy and an identity we no longer claim. It is perfectly true that when we say:

I said shut the window

we can mean almost exactly what we would have meant had we uttered the unadorned version:

Shut the window

as a repetition of a prior command. But if we happen to be recounting a tale of something that happened many years ago, when we were a person we consider we no longer are, then the 'I' in 'I said shut the window' is linked to us – the person present – merely through biographical continuity, something that much or little can be made of, and nothing more immediate than that. In which case, two animators can be said to be involved: the one who is physically animating the sounds that are heard, and an embedded animator, a figure in a statement who is present only in a world that is being told about, not in the world in which the current telling takes place. (Embedded authors and principals are also possible.) Following the same argument, one can see that by using second or third person in place of first person we can tell of something someone *else* said, someone present or absent, someone human or mythical. We can embed an entirely different speaker into our utterance. For it is as easy to cite what someone else said as to cite oneself. Indeed, when queried as to precisely what someone said, we can reply quotatively:

Shut the window

and, although quite unadorned, this statement will be understood as something someone other than we, the current and actual animator, said. Presumably, 'He (or "she") said' is implied but not necessarily stated.

Once embedding is admitted as a possibility, then it is an easy step to see that multiple embeddings will be possible, as in the following:

To the best of my recollection,
(1)   I think that
(2)   I said
(3)   I once lived that sort of life.

where (1) reflects something that is currently true of the individual who animates (the 'addressing self'), (2) an embedded animator who is an earlier incarnation of the present speaker and (3) is a doubly embedded figure, namely, a still earlier incarnation of an earlier incarnation.

Although linguists have provided us with very useful treatments of direct and indirect quotation, they have been less helpful in the question of how else, as animators, we can convey words that are not our own. For example, if someone repeatedly tells us to shut the window, we can finally respond by repeating his words in a strident pitch, enacting a satirical version of his utterance ('say-foring'). In a similar way we can mock an accent or dialect, projecting a stereotyped figure more in the manner that stage actors do than in the manner that mere quotation provides. So, too, without much warning, we can corroborate our own words with an adage or saying, the understanding being that fresh talk has momentarily ceased and an anonymous authority wider and different from ourselves is being suddenly invoked (Laberge and Sankoff, 1979; esp. sec. 3). If these playful projections are to be thought of in terms of embeddings, then stage acting and recitation must be thought of as forms of embedded action, too. Interestingly, it seems very much the case that in socializing infants linguistically, in introducing them to words and utterances, we from the very beginning teach them to use talk in this self-dissociated, fanciful way.

It should be clear, then, that the significance of production format cannot be dealt with unless one faces up to the embedding function of much talk. For obviously, when we shift from saying something ourselves to reporting what someone else said, we are changing our footing. And so, too, when we shift from reporting our current feelings, the feelings of the 'addressing self', to the feelings we once had but no longer espouse. (Indeed, a code switch sometimes functions as a mark of this shift.)

Final points. As suggested, when as speaker we project ourselves in a current and locally active capacity, then our coparticipants in the encounter are the ones who will have their selves partly determined correspondingly. But in the case of a replay of a past event, the self we select for ourself can only 'altercast' the other figures *in the story*, leaving the hearers of the replay undetermined in that regard. *They* are cast into recipients of a bit of narrative, and this will be much the same sort of self whomsoever we people our narrative with, and in whatsoever capacity they are there active. The statuses 'narrator' and 'story listener', which would seem to be of small significance in terms of the overall social structure, turn out, then, to be of considerable importance in conversation, for they provide a footing to which a very wide range of speakers and hearers can briefly shift. (Admittedly, if a listener is also a character in the story he is listening to, as in the millions of mild recriminations communicated between intimates, then he is likely to have more than a mere listener's concern with the tale.)

[. . .]

It was recommended that one can get at the structural basis of footing by breaking up the primitive notions of hearer and speaker into more differentiated parts, namely, participation framework and production format. Then it was suggested that this picture must itself be complicated by the concept of embedding and an understanding of the layering effect that seems to be an essential outcome of the production process in speaking. But this complication itself cannot be clearly seen unless one appreciates another aspect of embedding, one that linguistic analysis hasn't much prepared us for, namely, the sense in which participation frameworks are subject to transformation. For it turns out that, in something like the ethological sense, we quite routinely ritualize participation frameworks; that is, we self-consciously transplant the participation arrangement that is natural in one social situation into an interactional environment in which it isn't. In linguistic terms, we not only embed utterances, we embed interaction arrangements.

Take collusion, for example. This arrangement may not itself be common, but common, surely, is apparently unserious collusion broadly played out with winks and elbow nudges in the obviously open presence of the excolluded. Innuendo is also a common candidate for playful transformation, the target of the slight meant to understand that a form is being used unseriously – a practice sometimes employed to convey an opinion that could not safely be conveyed through actual innuendo, let alone direct statement. The shielding of the mouth with the hand, already a ritualized way of marking a byplay during large meetings, is brought into small conversational circles to mark a communication as having the character of an aside but here with no one to be excluded from it. (I have seen an elderly woman in a quiet street talking about neighbourhood business to the man next door and then, in termination of the encounter, bisect her mouth with the five stiff fingers of her right hand and out of one side remark on how his geraniums were growing, the use of this gesture, apparently, marking her appreciation that to play her inquiry straight would be directly to invoke a shared interest and competency, not a particularly masculine one, and hence a similarity her neighbour might be disinclined to confront.) Or witness the way in which the physical contact, focusing tone, and loving endearments appropriate within the privacy of a courtship encounter can be performed in fun to an unsuitable candidate as a set piece to set into the focus of attention of a wider convivial circle. Or, in the same sort of circle, how we can respond to what a speaker says to an addressed recipient as though we weren't ratified coparticipants, but bystanders engaged in irreverent sideplay. Or, even when two individuals are quite alone together and cannot possibly be overheard, how one may mark the confidential and disclosive status of a bit of gossip by switching into a whisper voice. I think there is no doubt that a considerable amount of natural conversation is laminated in the manner these illustrations suggest; in any case, conversation is certainly vulnerable to such lamination. And each increase or decrease in layering – each movement closer to or further from the 'literal' – carries with it a change in footing.

Once it is seen that a participation framework can be parenthesized and set into an alien environment, it should be evident that all the participation frameworks earlier described as occurring outside of conversation – that is, arrangements involving an audience or no official recipient at all – are themselves candidates for this reframing process; they, too, can be reset into conversational talk. And, of course, with each such embedding a change of footing occurs. The private, ruminative self-talk we may employ among strangers when our circumstances suddenly require explaining, we can playfully restage in conversation, not so much projecting the words, but projecting a dumbfounded person projecting the words. So, too, on such occasions, we can momentarily affect a podium speech register, or provide a theatrical version (burlesqued, melodramatic) of an aside. All of which, of course, provides extra warrant – indeed, perhaps, the main warrant – for differentiating various participation frameworks in the first place.

It is true, then, that the frameworks in which words are spoken pass far beyond ordinary conversation. But it is just as true that these frameworks are brought back into conversation, acted out in a setting which they initially transcended. What nature divides, talk frivolously embeds, insets, and intermingles. As dramatists can put any world on their stage, so we can enact any participation framework and production format in our conversation.

I have dealt till now with *changes* in footing as though the individual were involved merely in switching from one stance or alignment to another. But this image is itself too mechanical and too easy. It is insufficiently responsive to the way embedding and ritualization work. For often it seems that when we change voice – whether to speak for another aspect of ourselves or for someone else, or to lighten our discourse with a darted enactment of some alien interaction arrangement – we are not so much terminating the prior alignment as holding it in abeyance with the understanding that it will almost immediately be reengaged. So, too, when we give up the floor in a conversation, thereby taking up the footing of a recipient (addressed or otherwise), we can be warranted in expecting to reenter the speaker role on the same footing from which we left it. As suggested, this is clearly the case when a narrator allows hearers to 'chip in', but such perceivedly temporary foregoing of one's position is also to be found when storytelling isn't featured. So it must be allowed that we can hold the same footing across several of our turns at talk. And within one alignment, another can be fully enclosed. In truth, in talk it seems routine that, while firmly standing on two feet, we jump up and down on another.

Which should prepare us for those institutional niches in which a hard-pressed functionary is constrained to routinely sustain more than one state of talk simultaneously. Thus, throughout an auction, an auctioneer may intersperse the utterances he directs to the bidding audience with several streams of out-of-frame communication – reports on each sale spoken through a microphone to a recording clerk in another room, instructions to assistants on the floor, and (less routinely) greetings to friends and responses to individual buyers who approach with quiet requests for an updating. Nor need there be one dominant state of talk and the rest styled as asides respectfully inserted at junctures. For example, in a medical research/training facility (as reported in a forthcoming paper by Tannen and Wallat), a pediatrician may find she must continuously switch code, now addressing her youthful patient in 'motherese', now sustaining a conversation-like exchange with the mother, now turning to the video camera to provide her trainee audience with a running account couched in the register of medical reporting. Here one deals with the capacity of different classes of participants to by-stand the current stream of communication whilst 'on hold' for the attention of the pivotal person to reengage them. And one deals with the capacity of a dexterous speaker to jump back and forth, keeping different circles in play.

Notes

1   Grateful acknowledgement is made to *Semiotica*, where this paper first appeared (25[1979]: 1–29).
2   An initial statement appears in Goffman (1974: 496–559).

References

Abercrombie, D. (1965) *Conversation and Spoken Prose: Studies in Phonetics and Linguistics*, London, Oxford University Press.

Blom, J-P. and Gumperz, J.J. (1972) 'Social meaning in linguistic structure: code-switching in Norway' in J. Gumperz and D. Hymes (eds) *Directions in Sociolinguistics*, New York, Holt, Rinehart and Winston.

Cook-Gumperz, J. and Gumperz, J. (1976) 'Context in children's speech' in J. Cook-Gumperz and J. Gumperz, *Papers on Language and Context* (Working Paper 46), Berkeley, Language Behavior Research Laboratory, University of California, Berkeley.

The Evening Bulletin (Philadelphia), (1973) August 7.

Fisher, L.E. (1976) 'Dropping remarks and the Barbadian audience', *American Ethnologist*, vol. 3, pp. 227–42.

Goffman, E. (1974) *Frame Analysis*, New York, Harper and Row.

Goffman, E. (1976) 'Replies and responses', *Language in Society*, vol. 5, pp. 257–313.

Goffman, E. (1978) 'Response cries', *Language*, vol. 54, no. 4.

Gossen, G.H. (1976) 'Verbal dueling in Chamula' in B. Kirshenblatt-Gimblett (ed.) *Speech Play*, Philadelphia, University of Pennsylvania Press.

Gumperz, J. (1976) 'Social networks and language shift' in J. Cook-Gumperz and J. Gumperz, *Papers on Language and Context* (Working Paper 46), Berkeley, Language Behavior Research Laboratory, University of California, Berkeley.

Hockett, C. (1963) 'The problem of universals in language' in J. Greenberg (ed.) *Universals of Language*, Cambridge, MIT Press.

Hymes, D.H. (1974) *Foundations in Sociolinguistics*, Philadelphia, University of Pennsylvania Press.

Laberge, S. and Sankoff, G. (1979) 'Anything *you* can do' in T. Givón and C. Li (eds) *Discourse and Syntax*, New York, Academic Press.

Moerman, M. (1968) 'Being Lue: uses and abuses of ethnic identification.' in J. Helm (ed.) *Essays on the Problem of Tribe*, Seattle, University of Washington Press.

Spiegelberg, H. (1973) 'On the right to say "we": a linguistic and phenomenological analysis' in G. Psathas (ed.) *Phenomenological Sociology*, New York, John Wiley and Sons.

Strong, P.M. (1979) *The ceremonial order of the clinic*, London, Routledge and Kegan Paul.

Tannen, D. and Wallat, C. (forthcoming) 'A sociolinguistic analysis of multiple demands on the pediatrician in doctor/mother/child interaction'.

Weinstein, E. and Deutschberger, P. (1963) 'Some dimensions of altercasting', *Sociometry*, vol. 26, pp. 454–66.

Lecture 1: Rules of Conversational Sequence

Harvey Sacks

Source: Sacks, H. (1992) 'Lecture 1: rules of conversational sequence', in H. Sacks *Lectures on Conversation*, vol. 1, ed. E. Jefferson, Oxford, Blackwell.

I'll start off by giving some quotations.

(1) **A** Hello
     B Hello

(2) **A** This is Mr Smith may I help you
     B Yes, this is Mr Brown

(3) **A** This is Mr Smith may I help you
     B I can't hear you.
     A This is Mr <u>Smith</u>.
     B Sm*i*th.

These are some first exchanges in telephone conversations collected at an emergency psychiatric hospital. They are occurring between persons who haven't talked to each other before. One of them, A, is a staff member of this psychiatric hospital. B can be either somebody calling about themselves, that is to say in trouble in one way or another, or somebody calling about somebody else.

I have a large collection of these conversations, and I got started looking at these first exchanges as follows. A series of persons who called this place would not give their names. The hospital's concern was, can anything be done about it? One question I wanted to address was, where in the course of the conversation could you tell that somebody would not give their name? So I began to look at the materials. It was in fact on the basis of that question that I began to try to deal in detail with conversations.

I found something that struck me as fairly interesting quite early. And that was that if the staff member used 'This is Mr Smith may I help you' as their opening line, then overwhelmingly, any answer other than 'Yes, this is Mr Brown' (for example, 'I can't hear you', 'I don't know', 'How do you spell your name?') meant that you would have serious trouble getting the caller's name, if you got the name at all.

I'm going to show some of the ways that I've been developing of analysing stuff like this. There will be series of ways fitted to each other, as though one were constructing a multi-dimensional jigsaw puzzle. One or another piece can be isolated and studied, and also the various pieces can be studied as to how they fit together. I'll be focussing on a variety of things, starting off with what I'll call 'rules of conversational sequence'.

Looking at the first exchange compared to the second, we can be struck by two things. First of all, there seems to be a fit between what the first person who speaks uses as their greeting, and what the person who is given that greeting returns. So that if A says, 'Hello,' then B tends to say, 'Hello.' If A says 'This is Mr Smith, may I help you, B tends to say, "Yes, this is Mr Brown." We can say there's a procedural rule there, that a person who speaks first in a telephone conversation can choose their form of address, and in choosing their form of address they can thereby choose the form of address the other uses.

By 'form' I mean in part that the exchanges occur as 'units.' That is, 'Hello' 'Hello' is a unit, and 'This is Mr Smith, may I help you' 'Yes, this is Mr Brown' is a unit. They come in pairs. Saying 'This is Mr Smith, may I help you' thereby provides a 'slot' to the other wherein they properly would answer: 'Yes, this is Mr Brown.' The procedural rule would describe the occurrences in the first two exchanges. It won't describe the third exchange, but we'll come to see what is involved in such materials.

Secondly, if it is so that there is a rule that the person who goes first can choose their form of address and thereby choose the other's, then for the unit, 'This is Mr Smith, may I help you' 'Yes, this is Mr Brown,' if a person uses 'This is Mr Smith . . .' they have a way of asking for the other's name – without, however, asking the question, 'What is your name?' And there is a difference between saying 'This is Mr Smith, may I help you' – thereby providing a slot to the other wherein they properly would answer, 'Yes, this is Mr Brown' – and asking the question 'What is your name?' at some point in the conversation. They are very different phenomena.

For one, in almost all of the cases where the person doesn't give their name originally, then at some point in the conversation they're asked for their name. One way of asking is just the question, 'Would you give me your name?' To that, there are alternative returns, including 'No' and 'Why?' If a caller says 'Why?' the staff member may say something like, 'I want to have something to call you' or 'It's just for our records.' If a caller says 'No,' then the staff member says 'Why?' and may get something like 'I'm not ready to do that' or 'I'm ashamed.'

Now, I'll consider many times the use of 'Why?' What I want to say about it just to begin with, is that what one does with 'Why?' is to propose about some action that it is an 'accountable action.' That is to say, 'Why?' is a way of asking for an account. Accounts are most extraordinary. And the use of accounts and the use of requests for accounts are very highly regulated phenomena. We can begin to cut into these regularities by looking at what happens when 'May I have your name?' is followed by 'Why?' Then you get an account; for example, 'I need something to call you.' The other might then say, 'I don't mind.' Or you might get an account, 'It's just for our records.' To which the other might say, 'Well I'm not sure I want to do anything with you, I just want to find out what you do' – so that the records are not relevant.

What we can see is that there are ways that accounts seem to be dealable with. If a person offers an account, which they take it provides for the action in question being done – for example, the caller's name being given – then if the other can show that the interest of that account can be satisfied without the name being given, the name doesn't have to be given. That is, if the account is to control the action, then if you can find a way that the account controls the alternative action than it proposed to control, you can use it that way.

It seems to be quite important, then, who it is that offers the account. Because the task of the person who is offered the account can then be to, in some way, counter it. Where, alternatively, persons who offer an account seem to feel that they're somehow committed to it, and if it turns out to be, for example, inadequate, then they have to stand by it.

[. . .]

We see, then, one clear difference between providing a slot for a name, and asking for a name. Asking for a name tends to generate accounts and counters. By providing a slot for a name, those activities do not arise.

We can also notice that, as a way of asking for the other's name, 'This is Mr Smith . . .' is, in the first place, not an accountable action. By that I mean to say, it's not required that staff members use it and they don't always use it, but when they do, the caller doesn't ask why. 'This is Mr Smith . . .' gets its character as a non-accountable action simply by virtue of the fact that this is a place where, routinely, two persons speak who haven't met. In such places the person who speaks first can use that object. And we could say about that kind of item that the matters discriminated by its proper use are very restricted. That is to say, a call is made; the only issue is that two persons are speaking who presumably haven't met, and this object can be used.

Furthermore, the matters are discriminated in different terms than those which the agency is constructed for. That is, they are discriminated in terms of 'two people who haven't met' rather than, for example, that an agency staff member is speaking to someone calling the agency for help. And where one has some organization of activities which sets out to do some task – and in this case it's important for the agency to get names – then if you find a device which discriminates in such a restricted fashion, you can use that device to do tasks for you.

Now, given the fact that such a greeting as 'This is Mr Smith . . .' provides for the other giving his own name as an answer, one can see what the advantage of 'Hello' is for someone who doesn't want to give their name. And I found in the first instance that while sometimes the staff members use 'Hello' as their opening line, if it ever occurred that the persons calling the agency spoke first, they always said 'Hello.'

Persons calling could come to speak first because at this agency, caller and staff member are connected by an operator. The operator says 'Go ahead please' and now the two parties are on an open line, and one can start talking or the other can start talking. This stands in contrast to, for example, calling someone's home. There, the rights are clearly assigned; the person who answers the phone speaks first. If they speak first, they have the right to choose their form. If they have the right to choose their form, they have the right thereby to choose the other's. Here, where the rights are not clearly assigned, the caller could move to speak first and thereby choose the form. And when callers to this agency speak first, the form they choose is the unit 'Hello' 'Hello'. Since such a unit involves no exchange of names, they can speak without giving their name and be going about things in a perfectly appropriate way.

Now, there are variant returns to 'This is Mr Smith may I help you?' one of which is in our set of three exchanges: 'I can't hear you'. I want to talk of that as an 'occasionally usable' device. That is to say, there doesn't have to be a particular sort of thing preceding it; it can come at any place in a conversation. Here is one from the middle of a conversation, from a different bunch of materials.

A   Hey you got a cigarette Axum. I ain't got, I ain't got a good cigarette, and I can't roll one right now. Think you can afford it maybe?
B   I am not here to support your habits.
A   Huh? My helplessness?
B   I am not responsible for supporting your habits ( )
A   My habits ((laughing))

Our third exchange from the psychiatric hospital has the device used at the beginning of the conversation.

A   This is Mr Smith may I help you
B   I can't hear you.
A   This is Mr <u>Smith</u>.
B   Sm<u>i</u>th.

What kind of a device is it? What you can see is this. When you say 'I can't hear you,' you provide that the other person can repeat what they said. Now what does that repetition do for you? Imagine you're in a game. One of the questions relevant to the game would be, is there a way in that game of skipping a move? It seems that something like 'I can't hear you' can do such a job. If you introduce it you provide for the other to do some version of a repeat following which you yourself can repeat. And then it's the other's turn to talk again. What we find is that the slot where the return would go – your name in return to 'This is Mr Smith . . .' – never occurs.

It is not simply that the caller ignores what they properly ought to do, but something rather more exquisite. That is, they have ways of providing that the place where the return name fits is never opened. So that their name is not absent. Their name would be absent if they just went ahead and talked. But that very rarely occurs. The rules of etiquette – if you want to call them that, though we take etiquette to be something very light and uninteresting and to be breached as you please – seem to be quite strong. Persons will use ways to not ignore what they properly ought to do by providing that the place for them to do it is never opened.

I hope it can also be seen that a device like 'I can't hear you' – the repeat device, providing for a repetition of the thing that was first said, which is then repeated by the person who said 'I can't hear you' – is not necessarily designed for skipping a move. It is not specific to providing a way of keeping in the conversation and behaving properly while not giving one's name. It can be used for other purposes and do other tasks, and it can be used with other items. That's why I talk about it as an 'occasional device.' But where that is what one is trying to do, it's a rather neat device.

Let me turn now to a consideration which deals with a variant return to 'May I help you?' That is, not 'Yes . . .' but 'I don't know'. I'll show a rather elaborate exchange in which the staff member opens with a version of 'This is Mr Smith may I help you' but the combination gets split. The name is dealt with, and when the 'can I help you' is offered, it occurs in such a way that it can be answered independent of the name.[1]

Op Go ahead please
A This is Mr Smith (B: Hello) of the Emergency Psychiatric Center can I help you.
B Hello?
A Hello
B I can't hear you.
A I see. Can you hear me now?
B Barely. Where are you, in the womb?
A Where are you calling from?
B Hollywood.
A Hollywood.
B I can hear you a little better.
A Okay. Uh I was saying my name is Smith and I'm with the Emergency Psychiatric Center.
B Your name is what?
A Smith.
B Smith?
A Yes.
A Can I help you?
B I don't know hhheh   I hope you can.
A Uh hah   Tell me about your problems.
B I uh   Now that you're here I'm embarrassed to talk about it. I don't want you telling me I'm emotionally immature 'cause I know I am

I was very puzzled by 'I don't know' in return to 'May I help you.' I couldn't figure out what they were doing with it. And the reason I was puzzled was that having listened to so many of these things and having been through the scene so many times, I heard 'May I help you' as something like an idiom. I'm going to call these idiom-like things 'composites.' That means you hear the whole thing as a form, a single unit. And as a single unit, it has a proper return. As a composite, 'May I help you' is a piece of etiquette; a way of introducing oneself as someone who is in the business of helping somebody, the answer to which is 'Yes' and then some statement of what it is one wants. We can consider this item in terms of what I'll call the 'base environment' of its use.

By 'base environment' I mean, if you go into a department store, somebody is liable to come up to you and say 'May I help you.' And in business-type phone calls this item is routinely used. And if you come into a place and you don't know what it's like, and somebody comes up to you and uses such an item, that's one way of informing you what kind of a place it is. So, if a new institution is being set up, then there are available in the society whole sets of ways that persons go about beginning conversations, and one could, for example, adopt one or another of a series of them as the ones that are going to be used in this place.

Now the thing about at least some composites is that they can be heard not only as composites, but as ordinary sentences, which we could call 'constructives,' which are understood by taking the pieces and adding them up in some way. As a composite 'May I help you' is a piece of etiquette, a signal for stating your request – what you want to be helped with. Alternatively, as a constructive, 'May I help you' is a question. If one hears it as a question, the piece of etiquette and its work hasn't come up, and 'I don't know' is a perfectly proper answer.

Further, 'I don't know' may be locating a problem which 'May I help you' is designed, in the first place, to avoid. In its base environment, for example a department store, it's pretty much the case that for a customer, the question of whether some person 'can help' is a matter of the department store having made them the person who does that. That is to say, lots of things, like telling you whether you can find lingerie in a certain size, is something anybody can do, and as long as the department store says this person is going to do it, that's enough. But we're dealing with a psychiatric hospital. In a department store, being selected to do a job and having credentials to do it are essentially the same thing. In a psychiatric hospital and lots of other places, however, they are very different things. That is, whether somebody can help you if you have a mental disorder, is not solved or is not even presumptively solved by the fact that they've been selected by somebody to do that job. The way it's solved in this society is by reference to such things as having been trained in a particular fashion, having gotten degrees, having passed Board examinations, etc.

Now, in the base environment of the use of 'May I help you?' there is, as I say, no difference essentially between having credentials and being selected. If one can formulate the matter in a psychiatric hospital such that those things come on as being the same, then one needn't start off by producing one's credentials at the beginning of the conversation. And in my materials, again and again, when 'May I help you' is used the person calling says 'Yes' and begins to state their troubles.

As a general matter, then, one can begin to look for kinds of objects that have a base environment, that, when they get used in that environment perform a rather simple task, but that can be used in quite different environments to do quite other tasks. So, a matter like 'credentials' can be handled by this 'May I help you' device. There will be lots of other devices which have a base environment, which do some other task in some other environment.

Before moving off of 'May I help you' I want to mention one other thing about it. If the base environment is something like a department store, then, when it's used in other places – for example, a psychiatric hospital – one of the pieces of information it seems to convey is that whatever it is you propose to do, you do routinely. To whomsoever that calls. That is, it's heard as a standardized utterance. How is that relevant? It can be relevant in alternative ways. First of all, it can be a very reassuring thing to hear. Some persons feel that they have troubles, and they don't know if anybody else has those troubles; or, if others do have those troubles, whether anybody knows about them. If someone knows about them, then there may be a known solution to them. Also and relatedly, a lot of troubles – like mental diseases – are things that persons feel very ambivalent about. That is, they're not sure whether it's some defect of their character, or something else. That, in part, is why they're hesitant to talk about it. And it seems that one of the ways one begins to tell people that they can talk, that you know what they have and that you routinely deal with such matters, is to use manifestly organizational talk.

'May I help you,' then, can be a reassuring way to begin. It can alternatively be something else. Consider the exchange I just showed, in which such standardized utterances as 'May I help you' and 'Tell me about your problems' are used.

> **A**   Can I help you?
> **B**   I don't know hhheh   I hope you can
> **A**   Uh hah   Tell me about your problems
> **B**   I uh   Now that you're here I'm embarrassed to talk about it. I don't want you telling me I'm emotionally immature 'cause I know I am

That is, the use of standardized, manifestly organizational talk can provide for the person calling that they're going to get routine treatment. But 'routine', for them, may not be such a happy thing. Because, for example, they've been through it before. But they may have gone through it, as psychiatrists would say, part way. For example, they were in analysis for three years and ran out of money, or the psychiatrist wouldn't keep them on, or they didn't want to stay. Part way, they may have come to some point in the analysis where they 'knew what was wrong with them.' That is, they knew the diagnostic term. But that diagnostic term may have had a lay affiliate. By that I mean, if a psychiatrist says you're regressed, it's a technical term. But 'regressed' is also a lay term, and as a lay term it doesn't have a great deal of attractiveness. If one finds oneself living with a lay understanding of such a term, where the term is not a very nice thing to have in its lay sense, then when you hear someone using such an item as 'May I help you,' you can hear that some procedure will be gone through, the upshot of which will be the discovery of what you 'already know' – the knowing of which doesn't do you any good.

Related to that are such things as, some people seem to feel very much disturbed about the fact that their relationship to a psychiatrist or to other doctors is monetary. What they want, they say, is a personal solution. Ask them what they want, 'Well, that you don't have to pay for it.' When they hear 'May I help you,' they hear 'a professional.' But they feel that the way you get cured is by getting an affiliation to somebody which is like the affiliations that they failed to get in their lives. That is, they may already have come to learn from some other psychiatrist that the failure of love by their parents is the cause of their troubles. Then, what they come to see is that they need the love of somebody else. And they can't get that from a therapist. Because as soon as they don't pay, that's the end of the relationship.

Now let me just make a few general points. Clearly enough, things like 'This is Mr Smith,' 'May I help you?' and 'I can't hear you' are social objects. And if you begin to look at what they do, you can see that they, and things like them, provide the makings of activities. You assemble activities by using these things. And now when you, or I, or sociologists, watching people do things, engage in trying to find out what they do and how they do it, one fix which can be used is:

Of the enormous range of activities that people do, all of them are done with something. Someone says 'This is Mr Smith' and the other supplies his own name. Someone says 'May I help you' and the other states his business. Someone says 'Huh?' or 'What did you say?' or 'I can't hear you,' and then the thing said before gets repeated. What we want then to find out is, can we first of all construct the objects that get used to make up ranges of activities, and then see how it is those objects do get used.

Some of these objects can be used for whole ranges of activities, where for different ones a variety of the properties of those objects will get employed. And we begin to see alternative properties of those objects. That's one way we can go about beginning to collect the alternative methods that persons use in going about doing whatever they have to do. And we can see that these methods will be reproducible descriptions in the sense that any scientific description might be, such that the natural occurrences that we're describing can yield abstract or general phenomena which need not rely on statistical observability for their abstractness or generality.

There was a very classical argument that it would not be that way; that singular events were singular events, given a historian's sort of argument, that they just happen and they get more or less accidentally thrown together. But if we could find that there are analytically hard ways of describing these things – where, that is, we're talking about objects that can be found elsewhere, that get placed, that have ways of being used; that are abstract objects which get used on singular occasions and describe singular courses of activity – then that's something which is exceedingly non-trivial to know.

One final note. When people start to analyse social phenomena, if it looks like things occur with the sort of immediacy we find in some of these exchanges, then, if you have to make an elaborate analysis of it – that is to say, show that they did something as involved as some of the things I have proposed – then you figure that they couldn't have thought that fast. I want to suggest that you have to forget that completely. Don't worry about how fast they're thinking. First of all, don't worry about whether they're 'thinking'. Just try to come to terms with how it is that the thing comes off. Because you'll find that they can do these things. Just take any other area of natural science and see, for example, how fast molecules do things. And they don't have very good brains. So just let the materials fall as they may. Look to see how it is that persons go about producing what they do produce.

Note

1   The fragment of data is reproduced pretty much as Sacks transcribed it, preserving his attempts to deal with simultaneous talk (i.e., A: This is Mr Smith (B: Hello) of the Emergency Psychiatric Center) and silence (e.g., B: I uh Now that you're here . . .).

The Construction of 'Delicate' Objects in Counselling

David Silverman

Source: Silverman, D. (1997) *Discourses of Counselling: HIV Counselling as Social Interaction*, London, Sage, Chapter 4.

[. . .]

Sex and death are culturally constituted as central human experiences. Yet the descriptive apparatus through which we understand them has been more the topic of fiction writers than of scientific work (for recent exceptions see Foucault, 1979; Prior, 1987). Perhaps the romantic impulse which threatens to engulf certain parts of the human sciences (see Silverman, 1989; Strong and Dingwall, 1989) makes us reluctant to treat them as simply language games among others.

Yet the legal requirement that HIV testing should be preceded by counselling guarantees, tragically, that 'sex' and the prospect of death should become topicalized in large numbers of professional–client exchanges which, if the patient is seropositive, are likely to be lifelong.[1] A social force, even prior to HIV, counselling now offers more people than ever the opportunity to 'learn what we are like, what our experience is, how things are with us' (Taylor, 1986: 78).

[. . .]

In the context of HIV, we may assume that part of the difficulty resides in broaching the topic of safer sex with partners.

Yet we lack knowledge of how people talk about their sexual behaviour in naturally occurring situations.

[. . .]

The discussion of sexual matters may sometimes be marked as a 'delicate' matter. In part, this may relate to the social context in which this topic arises. For instance, where parties are routinely or professionally concerned with matters related to sexuality or death (e.g. in case conferences of surgeons treating transsexual people or discussion between workers in funeral parlours), one need not expect to find delicacy markers.

However, such speculation is fruitless. In particular, it would limit us to a social psychology of how people respond to 'embarrassing' situations which would have to take it on trust that this is how the participants are orienting to the context. As it turns out, what is a 'delicate' matter is something that is locally produced and managed as participants themselves assemble some context for their talk.

The production of 'delicate' matters

The management of 'embarrassing' or 'delicate' situations is addressed both in the theoretical gaze of books of etiquette and in the practical organization of everyday life. For instance, in the context of doctors' conduct of physical examinations of their patients, both parties organize the marking and management of potentially 'delicate' items. In general practice consultations, Heath (1988) has shown how patients position themselves and organize their gaze to mark their disattendance to the parts of their body being examined.

[. . .] Heath shows how we can analyse the cooperative marking and management of 'delicate' objects without attributing psychological states, like 'embarrassment', to the individuals concerned.

Research on the local organization of 'delicacy' reveals that it may be functional to proceed 'cautiously'. For instance, Maynard (1991) has noted that conversationalists may seek to elicit an opinion from someone else before making their own statement. Maynard gives an example:

Extract 1 (Maynard, 1991: 459)

```
1  Bob    Have you ever heard anything about wire wheels?
2  Al     They can be a real pain. They you know they go outta
3         line and—
4  Bob    Yeah the – if ya get a flat you hafta take it to a
5         special place ta get the flat repaired.
6  Al     Uh – why's that?
```

Maynard concludes that the PDS (prospective display sequence) has a special function in circumstances requiring *caution*. In ordinary conversations, this may explain why it is seen most frequently in conversations between strangers or acquaintances where the person about to deliver an opinion is unlikely to know about the other person's views.[2]

[. . .]

The management of delicacy is not confined to medical encounters. For instance, Clayman (1992) characterizes TV news interviewing as a site for much 'expressive caution', given that news interviewers are supposed to be neutral or objective.

Clayman investigates how interviewers shift footing when they come on to relatively controversial opinion statements. Look at the interviewer's utterance in Extract 10.2, Line 4 below:

Extract 2 (Clayman, 1992) [Meet the Press] (IV = Interviewer)

```
1  IV     Senator, (0.5) uh: President Reagan's elected
2         thirteen months ago: an enormous landslide.
3         (0.8)
4  IV     It is s::aid that his programs are in trouble
```

In Lines 1–2, a footing is constructed whereby IV is the author of a factual statement. However, at Line 4, the footing shifts to what 'it is said'. As Clayman suggests, such a formulation indicates that IV is no longer the author of the assertion. This serves to mark the item as possibly 'controversial' and to preserve IV's position of 'neutrality' towards such matters. Once more, expressive caution is being used to mark and manage 'delicate' items.

Expressive caution in HIV counselling

Counselling around the antibody test routinely involves Patients (Ps) being asked to describe their reasons for wanting a test. We present below extracts from several transcripts where the Counsellor (C) asks such a question. Although these transcripts derive from recordings at three different testing centres (two in England and one in the USA), our analysis will show that certain phenomena are massively recurrent in how Ps answer this question. Let us examine Extract 3 below:

Extract 3 (US1)

```
1   C   erm: what made you decide to come in then [softer]
2       to be tested?
3       (1.0)
4   P   er: well I (1.2) actually I'd been thinking about
5       doing it for some ti:me er:: (0.5) I had (.) I was
6       in a relationship about er six or eight months ago
7       (0.7) which lasted (1.0) well it ended six or eight
8       months ago it lasted for about three years and er
9       (1.0) er we had engaged in some unsafe sex
10      activities and er I later found that er my partner
11      had been having (.) sex with other people
```

P begins his answer in a flow of perturbed speech (a hesitation and a 1.2 second pause, followed by a repair). Again, when P begins to describe a relationship in Line 5, he hesitates ('er::'), pauses and then repairs ('I had (.) I was in a relationship').

P here attends to the issue of the length of time he had given to thinking about having an HIV test. Two functions seem to be served by introducing this topic. First, it may put P in a favourable light since 'thinking about doing [things] for some time' may be hearable as an activity which suggests the category 'responsible person'. Second, it avoids P getting straight into the issue of his risky activities. This expressive caution is underlined since P's initial utterance ('er: well I (1.2) actually') *might* have led to an immediate disclosure of his sexual activities but is forestalled by its repair.

Such caution allows P to set up a 'good news' sequence prior to what may be the delivery of delayed (and hence dispreferred, that is, problematic in one way or another) 'bad news'. Already hearable as a 'responsible person', P initially uses description of others, with whom he participated in sexual activities, which imply a long-term involvement ('a relationship' and, at the end, 'my partner' – also delivered after a hesitation).

Extract 3 shows that the phenomenon of delay extends to descriptions of activities as well as relationships. Observe P's hesitations and pause which make his activity-description of 'unsafe sexual activities' and the micro-pause in 'having (.) sex with other people' hearable as dispreferred.

Notice also that P's failure to specify the people involved or the nature of their activities may invite C to treat his description as an 'indefinite' reference and to request that he should specify it further. Should C request such specification, then C shares the responsibility for any potentially delicate items that P delivers.

So, by postponing specification, until requested by C, patients neatly find a solution to two interactional problems. First, they avoid the potentially morally dubious activity of volunteering details of sexual activities. Second, not knowing what is appropriate in such a consultation, they give the professional an option about whether specification is in order.

The apparatus of description

The extracts above contain a more general message: participants as well as sociological analysts skilfully manage their descriptions of events. As Harvey Sacks noted, this raises some vital methodological questions for ethnographers and anyone else attempting to construct sociology as an 'observational' discipline. Sacks puts the issue succinctly:

> Suppose you're an anthropologist or sociologist standing somewhere. You see somebody do some action, and you see it to be some activity. How can you go about formulating who it is that did it, for the purposes of your report? Can you use at least what you might take to be the most conservative formulation – his name? Knowing, of course, that any category you choose would have the [se] kinds of systematic problems: how would you go about selecting a given category from the set that would equally well characterise or identify that person at hand?
>
> (1992, Vol. 1: 467–468).

Sacks shows how you cannot resolve such problems simply 'by taking the best possible notes at the time and making your decisions afterwards' (ibid.: 468). Instead, our aim should be to try to understand when and how members do descriptions, seeking thereby to describe the apparatus through which members' descriptions are properly produced.

Consider this description in which the identities of the parties are concealed:

> The X cried. The Y picked it up.

Why is it that we are likely to hear the X as, say, a baby but not a teacher? Furthermore, given that we hear X as a baby, why are we tempted to hear Y as an adult (possibly as the baby's mother)?

In this chapter, I draw upon some of the concepts that Sacks uses to answer such questions. For simplicity, I will only refer to two such concepts:

Membership categorization devices (MCDs)

Each identity is heard as a category from some collection of categories which

Sacks calls a membership categorization device. For instance, in the example above, we hear 'mother' as a category from the collection 'family'. The implication is that to choose one category from an MCD excludes someone being identified with some other category from the same device.

Category-bound activities (CBAs)

Many kinds of activity are common-sensically associated with certain membership categories. So, by identifying a person's activity (say, 'crying'), we provide for what their social identity is likely to be (in this case a 'baby'). Moreover, we can establish negative moral assessments of people by describing their behaviour in terms of performing or avoiding activities inappropriate to their social identity. For instance, it may be acceptable for a parent to 'punish' a child, but it will be unacceptable for a child to 'punish' a parent. Notice that, in both cases, 'punish' serves as a powerful picture of an activity which could be described in innumerable ways. Categories can usually be read off the activities in which people engage. Thus, to hear a report of someone crying *may* be heard as the activity of a baby. Similarly, a person who properly picks a baby up *may* be hearable as a 'mother'. Moreover, if both baby and mother are mentioned, we will try to hear them as a 'team' – so that, if the mother picks up the baby, we will hear the mother as not any mother but as the mother of this baby.

Using Sacks's (1972) account of how descriptions are organized, we can show how the marking of potentially delicate items carries strong implications about the moral status of clients. Following Heath's (1988) work on 'embarrassment' in the context of doctors' conduct of physical examinations of their patients, we have also demonstrated how, having marked an item as delicate, both parties cooperatively restore a life-as-normal framework.

Expressive caution in one counselling interview

Let us try to demonstrate these processes using an extended example taken from a pre-test counselling interview in a British testing centre. The extract begins about three minutes after the start of the consultation.

Extract 4 (UK1)

```
1    C   Let's finish this HIV thing . . . hhhhh So (.) do you
2        understand about the antibodies.=
3    P   =Yes I [do:.
4    C          [Ri:ght. .hh So: .h how lo:ng is it since you
5        think (.) you might have been at ri:sk (.) of being
6        infected with HIV.
7    P   Well uh- (0.4) uhuh to tell you the truth it's only
8        I- like er Friday I had a phone call from a .h ex-
9        girlfriend- my boyfriend's ex-girlfriend .hh to say
10       that uh:m (0.5) she'd been to the VD clinic (0.2)
11       and uhm she thought that I should go:, (0.2) bu:t
12       (.) (since) then I've never worried. It was only (.)
```

```
13        after the phone-ca:ll.
14   C    Oh ri:ght.=
15   P    =That I thought that well I'd better go check it
16        o(h)u(h)t. .hhhh You kno: [w.
17   C                              [So: the thing is you see
18        w- wh- what abou:t contacts before your present
19        boyfriend if I might ask about (tha:[:t.
20   P                                       [Well I had (.)
21        since my: divorce in eighty-two (.) I've only had
22        two relationships.
23   C    Right.
24   P    And uh:m (0.2) one lasted for eight years and one
25        lasted for three year:s.
26   C    Uh huh
27   P    So I don't- I haven't worried
28   C    No sure.
29   P    you know because uh- those are the only two me:n.
30        Bu:t (.) on saying tha::t (0.2) my latest boyfriend
31        (.) is the only one that I've well had to worry
32        about because of the phone-ca:ll.
33        I'v[e never worried before.
34   C       [(Yea:h).
35   C    How long have you been with your latest boyfriend.
36   P    Three months.
37   C    Three months.
38   P    Yea:h.
39   C    Right. .hhhhh So: (.) we are only just really on the
40        time limit for this HIV for your present boyfriend
41        [then aren't u- aren't we.
42   P    [Yea:h.
43   P    [Mm hm
```

Extract 4 begins just as C has completed a long sequence of information about the nature of an HIV test (data not shown). By Line 7 of this extract, however, P is into a much longer turn at talk. This is tied into a question asked by C which sets off the long question–answer chain shown in this extract.

Let us look first at how P sets up her reply to C's question beginning at Line 7 compared to her answer at Line 3. P was quickly into her earlier answer – indeed the transcript indicates the absence of even the slightest pause between the answer and the preceding question. Here, by contrast, there is considerable hesitation before P gets into her answer.

At Line 3, P can latch her 'yes' immediately to the completion of C's turn because this is the candidate answer hearable from the question's juxtapositioning with the agenda statement. This is not to say that P could *not* have said that she didn't understand about antibodies, merely that what is, in this context, a problematic answer would normally be marked. However, in Lines 7–8, P precisely does mark her answer as problematic through considerable expressive caution which includes two hesitations (uh, uhuh), a pause, two downgrades (well, only), a repair (I like er) and a preface (to tell you the truth). P's use of 'only' to describe how long she has been worried suggests that she is setting up her answer as delicate because she hears C's question as implying that most people will spend a lot of time deliberating before coming for an HIV test.

However, I am more concerned here with such expressive caution in the description of sexual activities. Note, once again, that I do not begin from the assumption that sexual matters and the like are intrinsically 'delicate' because of cultural taboos. Any such assumption is defeasible since we can visualize sequential features and other local circumstances where such taboos do not operate. Instead, I am concerned with how expressive caution works in the *local* production of delicacy.

Let us begin by looking further at P's utterance in Line 7 'to tell you the truth'. As we will see, the story that P tells between Lines 7 and 13 involves a highly organized set of disclosures which delay certain items. Before making a set of observations, I will reproduce this passage below:

Extract 4 (part of)

```
7    P    Well uh- (0.4) uhuh to tell you the truth it's only
8         I- like er Friday I had a phone call from a .h ex-
9         girlfriend- my boyfriend's ex-girlfriend .hh to say
10        that uh:m (0.5) she'd been to the VD clinic (0.2)
11        and uhm she thought that I should go:, (0.2) bu:t
12        (.) (since) then I've never worried. It was only (.)
13        after the phone-ca:ll.
14   C    Oh ri:ght.=
15   P    =That I thought that well I'd better go check it
16        o(h)u(h)t. .hhhh You kno:[w.
```

The story begins with the report of a phone call. Straight off we can remark that phone calls are a routine part of ordinary modern existence. This sets up a nice contrast with C's question about the relatively extraordinary topic of thinking about one's risk of being infected with HIV. How do we account for this contrast? We can find a parallel in the reports of witnesses to the assassination of President Kennedy who typically prefaced their accounts by referring to their original thoughts that perhaps what they had heard were the sounds of an ordinary event, such as a car backfiring. As Sacks has observed:

> there is a preference for descriptions which start off by exploring routine, normal or non-problematic explanations of unexpected events: members are 'engaged in finding out only how it is that what is going on is usual'.
>
> (Sacks, 1984: 419)

After the phone call is reported in speech which exhibits none of the perturbations present in the beginning of the turn, P moves once again into a very turbulent delivery pattern from the end of Line 8 to the end of Line 10. Before she says 'ex-girlfriend', P takes an in breath and then after a short pause she repairs her description into 'my boyfriend's ex-girlfriend'. Clearly, expressive caution is being displayed here. What work is being done in the production of such perturbations? First, in naming an associate (here boyfriend's ex-girlfriend), one implies a description of oneself – in this case the standardized relational pair (SRP) (Sacks, 1972) of boyfriend:girlfriend. Because of this self-involvement, descriptions of certain types of associates may be foreshadowed as delicate matters. By referring to the ex-girlfriend of your boyfriend, you describe yourself as having a boyfriend who has had at least one earlier partner. Now the fact of having a relationship with someone who has had at least another partner may not be extraordinary. However, *reporting* such a fact may be heard as a category-bound activity with potentially delicate implications (casting doubt on whether this present relationship may be temporary, etc.). Indeed, P's use of 'ex' in the description 'ex-girlfriend' suggests that we are to hear her boyfriend as engaged in serial monogamy (i.e. as not promiscuous) which creates, by implication, the SRP of 'faithful partners'. This may have something to do with her repair from her original formulation of 'a .h ex-girlfriend'.

The hesitation and repair prior to this report thus constitute a nice solution to the problems of delicacy which may arise in describing one's sexual partners – proceed with expressive caution by delaying such descriptions. Moreover, such caution is not just self-interested. It shows a fine attention to what a recipient may want to hear. By producing a minimal amount of potentially delicate items at a first turn after a question, one leaves it up to the recipient to decide whether to treat it as a gloss which needs unpacking, for example via a probe or a demand for specification. Such requests provide a favourable environment for disclosing items marked as delicate because such items can now be produced as demanded by C rather than as volunteered by P.

Further turbulences (a hesitation and a half-second pause) occur in P's delivery of the item 'she'd been to the VD clinic' (Line 10). Here we are concerned with a description of an activity rather than an associate. As Sacks (ibid.) also notes, activities are category-bound because they imply the kind of persons who might engage in them, e.g. 'crying' may be heard as being done by a baby. However, while a baby crying may be heard as 'normal', this is unlikely to be the case with going 'to the VD clinic'. P's expressive caution in the delivery of this item nicely marks the delicate implications of having a boyfriend who has had an affair with someone who has gone to a VD clinic. The delay also marks out the speaker as someone-who-does-not-normally-talk-about-people-going-to-VD-clinics. Throughout, P's own visit for an HIV test (in what may be described as 'a VD clinic' is produced as something that arises from someone else's suggestion (her boyfriend's ex-girlfriend) and from someone else's actions (her boyfriend who presumably had infected the ex-girlfriend).

Now P produces her reasons for seeking a test in terms of her caller's wishes ('she thought that I should go') (Line 11) and her own sense of the situation ('I thought that well I'd better go check it o(h)u(h)t') (Lines 15–16). Note the appeal to doing what someone else thinks best and to the responsibility of 'checking out' things. Both delay the description of one's own sexual activities while trading off life-as-usual situations which serve to downgrade the unusual and delicate business of seeking an HIV test. Now P's rapid visit for an HIV test is reconstituted as depicting a responsible person (who realizes she must rapidly 'check it out') rather than someone who has not reflected sufficiently (recognized in her earlier 'it's only 1- like er Friday').

In the passage above, we have seen how both parties steer away from problematic explanations of such an unexpected event as seeking an HIV test. As Sacks (1984: 419) puts it, members are 'engaged in finding out only how it is that what is going on is usual'. But the cooperative accomplishment of expressive caution sits uneasily with the prescribed tasks of HIV counselling which require that clients address their risks in specific terms (see Peräkylä and Bor, 1990).

While Ps' initial descriptions can appear perfectly adequate at the time, C's follow-up questions and/or requests for specification redefine P's answers. These answers are then transformed into indefinite references requiring further specification.

Bearing in mind the expressive caution about delicate items, two questions remain: (1) how do Cs set up their requests for specification?; and (2) how do Ps expand (what are now received as) insufficiently precise references? The next nine lines of the extract bear upon these questions:

Extract 5 (part of)

```
17  C                              [So: the thing is you see
18      w- wh- what abou:t contacts before your present
19      boyfriend if I might ask about (tha:[:t).
20  P                                          [Well I had (.)
21      since my: divorce in eighty-two (.) I've only had
22      two relationships.
23  C   Right.
24  P   And uh:m (0.2) one lasted for eight years and one
25      lasted for three year:s.
```

C's 'so' (Line 17) locates her upcoming question as the natural upshot of P's account, while her reference to P's boyfriend (Line 19) nicely ties her question to P's own description. Moreover, C's initial question: 'how lo:ng is it since you think (.) you might have been at ri:sk' has already provided for the possibility that P may have been at risk longer than she suspects and thus warrants the line of questioning beginning here.

Before introducing her own term 'contacts', C marks its potentially delicate character by a set of perturbations ('w- wh- what abou:t contacts'). Having 'contacts', while the standard term used by professionals in STD clinics, can be heard by clients as an activity bound to the category of 'promiscuous person'. Indeed, we shall see that this is a deviant case since elsewhere both parties recurrently strive to locate patients' sexual activities in the context of long-term relationships.

As Schegloff (1980) points out, various types of action projection can serve to mark out and request formal permission for potentially delicate or risqué actions. So here C adds a little rider to her question ('if I might ask about (tha:[:t).'). Although, unlike question projections, this request comes after, rather than before, the question, it serves the same function of marking out that C understands that this may be heard as a delicate topic.

Here, then, C has skilfully prepared the ground for exploring a potentially delicate topic. In doing so, she has provided some kind of a favourable environment in which P can specify her indefinite reference.

Faced with C's request for specification, P does tell more in relatively undisturbed speech. But note two things. First, she converts the C's professional item 'contacts' into 'relationships'. This transforms the relational pairs involved: compare the description of sexual partners as contacts (for sexually transmitted diseases) to ones involved in relationships (implying that the sexual activity is necessarily contexted in 'commitments' and other non-sexual matters).

Second, note that the P prefaces her response by 'since my: divorce'. This does a lot of interesting work:

– it gives us a favourable context to read her upcoming MCD 'relationships' (by implying that prior to her divorce she was only involved in one relationship);

– it makes several relationships permissible to a 'single' woman (but only one after the other, as she later makes clear). Even though the years do not add up (eight plus three years from 1982 takes us to 1991 and the interview takes place in 1989), we hear her as engaged in consecutive monogamy – just as in her earlier description of her boyfriend's 'ex-girlfriend'.

As C's disturbed delivery of the term 'contacts' showed, professionals display caution in organizing questions about potentially delicate matters. In turn, one of the strategies available to clients is to portray themselves in a favourable light – as in P's appeal to a pattern of serial monogamy. However, we should not emphasize the separate strategies of each party since the identification and management of delicacy tends to be a cooperative matter. This is nicely shown as the interview continues:

Extract 5 (UK1) [Extract 4 continued]

```
44   C   [.hhh Uhm .hhh d'you know if any of your: your er
45       partners have been drug users. =Intra[venous drug =
46   P                                    [No:.
47   C   =[users is our main [uhm you- you've never used =
48   P   [They haven't.       [Mm
49   C   =needles for yourself [(either. = No). .hh I ask =
50   P                         [No:
51   C   =everybody those questions. =I haven't saved them
52       [up for you..hhhh Obviously when we're talking=
53   P   [(That's okay yeah).
54   C   =about HIV .hhhh uhm (.) the intravenous drug using
55       population are a population that are at ri:sk.
56   P   Yea[:h.
57   C       [Because (.) if they share needles (.) then
58       they're sharing (.) infection with the blood on the
59       needles obvious[ly.
```

```
60  P                [Mm h[m
61  C                       [.hhhhhh Uhm (0.5) d'you know if
62      any of your partners have been bisexual.
63  P   No they haven't.=
```

The task of pre-test counselling involves asking clients to assess the nature of their risk of having been exposed to HIV. In this passage, both parties have to cope with the implications of discussing potentially delicate aspects of the status of P's sexual contacts.

The extract is closely analysed below to show how delicacy is nicely marked and managed. C prefaces her question at Line 44 by 'd'you know'. We can see the power of this preface by imagining an alternative way of posing the question:

   *C   Have any of your partners been drug users

Putting the question this way would imply that P is the kind of person who *knowingly* might associate with drug users. So this form of the question can be a category-bound activity, where its recipient is to be heard in the category of a-person-who-might-consort-with-drug-users. The C's preface is a neat device to overcome this hearing. It allows P, if necessary, to reveal that she had subsequently discovered that a partner was a drug user, without any kind of implication that she would knowingly associate with that category of person.

In Line 45, C uses the category 'partner'. Note the expressive caution ('er') that precedes it. Massively recurrent in these materials are such delays in the first delivery (by both professionals and clients) of descriptive categories relating to sexual associates and activities. However, note that the category 'partner' may be less damaging to the propriety of P's behaviour than 'contact' – C's earlier term. Although both relate to sexual activity, the SRP 'partner – partner' is less implicative of promiscuity than the pair 'contact – contact'. Again, both professionals and clients in these sessions strive to present client behaviour in the best possible light.

Note how, in Line 50, P overlaps with C's talk in order to produce a reply at the first available turn-transition point. In this way, non-delicate matters are marked by unqualified delivery at the first opportunity.

Equally, at Lines 46–8, P marks her answer ('no . . . they haven't') as preferred by producing it early and without qualification, overlapping with C's elaboration of her question. Moreover, at Line 46, P does not embed her 'no' in C's 'd'you know' format. Thereby, she elides the possibility that she could be the sort of person who did not fully 'know' all her partners.

Again, see how, in Lines 47–9, C redesigns her next question. This may be in order to re-orient towards P's presentation of herself, dropping the 'd'you know' format and offering a negative answer as the preferred one.

More plausibly, C is now asking about P herself, not some other about whom her knowledge might be incomplete.

C's justification of her line of questioning ('Intra[venous drug users is our main; I ask everybody those questions. =I haven't saved them up for you') works as a retrospective justification for asking such a question. It serves neatly to

counter the category-bound implications of the activity of asking someone if they
have had sex with drug users. Without the elaboration, the implication might be
that C had reason to suspect that P might be the sort of person who would
engage in such an activity. The elaboration, however, seems to be about to make
clear that the question has not been generated by anything that P has said or
done – other than presenting herself at a clinic in which 'intravenous drug users
is our main' (client population?). This is underlined by C's observation 'I haven't
saved them up for you'.

P's agreement tokens on Line 53 ('that's okay yeah') show her acceptance of
C's elaboration and thus mark her continued recipiency for this line of
questioning. This allows C to tag on a further question (about 'bisexual partners')
whose delicacy is nicely marked and managed by the same 'd'you know' format
as used on Line 44.

Extracts 4 and 5 have allowed us to distinguish a number of practices involved
in the local production and management of 'delicate' items by counsellors (C)
and their patients (P). These are set out in Table 10.1.

Table 1 *Delicacy, description and expressive caution: some findings*

---

1 Cs and Ps use 'expressive caution' to mark potentially delicate objects: i.e. they delay
   their delivery, engage in various speech perturbations, and use elaborations and story-
   prefaces to mark and manage delicate items.
2 Ps produce a minimal amount of potentially delicate items at a first turn after a
   question, leaving it up to the recipient to decide whether to treat it as a gloss which
   needs unpacking.
3 Cs provide a favourable environment for disclosing delicate information by using
   perspective display sequences, downgrades, ambiguous and indirect questions
   and prospective and retrospective justifications for questions and requests for
   specification.
4 Cs and Ps show a preference for descriptions which start off by exploring routine,
   normal or non-problematic explanations of unexpected events.
5 Cs and Ps endeavour to put Ps in a 'positive' light, e.g. by countering implications of
   P promiscuity.

However, as I have argued elsewhere (Silverman, 1993), we must guard against
the ease with which we can select instances from qualitative data which confirm
an initial hypothesis. One check on such anecdotal use of data is deviant-case
analysis.

Inspection of 50 transcripts from our corpus of almost 200 consultations has so
far revealed three apparently deviant cases. Space allows us only to deal with
one of them. Extract 6 is unique in our corpus of data in that a patient seems to
produce straight off a description which implies that he engages in casual sex:

Extract 6 (US1)

1   **P**   Well I've- I've (0.5) I have been out with a (0.7)
2   er: hhh (1.7) you know I have paid for sex you know
3   o[ff- off <u>street</u>walkers[s I think I =

```
4    C    [Mm hm                    [Uh huh
5    P    = might have got it (that way because)
```

Note how P produces the category-bound activity 'paid for sex' and the MCD 'streetwalkers' in his first turn. However, a closer reading of this extract shows that 'streetwalker' is *not* P's first description of his partner. Notice that P begins with this description: 'I have been out with a (0.7) er:'. Although this first description is not completed, it may appeal to an activity, very different to that of 'paying for sex'. After all, 'being out with [someone]' is a description which can be heard as bound to the 'life-as-usual' activity of 'dating'. Like the standard examples, then, Extract 6 shows how objects can be marked as potentially delicate by being offered as disturbed second descriptions.

Nonetheless, when a speaker does use a description which does not respect this preference, (s)he marks it.[3] In Extract 6, note the turbulent delivery before the MCD 'streetwalker' is produced – the aborted initial delivery (after a repair and two pauses), the further turbulences before the activity-description ('I have paid for sex') and the repair immediately before 'streetwalkers'. These multiple speech perturbations mark the account as particularly extra-ordinary and delicate.

[. . .]

Not sexuality but morality

Ironically, as always, interactional solutions are solutions to the very problems that members locally produce for themselves.[4] This means that both problems and solutions arise in the sequential organization of talk. It also means that much more is potentially at stake in these interviews than mere issues of sexual behaviour. As it turns out, such behaviour is only relevant in the context of an indefinite series of other matters that may be held to pertain to the moral standing of clients and their partners. I will demonstrate this point through a turn-by-turn analysis of one further long extract set out below.

Extract 10.7 is taken from the very beginning of a pre-HIV test counselling interview held at the sexually transmitted disease department of a hospital in a provincial British city:

Extract 7 (UK3)

```
1    C    righty ho (0.2) could you tell us (.) why you've
2         come for an HIV test today=
3    P    =well basically (.) because I'm: worried that I
4         might have AIDS (0.2) er: (0.2) when my girlfriend
5         (.) like she was on holiday in: (.) [X]* (0.2) in
6         April with her friend
7    C    mm hm
8    P    I didn't go because I was busy (1.0) er:: (0.6) she
9         came back but she was away for three weeks she came
10        back (0.6) er: April (   ) May (.) April (.) May
```

11   June July August September October November (0.8)
12   and it's now November she's just told me (.) that
13   she had sex with (.) a [Xian]* when she was out there
14   well not actually had sex with but this she said
15   that this guy (0.2) this is what she told me this
16   guy had (.) forced herself (.) hisself upon her you
17   know (0.6) er:: [further details of what happened]
18   P   so: that's what I'm worried about
19   (0.8)
20   C   [mm
21   P   [and it's been unprotected sex as well
22   C   right: so obviously someone had forced (0.2) himself
23   on her=
24   P   =yeah=
25   C   =hh there was: nothing she could do
26   P   mm hm
27   C   (   ) hh
28   P   but apparently that's what they're like out there:
29   you know
30   (0.6)
31   C   mm
32   P   so:: (0.6) that's what the score is (0.4) that's
33   what I'm worried about

* I have deleted the country referred to in Line 5 and the nationality in Line 13 in order to preserve P's anonymity.

In Extract 7, as in the other extracts, category-bound activities and membership categorization devices are used to confirm each other. So being 'worried' about 'AIDS' (Lines 3–4) is appropriate to the implied category 'patient' who has 'come for an HIV test today'. Moreover, descriptions construct a profoundly *moral* universe of 'reasonable' activities conducted and perceived by 'reasonable' people. So, for instance, coming today for an HIV test is not only an 'appropriate' activity if you are 'worried', it is also a sensible and reasonable activity, serving to protect yourself (against further 'worry') and the community (because it shows you are aware of the dangers of receiving and transmitting the HIV virus).

Since HIV is hearable as a sexually transmitted disease, answering why one wants an HIV test often involves references to relationships with others. As Sacks tells us, how one describes a related other and their activities is deeply morally implicative of oneself and one's own activities. Let us now look at how this moral universe is constructed as P tells his story.

'My girlfriend' (Line 4) tells us that P is heterosexual or at least bisexual. Moreover, by choosing 'girlfriend' rather than 'girl', 'woman', etc., P implies that, at least in this case, he is someone who has a 'relationship' rather than other alternatives (a 'one-night stand', commercial sex, etc.).

'She was on holiday' (Line 5) is a CBA tied to the category 'holidaymaker' but also associated with other activities such as holiday 'romances', holiday 'flings'. Because we know that holidays are a time when moral inhibitions may be temporarily lifted, the upcoming description of potentially 'promiscuous' behaviour is potentially downgraded or at least made comprehensible.

'With her friend' (Line 6) tells us that she had not gone away on her own, where going away on your own may be heard as implying a problem with a relationship, although it does leave a question hanging about why P had not accompanied his girlfriend. 'Her friend' does not tell us the gender of the 'friend'. However, we know that, if that gender had been male, it would have massive implications for the story that is being told and, therefore, P would have been obliged to tell us. Given that he doesn't, we must assume that 'her friend' is female. Moreover, we can also assume, for the same reason, that it is not a sexual relationship.

'I didn't go because I was busy' (Line 8) attends to the question that is hanging about why P didn't accompany his girlfriend, given that 'going on holiday together' is a CBA appropriate to the SRP girlfriend/boyfriend. Here P shows that he analyses these inferences in exactly this way. First, he underlines what we had inferred in his original description: 'I didn't go'. Second, he shows that this 'not going' is accountable and provides its warrant: 'because I was busy'.

'She's just told me (.) that she had sex with (.) a [Xian] when she was out there' (Line 13) consists of a series of highly implicative CBAs. Having 'sex' with a third party is category-bound to the category 'being unfaithful'. Although the earlier CBA being 'on holiday' (confirmed by the place-locater 'when she was out there') may make this description understandable, it may not make it excusable. As we shall see, first P and then C engage in considerable interpretive work to preserve the moral status of P's girlfriend.

However, the 'telling' of a story which reflects badly on oneself can itself be a praiseworthy activity.[5] Moreover, given that we are not told that the 'girlfriend' was not forced to tell her story or 'found out', we must assume that her admission was voluntary – itself a praiseworthy activity as we learn from the sentencing policy of most criminal courts.

One aspect of the content of this description, namely having 'sex with a [Xian]', where an Xian may be known to be category-bound to the description 'possible HIV carrier' and the CBA 'risky activity' neatly provides the warrant for P wanting an HIV test.

The account also creates a standardized relational pair of news-teller/news-receiver. This SRP has an implication for P's own moral status. Because he has only 'just' (Line 12) heard about his girlfriend's implied risky activity (and hence his own risk), the delay between his being at risk and coming for a test is explained and, indeed, his immediate appearance at the clinic is implicitly 'praiseworthy'.

'Well not actually had sex with' (Line 14): here the damaging CBA 'having sex (with a third party)' is immediately repaired by B. Thus we have to suspend the category-bound implication 'unfaithful girlfriend'. But this repaired description is ambiguous. For instance, are we to hear 'not actually sex' as a physical or social description of the activity?[6]

'She said that this guy (0.2) this is what she told me this guy had (.) forced herself (.) hisself upon her you know' (Lines 14–17). It is clear from his next utterance that P is attending to this ambiguity as something in need of further explication. If 'he forced . . . hisself upon her', then we are given a CBA implying the categories rapist/victim where 'victim' implies the activity of not giving consent. So P reworks his original category 'having sex', with its damaging implications, by positing the absence of consent and thus a withdrawal of the warrant of the charge 'unfaithful girlfriend'. Later, in a different portion of the transcript, he attends to the physical nature of the act to warrant his description of 'not actually having sex'.

There is a further nice feature embedded in P's description. It arises in its preface: 'she said that this guy (0.2) this is what she told me'. P's story of these events is thus doubly embedded (both in 'she said' and in 'this is what she told me'). How does 'this is what she told me' serve to repair 'she said'?

We can unpick the nature of this repair by recognizing that when somebody offers an account the upshot of which puts them in an unfavourable light, we may suspect that they have organized their description in order to put themselves in a more favourable light. So, if P had simply reported what his 'girlfriend' had said about this incident, then, although he would be implying that he was a 'trusting partner', he could be seen as 'too trusting', i.e. as a dope.

Now we see that 'this is what she told me' makes him into an astute witness by drawing attention to the potential credibility problem about his girlfriend's account. As one of the people involved in a British sex scandal of the 1960s said about the story of another participant: 'He would say that, wouldn't he?' However, note that, unlike this comment, P is *not* directly stating that his girlfriend is to be disbelieved. Rather her story is offered just as that – as her *story* without the implication that P knows it to be true or false.

The beauty of P's repair into 'this is what she told me' is that it puts him in a favourable light (as an astute observer), while not making a direct charge against his girlfriend's veracity (an activity category-bound to the description 'disloyal partner'). This allows a hearer of his story to believe or disbelieve his girlfriend's account and allows him to go along with either conclusion. And this is precisely what happens.

'So obviously someone had forced (0.2) himself on her' (Lines 22–3): note how, in this formulation of the upshot of P's account, C elects to believe his girlfriend's reported account. C's use of 'obviously' makes such belief apparently natural and inevitable. Yet how can this be? After all, P has distanced himself from the story by his repair into 'this is what she told me'.

We can resolve this problem by considering the interactional consequences of a recipient of P's story doubting his girlfriend's account. This would transform P's general doubt about such accounts into a specific charge against someone whom C didn't know. Moreover, it would not be a charge against any stranger but a stranger with close ties to the story-teller. Were C to disbelieve P's girlfriend's reported account, then this would make the friend into a recognizably disreputable character and, by implication, cast doubt on P (as someone-involved-with-a-disreputable character). None of this would be desirable if the interview is to proceed. There are strong interactional grounds here for hearers of P's story to suspend disbelief.[7]

From now on, this version of P's girlfriend as both the innocent victim and the teller of truthful stories is cooperatively developed. At Line 24, P supports C's version at the earliest opportunity, despite his previous attempt to distance himself from it.

Consider the implications of P contesting C's account. First, he would be doubting the upshot-formulation of an impartial hearer. Second, he would have to move from the sensible doubt about the testimony of any interested party to making a specific charge against his girlfriend's veracity and faithfulness. Immediate agreement thus serves as a CBA which allows him to be described as 'loyal'. As C embroiders her account, 'there was nothing she could do' (Line 25), P continues not to contest it, offering a response-token at Line 26.

'But apparently that's what they're like out there' (Line 28): now, when C has apparently passed her turn, P himself continues the embroidery, finding a reason to explain why an [Xian] might have 'forced himself' on a woman.

However, remarks like this *can* be heard not simply as explanations of particular conduct but as an activity which is category-bound to the category 'racist'. Notice now that, while C does offer a response-token (Line 31), it is delayed. Of course, response-tokens like 'mm' are hearable as anything from indications of co-presence, coupled with a passing of one's turn, to agreement. However, if C's 'mm' is hearable as an agreement, given the preference for agreement, its delay is highly implicative of (suppressed) disagreement. And, of course, there is evidence that P hears it this way too – notice his exit from the topic via a summary statement (32–3).

Our analysis of this extract has revealed that hearably 'delicate' matters extend far beyond the sphere of sexual behaviour. Rather, as Sacks has suggested, the description of *any* matter involves both speakers and hearers in a profoundly moral universe in which they can be held to account for a huge number of inferences of their viewings and hearings.

We have seen how both parties attend to such matters as explaining particular courses of action, the warrant for believing other people's stories and taking action on hearing such stories. As speakers modify and embellish each other's accounts, the moral universe they inhabit is both locally and sequentially established.

[. . .]

Summary

Throughout these extracts, we have seen how both speakers fashion their account in a way which attends to the implications of their descriptions. Those implications derive from the machinery of interaction: i.e. *both* that of the apparatus of description (notably in the form of category-bound activities) and the sequential organization of turn-taking. Through this apparatus and this organization, people cooperatively organize and discover anew what it is that they must have meant.

This serves to underline rather than evade the locally organized employment of such an apparatus. While we might assume that presenting oneself as reasonably non-promiscuous might be a shared norm in professional – client interactions, local considerations cause some variance. Therefore, while it is tempting to appeal to apparently self-evident norms of interaction, close investigation of such local practices reveals that people are far from being 'judgemental dopes'. Consequently, the appealing prospect of a sociology of the moral order must begin by clearly delineating the local production of the phenomenon itself.

[. . .]

Notes

1   This chapter concerns itself with how 'risk behaviour' is discussed in HIV counselling. For extended discussion of how 'death' is discussed as a 'dreaded issue' in family-therapy-based counselling see Peräkylä, 1993 and 1995.
2   In the paediatric setting discussed, the functions of the PDS are obvious:

> By adducing a display of their recipients' knowledge or beliefs, clinicians can potentially deliver the news in a hospitable conversational environment, confirm the parents' understanding, coimplicate their perspective in the news delivery, and thereby present assessments in a publicly affirmative and nonconflicting manner. (Maynard, 1991: 484)

3   When people straight off produce a non-routine description, they mark it' (Jefferson, 1985: 450).
4   This, of course, is part of the phenomenon of 'reflexivity' (Garfinkel, 1967).
5   As Cuff (1980) remarks, delivering news about a hearably 'bad' feature of oneself may serve as a pre-emptive strike by showing that, at least, the teller is aware of her culpability. Note, for instance, how it is always newsworthy when criminals show 'no remorse'.
6   Anssi Peräkylä (personal communication) has suggested that the ambiguity created by P's repair nicely serves to present the reported events in a way which constitutes their 'real nature' as unclear to the teller. When wedded to P's use of 'this is what she told me', there is perhaps then a double layer of cautiousness about P's account.
7   Given that C's job is to assess the degree of risk involved in P's sexual relations, the 'truth' of his girlfriend's sexual episode is not primarily relevant for C's task at hand. Hence C opts for the interactionally least complicated 'hearing' of P's ambiguous description.

References

Clayman, S.C. (1992) 'Footing in the achievement of neutrality: the case of news-interview discourse', in P. Drew and J. Heritage (eds) *Talk at Work*, Cambridge, Cambridge University Press.

Cuff, E.C. (1980) 'Some issues in studying the problem of versions in everyday life', (Manchester Sociology Occasional Paper, No. 3), Department of Sociology, Manchester University.

Foucault, M. (1979) *The History of Sexuality: Volume 1*, trans. Robert Hurley, Harmondsworth, Penguin.

Garfinkel, E. (1967) *Studies in Ethnomethodology*. Englewood Cliffs, NJ: Prentice-Hall.

Heath, C. (1988) 'Embarrassment and interactional organization', in P. Drew and A. Wootton (eds) *Erving Goffman: Exploring the Interaction Order*, Cambridge, Polity Press.

Jefferson, G. (1985) 'On the interactioanal unpackaging of a "gloss"', *Language in Society*, vol. 14, pp. 435–66.

Maynard, D.W. (1991) 'Interaction and asymmetry in clinical discourse', *American Journal of Sociology*, Vol. 97, pp. 448–95.

Peräkylä, A. (1993) 'Invoking a hostile world: patients' future in AIDS counselling', *Text*, vol. 13, pp. 291–316.

Peräkylä, A. (1995) *AIDS Counselling: Institutional Interaction and Clinical Practice*, Cambridge, Cambridge University Press.

Peräkylä, A. and Bor, R. (1990) 'Interactional problems of addressing "dreaded issues" in HIV counselling', *AIDS Care*, vol. 2, pp. 325–38.

Prior, L. (1987) 'Policing the dead: a sociology of the mortuary', *Sociology*, 21(3), pp. 355–76.

Sacks, H. (1972) 'On the analysability of stories by children' in J. Gumperz and D. Hymes (eds) *Directions in Sociolinguistics*, New York, Holt, Rinehart and Winston.

Sacks, H. (1984) 'On doing "being ordinary"' in J.M. Atkinson and J. Heritage (eds) *Structures of Social Action*, Cambridge, Cambridge University Press.

Sacks, H. (1992) *Lectures on Conversation*, 2 vols, ed. Gail Jefferson with an Introduction by Emmanuel Schegloff, Oxford, Basil Blackwell.

Schegloff, E.A. (1980) 'Preliminaries to preliminaries: "can I ask you a question?"', *Sociological Inquiry*, vol. 50, pp. 104–52.

Silverman, D. (1989) 'The impossible dreams of reformism and romanticism' in J. Gubrium and D. Silverman (eds) *The Politics of Field Research: Sociology beyond Enlightenment*, London, Sage.

Silverman, D. (1993) *Interpreting Qualitative Data: Methods for Analysing Talk, Text and Interaction*, London, Sage.

Strong, P.M. and Dingwall, R. (1989) 'Romantics and stoics', in J. Gubrium and D. Silverman (eds) *The Politics of Field Research: Sociology beyond Enlightenment*, London, Sage.

Taylor, C. (1986) 'Foucault on freedom and truth' in D. Hoy (ed.) *Foucault: A Critical Reader*, Oxford, Basil Blackwell.

Interethnic Communication

John Gumperz

Source: Gumperz, J.J. (1982) *Discourse Strategies*, Cambridge, Cambridge University, Chapter 8.

[This chapter employs a perspective that] can account for both shared grammatical knowledge and for differences in communicative style that characterize our modern culturally diverse societies.

This approach to speaking has both theoretical and practical significance. On the theoretical level it suggests a way of carrying out Garfinkel's programme for studying naturally organized activities through language without relying on a priori and generally untestable assumptions about what is or is not culturally appropriate. Although it might seem at first glance that contextualization cues are surface phenomena, their systematic analysis can lay the foundation for research strategies to gain insights into otherwise inaccessible symbolic processes of interpretation.

On the practical level, the study of conversational inference may lead to an explanation for the endemic and increasingly serious communication problems that affect private and public affairs in our society. We can begin to see why individuals who speak English well and have no difficulty in producing grammatical English sentences may nevertheless differ significantly in what they perceive as meaningful discourse cues. Accordingly, their assumptions about what information is to be conveyed, how it is to be ordered and put into words and their ability to fill in the unverbalized information they need to make sense of what transpires may also vary. This may lead to misunderstandings that go unnoticed in the course of an interaction, but can be revealed and studied empirically through conversational analysis.

[. . .]

In a staff cafeteria at a major British airport, newly hired Indian and Pakistani women were perceived as surly and uncooperative by their supervisor as well as by the cargo handlers whom they served. Observation revealed that while relatively few words were exchanged, the intonation and manner in which these words were pronounced were interpreted negatively. For example, when a cargo handler who had chosen meat was asked whether he wanted gravy, a British assistant would say 'Gravy?' using rising intonation. The Indian assistants, on the other hand, would say the word using falling intonation: 'Gravy'. We taped relevant sequences, including interchanges like these, and asked the employees to paraphrase what was meant in each case. At first the Indian workers saw no difference. However, the English teacher and the cafeteria supervisor could point out that 'Gravy', said with a falling intonation, is likely to be interpreted as 'This is gravy', i.e. not interpreted as an offer but rather as a statement, which in the context seems redundant and consequently rude. When the Indian women heard this, they began to understand the reactions they had been getting all along which had until then seemed incomprehensible. They then spontaneously recalled intonation patterns which had seemed strange to them when spoken by native English speakers. At the same time, supervisors learned that the Indian women's falling intonation was their normal way of asking questions in that situation, and that no rudeness or indifference was intended.

After several discussion/teaching sessions of this sort, both the teacher and the cafeteria supervisor reported a distinct improvement in the attitude of the Indian workers both to their work and to their customers. It seemed that the Indian workers had long sensed they had been misunderstood but, having no way of talking about this in objective terms, they had felt they were being discriminated against. We had not taught the cafeteria workers to speak appropriate English; rather, by discussing the results of our analysis in mixed sessions and focusing on context bound interpretive preferences rather than on attitudes and stereotypes, we have suggested a strategy for self-diagnosis of communication difficulties. In short, they regained confidence in their own innate ability to learn.

The first of the longer case studies examines excerpts from an interview – counselling session recorded in an industrial suburb in London. The participants are both educated speakers of English; one is a Pakistani teacher of mathematics, who although born in South Asia went to secondary school and university in England. The other is a staff member of a centre funded by the Department of Employment to deal with interethnic communication problems in British industry. The teacher has been unable to secure permanent employment and having been told that he lacks communication skills for high school teaching, he has been referred to the centre. While both participants agree on the general definition of the event as an interview – counselling session, their expectations of what is to be accomplished, and especially about what needs to be said, differ radically. Such differences in expectation are of course not unusual even where conversationalists have similar cultural backgrounds. Conversations often begin with an introductory phase where common themes are negotiated and differences in expectation adjusted. What is unusual about this situation is that participants, in spite of repeated attempts at adjustment over a period of more than an hour, utterly fail to achieve such negotiation. Our analysis concentrates on the reasons for this failure and shows how it is based on differences in linguistic and socio-cultural knowledge.

[. . .] [Methods] rely partly on comparative analysis of a wide variety of ethnically homogeneous in-group and ethnically mixed encounters. Indirect elicitation procedures are used along with experiments in which participants in a conversation or others of similar background listen to tape recorded passages and are questioned to discover the perceptual cues they use in arriving at their interpretation.

Case study 1

    A Indian male speaker
    B British female speaker

The recording begins almost immediately after the initial greetings. B has just asked A for permission to record the interview, and A's first utterance is in reply to her request.

1 **A** exactly the same way as you, as you would like
2   ⌈to put on
3 **B** ⌊Oh no, no
4 **A** there will be some of ⌈the things you would like to
5 **B**   ⌊yes
6 **A** write it down
7 **B** that's right, that's right (laughs)
8 **A** but, uh . . . anyway it's up to you
        (pause, about 1 second)
9 **B** um, (high pitch) . . . well . . . ⌈I I Miss C.
10 **A**   ⌊first of all
11 **B** hasn't said anything to me you see
        (pause, about 2 seconds)
12 **A** I am very sorry if ⌈she hasn't spoken anything
13 **B** (softly)   ⌊doesn't matter
14 **A** on the telephone at least,
15 **B** doesn't matter
16 **A** but ah . . . it was very important uh thing for me
17 **B** ye:s. Tell, tell me what it ⌈is you want
18 **A**   ⌊umm
19   Um, may I first of all request for the introduction please
20 **B** Oh yes sorry ⌈
21 **A**   ⌊I am sorry
        (Pause, about 1 second)
22 **B** I am E.
23 **A** Oh yes   ⌈(breathy) I see . . . oh yes . . . very nice
24 **B** | and I am a teacher here in the Center
25 **A** very nice |
26 **B** ⌊and we run⌈
27 **A**   ⌊pleased to meet you (laughs)⌈
28 **B**   ⌊different
29   courses (A laughs) yes, and you are Mr. A?
30 **A** N.A.
31 **B** N.A. yes, yes, I see (laughs). Okay, that's the
32   introduction (laughs)
33 **A** Would it be enough introduction?

Note that apart from a few seemingly odd phrases the passage shows no readily apparent differences in linguistic code, yet the oddness of A's question, (33) 'Would it be enough introduction?' coming as it does after B's (31) 'Okay, that's the introduction,' clearly suggests that something is going wrong. Normally one might explain this sort of utterance and the awkward exchanges that precede it in psychological terms as odd behavior, reflecting participants' personal motives. But a closer examination of the interactive synchrony of the entire passage, as revealed in the coordination of speakers' messages with back-channel cues such as 'um', 'yes' or 'no no' suggests that the problem is more complex than that.

Studies of interactive synchrony (Erickson and Schultz, 1982), focusing primarily on nonverbal signs, have shown that in conversation of all kinds, speakers' moves and listeners' responses are synchronized in such a way as to conform to a regular and measurable rhythmic beat. Most longer encounters alternate between synchronous or smooth phases exhibiting a high degree of coordination and phases of asynchrony which Erickson calls 'uncomfortable moments'. Experiments carried on at Berkeley (Bennett, 1981; Bennett, Erickson and Gumperz, 1976) with ethnically mixed student groups reveal that the relationship of back-channel signals to speakers' utterances is closely related to interactional synchrony at the nonverbal level. In synchronous phases back-channel signals stand in regular relationship to points of maximum information content in the speaker's message, as marked by stress and intonation contour. Asynchronous phases lack such coordination. It has furthermore been noted that when participants are asked to monitor video or audio tapes of their own encounters, they have little difficulty in agreeing on the boundaries between synchronous and asynchronous phases. But when they are asked to interpret what was going on in these phases, their interpretations tend to differ. Conversational synchrony thus yields empirical measures of conversational cooperation which reflect automatic behavior, independent of prior semantic assumptions about the content or function of what was said. Analysis of conversational synchrony can form a useful starting point for comparative analysis of interpretive processes.

In interactions among individuals who share socio-cultural background, which are not marked by other overt signs of disagreement, asynchronous movements tend to reflect the initial negotiation transitions in verbal activity or routines, or unexpected moves by one or another participant, and are relatively brief. In our passage here, however, lack of coordination is evident throughout.

Note, for example, the placement of B's 'oh no' (3). In a coordinated exchange this should appear shortly after A's verb phrase 'write it down' (6). Here it occurs after the auxiliary 'like'. Similarly B's 'yes' (5) overlaps with A's 'the' (4). The same is true of B's 'doesn't matter' (13) and A's 'umm' (18). Similar asynchronous overlaps are found throughout the tape. In Line 9 B shifts to a high-pitched 'um, well', and as she is about to go into her message, A simultaneously begins with 'first of all'. In addition there are premature starts, i.e. starts which lack the usual rhythmic interval, in Lines 21, 23 and 25; in Lines 8, 11 and 21, we find arhythmic pauses of one, two, and one seconds respectively.

Lack of coordination seems to increase rather than decrease with the progress of the interaction, culminating in several bursts of nervous laughter (27, 29, 31, 32) which suggest that both participants are becoming increasingly ill at ease. Given what we know about conversational rhythm and synchrony there is strong evidence for systematic differences in contextualization and interpretive strategies in this interaction.

To find out what these differences are, we must turn to content. The passage divides into roughly three sequentially ordered subepisodes. These are distinct in manifest topic. But beyond that, they also have semantic import in terms of the role relations and expected outcomes they imply, and can thus be seen as reflecting distinct activity types.

The first subepisode begins with A's response to B's request for permission to tape record. This gives A the option either to agree or to refuse, and further to explain or justify his decision. His words here indirectly suggest that he is agreeing and is taking advantage of his option, in order to comment on the importance of his problem. B, however, does not seem to understand what he's trying to do. Her 'no, no' (3) suggests she is defensive about her request to record, and her 'that's right' (7) seems intended to cut short the preliminaries. In Line 9, B attempts to lead into the interview proper. Her rise in pitch is of the type English speakers use elsewhere in our comparative tapes to mark shifts in focus to introduce important new information. A's interruption here suggests that he either does not recognize or disagrees with her change in focus.

Subepisode 2, Lines 9–17, consists of B's indirect attempts to get A to state his problem. These are temporarily sidetracked by his responses. In subepisode 3 B once more tries to get started with the interview proper, whereupon A responds with an asynchronous 'umm' and counters by asking for an introduction. The remainder of the passage then focuses on that introduction.

Looking in more detail at the process of speaker – listener coordination, we note that in Line 11, B simply ignores A's interruption. Her message is followed by a long pause of two seconds. A's statement following that pause is marked by what, when compared to his preceding and following statements, is unusually slow rhythm and highly contoured intonation. 'Very sorry' (12) and 'very important' (16) are stressed. Many Indian English speakers readily identify the prosody here as signalling that the speaker is seriously concerned and wants the listener to understand the gravity of his situation before he goes on to give more detail. Similar contouring occurs in a number of other interethnic encounters as well as elsewhere in the present interview. Listeners of English background tend not to be attuned to the signalling value of such cues; those who notice this shift in prosody tend to dismiss it as a rather minor and somewhat misplaced indication of affect. What we seem to be faced with is an ethnically specific signalling system where contoured prosody and slowed rhythm contrast with flattened contours and normal rhythm to suggest personal concern.

In this episode, B is either unaware of this signalling convention or has decided to ignore it, since she fails to respond. In Western English conventions her statement 'Miss C. hasn't said anything to me' counts as an indirect request for more detail as to what the problem is. She seems to want to go on with the interview and when A does not respond as expected she twice interrupts with 'doesn't matter' (13, 15). Both her interruptions are asynchronous with A's talk. She seems to be interpreting A's statement as a somewhat irrelevant formulaic excuse, rather than as a preamble, or an attempt to prepare the ground for what is to come. As A continues, 'it was very important,' she responds with a 'yes' spoken with normal intonation, and without raising her pitch at all she attempts once more to begin the interview proper. When A then asks for the introduction, she counters with 'oh yes sorry', whereupon A immediately, i.e. without the normal rhythmic interval, says: 'I am sorry'. Now B seems thrown off balance. She takes a full second to formulate her reply, and it is easy to see why. Her own 'sorry' indicates that she interprets A's preceding remark as implying she has been remiss, but when he himself then replies with 'I am sorry' he seems to be suggesting it is his own fault.

When B then gives her name in Line 22, A replies with a very breathy and contoured 'very nice'. Indian English speakers who listen to the tape will readily identify this last as a formulaic utterance. It is the Indian English equivalent of Urdu *bəhut əccha* which is used as a back-channel sign of interest similar to our 'O.K. go on'. The breathy enunciation and contoured intonation are signs of polite emphasis. For Western English speakers, however, the meaning is quite different. 'Very nice' is used to respond to children who behave properly. In this situation moreover, it might be interpreted as having sexual overtones. In any case, B ignores the remark and in Line 26 attempts to shift the focus away from herself to talk about the centre where she works. A does not follow her shift in focus however. His 'pleased to meet you' focuses once more on her as a person. This is either intentional or it could be the result of his slowness in following her shift in focus. In any case his laughing now suggests lack of ease or nervousness.

B continues as if he hadn't spoken and then when A laughs again asks 'and you are Mr. A?' When A then gives his name she repeats it. Her subsequent laugh and her concluding statement, 'Okay, that's the introduction,' indicate that she has interpreted A's original suggestion that they introduce each other as simply a request to exchange names, which given her frame of reference she regards as somewhat superfluous in this situation.

A's subsequent 'would it be enough introduction?' in Line 33, however, shows that he has quite different expectations of what the introduction was to accomplish. We can begin to see what these expectations are by examining the following exchange which takes place much later in the interview.

Case study 2

```
1    A    then I had decided because I felt all the
2         way that whatever happened that was totally
3         wrong that was not, there was no trace of
4         truth in it. I needed teaching. I wanted
5         teaching,  ⌈I want teaching
6    B              ⌊hu
7    A    I want to um um to waive ⌈that
8    B                             ⌊hu
9    A    ⌈condition so that by doing,
10   B    ⌊hu
11   A    some sort of training ⌈language training
12   B                          ⌊hu
13   A    I can fulfill the condition and then I can
14        come back
15   B    hu
16   A    and reinstate in ⌈teaching condition
17   B                     ⌊hu
```

18 **A** this is what I had the view to write to
19   the Department of ⌈Education and Science and
20 **B**   ⌊yes I see
21 **A** with the same view I approached
22 **B** Twickenham
23 **A** Twickenham as well as Uxbridge ⌈University
24 **B**   ⌊yes
25 **A** as well as Ealing Technical College
26 **B** college
27 **A** and at the end they had directed me to
28   ⌈give the ⌈best possible advice
29 **B** ⌊yes   ⌊yes
30 **A** by doing some sort of language course in
31   which I could best help, so I can be reinstated
32   and I can do something productive rather
33   than wasting my time ⌈and the provincial and
34 **B**   ⌊yes I see, yes I understand
35 **A** the money and time
36 **B** Okay now the thing is Mr A. there is no course here
37   which is suitable for you at the moment
38 **A** this I had seen the ⌈pro . . . prospectus ⌈this
39 **B**   ⌊yes   ⌊yes
40 **A** teachers' training ⌈(   )
41 **B**   ⌊yes that's teachers' training
42   is for teachers who are employed doing language
43   training in factories
44 **A**   per . . . perhaps perhaps there will be
45   some way out for you for to for to to
46   ⌈to help me
47 **B** ⌊to help there might be but I can't tell you now
48   because I shall have to, you see at the moment there
49   is no course sui . . . suitable for you ⌈the
50 **A**   ⌊um
51 **B** Teachers' training course is run one day here, one
52   day there, two days here, two days there and these are
53   connected with a specific project
54 **A** I don't mind doing any sort of ⌈pro . . . project but
55 **B**   ⌊no but th . . .
56   th . . . that's not suitable, I can tell you honestly
57   you won't find it suitable for you, ⌈it won't
58 **A**   ⌊but
59 **B** is is ⌈nothing to do what you want
60 **A**   ⌊but no it is not what actually I want I want
61   only to waive the condition, waive the condition
62   which I have been ⌈restricted from the admission
63 **B**   ⌊but you see it it
64   would only be may five days a year, it's only
65   conferences, we don't have a teachers' training

66		course here
67	**A**	nothing (looks at program)
68	**B**	Yes, oh that's the RSA course
69	**A**	Yes
70	**B**	that's at Ealing Technical College, that isn't here
71	**A**	But it's it's given here
72	**B**	Yes that's ⌈right it's at Ealing Technical College
73	**A**	⌊it's it's

A has here completed his story of the experiences that led to his present predicament, and begins to explain what he wants. The phrase 'I want to waive that condition' (7,9) and his repeated use of the word 'condition' (13, 16) are his references to the fact that he has been told that he needs additional communication skills. He then proceeds to ask to be admitted to a training course. When, in Line 36, B tells him that there is no course which is suitable for him, he disputes this by mentioning the centre's prospectus. Then in response to B's remarks in Lines 51–3, he says 'I don't mind doing any sort of project.' When B then insists that this would not be suitable, and is not what he wants, he says once more, repeating the same phrase twice, that all he wants to do is to 'waive the condition'. In other words he wants another certificate, not more training.

From this, from our analysis of similar situations, and from our interviews with Asians in British industry, we can see that A, along with many others of similar background, views these counselling situations in terms which are similar to the way many Indians view contracts between government functionaries and members of the lay public in general. Following a type of cultural logic which is perhaps best illustrated in Dumont (1970), these situations are seen as basically hierarchical situations in which the counselee acts as a petitioner requesting the counsellor to facilitate or grant access to a position. It is the petitioner's role in such situations to plead or present arguments based on personal need or hardship (as in A's expressions of concern in case study 1, Lines 12ff.), which the functionary then either grants or refuses.

In the present case, having been told he lacks communication skills, A interprets this to mean that he needs to get another certificate to qualify for a new teaching post. What he wants to ask of B is that she help him get such a certificate. Before he can make his request, however, he needs to find out what her position in the organization is so that he can judge the extent to which she is able to help him. This is what he wants to accomplish with his request for introductions. His awkward-sounding comments are simply attempts at using indirect verbal strategies to get the information he needs.

Seen from this perspective B's response is clearly insufficient. We know, for example, that although B is a trained teacher and does occasionally teach, her main function is that of assistant director of the centre in charge of curriculum planning. In identifying herself as a teacher she follows the common English practice of slightly understating her actual rank. Most of us would do likewise in similar situations. If someone were to ask me to introduce myself, I might say that I teach anthropology at Berkeley, but I would certainly not identify myself directly as a full professor, and list my administrative responsibilities. Anyone who needs this type of information would have to elicit it from me. To do so requires command of indirect strategies which could induce me to volunteer the required information, strategies which are dependent on socio-culturally specific background knowledge. A's probes in case study 1, Lines 23, 25, 27 and 33 fail because he has neither the socio-cultural knowledge to know what to expect, nor the contextualization strategies needed to elicit information not freely offered.

What B's expectations are emerges from the following passage which in the actual interview follows immediately after case study 1.

Case study 3

1	**B**	well tell me what you have been studying . . .
2	**A**	um . . .
3	**B**	up till now
4	**A**	um, I have done my M.Sc. from N. University
5	**B**	huh
6	**A**	I have done my graduate certificate in Education from L. University.
7		I had been teaching after getting that teachers' training in
8		H., in H.
9	**B**	Oh, so you have *done* some teaching
10	**A**	Some ⎡I have done I have done some ⎡teaching
11	**B**	⎣in H. ⎣I see
12	**A**	Um . . . I completed two terms . . . uh, unfortunately I had to
13		leave from that place because ⎡uh I was appointed only
14	**B**	⎣oh
15	**A**	for two terms
16	**B**	Oh so you didn't get to finish your probation, I suppose
17	**A**	(sighs) so that is uh ⎡my start was alright but later
18	**B**	⎣oh
19	**A**	on what happened it is a mi—a great chaos, I don't know
20		where I stand or what I can do . . . um, ⎡after
21	**B**	⎣and now you find
22		you can't get a job
23	**A**	no this is not actually the situation, ⎡I have not
24	**B**	⎣oh
25	**A**	completely explained ⎡my position
26	**B**	⎣yes yes
27	**A**	After um completing two um um terms of my probation ⎡teaching
28	**B**	⎣huh huh
29	**A**	I had to apply somewhere else. I, there was a job in the borough,
30		London borough of H., I applied and there that was first application
31		which I made and I got the job, but since the beginning the
32		teach – teaching situation was not suitable for a probationary
33		teacher.

The initial question here calls for information about the subjects A has studied. Yet A responds first with an asynchronous 'um' and then, following the amplification, 'up till now', he gives a list of his degrees starting with his first degree. B's 'so you have done some teaching' (9) focuses on 'done' and is thus an indirect probe for more details on A's actual work experience. A's response to this probe is rhythmically premature and simply copies the last phrase of her remark. It almost sounds as if he were mimicking her, rather than responding to the question.

When interpreted in the light of what transpired later, A's next remarks (12–15) are intended to lead into a longer narrative. He starts by mentioning the first of several teaching posts he has held, a temporary appointment which lasted for two terms. However his contextualization practices create problems. Following the initial stressed sentence, 'I completed two terms,' his voice drops and the tempo speeds up. Thus the key bit of information about the limited nature of this first appointment is appended to what to English ears must sound like a qualifying remark, which moreover starts with the word 'unfortunately'.

In the present case B clearly does not respond to what is intended. Being familiar with personnel policies in British education, she knows that new graduates usually begin probationary appointments which last for three terms. Her asynchronous 'oh' (14) and the subsequent response in (16) show that she assumes that A is talking about such a post and that something may have happened to cause his premature dismissal. Given A's prosody and his use of 'unfortunately', her conclusion seems justified. When A continues with, 'so that is uh my start was alright' (17), she interjects another surprised 'oh'. Viewed purely in terms of its propositional content, A's remark could count as a repair or a correction. What he is saying is that the teaching experience he has just referred to was satisfactory. But his choice of words and prosody again go counter to English speakers' expectations. Repairs and corrections imply that new or nonshared information is being introduced. Ordinarily this is conventionally marked by accent or rise in pitch and by lexicalized transitions such as 'no' or 'I mean'. In the Western English system his initial 'so that is . . .' implies that he thinks that what he is saying follows from his previous remarks. He seems to be inconsistent and moreover he is not responding to B's reply. This explains her second interjection.

In Line 19 A continues once more with unmarked prosody, but after the initial phrase ending with 'chaos' there is a short pause. This is followed by 'I don't know where I stand or what I can do' spoken with contoured intonation similar to that found in case study 1 (Lines 12–16). As was pointed out before, Indian English speakers interpret this type of contouring as a signal that what is to come is of great concern to the speaker. In other words A would seem to be saying: 'now listen to what I have to say next, it's important.' But when he is about to go on to his next point and starts with 'after', B interrupts to continue her own line of reasoning with 'and now you find you can't get a job.'

Notice that the 'can't' here can refer either to the addressee's qualifications or to outside circumstances which prevent the desired condition from coming about. A, having been interrupted and recognizing that he is not being listened to, seems to adopt the first interpretation. His reply 'no this is not the actual situation' has the prosodic characteristics of his earlier phrase 'Would it be enough introduction?' (case study 1, Line 33) and suggests annoyance. He then goes on to insist on explaining his case in minute detail.

Line 29 marks the beginning of his narrative which lasts for more than half an hour. Throughout this period B makes regular attempts to get him to concentrate on what she thinks is the point of the interview: talk about the skills he has acquired, about his classroom experiences and about the kind of training he might still need to improve his skills. But the interaction is punctuated by long asides, misunderstandings of fact and misreadings of intent. A, on the other hand, finds he is not being listened to and not given a chance to explain his problem. Neither participant can control the interview. More importantly the fundamental differences in conceptions of what the interview is about that emerge from our discussion of case study 2 are never confronted.

[. . .] What is important about this case is not the misunderstanding as such but the fact that, in spite of repeated attempts, both speakers utterly fail in their efforts to negotiate a common frame in terms of which to decide on what is being focused on and where the argument is going at any one time. As one Indian English speaker put it in connection with a similar case study, 'they're on parallel tracks which don't meet' (Gumperz and Roberts, 1980).

The fact that two speakers whose sentences are quite grammatical can differ radically in their interpretation of each other's verbal strategies indicates that conversational management does rest on linguistic knowledge. But to find out what that knowledge is we must abandon the existing views of communication which draw a basic distinction between cultural or social knowledge on the one hand and linguistic signalling processes on the other. We cannot regard meaning as the output of nonlinear processing in which sounds are mapped into morphemes, clauses and sentences by application of the grammatical and semantic rules of sentence-level linguistic analysis, and look at social norms as extralinguistic forces which merely determine how and under what conditions such meaning units are used. Socio-cultural conventions affect all levels of speech production and interpretation from the abstract cultural logic that underlies all interpretation to the division of speech into episodes; from their categorization in terms of semantically relevant activities and interpretive frames, to the mapping of prosodic contours into syntactic strings and to selection among lexical and grammatical options. The failure to recognize this is another consequence of the fact that linguistic analysis has been sentence-based and influenced by the culture of literacy.

This view of social knowledge is implicit in modern theories of discourse. But work in this tradition has been limited by an unnecessarily diffuse view of extralinguistic knowledge as 'knowledge of the world' and by its failure to account for the interactive nature of interpretive processes and the role of linguistic contextualization processes in retrieving information and in processing of verbal messages. We can avoid some of the ambiguities inherent in linguists' notions of meaning and intent by concentrating on what participants have to know in order to enter into a conversation and on the inferences they must make to maintain thematic progression. This is essentially what sociologists concerned with conversational analysis have begun to do. But in dealing with these problems we cannot assume that interpretive processes are shared. Only by looking at the whole range of linguistic phenomena that enter into conversational management can we understand what goes on in an interaction.

References

Bennett, A. (1981) 'Everybody's got rhythm' in W. von Raffler-Engel and B. Hoffer (eds) *Aspects of Non-Verbal Communication*, San Antonio, Texas, Trinity University Press.

Bennett, A.F., Erickson, F. and Gumperz, J.J. (1976) Coordination of verbal and non-verbal cues in conversation. Ms. Report on Workshop at the University of California, Berkeley, January 1976.

Dumont, L. (1970) *Homo Hierarchicus*, London, Weidenfeld and Nicolson.

Erickson, F. and Schultz, J.J. (eds) (1982) *The Counselor as Gatekeeper: social and cultural organization of communication in counselling interviews*, New York, Academic Press.

Gumperz, J.J. and Roberts, C. (1980) 'Developing awareness skills for interethnic communication' in *Occasional Papers*, no. 12. Seameo Regional Language Center, Singapore.

The Relativity of Linguistic Strategies: Rethinking Power and Solidarity in Gender and Dominance

Deborah Tannen

Source: Tannen, D. (1993) The relativists of linguistic strategies: rethinking power and solidarity in gender and dominance, in D. Tannen (ed.) *Gender and Conversational Interaction*, New York, Oxford University Press, Chapter 7.

In analysing discourse, many researchers operate on the unstated assumption that all speakers proceed along similar lines of interpretation, so a particular example of discourse can be taken to represent how discourse works for all speakers. For some aspects of discourse, this is undoubtedly true. Yet a large body of sociolinguistic literature makes clear that, for many aspects of discourse, this is so only to the extent that cultural background is shared. To the extent that cultural backgrounds differ, lines of interpretation and habitual use of many linguistic strategies are likely to diverge. One thinks immediately and minimally of the work of Gumperz (1982), Erickson and Shultz (1982), Scollon and Scollon (1981), and Philips (1983). My own research shows that cultural difference is not limited to the gross and apparent levels of country of origin and native language, but also exists at the subcultural levels of ethnic heritage, class, geographic region, age, and gender. My earlier work (Tannen, 1984, 1986) focuses on ethnic and regional style; my most recent work (Tannen, 1990b) focuses on gender-related stylistic variation. I draw on this work here to demonstrate that specific linguistic strategies have widely divergent potential meanings.

This insight is particularly significant for research on language and gender, much of which has sought to describe the linguistic means by which men dominate women in interaction. That men dominate women as a class, and that individual men often dominate individual women in interaction, are not in question; what I am problematizing is the source and workings of domination and other intentions and effects. I will show that one cannot locate the source of domination, or of any interpersonal intention or effect, in linguistic strategies such as interruption, volubility, silence, and topic raising, as has been claimed. Similarly, one cannot locate the source of women's powerlessness in such linguistic strategies as indirectness, taciturnity, silence, and tag questions, as has also been claimed. The reason one cannot do this is that the same linguistic means can be used for different, even opposite, purposes and can have different, even opposite, effects in different contexts. Thus, a strategy that seems, or is, intended to dominate may in another context or in the mouth of another speaker be intended or used to establish connection. Similarly, a strategy that seems, or is, intended to create connection can in another context or in the mouth of another speaker be intended or used to establish dominance.

Put another way, the 'true' intention or motive of any utterance cannot be determined from examination of linguistic form alone. For one thing, intentions and effects are not identical. For another, as the sociolinguistic literature has dramatized repeatedly (see especially Duranti and Brenneis, 1986; Erickson, 1986; Schegloff, 1982, 1988; McDermott and Tylbor, 1983), human interaction is a 'joint production': everything that occurs results from the interaction of all participants. [. . .]

Theoretical background

Power and solidarity

Since Brown and Gilman's (1960) introduction of the concept and subsequent elaborations of it, especially those of Friedrich (1972) and Brown and Levinson ([1978] 1987), the dynamics of power and solidarity have been fundamental to sociolinguistic theory. (Fasold, 1990 provides an overview.) Brown and Gilman based their framework on analysis of the use of pronouns in European languages which have two forms of the second-person pronoun, such as the French *tu* and *vous*. In English the closest parallel is to be found in forms of address: first name versus title-last name. In Brown and Gilman's system, power is associated with nonreciprocal use of pronouns; in English, the parallel would be a situation in which one speaker addresses the other by first name but is addressed by title-last name (for example, doctor and patient, teacher and student, boss and secretary, building resident and elevator operator). Solidarity is associated with reciprocal pronoun use or symmetrical forms of address: both speakers address each other by *tu* or by *vous* (in English, by title-last name or by first name). Power governs asymmetrical relationships where one is subordinate to another; solidarity governs symmetrical relationships characterized by social equality and similarity.

In my previous work exploring the relationship between power and solidarity as it emerges in conversational discourse (Tannen 1984, 1986), I note that power and solidarity are in paradoxical relation to each other. That is, although power and solidarity, closeness and distance, seem at first to be opposites, each also entails the other. Any show of solidarity necessarily entails power, in that the requirement of similarity and closeness limits freedom and independence. At the same time, any show of power entails solidarity by involving participants in relation to each other. This creates a closeness that can be contrasted with the distance of individuals who have no relation to each other at all.

[. . .]

The ambiguity of linguistic strategies

The same symbol – a three-piece suit – can signal either power or solidarity, depending on, at least, the setting (e.g. board meeting or student demonstration), the habitual dress style of the individual, and the comparison of his clothing with that worn by others in the interaction. (I say 'his' intentionally; the range of meanings would be quite different if a man's three-piece suit were worn by a woman.) This provides an analogue to the ambiguity of linguistic strategies, which are signals in the semiotic system of language. As I have demonstrated at length in previous books, all linguistic strategies are potentially ambiguous. The power – solidarity dynamic is one fundamental source of ambiguity. What appear as attempts to dominate a conversation (an exercise of power) may actually be intended to establish rapport (an exercise of solidarity). This occurs because (as I have worded it elsewhere) power and solidarity are bought with the same currency: the same linguistic means can be used to create either or both.

This ambiguity can be seen in the following fleeting conversation. Two women were walking together from one building to another in order to attend a meeting. They were joined by a man they both knew who had just exited a third building on his way to the same meeting. One of the women greeted the man and remarked, 'Where's your coat?' The man responded, 'Thanks, Mom.' His response framed the woman's remark as a gambit in a power exchange: a mother tells a child to put on his coat. Yet the woman might have intended the remark as showing friendly concern rather than parental caretaking. Was it power (condescending, on the model of parent to child) or solidarity (friendly, on the model of intimate peers)? Though the man's uptake is clear, the woman's intention in making the remark is not.

[. . .]

The polysemy of power and solidarity

The preceding example could be interpreted as not only ambiguous but polysemous. The question 'Where's your coat?' shows concern *and* suggests a parent-child constellation.

[. . .]

Brown and Gilman are explicit in their assumption that power is associated with asymmetrical relationships in which the power is held by the person in the one-up position. This is stated in their definition: 'One person may be said to have power over another to the degree that he is able to control the behavior of the other. Power is a relationship between at least two persons, and it is nonreciprocal in the sense that both cannot have power in the same area of behavior' (1960: 254). I have called attention, however, to the extent to which solidarity in itself can be a form of control. For example, a young woman complained about friends who 'don't let you be different'. If the friend says she has a particular problem and the woman says. 'I don't have that problem,' her friend is hurt and accuses her of putting her down, of acting superior. The assumption of similarity requires the friend to have a matching problem (Tannen, 1990b).

Furthermore, although Brown and Gilman acknowledge that 'power superiors may be solidary (parents, elder siblings)' and 'power inferiors, similarly, may be as solidary as the old family retainer' (1960: 254), most Americans are inclined to assume that solidarity implies closeness, whereas power implies distance. Thus Americans regard the sibling relationship as the ultimate in solidarity: 'sister' or 'brother' can be used metaphorically to indicate closeness and equality. In contrast, it is often assumed that hierarchy precludes closeness: employers and employees cannot 'really' be friends. But being linked in a hierarchy necessarily brings individuals closer. This is an assumption underlying Watanabe's (1993) observation, in comparing American and Japanese group discussions, that whereas the Americans in her study saw themselves as individuals participating

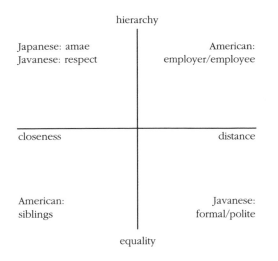

Figure 1   *The intersecting dimensions of closeness/distance and hierarchy/ equality*

in a joint activity, the Japanese saw themselves as members of a group united by hierarchy. When reading Watanabe, I was caught up short by the term 'united'. My inclination had been to assume that hierarchy is distancing, not uniting.

[. . .]

We can display these dynamics as a multidimensional grid of at least (and, potentially and probably, more) intersecting continua. The closeness/distance dimension can be placed on one axis and the hierarchy/equality one on another (See Figure 1). Indeed, the intersection of these dimensions – that is, the co-incidence of hierarchy and closeness – may account, at least in part, for what I am calling the ambiguity and polysemy of power and solidarity.

Similarity/difference

There is one more aspect of the dynamics of power and solidarity that bears discussion before I demonstrate the relativity of linguistic strategies. That is the similarity/difference continuum and its relation to the other dynamics discussed.

For Brown and Gilman solidarity implies sameness, in contrast to power, about which they observe, 'In general terms, the *V* form is linked with differences between persons' (1960: 256). This is explicit in their definition of 'the solidarity semantic':

> Now we are concerned with a new set of relations which are symmetrical; for example, *attended the same school* or *have the same parents* or *practice the same profession*. If A has the same parents as B, B has the same parents as A. Solidarity is the name we give to the general relationship and solidarity is symmetrical.
>
> (1960: 257; italics in original)

The similarity/difference continuum calls to mind what I have discussed elsewhere (Tannen 1984, 1986) as the double bind of communication. In some ways, we are all the same. But in other ways we are all different. Communication is a double bind in the sense that anything we say to honour our similarity violates our difference, and anything we say to honour our difference violates our sameness. Thus a complaint can be lodged: 'Don't think I'm different.' ('If you prick me, do I not bleed?' one might protest, like Shylock.) But a complaint can also be lodged: 'Don't think I'm the same.' (Thus, for example, women who have primary responsibility for the care of small children will be effectively excluded from activities or events at which day care is not provided.) Becker (1982: 125) expresses this double bind as 'a matter of continual self-correction between exuberance (i.e. friendliness: you are like me) and deficiency (i.e., respect: you are not me).' All these formulations elaborate on the tension between similarity and difference, or what Becker and Oka (1974) call 'the cline of person', a semantic dimension they suggest may be the one most basic to language: that is, one deals with the world and the objects and people in it in terms of how close (and I would add, similar) they are to oneself.

As a result of these dynamics, similarity is a threat to hierarchy. This is dramatized in Harold Pinter's play *Mountain Language*. Composed of four brief scenes, the play is set in a political prison in the capital city of an unnamed country that is under dictatorial siege. In the second scene, an old mountain woman is finally allowed to visit her son across a table as a guard stands over them. But whenever she tries to speak to her son, the guard silences her, telling the prisoner to tell his mother that it is forbidden to speak their mountain language in the capital. Then he continues:

GUARD

. . . And I'll tell you another thing. I've got a wife and three kids. And you're all a pile of shit.
Silence.

PRISONER

I've got a wife and three kids.

GUARD

You've what?
Silence.
You've got what?
Silence.
What did you say to me? You've got what?
Silence.
You've got *what?*
He picks up the telephone and dials one digit.
Sergeant? I'm in the Blue Room . . . yes . . . I thought I should report, Sergeant . . . I think I've got a joker in here.

The Sergeant soon enters and asks, 'What joker?' The stage darkens and the scene ends. The final scene opens on the same setting, with the prisoner bloody and shaking, his mother shocked into speechlessness. The prisoner was beaten for saying, 'I've got a wife and three kids.' This quotidian statement, which would be unremarkable in casual conversation, was insubordinate in the hierarchical context of brutal oppression because the guard had just made the same statement. When the guard said, 'I've got a wife and three kids. And you're a pile of shit,' he was claiming, 'I am different from you.' One could further interpret his words to imply, 'I'm human, and you're not. Therefore I have a right to dominate and abuse you.' By repeating the guard's words verbatim, the prisoner was then saying, 'I am the same as you.' By claiming *his* humanity and implicitly denying the guard's assertion that he is 'a pile of shit,' the prisoner challenged the guard's right to dominate him. Similarity is antithetical to hierarchy.

The ambiguity of closeness, a spatial metaphor representing similarity or involvement, emerges in a nonverbal aspect of this scene. In the performance I saw, the guard repeated the question 'You've got what?' while moving steadily closer to the prisoner, until he was bending over him, nose to nose. The guard's moving closer was a kinesic/proxemic analogue to the prisoner's statement, but with opposite effect: he was 'closing in'. The guard moved closer and brought his face into contact with the prisoner's not as a sign of affection (which such actions could signify in another context) but as a threat. Closeness, then, can mean aggression rather than affiliation in the context of a hierarchical rather than symmetrical relationship.

The relativity of linguistic strategies

The potential ambiguity of linguistic strategies to mark both power and solidarity in face-to-face interaction has made mischief in language and gender research, wherein it is tempting to assume that whatever women do results from, or creates, their powerlessness and whatever men do results from, or creates, their dominance. But all the linguistic strategies that have been taken by analysts as evidence of dominance can in some circumstances be instruments of affiliation. For the remainder of this chapter I demonstrate the relativity of linguistic strategies by considering each of the following strategies in turn: indirectness, interruption, silence versus volubility, topic raising, and adversativeness, or verbal conflict. All of these strategies have been 'found' by researchers to express or create dominance. I will demonstrate that they are ambiguous or polysemous with regard to dominance or closeness. Once again I am not arguing that these strategies *cannot* be used to create dominance or powerlessness, much less that dominance and powerlessness do not exist. Rather, my purpose is to demonstrate that the 'meaning' of any linguistic strategy can vary, depending at least on context, the conversational styles of participants, and the interaction of participants' styles and strategies. Therefore we will have to study the operation of specific linguistic strategies more closely to understand how dominance and powerlessness are expressed and created in interaction.

Indirectness
Lakoff (1975) identifies two benefits of indirectness: defensiveness and rapport. Defensiveness refers to a speaker's preference not to go on record with an idea in order to be able to disclaim, rescind, or modify it if it does not meet with a positive response. The rapport benefit of indirectness results from the pleasant experience of getting one's way not because one demanded it (power) but because the other person wanted the same thing (solidarity). Many researchers

have focused on the defensive or power benefit of indirectness and ignored the payoff in rapport or solidarity.

The claim by Conley, O'Barr and Lind (1979) that women's language is really powerless language has been particularly influential. In this view women's tendency to be indirect is taken as evidence that women don't feel entitled to make demands. Surely there are cases in which this is true. Yet it can easily be demonstrated that those who feel entitled to make demands may prefer not to, seeking the payoff in rapport. Furthermore, the ability to get one's demands met without expressing them directly can be a sign of power rather than of the lack of it. An example I have used elsewhere (Tannen, 1986) is the Greek father who answers, 'If you want, you can go,' to his daughter's inquiry about going to a party. Because of the lack of enthusiasm of his response, the Greek daughter understands that her father would prefer she not go and 'chooses' not to go. (A 'real' approval would have been 'Yes, of course, you should go.') I argue that this father did not feel powerless to give his daughter orders. Rather, a communicative system was conventionalized by which he and she could both preserve the appearance, and possibly the belief, that she chose not to go rather than simply obeying his command.

Far from being powerless, this father felt so powerful that he did not need to give his daughter orders; he simply needed to let her know his preference, and she would accommodate to it. By this reasoning, indirectness is a prerogative of the powerful. By the same reasoning, a master who says, 'It's cold in here,' may expect a servant to make a move to close a window, but a servant who says the same thing is not likely to see his employer rise to correct the situation and make him more comfortable. Indeed, a Frenchman who was raised in Brittany tells me that his family never gave bald commands to their servants but always communicated orders in indirect and superpolite form. This pattern renders less surprising the finding of Bellinger and Gleason (1982, reported in Gleason, 1987) that fathers' speech to their young children had a higher incidence than mothers' of both direct imperatives (such as 'Turn the bolt with the wrench') *and* implied indirect imperatives (for example, 'The wheel is going to fall off').

The use of indirectness can hardly be understood without the cross-cultural perspective. Many Americans find it self-evident that directness is logical and aligned with power whereas indirectness is akin to dishonesty as well as subservience. But for speakers raised in most of the world's cultures, varieties of indirectness are the norm in communication. In Japanese interaction, for example, it is well known that saying 'no' is considered too face-threatening to risk, so negative responses are phrased as positive ones: one never says 'no' but initiates understanding from the form of the 'yes' whether it is truly a 'yes' or a polite 'no'. And this applies to men as well as women.

The American association of indirectness with female style is not culturally universal. Keenan (1974) found that in a Malagasy-speaking village on the island of Madagascar, women are direct and men indirect. But this in no way implies that the women are more powerful than men in this society. Quite the contrary, Malagasy men are socially dominant – and their indirect style is more highly valued. Keenan found that women were widely believed to debase the language with their artless directness, whereas men's elaborate indirectness was widely admired. In my own research (Tannen, 1981) I compared Greeks and Americans with regard to their tendency to interpret a question as an indirect means of making a request. I found that whereas American women were more likely to take an indirect interpretation of a sample conversation, Greek men were as likely as Greek women, and more likely than American men *or women*, to take an indirect interpretation. Greek men, of course, are not less powerful vis-à-vis women than American men.

[. . .]

Interruption

That interruption is a sign of dominance has been as widespread an assumption in research as in conventional wisdom. Most frequently cited is West and Zimmerman's (1983) finding that men dominate women by interrupting them in conversation. Tellingly, however, Deborah James and Sandra Clarke (in Tannen, 1993), reviewing research on gender and interruption, do not find a clear pattern of males interrupting females. Especially significant is their discovery that studies comparing amount of interruption in all-female versus all-male conversations find more interruption, not less, in all-female groups. Though initially surprising, this finding reinforces the need to distinguish linguistic strategies by their interactional purpose. Does the overlap show support for the speaker, or does it contradict or change the topic? I explore this phenomenon in detail elsewhere (Tannen, 1989b) but I will include a brief summary of the argument here.

The phenomenon commonly referred to as 'interruption', but more properly referred to as 'overlap', is a paradigm case of the ambiguity of power and solidarity. This is clearly demonstrated with reference to a two and a half hour dinner-table conversation that I have analysed at length (Tannen, 1984). My analysis makes clear that some speakers consider talking along with another a show of enthusiastic participation in the conversation (solidarity, creating connections); others, however, assume that only one voice should be heard at a time, so for them any overlap is an interruption (an attempt to wrest the floor, a power play). The result, in the conversation I analysed, was that enthusiastic listeners who overlapped cooperatively, talking along to establish rapport, were perceived by overlap-resistant speakers as interrupting. This doubtless contributed to the impression reported by the overlap-resistant speakers that the cooperative overlappers had 'dominated' the conversation. Indeed, the tape and transcript also give the impression that the cooperative overlappers had dominated, because the overlap-aversant participants tended to stop speaking as soon as another voice began.

[. . .]

Thus, to understand whether an overlap is an interruption, one must consider the context (for example, cooperative overlapping is more likely to occur in casual conversation among friends than in a job interview), the speakers' habitual styles (for example, overlaps are more likely not to be interruptions among those with a style I call 'high-involvement'), and the interaction of their styles (for example, an interruption is more likely to occur between speakers whose styles differ with regard to pausing and overlap). This is not to say that one cannot use interruption to dominate a conversation or a person, only that it is not self-evident from the observation of overlap that an interruption has occurred, or was intended, or was intended to dominate.

Silence versus volubility

The excerpt from Pinter's *Mountain Language* dramatizes the assumption that powerful people do the talking and powerless people are silenced. This is the trope that underlies the play's title and its central theme: by outlawing their language, the oppressors silence the mountain people, robbing them of their ability to speak and hence of their humanity. In the same spirit, many scholars (for example, Spender, 1980) have claimed that men dominate women by silencing them. There are obviously circumstances in which this is accurate. Coates (1986) notes numerous proverbs that instruct women, like children, to be silent.

Silence alone, however, is not a self-evident sign of powerlessness, nor volubility a self-evident sign of domination. A theme running through Komarovsky's (1962) classic study, *Blue-collar Marriage*, is that many of the wives interviewed said they talked more than their husbands: 'He's tongue-tied,' one woman said (1962: 13); 'My husband has a great habit of not talking,' said another (1962: 162); 'He doesn't say much but he means what he says and the children mind him,' said a third (1962: 353). Yet there is no question that these husbands are dominant in their marriages, as the last of these quotes indicates.

Indeed, taciturnity itself can be an instrument of power. This is precisely the claim of Sattel (1983), who argues that men use silence to exercise power over women. Sattel illustrates with a scene from Erica Jong's novel *Fear of Flying*, only a brief part of which is presented here. The first line of dialogue is spoken by Isadora, the second by her husband, Bennett. (Spaced dots indicate omitted text; unspaced dots are a form of punctuation included in the original text.)

> 'Why do you turn on me? What did I do?'
> Silence.
> 'What did I do?'
> He looks at her as if her not knowing were another injury.
> 'Look, let's just go to sleep now. Let's just forget it.'
> 'Forget what?'
> He says nothing.
>
> 'It was something in the movie, wasn't it?'
> 'What, in the movie?'
> '. . . It was the funeral scene. . . . The little boy looking at his dead mother.
> Something got you there. That was when you got depressed.'
> Silence.
> 'Well, *wasn't* it?'
> Silence.
> 'Oh come on, Bennett, you're making me *furious*. Please tell me. Please.'

The painful scene continues in this vein until Bennett tries to leave the room and Isadora tries to detain him. The excerpt certainly seems to support Sattel's claim that Bennett's silence subjugates his wife, as the scene ends with her literally lowered to the floor, clinging to his pajama leg. But the reason his silence is an effective weapon is her insistence that he tell her what's wrong. If *she* receded into silence, leaving the room or refusing to talk to him, his silence would be disarmed. The devastation results not from his silence alone but from the combination of his silence and her insistence on talking, in other words, the interaction of their differing styles.

Researchers have counted numbers of words spoken or timed length of talk in order to demonstrate that men talk more than women and thereby dominate interactions. Undoubtedly there is truth to this observation in some settings. But the association of volubility with dominance does not hold for all settings and all cultures. Imagine, for example, an interrogation, in which the interrogator does little of the talking but holds all the power.

The relativity of the 'meaning' of taciturnity and volubility is high-lighted in Margaret Mead's (1977) discussion of 'end linkage', a concept developed jointly by Mead, Gregory Bateson, and Geoffrey Gorer. Their claim is that universal and biologically constructed relationships, such as parent–child, are linked to different behaviours in different cultures. One of their paradigm examples is the apportionment of spectatorship and exhibitionism. In middle-class American culture, children, who are obviously the weaker party in the constellation, are expected to exhibit while their more powerful parents are spectators; in contrast, in middle- and upper-class British culture, exhibition is associated with the parental role and spectatorship with children, who are expected to be seen and not heard.

Furthermore, volubility and taciturnity, too, can result from style differences rather than speakers' intentions. As I (Tannen, 1984, 1985) and others (Scollon and Scollon 1981; Scollon, 1985) have discussed at length, there are cultural and subcultural differences in the length of pauses expected between and within speaking turns. In my study of the dinner table conversation, those who expected shorter pauses between conversational turns began to feel an uncomfortable silence ensuing while their longer-pausing friends were simply waiting for what they regarded as the 'normal' end-of-turn pause. The result was that the shorter pausers ended up doing most of the talking, another sign interpreted by their interlocutors as dominating the conversation. But their intentions had been to fill in what to them were potentially uncomfortable silences, that is, to grease the conversational wheels and ensure the success of the conversation. In their view, the taciturn participants were uncooperative, failing to do their part to maintain the conversation.

Thus silence and volubility, too, cannot be taken to 'mean' power or powerlessness, domination or subjugation. Rather, both may imply either power or solidarity, depending on the criteria discussed.

Topic raising

Shuy (1982) is typical in assuming that the speaker who raises the most topics is dominating a conversation. However, in a study I conducted (Tannen, 1990a) of videotaped conversations among friends of varying ages recorded by Dorval (1990), it emerged that the speaker who raised the most topics was not always dominant, as judged by other criteria (for example, who took the lead in addressing the investigator when he entered the room). In a twenty-minute conversation between a pair of sixth-grade girls who identified themselves as best friends, Shannon raised the topic of Julia's relationship with Mary by saying, 'Too bad you and Mary are not good friends anymore.' The conversation

proceeded and continued to focus almost exclusively on Julia's troubled
relationship with Mary.

Similarly, most of the conversation between two tenth-grade girls was about
Nancy, but Sally raised the topic of Nancy's problems. In response to Nancy's
question 'Well, what do you want to talk about?' Sally said, 'Your mama. Did you
talk to your mama?' The ensuing conversation focuses on happenings involving
Nancy's mother and boyfriend. Overall, Sally raised nine topics, Nancy seven.
However, all but one of the topics Sally raised were questions focused on Nancy.
If raising more topics is a sign of dominance, Sally controlled the conversation
when she raised topics, although even this was subject to Nancy's collaboration
by picking them up. It may or may not be the case that Sally controlled the
conversation, but the nature of her dominance is surely other than what is
normally assumed by that term if the topics she raised were all about Nancy.

Finally, the effect of raising topics may also be an effect of differences in
pacing and pausing, as discussed with regard to my study of dinner-table
conversation. A speaker who thinks the other has no more to say on a given
topic may try to contribute to the conversation by raising another topic. But a
speaker who was intending to say more and was simply waiting for the
appropriate turn-exchange pause will feel that the floor was taken away and the
topic aggressively switched. Yet again, the impression of dominance might
simply result from style differences.

Adversativeness: conflict and verbal aggression

Research on gender and language has consistently found male speakers to be
competitive and more likely to engage in conflict (for example, by arguing,
issuing commands, and taking opposing stands) and females to be cooperative
and more likely to avoid conflict (for example, by agreeing, supporting, and
making suggestions rather than commands). (Maltz and Borker, 1982 summarize
some of this research.) Ong (1981: 51) argues that 'adversativeness' is universal,
but 'conspicuous or expressed adversativeness is a larger element in the lives of
males than of females.'

In my analysis of videotapes of male and female friends talking to each other
(Tannen, 1990a), I have begun to investigate how male adversativeness and
female cooperation are played out, complicated, and contradicted in
conversational discourse. In analysing videotapes of friends talking, for example,
I found a sixth-grade boy saying to his best friend,

> Seems like, if there's a fight, me and you are automatically in it. And everyone else
> wants to go against you and everything. It's hard to agree without someone saying
> something to you.

In contrast, girls of the same age (and also of most other ages whose talk I
examined) spent a great deal of time discussing the dangers of anger and
contention. In affirming their own friendship, one girl told her friend,

> Me and you <u>never</u> get in fights hardly,

and

I mean like if I try to talk to you, you'll say, 'Talk to me!' And if you try to talk to me, I'll talk to you.

These examples of gendered styles of interaction are illuminated by the insight that power and solidarity are mutually evocative. As seen in the statement of the sixth-grade boy, opposing other boys in teams entails affiliation within the team. The most dramatic instance of male affiliation resulting from conflict with others is bonding among soldiers, a phenomenon explored by Norman (1990).

By the same token, girls' efforts to support their friends necessarily entail exclusion of or opposition to other girls. This emerges in Hughes's (1988) study of girls playing a street game called foursquare, in which four players occupy one square each and bounce a ball into each other's squares. The object of the game is to eliminate players by hitting the ball into their square in such a way that they fail to hit it back. But this effort to 'get people out' is at odds with the social injunction under which the girls operate, to be 'nice' and not 'mean'. The girls resolved the conflict, and formed 'incipient teams' composed of friends, by claiming that their motivation in eliminating some players was to enable others (their friends) to enter the game, since eliminated players are replaced by awaiting players. In the girls' terms 'getting someone out' was 'nice-mean' because it was reframed as 'getting someone [a friend] in.' This dynamic is also supported by my analysis of the sixth-grade girls' conversation: Most of their talk was devoted to allying themselves with each other in opposition to another girl who was not present. So their cooperation (solidarity) also entails opposition (power).

For boys power entails solidarity not only by opposition to another team, but by opposition to each other. In the videotapes of friends talking, I found that all the conversations between young boys (and none between young girls) had numerous examples of teasing and mock attack. In examining preschool conversations transcribed and analysed by Corsaro and Rizzo (1990: 34), I was amazed to discover that a fight could initiate rather than preclude friendship. In the following episode, a little boy intrudes on two others and an angry fight ensues. This is the way Corsaro and Rizzo present the dialogue:

> Two boys (Richard and Denny) have been playing with a slinky on the stairway leading to the upstairs playhouse in the school. During their play two other boys (Joseph and Martin) enter and stand near the bottom of the stairs.

DENNY   Go!

(Martin now runs off, but Joseph remains and he eventually moves halfway up the stairs.)

JOSEPH   These are big shoes.
RICHARD   I'll punch him right in the eye.
JOSEPH   I'll punch you right in the nose.
DENNY   I'll punch him with my big fist.
JOSEPH   I'll- I- I-

RICHARD	And he'll be bumpety, bumpety and punched out all the way down the stairs.
JOSEPH	I- I- I'll- I could poke your eyes out with my gun. I have a gun.
DENNY	A gun! I'll- I- I- even if-
RICHARD	I have a gun too.
DENNY	And I have guns too and it's bigger than yours and it poo-poo down. That's poo-poo.

(All three boys laugh at Denny's reference to poo-poo.)

RICHARD	Now leave.
JOSEPH	Un-uh. I gonna tell you to put on- on the gun on your hair and the poop will come right out on his face.
DENNY	Well.
RICHARD	Slinky will snap right on your face too.
DENNY	And my gun will snap right-

Up until this point I had no difficulty interpreting the interaction: the boys were engaged in a fight occasioned by Joseph's intrusion into Richard and Denny's play. But what happened next surprised and, at first, perplexed me. Corsaro and Rizzo describe it this way:

> At this point a girl (Debbie) enters, says she is Batgirl, and asks if they have seen Robin. Joseph says he is Robin, but she says she is looking for a different Robin and then runs off. After Debbie leaves, Denny and Richard move into the playhouse and Joseph follows. From this point to the end of the episode the three boys play together.

At first I was incredulous that so soon after their seemingly hostile encounter, the boys played amicably together. Finally I came to the conclusion that for Joseph picking a fight was a way to enter into interaction with the other boys, and engaging him in the fight was Richard and Denny's way of accepting him into their interaction – at least after he acquitted himself satisfactorily in the fight. In this light, I could see that the reference to poo-poo, which occasioned general laughter, was the beginning of a reframing from fighting to playing.

Folklore provides numerous stories in which fighting precipitates friendship among men. One example is the Sumerian Gilgamesh epic, as recounted by Campbell (1964: 87–92). Enkidu, a hairy man who lives with wild animals, is created by the mother-goddess to tame Gilgamesh, a god-king who has grown too arrogant and tyrannical. A hunter who encounters Enkidu appeals to Gilgamesh for help in subduing him. Gilgamesh sends the temple prostitute to lure Enkidu away from his wild animal companions. When the prostitute tells Enkidu about Gilgamesh,

> his heart grew light. He yearned for a friend. 'Very well!' he said. 'And I shall challenge him.'

When they meet:

> They grappled, locked like bulls. The doorpost of the temple shattered; the wall shook. And, at last, Gilgamesh relented. His fury gone, he turned away. And the two, thereafter, were inseparable friends.
>
> (1964: 89)

When Enkidu dies, Gilgamesh is distraught. In this legend, fighting each other is the means to establishing lifelong friendship

A modern-day academic equivalent is to be found in the situation of fruitful collaborations that began when an audience member publicly challenged a speaker after his talk. Finally, Penelope Eckert (p.c.) informs me that in her research on high school students (Eckert, 1990) she was told by boys, but never by girls, that their close friendships began by fighting.

These examples call into question the correlation of aggression and power on one hand, and cooperation and solidarity on the other. Again the cross-cultural perspective provides an invaluable corrective to the temptation to align aggression with power as distinguished from solidarity. Many cultures of the world see arguing as a pleasurable sign of intimacy. Schiffrin (1984) shows that among lower-middle-class men *and women* of East European Jewish background, friendly argument is a means of being sociable. Frank (1988) shows a Jewish couple who tend to polarize and take argumentative positions, but they are not fighting; they are staging a kind of public sparring, where both fighters are on the same team. Byrnes (1986) claims that Germans find American students uninformed and uncommitted because they are reluctant to argue politics with new acquaintances. For their part Americans find German students belligerent because they provoke arguments about American foreign policy with Americans they have just met.

[. . .]

Conclusion

The intersection of language and gender provides a rich site for analysing how power and solidarity are created in discourse. But prior research in this area evidences the danger of linking linguistic forms with interactional intentions such as dominance. In trying to understand how speakers use language, we must consider the context (in every sense, including at least textual, relational, and institutional constraints), the speakers' conversational styles, and, most crucially, the interaction of their styles with each other.

Attempts to understand what goes on between women and men in conversation are muddled by the ambiguity of power and solidarity. The same linguistic means can accomplish either, and every utterance combines elements of both: Scholars, however, like individuals in interaction, are likely to see only one and not the other, like the picture that cannot be seen for what it is – simultaneously a chalice and two faces – but can only be seen alternately as one or the other. In attempting the impossible task of keeping both images in focus at once, we may at least succeed in switching from one to the other rapidly and regularly enough to deepen our understanding of the dynamics underlying interaction such as power and solidarity as well as gender and language use.

Note

This chapter is a significantly revised, rewritten, and enlarged version of a paper entitled 'Rethinking power and solidarity in gender and dominance,' in Kira Hall, Jean–Pierre Koenig, Michael Meacham, Sondra Reinman, and Laurel A. Sutton (eds) *Proceedings of the 16th Annual Meeting of the Berkeley Linguistic Society* (519–529), Berkeley, Linguistics Department, University of California, 1990. The rethinking and rewriting were carried out while I was in residence at the Institute for Advanced Study in Princeton. New Jersey, for which I am grateful to Clifford Geertz and the other faculty members of the Institute's School of Social Science.

References

Becker, A.L. (1982) 'Beyond translation: esthetics and language description' in H. Byrnes (ed.) *Contemporary perceptions of language: Interdisciplinary dimensions. Georgetown University Round Table on Languages and Linguistics 1982*, Washington, DC, Georgetown University Press.

Becker, A.L. and Oka, I Gusti Ngurah (1974) 'Person in Kawi: exploration of an elementary semantic dimension', *Oceanic Linguistics*, vol. 13, pp. 229–55.

Bellinger, D. and Gleason, J.B. (1982) 'Sex differences in parental directives to young children', *Sex Roles*, vol. 8, pp. 1123–39.

Brown, R. and Gilman, A. (1960) 'The pronouns of power and solidarity' in Thomas Sebeok (ed.) *Style in Language*, Cambridge, MA, M.I.T. Press.

Brown, P. and Levinson, S. (1987 [1978]) *Politeness: Some Universals in Language Usage*, Cambridge, Cambridge University Press.

Byrnes, H. (1986) 'Interactional style in German and American conversations,' *Text*, vol. 6, pp. 189–206.

Campbell, J (1964) *The Masks of God: Occidental Mythology*, New York, Viking.

Coates, J. (1986) *Women, Men and Language*, London, Longman.

Conley, J.M., O'Barr, W.M., and Lind, E.A. (1979) 'The power of language: presentational style in the courtroom,' *Duke Law Journal*, vol. 1978, no. 6.

Corsaro, W. and Rizzo, T. (1990) 'Disputes in the peer culture of American and Italian nursery school children' in A. Grimshaw (ed.) *Conflict Talk*, Cambridge, Cambridge University Press.

Dorval, B. (ed.) (1990) *Conversational Coherence and its Development*, Norwood, NJ, Ablex.

Duranti, A. and Brenneis, D. (eds) (1986) *The Audience as Co-author*, Special issue of *Text* 6, pp. 239–47.

Eckert, P. (1990) Personal communication.

Erickson, Frederick (1986) 'Listening and speaking' in D. Tannen (ed.) *Languages and Linguistics: The Interdependence of Theory, Data, and Application, Georgetown University Round Table on Languages and Linguistics 1985*, Washington, DC, Georgetown University Press.

Erickson, F. and Shultz, J. (1982) *The Counseler as Gatekeeper: Social Interaction in Interviews*, New York, Academic Press.

Fasold, R.W. (1990) *The Sociolinguistics of Language*, Oxford, Basil Blackwell.

Frank, J. (1988) 'Communicating "by pairs": agreeing and disagreeing among married couples', Manuscript, Georgetown University.

Friedrich, P. (1972) 'Social context and semantic features: the Russian pronominal usage' in J.J. Gumperz and D. Hymes (eds) *Directions in Sociolinguistics*, New York, Holt, Rinehart and Winston.

Gleason, J.B. (1987) 'Sex differences in parent-child interaction' in S.U. Philips, S. Steele and C. Tanz (eds) *Language, Gender, and Sex in Comparative Perspective*, Cambridge, Cambridge University Press.

Gumperz, J.J. (1982) *Discourse strategies*, Cambridge, Cambridge University Press.

Hughes, L.A. (1988) '"But that's not *really* mean": competing in a cooperative mode', *Sex Roles*, vol. 19, pp. 669–87.

Kakava, C. (1989) 'Argumentative conversation in a Greek family', Paper presented at the Annual Meeting of the Linguistic Society of America, Washington, DC.

Keenan, E. (1974) 'Norm-makers, norm-breakers: uses of speech by men and women in a Malagasy community' in R. Bauman and J. Sherzer (eds) *Explorations in the Ethnography of Speaking*, Cambridge, Cambridge University Press.

Klagsbrun, F. (1992) *Mixed Feelings: Love, Hate, Rivalry, and Reconciliation Among Brothers and Sisters*, New York, Bantam.

Komarovsky, M. (1962) *Blue-collar Marriage*, New York, Vintage.

Lakoff, R. (1975) *Language and Woman's Place*, New York, Harper and Row.

Maltz, D.N. and Borker, R.A. (1982) 'A cultural approach to male-female miscommunication' in J.J. Gumperz (ed.) *Language and Social Identity*, Cambridge, Cambridge University Press.

McDermott, R.P. and Tylbor, H. (1983) 'On the necessity of collusion in conversation', *Text*, vol. 3, pp. 277–97.

Mead, M. (1977) 'End linkage: a tool for cross-cultural analysis' in J. Brockman (ed.) *About Bateson*, New York, Dutton.

Norman, M. (1990) *These Good Men: Friendships Forged from War*, New York, Crown.

Ong, W.J. (1981) *Fighting for Life: Contest, Sexuality, and Consciousness*, Ithaca, Cornell University Press, Amherst, University of Massachusetts Press.

Philips, S.U. (1983) *The Invisible Culture: Communication in Classroom and Community on the Warm Springs Indian Reservation*, New York and London, Longman; rpt. Waveland Press.

Pinter, H. (1988) *Mountain Language*, New York, Grove Press.

Sattel, J.W. (1983) 'Men, inexpressiveness and power' in B. Thorne, C. Kramarae and N. Henley (eds) *Language, Gender and Society*, Rowley, MA, Newbury House.

Schegloff, E. (1982) 'Discourse as an interactional achievement: some uses of 'uhuh' and other things that come between sentences' in D. Tannen (ed.) *Analysing Discourse: Text and Talk. Georgetown University Round Table on Languages and Linguistics 1981*, Washington, DC, Georgetown University Press.

Schegloff, E. (1988) 'Discourse as an interactional achievement II. An exercise in conversation analysis' in D. Tannen (ed.) *Linguistics in Context: Connecting Observation and Understanding*, Norwood, NJ, Ablex.

Schiffrin, D. (1984) 'Jewish argument as sociability,' *Language in Society*, vol. 13, pp. 311–35.

Scollon, R. 1985. 'The machine stops: silence in the metaphor of malfunction' in D. Tannen and M. Saville-Troike (eds) *Perspectives on Silence*, Norwood, NJ, Ablex.

Scollon, R. and Scollon, S.B.K. (1981) *Narrative literacy and face in interethnic communication*. Norwood, NJ: Ablex.

Shuy, R.W. (1982) 'Topic as the unit of analysis in a criminal law case' in D. Tannen (ed.) *Analysing Discourse: Text and Talk, Georgetown University Round table on Languages and Linguistics 1981*, Washington, DC, Georgetown University Press.

Sifianou, M. (1992) 'The use of diminutives in expressing politeness: modern Greek versus English', *Journal of Pragmatics*, vol. 17, pp. 155–73.

Spender, D. (1980) *Man made language*, London, Routledge and Kegan Paul.

Tannen, D. (1981) 'Indirectness in discourse: ethnicity as conversational style,' *Discourse Processes*, vol. 4, pp. 221–38.

Tannen, D. (1984) *Conversational style: Analysing Talk Among Friends*, Norwood, NJ, Ablex.

Tannen, D. (1985) 'Silence: anything but' in D. Tannen and M. Saville-Troike (eds) *Perspectives on Silence*, Norwood, NJ, Ablex.

Tannen, D. (1986) *That's Not What I Meant!: How Conversational Style Makes or Breaks Your Relations with Others*, New York, Ballantine.

Tannen, D. (1987) 'Repetition in conversation: toward a poetics of talk,' *Language*, vol. 63, pp. 574–605.

Tannen, D. (1989a) *Talking Voices: Repetition, Dialogue and Imagery in Conversational Discourse*, Cambridge, Cambridge University Press.

Tannen, D. (1989b) 'Interpreting interruption in conversation' in B. Music, R. Graczyk and C. Wiltshire (eds) *Papers from the 25th Annual Regional Meeting of the Chicago Linguistic Society. Part Two: Parasession on Language in Context*, Chicago, Chicago Linguistic Society. Rpt. in *Gender and Discourse*, New York and Oxford, Oxford University Press, in preparation.

Tannen, D. (1990a) 'Gender differences in conversational coherence: physical alignment and topical cohesion' in B. Dorval (ed.) *Conversational Coherence and its Development*, Norwood, NJ, Ablex. Rpt. in *Gender and Discourse*, New York and Oxford, Oxford University Press, in preparation.

Tannen, D. (1990b) *You Just Don't Understand: Women and Men in Conversation*. New York, Ballantine.

Tannen, D. and Kakava, C. (1992) Power and solidarity in modern Greek conversation: Disagreeing to agree. *Journal of Modern Greek Studies*, vol. 10, pp. 12–29.

Watanabe, S. (1993) 'Cultural differences in framing: American and Japanese group discussions' in Deborah Tannen (ed.) *Framing in Discourse*, New York and Oxford, Oxford University Press.

West, C. and Zimmerman, D.H. (1983) 'Small insults: a study of interruptions in cross-sex conversations between unacquinted persons' in B. Thorne, C. Kramarae, and N. Henley (eds) *Language, Gender and Society*, Rowley, MA, Newbury House.

Just Say No? The Use of Conversation Analysis in Developing a Feminist Perspective on Sexual Refusal

Celia Kitzinger and Hannah Frith

Source: Kitzinger, C. and Frith, H. (1999) 'Just say no? The use of conversation analysis in developing a feminist perspective on sexual refusal', in *Discourse and Society*, vol. 10, pp. 293–317.

The teaching of 'refusal skills' is common to many date rape prevention, assertiveness training and social skills programmes for young women. The assumption underlying such programmes is that young women find it difficult to refuse unwanted sexual activity. A common goal of such programmes is to teach women to 'just say no', clearly, directly, and unapologetically: they aim to 'provide women with the skills to avoid victimization by learning to say "no" effectively' (Kidder *et al.*, 1983: 159).

The aim of this article is to show the value of conversation analysis (CA) for feminist theory and practice in the area of refusal skills training and date rape prevention. We review the existing CA literature on how people 'say no' in ordinary everyday interactions, and consider what we know about how such refusals are done both in relation to what young women already know about 'saying no' and in relation to the educational literature on refusal skills. Illustrating our argument with our own data, we first support the claim that young women *do* indeed find it difficult to 'just say no' to unwanted sex, and we outline some of the explanations commonly offered for why this might be the case. Second, we draw upon CA to offer an alternative explanation for this difficulty. We show that the empirical findings of CA demonstrate that refusals are complex and finely organized conversational interactions, and are not appropriately summarized by the advice to 'just say no'. Third, we use our data to show that young women already have, and can explicitly articulate, a sophisticated awareness of these culturally normative ways of doing refusals and we suggest that it is precisely their knowledge of the cultural rules documented by conversation analysts which explains why they do not 'just say no' in response to unwanted sex. We suggest that date rape prevention (and similar) programmes which insist upon 'just saying no' as appropriate behaviour are deeply problematic in that they ignore and override culturally normative ways of indicating refusal. Fourth (and with important consequences for education in refusal skills), we use the conversation analytic research on refusals to show that *it should not in fact be necessary for a woman to say 'no' for her to be understood as refusing sex* and that insistence upon 'just say no' may be counter-productive insofar as it implies that other ways of doing refusals (which do not include the word 'no') are less than adequate. [. . .]

We would like to emphasize that our focus here on the conversational problems entailed in 'just saying no' does not mean that we have no *other* criticisms of date rape education and refusal skills programmes and their theoretical/political rationale. [. . .] In particular, we would draw attention to their implicit (sometimes explicit) reliance on 'miscommunication' theory (Tannen, 1991), according to which date rape is often the result of miscommunication between the sexes: he misinterprets her verbal and non-verbal communication, falsely believing that she wants sex; she fails to say 'no' clearly and effectively. As Carole Cocoran (1992: 135) points out, 'most acquaintance rape programs stress misinterpretation as the cause of date rape and therefore suggest that the remedy lies in assertive verbal communication on the part of the female'. For example, assuming that there are differences of interpretation between men and women, the American College Health Association (cited in Turner and Rubinson, 1993: 605) advises women that 'often most men interpret timidity as permission' (which is why it is important to 'say no when you mean no'). Consequently, women's 'undercommunication of disinclination to have sex' is viewed as a contributing factor in date rape (Allgeier, 1986, cited in Murnen *et al.*, 1989) and psychologists conclude that 'if more women were able to communicate their disinterest [sic], more of the unwanted sex would be eliminated' (Murnen *et al.*, 1989). As we have noted elsewhere (Frith and Kitzinger, 1997), this theory places the burden of responsibility for date rape back on to women and obscures institutionalized gender power relations. As Ehrlich (1998) demonstrates, the miscommunication model of date rape is a useful resource for defendants in sexual assault tribunals seeking to construct themselves as innocent: complainants are represented as deficient in their efforts to signal non-consent.

Our argument here does *not* rely upon the idea that there are gender differences in the expression or understanding of refusals. Rather than attempting to define gender differences in talk, or to characterize the interactional styles of men and women, we explore the ways in which young women themselves talk about sexual refusals. Drawing on the conversation analytic literature, and on our own data, we claim that both men and women have a sophisticated ability to convey and to comprehend refusals, including refusals which do not include the word 'no', and we suggest that male claims not to have 'understood' refusals which conform to culturally normative patterns can only be heard as self-interested justifications for coercive behaviour.

Young women find it difficult to 'just say no' to unwanted sex

It is common for women to report that they find it difficult to refuse unwanted sex (e.g. Campbell and Barnlund, 1977; Howard, 1985a, 1985b; Warzak and Page, 1990), and victims of sexual assault often report feeling that they had 'failed to make their refusal sufficiently clear' (Cairns, 1993: 205). Forty-five per cent of participants in one study (Warzak *et al.*, 1995) 'reported that they lacked effective refusal skills' and 77 per cent of all participants in the study 'responded in the affirmative when asked if they had an interest in learning more effective refusal skills'.

Our own data from focus groups (cf. Wilkinson, 1999) with 58 female school and university students support these findings. There are many discussions throughout our data about the difficulty of saying no (see Frith and Kitzinger, 1998; Frith, 1997, for more details). For example, in the following extract, Tara and Pat recount how difficult they find it to reject someone sexually, even at a fairly early stage in the proceedings.

TARA   My male friends are always thinking, you know, that I've . . . I've got that sort of problem where somebody's keen, I just can't . . . I just can't say to somebody, 'look, sorry, I'm not', and I'll end up . . . I'll avoid it in the end, but I'll quite often end up speaking to them for hours and hours, and I'm just thinking like, 'I really don't want to be here; I want to be doing something else' [. . .] I just can't drop it.

INT   Why?

PAT   You don't want to hurt their feelings. [. . .] I really try and avoid ever having to be in the situation of having to say to somebody, 'look, no, I'm sorry' [. . .] I wouldn't really risk to have a sort of a flirty jokey sort of conversation with someone that I don't know very well in case they suddenly just say, 'okay, how about it?', and then it would just be like 'uuuuhhhhh!'.

For both Tara and Pat, then, saying 'no' is so difficult that they try to avoid ever having to do it. In the following extract, another young woman describes the problem of trying to refuse particular sexual activities once a sexual encounter has commenced.

LIZ   You've sat there and all through it you've been thinking 'I don't want to do this, I should have said no, I should have stopped him before, and I can't stop him now, because we're half way through the swing of it all, and I'm just so stupid. Next time I'm just going to sort it all out. . .' [. . .] But you never do. . .

Asked how one might go about refusing sex with men, one young woman resorts to fantasy as the only way she can imagine of doing this successfully.

SARA   Have a supersonic button, right (laughter), and then, just before you have sex, and you didn't want to, you could press it and vaporize them.

Of course, this is not the only way in which young women talked about refusing sex. Sometimes, they say, refusing sex is a relatively simple matter of just saying no: 'you just get straight to the point' (Jane); 'I personally feel that I could say no, and I have done' (Jan). Quantification of our data (i.e. what percentage of women report finding it difficult to refuse sex and what percentage report finding it easy) is, however, not a straightforward counting exercise. Some women avoid ever commenting directly on the relative ease or difficulty of refusing sex, and many say at one point in the group discussion that it is easy, and at another that it is difficult. On one occasion, for example, Liz comments that a forthright no is simple and effective ('that's what I said to my present boyfriend, "I'm not having sex with you"'); later she talks about finding refusals difficult and embarrassing ('it just doesn't seem right to say no when you're up there in the situation'). These contradictions and ambiguities arise, we believe, because talk is not simply a transparent report of experience; rather it is doing interactive business between focus group participants. [. . .] For the purposes of this article, we consider it sufficient to note that there are relatively few occasions on which the 58 young women in our study reported that they felt able to say a clear and direct 'no', and fewer still instances of actual examples from their own experience of times when they had done this. Many researchers would see young women like these as prime candidates for sexual assertiveness training courses where they can be taught how to 'just say no'.

Why is it apparently so difficult for young women to refuse unwanted sex? A wide range of explanations is offered in the literature. The failure to 'just say no' is often attributed to internal personality characteristics such as low self-esteem (Stere, 1985), lack of assertiveness (McConnch, 1990) or lack of perseverance (Sandler *et al.*, 1992). According to Murnen *et al.* (1989) internalization of traditionally feminine gender role stereotypes ('passivity, submissiveness, nurturance, acquiescence to male needs and helpfulness') means that 'women are often trained to be ineffective communicators in a sexual relationship'. Other researchers suggest that young women find it hard to 'just say no' because they are concerned about the damage to their reputations if they do not comply with male sexual demands (e.g. fear of being labelled 'frigid' or 'lesbian'; Muehlenhard and Cook, 1988); because they are committed to safeguarding the emotional and sexual well-being of their partners (Duncombe and Marsden, 1993, 1996): or because they are the victims of sexual scripts according to which (for example) 'going too far' in some assumed sexual sequence means that a woman then forfeits the right to say 'no' (e.g. Goodchilds *et al.*, 1988; Quinn *et al.*, 1991). It is also often suggested that sexuality is a particularly difficult topic for open and clear communication, and that young women who might be fully able to communicate their desires (or lack of them) in other situations, are unable to do so in the sexual situation, with its heavy cultural loading and high level of personal investment. We think all of these explanations may sometimes be useful, and our own data indicate that young women themselves often use explanations like these to account for their own (and other people's) difficulties in refusing unwanted sex.

However, what these explanations leave out is the simple fact that saying no is difficult in *any* context. These young women's reported discomfort with, and inability to say, open, clear and direct 'no's is not specific to their age, to the situation, or even to their gender. It is common for people to experience difficulty in refusing invitations or declining offers, at whatever age, and across a wide variety of situations. Advice on how to say no is widely available in Anglo–American culture – even on the Web ('How to say no with style' from www.synapsenet/-oracle). Assertiveness books routinely include role play exercises in saying no (e.g. Fensterheim and Baer, 1975; McConnch, 1990) and management books have sections with titles like 'Knowing How to Say No' (Burley-Allen, 1983), or lists of techniques for helping people to say no in the work environment (Stubbs, 1986). Saying no 'nicely' has always been a key question of etiquette (e.g. Coudert, 1993; Martin, 1982: 87–9) and therapists and counsellors also often find themselves giving advice on how to say no. Such advice would not be so widely available if most people experienced saying no as unproblematic. The difficulty of 'saying no' is so well known that it has generated an endless stream of 'jokes' (see Crombie, 1994, for examples) which underscore the apparent need people feel to come up with (sometimes implausible) excuses and justifications to explain their refusals [. . .]

Refusal skills training is one of a set of 'verbal hygiene practices' (Cameron, 1995) which has been directed disproportionately at women, commonly seen as suffering from gendered linguistic problems associated with oppressive expectations about 'feminine' or 'ladylike' speech. Deborah Cameron quotes a feature on assertiveness training in the US feminist magazine *Ms.* of March 1975 which began by relating the experiences of women involved in what they described as 'the first course of its kind in Seattle':

> We are 10 women who find it difficult to say No or to express an opinion at all. Education, experience and feminism may make us *feel* equal. But learning how to speak up for ourselves and what we believe in is something else again. That is why we have signed up for a course in verbal self-assertion.
>
> (Withers, 1975, quoted in Cameron, 1995: 178)

Assertiveness training and other types of refusal skills courses address this widespread difficulty in 'saying no' by routinely advising that refusals are best accomplished through plain unvarnished 'no's. For example, the authors of the classic handbook. *The Assertive Woman* (Phelps and Austin, 1987) devote an entire chapter to 'Saying "No"', and claim that:

> It is crucial that you give a simple 'no' rather than a long-winded statement filled with excuses, justifications, and rationalizations about why you are saying 'no'. It is enough that you do not want to do this, simply because you do not want to do it.
>
> (Phelps and Austin, 1987: 123–4)

Refusal skills training routinely emphasizes the importance of the unvarnished, direct, unhesitating word 'no' in communicating refusals. Many books recommend *repeated* 'no's (as in the so-called 'cracked record' technique, e.g. Phelps and Austin. 1987) – and many labour the point that refusals should not normally be accompanied by explanations. Writing for physicians concerned to help teenagers to postpone sexual involvement, Marion Howard (1985a: 82) counsels them to 'emphasise to young teenagers that they have the right to say "no"' and 'to reinforce the idea that they do not have to give a reason or explanation': they should just 'say "no" and keep repeating it' (p. 87).

In sum, then, refusals skills training of the sort employed in date rape prevention and other similar programmes aimed at young women routinely teach that refusals are best accomplished with clear, direct, straightforward 'no's.

Conversation analysis shows that refusals are complex and finely organized interactional accomplishments

[. . .]

Conversation analysts have built up a considerable body of work about the structure of refusals in ordinary everyday conversation (Atkinson and Heritage,

1984; Davidson, 1984; Drew, 1984; Pomerantz, 1984). This body of work (like all of that in CA) relies upon careful attention to small details of talk, such as short pauses, hesitations, false starts, and self-corrections. One important finding of CA is that speakers (and listeners) are very finely tuned in to these small details such that all of these micro-level features have interactional relevance. For example, 'mm hm' and 'yeah' are both used as ways in which one person acknowledges what another is saying, but they have been shown to have very different functions (Jefferson, 1984); and very short pauses (of less than a second) between one person finishing speaking and the next person starting to speak have been shown routinely to influence the first person's perception of what the second person is about to say (Heritage, 1984; Levinson, 1983; Pomerantz, 1984). For conversation analysts, then, 'even the finest levels of conversational detail, every speech error, pause, overlap or lexical correction, might be there as a "designed" or consequential feature of social action' (Edwards and Potter, 1992: 6).

[. . .]

Analysis of naturally occurring conversations in which people either accept or refuse invitations (offers, proposals, etc.) shows that acceptances and refusals follow very different patterns: acceptances do, indeed, often involve simply 'just saying yes', but refusals very rarely involve 'just saying no'. Acceptances generally involve (i) simple acceptance; and (ii) no delay (Heritage, 1984; 266–7), as in the following examples. (Note that the '[' symbol indicates overlapping speech.)

Example 1

A   Why don't you come up and <u>see</u> me some ⌈time
B   ⌊I would like to

(Atkinson and Drew, 1979: 58)

Example 2

A   <u>We</u>:ll, will you help me ⌈<u>ou</u>:t.
B   ⌊[I certainly wi:ll.

(Davidson, 1984: 116)

These acceptances are typical in being immediate and direct. There is no pause between the request and the acceptance (in fact, the person providing the acceptance often produces speech which overlaps with that of the person making the request) and the acceptance itself is simple and straightforward. (It is possible that *sexual* acceptances – especially from women – may be somewhat different in form; for example, there is some evidence that sexual agreement is often conveyed nonverbally, and may even be communicated via a token refusal, cf. Muehlenhard and Hollabaugh (1988). We are not aware of any research

which has used as data actual naturalistically occurring acceptances – or refusals
– of sexual interaction.)

In contrast with the 'unvarnished acceptances' (Heritage, 1984: 266), typical in
the non-sexual domain, non-sexual refusals are typically neither immediate nor
direct. Here are two examples of refusals, incorporating those features which
conversation analysts have identified as typical. [. . .]

Example 3

MARK   We were wondering if you wanted to come over Saturday, f'r dinner.
             (0.4)
JANE   Well (.) .hh it'd be great but we promised Carol already.

(Potter and Wetherell, 1987: 86)

Example 4

A   Uh if you'd care to come and visit a little while this
          morning I'll give you a cup of *cof*fee.
B   hehh Well that's awfully sweet of you, I don't think I can
          make it this morning. .hh uhm I'm running an ad in the
          paper and-and uh I have to stay near the phone.

(Atkinson and Drew, 1979: 58)

Conversation analysis shows that refusals are routinely designed to
incorporate at least some of the following features:

(i)   delays, e.g. pauses and hesitations, like the four-tenths of a second pause in
        Example 3, and the filled pause 'hehh' in Example 4;

(ii)   prefaces (also referred to as 'hedges') e.g. use of markers like 'uh' or 'well'
        ('well' is used in both the preceding extracts);

(iii)   palliatives, e.g. appreciations, apologies, token agreements etc. which serve
        to alleviate the pain caused by the refusal; compliments such as 'it'd be
        great' or 'that's awfully sweet of you' are both examples of palliatives. Other
        possible palliatives would include accompanying a refusal with a delayed
        acceptance ('not today, but tomorrow'), or with the offer of an alternative
        ('I can't come round to your place, but why don't you come round to me?')
        (Antaki, 1994: 79); and/or

(iv)   accounts, i.e. explanations/justifications/excuses for why the invitation is
        not being accepted such as a prior engagement or commitment as in
        Examples 3 and 4. It is common (as in the preceding examples) for people
        to present accounts which suggest that the person refusing the invitation
        cannot accept it (rather than that s/he *chooses* not to), i.e. that they are
        un*able* rather than un*willing*. The advantage of this account is that it has a
        'no blame' quality, which avoids the implication that the invitation is

unattractive or unwanted: it functions to constitute a refusal while avoiding
negative or critical consequences (Potter and Wetherell, 1987: 86). It is also
common for refusals to be qualified or mitigated in some way (as in 'I don't
think I can make it this morning' in Example 4).

In sum, then, careful attention to the details of naturally occurring conversation
shows that it is conversationally most unusual to 'just say no'. Rejections and
refusals are commonly delayed and indirect and follow a typical pattern which
generally includes *delay* in responding, some kind of *prefacing* of the refusal
(with words like, 'well', or 'ahhh . . .'), a *palliative* remark, and some kind of
account aimed at softening, explaining, justifying, excusing, or redefining the
rejection. It is important to note that refusals are almost always accompanied by
explanations or justifications (Labov and Fanshel, 1977: 86–8). This is what
conversation analysts mean when they describe rejections as 'dispreferred'
actions. Actions which are characteristically performed straightforwardly and
without delay (like acceptances) are termed 'preferred' actions, while those which
are delayed, qualified and accounted for are termed 'dispreferred'. The concept of
'preference structure' is widely used in CA: another example of a 'preferred action'
is agreeing (e.g. with someone's opinion), which, like accepting an invitation, is
usually carried out quickly and directly; disagreeing, by contrast is described as
'dispreferred', because it is characteristically marked by the same pattern (of
delay, prefacing etc.) that we have noted in refusals. Note that the terms
'preferred' and 'dispreferred' are not intended in any way to refer to the private
desires or psychological proclivities of individual speakers: they are simply
descriptive of the different ways in which acceptances and refusals are routinely
done in ordinary talk (including the acceptance of invitations the individual may
actually want to reject, or the refusal of invitations s/he may wish to accept).

[. . .] As we have seen, refusals are usually delayed and indirect, and this
means that immediate and direct no's, particularly those for which no
explanations are provided, are often experienced as rude or hostile (Heritage,
1984: 268). Advising someone to 'just say no', then, may not be very good advice.
[. . .]

Young women talking about refusals display their knowledge of the cultural rules documented by conversation analysts

The data we have collected are based on tape-recorded interactions in which
young women *talk about doing refusals*. Data in which refusals were actually
being done by young women would show that they, like other competent
members of their language community, have an *implicit* understanding of the
culturally accepted rules for refusals, as documented by conversation analysts.
Our data, by contrast, in which young women *talk about doing refusals*
illustrates the extent to which they are able to articulate and to make *explicit*
these normative conversational patterns.

Of course, young women describing the doing of refusals do not sound like
academic conversation analysts. We would be very surprised if one of the young
women in our focus groups used terms like 'dispreferred', or 'palliative', in

discussing the refusal of unwanted sex. Nonetheless, we show here that it is possible to identify, in young women's talk about the doing of refusals, a great deal of 'common-sense' knowledge about how refusals are normatively done – and that this can be characterized as a lay version of conversation analytic theory. (For a more detailed discussion of the relationship between 'common-sense' and 'expert', e.g. conversation analytic, knowledge about communicative norms, see Kitzinger, 1998.) In this section we show how young women's talk about refusals demonstrates their sophisticated understanding of culturally acceptable ways of refusing – understandings which map on to the empirical findings of CA, but which are often at variance with the simplistic prescriptions of date rape education (and similar) programmes.

First, although young women do not, of course, use the term, they know that refusals are *dispreferred* conversational actions, i.e. that they necessitate a great deal more interactional work than do, for example, acceptances. Whereas date rape prevention programmes insist on direct and straightforward no's, young women display their sophisticated knowledge about talk in interaction by describing feelings akin to wrongness, rudeness or foolishness which accompany the unvarnished 'no', and by insisting on the need to explain and justify their refusals.

> **LIZ** It just doesn't seem right to say no when you're up there in the situation.
> **SARA** It's not rude, it's not rude – it sounds awful to say this, doesn't it.
> **LIZ** I know.
> **SARA** It's not rude, but it's the same sort of feeling. It's like, 'oh my god, I can't say no now, can I?'

In general, the young women in our focus groups characterized explicit refusals of sex as having negative implications for them. [. . .] In sum, these young women's talk about the rudeness and arrogance which would be attributed to them, and the foolishness they would feel, in saying clear and direct 'no's, indicates their awareness that such behaviour violates culturally accepted norms according to which refusals are dispreferred actions.

Second, in line with their understanding that refusals are dispreferreds, young women often insist that it is necessary to offer *accounts* (reasons or excuses) for their refusals. This again runs counter to the advice offered by many date rape and refusal skills training programmes. The slogan 'just say no' implies that nothing other than 'no' needs to be said. Consider, for example, the 'positive self-statement' offered by Muehlenhard *et al.* (1989) as part of their cognitive-behavioural treatment programme for women at high risk of acquaintance rape: 'I have a right to say no without explaining my reasons' (Muehlenhard *et al.*, 1989). As a statement of the rights of an individual, this is certainly true, but it is equally true that to say no without explaining one's reasons is conversationally very abnormal. Young women are clear that refusing sex *is* something for which reasons are needed. They point out that 'just saying no in a relationship is not enough if you've got a good relationship' (Wendy); Jan says, 'I think it's better if you try to be nice and explain why [you are refusing sex]'; and Jill describes how she would respond to unwanted sexual pressure by saying '"oh no, I don't want to have sex with you because . . ." and then explain it'.

Third, as conversation analysts have also claimed, young women talk about good excuses as being those which assert their *inability* (rather than their unwillingness) to comply with the demand that they engage in sexual intercourse: from the vague (and perhaps, for that reason, irrefutable) statement that they are 'not ready', through to sickness and menstruation. Several women reported that they relied on some kind of illness as an excuse: a 'headache' (Karen and Cath), feeling 'tired' (Cath), 'knackered' (Jane and Pam) or just feeling 'really ill' (Wendy). Other excuses which emphasized the practical difficulties which made them *unable* (rather than unwilling) to have sex were 'you've got nowhere to do it' (Ros), 'you could get expelled' (Zoe) or 'you're scared of getting pregnant' (Rose). Note that these were offered by the young women not as genuine reasons for their not wanting sex, but as excuses which they believed young men would find relatively acceptable – and they sometimes made explicit their belief that the relative acceptability of these excuses derives from their focus on *inability* rather than *unwillingness* to have sex. Jill explains that saying no to sex with a boyfriend 'not for any reason, but if you just didn't want to' could result in a partner becoming 'really upset about it'. In order to avoid such an outcome, a plausible excuse is necessary. Pretending to be menstruating was one much-discussed excuse: 'being on your period' was seen as an effective excuse, at least in the short term, because 'that would stop the boy from blaming you' (Jill). These young women's view that effective excuses are those rooted in inability rather than unwillingness conforms with the empirical findings of CA, but is at variance with the advice of refusal skills training programmes which often model statements of *unwillingness* as paradigmatic assertive behaviour (e.g. 'I don't feel like making out tonight', 'I don't want to get in bed with you tonight'. 'I just don't want to', all from Smith. 1975: 246–7)

Their refusals are also often qualified or mitigated in some way. One form of refusal which was very often recommended by young women in our focus groups was the 'delayed acceptance', i.e. the statement that one is 'not ready' for sex, or 'not ready *yet*'. Cath comments that 'one way is not to say "no" as in you never want to. but "no" as in "not now"', and this was a very commonly reported strategy: 'I'd say, "look, maybe sometime in the future"' (Michelle); 'I'm not ready yet; can we wait a while?' (Sam); 'I start by telling him that it is all too soon' (Maggie); 'just say you're not ready yet, or you want to keep it for a special time' (Zoe). The *dis*advantages of giving delayed acceptances as a form of refusal were also discussed at some length by the young women in our groups; the young women shared, however, a sense that delayed acceptances, whatever longer term problems follow in their wake, are more interactionally acceptable ways of avoiding sex than are explicit 'no's. Again, young women's views about how refusals are done, while mapping nicely on to the conversation analytic literature, run counter to the recommendations of the refusal skills literature which warns:

> Telling the man that you do not want to have sex by saying things like 'I really don't know if we should do this', 'Not now, can't we wait?' or 'I really like you but I'm not sure' is not effective. All these statements can be misconstrued as meaning that you need a little more urging to be cooperative.
>
> (Wiseman, 1994: 65)

Fourth, young women explicitly state that it is a good idea to offer (what conversation analysts call) *palliatives* in refusing sex. Young women report refusing sexual activity with phrases such as: 'well, it's very flattering of you to ask' (Sharon), or 'look, you're a really nice guy and I do like you, but that's it' (Pat). Phrases like these serve to 'soften' the refusal; as Judy says 'you've got to soften the blow somehow, haven't you'. This search for palliatives or attempt to 'soften' refusals is often expressed as a concern to find ways of refusing sex 'without hurting his feelings' (Carla), and other research on young women's sexuality has documented the extent to which this is a major concern for them (e.g. Frith and Kitzinger, 1998; Howard and McCabe, 1990). According to Sharon: 'If you have to reject someone sexually, then the best thing to do is to make it up to them in some other direction, so that you can reject someone sexually by offering them friendship back'. Again, as the extract from Wiseman (1994: 65) quoted here ('I really like you . . .', etc) indicates, palliatives are actively criticized in the refusal skills literature.

What these data illustrate, then, is that the young women in our focus groups have a sophisticated awareness of normative communication patterns around refusal which permit them not only (presumably) to do refusals in the culturally appropriate way, but also to verbalize some aspects of what is involved in doing this. Our data suggest that young women's concerns about appropriate refusal technique are fairly sophisticated compared with the crass advice to 'just say no'. Date rape education (and similar) programmes are prescribing behaviour which violates basic cultural norms and social etiquette, and young women know this. Our claim here is supported by the findings of Amy Gervasio and Mary Crawford (1989) who have reviewed research on how people evaluate so-called 'assertive' behaviour. It seems that what experts think is healthy assertion strikes others as 'aggressive' and 'rude', and they suggest that one reason for this is because it breaks the rules of normal conversation. The evidence is that 'just saying no' is rude, and that young women know this. Date rape prevention (and similar) programmes which insist upon 'just saying no' as appropriate behaviour are deeply problematic in that they ignore and override culturally normative ways of indicating refusal.

It should not be necessary for a woman to say 'no' in order for her to be understood as refusing sex

Thus far we have shown that conversation analysts have demonstrated that refusals follow a normative pattern, and that young women are able to articulate at least some features of this pattern in their own talk about refusals. There is, however, a crucial feature of refusing which we have not yet mentioned, although it has important implications for refusal skills training programmes based on the slogan, 'Just say no'. Simply put, the word 'no' is neither sufficient, nor necessary, for a refusal to be heard as such.

Most date rape (and similar) prevention programmes have incorporated the idea that saying 'no' is not *sufficient* for a refusal to be heard as a refusal. The widespread use of 'token resistance' (saying 'no' but meaning 'yes') has been well-documented and studies have repeatedly found that about 40 per cent of US female undergraduates report saying to their dates that they did not want to have sex when actually they 'had every intention to' and were 'willing to engage in sexual intercourse' (Muehlenhard and Hollabaugh, 1988; Muehlenhard and McCoy, 1991; Sprecher *et al.*, 1994). Because women sometimes apparently mean 'yes' but say 'no', refusal skills teaching often encourages women to disambiguate genuinely meant no's by reinforcing their meaning with (for example) a firm tone, eye contact, or other forms of non-verbal communication (e.g. physically leaving the room, slapping the man). A 'genuine' no is supposed to be clear and definite in order to distinguish it from token refusals.

But while refusal skills education acknowledges that saying 'no' is not *sufficient* for refusal what it does *not* usually acknowledge is that saying no is also not *necessary* for refusal. Indeed, the slogan, 'just say no' puts the word 'no' in pride of place as the key semantic component of a refusal. This is mirrored in virtually *all* date rape education (and other refusal skills) programmes; an 'explicit and audible NO' is part of the operational definition of a 'refusal' in the study by Warzak and Page (1990), and the teaching of 'how to assertively yet emphatically say "No"' is the key pedagogic aim of the self-help book by Smith (1975). Yet, CA demonstrates conclusively that it is not necessary to say 'no' in order to refuse a request effectively, and to have a refusal heard *as* a refusal.

In fact, neither of the data extracts quoted earlier (Examples 3 and 4) to illustrate the key components of refusals includes the word 'no'. In both cases, however, the person addressed apparently understood them to be refusals, and responded as though the speaker were refusing the invitation. Let us look at another example in more detail:

Example 5

A If you wanted to: 'hh you could meet me at UCB an' I could show you some a' the other things on the computer.
(.)
maybe even teach you how to programme Basic or something
B (0.6) Well I don't know if I'd wanna get all <u>that</u> invo:lved, hh'hhh!

(Davidson, 1984: 108, transcription simplified)

In this extract, A's offer to show B some things on the computer is not immediately accepted (note the short pause '(.)' which follows it). A then modifies the invitation, offering to even teach B how to programme Basic. But still, B doesn't respond immediately: A's offer is met first with a short pause, then with the word 'well' (the preface), and then with the statement, 'I don't know if I'd wanna get all <u>that</u> involved'. Note that B does not say 'no'. Nonetheless, most of us will recognize that this is what B means – as, indeed, A does. The extract continues:

A It's really <u>interesti:ng.</u>

In other words, A 'hears' B as refusing (even though B hasn't actually said the word 'no'), and tries to persuade B ('it's really interesting'): the effort to persuade someone indicates (obviously) that you understand that they don't want to do it, but that you hope you can change their mind. So, B has successfully communicated a refusal, despite not saying a direct, clear, and immediate 'no'.[1] Conversation analysis shows that this is absolutely normal: this is the way most refusals are done, and they are heard (or, as conversation analysts say, 'oriented to') *as* refusals in the course of ordinary conversation. (For other examples see Antaki, 1994; Davidson, 1984; Heritage, 1989). [. . .]

So, the evidence is that people usually hear refusals without the word 'no' necessarily being uttered. In fact, people often respond to just one part of the refusal sequence as signalling refusal in and of itself. For example, one of the most potent indicators of refusal is a delay in responding. According to Davidson (1984: 103) 'a silence offering immediately after an invitation, offer, request or proposal may be taken as displaying that it is possibly going to be rejected'. In fact, a pause of two-tenths of a second seems to be taken as evidence for an invitation rejection coming up (Levinson, 1983: 336). The following examples illustrate the way in which speakers, having issued requests or invitations, attend to pauses (in which their conversational partners *could* speak, but do not), as foreshadowing refusals. (Remember that (.) means a pause of less than two-tenths of a second, and longer pauses are indicated in seconds and tenths of seconds.)

Example 6

C   So I was wondering would you be in your office
      on Monday (.) by any chance?
      (2.0)
      Probably not

(Levinson, 1983: 320)

Example 7

R   What about coming here on the way
      (.)
      Or doesn't that give you enough time?

(Levinson, 1983: 335)

Example 8

C   Well you can both stay.
      (0.4)
      Got plenty a' room.

(Davidson, 1984: 10; transcription simplified)

In these three examples, speakers, hearing the silences which follow their requests or invitations, indicate that they are anticipating refusals. The third example is interesting because the speaker attempts to forestall rejection by dealing with what might be causing it (the belief that perhaps there isn't enough room for her guests). It is common to find that when people issue invitations, offers, requests or proposals and are met with brief silences, they reformulate or elaborate on the original invitation so as to make an acceptance more likely – as A also does in Example 5. The very fact that these 'subsequent versions' (Davidson, 1984) are produced demonstrates, of course, that the initial silence was heard as heralding a refusal. So CA indicates that a brief pause (of no more than two-tenths of a second) following a request or invitation is often, in and of itself, heard as implying refusal.

The production of palliatives in response to an invitation, offer or request is also generally heard as a refusal in and of itself. In an example cited by Antaki (1994: 81), N responds to a lunch invitation (after the short pause we know to be typical of refusals), 'well, you're real sweet, hon:, uh::m': note the preface ('well') and the palliative, which in this case takes the form of a compliment. This is *all* N says, but it is enough to constitute an implied refusal, as we can see from the response of the person making the invitation: 'or do you have something else'. If, in everyday conversation, a simple palliative is heard as implying refusal, then young women who respond to sexual invitations with palliatives like 'well, I do like you' or 'it's flattering to be asked' should likewise be heard as implying refusal – especially if these responses are preceded by a couple of tenths of a second of silence.

Furthermore, in ordinary, naturally occurring speech, weak *agreements* (such as half hearted 'yeah's or 'uh huh's) are often heard and reacted to as if they imply *dis*agreement or refusal (Pomerantz, 1984). In the extract which follows, A asks B to telephone someone tonight. Notice that B says 'yeah' (which sounds like a – not very enthusiastic – agreement), but A (after waiting a short time, perhaps to offer B the opportunity to say why s/he isn't keen to make the call), reacts *as though* B had said 'no': 'Plea::se', A begs.

Example 9

A   'hhhhh Uh will you call 'im tuhnight for me,=
B   =eYea:h,
          (.)
A   Plea::se,

(Davidson, 1984: 113)

Here we have a 'yes', which is understood by the person making the request as if it were a refusal. We can see why this is if we compare it with conversations in which requests are accepted (see Examples 1 and 2 cited earlier): the evidence is that acceptances (real ones – that is, ones which are understood as such by the person making the request) occur quickly and without delay. This explains why, in Example 9, A understands the delayed and weak 'acceptance' as a refusal. In sexual situations, too, then, we might expect weak or delayed acceptances to be heard as refusals.

In sum, refusals do not have to be – and generally are not – emphatic, direct, and immediate 'no's. In ordinary conversation they are signalled by relatively subtle cues such as pauses, palliatives, and even weak agreements. It is clear that the word 'no' is not a necessary semantic component of refusals. It is not normally necessary to say 'no' in order to be heard as refusing an offer or invitation – pausing, hedging, producing a palliative, and even delayed or weak 'acceptances' are typically understood as refusals in everyday talk.

Conclusion and implications

To conclude, then, if we read the literature on young women's sexual negotiation in conjunction with the conversation analytic work on refusals, then it seems that young women responding to unwanted sexual pressure are using absolutely normal conversational patterns for refusals: that is, according to the research literature (and our own data) on young women and sexual communication, they are communicating their refusals indirectly; their refusals rarely refer to their own lack of desire for sex and more often to external circumstances which make sex impossible; their refusals are often qualified ('maybe later'), and are accompanied by compliments ('I really like you, but . . .') or by appreciations of the invitation ('it's very flattering of you to ask, but . . .'); and sometimes they refuse sex with the kind of 'yes's which are normatively understood as communicating refusal. These features are all part of what are commonly understood to be refusals. Yet the feminist and the date rape prevention literatures (and refusal skills training programmes more generally) present refusals of this kind as inadequate and insufficiently communicative. By contrast, we would suggest that young women are communicating in ways which are usually understood to mean refusal in other contexts and it is not the adequacy of their communication that should be questioned, but rather their male partners' claims not to understand that these women are refusing sex. As conversation analyst Michael Moerman (1988: 45) puts it:

> In any society, the recurrent and systematic attainment of misunderstanding between members of social categories who regularly converse with one another must thus be regarded as an artful, complicit, and damning accomplishment.

The conversation analytic literature leads us to question the source of men's alleged failure to 'understand' women's refusals.

If there is an organized and normative way of doing indirect refusal, which provides for culturally understood ways in which (for example) 'maybe later' means 'no', then men who claim not to have understood an indirect refusal (as in, 'she didn't actually say no') are claiming to be cultural dopes, and playing rather disingenuously on how refusals are usually done and understood to be done. They are claiming not to understand perfectly normal conversational interaction, and to be ignorant of ways of expressing refusal which they themselves routinely use in other areas of their lives.

While feminists have enthusiastically embraced the slogan 'yes means yes, and no means no', some anti-feminists have been virulent in opposition. For example, Gilbert (1991), criticizing the 'radical feminist effort to impose new norms governing intimacy between the sexes' (p. 61) complains that 'the awesome complexity of human interaction is reduced to "No means no"'. Conversation analytic research (like the work on token resistance) suggests that Gilbert is right: human conversational interaction is indeed intricately complex: 'yes' may sometimes mean 'no', 'no' may sometimes mean 'yes', and the word 'no' is not necessarily part of a refusal. What are the implications of this for feminism?

This article has argued that young women find it difficult to say 'no' to sex at least partly because saying immediate clear and direct 'no's (to anything) is not a normal conversational activity. Young women who do not use the word 'no', but who refuse sex with delays, prefaces, palliatives and accounts are using conversational patterns which are normatively recognized as refusals in everyday life. For men to claim that they do not 'understand' such refusals to be refusals (because, for example, they do not include the word 'no') is to lay claim to an astounding and implausible ignorance of normative conversational patterns. We have suggested that the insistence of date rape prevention (and other refusal skills) educators on the importance of saying 'no' is counter-productive in that it demands that women engage in conversationally abnormal actions which breach conventional social etiquette, and in that it allows rapists to persist with the claim that if a woman has not actually said 'NO' (in the right tone of voice, with the right body language, at the right time) then she hasn't refused to have sex with him.

Our analysis in this article supports the belief that the root of the problem is not that men do not understand sexual refusals, but that they do not like them. Confronted with a date rape education 'no means no' poster campaign, seeking to disambiguate women's refusals, nine male students at Queens University in Canada responded with posters of their own including slogans such as 'no means kick her in the teeth', 'no means on your knees bitch', 'no means tie her up', 'no means more beer' and 'no means she's a dyke' (cf. Mahood and Littlewood, 1997). Similar evidence comes from a recent study of 16-year-old boys who were asked 'if you wanted to have sex and your partner did not, would you try to persuade them to have sex? How?': the researchers comment that there was 'clear evidence of aggression towards girls who were not prepared to be sexually accommodating' and quote interview extracts in which boys say that in such situations they would 'root the fucking bitch in the fucking arse', 'give her a stern talking to', or just 'shove it in' (Moore and Rosenthal, 1992, cited in Moore and Rosenthal, 1993: 179). The problem of sexual coercion cannot be fixed by changing the way women talk.

In the present study, CA has made clear that there are normatively understood ways of doing refusals which are generally understood to *be* refusals, and consequently we believe that there is no reason why feminists concerned about sexual coercion should respond to men's allegations of their 'ambiguity' by taking upon ourselves the task of inventing new ways of doing refusals. As feminists, we have allowed men (disingenuously claiming not to understand normative conversational conventions) to set the agenda, such that we have accepted the need to educate women to produce refusals which men cannot claim to have 'misunderstood'. This, in turn, has led only to an escalation of men's claims to have 'misunderstood', to *be* 'misunderstood', and, in general, to be 'ignorant' about women's (allegedly different and special) ways of communicating. Men's self-interested capacity for 'misunderstanding' will always outstrip women's earnest attempts to clarify and explain.

[. . .]

Appendix: transcription notation

Most conversation analysts use a version of the transcription notation developed by Gail Jefferson (for a complete description see Atkinson and Heritage, 1984). We have provided here only what the reader needs to make sense of the extracts cited in this article.

[	indicates onset of overlapping speech
:	indicates that the preceeding sound is lengthened or drawn out (more colons indicate greater prolongation, e.g. Ah::::::)
underlining	indicates emphasis
(.)	pause less than 0.2 of a second
(0.3)	pause, timed in tenths of a second
.hhh	inbreath (more 'h's indicate a longer inbreath)
hhh	outbreath (more 'h's indicate a longer outbreath)
=	indicates no pause between speakers; one turn runs into another with no discernible pause
,(comma)	not used as a punctuation mark, but to indicate a slightly rising 'continuing' intonation

Notes

The authors would like to thank the members of Loughborough University's Discourse and Rhetoric Group (especially Derek Edwards, Jonathan Potter, Mick Billig and Charles Antaki) and Women's Studies Research Group (especially Sue Wilkinson and Cath Benson) for stimulating discussions which informed our writing of this article.

1   To be absolutely accurate here, we should note that we do not in fact know anything about what B *intended* to communicate – and indeed B's intentions and desires are unknowable by, and irrelevant to, conversation analysts. Conversation analysts do not claim to be able to use what people say to read off psychological phenomena like intentions, desires, emotions, or other cognitions. The claim is only that A *reacts* to what B says as though B were refusing the invitation, and hence that the structure of B's speech is the kind of structure which ordinary members of the speech community commonly orient to *as a refusal*. See Edwards (1997) for a comprehensive discussion of the relationship between talk and cognition.

References

Antaki, C. (1994) *Explaining and Arguing: The Social Organisation of Accounts*, London, Sage.
Atkinson, J.M. and Drew, P. (eds) (1979) *Order in Court: The Organization of Verbal Interaction in Judicial Settings*, London, Social Sciences Research Council.
Atkinson, J.M. and Heritage, J., (eds) (1984) *Structures of Social Action: Studies in Conversation Analysis*, Cambridge, Cambridge University Press.
Burley-Allen, M. (1983) *Managing Assertively: How to Improve your People Skills*, New York, Wiley.

Cairns, K. (1993) 'Sexual entitlement and sexual accommodation: male and female responses to sexual coercion', *Canadian Journal of Human Sexuality*, vol. 2, pp. 203–14.

Cameron, D. (1995) *Verbal Hygiene*, London, Routledge.

Campbell, B.K. and Barnlund, D.C. (1977) 'Communication patterns and problems of pregnancy', *American Journal of Orthopsychiatry*, vol. 47, pp. 134–9.

Cocoran, C. (1992) 'From victim control to social change: a feminist perspective on campus rape prevention programmes' in J.C. Chrisler and D. Howard (eds) *New Directions in Feminist Psychology: Practice, Theory and Research*, New York, Springer.

Coudert, J. (1993) 'Nice ways to say no' *Readers Digest*, Feb., pp. 56–8.

Crombie, A.B. (1994) *The Art of Saying No: Creative Escapology*, London, Golden Rule Publications.

Cvetkovitch, G., Grote, B., Lieverman, E.S. and Miller, W. (1978) 'Sex role development and teenage fertility-related behavior', *Adolescence*, vol. 8, pp. 231–6.

Davidson, J. (1984) 'Subsequent versions of invitations, offers, requests, and proposals dealing with potential or actual rejection' in J.M. Atkinson and J. Heritage (eds) *Structures of Social Action: Studies in Conversation Analysis*, Cambridge, Cambridge University Press.

Drew, P. (1984) 'Speakers' reportings in invitation sequences' in J.M. Atkinson and J. Heritage (eds) *Structures of Social Action: Studies in Conversation Analysis*, Cambridge, Cambridge University Press.

Duncombe, J. and Marsden, D. (1993) 'Love and intimacy: The gender division of emotion and emotion work: A neglected aspect of sociological discussion of heterosexual relationships', *Sociology*, vol. 27, pp. 221–41.

Duncombe, J. and Marsden, D. (1996) 'Whose orgasm is this anyway? "sex work" in long term heterosexual couple relationships' in J. Weeks and J. Holland (eds) *Sexual Cultures: Communities, Values and Intimacy*, London, Macmillan Press.

Edwards, D. (1997) *Discourse and Cognition*, London, Sage.

Edwards, D. and Potter, J. (1992) *Discursive Psychology*, London, Sage.

Ehrlich, S. (1998) 'The discursive reconstruction of sexual consent', *Discourse & Society*, Vol. 9, pp. 149–71.

Fensterheim, H. and Baer, J. (1975) *Don't Say Yes When You Want to Say No*, New York, David McKay.

Frith, H. (1997) *Young Women Refusing Sex: The Epistemological Adventures of a Feminist*, unpublished PhD thesis, Loughborough University, UK.

Frith, H. and Kitzinger, C. (1997) 'Talk about sexual miscommunication', *Women's Studies International Forum*, vol. 20, pp. 517–28.

Frith, H. and Kitzinger, C. (1998) '"Emotion work" as a participant resource: A feminist analysis of young women's talk-in-interaction', *Sociology*, vol. 32, pp. 299–320.

Gervasio, A.H. and Crawford, M. (1989) 'Social evaluations of assertiveness: a critique and speech act reformulation', *Psychology of Women Quarterly*, vol. 13, pp. 1–25.

Gilbert, N. (1991) 'The phantom epidemic of sexual assault', *The Public Interest*, vol. 103, pp. 54–65.

Goodchilds, J.G., Zellman, G.L., Johnson, P.B. and Giarrusso, R. (1988) 'Adolescents and their perceptions of sexual interactions' in A.W. Burgess (ed.) *Rape and Sexual Assault*, New York, Garland.

Heritage, J. (1984) *Garfinkel and Ethnomethodology*, Cambridge, Polity Press.

Heritage, J. (1989) 'Current developments in conversation analysis' in D. Roger and P. Bull (eds) *Conversation: An Interdisciplinary Perspective*, Clevedon, PA, Multilingual Matters.

Howard, M. (1985a) 'How the family physician can help young teenagers postpone sexual involvement', *Medical Aspects of Human Sexuality*, vol. 19, pp. 76–87.

Howard, M. (1985b) 'Postponing sexual involvement among adolescents: an alternative approach to prevention of sexually transmitted diseases', *Journal of Adolescent Health Care*, vol. 6, pp. 271–7.

Howard, M. and McCabe, J.B. (1990) 'Helping teenagers postpone sexual involvement', *Family Planning Perspectives*, vol. 22, pp. 21–6.

Jefferson, G. (1984) 'Notes on a systematic deployment of the acknowledgement tokens "yeah" and "mm hm"', *Papers in Linguistics*, vol. 17, pp. 197–216.

Kidder, L.H., Boell, J.L. and Moyer, M.M. (1983) 'Rights consciousness and victimization prevention: personal defence and assertiveness training', *Journal of Social Issues*, vol. 39, pp. 155–70.

Kitzinger, C. (1998) 'Expertise vs commonsense: theory and rhetoric in editorial discourse', *Discourse & Society*, vol. 9, pp. 143–6.

Labov, W. and Fanshel, D. (1977) *Therapeutic Discourse*, New York, Academic Press.

Levinson, S.C. (1983) *Pragmatics*, Cambridge, Cambridge University Press.

McConnch, S. (1990) *Assertiveness: A Personal Skills Course for Young People*, Basingstoke, Macmillan Education.

Mahood, L. and Littlewood, B. (1997) 'Daughters in danger: the case of "campus sex crimes"' in A.M. Thomas and C. Kitzinger (eds) *Sexual Harassment: Contemporary Feminist Perspectives*, Milton Keynes, Open University Press.

Martin, J. (1982) *Miss Manners' Guide to Excruciatingly Correct Behavior*, New York, Atheneum.

Moerman, M. (1988) *Talking Culture: Ethnography and Conversation Analysis*, Philadelphia, University of Pennsylvania Press.

Moore, S. and Rosenthal, D. (1992) 'The social context of adolescent sexuality: safe sex implications', *Journal of Adolescence*, vol. 15, pp. 415–35.

Moore, S. and Rosenthal, D. (1993) *Sexuality in Adolescence*, London, Routledge.

Morgan, D.L. (1996) 'Focus groups', *Annual Review of Sociology*, vol. 22, pp. 129–52.

Muehlenhard, C.L. and Cook, S.W. (1988) 'Men's self reports of unwanted sexual activity', *Journal of Sex Research*, vol. 24, pp. 58–72.

Muehlenhard, C.L. and Hollabaugh, L.C. (1988) 'Do women sometimes say no when they mean yes? The prevalence and correlates of women's token resistance to sex', *Journal of Personality and Social Psychology*, vol. 54, pp. 872–9.

Muehlenhard, C.L. and McCoy, M.L. (1991) 'Double standards/double bind: the sexual double standard and women's communication about sex', *Psychology of Women Quarterly*, vol. 15, pp. 447–61.

Muehlenhard, C., Julsonnet, S., Carson, M. and Falrity-White, L.A. (1989) 'A cognitive-behavioral programme for preventing sexual coercion', *Behavior Therapist*, vol. 12, pp. 211–14.

Murnen, S.K., Perot, A. and Byrne, D. (1989) 'Coping with unwanted sexual activity: normative responses, situation determinants, and individual differences', *Journal of Sex Research*, vol. 26, pp. 85–106.

Phelps, S. and Austin, N. (1987) *The Assertive Woman*, 2nd edn., San Luis, CA, Impact Publishers.

Pomerantz, A.M. (1984) 'Agreeing and disagreeing with assessments: some features of preferred/dispreferred turn shapes' in J.M. Atkinson and J. Heritage (eds) *Structures of Social Action: Studies in Conversation Analysis*, Cambridge, Cambridge University Press.

Potter, J. and Wetherell, M. (1987) *Discourse and Social Psychology*, London, Sage.

Psathas, G. and Anderson, T. (1990) 'The "practices" of transcription in conversation analysis', *Semiotica*, vol. 78, pp. 75–99.

Quinn, K., Sanchex-Hucles, J., Coates, G. and Gillen, B. (1991) 'Men's compliance with a woman's resistance to unwanted sexual advances', *Journal of Offender Rehabilitation*, vol. 17, pp. 13–31.

Sandler, A.D., Watson, T.E. and Levine, M.D. (1992) 'A study of the cognitive aspects of sexual decision making in adolescent females', *Developmental and Behavioral Pediatrics*, vol. 13, pp. 202–7.

Smith, M.J. (1975) *When I Say No, I Feel Guilty*, New York, Dial Press.

Sprecher, S., Hatfield, E., Cortese, A., Potapova, E. and Levitskaya, A. (1994) 'Token resistance to sexual intercourse and consent to unwanted sexual intercourse', *Journal of Sex Research*, vol. 31, pp. 125–32.

Stere, L.K. (1985) 'Feminist assertiveness training: self-esteem groups as skill training for women' in L.B. Rosewater and L.G.A. Walker (eds) *Handbook of Feminist Theory*, New York, Springer.

Stubbs, D.R. (1986) *Assertiveness at Work: A Necessary Guide to an Essential Skill*, London, Pan.

Tannen, D. (1991) *You Just Don't Understand: Women and Men in Conversation*, London: Virago.

Turner, J.S. and Rubinson, L. (1993) *Contemporary Human Sexuality*, Englewood Cliffs, NJ, Prentice Hall.

Warzak, W.J. and Page, T.J. (1990) 'Teaching refusal skills to sexually active adolescents', *Journal of Behavioral Therapy and Experimental Psychiatry*, vol. 21, pp. 133–9.

Warzak, W.J., Grow, C.R., Poler, M.M. and Walburn, J.N. (1995) 'Enhancing refusal skills: identifying contexts that place adolescents at risk for unwanted sexual activity', *Developmental and Behavioral Pediatrics*, vol. 16, pp. 98–100.

Wilkinson, S. (1999) 'Focus groups: a feminist method', *Psychology of Women Quarterly*, Special issue on innovative methods, M. Crawford and E. Kimmel (eds), vol. 23, pp. 221–44.

Wiseman, R. (1994) *Defending Ourselves: A Guide to Prevention, Self-Defense, and Recovery from Rape*, New York, Farrar, Straus and Giroux.

PART THREE
MINDS, SELVES AND SENSE-MAKING

Editor's Introduction

Margaret Wetherell

Reading One in Part One suggested that pieces of discourse like the *Panorama* interview with Princess Diana present a wide range of hooks or themes for discourse researchers. The nature of social interaction, explored in depth in Part Two, was just one of these entry points. A further entry point was the psychological – Diana as a person, the speaking subject. What can discourse research tell us about the construction of identity and subjectivity, about mind in talk and the ways in which people come to make sense of their social worlds? Part Three of the Reader focuses on these themes and the role of discourse in the production of social actors. How does the new thinking about language and social life reviewed in Part One alter our conception of the person?

At its most basic, the study of discourse and persons investigates how people tell stories about themselves and how they present themselves in talk. We can look at how people put together an account, the discursive practices and routines they use and the consequences of choosing one way of talking about oneself over another. But this study also raises a number of theoretical questions. It changes our understanding of individuals, their internal states, how people form their views of the world, their emotions, desires and innermost selves. It alters the ways in which the relationship between the psychological and the social is formulated.

Some hints of the broader issues at stake emerged in a number of readings in Part Two. Goffman's notion of footing, for example (see Reading Eight), suggests the ways in which discursive practices fragment, multiply and decentre the self. Which is the 'real me' – the character I construct for myself as I tell a story of some event in my life (the principal) or is the 'real me' best understood as the animator, the speaking voice? Questions proliferate from here. What counts as 'real' anyway, when it comes to persons? What is identity? Is it a set of stable and semi-permanent traits and attributes which express a natural state of being? Or, is identity a set of culturally available performances (footings) sanctioned through power relations?

Equally, Silverman's work on HIV counselling sessions (see Reading Ten) demonstrated people's dependence on others for self-definition. Identity seems to be emergent and co-constructed. It is partly a matter of what one can create for oneself and partly a matter of the positions made available by others in the preceding turns of the conversation. Consider, for instance, how the counsellor sets the scene for the patient's construction of their identity as they move on to the 'delicate object' of sexual history. But, how does this mutuality and the interdependence of speakers square with our preferred self-image in Western societies as detached, independent, rational, self-contained and consistent thinkers?

One consequence of the turn to discourse for the study of persons has been a radical questioning of this image of the solitary self-contained individual – the traditional reference point for much of psychology. Much psychological research (and this view also seems simple common sense) assumes the individual is behind and beyond language. As Michael Billig (1999) has argued, the dominant perspective is that people operate rather like Rodin's famous statue of 'The Thinker' ('Le Penseur'). The statue depicts a man alone, naked, head in hand, sitting on a rock, obviously deep in thought. The assumption is that we are bombarded with sensory impressions and experiences and like 'Le Penseur' we then sit and process these in solitary contemplation and introspection, working out our beliefs, our line, our emotions before we talk and act on the world. Billig argues that while we may well sit alone to think, thought itself is never a solitary process. It is suffused with dialogue, with the words of others. 'Le Penseur' may be alone with his thoughts but those thoughts bear the marks of social contexts and historical struggles over meaning. Minds and selves are constructed from cultural, social and communal resources.

As Edwards (1997) notes, discourse research takes apart the everyday assumption that talk is a best sense or best efforts expression of the internal states of the thinking individual. It takes apart the notion, in other words, that language and thought are separate – that thinking is cognitive, a mental sorting out in our heads, while talking is about language, a struggle to find just the right words which most accurately express the mental states and conclusions. Instead, it is argued that internal states (such as feelings, intentions, motives, beliefs) are constructed as particular entities in discourse (both in the discourse produced for ourselves and discourse for others).

This critique of traditional psychological assumptions is inspired by a number of the developments in the history of language research reviewed in Part One. A central point Wittgenstein makes, for instance, is that the meaning of words depends on their contexts of use (see Reading Three). What it means to 'have your train of thought disrupted' or 'be hopping mad' or 'wildly infatuated' or 'emotionally fragile' or 'away in a dream' is guaranteed not by reference to a range of discrete underlying mental states which these words purport to describe but through the contexts of use of these terms in the language communities to which we belong.

In this view it is not so much that we have the experience and then generate the most accurate terms to describe the experience. Rather we come to know what the experience is because we have the words or language games available to us. It would be a mistake, then, according to Wittgenstein, to try to understand 'away in a dream' through careful introspection of our pure feelings and experiences. We understand what this means because we are embedded in the linguistic history of our communities and are familiar with the different uses and connotations the phrase has acquired which determine when it is an appropriate and plausible thing to say. Conversation analytic and ethnomethodological research (see Reading Four) have since sustained and elaborated upon these conclusions.

Further, Bakhtin and Volosinov (see Reading Six) reinforce Billig's point that an internal subjective life built from discourse is never solitary. Discourse is dialogical. Our minds are organized around collective resources so that the voices of others are embedded internally in our modes of representing. This has radical implications for understanding how children become socialized. It is argued that children acquire a mental life as they acquire a language and become competent members of their culture. Our minds are partly constituted from discourse as conversations with others become internalized as private mental operations. Foucault, of course, adds to this the dimension of power (see Reading Seven). If our minds are a record and accumulation of discursive history and that history is a record of power then we are subjected to certain epistemic regimes and disciplined as we are constituted. All of these points question the notion of social actors as whole and coherent and standing behind language, operating it and expressing themselves as they talk, but remaining essentially independent – language users rather than products of discourse.

What are some of the further consequences of the 'turn to discourse' for the study of psychological issues? Another issue which was implicitly raised in some of the readings in Part One concerns methodology. The data of psychology are varied but include people's self-reports, their paper and pencil responses to questionnaires, written observations of behaviour, diary records, interviews and accounts of actions performed in experiments. If language, however, is constructive and constituting, performative as well as referential, then any simple notion of good data as neutral and transparent descriptions of states of mind or events in the world becomes complicated. The turn to discourse in psychology, therefore, has involved a shift to studying talk in itself rather than quick detours past the words and the doing with words to some assumed mental state or underlying behavioural pattern. Discourse has become interesting *per se* rather than being taken for granted as a direct access route to the real psychological business.

The readings in Part Three exemplify a varied tradition of work on discourse which has come to be known as 'discursive psychology' (see Edwards and Potter, 1992; Harré and Gillett, 1994 for programmatic overviews). This tradition of research began in the UK in the 1980s as psychologists began to think through the implications of new emphases on discourse and related epistemological debates for psychology. There were several strands to this early work. One strand was the social constructionist movement in psychology which set the scene for the development of discourse analysis in social psychology and sustains the current context for discursive psychology (Gergen, 1985; Gergen and Davis, 1985; Harré, 1979; Shotter, 1984). Social constructionists developed a passionate critique of experimental and other quantitative methods in psychology and the theory of the person and epistemology these methods assumed, which led to new thinking on the formation of self and subjectivity.

A second crucial intellectual movement was the development of critical psychology (Henriques *et al.*, 1984). Henriques *et al.* were some of the first psychologists to recognize the importance of Foucault's work for studies of subjectivity (see Hollway, Reading Twenty). Meanwhile other researchers in the same period (Potter and Wetherell, 1987) began a self-conscious attempt to develop a viable theory and method of discourse analysis for empirical research on psychological topics. And, Billig's (1987) work introduced ancient and modern work on rhetoric to psychology.

Potter and Wetherell re-worked a range of previous discourse research including ethnomethodology and its use of Wittgenstein (Coulter, 1979, 1983; Heritage, 1984), discourse work in the sociology of science (Gilbert and Mulkay, 1984), speech act theory (Austin, 1962) and semiology (Barthes, 1972), and from these sources formed their method of discourse analysis. Subsequent research and theoretical development have added further threads to the general project of discursive psychology including Bakhtinian discourse research (see Billig in Reading Fifteen; Shotter, 1993), further incorporation of conversation analysis (Antaki, 1994; see Edwards in Reading Seventeen; Edwards and Potter, 1992; Widdicombe and Wooffitt, 1995) and has elaborated upon the Foucauldian themes (Burman and Parker, 1993; Parker, 1992; Wetherell and Potter, 1992).

In parallel developments, studies (mostly in the USA) of 'narrative psychology' (Sarbin, 1986) have added a stronger emphasis on people's autobiographical constructions of identity whether in life history interviews (see Gergen in Reading Eighteen; Gergen and Gergen, 1993; Josselson and Lieblich, 1993; Mishler, 1995), in the conversations which make up therapy (White and Epston, 1990) or in the storytelling characteristic of everyday life (Bruner, 1987; Gee, 1991, 1992). Van Dijk's work (1989; Van Dijk and Kintsch, 1983), particularly on racism, has offered a contrasting model of discourse and cognition which sees an autonomous role for cognitive processes in discourse and text processing.

Discursive psychology, more than the other discourse traditions covered in this Reader, is a hybrid approach and embodies many of the tensions between fine-grain analysis and more macro-social discourse work. In this Reader it is defined inclusively rather than narrowly including both Foucauldian and conversation analytic research on psychological issues.

The readings

The reading from **Potter and Wetherell** which opens Part Three is, as noted, one of the first attempts to explore discourse analysis in a psychological context. Potter and Wetherell outline three principles in their approach to discourse analysis: function, construction and variation. These principles exemplify and can be deduced from the critique of language as transparent, neutral and a 'do nothing' domain and Potter and Wetherell explicitly develop this critique. They go on to consider the implications of function, construction and variation for a key psychological concept: the notion of attitude (see also Potter, 1996a). Attitudes fit within the sense-making theme of Part Three. It is one of the principal concepts social psychologists use to understand how people process and hold information about the social world. The measurement of attitudes is, of course, now a major industry found in market research, for instance, in polling on political issues and as a barometer of public opinion, as well as providing the rationale for survey research in psychology more generally.

Potter and Wetherell suggest an alternative perspective on the ways in which people represent and make sense of social reality. Traditional attitude theory in psychology falls prey to some of the problems Wittgenstein's perspective on language highlights (see Reading Three). The notion of attitude tends to assume, for instance, that mind is independent of language so that an attitude is a description of a pre-existing mental state as opposed to a speech act produced in context for a purpose.

As they explore these themes, Potter and Wetherell consider some of the methodological implications of the slipperiness and flexibility discourse analysis reveals. They show how survey research and questionnaire studies of attitudes work by constraining and circumventing natural language use and discuss some of the techniques researchers use for producing 'good' but, arguably, misleading data. The implications of these claims about attitudes were later developed in a detailed empirical investigation of racist discourse (Wetherell and Potter, 1992) and views on egalitarianism and gender (Wetherell *et al.*, 1987), while the style of discourse analysis emerging here was applied to other topics such as the notion of 'community' (Potter and Reicher, 1987) and violent identities (Wetherell and Potter, 1989).

The second reading from **Billig** carries on the theme of attitudes and the question of how best to conceptualize people's sense-making. Potter and Wetherell note the variability in people's accounts of the world. Billig (Billig, 1987, 1991, 1995; Billig *et al.*, 1988) has also explored this aspect of discourse in use extensively and developed a new perspective on ideology incorporating insights from the study of rhetoric. One view of the social actor is as a relatively rational information processer so the individual observes the social world and arrives at opinions and beliefs which are coherent, enduring and consistent. An alternative view has the social actor as a kind of 'social dope' or tool of political interests so that any beliefs and opinions simply parrot the received ideas of the ruling groups in a historical period. Against both these views, Billig counterposes a different image of ideology and sense-making. Billig and his colleagues (Billig *et al.*, 1988) stress the ways in which beliefs and opinions are dilemmatic in character, organized around competing versions and principles. He emphasizes the role of argument, debate and persuasion in social life and so the social actor is not a passive imbiber of received views but actively engaged in puzzling. Crucially, the social actor is engaged in rhetoric, in organizing accounts and versions into 'winning arguments'. People's world views are thus built up from a 'patchwork' or 'kaleidoscope' of often highly inconsistent interpretative resources.

In addition to this theme, this reading from Billig also demonstrates the application of ideas encountered in Part One from Bakhtin and Volosinov (Reading Six), Wittgenstein and Austin (Reading Three) and conversation analysis (Reading Four). Billig looks at other internal mental states, such as memory, in addition to attitudes and applies the logic derived from these philosophical and other sources to argue against traditional psychological views of how memory functions in social life drawing on the work of Middleton and Edwards (1990). Billig also explores the relationship between words and actions, claiming that words are actions, a move inspired by Austin's speech act theory.

The next reading from **Wertsch** also takes up Bakhtin's ideas and returns the discussion to issues concerning selves and identity more generally along with the question of socialization. How do children learn their culture? How do they become competent members? Wertsch's exploration here is part of an attempt to work with and develop the theory of the Russian developmental psychologist, Vygotsky, of mediated action (see also Wertsch, 1985). Wertsch asks two fascinating and provoking questions: who is doing the talking and who owns meaning? To answer these questions he draws on Bakhtin's notion of 'ventriloquation', the concept of dialogicality and Bakhtin's work on reported speech (see also Maybin, 1993, for an application of Bakhtin's work on voice to children's talk).

Wertsch shows how this work opposes two very common views of the individual and communication in Western society. One is the view of the individual as disengaged from society – the rational, independent, self-contained actor referred to earlier. The second is the metaphor of language as a conduit and communication as the processes of encoding and decoding. Encoding and decoding are assumed to work as follows: the individual has a thought, she or he searches for the best words to convey this thought and encodes the thought into words; the listener hears the words and decodes them to find the original thought. Bakhtin argued that the individual is more thoroughly bound into the social world. Further, a message may be delivered through one speaking voice but it bears the marks of many voices – the message is not a possession of the solitary individual but is marked by its passage through culture. The speaker is ventriloquating – speaking their culture as they communicate. The image of two separated speakers with a uni-directional message passing from one to another misses many other important dimensions of discourse in use. It misses, for instance, the way in which the reader or the listener actively constructs and thus constitutes the nature of the message.

Wertsch presents a worked example of a dialogue between a mother and a child which illustrates these points and demonstrates how discursive and other activities which occur first on the inter-mental plane of functioning between people can be then taken in by the child to form the intra-mental plane of functioning as they make their culture and the voices of others part of their own mental apparatus (see also Cole, 1994; Miller and Hoogstra, 1992; Miller *et al.*, 1992 for similar explorations of children's talk). Such an example turns our attention to questions of power and Wertsch discusses Bakhtin's views on how the authoritative voice operates.

In the next reading, **Edwards** takes the foundations of discursive psychology emerging here – notions of rhetoric; words as actions; construction, function and variation (the building blocks provided by Wittgenstein, Sacks, Austin and Bakhtin) – and in an extract taken from his path-breaking book, *Discourse and Cognition* (1997), applies these to develop a discursive psychology of the emotions. With Jonathan Potter, Edwards was responsible for constructing a second stage of discursive psychology (Edwards and Potter, 1992; Potter, 1996b). This work on the emotions is part of their general project to re-conceptualize the study of psychological states particularly those investigated by cognitive psychology (Edwards, 1991; Edwards and Potter, 1993; Potter and Edwards, 1990).

Emotions represent a good test case for a re-working of traditional psychological topics in discursive terms. What could be more visceral, more experiential, less wordy than feelings? Edwards shows how wrong this view is:

emotions have to be communicated and the study of emotion talk tells us a great deal about what emotions are. The move is becoming a familiar one. The focus is not on incohate mental states but on talk-in-action. In studying emotion talk, Edwards develops a more fine-grain form of analysis than seen so far in Part Three and indicates the debt his branch of discursive psychology owes to conversation analysis (see Reading Four and Horton-Salway, 2001, for a worked example showing the stages in Edwards and Potter's approach to discursive psychology).

In particular, Edwards' work is distinguished by the application of the conversation analytic principle that the task is to clarify the endogenous sense-making of the participants to the interaction and in this way attempt to stay with the discursive patterns. He is critical of psychological research which attempts to go beyond the logic of the interaction or read it as merely ephemeral, reflective or symptomatic of some determining underlying mental state presumed to cause the patterns in talk. This rooting of discursive psychology in conversation analysis can be contrasted with Billig's more social and political concerns in Reading Fifteen and with other more recent empirical work in discursive psychology which has focused on the social context to the construction of identity (see the articles in Burman and Parker, 1993; Edley and Wetherell, 1997; Wetherell, 1998; Wetherell and Edley, 1998).

From emotions we turn to the concept of the self in the next reading. Again what could be more private, hidden and inaccessible? In contrast to this view, **Gergen** argues for the centrality of discourse, specifically narrative, to self-experience and the performance of identity. He argues that narratives and stories are the means by which we make ourselves intelligible – how people know who they are and communicate their identities to others. Gergen considers the characteristics of well-formed narratives and various types which are likely to emerge in everyday discourse such as the comedy-romance (see also Gergen and Gergen, 1988).

Several points are worth noting here. First, Gergen is rejecting the view of humanistic psychology that there is a real, authentic or true self which can be discovered so that a person could be said to have 'found themselves' after sufficient introspection. This implies a pre-existent self, already there, which just needs the words to describe it. In line with the perspective on language which is characteristic of discourse research, Gergen argues instead that who we are emerges in a contingent, variable and flexible fashion as we talk ourselves into being. This does not mean there is no continuity to the self. Rather, old, already familiar stories (large-scale significant autobiographical narratives and the tiny anecdotes of everyday life) contextualize the new stories. Crucially some of the discursive properties of narratives (that there should be a stable protagonist) also ground us.

You will recognize many parallels with themes from earlier readings: the centrality of variation, construction and function in the performance of narrative and in talk in general, for instance, introduced by Potter and Wetherell in Reading Fourteen, and the importance of rhetoric in everyday life, introduced by Billig in Reading Fifteen. Stories are for an audience, they are relational, oriented to others, dialogical, worked up in contexts and designed pragmatically. Gergen (1985, 1991, 1994) is a leading exponent of social constructionism within psychology. Social constructionist themes were introduced in Edwards' discussion of emotion and are reiterated here. In particular, communal resources are emphasized. Thus, it is not the case that individuals consult the contents of their own minds and produce anew each time a fresh idiosyncratic description of themselves. Rather, people creatively work with discursive history. Gergen notes two senses in which this is the case. We are constrained and empowered by our existing cultural conceptions of the form of a good narrative and the content of our narratives is also socially constructed. What is particularly exciting about Gergen's work is that the study of narrative suggests a method or a way into the concrete analysis of people's accounts of their life histories and narrative research in this sense has become a major research tool in psychology (e.g. Bruner, 1987; Gee, 1991; Mishler, 1995; Sarbin, 1986).

Although a chronologically earlier account, the next reading from **Davies and Harré** fits well within the general framework of the discursive self sketched out by Gergen. This reading focuses on one crucial property of narratives and stories: they position people (see also Harré, 1998; Harré and Van Langenhove, 1991). In other words, to talk is to take a line of some kind and to take on a narrative is also to take on a position from which one speaks. Such positions construct character. Positioning, moreover, is mutual and reciprocal. When we are addressed by others we have to deal with the positions they construct for us and as we speak we in turn position them. Davies and Harré develop a hypothetical example of two characters, Sano and Enfermada, to illustrate these points. This notion of positioning has a long intellectual history and similar arguments can be found in Foucault's work (see Reading Seven) and there are echoes of Althusser's notion of 'interpellation' (Hall, 1996) (see also Edley, 2001, for a worked example which demonstrates how the concept of subject position might be used in empirical research).

Like other authors in Part Three, Davies and Harré locate themselves as part of the larger social constructionist movement within psychology which is attentive to new views on language. Indeed, Harré's (1979, 1983) theoretical work in psychology was central in establishing this approach. Davies and Harré refer also to 'new paradigm psychology' and 'ethogenics' (Harré, 1977; Harré et al., 1985) which were precursors of social constructionism. They coin a phrase – 'psycho-socio-linguistics' – to sum up the emerging discursive work in psychology. This term has been superseded by the notion of 'discursive psychology' (see Harré and Gillett, 1994).

It is worth noting the authors' definition of 'discourse' and 'discursive practice'. Discursive practice is 'all the ways in which people actively produce social and psychological realities', while discourse is 'the institutionalized use of language'. This definition of discourse indicates the Foucauldian and feminist poststructuralist influences on Davies and Harré signalled by the concern with the connections between knowledge, power and social relations. This way of thinking about discourse, and the feminist influence, is developed further in the next reading. Like many influenced by but sceptical of this tradition, Davies and Harré are concerned to retain some sense of human agency – in their view people actively produce social realities. They argue that the contradictions between people's multiple positions promote choice. They note, however, some of the features of positioning and ideologies of selfhood in Western societies which encourage the sense of the independent, originating, consistent and authentic subject. Perhaps our assumptions about what we are 'foundationally', 'really' and 'ontologically' are the strongest effect of language.

Finally, it is worth noting the ways in which Davies and Harré draw on some themes from the histories of language research developed in Part One of this Reader. They stress *parole*, for instance, at the expense of *langue* (see Reading Two) and use Austin's speech act theory (see Reading Three) to highlight the functional force of utterances. A further distinction is made between transcendentalist and immanentist views to contrast two notions of the origins of pattern and structure in talk. The immanentist view argues that order is normative, produced and reproduced by people in an on-going fashion. Order is emergent and open to revision and needs to be constantly done over and over in practice to retain its force. The transcendentalist view instead looks for an underlying determining structure outside concrete examples of human practice. Conversation analysis is an excellent example of an immanentist view (see Reading Four).

The final reading in Part Three from **Hollway** more explicitly introduces a Foucauldian perspective into the study of subjectivity and discourse and, as noted, Hollway was one of the first to consider the relevance of this perspective to psychology (see Rose, 1996, for a discussion of the implications of Foucault's later work for the study of identity such as the notion of 'technologies of the self'). One key advantage of Foucault's approach is the attention paid to power and inequality which was left implicit in Gergen's account, for instance. Discourse is not seen as neutral but as producing power relations as people are positioned in talk. Hollway focuses on sexuality and gender differentiated ways of talking about sexual relations to demonstrate this point (see Carabine, 2001, for a further worked example of a genealogical analysis of sexuality).

Note that the connotation of the term 'discourse' is continuing to change here. Whereas in previous readings, discourse often tended to be understood as a verb ('to discourse'), in Foucauldian work, discourse becomes a noun (Potter *et al.*, 1990). In other words, a discourse is defined as a recognizable collection of statements which cohere together. Thus Hollway identifies, for instance, a 'have and hold' discourse of sexuality, meaning a connected set of ways of making sense which have a particular geneaology or history. This distinction between 'discourse as a verb' and 'discourse as a noun' styles of analysis can be rather simplistic, however, if taken too literally. Hollway is also at pains to stress that discourses are practices and therefore are mobile, flexible, instantiated differently in different contexts and always in transformation.

Like Davies and Harré, Hollway is interested in positioning or the identities each discourse of sexuality offers to those who adopt it. In a fascinating analysis she argues that the positions within sexuality discourses are not equally available to men and women. Men, for instance, take up characteristic positions – they tend to talk about themselves as the *subjects* of 'male sex drive discourse' and the *objects* of 'have and hold' discourse. Hollway explains this in terms of gender power – as a consequence of the power men gain from these moves – in particular they avoid vulnerability and dependence.

Although Hollway draws extensively on Foucauldian notions, she is critical of Foucault's theory of subjectivity. She notes a point often made about Foucault's work that he has little space for agency or choice and implies a somewhat mechanical reproduction of discourses as though discourse is the main motor of social life with human agents following haplessly behind, forever caught in the available positions. Hollway argues that it is all much more contingent than this. In particular, meanings are multiple, people are constituted from many contradictory discourses and this alone gives considerable flexibility, reflexivity, dialogue and scope for interrogating one position from the perspective of another. This theme runs through all the readings in Part Three.

Secondly, Hollway turns to psychoanalytic explanations and the question of investment to preserve some autonomy for subjectivity (see also Hollway, 1989). She asks the reader to think about investment and motivation and continually comes back to the question: what is in it for men and women, what do each gain from the positions they take up and how is this related to the complex patterning of desire for the Other laid down in childhood. This appeal to the complex non-unitary subjectivity characteristic of psychoanalytic theory also provides some sense of agency and the human being living the discourse. Hollway's work initiated and reflects a fascinating and now quite extensive body of work by psychologists which draws on both psychoanalysis and discourse theory (see Frosh, 1997; Hollway and Featherstone, 1997; Hollway and Jefferson, 2000; Walkerdine, 1990, 1997). A final theme in the reading is that of politics. As a feminist, Hollway is interested in social change and thus relates her discussion of agency and the scope for multiple positioning to the possibilities for political action.

References

Antaki, C. (1994) *Explaining and Arguing: The Social Organisation of Accounts*, London, Sage.

Austin, J. (1962) *How to do Things with Words*, London, Oxford University Press.

Barthes, R. (1972) *Mythologies*, London, Paladin.

Billig, M. (1987) *Arguing and Thinking: A Rhetorical Approach to Social Psychology*, Cambridge, Cambridge University Press.

Billig, M. (1991) *Ideology, Rhetoric and Opinion*, London, Sage.

Billig, M. (1995) *Banal Nationalism*, London, Sage.

Billig, M. (1999) *Freudian Repression: Conversation Creating the Unconscious*, Cambridge, Cambridge University Press.

Billig, M., Condor, S., Edwards, D., Gane, M., Middleton, D. and Radley, A. (1988) *Ideological Dilemmas*, London, Sage.

Bruner, J. (1987) 'Life as narrative', *Social Research*, vol. 54, pp. 11–32.

Burman, E. and Parker, I. (eds) (1993) *Discourse Analytic Research*, London, Routledge.

Carabine, J. (2001) 'Unmarried motherhood 1830–1990: a genealogical analysis' in M. Wetherell, S. Taylor and S.J. Yates (eds) *Discourse as Data: A Guide to Analysis*, London, Sage in association with the Open University.

Cole, M. (1994) 'Culture and cognitive development: from cross-cultural research to creating systems of cultural mediation', *Culture and Psychology*, vol. 1, pp. 25–54.

Coulter, J. (1979) *The Social Construction of Mind*, London, Macmillan.

Coulter, J. (1983) *Rethinking Cognitive Theory*, London, Macmillan.

Edley, N. (2001) 'Analysing masculinity: interpretative repertoires, subject positions and ideological dilemmas' in M. Wetherell, S. Taylor and S.J. Yates (eds) *Discourse as Data: A Guide to Analysis*, London, Sage in association with the Open University.

Edley, N. and Wetherell, M. (1997) 'Jockeying for position: the construction of masculine identities', *Discourse and Society*, vol. 8, pp. 203–17.

Edwards, D. (1991) 'Categories are for talking', *Theory and Psychology*, vol. 1, pp. 515–42.

Edwards, D. (1997) *Discourse and Cognition*, London, Sage.

Edwards, D. and Potter, J. (1992) *Discursive Psychology*, London, Sage.

Edwards, D. and Potter, J. (1993) 'Language and causation: a discursive action model of description and attribution', *Psychological Review*, vol. 100, pp. 23–41.

Frosh, S. (1997) 'Screaming under the bridge: masculinity, rationality and psychotherapy' in J. Ussher (ed.) *Body Talk*, London, Routledge.

Gee, J.P. (1991) 'A linguistic approach to narrative', *Journal of Narrative and Life History*, vol. 1, pp. 15–39.

Gee, J.P. (1992) *The Social Mind: Language, Ideology and Social Practice*, New York, Bergin and Garvey.

Gergen, K. (1985) 'The social constructionist movement in modern psychology', *American Psychologist*, vol. 40, pp. 266–75.

Gergen, K. (1991) *The Saturated Self*, New York, Basic Books.

Gergen, K. (1994) *Toward Transformation in Social Knowledge*, Second Edn, London, Sage.

Gergen, K. and Davis, K. (eds) (1985) *The Social Construction of the Person*, New York, Springer-Verlag.

Gergen, K. and Gergen, M. (1988) 'Narrative and the self as relationship' in L. Berkowitz (ed.) *Advances in Experimental Social Psychology*, vol. 21, New York, Academic Press.

Gergen, M. and Gergen, K. (1993) 'Narratives of the gendered body in popular autobiography' in R. Josselson and A. Lieblich (eds) (1993) *The Narrative Study of Lives*, London, Sage.

Gilbert, N. and Mulkay, M. (1984) *Opening Pandora's Box: A Sociological Analysis of Scientists' Discourse*, Cambridge, Cambridge University Press.

Hall, S. (1996) 'Introduction: who needs "identity"?' in S. Hall and P. du Gay (eds) *Questions of Cultural Identity*, London, Sage.

Harré, R. (1977) 'The ethogenic approach: theory and practice' in L. Berkowitz (ed.) *Advances in Experimental Social Psychology*, vol. 10, London, Academic Press.

Harré, R. (1979) *Social Being*, Oxford, Blackwell.

Harré, R. (1983) *Personal Being*, Oxford, Blackwell.

Harré, R. (1998) *The Singular Self*, London, Sage.

Harré, R., Clarke, D. and de Carlo, N. (1985) *Motives and Mechanisms: An Introduction to the Psychology of Action*, London, Methuen.

Harré, R. and Gillett, G. (1994) *The Discursive Mind*, Thousand Oaks, California: Sage.

Harré, R. and Van Langenhove, L. (1991) 'Varieties of positioning', *Journal for the Theory of Social Behaviour*, vol. 21, pp. 393–407.

Henriques, J., Hollway, W., Urwin, C., Venn, C. and Walkerdine, V. (1984) *Changing the Subject: Psychology, Social Regulation and Subjectivity*, London, Methuen.

Heritage, J. (1984) *Garfinkel and Ethnomethodology*, Cambridge, Polity.

Hollway, W. (1989) *Subjectivity and Method in Psychology*, London, Sage.

Hollway, W. and Featherstone, B. (eds) (1997) *Mothering and Ambivalence*, London, Routledge.

Hollway, W. and Jefferson, T. (2000) *Doing Qualitative Research Differently: Free Association, Narrative and the Interview Method*, London, Sage.

Horton-Salway, M. (2001) 'The construction of ME: the discursive action model' in M. Wetherell, S. Taylor and S.J. Yates (eds) *Discourse as Data: A Guide to Analysis*, London, Sage in association with the Open University.

Josselson, R. and Lieblich, A. (eds) (1993) *The Narrative Study of Lives*, London, Sage.

Maybin, J. (1993) 'Children's voices: Talk, knowledge and identity' in D. Graddol, J. Maybin and B. Stierer (eds) *Researching Language and Literacy in Social Context*, Clevedon, Multilingual Matters.

Middleton, D. and Edwards, D. (eds) (1990) *Collective Remembering*, London, Sage.

Miller, P.J. and Hoogstra, L. (1992) 'Language as tool in the socialisation and apprehension of cultural meanings' in T. Schwartz, G. White and C. Lutz (eds) *New Directions in Psychological Anthropology*, Cambridge, Cambridge University Press.

Miller, P.J., Mintz, J., Hoogstra, L., Fung, H. and Potts, R. (1992) 'The narrated self: young children's construction of self in relation to others in conversational stories of personal experience', *Merrill Palmer Quarterly*, vol. 38, pp. 45–67.

Mishler, E. (1995) 'Models of narrative analysis: a typology', *Journal of Narrative and Life History*, vol. 5, pp. 87–123.

Parker, I. (1992) *Discourse Dynamics: Critical Analysis for Social and Individual Psychology*, London, Routledge.

Potter, J. (1996a) 'Attitudes, social representations and discursive psychology' in M. Wetherell (ed.) *Identities, Groups and Social Issues*, London, Sage in association with the Open University.

Potter, J. (1996b) *Representing Reality: Discourse, Rhetoric and Social Constructionism*, London, Sage.

Potter, J. and Edwards, D. (1990) 'Nigel Lawson's tent: attribution theory, discourse analysis and the social psychology of factual discourse', *European Journal of Social Psychology*, vol. 20, pp. 405–24.

Potter, J. and Reicher, S. (1987) 'Discourses of community and conflict: the organisation of social categories in accounts of a "riot"', *British Journal of Social Psychology*, vol. 26, pp. 25–40.

Potter, J. and Wetherell, M. (1987) *Discourse and Social Psychology*, London, Sage.

Potter, J., Wetherell, M., Gill, R., and Edwards, D. (1990) 'Discourse: noun, verb or social practice?', *Philosophical Psychology*, vol. 3, pp. 205–17.

Rose, N. (1996) 'Identity, genealogy, history' in S. Hall and P. Du Gay (eds) *Questions of Cultural Identity*, London, Sage.

Sarbin, T. (ed.) (1986) *Narrative Psychology – the Storied Nature of Human Conduct*, New York, Praeger.

Shotter, J. (1984) *Social Accountability and Selfhood*, Oxford, Blackwell.

Shotter, J. (1993) *Conversational Realities*, London, Sage.

Van Dijk, T. (1989) 'Social cognition and discourse' in H. Giles and P. Robinson (eds) *Handbook of Social Psychology and Language*, Chichester, Wiley.

Van Dijk, T. and Kintsch, W. (1983) *Strategies of Discourse Comprehension*, New York, Academic Press.

Walkerdine, V. (1990) *Schoolgirl Fictions*, London, Verso.

Walkerdine, V. (1997) *Daddy's Girl: Young Girls and Popular Culture*, London, Macmillan.

Wertsch, J. (1985) *Vygotsky and the Social Formation of Mind*, Cambridge, Mass, Harvard University Press.

Wetherell, M. (1998) ' Positioning and interpretative repertoires: Conversation analysis and post-structuralism in dialogue', *Discourse and Society*, vol. 9, pp. 431–56.

Wetherell, M. and Edley, N. (1998) 'Gender practices: steps in the analysis of men and masculinities' in K. Henwood, C. Griffin and A. Phoenix (eds) *Standpoints and Differences: Essays in the Practice of Feminist Psychology*, London, Sage.

Wetherell, M. and Potter, J. (1989) 'Narrative characters and accounting for violence' in J. Shotter and K. Gergen (eds) *Texts of Identity*, London, Sage.

Wetherell, M. and Potter, J. (1992) *Mapping the Language of Racism: Discourse and the Legitimation of Exploitation*, London, Harvester Wheatsheaf.

Wetherell, M., Stiven, H. and Potter, J. (1987) 'Unequal egalitarianism: a preliminary study of discourses concerning gender and employment opportunities', *British Journal of Social Psychology*, vol. 26, pp. 59–71.

White, M. and Epston, D. (1990) *Narrative Means to Therapeutic Ends*, New York, Norton.

Widdicombe, S. and Wooffitt, R. (1995) *The Language of Youth Sub-Cultures: Social Identity in Action*, London, Harvester Wheatsheaf.

Unfolding Discourse Analysis

Jonathan Potter and Margaret Wetherell

Source: Potter, J. and Wetherell, M. (1987) *Discourse and Social Psychology: Beyond Attitudes and Behaviour*, London, Sage, Chapter 2.

In the first part of this chapter we would like to begin the process of describing what we mean by discourse analysis [. . .]. We hope to indicate how a new style of socio-psychological research can be erected on the foundations of speech act theory, ethnomethodology and semiotics.

Throughout, we will be assuming that discourse analysis will become more than a new field of study in social psychology – that is, discourse added to the list of attributions, altruism, bystander apathy and all the other topics which have interested social psychologists over the last thirty years. Discourse analysis is a radical new perspective with implications for all socio-psychological topics. The second part of this chapter will try to make this claim come alive through demonstrating how other socio-psychological methodologies have ignored or covered over the constructive, active use of language in everyday life and then the implications of this repression for the central socio-psychological concept of attitude. [. . .]

Some major components of discourse analysis

Function, construction and variation

One of the themes strongly stressed by both speech act theory and ethnomethodology was that people use their language to *do* things: to order and request, persuade and accuse. This focus on language function is also one of the major components of discourse analysis. Function, however, cannot be understood in a mechanical way. Unfortunately, as we all know, when people are persuading, accusing, requesting etc. they do not always do so explicitly. When someone makes a request – perhaps they want to borrow your calculator – they do not always politely but explicitly ask: 'could I borrow your calculator this evening, please?'. Often they are less direct than this, perhaps couching the request as an abstract question: 'would you mind if I borrowed your calculator this evening?' or even more obliquely: 'it is going to drive me mad doing all those statistics by hand tonight' (Brown and Levinson, 1978). It may be to the speaker's advantage to make a request indirectly because it allows the recipient to reject it without making the rejection obvious (Drew, 1984). On the whole, people prefer to head off undesirable acts like rejections before they happen (Drew, 1986).

The analysis of function thus cannot be seen as a simple matter of categorizing pieces of speech, it depends upon the analyst 'reading' the context. There is nothing intrinsic to a complaint about doing statistics by hand that makes it a request. It can only be recognized as this from the context.

In the calculator example one specific function is being performed: requesting. However, functions can also be more global, and this is the second point to make. A person may wish to present himself or herself in a favourable light, for example, or to present someone they dislike in a poor light. Global self-presentations can be achieved with particular kinds of formulations which emphasize either good or bad features. As with the previous example, it can be sensible to be inexplicit. For one thing, explicitness risks being less persuasive. To present yourself as a wonderful human being to someone, you perhaps should not say 'I am a wonderful human being', but you might modestly slip into the conversation at some 'natural' point that you work for charities, have won an academic prize, read Goethe and so on.

In general, we find that if talk is orientated to many different functions, global and specific, any examination of language over time reveals considerable *variation*. A person's account will vary according to its function. That is, it will vary according to the purpose of the talk. For example, if we take two descriptions of a particular individual, we will expect them to vary in accordance with the feelings of the person doing the describing. If you like a person you may, in the course of everyday gossip, describe particularly likeable characteristics out of the many available. Someone who dislikes that person may emphasize very different characteristics, or the same likeable characteristics may now become disagreeable. Alternatively, imagine you have to describe a person to a close friend on one occasion and to a parent on another. Again, what will be picked out for description will vary. For instance, you are probably not going to focus the parental account on this person's daring acts of delinquency, but this might be a more appropriate focus for a close friend.

What is happening in these cases is that people are using their language to *construct* versions of the social world. The principal tenet of discourse analysis is that function involves construction of versions, and is demonstrated by language variation. The term 'construction' is apposite for three reasons. First, it reminds us that accounts of events are built out of a variety of pre-existing linguistic resources, almost as a house is constructed from bricks, beams and so on. Second, construction implies active selection: some resources are included, some omitted. Finally, the notion of construction emphasizes the potent, consequential nature of accounts. Much of social interaction is based around dealings with events and people which are experienced *only* in terms of specific linguistic versions. In a profound sense, accounts 'construct' reality.

We do not wish, however, to make the process seem necessarily deliberate or intentional. It may be that the person providing the account is not consciously constructing, but a construction emerges as they merely try to make sense of a phenomenon or engage in unselfconscious social activities like blaming or justifying. It is important to note that in these cases, too, there is variability in accounts, because different forms of description may be right for different occasions, but the person may be just 'doing what comes naturally' rather than intentionally deciding this rather than that form of language will be appropriate. Indeed, we expect this to be the much more common situation in the hurly-burly of ordinary language use, and we are not beguiled into thinking that some classes of talk are merely descriptive while others are deliberately constructive. All language, even language which passes as simple description, is constructive and consequential for the discourse analyst.

Overall, then, discourse analysts propose that people's language use is much more variable than is indicated by the widely held 'realistic' descriptive model of language – which treats discourse as a relatively unambiguous pathway to actions, beliefs or actual events. Researchers who presuppose the realistic mode assume that when people describe the same event, action or belief, their accounts will, broadly speaking, be consistent. And, for methodological purposes, they will take consistent accounts to mean that events did happen as described. [. . .]

There are two basic problems with this. First, consistency in accounts is often overstated by the various aggregating techniques commonly used by psychologists. Second, there is no reason to suppose that consistency in accounts is a sure indicator of descriptive validity. This consistency may be a product of accounts sharing the same function; that is, two people may put their discourse together in the same way because they are doing the same thing with it.

Discourse as topic

Discourse analysts have responded to the all-encompassing functional/ constructive nature of accounts by suspending the realistic approach and focusing on discourse as a topic in its own right. That is, we are not trying to recover events, beliefs and cognitive processes from participants' discourse, or treat language as an indicator or signpost to some other state of affairs but looking at the analytically prior question of how discourse or accounts of these things are manufactured (Gilbert and Mulkay, 1984; Potter, Stringer and Wetherell, 1984).

Take the idea of attitudes. If someone espouses attitude x on one occasion and the contradictory attitude y on another, the analyst clearly cannot treat the existence of attitude x or y as an unproblematic guide to what the person actually believes. But it is possible to treat the account containing the expression of the attitude as the focus itself, asking: on what occasions is attitude x rather than attitude y espoused? How are these attitude accounts constructed? And what functions or purposes do they achieve? It is questions of this kind which are at the heart of discourse analysis.

To summarize, then, this first stage, discourse analysts are suggesting that:

1 language is used for a variety of functions and its use has a variety of consequences;

2 language is both constructed and constructive;

3 the same phenomenon can be described in a number of different ways;

4 there will, therefore, be considerable variation in accounts;

5 there is, as yet, no foolproof way to deal with this variation and to sift accounts which are 'literal' or 'accurate' from those which are rhetorical or merely misguided thereby escaping the problems variation raises for researchers with a 'realistic' model of language;

6 the constructive and flexible ways in which language is used should
   themselves become a central topic of study.

So far we have illustrated the need for an analysis of participants' discourse
from theoretical principles. Nevertheless, it is clear that our perspective depends
on an empirical claim as its mainstay, namely that there is considerable variation
in participants' accounts; or, more specifically, that there is sufficient variation in
accounts to cause problems for the realistic approach.
      [. . .]

Attitudes in discourse

Our approach to attitudes should reveal the distinctiveness of the discourse
position and put some flesh on the notion of variability in accounts along with
the idea that accounts are constructed to have specific consequences. First, let us
clarify what social psychologists mean by the term 'attitude'.

The concept of attitude is one of the oldest theoretical ideas in social
psychology and, in manifold ways, has supported a huge body of sometimes
disparate research. Despite this history, the exact meaning of the notion has
remained somewhat obscure. [. . .]

McGuire claims that empirical studies of attitudes work with, at least implicitly,
the following basic definition. When people are expressing attitudes they are
giving responses which 'locate "objects of thought" on "dimensions of
judgment"' (McGuire, 1985: 239). That is, when they are speaking or acting,
people are taking some idea or object of interest and giving it a position in an
evaluative hierarchy. We will describe a concrete example to make this concept
sharper.

Traditional approaches to attitudes and racism
In 1976 a British researcher, Alan Marsh, asked a random sample of 1,785 people
to express their attitude to 'coloured immigrants' by placing a mark on a scale
which ran from 'completely sympathetic', through to 'no feelings about them
either way', to 'completely unsympathetic'. In McGuire's terms the object of
thought would be the 'coloured immigrants', while the dimension of judgement
would consist of the 'sympathy' which the respondent can offer or refuse.
Marsh's survey resembles myriads of other surveys, the techniques he used are
extremely common in attitude research. Having collected his responses, Marsh
went on to split his scale up 'logically' into categories. These are labelled 'very
hostile', 'hostile', 'neutral' and so on (see Table 1).

From the point of view of a discourse analyst, there are a number of
interesting points to be made, both about McGuire's minimal definition of
attitudes and the kind of practical research procedures illustrated by Marsh's
scale; we will concentrate on three issues.

First, there are obvious problems with the status of 'coloured immigrants' as an
object of thought. One way of looking at the term 'coloured immigrants' would
be as a simple category label for a group of people, in fact those people who fit
the descriptions 'coloured' and 'immigrant'. However, things are a lot more

Table 14.1   *Distribution of sympathetic and unsympathetic feelings towards coloured immigrants*

Completely unsympathetic		No feelings about them either way				Completely sympathetic
0	1–20	21–45	46–55	56–79	80–99	100
12%	13%	17%	25%	20%	10%	3%
Very hostile	Hostile	Unsympathetic	Neutral	Sympathetic	Positive	Very positive

No. in sample: unweighted = 1,785, weighted = 1,482; 'don't know' (excluded = 4%).
Source: Marsh, 1976.

complex than this. For example, there is no clear-cut neutral way of deciding how to apply the category 'coloured immigrant'. That is, there are no objective criteria for category membership.

The proper application of 'coloured' is dependent on unstated theories of race and biology. But modern theories of genetics and population give no support to the idea that 'races' of people can be distinguished in terms of unambiguous, underlying physical, and ultimately genetic, differences (Husband, 1982). In addition, 'immigrant' means (in the dictionary sense) a person who comes into a foreign country as a settler. Yet Marsh (1976) does not address the problem of splitting 'coloured immigrants' from 'coloured residents', and it is clear that he takes the term 'coloured immigrant' as a bland descriptive category covering both these groups. In fact this is reflected in the very title of his article, which is called 'Who hates the Blacks?' not 'Who hates those people who are both recent settlers in Britain and black defined?'. His terminology is not neutral. If you have lived in a country for the whole of your life you might be concerned if people start calling you an immigrant – a term often used to connote aliens or outsiders (Reeves, 1983; Sykes, 1985).

A second problem arises when we examine the transformations which Marsh makes to his subjects' responses. If we look at Table 1 we can see that Marsh has transformed one dimension, running from 'completely unsympathetic' to 'completely sympathetic', into a more complex set of labels: 'very hostile', 'hostile', 'unsympathetic' etc. There is no coherent justification for making transformations of this kind. For example, it is probably wrong to suggest respondents mean the same thing by the words 'very hostile' and 'completely unsympathetic'. For one thing, the term hostility is often used to imply an *active* disposition, while if someone lacks sympathy, they are *without* a certain kind of active disposition. By making this transformation the analyst is riding roughshod over subtle distinctions that may play a crucial role in the participants' discourse, and certainly in their methods of making sense of the survey questions.

A third problem also concerns translation: in this case the researchers' translation of participants' responses into the underlying theoretical category of attitude. The aim of attitude scales is not merely to show how people fill in these scales, but to identify attitudes. That is, in McGuire's terms, to identify where on a specific dimension a person locates an object of thought; in the current example, where the respondents locate 'coloured immigrants' on the dimension of 'sympathy'. The crucial assumption of attitude researchers is that there is something enduring within people which the scale is measuring – the attitude.

Discourse analysis points to many difficulties with this. We need to ask, for instance, whether people filling in an attitude scale are performing a neutral act of describing or expressing an internal mental state, their attitude, or whether they are engaged in producing a specific linguistic formulation tuned to the context at hand. From the discourse analytic perspective, given different purposes or a different context a very different 'attitude' may be espoused. Put another way, if a certain attitude is expressed on one occasion it should not necessarily lead us to expect that the same attitude will be expressed on another. Instead there may be systematic variations in what is said, which cast doubt on the enduring homogeneous nature of the supposed internal mental attitude.

How, then, should we deal with these three problems which are by no means unique to Marsh? First, the meaning or interpretation given to the terms in the attitude scale; second, the translation between participants' discourse and analysts' categories; and third, the treatment of linguistic products as transparent indicators of underlying objects or dispositions. More generally, what might a study of participants' discourse tell us about phenomena traditionally understood in terms of attitudes? The time has come to get down to the nitty-gritty of accounts and perform our own analysis.

Discourses of immigration

In the remainder of this chapter we will indicate how a discourse analyst might go about researching attitudes to constructed categories such as 'coloured immigrants'. We will closely examine some accounts produced in a less organized environment than Marsh's survey, but which, nonetheless, are easily recognizable as evaluative expressions concerning race and immigration. All the accounts we shall analyse have been extracted from open-ended interviews with white, middle-class New Zealanders. These interviews discussed generally 'controversial' issues in New Zealand society.

The goals of our analysis will obviously differ from those determining traditional attitude research. Broadly speaking, discourse analysts are interested in the different ways in which texts are organized, and the consequences of using some organizations rather than others. So our aim will be to look at the different forms taken by evaluative discourse about minority groups, and the effects of these forms. At the same time, the analysis will try to avoid the three problems we identified as endemic in traditional attitude research, namely presupposing the existence of the 'attitudinal object', making translations from unexplicated participants' discourse to unexplicated analysts' discourse, and treating utterances as indicators of the presence of enduring, underlying attitudes. We shall try to show why the concept of an enduring attitude is theoretically redundant.

Context

Perhaps the first thing which becomes apparent when embarking on this task is the sheer complexity of working with extended sequences of talk rather than the brief isolated utterances which make up responses to attitude questionnaires. Take the following interview extract for example.

1   Respondent. I'm not anti them at all you know

(Benton: 26).

We do not have any trouble in reading this as a relatively positive statement of
the speaker's position on 'them' – in this case, in the New Zealand context,
'Polynesian immigrants'. In attitude terms, the 'object of thought' is 'Polynesian
immigrants', the 'dimension of judgment' lies from pro to anti, and the position
espoused is pro. Following standard attitude theory, we would treat this speaker
as possessing a specific attitude. If they had to fill in Marsh's questionnaire they
might endorse the 'sympathetic' end of the scale – or so the traditional account
would have it.

Yet, when we look at more of this sequence, the simplicity starts to fall away.
Here is the entire turn of talk from which Extract One was taken.

2   Respondent. I'm not anti them at all you know, I, if they're willing to get on
    and be like us; but if they're just going to come here, just to be able to use our
    social welfares and stuff like that, then why don't they stay home?

(Benton: 26).

There are a number of interesting features here which immediately question
our first interpretation. To begin with, the 'pro immigrants' claim is made
contingent on immigrants exhibiting a willingness 'to be like us'. Thus we can no
longer read it as an unqualified expression of sympathy. Moreover, the whole
statement is organized within a complex linguistic structure of conditionals and
contrasts. This can be shown clearly if we rearrange the extract.

2b   **A1**   If [they're willing to get on and be like us]
     A2   then [I'm not anti them]
              but
     B1   if [they're just going . . . to use our social welfares]
     B2   then [why don't they stay home]

In technical terms, contrast structures are now revealed. Taken in isolation, the
consequences of these kinds of contrast structures are not easy to ascertain.
However, it is notable that studies of the way public speakers, such as Margaret
Thatcher and other politicians, elicit applause have found that constructions of
this sort are very effective in producing audience appreciation (Atkinson, 1984;
Heritage and Greatbatch, 1986). And it may well be that this kind of construction
is commonplace in everyday discourse because it helps package the message to
make it more convincing.

A further feature of Extract Two also highlights its persuasive orientation. It
draws upon what Pomerantz (1986) has called the *extreme case* formulation. For
example, if someone is asked why they carry a gun and they respond, '*everybody*
carries a gun', they are providing an effective warrant. Gun-toting is depicted not
as a notable or restricted activity but as normative, something shared by
everybody. Extreme case formulations take whatever evaluative dimension is
being adopted to its extreme limits. Thus if it is a question of numbers, then it is
'everybody' or 'only one', things are 'very' or 'terribly' bad etc. In the second part

of Extract Two the speaker produces an extreme case formulation of this type: 'if they are *just* going to come here, *just* to be able to use our social welfares and stuff'. The repeated use of the word 'just' paints a picture of people whose *sole* purpose in coming to New Zealand is the collection of social security, a selfish motive much more blameworthy than, say, coming to provide essential labour but being laid off due to economic recession. By representing it in this extreme way the criticisms are made to appear more justifiable.

Finally, if we look back to the first part of Extract Two – 'I am not anti them at all' – we can see that this operates as a *disclaimer*. Hewitt and Stokes (1975) define a disclaimer as a verbal device which is used to ward off potentially obnoxious attributions. Thus, if someone says 'I am no sexist but . . .' they are aware that what they are about to say may sound sexist, but are trying to head off such an attribution. In this case, the speaker is disclaiming possible attributions of racism consequent on the suggestion that immigrants should 'stay home'.

Now, these interpretations of Extract Two are tentative. They are not based on a systematic study of many instances but on a detailed reading of a single one. But they suggest two things. First, that even a small amount of additional information about context can throw into question what, at first, appears to be a reasonable interpretation of a person's utterance. Second, that discourse has an action orientation; it is constructed in such a way that particular tasks – in this case blaming and disclaiming responsibility for the obnoxious effects of this blaming – are facilitated.

These points have important implications for attitude scale research. If the person filling in the scale is viewed as merely *describing* or *expressing* their attitude, things seem quite clear-cut. Yet, if we start to view their response as a discursive act, which it always is, things become murkier, because there is a great deal of scope to perform different kinds of acts when filling in the scale. For example, a person might fill in the scale to perform the task of disclaiming by marking the 'sympathetic' pole; or they might perform the task of blaming by marking the 'unsympathetic' pole. They might hesitate because they see themselves as sympathetic and unsympathetic at the same time – 'I'm not anti but . . .'. Two people putting the same mark on the scale could well be doing very different things with their discourse. If the opinion pollster is coordinating an interview rather than requiring paper and pen responses the person might offer the whole utterance to the pollster and how it emerges, in terms of the category scales, will depend on the pollster's current method of scaling.

One way we could proceed, given this line of argument, is to suggest that attitude measurement might survive in its present form if it became a more subtle business, more sensitive to the different acts performed. We should note, however, that this continues to assume that there is such a thing as 'an attitude' or an enduring, underlying state expressed in talk and behaviour. This position becomes extremely difficult to maintain when we look at the variations which appear in participants' accounts.

Variability

The following example is typical of the sort of variation in accounts which has now been documented in a wide swathe of different kinds of discourse. These two extracts are taken from subsequent pages of the interview transcript.

3   *Respondent.* What I would li..rather see is that, sure, bring them ['Polynesian immigrants'] into New Zealand, right, try and train them in a skill, and encourage them to go back again (Pond: 17).

4   *Respondent.* I think that if we encouraged more Polynesians and Maoris to be skilled people they would want to stay here, they're not um as uh nomadic as New Zealanders are (*Interviewer.* Haha.) so I think that would be better (Pond: 18).

The contradiction is stark. In Extract Three the respondent states that they would like Polynesian immigrants to be trained in New Zealand and then to return to the Pacific Islands. In Extract Four the respondent claims it would be better if Polynesians were encouraged to become skilled and then stay in New Zealand. What are we to make of this variability? The problem is particularly acute for the attitude researcher because of the conflict between versions. An attempt to recover the person's 'underlying attitude' is not going to get very far.

The discourse analyst's response is rather different from the attitude researcher. We do not intend to use the discourse as a pathway to entities or phenomena lying 'beyond' the text. Discourse analysis does not take for granted that accounts reflect underlying attitudes or dispositions and therefore we do not expect that an individual's discourse will be consistent and coherent. Rather, the focus is on the discourse *itself*: how it is organized and what it is doing. Orderliness in discourse will be viewed as a product of the orderly *functions* to which discourse is put.

If we return to the accounts quoted above, and provide a bit more of the context, we can illustrate how a functional analysis might begin.

5   *Interviewer.* [Do] you think that, say, immigration from the Pacific Islands should be encouraged [   ] to a much larger extent than it is? It's fairly restricted at the moment.
    Respondent. Yes. Um, I think there's some problems in, in encouraging that too much, is that they come in uneducated about our ways, and I think it's important they understand what they're coming to. I, what I would li..rather see is that, sure, bring them into New Zealand, right, try and train them in a skill, and encourage them to go back again because their dependence on us will be lesser. I mean [ ] while the people back there are dependent on the people being here earning money to send it back, I mean, that's a very very negative way of looking at something. [ ] people really should be trying, they should be trying to help their own nation first. (Pond: 17–18)

6   Polynesians, they are doing jobs now that white people wouldn't do. So in many sectors of of the community or or life, um, we would be very much at a loss without them, I think. Um, what I would like to see is more effort being made to train them into skills, skilled jobs, because we are without skilled people and a lot of our skilled people, white people, have left the country to go to other places. I think that if we encouraged more Polynesians and Maoris to be skilled people they would want to stay here, they're not as, uh, nomadic as New Zealanders are (*Interviewer.* Haha.) so I think that would be better. (Pond: 18)

Now we have a bit more of the context available we can see that the question of Polynesians returning to the Islands is related to a different issue in each extract. In Extract Five returning is related to the problem of 'dependence'. The speaker expresses concern that if Polynesians stay in New Zealand they will become dependent upon their incomes to support people in the Pacific Islands. The speaker suggests it would be better if they returned with skills to contribute to their 'own nation'.

In Extract Six, on the other hand, returning is related to problems with the New Zealand workforce. The speaker suggests that Polynesians are doing dirty jobs disliked by 'whites', so their leaving would precipitate economic problems. Moreover, she goes on to claim, the emigration of skilled whites has left a hole in the labour market which Polynesians should be trained to fill. So the speaker's two different versions of whether Polynesians ought to stay or not can be seen to flow logically and naturally from the formulations in the surrounding text. It is, of course, only sensible to adjust one's response to a topic according to the context. However, this kind of adjustment tends to be overlooked by the attitude researcher who would expect the speaker to be able to articulate on a decontextualized scale a static constant attitude regarding whether Polynesians should stay or return. If it is not static and constant then much of the point of this kind of measurement technology disappears.

Constitution

In traditional attitude theory, the attitude is considered to be separate from the 'object of thought'. The entire logic of attitude measurement, where a scale is used to compare different people's attitudes to the same object, is based upon this. If the object is not the same for different people there is no sense in comparing attitudes and the notion ceases to have utility. However, when we come to look at the detail of people's accounts this separation becomes virtually impossible to sustain. Far from the object of thought being a simple already present entity, the object is formulated and constructed in discourse in the course of doing evaluation.

Take the following extract, for example, which is part of an answer to a question about Polynesian crime.

> 7   *Respondent.* Then again, it's a problem of their racial integration. They've got a big racial minority coming in now and so they've got to get used to the way of life and, er, perhaps rape is accepted over in Samoa and Polynesia, but not in Auckland. They've got to learn that. And the problem's that a lot of people coming in with mental disease I think it is, because there is a lot of interbreeding in those islan..islands. And that brings a big, high increase of retards and then people who come over here, retards perhaps and they//
> *Interviewer.* // and that causes problems?
> *Respondent.* And that's pretty general I know (Johnston: 20–1).

In this passage the speaker is not just giving his views *about* 'Polynesian immigrants', he is formulating the very nature of the Polynesian immigrant. That is, he is not working with a neutral description of an object and then saying how he feels about it; he is constructing a *version* of the object. It is in this way evaluation is displayed. His version of the object carries off his evaluation. Polynesian immigrants are floridly depicted as a group who are involved in rapes and are carriers of 'mental disease'. It is implied they are from a culture which cannot control its desires properly, something they will have to learn to do before settling in New Zealand.

A central feature in this speaker's construction of 'Polynesian immigrants' is his use of broad explanatory principles. He does not rest at merely describing phenomena, he explains them too. Specifically he accounts for the prevalence of mental disease in terms of simple farmyard genetics; it is a consequence of 'interbreeding'. This drawing together of description, evaluation and broad systems of explanation is dramatically illustrated in the next extract from another speaker.

> 8   *Interviewer*. Yeah, so [crime] is partly sort of immig., its related to immigration?
>   *Respondent*. Yeah, we don't, seeing them coming through, off the aircraft at night, half of them can't speak English. Um, if they can't speak English they're not going to be able to get a job, they're going to go and be in their little communities and they're not going to be able to contribute anything. And they're going to get frustrated because they're going to get bored. And they're going to, you know, there's nothing for them to do so the kids are going to start hanging around in the streets. At home Mum and Dad can't speak English and so the kids can't speak English. They go to school and suddenly they are confronted with English – 'we can't speak that, and what do we do?' – nothing. And so by the time they get to fifteen they just drop out. They have had it up to here with school and it's not the school's fault. They have brilliant lives, they have brilliant lives back in, family lives, back in the Islands and that is where they should be. (Jones: 16)

There are many fascinating features of this passage as a rhetorical construction. But the central thing to note is the way the final claim – that potential immigrants should stay in the Islands – is warranted through the use of an elaborate psychological and sociological story starting with a charged image of Polynesian slipping off the plane at night, going through language difficulties encountered by immigrants, which is taken to cause unemployment, and, eventually, the children's alienation from school. All this is contrasted with the 'brilliant family lives' available if they had not come to New Zealand. Throughout the passage we see a complex intertwining of description, explanation and evaluation.

Crucially, what we find when we examine naturally occurring discourse in detail is that the distinction between 'object of thought' and position on a 'dimension of judgment' becomes virtually impossible to make. It seems this distinction is an *artifact* of the way attitude scales are put together: all respondents are supposedly reacting to the same object of thought. Yet, as we can see from the extracts discussed in this chapter, sameness of wording does not necessarily mean that respondents will understand the terms or formulate the object of thought in an identical way. We have seen how different respondents formulate 'Polynesian immigrants', and how the *same* respondent might reformulate this notion on different occasions. If a researcher really wishes to get to grips with racism then a vital part of their activity must be the investigation of how description and explanation are meshed together and how different kinds of explanations assume different kinds of objects or supply the social world with varying objects.

    [. . .]

References

Atkinson, J.M. (1984) *Our Master's Voices: The Language and Body Language of Politics*, London, Methuen.

Brown, D. and Levinson, S. (1978) 'Universals in language use: politeness phenomena' in E. Goody (ed.) *Questions and Politeness: Strategies in Social Interaction*, Cambridge, Cambridge University Press.

Drew, P. (1984) 'Speakers' reportings in invitation sequences' in J.M. Atkinson and J. Heritage (eds) *Structures of Social Action: Studies in Conversation Analysis*, Cambridge, Cambridge University Press.

Drew, P. (1986) 'A comment on Taylor and Johnson', *British Journal of Social Psychology*, vol. 25, pp. 197–8.

Gilbert, G.N. and Mulkay, M. (1984) *Opening Pandora's Box: A Sociological Analysis of Scientists' Discourse*, Cambridge, Cambridge University Press.

Heritage, J. and Greatbatch, D. (1986) 'Generating applause: a study of rhetoric and response at party political conferences', *American Sociological Review*, vol. 92, pp. 110–57.

Hewitt, J.P. and Stokes, R. (1975) 'Disclaimers', *American Sociological Review*, 40, pp. 1–11.

Husband, C. (1982) 'Introduction: "race", the continuity of a concept' in C. Husband (ed.) *'Race' in Britain: Continuity and Change*, London, Hutchinson.

McGuire, W.J. (1985) 'Attitudes and attitude change' in G. Lindzey and E. Aronson (eds) *Handbook of Social Psychology*, 3rd Edn, Vol. 2, New York, Random House.

Marsh, A. (1976) 'Who hates the blacks?', *New Society*, vol. 23 September, pp. 649–52.

Pomerantz, A. (1986) 'Extreme case formulations: a new way of legitimating claims' in G. Button, P. Drew and J. Heritage (eds) *Human Studies*, (Interaction and Language Use Special Issue), vol. 9, pp. 219–30.

Potter, J., Stringer, P. and Wetherell, M. (1984) *Social Texts and Context: Literature and Social Psychology*, London, Routledge and Kegan Paul.

Reeves, W. (1983) *British Racial Discourse: A Study of British Political Discourse about Race and Race-Related Matters*, Cambridge, Cambridge University Press.

Sykes, M. (1985) 'Discrimination in discourse' in T.A. van Dijk (ed.) *Handbook of Discourse Analysis*, vol. 4, London, Academic Press.

Discursive, Rhetorical and Ideological Messages

Michael Billig

Source: Billig, M. (1997) 'Discursive, rhetorical and ideological messages' in C. McGarty and A. Haslam (eds) *The Message of Social Psychology*, Oxford, Blackwell.

[. . .] By and large, conventional social psychologists assume that the subject matter of social psychology comprises internal states or processes, which are themselves unobservable but which have to be inferred from outward behaviour. For example, social psychologists, who study attitudes, might assume that their goal is to discover the 'attitudinal systems' of individuals and to outline what effect such systems have on outward behaviour. An 'attitudinal system' does not, and cannot, exist in the way that a table or chair might exist. One cannot claim to touch or see an 'attitudinal system'. It is presumed to be hidden within the individual's head, governing the way that the individual organizes thoughts, experiences and reactions. By studying systematically the individual's reactions, the psychologist hopes to construct a picture of the hidden 'attitudinal system'. What the social psychologist cannot do is to study the 'system' directly, because it is unobservable, like all the cognitive structures which are assumed to intervene between stimuli and response. Thus, much of social psychology, especially cognitive social psychology, has objects of study – whether 'attitude systems', 'social identities' or 'cognitive schemata' which are presumed to be internal processes and, as such, hidden from view. These objects are the focus of considerable social psychological investigation, but are ghostly essences, lying behind and supposedly controlling what can be directly observed.

Discursive and rhetorical psychology does not take these hidden essences as its object of study. Instead, discursive social psychologists claim that the phenomena of social psychology are constituted through social interaction, especially discursive interaction. Thus, social psychologists should study that interaction, examining in particular the ways that language is used in practice by participants. In so doing, they will be able to observe directly what now appears to be hidden and secret.

In itself, this is not novel. Seventy years ago the great Russian linguist and philosopher, Mikhail Bakhtin, was saying similar things. In *Marxism and the Philosophy of Language*, which he published for political reasons under the name of Volosinov, Bakhtin criticized the idea that the objects of social psychology were inner states (or 'within' the individual):

> Social psychology in fact is not located anywhere within (in the 'souls' of communicating subjects) but entirely and completely without – in the words, the gesture, the act. There is nothing left unexpressed in it, nothing 'inner' about it – it is

wholly on the outside, wholly brought out in exchanges, wholly taken up in
material, above all in the material of the world.

(Volosinov, 1973: 19)

In Bakhtin's vision of social psychology, prime importance should be paid to the
study of language as it is actually used in practice. Often linguists have
considered language as some sort of abstract system of grammatical rules,
whereas Bakhtin proposed a practical linguistics to examine language in action.
Thus, Bakhtin/Volosinov continued: 'Social psychology is first and foremost an
atmosphere made up of multifarious speech performances' and, as such, 'social
psychology exists primarily in a wide variety of forms of "utterance" of little
speech genres of internal and external kinds'. (Volosinov, 1973: 19–20)

Bakhtin was suggesting that psychological states, as commonly understood,
are formed in interaction, especially interaction involving the use of language. If
one wishes to study such states, then one should study interaction and utterances.
Similar points were made by the philosopher Wittgenstein, who has provided the
intellectual inspiration for important strands of critical social psychology, as John
Shotter's (1993a and 1993b) scholarly and important analyses make clear.
Wittgenstein, in his later philosophy, advocated that close attention should be
paid to the use of language. Philosophers, Wittgenstein argued, are prone to
muddle if they do not understand the customary practices of language, or what he
called 'language games'. Given that language is socially shared, there must be
public criteria for the use of words. We learn how to use words such as 'table' and
'chair' by observing how these words are used: in this way, we learn to play
the appropriate language games, in which such words are used. One of
Wittgenstein's great insights was to claim that precisely the same happens with
the use of psychological words, such as 'remember', 'feel' or 'see'. These words
are used in various 'language games' and their sense must be understood in terms
of the practices of their usage. Wittgenstein warned against assuming that such
psychological words stand for internal processes, which provide their criteria of
usage. Children learn to use language such as 'I remember' or 'I have a pain' in
the same way that they learn other concepts; and they can be corrected if their
usage is incorrect. The criteria for using such words cannot be internal, private
states. As Wittgenstein stated in *Philosophical Investigations*, 'an "inner process"
stands in need of outward criteria' (1953: remark 580).

In consequence, if we wish to study 'memory', 'perception', 'emotion', we
should not be searching for the hidden inner processes, which are assumed to
stand behind the use of these words. To search for such entities is a mistake.
As Wittgenstein wrote, it is a 'misleading parallel' to say that 'psychology treats
of processes in the psychical sphere, as does physics in the physical' (1953:
remark 571). Seeing, hearing, thinking and feeling are not 'the subject of
psychology in the same sense' as the physical movements are the subject
matter of physics; physicists see, hear, think about and inform us about the
subjects of their research, whereas 'the psychologist observes the external
reactions (the behaviour) of the subject' (Wittgenstein, 1953: remark 571;
emphasis in original).

The implication is that we should study memory, perception or emotion by
investigating the relevant 'language games', or what Bakhtin called the 'genres of

utterance'. Attention should be paid to the ways in which people talk about their memories, perceptions and emotions. In so doing, we will discover the outward criteria for the social usage of these words. These criteria will be rooted in social practices. As will be suggested, more is involved. By taking seriously the idea that psychology is constituted in language, it will then become possible to study directly the processes of thinking.

Collective memory

The insights of Bakhtin and Wittgenstein can be used to construct a very different sort of empirical social psychology than that which is conventionally practised. This can be illustrated briefly with respect to two topics, which have long been important in the conventional study of social psychology: memory and attitudes. Both topics have also been studied in detail by discursive/rhetorical psychologists. And on both topics, Wittgenstein made important remarks in *Philosophical Investigations*.

Psychologists often discuss the topic of memory in terms of the storing and retrieving of stimulus information. Much effort has been devoted to discovering whether the processes of storage and retrieval differ when stimulus information is accurately, as opposed to inaccurately, remembered. In these investigations, the retrieval and storage 'systems' cannot be observed directly: they have to be inferred from the tasks which subjects are instructed to perform under experimental conditions. For example, cognitive psychologists might talk about 'Memory Organization Packets' or MOPs (Stevenson, 1993), but these are not physical packets, which can be put under the microscope as neurones can be. No one can claim to see a MOP, although MOPs are presumed to determine the business of remembering.

Because psychologists are searching for unknowable entities, they tend to pay little attention to the social activity which is occurring when remembering is taking place both naturally and in the psychological laboratory. That this activity – which typically is glossed over in the descriptions of procedure in the experimental reports – may be crucial is implied by one of Wittgenstein's remarks in *Philosophical Investigations* (remark 305). Wittgenstein was discussing the supposed role of 'inner processes' in memory. He suggested that the issue is not whether 'inner processes' occur, when people claim to remember things; the point was to specify what it means to claim that such inner processes occur. He stressed that the activity of remembering should not be understood as an inner process (for example, the hidden MOPs locked away in the individual's head). Wittgenstein states that he does not deny that there might be 'inner processes'. Quite the contrary:

> What we deny is that the picture of the inner process gives us the correct idea of the use of the word 'to remember'. We say that this picture with its ramifications stands in the way of our seeing the use of the word as it is.
>
> (Wittgenstein, 1953: 102)

For Wittgenstein, to understand 'remembering' one must investigate how the word 'remember' is used, when people are said to be 'remembering'.

Wittgenstein, in common with other linguistic philosophers, tended to analyse hypothetical examples. However, his insights lead the way to the empirical analysis of word-use in actual social interaction. Conversation analysts have developed techniques and theoretical concepts for the micro-analysis of conversational data (Antaki, 1994; Heritage, 1984). Much of the intellectual impetus for such work was derived from the pioneering work of Harvey Sacks (e.g. Sacks, 1972a and 1972b). Conversation analysts have revealed the enormous complexity of the most trivial-seeming exchanges. [. . .]

Many of the techniques of conversation analysis were developed initially for the analysis of routine exchanges rather than for discourse, which uses psychological words. Discursive psychologists have been able to show how these techniques could be applied to talk about psychological phenomena, such as claims to remember things. When such talk is analysed then psychological phenomena, such as remembering, are not seen to be located in hidden mental entities, but are rooted in social and discursive activity.

Edwards and Middleton (1986) observed mothers looking at photo albums with their young children. As they talked, the mothers were telling the children about memory. Not only were they recalling the events of the past, and providing memory-stories for the children to repeat, but they were also communicating the sorts of things which should be remembered, or considered memorable. In so doing they were instructing the children how the events of the past should be remembered and, thus, what it means 'to remember'. In this way, remembering is not an individual psychological process, which happens spontaneously; it is a social activity, which, like other social activities, has to be learnt in order to be performed proficiently.

Discursive psychologists are particularly interested in observing what people are doing when they make memory-claims. In conversations, people's claims about memory do not suddenly pop up, as if out of the blue. Often memory-claims are made when matters are in dispute. In this sense, the business of remembering can be a highly rhetorical or controversial business, so that the memory-claims might be accomplishing a variety of interactive business (Edwards and Potter, 1992; Potter and Edwards, 1990).
[. . .]

The social activity of remembering is not tied to the recall of directly experienced stimuli for we can, and continually do, claim to remember events at which we were not personally present. Thus, a present generation can 'remember' a previous generation's sacrifice. Such memories can be passed across time, rather as the mothers, talking about family photographs with their children, were transmitting the family memories across time. In this sense, memory is not to be located within the individual's head in hypothetical MOPs. As Maurice Halbwachs wrote many years ago, memory is 'collective' rather than individual (Halbwachs, 1980; see also Middleton and Edwards, 1990). It is something which is shared and the activity of remembering can also be collectively and discursively accomplished. As such, remembering is pre-eminently a social psychological topic, especially if social psychology is understood to be the analysis of collective activity, rather than the search for internal processes which are hidden within the individual.

Attitudes and arguments

[. . .]

Just as the activity of remembering deserves close social psychological attention so does the business of giving opinions. Again, a turn from the internal to the external is called for. Social psychologists have traditionally viewed attitudes as internal states of mind or feeling. By contrast, the discursive approach analyses the giving of opinions in terms of discursive action. In this, a particular form of discourse is involved – rhetorical discourse. Rhetoric refers to discourse which is argumentative and which seeks to persuade; as such the activities of criticism and justification are central to rhetorical discourse (Antaki, 1994; Billig, 1987; Edwards and Potter, 1992). Attitudes, far from being mysterious inner events, are constituted within the business of justification and criticism.

[. . .]

Discursive psychologists, who have studied the circumstances in which people give opinions in conversation, stress the rhetorical nature of opinion-giving (e.g., Billig, 1991; Edwards and Potter, 1992). Rarely, if ever, is the giving of an opinion merely a spontaneous report of an internal state. If someone says 'I feel that capital punishment is wrong' they are unlikely to be making a claim to be reporting a particular internal state of feeling, which only occurs when the topic of capital punishment arises and which is attached to no other topic. Their utterance is likely to be part of a conversation and its meaning should be analysed in terms of the conversational context.

Bakhtin (1986) claimed that all utterances are dialogic in that they are responses to other utterances and their meaning has to be understood in relation to these other utterances. This is particularly relevant for attitude-statements. Rather than being simple reports of internal states, attitude-statements tend to be uttered as stances in matters of public controversy. Thus, people generally are not said to have 'attitudes' on issues which are seen to be beyond public doubt. For example, McGuire (1964), in a classic social psychological study, investigated 'cultural truisms', or beliefs which no-one in a given culture seriously doubted (for example, the belief in contemporary Western society that one should clean one's teeth). These beliefs tend not to be termed 'attitudes', unless they are challenged. As soon as someone doubts the value of cleaning teeth, then the issue becomes one on which attitudes can be expressed (Billig, 1987).

That being so, attitude-statements will typically bear a rhetorical meaning, which must be understood in terms of the contexts of their utterance. A statement in favour of capital punishment is not merely a report about the speaker's self-positioning on the issue. Nor is it merely a statement about what the speaker supports. It is also a positioning against counter positions, for instance against the abolitionists. More than this, it represents an intervention in the argument against the abolitionists. When people give their opinion in dialogue, they give typically arguments, justifying their own views and criticizing counter-views. In this sense, the statement of an opinion often indicates a readiness to argue on a matter of controversy (Billig, 1991).

[. . .]

Discursive psychologists have examined how people, in discussion, are continually making utterances which fit the rhetorical demands of the moment

(Potter and Wetherell, 1987; Wetherell and Potter, 1992). In the conversational thrust and counter-thrust, novel remarks are made. In analysing such conversations, social psychologists are not merely studying the processes of conversation; they are studying directly the traditional topic of cognitive psychology: the processes of thought (Billig, 1991). Cognitive psychologists have assumed that thinking is a mysterious process, lying behind outward behaviour. However, the response and counter-response of conversation is too quick for it to be the outward manifestation of the 'real' processes of thought. The remarks are the thoughts: one need not search for something extra, as if there is always something lying behind the words, which we should call the 'thought'. Wittgenstein put the point graphically: 'When I think in language, there aren't "meanings" going through my mind in addition to the verbal expressions: the language is itself the vehicle of thought (1953: remark 329).

When the language is spoken out loud, the thinking can, quite literally, be heard. And, if one wished to differentiate between a speaker, who might be said to be speaking thoughtfully and one who is not, then 'I could certainly not say that the difference lay in something that goes on or fails to go on while he is speaking' (Wittgenstein, 1967: remark 93). In short, to discover what is being thought, when words are uttered, the observer should analyse the rhetorical complexity of the utterances themselves. Thus, discussions, in which people are responding rapidly to new dialogic challenges and are in their turn creating such challenges, offer the psychologist a royal road to examining thinking in action.

This is not to deny that silent, solitary thinking does occur. However, the rhetorical position stresses that such thinking is typically modelled on outer dialogue. It is, to use the phrase of Bakhtin, 'inner speech'. When we think about a matter, we often are debating silently with ourselves, weighing up the pros and cons. This is only possible if this sort of thinking is publicly observable in dialogue. If thinking were locked mysteriously and unobservably within the brain, then we could never learn, or be taught, to think: it would be something which occurs unstoppably and unalterably (Billig, 1987). The Eleatic Stranger, in Plato's dialogue *The Sophist*, expressed an important insight: 'Thought and speech are the same: only the former, which is a silent inner conversation of the soul with itself, has been given the special name of thought' (Plato, 1948: 263e). In consequence, dialogic conversation can offer the social psychologist a direct glimpse at the social processes of thought.

Action, words and discrimination

So far, it might be thought that the discursive approach represents a turn from the study of behaviour to the study of talk. Discursive psychologists might be suspected of only taking words into account and not actions. However, that is not so, for the criticism assumes that in social behaviour there is a clear distinction between words and action. [. . .]

It is easy to exaggerate the difference between words and actions, as if the latter were more 'real' than the former. In social life words are rarely 'mere words'. Many important social actions are performed through utterances. This can be illustrated briefly by considering the topics of intergroup prejudice and discrimination, which have long formed a key part of social psychological research. It is easy to assume that prejudice is basically a matter of words, such as the verbal repetition of stereotypes, while discrimination involves behaviour, or the putting of prejudiced words into practice. However, if acts of discrimination are examined in detail, one can see that the distinction between words and actions soon collapses.

Philomena Essed (1988) examined how white male employers in the Dutch civil service discriminate against black female job seekers. The processes involve subtle and often unconscious details of interaction. In interviews, the employer might ask the sort of question, which implies that the black female has a pattern of behaviour which fits prevailing stereotypes and which is inappropriate for a high-level job. She, in turn, is discomfited and responds tensely. In consequence, the white male deems the interview unsatisfactory and offers the position elsewhere. All this is performed through utterances. Moreover, the very act of discrimination – the refusal to offer employment to the black female – is accomplished through words. Successful and unsuccessful candidates have to be informed; papers have to be signed, telephone calls made. All these verbal activities – written and spoken utterances – perform the discrimination. In our language-saturated society, actions such as racial and sexual discrimination do not exist apart from utterances. They are performed through complex sequences of utterances, including, typically, utterances which deny that discrimination and prejudice are taking place (Billig, 1991; van Dijk, 1992 and 1993; Wetherell and Potter, 1992).

The importance of utterances, and their comparative neglect in conventional social psychology, can be seen by looking at one of the famous studies in social psychology. The Sherif Boys Camp Experiments (Sherif, 1966; Sherif, 1981, Sherif and Sherif, 1953) are recognized to be classic studies of intergroup relations (see, for example, the tributes by Cherry, 1994; Taylor and Moghaddam, 1994). These studies observed intergroup behaviour *in situ*, as Muzafer and Carolyn Sherif divided the boys in a summer camp into two separate groups, organized competitions between the groups and observed the growth of intergroup hostilities and prejudices. The experiment is usually regarded as showing how prejudiced mental structures (such as group stereotypes) develop within the group members and, also how intergroup behaviour (such as pushing and shoving) occurs. A quick glance at Muzafer Sherif's description of events illustrates the importance of language.

At a crucial stage in the camp's activities, the boys were divided into two groups. This was accomplished by the camp authorities giving verbal instructions. Sherif (1981) reports how the groups developed. Words and speech were vital to the development of group identity:

> As the group became an organization, the boys coined nicknames . . . Each group developed its own jargon, special jokes, secrets and special ways of performing tasks. One group, after killing a snake near a place where it had gone to swim, named the place 'Moccasin Creek' and thereafter preferred this swimming hole to any other, though there were better ones nearby.
>
> (1981: 321)

Sherif does not describe the killing of the snake in detail. One can imagine how the boys called to each other to coordinate their activities, how they talked about it and how it became a mythic event in the history of the group. We do hear that the event becomes mythologized in a place name, although we are not provided with the transcripts of the conversations which made this possible. It makes no sense to ask whether the boys invented these names because they had internal feelings of identity, as if the real causes were hidden from view. The invention of the names – the performance of the group rituals – was the way of accomplishing and demonstrating the group loyalty (see also Widdicombe and Wooffitt, 1995).

Similarly, the intergroup hostilities were not set apart from utterances and rhetoric. Sherif recounts how the good sporting spirit of the tournament soon degenerated. Language was involved:

> The members of each group began to call their rivals 'stinkers', 'sneaks' and 'cheaters' . . . The rival groups made threatening posters, and planned raids, collecting hoards of green apples for ammunition . . . name-calling scuffles and raids were the rule of the day.
>
> (1981, 324).

Of course, the actual throwing of the ammunition itself is not a verbal act, but the planning, the interpretation, the coordinating, the mythologizing of the apple-throwing are all accomplished through utterances, as was the name-calling. Without such utterances, the activities could not have had their intergroup significance.

The Sherif experiments can be interpreted in many ways. In an obvious sense, the Sherifs had provided a metaphor for warfare, showing how easily group loyalties can be created and brought into conflict with each other. If language is necessary for all this, then a further moral can be drawn. It is no coincidence that the only species which possesses the ability of language (or what Pinker, 1994, has called 'the language instinct') is a species which engages in organized warfare. Utterance is necessary to kill and die for the honour of the group.

History and ideology

The stress on examining language in practice may give the impression that discursive/rhetorical psychology is primarily concerned with interpersonal dynamics, as if it all comes down to investigating what speakers are doing when they make utterances. [. . .] These matters can form an important part of discursive psychology (Edwards and Potter, 1992). However, more can be said about language, as the focus is shifted from the interpersonal to the historical and ideological. [. . .]

Individuals, when they speak, do not create their own language, but they use terms which are culturally, historically and ideologically available. Each act of utterance, although in itself novel, carries an ideological history. As Volosinov stressed in *Marxism and the Philosophy of Language*, social psychologists, by investigating acts of utterance, should be studying ideology. An ideology comprises the ways of thinking and behaving within a given society which make the ways of that society seem 'natural' or unquestioned to its members (Eagleton, 1991). In this way, ideology is the common-sense of the society. Through ideology, the inequalities of that society will appear as 'natural' or 'inevitable'. Thus, ideology comprises the habits of belief, which, for example, in former terms made it appear 'natural' that women should not be full citizens, or which, in our day, make it appear obvious that the street-sweeper be paid a fraction of the company director's remuneration. These ideological habits can be deeply rooted into language, and, thereby, into consciousness.

There is an important implication for the study of social psychology. If social psychological states are constituted within language and if languages are historical and ideological creations, then so are the topics of social psychology. It should then be possible to examine, through the study of utterance, how ideology creates the subjects of psychology. A number of discursive investigators have examined explicitly ideological themes, relating to social inequality. For example, several have investigated racist discourse (Billig, 1991; van Dijk, 1991, 1992, 1993; Wetherell and Potter, 1992) and also sexist discourse (Edley and Wetherell, 1995). [. . .] In such studies, investigators show how speakers use themes, which they take to be common-sense, but how, in using such themes speakers are making ideological utterances about themselves and society.

Often the utterances of ideology are not straightforward, but are 'dilemmatic' (Billig et al., 1988). It is the nature of common-sense that it contains contrary themes – for example there are maxims praising both caution and risk-taking, or praising both firmness and mercy. If ideologies did not contain contrary themes, they would not provide the resources for common-sense thinking, for thinking involves dialogic discussion, or the counter-positioning of contrary themes, which can both appear in their way to be reasonable. In discussions, one can hear people jostling with the contrary themes of common-sense. This is particularly so when the topics are explicitly ideological. Thus, those making racist remarks often assert their own lack of prejudice, even as they make their racist utterances. Or English speakers claim to want the Royal Family both to be ordinary and not ordinary, thereby simultaneously articulating themes in favour of both equality and inequality. Investigators, studying such discussions from a discursive/rhetorical perspective, are not aiming to describe the 'attitude-system' of each speaker, as if all speakers must possess a clearly demarcated internal system, before they speak. Rather the aim is to see how the themes of ideology are instantiated in ordinary talk, and how speakers are part of, and are continuing, the ideological history of the discursive themes which they are using.

This involves paying greater attention to the meaning of categories than social psychology has tended to do. For example, much cognitive social psychology, especially that concerned with intergroup relations, has been concerned with the process of categorization. It has been asserted that categorization is crucial for the development of group identity (i.e. Abrams and Hogg, 1990; Tajfel, 1981; Turner et al., 1987). Such investigators tend to treat categorization as if it were a universal process. They search for the common psychological factors involved in categorization. In consequence, different forms of group categories are treated as being similar and as exemplifying the supposed general processes of categorization. What is forgotten in such studies is that categories, as Edwards (1991) has written, are 'for talking': they should be studied in their discursive and rhetorical contexts. Moreover, categories carry meanings and not all categories – certainly not all group categories – carry identical meanings. A social psychology, which seeks to study how ideological forces shape psychological states, cannot afford to ignore these meanings.

The point can be illustrated by the example of national identity. National identities depend upon the creation and maintenance of national categories, such as 'French', 'German' or 'Bolivian'. In this respect, national identity resembles other group identities, including those formed by the young boys in the Sherif experiments. However, the national category also carries particular meanings, which relate to the historically particular ways in which nation-states have been created in the past two hundred and fifty years. The era of nation-states has seen national communities being 'imagined' in particular ways, which, for example, are very different from the ways communities were 'imagined' in the Middle Ages (Anderson, 1983; Billig, 1995; Gellner, 1983). When groups declare themselves to be national groups, they are making particular political statements, evoking an ideological history of entitlements and rights. For example, when Palestinians declare themselves to have a national identity, they are doing more than claiming a psychological feeling of commonality: they are making a claim about the rights to statehood and national territory, which follow from a group defining itself as a 'national group', rather than any other sort of group.

In the modern age, the notion of national identity has been bound up with the notion of the nation-state. Today, these notions appear common-place and solid, so that it is difficult to imagine that in previous ages communities were not imagined in this way. The assumptions of nationhood have seeped through contemporary consciousness, so that the nation-state appears as a 'natural' form of community. In established nation-states, such as the USA, the United Kingdom or France, there is what can be called a 'banal' form of nationalism (Billig, 1995). The link between people and soil, which was once articulated in mystical terms, has now become banal, even unnoticed. In routine ways, citizens of the state are reminded that they live in a nation within a world of nation-states. This reminding – or 'flagging' of the nation – takes place, for the most part, in taken-for-granted, unnoticed ways. The metaphor of the flag illustrates the banality of this nationalism. The political nationalist, who seeks to establish a new nation-state, might wave the national flag vigorously and self-consciously; by contrast, the citizen of the nation-state daily walks past, without a second glance, the flag flying outside the public building. Millions of such barely glanced-at flags are on display each day. All these unmindful reminders are necessary for the continuation of the nation-state and for their members' sense of belonging. In consequence, those who wish to study nationalism and 'national identity' in contemporary states should pay attention to the banal forms by which those states are reproduced (for details of 'banal nationalism', see Billig, 1995).

[. . .]

By examining these sorts of issues, the scope of social psychology will be widened. The traditional topics of social psychology are to be studied in terms of discursive utterances and language games. However, the analysis does not stop there. Discourses are not merely to be investigated in terms of their particular uses and immediate contexts. The ideological history of the discourses is to be sketched, in order to see how this history shapes and is continued by the local practices. In examining ideology – and the history of ideology – the analyst is decoding what is being taken for granted as common-sense, for ideology embraces the common-sense of each social period. Historical and anthropological dimensions can be directly added by making comparisons with other ages and with other types of community. By noting anthropological and historical differences in the use of psychological language, the analyst can show how social psychological phenomena differ according to place and period (Harré and Gillett, 1994).

In addition, the rhetorical analysis of argumentation can be used to investigate patterns of ideology, for it can reveal what is being taken for granted as common-sense. The analyst, in examining patterns of discussion and argument, observes not merely what issues are being overtly challenged by speakers and how these challenges are being discursively effected; the analyst can also note what is being left unchallenged or what is being presented as if unchallengeable. Commonly in discussions, speakers will attempt to justify their particular stances by appealing to common values (or rhetorical 'topoi'), which they will assume are acceptable to all (Billig, 1987, 1991). These appeals to what Perelman and Olbrechts-Tyteca (1971) called the 'universal audience' contain clues about the ideological common-sense of the times. In addition, the analyst should be alert to gaps. In investigating ideologies one is looking, not merely for the themes which are presented as 'common-sense', but also for what is common-sensically left unsaid and what is assumed to be beyond controversy.

If social psychologists take seriously the project to investigate ideology, then the nature of social psychology will be dramatically transformed. Not merely will such a social psychology have very different methodological procedures, but, more importantly, its intellectual reach will be expanded. By incorporating historical, anthropological and linguistic insights, this social psychology will draw closer to other social scientific investigations. In so doing, it will be addressing some of the most important issues in the contemporary social sciences.

References

Abrams, D. and Hogg, M.A. (eds) (1990) *Social Identity Theory*, New York, Springer Verlag.

Anderson, B. (1983) *Imagined Communities*, London, Verso.

Antaki, C. (1994) *Explaining and Arguing*, London, Sage.

Bakhtin, M.M. (1986) *Speech Genres and Other Late Essays*, Austin, University of Texas.

Billig, M. (1987) *Arguing and Thinking*, Cambridge, Cambridge University Press.

Billig, M. (1991) *Ideology and Opinions*, London, Sage.

Billig, M. (1995) *Banal Nationalism*, London, Sage.

Billig, M., Condor, S., Edwards, D., Gane, M., Middleton, D. and Radley, A.R. (1988) *Ideological Dilemmas: a Social Psychology of Everyday Thinking*, London, Sage.

Cherry, F. (1994) *The Stubborn Particulars of Social Psychology*, London, Routledge.

Eagleton, T. (1991) *Ideology: an Introduction*, London, Verso.

Edley, N. and Wetherell, M. (1995) *Men in Perspective*, London, Prentice Hall.

Edwards, D. (1991) 'Categories are for talking', *Theory and Psychology*, vol. 1, pp. 515–42.

Edwards, D. and Middleton, D. (1986) 'Conversational remembering and family relationships: how children learn to remember', *Journal of Social and Personal Relationships*, vol. 5, pp. 3–25.

Edwards, D. and Potter, J. (1992) *Discursive Psychology*, London, Sage.

Essed, P. (1988) 'Understanding verbal accounts of racism: politics and the heuristics of reality constructions', *Text*, vol. 8, pp. 5–40.

Gellner, E. (1983) *Nations and Nationalism*, Blackwell, Oxford.

Halbwachs, M. (1980) *The Collective Memory*, Harper and Row, New York.

Harré, R. and Gillet, G. (1994) *The Discursive Mind*, London, Sage.

Heritage, J. (1984) *Garfinkel and Ethnomethodology*, Cambridge, Polity Press.

McGuire, W.J. (1964) 'Inducing resistance to persuasion: some contemporary approaches' in L. Berkowitz (ed.) *Advances in Experimental Social Psychology*, vol. 1, New York, Academic Press.

Middleton, D. and Edwards, D. (eds) (1990) *Collective Remembering*, London, Sage.

Moscovici, S. (1984) 'The myth of the lonely paradigm: a rejoinder,' *Social Research*, vol. 51, pp. 939–67.

Perelman, C. and Olbrechts-Tyteca, L. (1971) *The New Rhetoric*, Indiana, University of Notre Dame Press.

Pinker, S. (1994) *The Language Instinct*, Harmondsworth, Penguin.

Plato (1948) *The Sophist*, London, Loeb Classical Library.

Potter, J. and Edwards, D. (1990) 'Nigel Lawson's tent: attribution theory, discourse analysis and the social psychology of factual discourse', *European Journal of Social Psychology*, vol. 20, pp. 405–24.

Potter, J. and Wetherell, M. (1987) *Discourse and Social Psychology*, London, Sage.

Sacks, H. (1972a) 'An initial investigation of the usability of conversational data for doing sociology' in D. Sudnow (ed.) *Studies in Social Interaction*, New York, Free Press.

Sacks, H. (1972b) 'Notes on police assessment of moral character' in D. Sudnow (ed.) *Studies in Social Interaction*, New York, Free Press.

Sherif, M. (1966) *Group Conflict and Co-operation*, London, Routledge and Kegan Paul.

Sherif, M. (1981) In *Readings about the Social Animal*, E. Aronson (ed.) New York, Freeman.

Sherif, M. and Sherif, C.W. (1953) *Groups in Harmony and Tension*, New York, Harper.

Shotter, J. (1993a) *The Cultural Politics of Everyday Life*, Milton Keynes, Open University Press.

Shotter, J. (1993b) *Conversational Realities: Studies in Social Constructionism*, London, Sage.

Stevenson, R.J. (1993) *Language, Thought and Representation*, Chichester, John Wiley.

Tajfel, H. (1981) *Human Groups and Social Categories*, Cambridge University Press, Cambridge.

Taylor, D.M. and Moghaddam, F.M. (1994) *Theories of Intergroup Relations*, Westport, Praeger.

Turner, J.C., Hogg, M.A., Oakes, P.J., Reicher, S.D. and Wetherell, M. (1987) *Rediscovering the Social Group*, Oxford, Blackwell.

van Dijk, T.A. (1991) *Racism and the Press*, London, Routledge.

van Dijk, T.A. (1992) 'Discourse and the denial of racism', *Discourse and Society*, vol. 3, pp. 87–118.

van Dijk, T.A. (1993) *Elite Discourse and Racism*, Newbury Park, Sage.

Volosinov, V.N. (1973) *Marxism and the Philosophy of Language*, New York, Seminar Press.

Wetherell, M. and Potter, J. (1992) *Mapping the Language of Racism*, Hemel Hempstead, Harvester/Wheatsheaf.

Widdicombe, S. and Wooffitt, R. (1995) *The Language of Youth Subcultures*, Hemel Hempstead, Harvester/Wheatsheaf.

Wittgenstein, L. (1953) *Philosophical Investigations*, Oxford, Blackwell.

Wittgenstein, L. (1967) *Zettel*, Oxford, Blackwell.

The Multivoicedness of Meaning

James Wertsch

Source: Wertsch, J. V. (1990) *Voices of the Mind: A Sociocultural Approach to Mediated Action*, London, Harvester Wheatsheaf, Chapter 4.

Bakhtin's ideas have major implications for a Vygotskian approach to mediated action. In this chapter I shall expand on some of these implications as they relate to the issue of meaning. A Bakhtinian orientation to meaning leads down paths not often traveled in social science analyses, paths that explore voices, social languages, speech genres, and dialogicality.

Meaning is central to the sociocultural approach to mediated action precisely because the notion of mediation is central. The processes and structures of semiotic mediation provide a crucial link between historical, cultural, and institutional contexts on the one hand and the mental functioning of the individual on the other. Of course, this does not mean that a semiotic orientation can automatically be equated with a focus on meaning. Many semiotic analyses concern themselves primarily with the issues of formal structure that are at the centre of much of contemporary linguistics.

Yet this was not the direction Vygotsky and Bakhtin took. Following in a longstanding Russian tradition grounded in the 'priority of semantics' (Clark and Holquist, 1984: 11), they focused on ways in which language and other semiotic systems could be used to produce meaning, especially meaning as it shapes human action.

A motivating force behind the priority Bakhtin gave to semantics and a force closely tied to the fundamental Bakhtinian question 'Who is doing the talking?' can be formulated in terms of 'Who owns meaning?' (Holquist, 1981). As Holquist has noted, views range from the claim that no one owns meaning – for example, deconstructionists claim that the 'human voice is conceived merely as another means for registering differences' – to the claim that particular individuals own meaning. Proponents of the former position have criticized those of the latter on the basis of the argument that 'the very conception of meaning, to say nothing of persons, invoked in most traditional epistemologies begins by illicitly assuming a presence whose end Nietzsche really was announcing when he let it be known that God had died in history' (pp. 164–5).

In Bakhtin's approach, we find an underlying claim that in some ways appears to be an intermediate one between the position that individuals own meaning and the position that no one owns meaning. But because it is grounded in processes of dialogicality it is not some kind of unprincipled compromise and, indeed, differs from both these positions in productive ways. In Bakhtin's view, users of language 'rent' meaning (Holquist, 1981: 164). In other words, 'I can mean what I say, but only *indirectly*, at a second remove, in the words I take and give back to the community according to the protocols it establishes. My voice can mean, but only with others: at times in chorus, but at the best of times in a dialogue' (p. 165).

This renting metaphor is, of course, another form of the claim that the answer to the Bakhtinian question 'Who is doing the talking?' always involves at least two voices. It is a metaphor that emerged more naturally and was more readily accepted in the sociocultural setting in which Bakhtin worked, which did not stress the individualism and atomism characteristic of the modern West. Instead of seeking the source of meaning production in the isolated individual, it follows the more collectivist orientation of Russian culture and assumes that meaning is always based in group life.

Holquist's metaphor is quite useful when it comes to specifying some of the concrete ways in which Bakhtin's theory of meaning is distinct from other theories that guide the thinking of western scholars, especially those raised in the Anglo–American tradition. I shall address these differences by mapping out three issues, all of which can be formulated as aspects of a Bakhtinian approach to meaning. These are (1) rejection of a 'disengaged image of the self' and the 'atomism' associated with it; (2) recognition of a 'dialogic' as well as a 'univocal' text function; and (3) recognition of the authority attached to a text.

Rejection of a 'disengaged image of the self'

My claims about the 'disengaged image of the self' stem primarily from the writings of Charles Taylor (1985a, 1985b, 1989). Taylor has been struck by the tenacity with which western scholars hold to the underlying assumptions of approaches such as behaviourism, in spite of what he sees as overwhelming evidence that these assumptions lead to untenable claims. Taylor ties the emergence of what he terms the disengaged image of the self to the major cosmological shift that occurred in the West in the seventeeth century, which was marked by a transition from viewing the world order in terms of ideas to viewing it in terms of mechanism. The resulting disengaged image of the self is part of a 'typically modern notion of freedom as the ability to act on one's own, without outside interference or subordination to outside authority' (1985a: 5).

Taylor argues that in addition to the 'understandable prestige of the natural science model,' the assumptions that underlie the disengaged image of the self spring from certain fundamental beliefs characteristic of our sociocultural and historical context. In particular, he argues that 'behind and supporting the impetus to naturalism . . . stands an attachment to a certain picture of the agent.' This picture holds great attraction for us; it is 'both flattering and inspiring [because] it shows us as capable of achieving a kind of disengagement from our world by objectifying it' (p. 4).

In Taylor's view, one of the most noteworthy (and detrimental) consequences of the disengaged image of the self is 'atomism'. The concept of atomism he has in mind is tied to an understanding of the individual as 'metaphysically independent of society'. Contemporary atomistic views clearly allow for processes whereby individuals are shaped by their social environment; indeed, as Taylor notes, 'the early atomism of the seventeenth century seems incredible to us'. What atomism 'hides from view is the way in which an individual is constituted by language and culture which can only be maintained and renewed in the communities he is part of' (1985a: 8).

Taylor has specific issues in mind when he writes of how an individual is constituted by language, and these are not always the same issues raised by Bakhtin. What these two thinkers have in common is their rejection of the idea that individuals are 'metaphysically independent of society', a point that is played out in Bakhtin's approach in relation to the question 'Who is doing the talking?' Bakhtin rejected the notion that isolated individuals create utterances and meaning. This rejection is implicit throughout his account of dialogicality, and scholars such as Holquist (1986) have made it quite explicit when comparing Bakhtin's account with Saussure's assumptions about *parole*. This does not mean that the speaker or writer must be or can be totally subordinated to outside authority; to do so would be to revert to a kind of monologism that Bakhtin criticized in his account of the 'authoritative word'. What it does mean is that for Bakhtin, a kind of 'interference' and 'subordination' is an inherent part of any utterance and its meaning, a fact that ultimately follows from the general observation that an utterance is always a link in the chain of speech communication.

In a Bakhtinian approach, interference and subordination come in many forms, but they are especially evident in the process of ventriloquation. The notion of ventriloquation presupposes that a voice is never solely responsible for creating an utterance or its meaning. It begins with the fact that 'the word in language is half someone else's.' (Bakhtin, 1981: 293–4). In a view grounded in ventriloquation, then, the very act of speaking precludes any claims about the individual's being 'metaphysically independent of society' (Taylor, 1985a: 8).

Among other things, Taylor's comments on the idea of the disengaged image of the self and on atomism are useful because they highlight the fact that problems in understanding a position such as Bakhtin's reflect the general sociocultural situatedness of those doing the understanding. Taylor reminds us that assumptions such as those underlying atomism are natural for modern western scholars because they are consistent with the pervasive, everyday assumptions in our sociocultural setting. In this view the image of the disengaged self is not created or manifested only in psychology or other social sciences. It 'is woven into a host of modern practices – economic, scientific, technological, psychotherapeutic, and so on' (p. 5). Indeed, one of Taylor's major points is that, despite their lack of intellectual or scientific merit, atomistic positions continue to appeal to us in the West because they are consistent with underlying, historically specific cultural assumptions.

[. . .]

The univocal and dialogic functions of texts

During the past few decades, a particular view of human communication has come to dominate much of the research in developmental psychology and other social sciences. According to this view, human communication can be conceptualized in terms of the *transmission* of information. This transmission model involves the translation (or 'encoding') of an idea into a signal by a sender, the transmission of this signal to a receiver, and the 'decoding' of the signal into a message by the receiver.

The origins of this approach can be traced to several sources. Per Linell (1988) notes precursors extending back at least to Locke (see also Harris, 1981; Parkinson, 1977). It is now generally recognized that in more recent times a major impetus for this model came from C. E. Shannon and Warren Weaver's (1949) mathematical information theory. Yet a close reading of their original theoretical statements reveals that their ideas cannot be equated to a simple transmission model. As theorists such as Michael Reddy (1979) have noted, however, the definition of information and communication that emerged from mathematical information theory soon came to be transformed through the influence of widely used metaphors (an aspect of scholars' mediational means) that shape our thinking and speaking about communication. These metaphors can be considered another major source (indeed, *the* major source if Reddy is right) of contemporary views about the transmission model of communication.

Reddy reviewed a wide range of metaphors concerned with communication in English, of which the following are a sample:

1 try to get your thought across better;

2 whenever you have a good idea practise capturing it in words;

3 can you actually extract coherent ideas from that prose?

On the basis of his analysis, he outlined the underlying 'conduit metaphor' that seems to shape a great deal of our understanding of human communication. The basic outlines of the conduit metaphor, at least in its 'major framework' version, consist of the following points: '(1) language functions like a conduit, transferring thoughts bodily from one person to another; (2) in writing and speaking, people insert their thoughts or feelings in the words; (3) words accomplish the transfer by containing the thoughts or feelings and conveying them to others; and (4) in listening or reading, people extract the thoughts and feelings once again from the words' (p. 290).

Reddy does not claim that the conduit metaphor makes it impossible to think about communication in other ways. Indeed, he views mathematical information theory as an example of how viable alternatives have been formulated and outlines one of his own. In his view, however, thinking about communication that avoids the conduit metaphor tends to 'remain brief, isolated, and fragmentary in the face of an entrenched system of opposing attitudes and assumptions' (pp. 297–8). The metaphors about communication in English are so heavily weighted in favour of conduit notions that 'practically speaking, if you try to avoid all obvious conduit metaphor expressions in your usage, you are nearly struck dumb when communication becomes the topic' (p. 299). According to Reddy, the power of this basic metaphor is largely responsible for the misinterpretation of information theory, even by its founders. Because 'English has a preferred framework for conceptualizing communication,' it ends up being 'its own worst enemy' (pp. 285, 286) in this respect.

The transmission model of communication that springs from the conduit metaphor is often represented schematically as in the accompanying diagram.

Figure 1   *Transmission model of communication*

One of the most common criticisms of the transmission model as schematized here concerns the unidirectionality of the arrows involved. Because they are unidirectional, the receiver is viewed as passive (note the very term *receiver*). As Reddy points out, 'in the framework of the conduit metaphor, the listener's task must be one of extraction. He must find the meaning "in the words" and take it out of them, so that it "gets into his head"' (p. 288). Because the receiver's task is viewed as being simply one of extraction, 'to the extent that the conduit metaphor does see communication as requiring some slight expenditure of energy, it localizes this expenditure almost totally in the speaker or writer. The function of the reader or listener is trivialized' (p. 308).

From a Bakhtinian perspective the schematization of the transmission model is problematic above all due to the inherently monologic assumptions that underlie it. These assumptions, reflected, among other places, in the schema's unidirectional arrows, run counter to Bakhtin's idea that understanding involves one voice's response to another, a process in which 'for each word of the utterance that we are in process of understanding, we, as it were, lay down a set of our answering words' (Volosinov, 1973: 102).

Furthermore, from a Bakhtinian perspective also, the assumption that it is possible to speak of a single, unaltered meaning or message is problematic. Again, instead of two voices coming into contact and interanimating one another, the communication model schematized above (at least as interpreted in terms of the conduit metaphor) assumes that the sender encodes, or packages, a single meaning and transmits it to the receiver, who passively decodes or fails to decode it. The 'it' remains the same throughout. Finally, instead of viewing senders as being influenced by past and future receivers, as a Bakhtinian approach suggests, models such as that sketched out above treat messages as if they can be understood outside the extended flow of speech communication.
    [. . .]

Authority and text

[I turn now to] Bakhtin's distinction between 'authoritative' and 'internally persuasive' discourse. In addition to univocality and dialogicality, Bakhtin characterized the difference in terms of the degree to which one voice has the authority to come into contact with and interanimate another. This notion of authority will turn out to have important implications in an account of meaning that is intended to deal with issues of how intermental and intramental functioning are socioculturally situated.

In Bakhtin's (1981) view, authoritative discourse is based on the assumption that utterances and their meanings are fixed, not modifiable as they come into contact with new voices: 'The authoritative word demands that we acknowledge it, that we make it our own; it binds us, quite independent of any power it might have to persuade us internally; we encounter it with its authority fused to it.' The 'static and dead' meaning structure of authoritative discourse allows no interanimation with other voices. Instead of functioning as a generator of meaning or as a thinking device, an authoritative text 'demands our unconditional allegiance,' and it allows 'no play with its borders, no gradual and flexible transitions, no spontaneously creative stylizing variants on it'.

As examples of authoritative texts, Bakhtin cited religious, political, and moral texts as well as 'the word of a father, of adults, of teachers, etc.' A text of this sort 'enters our verbal consciousness as a compact and indivisible mass; one must either totally affirm it, or totally reject it. It is indissolubly fused with its authority – with political power, an institution, a person – and it stands or falls together with that authority. One cannot divide it up – agree with one part, accept but not completely another part, reject utterly a third part' (pp. 342, 343). Throughout his account of authoritative discourse, Bakhtin emphasized its inability to enter into contact with other voices and social languages. It is for this reason that it gives rise to the kinds of univocal text presupposed by transmission models of communication. As Bakhtin noted, 'authoritative discourse cannot be represented – it is only transmitted' (p. 344).

In contrast to authoritative discourse, 'the internally persuasive word is half-ours and half-someone else's'; it allows dialogic interanimation. Indeed, 'its creativity and productiveness consist precisely in the fact that such a word awakens new and independent words, that it organizes masses of our words from within, and does not remain in an isolated and static condition . . . The semantic structure of an internally persuasive discourse is not *finite*, it is *open*; in each of the new contexts that dialogize it, this discourse is able to reveal ever new *ways to mean*' (pp. 345–6).

The major point of Bakhtin's comments is that transmission models of communication cannot adequately account for many of the social and individual processes we wish to address. Instead, the dynamics of dialogism will often come into play. This does not mean that one should simply dismiss the transmission model as inadequate. [. . .] Texts may simultaneously serve different functions.

In the final analysis, for any text the univocal and dialogic functions are best thought of as being in a kind of dynamic tension. There is always an element of univocality as envisioned in the transmission model and an element of response and retort as envisioned by Bakhtin. Put differently, for communication to occur, one must always listen to what the speaker says, but what the speaker says does not mechanistically generate an exclusive interpretation. This point about dynamic tension is tied to sociocultural contexts.

One of the criticisms most commonly leveled at Bakhtin is that he provided few detailed interpretations of texts and little concrete detail about the semiotic phenomena he had in mind. A phenomenon he did examine in some detail, however, and a phenomenon that is of use in trying to understand intermental and intramental functioning in sociocultural settings is 'reported speech'. Reported speech is the mechanism whereby one voice (the 'reporting voice') reports the utterance of another (the 'reported voice'). It was of particular interest to Bakhtin (Volosinov, 1973) because it is an arena in which voices come into contact in one of several ways. Hence it is an arena in which one can explore issues such as the univocality or dialogicality of texts, authoritative and internally persuasive discourse, and other related issues. In what follows, I shall make no attempt to provide a comprehensive review of the issues of reported speech. Furthermore, I shall make no attempt to deal with the myriad issues being taken up by contemporary authors as a result of Bakhtin's claims about reported speech (Hickmann, 1985; Lucy, in press). Instead, I shall limit my comments to outlining some basic issues that will be of use when dealing with social and psychological processes in sociocultural context.

As a way of explicating reported speech, consider (1) as an utterance to be reported.

(1)   I will be there!

In English, there are many possible ways to report this utterance. One of the basic forms involves 'direct discourse' (Volosinov, 1973) as in 2, and a second involves 'indirect discourse' as in (3).

(2)   He said, 'I will be there!'
(3)   He said enthusiastically that he would be here.

In 2 the reporting and reported voices are separated by the comma and quotation marks. Beyond the fact that utterances from the two voices are juxtaposed, there is little contact between them. As a result, the form of 1, including the intonation contour as marked by the exclamation point, is preserved in 2. In such cases the tendency in reporting speech is to 'maintain the integrity and authenticity' of the reported utterance. In Bakhtin's view

> [a] language may strive to forge hard and fast boundaries for reported speech. In such a case, the patterns and their modifications serve to demarcate the reported speech as clearly as possible, to screen it from penetration by the author's intonations, and to condense and enhance its individual linguistic characteristics.
>
> (Volosinov, 1973, p. 119)

In contrast, in 3 there are several points of contact and interanimation between the reporting and reported voices. In this case there is a tendency for the reporting voice to 'infiltrate' the reported utterance (Volosinov, 1973: 120). Such infiltration and the 'double voicedness' that ensues can occur in many guises. In 3, which is a relatively straightforward, unstylized case of indirect discourse, it appears in four places. The first is the second 'he', an expression that is coreferential with 'I' in the original utterance 1 but has a different form. Second, it appears in 'would' in 3, a term that replaces 'will' in 1. Third, the 'here' in 3 replaces the 'there' in 1 because the spatial coordinates of utterances 1 and 3 differ. Finally, the exclamation point in 1 is replaced with the adverb 'enthusiastically' in 3.

Not all the changes in 1 to form 3 need to take the particular form they have in this example. But changes of the sort I have outlined invariably do, and indeed (because of the grammar of English), must take place when using indirect discourse to report an utterance.

For my purposes the major point does not concern details of syntax and pragmatics; instead, it is how one would answer the Bakhtinian question 'Who is doing the talking?' in the case of utterance (3). Indirect discourse reveals a particular way in which the answer to this question is played out. For example, if one asks who is doing the talking in the case of the 'he', 'would', and 'here' in (3), the answer must be that at least two voices are simultaneously involved. The voice that produced the reported utterance specifies the referent in each case, and the voice that produced the reporting utterance provides the particular way of identifying the referent, the 'referential perspective' (Wertsch, 1980). One hears two voices in each case.

The use of 'enthusiastically' in (3) reflects another way in which voices can come into contact in indirect discourse. One cannot simply duplicate the intonation contour or use an exclamation point in (3) in order to portray the affective tone of (1). The use of these devices fails because their significance attaches to the reporting rather than the reported voice. Instead, indirect discourse relies on an 'analytic spirit' to represent this information. In Bakhtin's view, 'analysis is the heart and soul of indirect discourse' (Volosinov, 1973: 129). With regard to (3), this analytic orientation is manifested in the fact that the reporting voice infiltrates the reported voice by transforming the intonation contour or exclamation point of the reported voice into an analytic category. The reporting voice is allowed a wider range of options, and hence is given more responsibility in this case than in the case of the other three items, something that is revealed by the fact that expressions such as 'said excitedly' or 'shouted' could have been used in place of 'said enthusiastically'.

[. . .]

My major point is that reported speech provides a concrete example of how voices may or may not come into contact, interanimate, and infiltrate one another in various ways. Furthermore, this interanimation can be expected to occur to a greater or lesser degree depending on whether the reported utterance occurs in the form of authoritative or internally persuasive discourse. Whereas authoritative discourse tends to discourage contact, internally persuasive discourse encourages it.

An illustration

As a way of summarizing and coordinating my comments on the disengaged image of the self, the functional dualism of texts, and authority and text, I shall turn to an example concerned with the socialization of mental functioning. This example illustrates what Bakhtin labelled the 'primordial dialogism of discourse' (1981: 275). By this he meant the dialogic processes involved in concrete, face-to-face communication. In particular, the illustration concerns the ways in which the dialogic organization of speech on the intermental plane is mastered, thereby shaping the intramental plane of functioning.

The intramental functioning that results from this mastery, or 'internalization' (Wertsch and Stone, 1985), is closely related to what Bakhtin termed 'hidden dialogicality', which he characterized as follows:

Imagine a dialogue of two persons in which the statements of the second speaker are omitted, but in such a way that the general sense is not at all violated. The second speaker is present invisibly, his words are not there, but deep traces left by these words have a determining influence on all the present and visible words of the first speaker. We sense that this is a conversation, although only one person is speaking, and it is a conversation of the most intense kind, for each present, uttered word responds and reacts with its every fiber to the invisible speaker, points to something outside itself, beyond its own limits, to the unspoken words of another person.

(1984: 197)

The case of hidden dialogicality I shall examine involves the interaction of a two-and-a-half-year-old, middle-class American child and her mother in a problem-solving setting. The following excerpts reflect the microgenetic transitions that occurred over the course of one interactional session, whose object was to insert pieces from a 'pieces pile' into a 'copy' puzzle so that it would be identical with a 'model' puzzle. The data for this illustration come from three 'episodes' of interaction, which I shall define as verbal and nonverbal interaction in connection with the identification, selection, and insertion of a piece in the copy puzzle. In all three episodes the correct location of the piece in the copy puzzle could be determined only by consulting the model puzzle. I shall give special attention to the initial phase of each episode, which included the strategic substep of consulting the model puzzle in order to determine where the piece should go in the copy puzzle.

The initial segment of the first episode between this mother (M) and the child (C) proceeded as follows:

(1)   **C**   Oh. (C *glances at the model puzzle, C looks at the pieces pile.*) Oh, now where's this one go? (*C picks up a black piece from the pieces pile, C looks at the copy puzzle, C looks at the pieces pile.*)

(2)   **M**   Where does it go on this other one? (*C puts the black piece she is holding back down in the pieces pile. C looks at the pieces pile.*)

(3)   **M**   Look at the other truck and then you can tell. (*C looks at the model puzzle, C glances at the pieces pile, C looks at the model puzzle, C glances at the pieces pile.*)

(4)   **C**   Well . . . (*C looks at the copy puzzle, C looks at the model puzzle.*)

(5)   **C**   I look at it.

(6)   **C**   Um, this other puzzle has a black one over there. (*C points to the black piece in the model puzzle.*)

While it is true that the child glanced at the model puzzle at the very beginning of this episode, it does not appear that she did so at that point to determine where a piece should go in the copy puzzle. The first time she consulted the model for some clear purpose was in response to the mother's utterances (2) and (3). This response is part of a dialogue that occurred on the intermental plane of functioning. The child's responses (4), (5), and (6) indicate that in one sense she could respond appropriately to the mother's directive, while in another sense she apparently had not understood or incorporated the reasoning that motivated her mother's question because she did not see where her mother was going with the line of questioning.

The initial segment of a subsequent episode between this mother and child proceeded as follows:

(7) **C** (*C glances at the pieces pile, C looks at the copy puzzle, C picks up the orange piece from the pieces pile.*) Now where do you think the orange one goes?

(8) **M** Where does it go on the other truck? (*C looks at the model puzzle.*)

(9) **C** Right there. (*C points to the orange piece in the model puzzle.*) The orange one goes right there.

In this episode the child's action, consulting the model puzzle, was again part of the dialogue on the intermental plane. But the fact that the mother did not have to follow up her first directive with a second one, such as utterance (3) in the first episode, indicates that the child had begun to understand where the mother was going with her line of questioning.

A third episode in this problem-solving process began as follows:

(10) **C** (*C looks at the pieces pile, C picks up the yellow piece from the pieces pile, C looks at the copy puzzle.*) Now how . . . Now where . . . Now . . . (*C looks at the model puzzle.*)

(11) **C** You . . . you . . . the yellow on that side goes . . . One yellow one's right next there. (*C points to the yellow piece in the model puzzle, C looks at the yellow piece she is holding in her hand.*)

(12) **M** Okay.

In this episode the mother did not ask a question to guide the child's gaze to the model puzzle (intermental plane). Instead, it now appears that the child's egocentric and inner speech (intramental plane) guided this process. In Bakhtin's terminology, the child's speech has taken on the properties of hidden dialogicality. The 'statements of the second speaker [the mother] are omitted,' but the 'second speaker is present invisibly'; her 'words are not there, but deep traces left by these words have a determining influence on all the present and visible words of the first speaker [the child].' Furthermore, as predicted by Vygotsky (1987), the egocentric speech utterances have taken on an abbreviated, predicative form (Wertsch, 1979b). Instead of being fully developed answers, the child's responses to the 'unspoken words of another person' appear in the form of abbreviated utterances, a fact that reflects the beginning of the differentiation of speech for oneself and speech for others.

A comparison of these three episodes reveals several important microgenetic transitions in the child's mediated action. The first two began with the child's question about where a piece should go (utterances 1 and 7) and the mother's response, which directed the child's attention to the model puzzle (utterances 2, 3, and 8). In both of these episodes, the child's original questions led to the mother's response, which, in turn, led to the child's response, consulting the model. All of these communicative moves were carried out through external social dialogue (dialogue on the intermental plane). But the third episode began

232

quite differently. First, the child did not produce a fully expanded question about where a piece should go (although it appears that she began to do so in utterance 10). Second, and more important, when she looked at the model puzzle after utterance 10, it was not in response to an adult's directive in overt social dialogue. She did not rely on the adult to provide a regulative utterance but presupposed the utterance that would have occurred on the intermental plane and responded in egocentric and inner dialogue.

There are striking similarities between several of the child's utterances: (6) in the first episode, (9) in the second, and (11) in the third.

> *First episode*
> (6)   **C**   Um, this other puzzle has a black one over there. (*C points to the black piece in the model puzzle.*)
> *Second episode*
> (9)   **C**   Right there. (*C points to the orange piece in the model puzzle.*) The orange one goes right there.
> *Third episode*
> (11) **C**   You . . . you . . . the yellow on that side goes . . . One yellow one's right next there. (*C points to the yellow piece in the model puzzle, C looks at the yellow piece she is holding in her hand.*)

In all three cases, the verbal and nonverbal behaviours comprise a statement about the location of a particular piece in the model puzzle. In addition, in terms of the sequences of behaviours in the three episodes, (6), (9), and (11) mediate similar aspects of the problem-solving action. In all three cases the utterance serves to advance this action in the same way (all are concerned with consulting the model to determine where a piece from the pieces pile should go).

The striking similarity between utterance (11) and the previous two, despite the fact that (11) is part of intramental functioning and the others of intermental functioning, is due to the fact that all three utterances are responses to questions. In the case of (11), however, the question is posed by the child rather than the mother. An abbreviated form of this question appears in utterance (10). In subsequent episodes, the only utterances that appear in overt speech are the 'answers'; no questions surface, even in abbreviated form.

This tendency to see 'answers' in children's speech in the absence of questions is not uncommon in such problem-solving settings (Wertsch, 1979a). The fact that the utterances seem so obviously to be answers raises several issues that can be adequately addressed only if we invoke some notion of dialogicality. The main reason these utterances seem to be answers is that they mediate the action in ways that are similar to utterances in earlier episodes that *were* replies to concrete, overt questions. That is, the genetic precursor to these 'answers' on the intramental plane can be found in intermental functioning.

If this is so, how does one understand the notion of a question in such cases? Vygotsky's writings suggest that the questions to which the 'answers' correspond now occur in inner speech. This does not mean that a full-blown version of each question is somehow represented (perhaps subvocally) in internal mental functioning. Indeed, Vygotsky went to great pains in his account of the abbreviation that characterizes inner speech to preclude such a conclusion.

Instead, the question is *presupposed*. The meaning of the answer, as it occurs in the flow of problem-solving activity, changes to reflect the question that had formerly been part of an overt, social interaction.

This point has also been made by other Soviet investigators in their account of inner speech. In particular, P. Ya. Gal'perin (1969) has argued for the notion of presupposition in his account of the formation of mental acts. In his view, inner speech is inherently grounded in the notion of presupposition, which allows one to address the issue of how an utterance reflects the context of the other utterances among which it is situated.

Bakhtin's account of dialogicality can provide essential insights into several aspects of this interaction. His approach suggests that what comes to be incorporated into, or presupposed by, an utterance are voices that were formerly represented explicitly in intermental functioning. The issue is how one voice comes into contact with another, thereby changing the meaning of what it is saying by becoming increasingly dialogical, or multivoiced.

This conclusion is diametrically opposed to the notion that the process of microgenetic change can be understood simply as the shift from dialogue to monologue. While this may be a way of characterizing external, observable behaviours in the transition from intermental to intramental functioning, it fails to recognize the increasing dialogicality that characterizes intramental processes. Processes such as this (that is, 'dialogization') led Vygotsky (1981) to assert that even on the intramental plane, mental functioning retains a 'quasi-social' nature.

The process of dialogization poses a special set of problems for a theory of meaning. It calls on such a theory, for example, to account for the fact that in the mother–child interaction discussed above, utterances (6), (9), and (11) are overtly quite similar and mediate action in a similar way but are fundamentally different in the degree of dialogization they involve. This is a problem that most existing theories of meaning have no way of addressing, but it is a central one for a sociocultural approach to mind.

The implications of the process of dialogization can be summarized in terms of the issues outlined in this chapter. First, it is impossible to understand the transitions involved if one begins with an approach to meaning that rests on a disengaged image of the self and the atomism associated with it. These transitions involve changes in speech over the course of the interaction, changes which reflect the impact of what Taylor (1985a) terms 'outside interference' or 'subordination to outside authority'. As I outlined earlier, this outside authority can be understood in terms of Bakhtin's claim that the 'word is half someone else's'. If we ask the Bakhtinian question 'Who is doing the talking?', the hidden dialogicality found in the later episodes of the mother–child interaction I have described leads one to say that *both* the adult and child are speaking. In an important sense, then, the meaning of the child's utterances reflects the outside interference of another's voice.

Second, a transmission model of communication cannot alone account for these transitions. While it is certainly true that information is conveyed from adult to child and vice versa, it is obvious that the adult's utterances also served as a 'thinking device', a mechanism 'to generate new meanings' for the child. The text of the two participants' utterances is 'a semiotic space in which languages interact, interfere, and organize themselves hierarchically' (Lotman,

1988: 37). This is not to say that the influence occurs only in one direction, from the adult to the child; the adult's utterances can themselves only be understood as responses to the child's. But according to the hierarchical organization mentioned by Lotman, the main locus of change was in the child's speech and thinking.

This touches on a third issue, authority and text. Although the meanings of the child's utterances (and hence her understanding) underwent a major microgenetic transition over the course of the interaction, the meaning of the adult's utterances did not. The child's utterances changed in that they increasingly reflected the hidden dialogicality derived from incorporating the mother's meanings into her own. In contrast, the mother's voice remained relatively impermeable; she did not change her meanings or understanding of the strategic task as a result of her dialogue with the child. As in the case of the terms 'outside interference' and 'subordination to outside authority', the use of the term 'authoritative' here need not imply some kind of overt or potentially punitive force. Instead, these terms are concerned with the ways in which the dynamics between voices are played out as these voices come into contact.

[. . .]

References

Bakhtin, M.M. (1981) *The Dialogic Imagination: Four Essays by M.M. Bakhtin*, M. Holquist (ed.), C. Emerson and M. Holquist (trans), Austin, University of Texas Press.

Bakhtin, M.M. (1984) *Problems of Dostoevsky's Poetics*, C. Emerson (ed. and trans.) Minneapolis, University of Minnesota Press.

Clark, K. and Holquist, M. (1984) *Mikhail Bakhtin*, Cambridge, Mass, Harvard University Press.

Gal'perin, P. Ya. (1969) 'Stages in the development of mental acts' in M. Cole and I. Maltzman (eds) *A Hand-Book of Contemporary Soviet Psychology*, New York, Basic Books.

Harris, R. (1981) *The Language Myth*, London, Duckworth.

Hickmann, M. (1985) 'The implications of discourse skills in Vygotsky's developmental theory' in J.V. Wertsch (ed.) *Culture, Communication, and Cognition: Vygotskian Perspectives*, New York, Cambridge University Press.

Holquist, M. (1981) 'The politics of representation' in S. Greenblatt (ed.) *Allegory in Representation: Selected papers from the English Institute*, Baltimore, Johns Hopkins University Press.

Holquist, M. (1986) Introduction to *Speech Genres and Other Late Essays*, by M.M. Bakhtin, Austin, University of Texas Press.

Linell, P. (1988) 'The impact of literacy on the conception of language: The case of linguistics' in R. Saljo (ed.) *The Written Word: Studies in Literate Thought and Action*, Berlin, Springer-Verlag.

Lotman, Y.M. (1988) 'Text within a text', *Soviet Psychology*, vol. 26, pp. 32–51.

Lucy, J. (In press) *Reflexive Language: Reported Speech and Metapragmatics*, New York, Cambridge University Press.

Parkinson, G.H.R. (1977) 'The translation theory of understanding' in G. Vesey (ed.) *Communication and Understanding*, London, Hassocks.

Reddy, M.J. (1979) 'The conduit metaphor: a case of frame conflict in our language about language' in A. Ortony (ed.) *Metaphor and Thought*, Cambridge, Cambridge University Press.

Shannon, C.E., and Weaver, W. (1949) *The Mathematical Theory of Communication*, Urbana, University of Illinois Press.

Taylor, C. (1985a) *Human Agency and Language: Philosophical Papers 1*, New York, Cambridge University Press.

Taylor, C. (1985b) *Philosophy and the Human Sciences. Philosophical Papers 2*, New York, Cambridge University Press.

Taylor, C. (1989) *Sources of the Self: The Making of Modern Identity*, Cambridge, Mass., Harvard University Press.

Volosinov, V.N. (1973) *Marxism and the Philosophy of Language*, trans. L. Matejka and I.R. Titunik, New York, Seminar Press.

Vygotsky, L.S. (1981) 'The genesis of higher mental functions' in J.V. Wertsch (ed.) *The Concept of Activity in Soviet Psychology*, Armonk, NY, M.E. Sharpe.

Vygotsky, L.S. (1987) *Thinking and Speech*, N. Minick, (ed. and trans.) New York, Plenum.

Wertsch, J.V. (1979a) 'From social interaction to higher psychological processes: a clarification and application of Vygotsky's theory', *Human Development*, vol. 22, pp. 1–22.

Wertsch, J.V. (1979b) 'The regulation of human action and the given-new organization of private speech' in G. Zivin (ed.) *The Development of Self-regulation Through Private Speech*, New York, Wiley.

Wertsch, J.V. (1980) 'The significance of dialogue in Vygotsky's account of social, egocentric, and inner speech', *Contemporary Educational Psychology*, vol. 5, pp. 150–62.

Wertsch, J.V., and Stone, C.A. (1985) 'The concept of internalization in Vygotsky's account of the genesis of higher mental functions' in J.V. Wertsch (ed.) *Culture, Communication, and Cognition*, New York, Cambridge University Press.

Emotion

Derek Edwards

Source: Edwards, D. (1997) *Discourse and Cognition*, London, Sage, Chapter 7.

The emotions are often defined in contrast to rational thought. They are conceived to be natural bodily experiences and expressions, older than language, irrational and subjective, unconscious rather than deliberate, genuine rather than artificial, feelings rather than thoughts. Yet these categories and contrasts are precisely what signal their importance for discursive psychology. Their significance is in how they are *conceived*, how they may be *defined*, and especially in how various emotion categories contrast with alternative emotions, with non-emotional states, with rational conduct, and so on, within the discursive construction of reality and mind. Emotion discourse is rich and various, full of contrasts and alternatives, and marvellously useful in working up descriptions of human actions, interpersonal relations, and in handling accountability.

The discursive psychology of emotion deals with how people talk about emotions, whether 'avowing' their own or 'ascribing' them to other people, and how they use emotion categories when talking about other things. Emotion discourse is an integral feature of talk about events, mental states, mind and body, personal dispositions, and social relations. It is used to construct thoughts and actions as irrational, but, alternatively, emotions themselves may be treated as sensible and rationally based. Emotion categories are used in assigning causes and motives to actions, in blamings, excuses, and accounts. Emotional states may figure as things to be *accounted for* (in terms of prior causal events or dispositional tendencies, say), as *accounts* (of subsequent actions and events), and also as evidence of what *kind of events or actions* precede or follow them. [. . .]

As a glimpse at the kinds of phenomena under analysis, consider something Mary said about Jeff in the following extract. It is a snippet from her story about the events leading up to their coming for counselling. The counsellor has asked them both 'why: uh you went to Relate in the first place', and Mary's version is told first.

Extract 1

```
1    Mary    (. . .) so that's when I decided to (.) you know
2            to tell him. (1.0) U::m (1.0) and then::, (.)
3    →       obviously you went through your a:ngry stage,
4            didn't you?
5            (.)
```

6 →   Ve:ry upset <u>ob</u>viously, .hh an:d uh, (0.6)
7   we: started ar:guing a lot, an:d (0.6)
8   <u>just</u> drifted awa:y.

(DE-JF:C1:S1:4)

Mary provides, as part of her narrative, a time and place for, and specification of, Jeff's emotions on hearing about his wife's affair with another man (Lines 3 and 6). He was 'a:ngry' and 've:ry upset'. These descriptions characterize Jeff's reactions *as* emotional rather than, say, as having come to a damning but rational appraisal of Mary's actions and character. But the details I want to focus on are '<u>ob</u>viously' and 'stage'. The 'obviously' normalizes and somewhat endorses those emotional reactions as expectable, and sequentially proper within the story as told. Mary is displaying (here) an understanding, uncritical position on Jeff's reactions (though elsewhere, and soon after, she is more condemnatory).

The phrase 'your a:ngry stage' is exquisite. It employs a notion of anger as a temporary state with its proper occasions and durations. While Jeff's anger is proper in its place, one would not expect it to go on for ever, to endure unreasonably, beyond its 'stage'. Mary makes rhetorical room here for something she exploits soon afterwards, which is the notion that Jeff's reactions are starting to get in the way of progress, starting to become (instead of her infidelity, as Jeff insists) 'the problem' they have in their relationship. Indeed the *next thing she says* in her narrative (and implicationally, therefore, what not only follows but follows *from* Jeff's reactions), is how 'we: started ar:guing a lot, an:d (0.6) <u>just</u> drifted awa:y' (Lines 7–8). Their problems are now described as joint ones, arguments, and a kind of non-agentive, non-blaming, 'just' drifting apart. The implication that Mary develops in her subsequent discourse is that Jeff's reactions should end at some reasonable point. His 'stage' is already past tense ('you went through your a:ngry stage, <u>did</u>n't you?') and he starts to become accountable for continuing to be 'upset'.

Now, I have glossed in a condensed way quite a lot of what is going on between Jeff and Mary, rather than producing all of that through an analysis of further extracts from their talk. This is in order to succinctly point up the kinds of interactional business that emotion talk can perform. Emotions and cognitions (and the differences between them) are not just sitting there, inside Jeff's head and actions, waiting to be reported on. 'Anger' and 'upset' are *descriptions* that, first and easily missable, can be used to construct reactions *as* reactions, and *as* emotional ones, rather than, say, as something like coming to a view or an opinion. One of the uses of such talk is that emotions such as 'anger' and getting 'upset' permit talk of stages, of temporary inflammations of the passions, rather than the more enduring states of mind we might expect of things like conclusions or beliefs, or even 'the way things were' – events themselves. Similarly, emotion categories provide for rational (sequentially understandable, in Garfinkel's sense) accountability, though they can also be used to contrast with rational thought, to label behaviour as spontaneous and sequentially incoherent (unjustified by events), and even to pathologize it.

I have emphasized the *flexibility* of emotion discourse in providing the sense of events, of states of mind, and for managing issues of accountability. This is one of the advantages of examining emotion discourse *in use*, rather than relying solely on conceptual analysis or idealized cognitive models.

   [. . .]

Emotional etymology

Social constructionist studies of emotion can be grouped into three related kinds: historical, anthropological, and discursive. Each of these is concerned with exploring 'the ontological, conceptual, and temporal priority of the public realm' (Harré, 1983: 114). No clear distinction is drawn between emotion 'discourse' and emotions 'themselves', given that what emotions *are* is equivalent to what emotions are taken to be, how they are conceptualized, talked about, and interpreted, as intelligible social performances: 'look to see how the psychological vocabulary is actually used – then we will know of what it is used!' (Harré, 1983: 115; cf. Coulter, 1979, 1986). Both 'folk' psychology and its technical, professional counterpart are approachable as a set of practices, descriptions, and explanations that have their own cultural and historical trajectory, available to a constructionist analysis (Gergen, 1995).

Rom Harré notes that, whereas some emotions in current use can be historically dated to fairly recent times (he cites romantic love as an example, cf. Gillis, 1988), 'some emotions and moods which once had great importance for us have become extinct or obsolete . . . [for example] the extinct emotion *accidie* and the obsolete mood *melancholy*' (1983: 126). He goes on to draw a telling comparison and contrast between melancholy and 'one of its modern descendants, clinical depression' (1983: 126). Harré's argument is that the origin and extinction of emotions and emotion terms are at the same time rearrangements of the patterning of moral orders, social relations, and accountability. These are not just changes of vocabulary, while our inner (or outer) emotional life remains the same. Emotions 'themselves' are socially and historically defined.

Accidie was a mediaeval emotion, related to the religious sin *sloth*. It was associated with idleness and misery (or something approximating what those words now mean to us), with regard to the neglect of one's duties to God. The association between idleness and misery was part of a notion that performing one's duties to God ought to be a joyful matter, and not just a reluctant obligation, so that getting up and doing things and not being *behaviourally* slothful was not enough. The growth, change, and decline of the emotion was intrinsically linked to social patterns and religious beliefs (Wenzel, 1960), and defined with regard to a changing religious-moral order. So, 'idleness and procrastination are still amongst our failings but our emotions are differently engaged, defined against the background of a different moral order, roughly the ethics of a material production' (Harré, 1983: 129). Again, it is not merely that we feel the same things, but learn to call them by different names. It is that emotions and the names we call them are intrinsically tied to social conditions, rights, and responsibilities, which change historically and differ across cultures.

Historical studies of the changing meanings of emotion terms in English (Stearns and Stearns, 1988) are important in establishing the cultural relativity and specificity not only of current sets of emotion terms, but also of the general 'emotionology' that is built into psychology's most modern, technical 'models' (Gergen, 1995). For example, there is a common-sense notion, which can be traced etymologically, of emotions as private, subjective feelings that are expressed outwardly (and somewhat ambiguously, and subject to disguise) in behaviour.

A perusal of the marvellously informative *Oxford English Dictionary* (1994) reveals that subjective meanings of the word 'emotion' (from Latin *emovere* 'to move out') were preceded by physical, bodily and geographical meanings:

1. A moving out, migration, transference from one place to another. *Obs.*
1603 Knolles *Hist. Turks* (1621) 3 The divers emotions of that people [the Turks].
1695 Woodward *Nat. Hist. Earth* i. (1723) 45 Some accidental Emotion . . . of the Center of Gravity.

2. A moving, stirring, agitation, perturbation (in physical sense). *Obs.*
1692 Locke *Educ.* 7 When exercise has left any Emotion in his Blood or Pulse.
1708 O. Bridgman in *Phil. Trans.* XXVI. 138 Thunder . . . caused so great an Emotion in the Air.
1758 Ibid. L. 647 The waters continuing in the caverns . . . caused the emotion or earth-quake.

3. transf. A political or social agitation; a tumult, popular disturbance. *Obs.*
1579 Fenton *Guicciard.* ii, There were . . . great stirres and emocions in Lombardye.
1709 Addison *Tatler* No. 24 313 Accounts of Publick Emotions, occasion'd by the Want of Corn.

4. a. fig. Any agitation or disturbance of mind, feeling, passion; any vehement or excited mental state.
1762 Kames *Elem. Crit.* ii. §2. (1833) 37 The joy of gratification is properly called an emotion.
1785 Reid *Int. Powers* 725 The emotion raised by grand objects is awful.
1828 Scott *F.M. Perth*, Desirous that his emotion should not be read upon his countenance.

The current 'psychological' meaning is given as originating in the late eighteenth century, as follows:

Psychology. A mental 'feeling' or 'affection' (e.g. of pleasure or pain, desire or aversion, surprise, hope or fear, etc.), as distinguished from cognitive or volitional states of consciousness. Also *abstr.* 'feeling' as distinguished from the other classes of mental phenomena.

1808 *Med. Jrnl.* XIX. 422 Sea-sickness . . . is greatly under the dominion of emotion.
1841–4 Emerson *Ess. Friendship* Wks. (Bohn) I. 81 In poetry . . . the emotions of benevolence and complacency . . . are likened to the material effects of fire.

1842   Kingsley *Lett.* (1878) I. 61 The intellect is stilled, and the Emotions alone perform their . . . involuntary functions.

1875   Jowett *Plato* (ed. 2) I. 249 The . . . emotions of pity, wonder, sternness, stamped upon their countenances.

The original sense of 'emotion' is that of physical movement (cf. Harré and Gillett, 1994), such that the way the word has become associated with inner feelings would appear to be almost a historical recapitulation of Wittgenstein: felt emotions are the kinds of subjective experiences that have become descriptively associated with publicly described activities. The notion of a general class of 'emotions' as 'involuntary functions' of an inner mental life, conceptually distinguished from cognitive and volitional states, and 'stamped upon their countenances' coincides with the origins of psychology in the nineteenth century as a laboratory discipline founded in philosophical categories and the common-sense assumptions of contemporary linguistic usage.

Specific emotion words in English show a similar historical transformation, from overt social actions and public performances, to the inner life of the psyche.

[. . .]

It is important not to confuse a word's etymology with its current meaning. There is no suggestion that speakers of a language possess and use knowledge of its earlier history. Nevertheless, as Bakhtin (1981) has taught us, the past uses of a word leave residues in how it is currently used and understood, while the historical tracing of such meanings (even a study as casually performed as looking them up in an etymological dictionary) can be as informative as anthropological studies are in gaining a sense of cultural differences. Past meanings also bring the special bonus of looking 'developmentally' at how words for mental states might derive from situations of use with regard to public activities. According to Wittgensteinian and social constructionist perspectives on words, minds, and meanings, what we find in the etymological dictionary reflects an important principle of how all words, including mental process ones, come to mean things, and indeed are *learnable*. They are the coins of social exchange, used in the performance of social actions. It is only in and through that basic function that they can ever come to mean something ostensibly other than that, such as referring to a private, experiential, or personal subjectivity.

Cultural models, narrative, and rhetoric

In addition to historical perspectives, there is an extensive tradition of anthropological studies of emotion and emotion terms. (See Harré, 1986; Lutz and Abu-Lughod, 1990; and Shweder and Levine, 1984, for useful collections.) Catherine Lutz (1988, 1990) focuses on the 'emotion theories' of the Ifaluk people of Micronesia, in the Western Pacific. The notion that members of cultures possess 'theories' of how the world works, including an 'ethnopsychology' of persons and how they work, is a popular one in anthropology. Research on 'folk theories' examines how people talk about matters such as self, emotion, social relations, and the physical world, and constructs out of the patterns of that talk a coherent underlying cognitive model of local thought and social structure.

Lutz shows how the Ifaluk concept *song*, roughly translated as a kind of indignant and justified anger, functions within a hierarchically organized social life:

> . . . the everyday understanding of this emotion does not simply occur as a form of reflection on experience, but emerges as people justify and negotiate both cultural values and the prerogatives of power that some members of this society currently hold.
>
> (1990: 204)

Song expresses a moral judgment on another person's improper actions, generally when they have violated a social rule (such as against shouting aloud, spreading false rumours, or failing to share resources with others). Its very meaning is tied into, and reinforces, ideological patterns of power, obligation, and ownership: 'the direction in which "justifiable anger" flows is predominantly *down* the social scale' (1990: 218; original emphasis). *Song* is an emotion inseparable from the norms, expectations, and patterns of accountability of Ifaluk society; if you are not a member of that society, essentially you cannot have the emotion. In fact, it is part of a set of *inter-related* emotions specific to that culture, and the implication is that Western and other cultural patterns of emotions may be culturally systemic like that too, though we tend to think of them as basic, natural, and separate, merely because they are all we know.

For instance, *song* is an emotion Ifaluk people may express when something bad happens to a person for whom they feel *fago*, where *fago* is something like compassion, but not quite. It is felt for people who need help, or have suffered misfortune, and are socially subordinate, or are considered close to the kind of ideal Ifaluk sort of person – calm-natured and generous – so that, feeling *fago* for them, if something bad happens to them you feel *song*. Or you *should*, this being a moral or normative matter in Ifaluk society, just like English-speaking people are supposed to feel (or display) admiration, embarrassment, grief, or anger in some circumstances and not others.

The emotional interconnections multiply. Ifaluk people work to avoid the possibility of other people expressing *song* with regard to their conduct. But that work is undermined by displaying *ker* (a kind of excited happiness), in that *ker* conflicts with *metagu*, which is the sort of 'fear' that *song* properly elicits in those to whom it is applied. *Ker* is therefore subject to disapproval and moral condemnation, despite (from a Western point of view) its rough translation as 'happiness'. [. . .] Lutz's analysis provides an important insight into emotion terms as an interdependent set; one would probably have to understand *ker* and *metagu* (etc.) in order to experience *song*.

Lutz emphasizes the way *song* works as a description, as a word used on occasions of speaking. It is something people publicly *claim* to experience, and in doing so place a meaning on events that 'must be *negotiated* with the audience of such claims' (1990: 205; original emphasis). Thus for an Ifaluk person to display or report his or her *song* with regard to some state of affairs is to place a morally loaded construction on that state of affairs, and one that may be contested. Overt confrontation is nevertheless mostly avoided by means of a constant orientation to the possibility of *song*, such as when scarce resources are publicly evenly shared out: 'The daily anticipation of the "justifiable anger" of others is a fundamental regulator of the behaviour of individuals and a basic factor in the maintenance of the value of sharing' (1990: 211). This 'anticipation' of *song* is not merely Lutz's theory of underlying mental processes, but a feature of Ifaluk discourse in and of the events in question. Although the constellations of relationships and emotional alternatives are not the same, we can start to see a general parallel with the contentious, blaming, and mitigating business done by Jeff and Mary in their talk of emotions and events.

[. . .]

Lutz's ethnographic observations demonstrate the cultural workings of what we would call a discourse of the 'emotions': the use of verbal formulae for actions, feelings, and motives (our terms again), with regard to interpersonal judgements and attitudes, located within local moral orders of authority and responsibility. A key feature of emotion discourse is its deployment inside *narrative* and *rhetoric*. Emotion terms occur not merely as one-off descriptions of specific acts or reactions, but as parts of interrelated sets of terms that implicate each other in narrative sequences, and also in rhetorically potent contrasts between alternative descriptions. Narrative sequence and rhetorical contrast are *ways of talking* about things that perform social actions on the occasion of their production. Those social actions are discursive ones of a (by now) familiar kind: constructing the sense of events, orienting to normative and moral orders, to responsibility and blame, intentionality, and social evaluation. Emotion categories are not graspable merely as individual feelings or expressions, and nor is their discursive deployment reducible to a kind of detached, cognitive sense making. They are discursive phenomena and need to be studied as such, as part of how talk performs social actions.

[. . .]

Emotion metaphors as discursive resources

Emotion discourse includes not only terms such as *anger, surprise, fear,* and so on, but also a rich set of metaphors, such as 'boiling'. The notion of 'boiling' belongs to a set of anger metaphors, mainly to do with heat and internal pressure, that George Lakoff (1987) and Zoltan Kovecses (1986) have identified in American English, and which they trace to the emotion's bodily experience and physical manifestations. [. . .] Emotion metaphors can be considered *conceptual resources* that, where they occur in any language, whatever the metaphorical base, are available for discursive deployment. The concepts of anger as bodily heat, pressure, and agitation, for example, provide for a range of expressions such as (from Lakoff, 1987: 381–5): 'hot under the collar', 'burst a blood vessel', 'losing his cool', 'a heated argument', 'red with rage', 'hopping mad'. Then there are associations with distorted vision: 'blind with rage', 'see red', 'so mad I couldn't see straight'. Some metaphors are based on bodies imagined as strained containers: 'filled with anger', 'brimming with rage', 'bursting with anger', 'bottled up', 'outbursts', 'exploded'.

This is only a small part of anger's metaphorical thesaurus. But as well as raising questions about their conceptual origins, as Lakoff and Kovecses do, it is also useful to inquire into their discursive uses. The various metaphors are not equivalent and interchangeable, even those that are closely related, such that we should consider the grounds for choosing one rather than another, and what kinds of discursive business such choices may perform. Apart from heat, pressure, and container metaphors for anger, Lakoff (1987) lists madness, struggle, and dangerous animal metaphors. While it is possible to devise conceptual relationships between all these, they also have their own narrative implications and rhetorical uses. 'Contained heat' metaphors such as 'boiling with rage' are unlike wild animal metaphors such as 'bit her head off'. [. . .]

The point of all those alternative metaphorical expressions is, surely, to enable certain things to be *said* and not just *thought* (Edwards, 1991), such that the proliferation of metaphors may be motivated not only by their conceptual sense (as suggested by Gibbs, 1994; and Lakoff, 1987), but by what they allow us to say and do. [. . .]

Conclusions: emotion concepts and their rhetorical uses

[. . .]

It is possible to spell out a range of discursive resources concerning emotions, based on the examples and discussions in this chapter, in the form of a set of rhetorical positions and contrasts. These are not definitions of what emotion words 'mean', neither generally nor for individual words. Rather, they point to a range of things that emotion discourse can do, in everyday narrative and rhetoric (and, of course, in fiction), in discourses of events and accountability. They are not a definitive or discrete set. I am not proposing that there have to be ten of them, for instance, nor that they might be worked up into some kind of formal model. Their interrelatedness and flexibility are important features of how they work.

1 *Emotion versus cognition* – there is flexibility in how people's activities are described. Emotional descriptions are optional. We can formulate people's actions and words as expressions of their thoughts, their opinions, how they feel, and so on.

2 *Emotions as irrational versus rational* – emotions are not just irrational, they are an integral part of rational accountability; for example, the indignant anger of Ifaluk *song*.

3 *Emotion as cognitively grounded and/or cognitively consequential* – Ifaluk *song* implies prior cognitive assessments.

4 *Event-driven versus dispositional* –

5 *Dispositions versus temporary states* – Jeff's 'angry stage'.

6 Emotional behaviour as *controllable action or passive reaction* – the notion of emotions as 'feelings' that are 'expressed' or 'acted out' lends itself to a dichotomy between how someone felt and what he or she did about it; to the notion of controlling one's passions, and so on. Having emotional reactions can thus be split into how you unaccountably feel, and what you accountably do.

7 *Spontaneous versus externally caused* – 'spontaneous combustion . . .'; 'football induces anger . . .'. Note the marvellous flexibility here. The fact that emotions take intensional objects provides for ways of assigning causes: being angry *at* something can imply being angry *because* of it. But there is rhetorical scope for 'internal' and other causes to be induced: 'I can be . . . angry *at* little things *because* I am suffering from dyspepsia, where to know its object is not thereby to understand its cause' (Coulter, 1986: 129; original emphasis).

8 *Natural versus moral* – unconscious, automatic, bodily reactions versus social judgements; rather than these being parts of a comprehensive analysis of emotion terms, they can be selectively worked up and used.

9 *Internal states versus external behaviour: private* ('feelings') *versus public* ('expressions', 'displays') – a person's 'true' emotions can be those avowed on the basis of personal experience, as privileged reports from the inner life of the mind, or else ascriptions based on overt behaviour, which may be adduced to refute such avowals.

10 *Honest* (spontaneous, reactive) *versus faked*, artful, not 'true' – 'true lover'; 'self-belief masquerading as hatred'; 'sadness . . . but not the real thing'.

These sets of oppositions and contrasts are used discursively to construct (whether cooperatively or contentiously) the sense of events and their causes, and (thereby) to manage accountability. They may be used in various combinations. For example, the public–private dichotomy may be used in relation to active–passive and honest–fake. Thus, 'true' emotions may be those avowed from private experience, denying any impression based on superficial appearances. But such confessions might also be treated as fake, on the grounds that they contrast with actions (which can speak louder than words); or again, actions may be treated as insincere when they conflict with (ascribed) inner feelings.
[. . .]
It is a principle of ethnological and experimental studies of non-verbal communication (Argyle, 1988) that emotions are matters of public display, part of a rich interchange of verbal expressions and bodily signals. An interesting feature of studying situated discourse is that this notion of 'public display' may occur as a participant's descriptive category and interactional concern, rather than just what emotional life happens to be like. We see this in how people in relationship disputes claim to know each other's real feelings. A person's emotions can be treated discursively as private experiences, or as *anything but* his or her own private domain, and may even be strongly contrasted with cognition and language in this respect, such as in the popular idea that you can keep your thoughts to yourself, but not so easily your emotions.
What Buttny (1993: 88) calls a 'folk logic of affect' – experiences that happen to us beyond our control, and, thereby, prevent or inhibit adequate performance – is not so consistent and worked out as the term 'logic' implies. It might better be called a folk *rhetoric*. People may blame themselves, and be blamed, for having emotions, for 'expressing' them and for not expressing them, for not 'controlling' them or being too much in control, or for being emotionally

insincere. Emotions can be distinguished from their expression or control, and people can exploit their privacy and do things with 'confession'. The conceptual resources concerning emotions that are available for emotion discourse permit much more indexical and rhetorical variation than is implied by notions such as folk logic, folk theory, conceptual models, cognitive scenarios, and such. It is precisely because people's emotion displays can be treated either as involuntary reactions, or as under agentive control or rational accountability, that emotion discourse can perform flexible, accountability-oriented, rhetorical work. These are just the sorts of conceptual resources that people require for doing talk's business – inconsistent, contradictory, fuzzy, to-be-indexically-specified, rather than some kind of coherent cognitive model of the emotions.

It is a futile psychological enterprise to work up these conceptual resources into competing hypotheses about the true nature of emotional life and seek to choose between them. That misses the point of how all these fuzzy, overlapping, and contrastive resources are like that precisely so they can be put to work in locally specified ways, in situated talk. A discursive psychology of the emotions must try to examine, conceptually and empirically, the nature and uses of emotion discourse, rather than imagining that it adds up to something that could be called a folk theory, as if capable in some way of being not a very good one, and waiting to be improved on by professional psychology. From the perspective of discursive psychology, emotion talk is part of how people live their lives, rather than some kind of abstracted amateur theorizing. They cannot be 'wrong' about it, they can only do it differently.

[. . .]

References

Argyle, M. (1988) *Bodily Communication*, 2nd Edn., London, Routledge.

Bakhtin, M.M. (1981) *The Dialogic Imagination*, Austin, TX, University of Texas Press.

Buttny, R. (1993) *Social Accountability in Communication*, London, Sage.

Coulter, J. (1979). *The Social Construction of Mind: Studies in Ethnomethodology and Linguistic Philosophy*, London, Macmillan.

Coulter, J. (1986) 'Affect and social context: emotion definition as a social task' in R. Harré (ed.) *The Social Construction of Emotions*, Oxford, Blackwell.

Edwards, D. (1991) 'Categories are for talking: on the cognitive and discursive bases of categorization', *Theory and Psychology*, vol. 1, pp. 515–42.

Gergen, K.J. (1995) 'Metaphor and monophony in the 20th-century psychology of emotions' *History of the Human Sciences*, vol. 8, pp. 1–23.

Gibbs, R.W. (1994) *The Poetics of Mind: Figurative Thought, Language and Understanding*, Cambridge, Cambridge University Press.

Gillis, J.R. (1988) 'From ritual to romance' in C.Z. Stearns and P.W. Stearns (eds) *Emotions and Social Change: Towards a New Psychohistory*, New York, Holmes and Meier.

Harré, R. (1983) *Personal Being: a Theory for Individual Psychology*, Oxford, Blackwell.

Harré, R. (ed.) (1986) *The Social Construction of Emotions*, Oxford, Blackwell.

Harré, R. and Gillett, G. (1994) *The Discursive Mind*, London, Sage.

Kovecses, Z. (1986) *Metaphors of Anger, Pride, and Love*, Philadelphia, John Benjamins.

Lakoff, G. (1987) *Women, Fire and Dangerous Things: What Categories Reveal about the Mind*, Chicago, University of Chicago Press.

Lutz, C.A. (1988) *Unnatural Emotions: Everyday Sentiments on a Micronesian Atoll and Their Challenge to Western Theory*, Chicago, University of Chicago Press.

Lutz, C.A. (1990) 'Morality, domination and understandings of "justifiable" anger among the Ifaluk' in

G.R. Semin and K.J. Gergen (eds) *Everyday Understanding: Social and Scientific Implications*, London, Sage.

Lutz, C.A. and Abu-Lughod, L. (eds) (1990) *Language and the Politics of Emotion*, Cambridge, Cambridge University Press.

Oxford English Dictionary (1994) 2nd Edn on CD-ROM, Oxford, Oxford University Press.

Shweder, R.A. and Bourne, E.J. (1984) 'Does the concept of the person vary cross-culturally?' in R.A. Shweder and R. Levine (eds) *Culture Theory: Essays on Mind. Self and Emotion*, Cambridge, Cambridge University Press.

Stearns, C.Z. and Stearns, P.N. (eds) (1988) *Emotions and Social Change: Towards a New Psychohistory*, New York, Holmes and Meier.

Wenzel, S. (1960) *The Sin of Sloth: Acedia in Medieval Thought and Literature*, Chapel Hill, NC, University of North Carolina Press.

Self-Narration in Social Life

Kenneth Gergen

Source: Gergen, K.J. (1994) *Realities and Relationships: Soundings in Social Construction*, Cambridge, Mass., Harvard University Press, Chapter 8.

Enriching the range of theoretical discourse with the particular hope of expanding the potential for human practices is one of the central challenges for constructionist scholarship. One of the most inviting theoretical departures, because of its affinity with constructionist metatheory, arises from relational theory, the attempt to account for human action in terms of relational process. It attempts to move beyond the single individual to acknowledge the reality of relationship. Here, I want to propose a relational view of self-conception, one that views self-conception not as an individual's personal and private cognitive structure but as *discourse* about the self – the performance of languages available in the public sphere. I replace the traditional concern with conceptual categories (self-concepts, schemas, self-esteem), with the self as a narration rendered intelligible within ongoing relationships.

This, then, is a story about stories – and most particularly, stories of the self. Most of us begin our encounters with stories in childhood. Through fairy tales, folktales, and family stories we receive our first organized accounts of human action. Stories continue to absorb us as we read novels, biography, and history; they occupy us at the movies, at the theater, and before the television set. And, possibly because of this intimate and long-standing acquaintanceship, stories also serve as a critical means by which we make ourselves intelligible within the social world. We tell extended stories about our childhoods, our relations with family members, our years at school, our first love affair, the development of our thinking on a given subject, and so on. We also tell stories about last night's party, this morning's crisis, or lunch with a companion. We may even create a story about a near collision on the way to work or about scorching last night's dinner. In each case, we use the story form to identify ourselves to others and to ourselves. [. . .]

Yet, to say that we use stories to make ourselves comprehensible does not go far enough. Not only do we tell our lives as stories; there is also a significant sense in which our relationships with each other are lived out in narrative form. For White and Epston (1990), 'persons give meaning to their lives and relationships by *storying* their experience' (p. 13). The ideal life, Nietzsche proposed, is one that corresponds to the ideal story; each act is coherently related to all others with nothing to spare (Nehamas, 1985). More cogently, Hardy (1968) has written that 'we dream in narrative, daydream in narrative, remember, anticipate, hope, despair, believe, doubt, plan, revise, criticize, construct, gossip, learn, hate and love by narrative' (p. 5). Elaborating on this view, MacIntyre (1981) proposes that enacted narratives form the basis of moral character. My analysis will stop short of saying that lives *are* narrative events (in agreement with Mink, 1969). Stories are, after all, forms of accounting, and it seems misleading to equate the account with its putative object. However, narrative accounts are embedded within social action; they render events socially visible and typically establish expectations for future events. Because the events of daily life are immersed in narrative, they become laden with a storied sense: they acquire the reality of 'a beginning', 'a low point', 'a climax', 'an ending', and so on. People live out the events in this way and, along with others, they index them in just this way. This is not to say that life copies art, but rather, that art becomes the vehicle through which the reality of life is made manifest. In a significant sense, then, we live by stories – both in the telling and the realizing of the self.

[. . .]

The character of self-narrative

[. . .] For our purposes here, the term 'self-narrative' will refer to an individual's account of the relationship among self-relevant events across time. In developing a self-narrative we establish coherent connections among life events (Cohler, 1982; Kohli, 1981). Rather than see our life as simply 'one damned thing after another', we formulate a story in which life events are systematically related, rendered intelligible by their place in a sequence or 'unfolding process' (de Waele and Harré, 1976). Our present identity is thus not a sudden and mysterious event but a sensible result of a life story. [. . .]

Before embarking on this analysis I must say a word about the relationship between the concept of self-narrative and related theoretical notions. The concept of self-narrative in particular bears an affinity with a variety of constructs developed in other domains. First, in *cognitive psychology* the concepts of scripts (Schank and Abelson, 1977), story schema (Mandler, 1984), predictability tree (Kelly and Keil, 1985), and narrative thought (Britton and Pellegrini, 1990) have all been used to account for the psychological basis for understanding and/or directing sequences of action across time. In contrast to the cognitive program, with its search for universal cognitive processes, *rule-role* theorists (such as Harré and Secord, 1972) and *constructivists* (see, for example, Mancuso and Sarbin's [1983] treatment of 'narrative grammar') tend to emphasize the cultural contingency of various psychological states. Thus, the cognitivist's presumption of a narrative base of personal action is retained but with a greater sensitivity to the sociocultural basis of such narratives. Bruner's (1986, 1990) work on narratives falls somewhere between these two orientations, holding to a view of universal cognitive function while simultaneously placing strong emphasis on cultural meaning systems. *Phenomenologists* (see Carr, 1984; Josselson and Lieblich, 1993; Polkinghorne, 1988), *existentialists* (see Charme's [1984] analysis of Sartre), and *personologists* (McAdams, 1993) are also concerned with individual internal process (often indexed as 'experience') but typically eschew the cognitivist search for predication and control of individual behavior and replace the emphasis on cultural determination with a more humanistic investment in the self as author or agent.

In contrast to all these approaches, which place their major emphasis on the individual, I wish to consider self-narratives as forms of social accounting or public discourse. In this sense, narratives are conversational resources, constructions open to continuous alteration as interaction progresses. Persons in this case do not consult an internal script, cognitive structure, or apperceptive mass for information or guidance; they do not interpret or 'read the world' through narrative lenses; they do not author their own lives. Rather, the self-narrative is a linguistic implement embedded within conventional sequences of action and employed in relationships in such a way as to sustain, enhance, or impede various forms of action. As linguistic devices, narratives may be used to indicate future actions, but they are not themselves the cause or determinant basis for such actions. In this sense, self-narratives function much like oral histories or morality tales within a society. They are cultural resources that serve such social purposes as self-identification, self-justification, self-criticism, and social solidification. This approach joins with those that emphasize the sociocultural origins of narrative construction, though it is not intended to endorse a cultural determinism – it is through *interacting* with others that we acquire narrative skills, not through being acted upon. It also agrees with those concerned with personal engagement in narrative, but it replaces the emphasis on the self-determining ego with social interchange.

Scholars concerned with narratives are sharply divided on the issue of truth value: many hold that narratives have the potential to bear truth, while others argue that narratives do not reflect but construct reality. [. . .] Both in science and in daily life, the stories serve as communal resources that people use in ongoing relationships. From this standpoint narratives do not reflect so much as they create the sense of 'what is true'. Indeed, it is largely because of existing narrative forms that 'telling the truth' is an intelligible act. The special ways in which this is so will be further amplified in the following pages.

The structuring of narrative accounts

If narratives are demanded neither by cognition nor the world as it is, then what account can be given of their properties or forms? From the constructionist standpoint, the properties of well-formed narratives are culturally and historically situated. They are byproducts of people's attempts to relate through discourse, in much the same way that styles of painting serve as a means of mutual co-ordination within communities of artists or specific tactics and countertactics become fashionable within various sports. [. . .]

It is interesting in this context to inquire into contemporary narrative conventions. What are the requirements for telling an intelligible story within the present-day culture of the West? The question is particularly significant, since an elucidation of these conventions for structuring stories sensitizes us to the limits of self-identity. To understand how narratives must be structured within the culture is to press against the edges of identity's envelope – to discover the limits to identifying oneself as a human agent in good standing; it is also to determine what forms must be maintained in order to acquire credibility as a teller of truth. The structure of proper storytelling precedes the events about which 'truth is told'; to go beyond the conventions is to engage in an idiot's tale. If the narrative fails to approximate conventional forms, the telling becomes nonsensical. Thus, rather than being driven by facts truth telling is largely governed by a forestructure of narrative conventions.

[. . .]

The following criteria in particular appear to be central in constructing a narrative intelligible to significant segments of contemporary culture:

Establishing a valued endpoint

An acceptable story must first establish a goal, an event to be explained, a state to be reached or avoided, an outcome of significance or, more informally, a 'point'. To relate that one walked north for two blocks, east for three, and then turned left on Pine Street would constitute an impoverished story, but if this description were a prelude to finding an affordable apartment, it would approximate an acceptable story. The selected endpoint is typically saturated with value: it is understood to be desirable or undesirable. The endpoint may, for example, be the protagonist's well-being ('how I narrowly escaped death'), the discovery of something precious ('how he discovered his biological father'), personal loss ('how she lost her job'), and so on. Thus, if the story terminated on finding 404 Pine Street, it would lapse into insignificance. It is only when the search for a much-desired apartment is successful that we have a good story. In a related vein, MacIntyre (1981) proposes that 'narrative requires an evaluative framework in which good or bad character helps to produce unfortunate or happy outcomes' (p. 456). It is also clear that this demand for a valued endpoint introduces a strong cultural component (traditionally called 'subjective bias') into the story. Life itself could hardly be said to be composed of separable events, a subpopulation of which constitute endpoints. Rather, the articulation of an event and its position as an endpoint are derived from the culture's ontology and construction of value. Through verbal artistry, 'the brushing of her fingers on my sleeve' emerges as an event, and depending on the story, may serve as the beginning of or the conclusion to a romance. In addition, events as we define them do not contain intrinsic value. Fire in itself is neither good nor bad; we invest it with value depending generally on whether it serves what we take to be valuable functions (cooking food) or not (destroying the kitchen). Only within a cultural perspective can 'valued events' be made intelligible.

Selecting events relevant to the endpoint

Once an endpoint has been established it more or less dictates the kinds of events that can figure in the account, thus greatly reducing the myriad candidates for 'eventhood'. An intelligible story is one in which events serve to make the goal more or less probable, accessible, important, or vivid. Thus, if a story is about winning a soccer match ('how we won the game'), the most relevant events are those that bring that goal closer or make it more distant ('Tom's first kick bounced off the goal, but on the next attack he deflected the ball into the net with the twist of his head'). Only at the risk of inanity would one introduce a note on fifteenth-century monastic life or a hope for future space travel unless it could be shown that such matters were significantly related to winning the match ('Juan got his inspiration for the tactic from reading about fifteenth-century religious practices'). An account of the day ('It was crisp and sunny') would be acceptable in the narrative, since it makes the events more vivid, but a description of the weather in some remote country would seem idiosyncratic. Again we find that narrative demands have ontological consequences. One is not free to include all that takes place, but only that which is relevant to the story's conclusion.

The ordering of events

Once a goal has been established and relevant events selected, the events are usually placed in an ordered arrangement. As Ong (1982) indicates, the bases for such order (importance, interest value, timeliness, and so on) may change with history. The most widely used contemporary convention is perhaps that of a linear, temporal sequence. Certain events, for example, are said to occur at the beginning of the football match, and these precede the events that are said to take place toward the middle and at the end. It is tempting to say that the sequence of related events should match the actual sequence in which the events occurred, but this would be to confuse the rules of an intelligible rendering with what is indeed the case. Linear temporal ordering is, after all, a convention that employs an internally coherent system of signs; its features are not required by the world as it is. It may be applied to what is the case or not depending on one's purposes. Clock time may not be effective if one wishes to speak of one's 'experience of time passing in the dentist's chair', nor is it adequate if one wishes to describe relativity theory in physics or the circular rotation of seasons. In Bakhtin's (1981) terms, we may view temporal accounts as *chronotopes* – literary conventions governing space–time relationships or 'the ground essential for the . . . representability of events' (p. 250). That yesterday preceded today is a conclusion demanded only by a culturally specific chronotope.

Stability of identity

The well-formed narrative is typically one in which the characters (or objects) in the story possess a continuous or coherent identity across time. A given protagonist cannot felicitously serve as a villain at one moment and a hero in the next or demonstrate powers of genius unpredictably interspersed with moronic actions. Once defined by the storyteller, the individual (or object) will tend to retain its identity or function within the story. There are obvious exceptions to this general tendency, but most are cases in which the story attempts to explain the change itself – how the frog became a prince or the impoverished young man achieved financial success. Causal forces (such as war, poverty, education) may be introduced that bring about change in an individual (or object), and for dramatic effect a putative identity may give way to 'the real' (a trustworthy professor may turn out to be an arsonist). In general, however, the well-formed story does not tolerate protean personalities.

Causal linkages

By contemporary standards the ideal narrative is one that provides an explanation for the outcome. As it is said, 'The king died and then the queen died' is but a rudimentary story; 'The king died and then the queen died of grief' is the beginning of a veritable plot. As Ricoeur (1981) puts it, 'Explanations must . . . be woven into the narrative tissue' (p. 278). Explanation is typically achieved by selecting events that are by common standards causally linked. Each event should be a product of that which has preceded it ('Because the rain came we fled indoors'; 'As a result of his operation he couldn't meet his class'). This is not to presume that a universal conception of causality is insinuated into all well-formed stories: what may be included within the acceptable range of causal forms is historically and culturally dependent. Many scientists thus wish to limit discussions of causality to the Humean variety; social philosophers often prefer to see reason as the cause of human action; botanists often find it more convenient to employ teleological forms of causality. Regardless of one's preference in causal models, when events within a narrative are related in an interdependent fashion, the outcome approximates more closely the well-formed story.

Demarcation signs

Most properly formed stories employ signals to indicate the beginning and the end. As Young (1982) has proposed, the narrative is 'framed' by various rule-governed devices that indicate when one is entering the 'tale world', or the world of the story. 'Once upon a time . . .', 'Did you hear the one about . . .', 'You can't imagine what happened to me on the way over here . . .', or 'Let me tell you why I'm so happy . . .' would all signal the audience that a narrative is to follow. Endings may also be signalled by phrases ('That's it . . .', 'So now you know . . .') but need not be. Laughter at the end of a joke may indicate the exit from the tale world, and often the description of the story's point is sufficient to indicate that the tale world is terminated.

While in many contexts these criteria are essential to the well-formed narrative, it is important to note their cultural and historical contingency. As Mary Gergen's (1992) explorations of autobiography suggest, men are far more likely to accommodate themselves to the prevailing criteria for 'proper storytelling' than women. Women's autobiographies are more likely to be structured around multiple endpoints and to include materials unrelated to any particular endpoint. With the modernist explosion in literary experimentation, the demand for well-formed narratives in serious fiction has also diminished. In postmodern writing narratives may turn ironically self-referential, demonstrating their own artifice as texts and the ways in which their efficacy depends on still other narratives (Dipple, 1988).

Does it matter whether narratives are well formed in matters of daily living? As we have seen, the use of narrative components would appear to be vital in creating a sense of reality in accounts of self. As Rosenwald and Ochberg (1992) put it, 'How individuals recount their histories – what they emphasize and omit, their stance as protagonists or victims, the relationship the story establishes between teller and audience – all shape what individuals can claim of their own lives. Personal stories are not merely a way of telling someone (or oneself) about one's life; they are the means by which identities may be fashioned' (p. 1). The social utility of well-formed narrative is more concretely revealed in research on courtroom testimony. In *Reconstructing Reality in the Courtroom*, Bennett and Feldman (1981) subjected research participants to forty-seven testimonies that either attempted to recall actual events or were fictional contrivances. Although ratings of the stories revealed that the participants were unable to discriminate between the genuine and fictional accounts, an analysis of those accounts believed to be genuine as opposed to false proved interesting: participants made their judgements largely according to the approximation of the stories to well-formed narratives. Stories believed to be genuine were those in which events relevant to the endpoint were dominant and causal linkages among elements more numerous. In further research, Lippman (1986) experimentally varied the extent to which courtroom testimonies demonstrated the selection of events relevant to an endpoint, the causal linkages between one event and another, and the diachronic ordering of events. Testimonies that approximated the well-formed narrative in these ways were consistently found to be more intelligible and the witnesses to be more rational. Thus, the self-narratives of daily life may not always be well formed, but under certain circumstances their structure may be essential.

Varieties of narrative form

By using these narrative conventions we generate a sense of coherence and direction in our lives. They acquire meaning, and what happens is suffused with significance. Certain forms of narrative are broadly shared within the culture; they are frequently used, easily identified, and highly functional. In a sense, they constitute a syllabary of possible selves. What account can be given of these more stereotypic narratives? The question here is similar to that concerning fundamental plot lines. Since Aristotelian times philosophers and literary theorists, among others, have attempted to develop a formal vocabulary of plot. As is sometimes argued, there may be a foundational set of plots from which all stories are derived. To the extent that people live through narrative, a foundational family of plots would place a limit on the range of life trajectories.
   [. . .]
   As we have seen, a story's endpoint is weighted with value. Thus a victory, a consummated affair, a discovered fortune, or a prizewinning paper can all serve as proper story endings, while on the opposite pole of the evaluative continuum would fall a defeat, a lost love, and a squandered fortune, or a professional failure. We can view the various events that lead up to the story's end (the selection and ordering of events) as moving through two-dimensional, evaluative space. As one approaches the valued goal over time the storyline becomes more positive; as one approaches failure or disillusionment one moves in a negative direction. All plots, then, can be converted to a linear form in terms of their evaluative shifts over time. This allows us to isolate three rudimentary forms of narrative.
   The first may be described as a *stability narrative*, that is, one that links events so that the individual's trajectory remains essentially unchanged in relation to a goal or outcome; life simply goes on, neither better nor worse. The stability narrative could be developed at any level along the evaluative continuum. At the upper end an individual might conclude, for example, 'I am still as attractive as I used to be', or at the lower end, 'I continue to be haunted by feelings of failure.' As we can also see, each of these narrative summaries possesses inherent implications for the future: in the former, the individual might conclude that he or she will continue to be attractive for the foreseeable future, and in the latter, that feelings of failure will persist regardless of circumstance.

The stability narrative may be contrasted with two others, the *progressive narrative*, which links together events so that the movement along the evaluative dimension over time is incremental, and the *regressive narrative*, in which movement is decremental. The progressive narrative is the Panglossian account of life – ever better in every way. It could be represented by the statement, 'I am really learning to overcome my shyness and be more open and friendly with people.' The regressive narrative, in contrast, depicts a continued downward slide: 'I can't seem to control the events in my life anymore. It's been one series of catastrophes after another.' Each of these narratives also implies directionality, the former anticipating further increments and the latter further decrements.

As should be clear, these three narrative forms, stability, progressive, and regressive, exhaust the fundamental options for the direction of movement in evaluative space. As such, they may be considered rudimentary bases for other more complex variants. Theoretically one may envision a potential infinity of variations on these simple forms. However, in various historical conditions the culture may limit itself to a truncated repertoire of possibilities. Let us consider several prominent narrative forms in contemporary culture. There is first the *tragic narrative*. The tragedy, in this sense, would tell the story of the rapid downfall of one who had achieved high position: a progressive narrative is followed by a rapid regressive narrative. In contrast, in the *comedy-romance*, a regressive narrative is followed by a progressive narrative. Life events become increasingly problematic until the denouement, when happiness is restored to the major protagonists. This narrative is labelled comedy-romance because it conflates the Aristotelian forms. If a progressive narrative is followed by a stability narrative, we have what is commonly known as the *happily-ever-after myth*, which is widely exemplified in traditional courtship. And we also recognize the *heroic saga* as a series of progressive–regressive phases. In this case, the individual may characterize his or her past as a continuous array of battles against the powers of darkness. [. . .]

Narrative form in two populations: an application

As I pointed out, in order to maintain intelligibility in the culture, the story one tells about oneself must employ the commonly accepted rules of narrative construction. Narrative constructions of broad cultural usage form a set of ready-made intelligibilities; in effect, they offer a range of discursive resources for the social construction of the self. At first glance it would appear that narrative forms do not impose such constraints. Theoretically, as our analysis makes clear, the number of potential story forms approaches infinity. At the same time, it is also clear that there is a certain degree of agreement among analysts in Western culture, from Aristotle to the present, suggesting that certain story forms are more readily employed than others; in this sense, forms of self-narrative may likewise be constrained. Consider the person who characterizes him or herself by means of a stability narrative: life is directionless; it is merely moving in a steady, monotonous fashion neither toward nor away from a goal. Such a person would seem an apt candidate for psychotherapy. Similarly, one who characterizes his or her life as a repetitive pattern in which each positive occurrence is immediately followed by a negative one, and vice versa, would be regarded with suspicion.

We simply do not accept such life stories as approximating reality. In contrast, if one could make sense of one's life today as the result of 'a long struggle upward', a 'tragic decline', or a continuing saga in which one suffers defeats but rises from the ashes to achieve success, we are fully prepared to believe. One is not free to have simply any form of personal history. Narrative conventions do not, then, command identity, but they do invite certain actions and discourage others.

In this light it is interesting to explore how various American subcultures characterize their life histories. Let us consider two contrasting populations: adolescents and the elderly. In the former case, twenty-nine youths between the ages of nineteen and twenty-one were asked to chart their life history along a general evaluative dimension (Gergen and Gergen, 1988). Drawing on recollections from their earliest years to the present, how would they characterize their state of general well-being? The characterizations were to be made with a single 'life line' in a two-dimensional space. The most positive periods of their history were to be represented by an upward displacement of the line, the negative periods by a downward displacement. What graphic forms might these self-characterizations take? Do young adults generally portray themselves as part of a happily-ever-after story, a heroic saga in which they overcome one peril after another? More pessimistically, does life appear to be growing ever bleaker after the initially happy years of childhood? [. . .] The results show the general narrative form employed by this group of young adults is unlike any of those conjectured above; it is, rather, that of the comedy-romance. On the average, these young adults tended to view their lives as happy at an early age, beset with difficulty during the adolescent years, but now on an upward swing that bodes well for the future. They have confronted the tribulations of adolescence and emerged victorious.

In these accounts there is a sense in which the narrative form largely dictates memory. Life events don't seem to influence the selection of the story form; to a large degree it is the narrative form that sets the grounds for which events count as important. Let us consider the content through which these adolescents justified the use of the comedy-romance. They were asked to describe the events occurring at the most positive and the most negative periods on their life line. The content of these events proved highly diverse. The positive events included success in a school play, experiences with friends, owning a pet, and discovering music, while low periods resulted from such wide-ranging experiences as moving to a new town, failing at school, having parents with marital problems, and losing a friend. In effect, the 'adolescent crisis' does not appear to reflect any single objective factor. Instead, the participants seem to have used the available narrative form and employed whatever 'facts' they could to justify and vivify their selection.

More generally, it seems that when the typical young adult describes his or her life history in brief for an anonymous audience, it approximates the narrative form of what I described as the typical television drama (comedy-romance). An informative contrast to this preference is supplied by a sample of seventy-two persons ranging in age from sixty-three to ninety-three years (M. Gergen 1980). In this case, each respondent was interviewed about his or her life experiences. Respondents were asked to describe their general sense of well-being during various periods of life: when were the happiest days, why did things change, in what direction is life now progressing, and so on. These responses were coded so that the results were comparable to the young adult sample. The typical narrative of the older person follows the shape of a rainbow: the young adult years were difficult, but a progressive narrative enabled the achievement of a peak of well-being somewhere between the ages of fifty and sixty. Life since these 'golden years', however, has been on a downward trajectory. Aging is depicted as a regressive narrative.

Such results may seem reasonable, reflecting the natural physical decline in aging. But narratives are not the products of life itself, they are constructions of life – and they could be otherwise. 'Aging as decline' is but a cultural convention and so is subject to change. It is at this point that we must also question the role of the social sciences in fostering the view that the life course is a rainbow. The psychological literature is replete with factual accounts of early 'development' and late 'decline' (Gergen and Gergen, 1988). To the extent that such views make their way into public consciousness, they give the elderly little sense of hope or optimism. Different views of what is important in aging – such as those that have been adopted in many Asian cultures – would allow social scientists to articulate far more positive and enabling possibilities. [. . .]

Multiplicity in narration

[. . .]

The traditional view of self-conception presumes a core identity, an integrally coherent view of the self against which one can gauge whether actions are authentic or artificial. As it is said, an individual without a sense of core identity is without direction, without a sense of position or place, lacking the fundamental assurance that he or she is a worthy person. My argument here, however, throws all such assumptions into question. How often does one compare actions with some core image, for example, and why should we believe that there is but a single and enduring core? Why must one value a fixed sense of position or place and how often does one question one's worthiness? By shifting the emphasis from internal self-perceptions to the process of social intelligibility we can open new theoretical domains with different consequences for cultural life. Thus, even though it is common practice to view each person as possessing 'a life story', if selves are realized within social encounters there is good reason to believe that there is no *one* story to tell. Our common participation in the culture will typically expose us to a wide variety of narrative forms, from the rudimentary to the complex. We enter relationships with the potential to use any of a wide number of forms. Just as an experienced skier approaching an incline has a variety of techniques for an effective descent, so we can construct the relationship among our life experiences in a variety of ways. At a minimum, effective socialization should equip us to interpret our lives as stable, as improving, or as in decline. And with a little additional training, we can develop the capacity to envision our lives as tragedy, comedy, or heroic saga (see also Mancuso and Sarbin, 1983 on 'second-order selves' and Gubrium, Holstein, and Buckholdt, 1994 on multiple constructions of the life course). The more capable we are in constructing and reconstructing our self-narrative, the more broadly capable we are in effective relationships.

To illustrate this multiplicity, research participants were asked to draw graphs indicating their feelings of satisfaction in their relationships with their mother, their father, and their academic work over the years. These graph lines pose a striking contrast to the 'generalized well-being' account depicted earlier. There, the students portrayed their general life course as a comedy-romance – a positive childhood followed by an adolescent fall from grace and capped by a positive ascent. However, in the case of their father and their mother, participants tended most frequently to select progressive narratives – slow and continuous for the father but more sharply accelerated more recently for the mother. For both parents, they portrayed their relationships as steadily improving. Yet, although they were attending a highly competitive college, the students tended to depict their feeling of satisfaction with their academic work as one of steady decline – a regressive narrative that left them on the brink of despair in the present.

[. . .]

The interknitting of identities

In this chapter I have attempted to develop a view of narration as a discursive resource and of its richness and potentials as constituting a historical legacy available in varying degree to all within the culture. To possess an intelligible self – a recognizable being with both a past and a future, requires a borrowing from the cultural repository. In Bakhtin's (1981) sense, to be an intelligible person requires an act of *ventriloquation*. However, as developed here, there is also a strong emphasis on ongoing interchange. Narration may appear to be monologic, but its success in establishing identity will inevitably rely on dialogue. It is in this context that I wish finally to draw attention to ways in which narrated identities are interwoven within the culture. It is particularly useful to touch on self-narration and moral community, interminable negotiation, and reciprocal identities.

As I have suggested, self-narratives are immersed within processes of ongoing interchange. In a broad sense they serve to unite the past with the present and to signify future trajectories (Csikszentmihalyi and Beattie, 1979). It is their significance for the future that is of special interest here, because it sets the stage for moral evaluation. To maintain that one has always been an honest person (stability narrative) suggests that one can be trusted. To construct one's past as a success story (progressive narrative) implies a future of continued advancement. On the other hand, to portray oneself as losing one's abilities because of increasing age (regressive narrative) generates the expectation that one will be less energetic in the future. The important point here is that as these implications are realized in action they become subject to social appraisal. Others may find the actions and outcomes implied by these narratives (according to current conventions) coherent with or contradictory to the tellings. To the extent that such actions conflict with these accounts, they cast doubt on their validity, and social censure may result. In MacIntyre's (1981) terms, in matters of moral deliberation, 'I can only answer the question "What am I to do?" if I can answer the prior question "Of what story or stories do I find myself a part?"' (p. 201). What this means is that self-narrative is not simply a derivative of past encounters, reassembled within ongoing relationships; once used, it establishes the grounds for moral being within the community. It establishes reputation, and it is the community of reputations that form the core of a moral tradition. In effect, the performance of self-narrative secures a relational future.

[. . .]

This continuing negotiation of narrative identity is complicated by a final relational feature. So far I have treated narratives as if they were solely concerned with the temporal trajectory of the protagonist alone. This conception must be expanded. The incidents typically woven into a narrative are the actions not only of the protagonist but of others as well. In most instances the actions of others contribute vitally to the events linked in narrative sequence. For example, to justify his account of continuing honesty, an individual might describe how a friend unsuccessfully tempted him to cheat; to illustrate achievement, he might show how another person was vanquished in a competition; in speaking of lost capabilities he might point to the alacrity of a younger person's performance. In all cases, the actions of others become an integral part of narrative intelligibility. In this sense, constructions of the self require a supporting cast.

The implications of this need for context are broad indeed. First, in the same way that individuals usually command the privilege of self-definition ('I know myself better than others know me'), others also demand rights in defining their own actions. Thus, as one uses the actions of others to make oneself intelligible, one becomes reliant on their accord. In the simplest case, if the other is present, no account of one's actions can stand without the agreement that 'Yes, that's how it was.' If others are not willing to accede to their assigned parts, then one cannot rely on their actions within a narrative. If others fail to see their actions as 'offering temptation', the actor can scarcely boast of continued strong character; if others can show that they were not really vanquished in a competition, the actor can scarcely use the episode as a stepping-stone in a success story. Narrative validity, then, depends strongly on the affirmation of others.

This reliance on others places the actor in a position of precarious interdependence, for in the same way that self-intelligibility depends on whether others agree about their own place in the story, so their own identity depends on the actor's affirmation of them. An actor's success in sustaining a given self-narrative is fundamentally dependent on the willingness of others to play out certain pasts in relationship to him. In Schapp's (1976) terms, each of us is 'knitted into' the historical constructions of others just as they are into ours. As this delicate interdependence of constructed narratives suggests, a fundamental aspect of social life is the *network of reciprocating identities*. Because one's identity can be maintained for only so long as others play their proper supporting role, and because one is required in turn to play supporting roles in their constructions, the moment any participant chooses to renege, he or she threatens the array of interdependent constructions.

An adolescent may tell his mother that she has been a 'bad mother', thus potentially destroying her stability narrative as a 'good mother'. At the same time, however, he risks having his mother reply that she always felt his character was so inferior, he never merited her love; his continuing narrative of 'self as good' is thus in jeopardy. A lover may announce to her male partner that he no longer interests her as he once did, thus potentially crushing his stability narrative; however, he may reply that he has long been bored with her and is happy to be relieved of his lover's role. In such instances, when the parties in the relationship pull out of their supporting roles, the result is a general degeneration of identities. Identities, in this sense, are never individual; each is suspended in an array of precariously situated relationships. The reverberations of what takes place here and now – between us – may be infinite.

References

Bakhtin, M. (1981) *The Dialogic Imagination*, Austin, Texas, University of Texas Press.
Bennett, W.L. and Feldman, M.S. (1981) *Reconstructing Reality in the Courtroom*, New Brunswick, NJ., Rutgers University Press.
Britton, B.K. and Pellegrini, A.D. (eds) (1990) *Narrative Thought and Narrative Language*, Hillsdale, NJ., Erlbaum.
Bruner, J. (1986) *Actual Minds, Possible Worlds*, Cambridge, Harvard University Press.
Bruner, J. (1990) *Acts of Meaning*, Cambridge, Harvard University Press.
Carr, D. (1984) *Time, Narrative and History*, Bloomington, Indiana University Press.
Charme, S.L. (1984) *Meaning and Myth in the Study of Lives: A Sartrean Perspective*, Philadelphia, University of Pennsylvania Press.
Cohler, B.J. (1982) 'Personal narrative and the life-course' in P. Battles and O.G. Brim (eds) *Life-span Development and Behavior*, New York, Academic Press.
Csikszentmihalyi, M., and Beattie, O. (1979) 'Life themes: a theoretical and empirical explanation of their origins and effects', *Journal of Humanistic Psychology*, vol. 19, pp. 45–63.
de Waele, J.P. and Harré, R. (1976) 'The personality of individuals' in R. Harré (ed.) *Personality*, Oxford, Blackwell.
Dipple, E. (1988) *The Unresolvable Plot: Reading Contemporary Fiction*, London, Routledge.
Gergen, K.J. and Gergen, M.M. (1988) 'Narrative and the self as relationship' in L. Berkowitz, (ed.) *Advances in Experimental Social Psychology*, San Diego, Academic Press.
Gergen, M.M. (1980) 'Antecedents and consequences of self-attributional preferences in later life', PhD diss., Temple University.
Gergen, M.M. (1992) 'Life stories: pieces of a dream' in G. Rosenwald and R. Ochberg (eds) *Telling Lives*, New Haven, Yale University Press.
Gubrium, J., Holstein, J.A. and Buckholdt, D. (1994) *Constructing the Life Course*, Dix Hills, NY, General Hall.
Hardy, B. (1968) 'Towards a poetics of fiction: an approach through narrative', *Novel*, vol. 2, pp. 5–14.
Harré, R. and Secord, P. (1972) *The Explanation of Social Behaviour*, Oxford, Blackwell.
Josselson, R. and Lieblich, A. (1993) *The Narrative Study of Lives*, London, Sage.
Kelly, M.H. and Keil, F.C. (1985) 'The more things change . . .: metamorphoses and conceptual structure, *Cognitive Science*, vol. 9, pp. 403–16.
Kohli, M. (1981) 'Biography: account, text and method' in D. Bertaux, (ed.) *Biography and Society*, Beverly Hills, CA, Sage.
Lippman, S. (1986) 'Nothing but the facts, ma'am': the impact of testimony construction and narrative style on jury decisions'. Unpublished senior thesis, Swarthmore College.
MacIntyre, A. (1981) *After Virtue: A Study in Moral Theory*, London, Duckworth.
Mancuso, J.C. and Sarbin, T.R. (1983) 'The self-narrative in the enactment of roles' in T.R. Sarbin and K.E. Scheibe (eds) *Studies in Social Identity*, New York, Praeger.
Mandler, J.M. (1984) *Stories, Scripts and Scenes: Aspects of Schema Theory*, Hillsdale, NJ, Erlbaum.
McAdams, D.P. 1985. *Power, intimacy and the life story*. New York: Guilford.
McAdams, D.P. (1993) *The Stories We Live By*, New York, William Morrow and Sons.
Mink, L.A. (1969) 'History and fiction as modes of comprehension', *New Literary History*, vol. 1, pp. 556–69.
Nehamas, A. (1985) *Nietzsche: Life as Literature*, Cambridge, Harvard University Press.
Ong, W.J. (1982) *Orality and Literacy*, London, Methuen.
Polkinghorne, D.E. (1988) *Narrative Knowing and the Human Sciences*, Albany, State University of New York Press.
Ricoeur, P. (1981) *Hermeneutics and the Human Sciences*, trans. J. Thompson, New York, Cambridge University Press.

Rosenwald, G.C. and Ochberg, R.L. (1992) 'Introduction: life stories, cultural politics, and self-understanding' in G.C. Rosenwald and R.L. Ochberg (eds) *Storied Lives: The Cultural Politics of Self-understanding*, New Haven, Yale University Press.

Schank, R.C. and Abelson, R.P. (1977) *Scripts, Plans, Goals and Understanding*, Hillsdale, NJ, Erlbaum.

Schapp, W. (1976) *In Geschichten verstrickt zum Sein von Mensch und Ding*, Wiesbaden, Heymann.

White, M. and Epston, D. (1990) *Narrative Means to Therapeutic Ends*, New York, Norton.

Young, K. (1982) 'Edgework: frame and boundary in the phenomenology of narrative', *Semiotica*, vol. 41, pp. 277–315.

Positioning: The Discursive Production of Selves

Bronwyn Davies and Rom Harré

Source: Davies, B. and Harré, R. (1990) 'Positioning: the discursive production of selves', *Journal of the Theory of Social Behaviour*, vol. 20, pp. 43–65.

The idea for this paper emerged out of a discussion about the problems inherent in the use of the concept of role in developing a social psychology of selfhood. We explore the idea that the concept of 'positioning' can be used to facilitate the thinking of linguistically oriented social analysts in ways that the use of the concept of 'role' prevented. In particular, the new concept helps focus attention on dynamic aspects of encounters in contrast to the way in which the use of 'role' serves to highlight static, formal and ritualistic aspects. The view of language in which positioning is to be understood is the immanentist view expounded by Harris (1982), in which language exists only as concrete occasions of language in use. *La langue* is an intellectualizing myth – only *la parole* is psychologically and socially real. This position is developed in contrast to the linguistic tradition in which 'syntax', 'semantics' and 'pragmatics' are used in a way that implies an abstract realm of causally potent entities shaping actual speech. In our analysis and our explanation, we invoke concepts such as 'speech act', 'indexicality' and 'context', that is the concepts central to ethogenic or new *paradigm psychology* (Davies, 1982; Harré, 1979; Harré and Secord, 1973). Feminist poststructuralist theory has interesting parallels with this position. The recognition of the force of 'discursive practices', the ways in which people are 'positioned' through those practices and the way in which the individual's 'subjectivity' is generated through the learning and use of certain discursive practices are commensurate with the 'new psycho-socio-linguistics' (Davies, 1989; Henriques *et al.*, 1984; Potter and Wetherell, 1987; Weedon, 1987).

[. . .]

Conversation as joint action for the production of determinate speech acts

Since 'positioning' is largely a conversational phenomenon we must make clear at what level of analysis speaking together is to be taken as relevantly conversation. We take conversation to be a form of social interaction the products of which are also social, such as interpersonal relations. We must, therefore, select analytical concepts that serve to reveal conversation as a structured set of speech acts, that is as sayings and doings of types defined by reference to their social (illocutionary) force. This level of analysis must be extended to include non-verbal contributions to conversation. For example it has been found that there are phenomenologically identifiable markers by which people can distinguish telephone rings that are summoning them from those that are summoning others (Garfinkel, 1989). 'Summoning me' is an analytical concept of the speech act level.

Are we to think of conversation as a hazardous de-coding (by the hearers) of the individual social intentions of each speaker? Searle's (1979) version of Austin's (1975) speech act theory of conversation certainly tends in that direction, since he takes the type of a speech act to be defined by the social intention of the person who uttered it. We will argue here that, on the contrary, a conversation unfolds through the joint action of all the participants as they make (or attempt to make) their own and each other's actions socially determinate. A speech *action* can become a determinate speech *act* to the extent that it is taken up as such by all the participants. So what it is that has been said evolves and changes as the conversation develops. This way of thinking about speech acts allows for there to be multiple speech acts accomplished in any one saying and for any speech act hearing to remain essentially defeasible (cf. Muhlhausler and Harré, 1990; Pearce, 1989). As we develop our account of positioning we will argue for a productive interrelationship between 'position', and 'illocutionary force'. The social meaning of what has been said will be shown to depend upon the positioning of interlocutors which is itself a product of the social force a conversation action is taken 'to have'. We shall use the term 'discursive practice' for all the ways in which people actively produce social and psychological realities.

In this context a discourse is to be understood as an institutionalized use of language and language-like sign systems. Institutionalization can occur at the disciplinary, the political, the cultural and the small group level. There can also be discourses that develop around a specific topic, such as gender or class. Discourses can compete with each other or they can create distinct and incompatible versions of reality. To know anything is to know in terms of one or more discourses. As Frazer (1989) says of adolescent girls she interviewed: 'actors' understanding and experience of their social identity, the social world and their place in it, is discursively constructed. By this I mean that the girls' experience of gender, race, class, their personal–social identity, can only be expressed and understood through the categories available to them in discourse' (p. 282).

[. . .]

A particular strength of the poststructuralist research paradigm, to which we referred above, is that it recognizes both the constitutive force of discourse, and in particular of discursive practices and at the same time recognizes that people are capable of exercising choice in relation to those practices. We shall argue that the constitutive force of each discursive practice lies in its provision of subject positions. A subject position incorporates both a conceptual repertoire and a location for persons within the structure of rights for those that use that repertoire. Once having taken up a particular position as one's own, a person inevitably sees the world from the vantage point of that position and in terms of the particular images, metaphors, story lines and concepts which are made relevant within the particular discursive practice in which they are positioned. At least a possibility of notional choice is inevitably involved because there are many and contradictory discursive practices that each person could engage in. Among the products of discursive practices are the very persons who engage in them.

An individual emerges through the processes of social interaction, not as a relatively fixed end product but as one who is constituted and reconstituted through the various discursive practices in which they participate. Accordingly, who one is is always an open question with a shifting answer depending upon the positions made available within one's own and others' discursive practices and within those practices, the stories through which we make sense of our own and others' lives. Stories are located within a number of different discourses, and thus vary dramatically in terms of the language used, the concepts, issues and moral judgements made relevant and the subject positions made available within them. In this way poststructuralism shades into narratology.

[. . .]

The multiplicities of 'self'

Our aquisition or development of our own sense and of how the world is to be interpreted from the perspective of who we take ourselves to be, involves, we claim, the following processes:

1 Learning of the categories which include some people and exclude others, e.g. male/female, father/daughter;

2 Participating in the various discursive practices through which meanings are allocated to those categories. These include the story lines through which different subject positions are elaborated;

3 Positioning of self in terms of the categories and story lines. This involves imaginatively positioning oneself as if one belongs in one category and not in the other (e.g. as girl and not boy, or good girl and not bad girl);

4 Recognition of oneself as having the characteristics that locate oneself as a member of various sub classes of dichotomous categories and not of others – i.e. the development of a sense of oneself as belonging in the world in certain ways and thus seeing the world from the perspective of one so positioned. This recognition entails an emotional commitment to the category membership and the development of a moral system organized around the belonging.

5 All four processes arise in relation to a theory of the self embodied in pronoun grammar in which a person understands themselves as historically continuous and unitary. The experiencing of contradictory positions as problematic, as something to be reconciled or remedied, stems from this general feature of the way being a person is done in our society. Within feminist poststructuralist theory the focus has been on the experience of contradictions as important sites for gaining an understanding of what it means to be a gendered person. Such contradictions do not define different people – it is the fact that one person experiences themselves as contradictory that provides the dynamic for

understanding (Haug, 1987). We wish to defend the adoption of 'position' as the appropriate expression with which to talk about the discursive production of a diversity of selves – the fleeting panorama of Meadian 'me's' conjured up in the course of conversational interactions.

Smith (1988: xxxv) introduces the concept of positioning by distinguishing between 'a person' as an individual agent and 'the subject'. By the latter he means 'the series or conglomerate of positions, subject-positions, provisional and not necessarily indefeasible, in which a person is momentarily called by the discourses and the world he/she inhabits'. In speaking and acting from a position people are bringing to the particular situation their history as a subjective being, that is the history of one who has been in multiple positions and engaged in different forms of discourse. Self reflection should make it obvious that such a being is not inevitably caught in the subject position that the particular narrative and the related discursive practices might seem to dictate.

Positioning, as we will use it, is the discursive process whereby selves are located in conversations as observably and subjectively coherent participants in jointly produced story lines. There can be interactive positioning in which what one person says positions another. And there can be reflexive positioning in which one positions oneself. However it would be a mistake to assume that, in either case, positioning is necessarily intentional. One lives one's life in terms of one's ongoingly produced self, whoever might be responsible for its production.

Taking conversation as the starting point we proceed by assuming that every conversation is a discussion of a topic and the telling of, whether explicitly or implicitly, one or more personal stories whose force is made determinate for the participants by that aspect of the local expressive order which they presume is in use and towards which they orient themselves. The same anecdote might seem boastful according to one expressive convention, but an expression of proper pride according to another. In either reading the anecdote becomes a fragment of autobiography. People will therefore be taken to organize conversations so that they display two modes of organization: the 'logic' of the ostensible topic and the story lines which are embedded in fragments of the participants' autobiographies. Positions are identified in part by extracting the autobiographical aspects of a conversation in which it becomes possible to find out how each conversant conceives of themselves and of the other participants by seeing what position they take up and in what story, and how they are then positioned.

In telling a fragment of his or her autobiography a speaker assigns parts and characters in the episodes described, both to themselves and to other people, including those taking part in the conversation. In this respect the structure of an anecdote serving as a fragment of an autobiography is no different from a fairy tale or other work of narrative fiction. By giving people parts in a story, whether it be explicit or implicit, a speaker makes available a subject position which the other speaker in the normal course of events would take up. A person can be said thus to 'have been positioned' by another speaker. The interconnection between positioning and the making determinate of the illocutionary force of speech acts may also involve the creation of other positionings by a second speaker. By treating a remark as, say, 'condolence', in responding to that remark a second speaker positions themselves as, say, the bereaved. The first speaker may not have so intended what they said, that is, they may not wish to be positioned as one who would offer condolences on such an occasion.

When one speaker is said to position themselves and another in their talk, the following dimensions should be taken into account:

1 The words the speaker chooses inevitably contain images and metaphors which both assume and invoke the ways of being that the participants take themselves to be involved in.

2 Participants may not be aware of their assumptions nor the power of the images to invoke particular ways of being and may simply regard their words as 'the way one talks' on *this sort* of occasion. But the definition of the interaction being 'of this sort' and therefore one in which one speaks in this way, is to have made it into this sort of occasion.

3 The way in which 'this sort of occasion' is viewed by the participants may vary from one to another. Political and moral commitments, the sort of person one takes oneself to be, one's attitude to the other speakers, the availability of alternative discourses to the one invoked by the initial speaker (and particularly of discourses which offer a critique of the one invoked by the initial speaker) are all implicated in how the utterance of the initial speaker will be heard. This is also the case for any subsequent utterances, though the assumption is usually made by participants in a conversation that utterances by speakers subsequent to the initial speaker will be from within the same discourse.

4 The positions created for oneself and the other are not part of a linear non-contradictory autobiography (as autobiographies usually are in their written form), but rather, the cumulative fragments of a lived autobiography.

5 The positions may be seen by one or other of the participants in terms of known 'roles' (actual or metaphorical), or in terms of known characters in shared story lines, or they may be much more ephemeral and involve shifts in power, access, or blocking of access, to certain features of claimed or desired identity, and so on.

One way of grasping the concept of positioning as we wish to use it, is to think of someone listening to or reading a story. There is the narrative, say *Anna Karenina*, which incorporates a braided development of several story lines. Each story line is organized around various poles such as events, characters and moral dilemmas. Our interest focuses on the cast of characters (for instance, Anna, Karenin, Vronsky, Levin and Kitty). The story lines in the narrative describe fragments of lives. That there is a cast of characters from whose imagined points of view the events described in the narrative will be different opens up the possibility for multiple readings. Any reader may, for one reason or another, position themselves or be positioned as outside the story looking in. Such positioning may be created by how the reader perceives the narrator and/or author to be positioning them (as reader) or it may be created by the reader's perception of the characters themselves.

Transferring this conceptual system to our context of episodes of human interaction, we arrive at the following analogue: There is a conversation in which is created a braided development of several story lines. These are organized through conversation and around various poles, such as events, characters and moral dilemmas. Cultural stereotypes such as nurse/patient, conductor/orchestra, mother/son may be called on as a resource. It is important to remember that these cultural resources may be understood differently by different people.

The illocutionary forces of each speaker's contributions on concrete occasions of conversing can be expected to have the same multiplicity as that of the culturally available stereotypes as they are individually understood by *each* speaker. A conversation will be univocal only if the speakers severally adopt complementary subject positions which are organized around a shared interpretation of the relevant conversational locations. Even then, the fact that the conversation is seen from the vantage point of the two different positions, however complementary they are, militates against any easy assumption of shared understanding.

One speaker can position others by adopting a story line which incorporates a particular interpretation of cultural stereotypes to which they are 'invited' to conform, indeed are required to conform if they are to continue to converse with the first speaker in such a way as to contribute to that person's story line. Of course, they may not wish to do so for all sorts of reasons. Sometimes they may not contribute because they do not understand what the story line is meant to be, or they may pursue their own story line, quite blind to the story line implicit in the first speaker's utterance, or as an attempt to resist. Or they may conform because they do not define themselves as having choice, but feel angry or oppressed or affronted or some combination of these.

In our analysis of an actual conversation we will illustrate the importance of the insight that the same sentence can be used to perform several different speech acts. Which speech act it is will depend in part on which story line speakers take to be in use. It follows that several conversations can be proceeding simultaneously. It also follows that one speaker may not have access to a conversation as created by another or others, even though he or she contributes some of the sentences which serve as pegs for the speech acts the others create (Pearce and Cronen, 1981). Our analysis indicates that any version of what people take to be a determinate speech act is always open to further negotiation as to what the actual act (if there is such a thing) is.

To illustrate the use of the concept of 'positioning' for analysing real conversations we will describe a conversational event in which one speaker positioned another. What the positioning amounted to for each conversant will be shown to depend on the point of view from which the conversation is seen. Our example will draw on a case where a single attribute, namely powerlessness, was made salient rather than a typified role model. The main relevance of the concept of positioning for social psychology is that it serves to direct our attention to a process by which certain trains of consequences, intended or unintended, are set in motion. But these trains of consequences can be said to occur only if we give an account of how acts of positioning are made determinate for certain people. If we want to say that someone, say, A has been positioned as powerless we must be able to supply an account of how that position is 'taken up' by A, that is, from whence does A's understanding or grasp of powerlessness derive? We can raise the same issue by asking what psychological assumptions cluster around the single attribute, say powerlessness, which the act of positioning has fastened on A? We shall call this an extension of the significance of the attitude.

[. . .]

A lived narrative and its analysis using the concept of 'positioning'

The best way to recommend our proposal is to demonstrate its analytical power in a worked example.

In our story we have called ourselves Sano and Enfermada. Sano and Enfermada are, at the point the story begins, at a conference. It is a winter's day in a strange city and they are looking for a chemist's shop to try to buy some medicine for Enfermada. A subzero wind blows down the long street. Enfermada suggests they ask for directions rather than conducting a random search. Sano, as befits the one in good health, and accompanied by Enfermada, darts into shops to make enquiries. After some time it becomes clear that there is no such shop in the neighbourhood and they agree to call a halt to their search. Sano then says, 'I'm sorry to have dragged you all this way when you're not well.' His choice of words surprises Enfermada who replies, 'You didn't drag me, I chose to come,' occasioning some surprise in turn to Sano.

Sano and Enfermada offered separate glosses on this episode, whose differences are illustrative of the use of the concept of positioning and instructive in themselves since they reveal a third level of concepts beyond illocutionary force and positioning, namely moral orders. The subsequent debate between our protagonists ran as follows:

Sano protests that he feels responsible and Enfermada protests in return that she does not wish him to feel responsible since that places her in the position of one who is not responsible, and by implication, that she is one who is incapable of making decisions about her own well being. They then debate whether one taking responsibility deprives the other of responsibility. For Sano the network of obligations is paramount. He is at first unable to grasp the idea that anyone could suppose that the fulfilment of a taken-for-granted obligation on the healthy to take charge of the care of the ill could be construed as a threat to some freedom that he finds mythical. Enfermada is determined to refuse Sano's claim of responsibility, since in her feminist framework it is both unacceptable for another to position her as merely an accessory to their actions, rather than someone who has agency in her own right, *and* for her to accept such a positioning. Her concern is only in part for the unintended subject position that his words have apparently invited her to step into. She believes that his capacity to formulate their activity in such a way may be indicative of a general attitude towards her (and to women in general) as marginal, as other than central actors in their own life stories. She knows that he does not wish or intend to marginalize women and so she draws attention to the subject position made available in his talk and refuses to step into it. But her protest positions Sano as sexist, a positioning which he in turn finds offensive. His inclination is therefore to reject Enfermada's gloss as an incorrect reading of his words. But this of course only makes sense in his moral order of interpersonal obligations, not in the feminist moral order. Both speakers are committed to a pre-existing idea of themselves that they had prior to the interchange, Enfermada as a feminist and Sano as one who wishes to fulfil socially mandatory obligations. They are also both committed to their hearing of the interchange. Their protests are each aimed at sustaining these definitions and as such have strong emotional loading.

The episode went through a number of further cycles of reciprocal offence, too numerous to detail here. One of them involved Sano in accusing Enfermada of working off a worst interpretation principle which he claims is characteristic of the kind of ultra-sensitive response that feminists and members of minority groups engage in when responding to 'fancied slights'. Enfermada hears this as a claim that she is unnecessarily making life difficult for herself, alienating people (presumably including Sano) from her and her feminist views. This bothers Enfermada more than the original 'apology' because she sees herself not only robbed of agency but as trivialized and silly, an objectionable member of a minority group who, if they behaved properly, could have equitable membership of society along with Sano. The whole point of her original protest was that his words robbed her of access to that equitable world whether he intended it or not. Until that point she had believed that his intentions were in fact good, which was why it was worth raising the issue. Now she sees that even knowing how upsetting it is to be so positioned in his narrative, his wish is to allocate all responsibility for inequitable treatment that she receives to her own personal style. And so the story went, with claims and counter claims. The complexity, if not impossibility, of 'refusing the discourse' became more and more apparent, as did the subjective commitment to implicit story lines with their implications for the moral characters of each of the participants.

Leaving aside for one moment, the further cycles of offence that were generated around the original conversation, it is possible to render the episode in a symmetrical way and in terms of speech acts and illocutionary force as follows:

> Us: I'm sorry to have dragged you all this way when you are not well.
>
> Ue: You didn't drag me, I chose to come.
>
> Let us all call these utterances or speech actions Us and Ue respectively. We shall use the symbols A(Us) and A(Ue) for the corresponding speech actions which can be made determinate in the various story lines.
>
> What speech acts have occurred? To answer this question we have first to identify the story lines of which the utterances of S and E are moments. Only relative to those story lines can the speech actions crystallize as relatively determinate speech acts.
>
> SS *S's line as perceived by S*: medical treatment with associated positions of S = nurse and E = patient. In this story A (Us) = commiseration.
>
> SE *S's story line as perceived by E*: Paternalism with associated positions of S = independent powerful man and E = dependent helpless woman. In this story A(Us) = condescension. Indexical offence S to E.
>
> EE *E's story line as perceived by E*: joint adventure with associated positions of S and E as travellers in a foreign land. In this story A(Ue) is a reminder in relation to the story line.

ES *E's story line as perceived by S*: feminist protest with associated positions of S = chauvinist pig and E = righteous suffragette. In this story A(Ue) = complaint. Indexical offence E to S.

The importance of positioning as a real conversational phenomenon and not just an analyst's tool is evident in this example. Here are two well disposed people of good faith and reasonable intelligence conversing in such a way that they were entrapped into a quarrel engendered in the structural properties of the conversation and not at all in the intentions of the speakers. He was not being paternalistic and she was not being priggish yet each was driven by the power of the story lines and their associated positions towards the possibility of such mutual accusations.

There are several further points to be made in relation to this analysis.

It shows the way in which two people can be living quite different narratives without realizing that they are doing so. In the absence of any protest on Enfermada's part, Sano need never have questioned how his position as care giver would appear in the moral order of someone whose position was radically different from his. Without her particular reply he could not have realized that he could be heard as paternalistic. Her silence could only act as confirmation of his moral order.

Words themselves do not carry meaning. Sano's use of the apology-format is ambiguous. When it is placed in the context of Enfermada's narrative it causes indexical offence. Similarly, her protest at being 'made helpless' disturbs him since, in his story, it denies what he takes to be a ubiquitous moral obligation.

We have shown the relational nature of positioning – that is, in Enfermada's moral order, one who takes themselves up as responsible for joint lines of action, may position the other as not responsible. Or if one takes up the position of being aggrieved in relation to another then the other is a perpetrator of the injustice. We have shown that what seems obvious from one position, and readily available to any other person who would only behave or interpret in the correct way, is not necessarily so for the person in the 'other' position. The relative nature of positions not only to each other but to moral orders can make the perception of one almost impossible for the other, in the relational position, to grasp.

One's beliefs about the sorts of persons, including oneself, who are engaged in a conversation are central to how one understands what has been said. Exactly what is the force of any utterance on a particular occasion will depend on that understanding.

In demonstrating the shifting nature of positions, depending on the narrative/ metaphors/images through which the positioning is being constituted, we have shown how both the social act performed by the uttering of those words and the effect that action has is a function of the narratives employed by each speaker as well as the particular positions that each speaker perceives the other speaker to be taking up.

There are normative expectations at each level. Sano is surprised at Enfermada's protest because according to conventions of the nurse – patient narrative, there is a normative expectation that the poorly both need and accept care. Of course this narrative also includes the case of the difficult patient. Enfermada for her part is accustomed to being marginalized in men's talk. In hearing him as giving offence she is interpreting him as engaging in normative male behaviour. And of course within this narrative men are notoriously unable to recognize the ways in which their taking up of paternalistic positions negates the agency of the women they are interacting with.

We have shown the necessity of separating out intended meanings from hearable meanings in the process of developing discursive practices that are not paternalistic or discriminatory *in their effect*. The (personal) political implications of attending to the discursive practices through which one positions oneself and is positioned, are that one's speech-as-usual with its embedded metaphors, images, forms, etc, can be recognized as inappropriate to personal/political beliefs both of one's own and of others with whom one interacts.

Contradiction, choice and the possibility of agency

Persons as speakers acquire beliefs about themselves which do not necessarily form a unified coherent whole. They shift from one to another way of thinking about themselves as the discourse shifts and as their positions within varying story lines are taken up. Each of these possible selves can be internally contradictory or contradictory with other possible selves located in different story lines. Like the flux of past events, conceptions people have about themselves are disjointed until and unless they are located in a story. Since many stories can be told, even of the same event, then we each have many possible coherent selves. But to act rationally, those contradictions we are immediately aware of must be remedied, transcended, resolved or ignored. While it is logically impossible to act from a formally contradictory script – no-one could simultaneously go to Boston and go to New York – most people, most of the time wittingly or unwittingly accept that their beliefs about themselves and their environment are full of unresolved contradictions which one just lives with. This feature of being human in a Christian universe was much more openly acknowledged in the past, with the concept of 'God's mysterious ways'. How could a benevolent God create such an unjust world? and so on. The possibility of choice in a situation in which there are contradictory requirements provides people with the possibility of acting agentically.

In making choices between contradictory demands there is a complex weaving together of the positions (and the cultural/social/political meanings that are attached to those positions) that are available within any number of discourses; the emotional meaning attached to each of those positions which have developed as a result of personal experiences of being located in each position, or of relating to someone in that position; the stories through which those categories and emotions are being made sense of; and the moral system that links and legitimates the choices that are being made.

Because of the social/grammatical construction of the person as a unitary knowable identity, we tend to assume it is possible to have made a set of consistent choices located within only one discourse. And it is true we do struggle with the diversity of experience to produce a story of ourselves which is unitary and consistent. If we don't, others demand of us that we do. We also discursively produce ourselves as separate from the social world and are thus not aware of the way in which the taking up of one discursive practice or another (not originating in ourselves) shapes the knowing or telling we can do. Thus we experience these selves as if they were entirely our own production. We take on the discursive practices and story lines as if they were our own and make sense of them in terms of our own particular experiences. The sense of continuity that we have in relation to being a particular person is compounded out of continued embodiment and so of spatio-temporal continuity and shared interpretations of the subject positions and story lines available within them. How to do being a particular non-contradictory person within a consistent story line is learned both through textual and lived narratives.

References

Austin, J.L. (1975) *How to do Things With Words*, second edn, J.O. Urmson and M. Sbisn (eds) Oxford, Clarendon Press.

Davies, B. (1982) *Life in the Classroom and Playground: The Accounts of Primary School Children*, London, Routledge and Kegan Paul.

Davies, B. (1989) *Frogs and Snails and Feminist Tales: Preschool Children and Gender*, Sydney, Allen and Unwin.

Frazer, L. (1989) 'Feminist talk and talking about feminism', *Oxford Review of Education*, vol. 15, 2.

Harré, R. (1979) *Social Being*, Oxford, Blackwell.

Harré, R. and Secord, P.F. (1973) *The Explanation of Social Behaviour*, Oxford, Blackwell.

Harris, R. (1982) *The Language Makers*, London, Duckworth.

Haug, F. (1987) *Female Sexualisation*, London, Verso.

Henriques, J., Hollway, W., Urwin, C., Venn, C. and Walkerdine, V. (1984) *Changing the Subject: Psychology, Social Regulation and Subjectivity*, London, Methuen.

Muhlhausler, P. and Harré, R. (1990) *Pronouns and People*, Oxford, Blackwell.

Pearce, W.B. (1989) *Communication and the Human Condition*, Carbondale, Southern Illinois University Press.

Pearce, W.B. and Cronen, V. (1981) *Communication, Action and Meaning*, New York, Praeger.

Potter, J. and Wetherell, M. (1987) *Discourse and Social Psychology*, London, Sage.

Searle, J.R. (1979) *Expression and Meaning*, Cambridge, Cambridge University Press.

Smith, P. (1988) *Discerning the Subject*, Minneapolis, University of Minnesota Press.

Strawson, P.F. (1956) *Individuals*, London, Methuen.

Weedon, C. (1987) *Feminist Practice and Poststructuralist Theory*, Oxford, Blackwell.

Gender Difference and the Production of Subjectivity

Wendy Hollway

Source: Hollway, W. (1984) 'Gender difference and the production of subjectivity' in J. Henriques, W. Hollway, C. Urwin, C. Venn and V. Walkerdine (eds) *Changing the Subject*, London, Methuen.

In this chapter I attempt to analyse the construction of subjectivity in a specific area: heterosexual relations. My framework depends on three conceptual positions: the non-rational, non-unitary character of subjectivity; its social and historical production through signification; power relations and the re-production of systematic difference.

[. . .] I am interested in theorizing the practices and meanings which re-produce gendered subjectivity (what psychologists would call gender identity). My approach to subjectivity is through the meanings and incorporated values which attach to a person's practices and provide the powers through which he or she can position him- or herself in relation to others. Given the pervasive character of gender difference it is more than likely that all practices signify differently depending on the gender of their subject and object. However, I consider that heterosexual relations are the primary site where gender difference is re-produced. This claim will be substantiated in the detail of the analysis which follows.

[. . .]

The material comes from dialogues and discussions conducted in the course of my PhD research (Hollway, 1982). Participants talked about relationships, sexuality and gender. I talked to them singly and in groups, and without using a structured format of questions. They were not chosen to represent a range of social differences. Rather, it was my intention to make detailed readings of their accounts, recognizing their specific social location and its effectivity in the re-production of gender difference in discourse and subjectivity through power and signification.

[. . .]

Gender difference in three discourses concerning sexuality

[. . .]

In order to make a reading of the accounts I gathered concerning sexuality, I delineated three discourses: the male sexual drive discourse; the have/hold discourse; and the permissive discourse. I arrived at these three through a combination of my own knowledge and what was suggested by the data. Clearly my own assumptions and those of research participants share a largely common historical production; they will also be recognizable to most readers. Some assumptions are more widespread than others (indeed, some would say that the discourse of male sexual drive was universal and that this supports a claim that it is based on the biological 'fact' of male sexuality). It would be relatively easy to identify more discourses, with different boundaries. For my purposes, however, what is more important is the use I make of these three in my analysis of the effects of gender difference in positioning subjects.

The male sexual drive discourse

This needs little introduction because it is so familiar – so hegemonic, or dominant – in the production of meanings concerning sexuality. A man friend of mine captured it succinctly: 'I want to fuck. I *need* to fuck. I've always needed and wanted to fuck. From my teenage years, I've always longed after fucking.' Its key tenet is that men's sexuality is directly produced by a biological drive, the function of which is to ensure reproduction of the species. The discourse is everywhere in common-sense assumptions and is reproduced and legitimized by experts, including psychologists. For example Anthony Storr asserts that

> Male sexuality *because of the primitive necessity* of pursuit and penetration, does contain an important element of aggressiveness; an element which is both recognised and responded to by the female who yields and submits.
>
> (quoted in *The Observer*, 24 May 1981; my italics)

A more recent example of the discourse being made respectable by experts through recourse to scientific explanations is Glenn Wilson's (1979) use of sociobiology to attack feminist accounts of sex differences which are based on social theories of women's oppression. The effect and intention of his argument is to represent women's position as biologically determined and therefore unchangeable.

The have/hold discourse

This has as its focus not sexuality directly, but the Christian ideals associated with monogamy, partnership and family life. The split between wife and mistress, virgin and whore, Mary and Eve, indicates how this and the male sexual drive discourse coexist in constructing men's sexual practices. In some aspects the discourses are consistent; for example both share assumptions about sexuality being linked to reproductivity, and also that sex is heterosexual. Yet the two recommend different and contradictory standards of conduct for men.

This contradiction is resolved for men by visiting it upon women. Either women are divided into two types (as above), or more recently a woman is expected to be both things. In effect we end up with a double standard (the widespread recognition and criticism of which has not wholly changed the practices): men's sexuality is understood through the male sexual drive discourse: they are expected to be sexually incontinent and out of control – 'it's only natural'.

The following letter from a man in *Spare Rib* (a British feminist magazine) demonstrates how these discourses can coexist in the beliefs of one person:

As a mature male, I am in total support of the new 'women against violence against women' campaign, with the proviso that the supporters should realise that the majority of men are decent, of reasonably high principles and respect women as equal partners, and only a small proportion are grossly anti-social. But man being the animal he is, do you think that the answer to rape is well-ordered government-run brothels to cater for the large section of single, sexually-frustrated men in our society?

(*Spare Rib*, 104, March 1981)

The picture is more complicated for women. Underneath the insistence on our asexuality within this discourse is the belief that our sexuality is rabid and dangerous and must be controlled. This is far more explicit in Mediterranean cultures where women are traditionally seen as being in one of two categories: 'fallen' or 'not yet fallen' (Du Boulay, 1974). The implication is that women's sexuality is inevitable and dangerous. (It is not defined as a lack, as in post-Victorian northern Europe.) The only way to preserve the family honour is thus the total subservience of women to male control. Here men project onto women a rabid and ever-present sexuality, which leads to irrational jealousy (Moi, 1982). Later I shall approach the question in terms of men's 'desire for the Other' and the reasons for their projections, rather than falling into the assumption that this has something to do with women's sexuality.

According to the have/hold discourse, women's sexuality is seen as a lack, the possibility avoided by the stress on their relationship with husband and children. For example, Eustace Chesser, a liberal sexual reformer in the 1950s, argued that the sex act for women was only a prelude to satisfaction of the 'maternal instinct' and 'finding joy in family life' (quoted in Campbell, 1980).

Gender-differentiated positions

Before going on to comment on the permissive discourse, I will indicate the main implication of the coexistence of these two discourses for gender difference. It is not that women's sexuality is not constructed in the male sexual drive discourse. Rather woman is seen as its object. The position for a woman in this set of meanings is as the object that precipitates men's natural sexual urges:

[. . .]

However, in the practices of courtship and sexual activity, women are not just the hapless victims of this male sexual drive. Angela McRobbie in her work on adolescent working-class girls concludes that 'their goal is to attract and keep a man' (McRobbie, 1978). Commonly accepted practices of femininity take it for granted that there is status and power attached to being attractive to men. In order to attract them, women can take up the object position in the male sexual drive discourse. Women are often seen as 'trapping' men by their powers of sexual attraction. But sex can also derive its meaning from the have/hold discourse. For example:

Dot: The one time I did fuck with Charles, it felt really good, like there was an awful lot that was important going on. But I didn't have an orgasm . . . maybe the tension was too great or something. I don't know, I was very *turned on*. It was the idea of fucking with him rather than with someone else. The image I get makes me physically shudder with excitement. That reinforces my hunch that it's what's invested in the *idea*. I was in love with him. It's not fucking itself, it's something to do with the rights it gave me to see myself as having a relationship with him. I didn't have any of course.

Despite positioning herself in the permissive discourse (see below) by saying 'of course' she didn't have any rights to a relationship, Dot's reading of this one-off sexual encounter, and even her physical sexual response, were constructed through the set of meanings associated with the have/hold discourse. In another epoch, 'keeping a man' would have meant marriage. Here it is expressed as wanting a relationship. It entails positioning the woman as subject of the have/hold discourse. Although nothing was said on that matter between Dot and Charles, those meanings were an inalienable feature of her feelings. We don't know whether Charles positioned Dot through the have/hold discourse. When this is the case, in complementary fashion, the man is positioned as object of this discourse. This constructs the meanings, and affects the practices, of some men. For example Jim avoided casual sexual encounters because of what it might mean about commitment. Not specified, but a basic assumption in the following extract, is that a relationship was what the woman would want. The complementary position (that he does not) is also quite clear:

> *Jim*: Feeling that sex was kind of dangerous. If you had sex, it meant that you were committed in some way and I didn't want that. Also that if you *just* had sex without a relationship, it was a pretty shitty thing to do to have one part of it without the other.

The permissive discourse

The sexual practices of the participants in my study (aged on average around 30 in 1980) cannot be understood without recourse to a third discourse: the 'permissive' discourse. In this, the principle of monogamy is explicitly challenged, as is illustrated by this comment from the Student Christian Movement in 1966 speaking, predictably, from within the have/hold discourse: 'The teaching of the Christian church that sexual intercourse should be confined to marriage is frequently attacked as a theory and ignored in practice' (*Sex and Morality*, p. 4). In assuming that sexuality is entirely natural and therefore should not be repressed, the permissive discourse is the offspring of the male sexual drive discourse. Similarly it takes the individual as the locus of sexuality, rather than looking at it in terms of a relationship. In one important respect it differs from the male sexual drive discourse: it applies the same assumptions to women as to men. In other words it was – in principle at least – gender-blind. In 1968, a reviewer of Vance Packard's book *The Sexual Wilderness* summed up the characteristics of the permissive society in the following terms: 'On the whole the young of *both sexes* believe that they have a right to express their sexuality in any way they choose so long as nobody is hurt' (my italics). Women could now be subjects of a discourse in a way which meant active initiation of a sexual relationship based on the idea that our natural sexual drives were equal to (or the same as) men's. However, gender difference in sexuality was not suddenly transformed. That this was not the case demonstrates the importance of recognizing the historically specific nature of discourses, their relation to what has gone before and how practices – such as the one-night stands of the permissive era – are not the pure products of a single discourse.

The differences between men's and women's positions in the traditional discourses were never banished in permissive practices. Beatrix Campbell sums up what is commonly recognized now by women in the Women's Movement (many of whom were believers in the equality of sex in permissive practices at the time):

> [the permissive era] permitted sex for women too. What it did not do was defend women against the differential effects of permissiveness on men and women . . . It was about affirmation of young men's sexuality and promiscuity; it was indiscriminate, [so long as she was a woman]. The very affirmation of sexuality was a celebration of *masculine* sexuality.
>
> (Campbell, 1980: 1–2)

In the following extract Jo describes why permissive sex was alienating for her:

> *Jo*: I've fantasized it [the quickie] yes, but it's never functioned like that – even when that person was a complete stranger. Afterwards I just looked at that stranger and felt completely alienated from what I'd just done with him. I mean, really uncomfortable in the extreme. Why did I do it? I think in that situation I'd almost never come, because I'd just be too guarded. You know, there was too much, which I'm just not going to let go – with a complete stranger . . .
> *Colin*: Isn't that just the point? – Why the attraction? It's the fact that it's a stranger. It's nothing to do with the rest of your life. There's no damage that can be caused, you know, and all that kind of thing.
> *Piera*: Yes, you don't have to have a relationship with that person.
> *Jo*: But I don't think I can have sex without having a relationship. So if I haven't got one, it feels alienated, because to me, sex is expressing whatever the relationship is, and is going to be, and what can be built and how I feel with that person, and if it doesn't I really do feel awful. I do feel that if all I want is a quickie – that is some sexual tension released – then I'm much happier masturbating.
> *Colin*: I don't think that's the nature of a quickie, though.

The meanings of sex for Jo are inconsistent with the permissive discourse and therefore the practice which it promoted felt wrong. In contrast Colin's statements emanate from the assumptions of the permissive discourse. His account of the attraction of the quickie casts light on what Jim said above. In contrast to the have/hold discourse, the permissive discourse did not imply any commitment or responsibility. Had Jim been able to position himself by means of the permissive discourse rather than the have/hold discourse, sex would not have seemed so dangerous.

However, as I shall argue, the meanings of sex are more contradictory than that.

The practices that a discourse re-produces are not neutral. The liberating effects of the permissive discourse were particularly contradictory for women. Certainly the discourse enhanced men's powers (men's 'rights') to a heterosexual practice without emotional bonds. Later I shall return to the question of why men had more invested in this than women.

Summary and restatement of the approach

My treatment of these three discourses makes several points which are theoretically significant for the use of a discourse analysis to understand the relation of gender difference, subjectivity and change.

1   Discourses make available positions for subjects to take up. These positions are in relation to other people. Like the subject and object of a sentence (and indeed expressed through such a grammar), women and men are placed in relation to each other through the meanings which a particular discourse makes available: 'the female who yields and submits' to the man (Storr, 1971: 231).

2   Because traditional discourses concerning sexuality are gender-differentiated, taking up subject or object positions is not equally available to men and women. (Try out Storr's formulation in reverse: 'the man who yields and submits to the woman's aggressive pursuit'.) The same applies to practices understandable in terms of gender-differentiated discourses. For example, it's virtually impossible for women to put themselves in the position of subjects in the male sexual drive discourse when it comes to practices such as bottom-pinching or wolf-whistling.

3   The positions are specified for the category 'man' or 'woman' in general. None the less particular men and women fill these positions. Their practices in relation to each other are rendered meaningful according to gender-differentiated discourses.

4   Practices and meanings have histories, developed through the lives of the people concerned. These histories are not the product of a single discourse (though, depending on the hegemony of one discourse, meanings may be more or less homogeneous).

5   Because discourses do not exist independently of their reproduction through the practices and meanings of particular women and men, we must account for changes in the dominance of certain discourses, and the development of new ones (for example those being articulated by feminists) by taking account of men's and women's subjectivity. Why do men 'choose' to position themselves as subjects of the discourse of male sexual drive? Why do women continue to position themselves as its objects? What meanings might this have for women? How do the contradictions between the have/hold and male sexual drive discourses produce the practices of a particular heterosexual relationship? Do the practices signify differently for women and men, because they are being read through different discourses? Why and under what past and present circumstances are women more likely to read a sexual relationship through the have/hold discourse than men?

6   By posing such questions, it is possible to avoid an analysis which sees discourses as mechanically repeating themselves – an analysis which cannot account for change. By showing how subjects' investments, as well as the available positions offered by discourses, are socially constituted and constitutive of subjectivity, it is possible to avoid this deterministic analysis of action and change.

[. . .]

Foucault's genealogies – because they are based on empirical historical data – do not register the stasis of discourses, but rather their changes. However, there is a gap in the theory which he uses to account for such changes. He stresses the mutually constitutive relation between power and knowledge: how each constitutes the other to produce the truths of a particular epoch. Rather than power being equated with oppression and seen as a negative thing, which can be got rid of come the revolution, power is seen as productive, inherently neither positive nor negative: productive of knowledges, meanings and values, and of certain practices as opposed to others. He still does not account for how people are constituted as a result of certain truths being current rather than others. The advantage of the idea that current at any one time are competing, potentially contradictory discourses (concerning for example sexuality) rather than a single patriarchal ideology, is that we can then pose the question, how is it that people take up positions in one discourse rather than another? If the process is not a mechanical positioning, why is it that men take up the subject position in the discourse of male sexual drive? What's in it for them? Under what conditions do men cease to do this? What accounts for the differences between some men and others? These questions require that attention is paid to the histories of individuals in order to see the recursive positioning in certain positions in discourses. It also requires a question concerning the *investment* in that position.

[. . .] By claiming that people have investments (in this case gender-specific) in taking up certain positions in discourses, and consequently in relation to each other, I mean that there will be some satisfaction or pay-off or reward (these terms involve the same problems) for that person. The satisfaction may well be in contradiction with other resultant feelings. It is not necessarily conscious or rational. But there is a reason. In what follows, I theorize the reason for this investment in terms of power and the way it is historically inserted into individuals' subjectivity.

The suppressed in discourse and the multiple significations of sex

So far it might appear that men and women are so positioned by these different discourses that gender difference is well established and successful in producing men and women whose subjectivity is a unitary product of them. Is it not rather surprising, then, that men often stay in couple relationships – even hang on to them when the woman wants out – and find immediate replacements when a relationship ends? (I'm not saying women don't too, but this is consistent with women's positioning in discourses and inconsistent with men's.)

The meaning of sex is no more unitary than the discourses which compete to define the practice of sex. In this section I want to show how suppressed significations coexist with those expressed. [. . .] I will show how for men there are continued investments – to do with power – in defining women as subjects of the have/hold discourse, thereby suppressing their own wishes to have and to hold. One participant in my research wrote the following about the man she was in a relationship with:

If he's saying he has no expectations, no needs, then I can't let him down. If I can't
let him down, he has more power. He has the power to hurt me, but I don't have
the power to hurt him.

Her observation is a beautifully clear recognition of the relation between
knowledge (discourses) and power. As long as she and not he is positioned as
the subject of the have/hold discourse, unequal power is the consequence.

What does a man want?

It's obvious to men who have achieved a minimum of insight into their feelings
that men's wants are not made explicit in sexist discourses. One of the men who
participated in my research expresses needs more in keeping with women's as
they are articulated in the have/hold discourse, at the same time as being aware
of the contradictions:

> *Sam*: The thing that has caused me the most pain, and the most hope is the idea of
> actually living with Jane. And that's in the context of having tried to live with three
> other women before. And each time the relationship's been full of possibility. I don't
> want to live on my own. There's too many things all wrapped up in coupling.
> There's too many needs it potentially meets, and there are too many things it
> frustrates. I do want to have a close, a central-person relationship, but in the past,
> the negative aspects outweighed the positive aspects dramatically. Or my inability to
> work through them has led me to run.

What happens to men's needs for a 'close central-person relationship' as Sam
put it? The negative aspects, which occupy the other side of Sam's contradiction,
are not to do with free sexuality (although in the extract below he specifically
refers to that discourse in order to gainsay it):

> *Sam*: I'm very frightened of getting in deep – and then not being able to cope with
> the demands that the relationship's making. You see, a lot of these things aren't
> really to do with sexuality. They're to do with responsibility.

In this quotation from Sam, there is an elision between getting in deep and
responsibility. This occurs through the lack of clarity about whether Sam was
frightened of getting in deep himself, or of the women doing so. In the following
extract from Sam, the effect of the woman's position in the have/hold discourse
is to protect Sam's own deep feelings. It is a further illustration of the relation
between power and knowledge – the effect of discourse in action. It shows the
idea of women requiring commitment being reproduced as a result of men's
projected fears.

> *Sam*: I'll tell you something – which I don't know what it means but I'll say it
> anyway. When I say to somebody, who I'm making love to – I'm close to, when I
> say, 'I love you, I love you' it's a word that symbolizes letting go. The night before
> Carol went away, she was saying it, and then I started saying it to her, when we
> were making love. What frightens me is that word, it's an act of commitment.
> Somebody suddenly, expects something of me. They've said something, that's the

first word in a long rotten line towards marriage. That when you fall in love, you're caught up in the institution. And it's been an act of principle for me, that I can love somebody, and feel loved, without feeling any responsibility. That I can be free to say that I love somebody if I love them. Be free to feel. I can feel it quite unpredictably. It can hit me quite unexpectedly. And I think I worry about it because I can be quite sentimental.

The power of the meaning of 'I love you' for Sam was that he felt close to someone and it was a 'letting go' of his emotions. This is dangerous because of the power it confers on someone else; the other in the sexual relationship. As soon as Sam has said this, the signifier 'letting go' is suppressed by its capture in the discourse which positions women as requiring commitment. The fear which is generated because this can 'hit me quite unexpectedly' is sufficient to produce its repression, its falling to the level of the signified. Thus gender difference in the discourse 'women requiring commitment' is reproduced.

However, there is a contradiction which remains: men still have needs for the intimacy of a heterosexual relationship. A man writing in *Achilles Heel* (an anti-sexist men's magazine) suggests that this is the only place where men can get these needs met:

> For men (heterosexual) sex works out as a trap because it's the only place where men can really get tenderness and warmth. But they have no skills to evoke these things because there is nothing in the rest of our lives that trains us to do this. So we come into this where we want warmth and intimacy and we don't know how to get it. But it's the only place it exists so there's this tremendous tension for men, getting into bed with women.
>
> (*Achilles Heel*, 2, 1979: 9)

This quotation again illustrates that sex can be a cover for men's need for intimacy to be met. The reproduction of women as subjects of a discourse concerning the desire for intimate and secure relationships protects men from the risk associated with their own need (and the consequent power it would give women). Their own simultaneous position as object of the have/hold discourse and subject of the male sexual drive discourse enables them to engage in the practice of sex, and thus get what they want without recognizing those needs or risking exposure. 'Sex' as male drive therefore covers for the suppressed signification of 'sex' as intimacy and closeness. Because the practice itself does not require verbalization, the suppressed signification is not necessarily recognized. These significations (not necessarily conscious) are completely woven in to the practices of sex, suppressed as they are with the aid of the male sexual drive discourse. This is illustrated by Sam's immediate association when asked how a woman makes him feel: 'It's a closeness, isn't it . . . going to sleep, cuddling close. Feeling – I mean, I don't worry about burglars. I think I feel a lot more secure.'

Unlike a reply from within the discourse of male sexual drive, such as 'it turns me on', Sam's response captures significations normally suppressed through projection: closeness and security.

A man's fear of 'getting in deep' requires theorization in its own right. What are the strong feelings that are evoked by women with whom they have – or want – sexual relationships, which are invested in suppressing their own emotions and projecting them on to women?

Desire for the other, power relations and subjectivity

In the following extract, Martin describes forcefully what happens to him when he feels a little attracted to a woman. The account imposes on my analysis the question of the irrational in couple relations.

> *Martin*: People's needs for others are systematically denied in ordinary relationships. And in a love relationship you make the most fundamental admission about yourself – that you want somebody else. It seems to me that that is the greatest need, and the need which, in relationship to its power, is most strongly hidden and repressed. Once you've shown the other person that you need them, then you've made yourself incredibly vulnerable.
> *Wendy*: Yes, I agree. But I think there's a question about – how much you show yourself to be vulnerable.
> *Martin*: But you do, just by showing that you're soft on somebody. It seems to me what you've revealed that need, you put yourself in an incredibly insecure state. You've before managed by not showing anyone what you're like. By showing them only what is publicly acceptable. And as soon as you've shown that there is this terrible hole in you – that you want somebody else – then you're in an absolute state of insecurity. And you need much more than the empirical evidence that somebody likes you . . . You become neurotically worried that you're not accepted. Now you've let them see a little bit that's you. It'll be rejected. It's not so bad when a false exterior is rejected. The insecurity gives someone else power. I don't mean any viable self-exposure. I just mean any little indication that you like the other person.

Martin's experience of attraction leaves us with a pressing question: what is it that provides us with the irrational charge in sexual attraction? It is the quality of this experience which precipitates Martin's vulnerability and resistance. I call this experience 'desire for the Other', and by the use of this concept, link in to psychoanalytic theory for an explanation: desire for the mother is repressed but never extinguished. It reasserts itself in adult sexual relations.

I want to stress the effects of this subjective experience. Martin's 'desire for the Other' produces a feeling of intense vulnerability which in turn motivates him to exercise whatever powers he can muster in relation to women to whom he feels attracted. Sexist discourses serve this precise function. By reading himself as object of the have/hold discourse he can suppress the recognition of his dependence on a relationship with a woman. As long as he reads the woman as subject of the have/hold discourse he can camouflage his desire. If he succeeds, he can sustain the relationship and meet some of his needs while both remain unaware of them. That this has power effects, even when its suppression is not total, is illustrated in the following account by Martha, the woman with whom Martin has a relationship:

> *Martha*: All these things that we've been talking about hand such power to people. Martin and I go up and down like a see-saw. There are days when he's in another city, and needing me, and suddenly I'm powerful and can dictate terms. We're back

here, and I'm wanting a close, reciprocal, warm, working-out relationship, and suddenly he's powerful, because he doesn't want to give it. It really is dynamite . . . every day of our lives. It really is working less and less well. This business of having needs is so humiliating, because it makes one vulnerable.
Wendy: And shifts the power.
Martha: And shifts the power – exactly.

Her experience of the effects again bears witness to the way sexist discourse is productive of power – for men.

In the following extract Martha refers to the more general oppressive effects of Martin's resistance to the power he experiences her having in the relationship:

> *Martha*: I put up with it, rather than saying, 'No, this is not the way I want to be treated'. I want to be treated as a complete person, someone who has feelings and ideas and intuitions that are actually worth taking notice of. No room is allowed for me to be myself, fully because it might be too powerful an intrusion on his actions. To be accepted one hundred per cent means that the other person has to be strong enough . . . to keep their own integrity in the face of you being one hundred per cent yourself. It's so hard to find men who might be committed to taking those risks.

Her moving testimomy to the effects on her of Martin's power is a specific example of the experience of gender difference: it points to the psychological characteristics which are consistent with – and reproduce – sexist discourses where woman is the inferior 'other'.

[. . .]

Implications for changing gender difference

I have shown that the positions which are available in discourses do not determine people's subjectivity in any unitary way. Whilst gender-differentiated positions do overdetermine the meanings and practices and values which construct an individual's identity, they do not account for the complex, multiple and contradictory meanings which affect and are affected by people's practices. Specifically, men's sexuality is not plausibly accounted for by their positions as subject in the discourse of the male sexual drive and object in the have/hold discourse. 'Sex' signifies in many ways at once. The fact that a man succeeds in reading his sexual practices according to such sexist positions – locating the woman in the complementary positions – only means that the discourse provides the means whereby other significations can be suppressed. Yet 'desire for the Other' is present and affects practices. Thus the knowledge produced by the male sexual drive discourse confers power on men which, in a circular way, motivates them recurrently in taking up that position. This is a specific example of the power – knowledge relation that Foucault theorizes. If the woman is unable to resist her complementary positioning by having access to an alternative discourse and practice, or if her investment in being so positioned is paramount, the couple will reproduce the discourse and thus the existence of gender difference in practices and subjectivity.

What makes this analysis different from one which sees a mechanical circulation of discourses through practices is that there is an investment which, for reasons of an individual's history of positioning in discourses and consequent production of subjectivity, is relatively independent of contemporary positions available. According to my account this is an investment in exercising power on behalf of a subjectivity protecting itself from the vulnerability of desire for the Other. Otherwise power could only be seen as a determined feature of the reproduction of gender-differentiated discourses, which would be left untheorized or reduced to a biological or economic determinism. Instead I have tried to show by concrete example that the interest is specific and part of the history of men and women (in different ways).

[. . .]

The analysis is of political importance because it indicates the nature of the problem involved in changing gender difference. It is not only the social division of labour. Furthermore, it is not a problem to be addressed at the level of discourses alone, critical as that is. The reproduction of gender-differentiated practices depends on the circulation between subjectivities and discourses which are available. The possibility of interrupting this circle is contained in a grasp of the contradictions between discourses and thus of contradictory subjectivities. While one set of desires may be suppressed, along with their signification, by the dominant sexist discourses, the contradictions are never successfully eliminated. They are the weak points in the stronghold of gender difference: taking up gender-appropriate positions as women and men does not successfully express our multiple subjectivities.

[. . .]

References

Campbell, B. (1980) 'A feminist sexual politics: now you see it, now you don't', *Feminist Review*, vol. 5, pp. 1–18.

Du Boulay, J. (1974) *Portrait of a Greek Mountain Village*, Oxford, Clarendon Press.

Hollway, W. (1982) 'Identity and gender difference in adult social relations', unpublished PhD thesis, University of London.

McRobbie, A. (1978) '*Jackie*: An ideology of adolescent femininity', *Working Papers in Cultural Studies*, SP53, Birmingham Centre for Contemporary Cultural Studies.

Moi, T. (1982) 'Jealousy and sexual difference', *Feminist Review*, vol. 11, pp. 53–69.

Packard, V. (1968) *The Sexual Wilderness*, London, Pan.

Storr, A. (1971) *Human Aggression*, Harmondsworth, Penguin, quoted in *The Observer* (24 May 1981).

Student Christian Movement (1966) *Sex and Morality: A Report Presented to the British Council of Churches*, London, SCM Press.

Wilson, G. (1979) 'The sociobiology of sex differences' *Bulletin of the British Psychology Society*, vol. 32, pp. 350–3.

PART FOUR
CULTURE AND SOCIAL RELATIONS

Editor's Introduction

Margaret Wetherell

In this Part we turn to the third and final domain covered in the Reader – culture and social relations. In effect this is the territory of sociology, cultural studies, anthropology, social policy and the other social sciences such as politics, economics and geography. But what relevance might the study of language and discourse have to the more global concerns of these disciplines? Some answers to this question were prefigured in the foundational readings in Part One.

Historically, one of the reasons why those studying culture and society have been interested in language was that both language and culture seemed to have properties in common. Both can be treated as self-contained systems defined by rules for the combination of elements. Kress in Reading Two, for example, described Saussure's *structuralist* theory of language and this theory paralleled the model of culture found in the work of the anthropologist Lévi-Strauss which influenced a generation of social scientists (Culler, 1976).

We live now, however, in poststructuralist times. Kress explains why, in the end, the structuralist approach proved unsatisfactory. In effect, he argues that a more varied and interesting view of the relationship between language and the social context emerged when researchers began studying *practices* rather than *structures*. The focus turned to social action and actual lived realities. The writings of Bakhtin and Volosinov (see Reading Six) nicely exemplify the new understanding of meaning-making at issue here. As Maybin notes in Reading Six, for Bakhtin/Volosinov the meaning of words derives not from their place in a structure but from 'accumulated and dynamic social use'. This focus on practice has been reinforced by work on the ethnography of speaking (see Fitch in Reading Five). Cross-cultural research by anthropologists and linguists demonstrates the extent to which culture works through the construction of 'speech communities' and is marked by distinctive 'ways of speaking'.

Kress uses the example of a descriptive phrase from Australian politics – 'white invasion of the Coast' – to illustrate the relevance of this emerging perspective on language and meaning for the study of culture and social relations. He argues that 'the social conditions of the making of this utterance are . . . *in* the utterance, in its very form, in its shape'. Studying culture and social relations with an eye on discourse and language, then, involves studying how social relations are worked linguistically through the selection of vocabularies, genres, accents, lexical styles, and so on. Both language and social relations bear the marks of each other. Linguistic choices reflect power relations. Yet power is instantiated, maintained and reproduced and social relations become the kind of relations they are as the words are spoken. Bakhtin and Volosinov make a similar point: language carries an evaluative accent – it 'inevitably passes judgement on the world even as it describes it'.

A similar example is provided by the new linguistic forms which have emerged in the UK in recent years associated with the political dominance of 'New Labour' including terms such as 'New Labour' itself, the 'third way', the use of the term 'public–private partnership' for 'privatization', catch-phrases such as 'economic dynamism and social justice', and so on. The critical discourse analyst, Norman Fairclough, in his book *New Labour, New Language?* (2000) identifies and investigates this new way of speaking and argues that it both reflects trends in the development of capitalism, such as globalization and managerialism and, of course, is a crucial constituent of globalization and managerialism as social processes. The language is part of how these new forms of social relations are lived.

Two of the readings in this Part illustrate the ways in which linguists have worked with these ideas. Kress in Part One traced out some of its origins of critical linguistics as a tradition of discourse research. This approach emerged in the 1960s and 1970s in the work of scholars such as Labov (1972); Hymes (1972); Gumperz (1982) and Halliday (1978) as they responded to Saussurean linguistics. A further important development was Kress's own work with Robert Hodge (Hodge and Kress, 1979, 1988) and the highly influential studies of Roger Fowler (1981; Fowler *et al.*, 1979). Feminist linguistics was central also. This work was represented in Part Two with Reading Twelve from Deborah Tannen and has been developed by Deborah Cameron and Jennifer Coates among others (Cameron, 1992; Coates, 1986, 1996; Coates and Cameron, 1989).

The most recent newcomer in this field of linguistics is what has been called 'critical discourse analysis' developed, most notably, by scholars such as Norman Fairclough (1989, 1992, 1995), Teun Van Dijk (1984, 1991, 1998) and Ruth Wodak (1989, 1997). The readings we include to illustrate critical linguistics and critical discourse analysis consist of an example of critical linguistics from Hodge and Kress and a programmatic statement on critical discourse analysis from Teun Van Dijk. Readers are also recommended to look at the journal *Discourse and Society*, edited by Van Dijk, which presents many examples of empirical research on language and social relations from a critical perspective.

Linguistics offers us one mode of working with language and social relations. Another mode, more familiar to social scientists, has emerged from the work of Foucault and was also prefigured in Part One (see Reading Seven). Just as with critical discourse analysis in linguistics, Foucault's work represents the most recent twist in a much longer history of debate. Kress argued that before the study of discourse could properly begin, the ghost of Saussure (or structuralist interpretations of Saussure) had to be laid in linguistics. Until that point few linguists had much interest in the actual patterns of use of language in social contexts. A similar story can be told in social science. The laying of some of sociology's ghosts led to the development of cultural studies, intensive work on cultural forms, ideology, semiotics and signifying practices and thus to work on discourse.

Discourse research in the social sciences is based on the assumption that the study of culture matters – that ideas, ways of being, forms of knowledge are worth studying and are interesting and important in themselves. This seems an obvious position now. Yet one consequence of some early economistic interpretations of Marxist social theory was to marginalize culture and human meaning-making as ephemeral. Ideas and forms of knowledge were trivialized. They were seen as a super-structure, an effect of (determined by) modes of economic production. The emergence of cultural studies in Britain in the 1950s depended on the 'humanizing' of Marxism and the countering of this view. The work of Raymond Williams (1963, 1965) and Richard Hoggart (1969) in particular established the conditions for the study of popular culture. Culture was not something high-brow – English literature, opera and philosophy – but the everyday practices through which ordinary people lived their conditions of existence, and these had their own forms of organization and logics which didn't reduce to the economic. Indeed, culture came to be seen as relatively autonomous, playing a crucial role in defining the character of broader social relations along with modes of social organization such as social class and modes of economic production.

This new formulation of culture led to a burst of work on ideology in cultural studies evident in the work of Stuart Hall and the Centre for Contemporary Cultural Studies at Birmingham in the 1970s. Hall and his colleagues (CCCS, 1978, 1982; Hall, 1980, 1985) drew also on related developments in European social theory such as the work of Althusser (1969, 1971) and Barthes (1972) which took structuralist ideas such as Saussure and Lévi-Strauss's concepts of signification and devised new approaches and methods for the study of cultural phenomena (Culler, 1975). A further source was the work of the Italian political theorist Gramsci (1971) on the wars of position around ideas which occur in societies to produce hegemony for certain world views.

This work on ideology drew attention to the modes of representation found in a society and the politics of these. A number of themes were crucial here. First, there is the notion that the study of ideology investigates the ways in which people read themselves into social relations – the ways in which they make sense of the world and develop a taken-for-granted perspective, a feeling of 'that is just the way things are'. Second, ideologies provide identities and positions for people. This was very evident in the Readings in Part Three from Hollway and Davies and Harré. As we take on an ideology, we take on a position from which to speak. Third, ideology draws attention to the historical nature of ideas: that as we take on a belief system we join in, mostly unreflexively and unconsciously, a conversation which may have been going on for decades if not centuries. Finally, of course, ideas are about power. They are the methods through which ruling groups legitimate their dominance, such as ideologies of racism or sexism.

These themes inform contemporary Foucauldian discourse research. The new emphasis, however, is on 'discourse' rather than 'ideas'. In combination with the other trends reviewed in Part One, the focus is much more solidly on public modes of representation, talk and texts. Second, early Marxist work on ideology was concerned with testing ideas and statements for their truth value, or their accordance with reality. Foucault's work highlights instead the production of truth. The point of social sciences is not to pronounce on what forms of knowledge are true or false but to study how certain discourses become authoritative and to locate them historically. Furthermore, as Hall demonstrated in Reading Seven, the concept of power becomes both more personal and less personal. Less personal in the sense that Foucault saw patterns in discourse/ knowledge as the play of power and these were not seen as authored in the way that ideologies in Marxist work were seen as generated by ruling groups. Rather, for Foucault, what is interesting is how discursive formations formulate groups and bring populations and categories of people with defined characteristics (such as the madman, the witch, the tax inspector) into being. This process is also personal, however, because it creates subjectivities. Foucauldian discursive research places more stress on how discourse infiltrates mind and character.

The readings in Part Four include four examples of Foucauldian discourse work in the social sciences. These pick up characteristic themes such as 'government' – the surveillance, disciplining and construction of populations and permissible forms of subjectivity through, to use Foucault's phrase, 'technologies of the self'. And, also, themes such as power, struggle and contestation and the historical bases of contemporary representations which reflect older interests in ideology studies. There are some intriguing similarities and differences in the ways in which critical discourse analysts in linguistics and Foucauldian scholars theorize discourse and 'the social' and I will draw attention to these as I review each reading in greater depth.

The readings

The first reading comes from **Hodge and Kress**. It consists of two extracts, one in which they set out some of the analytic concepts of critical linguistics which constitute their 'social semiotics' and then a short illustrative analysis of text from a women's magazine. Hodge and Kress distinguish between two planes on which a message operates: the semiosic and the mimetic. The mimetic concerns what is represented while the semiosic concerns the social process by which meaning is constructed and exchanged. Thus in the analysis of Miss Seductress and Ms Winner which follows, Hodge and Kress argue that ideology operates on two dimensions. They examine the way the text constructs the character of Miss Seductress, describes her non-verbal codes and paints a picture. In effect they are examining how the text works mimetically. As they point out, however, it is not just through description or reference to ideologically charged phenomena that the text carries social messages for women about their place. It works also through the way the text is put together to address a reader and placed in conjunction with other texts such as Ms Winner. This is the semiosic plane.

Hodge and Kress define texts and discourse in interesting ways which both resonate with, and depart from, some of the Foucauldian perspectives on discourse evident in later readings. Kress and Hodge wish to investigate texts which they define as accumulations of messages. The form texts take is constrained by genres or the normative systems that specify, for instance, what a collection of words should look like before it would be taken as a magazine article or a parliamentary speech or as a family meal-time conversation. For Hodge and Kress texts are the realization of the broader systems of signs which make up a culture. They represent the manifestation of a culture's conventions and ways of organizing sense-making and communication. These systems of signs are constantly in transformation and flux, changing gradually over time and sometimes rapidly. A parliamentary speech, for instance, in the nineteenth century has some very different features and some continuity with such a speech in the twenty-first century. These differences and continuities reflect broader cultural and historical shifts and also stabilities in patterns of communication. Texts are the sites where change happens.

Discourse, on the other hand, is defined in Hodge and Kress's approach as 'the site where forms of social organization engage with systems of signs in the production of texts'. What does this mean? It suggests that Hodge and Kress see social relations and social practices as separate from culture or systems of signs, standing outside talk, writing and communication (texts). Such social relations might be, for example, the organization of the economy or social policies of welfare distribution or the gendered division of labour in households. These social practices and social relations interact with systems of signs and this is the discursive process.

Discourse, in other words, is the process that brings together human meaning-making and other human activities so that one reflects the other. Relations between signs, conventions in the ways humans communicate, genres, and so on, thus reflect patterns in the economic organization of society, or in organized relations between women and men, or the history of education, and so on. If systems of signs have changed, to continue our example, from the nineteenth to twenty-first centuries so that parliamentary speeches are now different, then those changes are not just internal to the history of communication in itself but reflect interactions at the level of discourse between those systems and social relations such as changes in capitalism, technological change, political changes, and so on.

The second reading in Part Four comes from **Van Dijk**. It outlines the principles of critical discourse analysis and provides an illustration analysing a speech from a parliamentary debate in the British House of Commons. Critical discourse analysts argue that their work should be judged by its ethical and political import. It should be evaluated by their success in attaining socio-political goals such as combating racism, for instance. These criteria for evaluation can be contrasted, for example, with those of conversation analysis where the goal is to clarify what an interaction is for the participants through the rigorous study of the evidence. We return to this issue of the political stance of the analyst in the Conclusion to the Reader.

In this reading Van Dijk offers an approach to discourse and a conceptualization of the relations between social actors, meaning-making and social relations which contrasts in interesting ways with a Foucauldian approach. For Van Dijk, discourse is defined broadly as the linguistic object of study – texts, talk, communication and words in use. He is concerned with the ways in which discourse interacts with two other categories: social relations and, then, human minds, particularly the cognitive operations which for Van Dijk guide the reception of messages. He presents these three categories as separate entities where he is interested in the relations between them.

This is against the thrust of much work in the Foucauldian tradition and in discursive psychology which argues that the dividing lines between these kinds of entities cannot be easily maintained, since discourse forms minds and constitutes the social world. Some of the specific differences with a Foucauldian approach are evident in Van Dijk's analysis of power. Whereas Foucault argued that power and knowledge are inseparable and, further, that power/knowledge constitutes social actors and forms the prior term, Van Dijk defines power as a property of groups and the relations between groups. Foucault was interested in how groups and defined populations (such as 'psychologists' or 'homosexuals') emerge through the operations of power/knowledge. Van Dijk's analysis, in contrast, tends to be much less interested in how groups are constituted and emerge historically and begins with groups or elites already in place and asks about their discursive strategies for maintaining power.

Van Dijk argues that one sign of power is access to discourse. Thus the control of discourse is a key topic in his analyses. When he examines, for example, newspaper discourse or racist discourse (1984, 1991) his strategy is to look at macro and micro levels and at three structures. One of these structures is 'the contextual, interactional, organizational and global forms of discourse control'. Who has access to expression and how is that controlled by different elite groups? He looks also at the micro-level expressions in texts and talk – how a text is put together – and he also studies structures of understanding. This last dimension refers to the way people receive and process messages and the cognitive strategies they adopt for understanding what is said.

The specimen analysis of the parliamentary speech Van Dijk presents indicates the analytic categories he recommends which include descriptions, among other things, of the setting, genre, participant positions and roles, style, local meaning and coherence. The critical dimension of critical discourse analysis is indicated in Van Dijk's decision to analyse the speech from an explicitly anti-racist stance. He aligns himself with those being criticized in the speech by Fox, and analyses the speech from their perspective.

The third reading in Part Four from **Shapiro** is the first of four readings which exemplify Foucauldian discourse research. Shapiro focuses on theory and introduces a number of themes which are then developed in the empirical case studies in the next three readings. Shapiro outlines, for instance, one of the core claims of discursive thinking in disciplines such as sociology, politics, cultural studies and social policy: social reality is not there simply to be apprehended, rather it is always constructed for us through human meaning-making. He refers to 'reality-making scripts' or world-making practices and the ways in which modes of representation construct social facts. His examples come from the study of international relations. Shapiro asks us to think, for instance, about the construction of global geographical spaces. When we talk about a country such as Guatemala, to what extent are we mapping what is already there? Are we instead not responding to a historical mode of representation which carves the world up in certain ways? Shapiro contrasts medieval views of world space derived from religious practices with contemporary understandings.

He makes a number of other important points about the process of reality making through discursive and representational practices. First, this is a process of contestation. Politics, he argues, involves contests over alternative understandings. Following Foucault he points out that what is most characteristic of discourse is that it is a 'value-producing' practice. In other words, as the world is described it is evaluated (see also Reading Six on Bakhtin/Volosinov). Good/bad binaries are constructed, some activities are institutionalized, others are marginalized. Discourse is a classifying and exclusionary practice and it is through these and other properties of knowledge making that power works. Crucially, as Foucault claimed, the value of statements is not determined by their truth but by their place in the knowledge-making process.

Shapiro also takes up the arguments of the deconstructionist, Jacques Derrida. Meaning, Derrida argues, cannot be owned. We have the illusion of control over meaning as we speak but this is an illusion since the meaning of utterances and statements is again determined by the place they hold in a discursive system and this is constantly open to slippage. Meaning can always be fixed and re-fixed in new ways. The practical and political consequences of this claim are elaborated in concrete terms by Stuart Hall in the reading which follows.

Finally, Shapiro also raises questions about our own writing practices as academics. How do we write our own texts: as factual statements, or as literary exercises? Should we draw attention to the constructive processes – our own reality making – as we write? This debate raises issues about the stance of the discourse analyst and about the validity claims discourse analysts might want to make for their work and we return to these in the Conclusion to the Reader. Shapiro distinguishes here between two kinds of investigations discourse analysts could conduct: 'structural' and historical. The historical focuses on the emergence of phenomena in language while the structural examines how a particular text is put together – the devices, strategies, tropes and rhetorics through which social reality is manufactured. As noted, social scientists interested in discourse have tended more towards historical analysis while critical linguists and sociolinguists have tended to pay more attention to developing tools for 'structural' analyses in the sense that they develop analytic concepts based on the properties of language *per se*, such as lexical and metaphorical forms.

The next reading from **Hall** looks at the consequences of the discursive turn for the understanding of race and ethnicity and the formation and construction of 'otherness'. Hall's meditations on this question provide a good example of the historical mode Shapiro delineates or 'genealogical' exploration. Hall is interested in the history of meaning-making practices and how different modes of representation emerge and the consequences of these for social relations. He begins, however, with an analysis of images of black sports people which demonstrates how representational practices attempt to fix meanings and privilege certain chains of association in racialized 'regimes of representation'. Hall then traces back some of the history of regimes around race through an examination of popular culture such as nineteenth-century advertising images and the filmic representation of black characters. Such analyses indicate that the techniques and perspectives of discourse analysis can be applied to all human meaning-making – to photographs, films and paintings as well as interview transcripts, documents and writings.

Various discursive techniques for dealing with those positioned as other become apparent through Hall's analysis, such as naturalization – the reading of social constructions as natural facts – and the pervasive tendency to formulate the world through binaries – black versus white, nature versus culture, good versus evil – which intensifies notions of otherness. A key reference point for Hall is the work of Edward Said on 'orientalism' which demonstrates how racialized epistemic regimes lubricate inequality, exploitation and imperial regulation. This is a good illustration of the connections Foucault postulates between discourse and power.

We noted in relation to the Readings in Part Three how social psychologists such as Davies and Harré and Hollway try to keep open a space for the active and creative subject through a sense of the multiple and contradictory ways in which people are positioned. A similar issue emerges for sociologists in relation to the scope for transformation, resistance and social change. Hall here implicitly takes up Derrida's argument reviewed by Shapiro. He examines some of the recent moves by black communities and artists to contest otherness and racialized regimes of representation. This is possible because meanings can never be fixed once and for all – the notion of 'black', for example, can be recovered from one chain of signification and re-embedded in another which changes radically its meaning. Hall describes this as a strategy of transcoding and notes other similar discursive techniques for resistance.

To explain why 'otherness' is such a potent theme in culture, Hall draws on four, connected but distinct, theoretical perspectives. Two of these involve theories of language. He describes Saussure's central insights about the relational nature of language and the centrality of difference in signification and then Bakhtin's notion of the dialogical. In these accounts otherness is built into the formation of meaning. The two other perspectives come from anthropology and psychoanalysis. Hall argues, following Mary Douglas, that binary oppositions are central to the classificatory systems of culture so that phenomena derive their sense from the way they are positioned in the symbolic order – the concept of 'raw' is only possible, for instance, because we have the notion of 'cooked'. Psychoanalysis offers a psychological take on this. Otherness is core to the formation of subjectivity. Difference creates identity – we only know who we are because we know who we are not. Difference can become a source of threat as well as self-definition as reactions to those defined as 'Other' pass through psychic processes such as projection and other defence mechanisms.

The fifth reading in Part Four from **Mehan** continues the theme of the politics of representation, the construction of 'otherness' and the construction of populations marked out as deficient in relation to a norm but with the difference that Mehan's interest is less in the broad historical sweep and more in the micro-organization of encounters. His concern is with the ways in which the big social pictures or knowledge regimes work through into the interactional details of institutional life. Mehan examines the discursive processes involved in the construction of one 'lexical label' – 'learning disabled' – and the procedures through which this identity is produced as a 'social fact'.

His work is informed by ethnomethodological and conversation analytic perspectives as well as Foucauldian ones. These emphases give him an interest in talk-in-action and in the practical projects of everyday life. Indeed Mehan distinguishes between two semiotic planes. To fully understand the construction of notions of 'learning disabled' it is necessary to work on the genealogical plane and develop a discursive history of the emergence of these categories, the forms of expertise which manage these categories and the power relations afforded by them. But also a complete analysis must look at what Mehan calls the 'indexical plane of the practical application of such attributes' and in this respect his work links with an earlier Reading in Part Two from Silverman.

Mehan describes his research methods in some detail and interestingly these involve ethnography. A particular theme in his work is the process of 'entextualization'. He is concerned with the ways in which texts are carried from site to site, so what may begin, for example, as an informal comment from a classroom teacher becomes textualized into an account which is then reproduced in a form such as a written document which can be 'devoiced', separated from its original context of production and carried into new interactions. Entextualization is related to the process through which authoritative voices emerge and the stratification of different modes of representation (and this was considered, too, by Wertsch in Reading Sixteen in Part Three). Mehan's work thus provides some analytic tools through which the process of fixing and then unfixing meanings described by Shapiro and Hall can be studied in the here and now.

The final reading from **Miller and Rose** broadens the picture once again. Mehan is concerned, in part, with the 'psychologization' of knowledge, with the ways in which psychologists have become expert commentators on categories which their expertise constructs, such as the 'learning disabled'. These are themes which social scientists have taken from Foucault and, in particular, from his interest in government and the new forms of managing and disciplining populations which emerged in the nineteenth and twentieth centuries. Miller and Rose provide an example of a large-scale analysis of this kind.

Their aim is to understand and describe the operations of a whole institution – the Tavistock Clinic and Tavistock Institute of Human Relations – as representative of changes in practices for managing people over time. They focus on the psychological and managerial vocabularies which constitute the forms of knowledge in which the Tavistock programme deals, the regulatory techniques and, crucially, the kinds of subjectivities (subject positions and narratives) which these 'technologies of the self' allow. One of Foucault's key contributions was to broaden the focus of our understanding of 'technology' and 'government'. Technology once implied the management of the physical, material and natural world. Foucault emphasized that the human, the subjective and the psychological are also managed in similar ways through routinized procedures. A new human invention such as therapy is a technique just as much as a new method of agriculture. Similarly, government refers to the large-scale management of the external features of populations but the term government also has an alternative meaning of self-control and self-management. Foucault's notions of 'governmentality' and 'techniques of the self' bring together these themes – large-scale management through expertise organizing something (the human, the subjective, the internal private world) once seen as outside of regulation and as belonging to a different order of things.

References

Althusser, L. (1969) *For Marx*, London, Allen Lane.
Althusser, L. (1971) *Lenin and Philosophy and Other Essays*, London, New Left Books.
Barthes, R. (1972) *Mythologies*, London, Jonathan Cape.
Cameron, D. (1992) *Feminism and Linguistic Theory*, second edn, London, Macmillan.
Centre for Contemporary Cultural Studies (1978) *On Ideology*, London, Hutchinson.
Centre for Contemporary Cultural Studies (1982) *The Empire Strikes Back*, London, Hutchinson.

Coates, J. (1986) *Women, Men and Language, A Sociolinguistic Account of Sex Differences in Language*, London, Longman.

Coates, J. (1996) *Women Talk: Conversation Between Female Friends*, Oxford, Blackwell.

Coates, J. and Cameron, D. (eds) (1989) *Women in Their Speech Communities*, London, Longman.

Culler, J. (1975) *Structuralist Poetics*, London, Routledge and Kegan Paul.

Culler, J. (1976) *Saussure*, London, Fontana.

Fairclough, N. (1989) *Language and Power*, London, Longmans.

Fairclough, N. (1992) *Discourse and Social Change*, Cambridge, Polity Press.

Fairclough, N. (1995) *Critical Discourse Analysis*, London, Longmans.

Fairclough, N. (2000) *New Labour, New Language?* London, Routledge.

Fowler, R. (1981) *Literature as Social DIscourse: The Practice of Linguistic Criticism*, London, Batsford Academic.

Fowler, R., Hodge, R., Kress, G.R., and Trew, T. (1979) *Language and Control*, London, Routledge.

Gramsci, A. (1971) *Selections from the Prison Notebooks*, London, Lawrence and Wishart.

Gumperz, J. (1982) *Language and Social Identity*, Harmondsworth, Penguin.

Hall, S. (1980) 'Cultural studies: two paradigms', *Media, Culture and Society*, vol. 2, pp. 57–72.

Hall, S. (1985) 'The rediscovery of "ideology": return of the repressed in media studies' in V. Beechey and J. Donald (eds) *Subjectivity and Social Relations*, Milton Keynes, Open University Press.

Halliday, M.A.K. (1978) *Language as Social Semiotic*, London, Edward Arnold.

Hodge, R. and Kress, G.R. (1979) *Language as Ideology*, London, Routledge.

Hodge, R. and Kress, G.R. (1988) *Social Semiotics*, Cambridge, Polity Press.

Hoggart, R. (1969) *The Uses of Literacy*, Harmondsworth, Penguin.

Hymes, D. (1972) 'Models of the interaction of language and social life' in J. Gumperz and D. Hymes (eds) *Directions in Sociolinguistics: The Ethnography of Communication*, New York, Holt, Rinehart and Winston.

Labov, W. (1972) *Language in the Inner City*, Philadelphia, University of Philadelphia Press.

Van Dijk, T. (1984) *Prejudice in Discourse*, Amsterdam, Benjamins.

Van Dijk, T. (1991) *Racism and the Press*, London, Routledge.

Van Dijk, T. (1998) *Ideology*, London, Sage.

Williams, R. (1963) *Culture and Society 1780–1950*, Harmondsworth, Penguin.

Williams, R. (1965) *The Long Revolution*, Harmondsworth, Penguin.

Wodak, R. (ed.) (1989) *Language, Power and Ideology*, Amsterdam, Benjamins.

Wodak, R. (ed.) (1997) *Gender and Discourse*, London, Sage.

Social Semiotics

Robert Hodge and Gunther Kress

Source: Hodge, R. and Kress, G. (1988) *Social Semiotics*, Cambridge, Polity Press, Chapters 1 and 3.

[. . .]

Message, text and discourse

In analysing semiotic structures and processes, social semiotics draws extensively on terms and concepts from mainstream semiotics. But semiotics has not arrived at a single agreed set of terms and concepts. Even if it had, social semiotics would need to redefine some of them, to reflect its emphasis on social action, context and use. In what follows, we give an outline of how we will understand the key terms we use.

The smallest semiotic form that has concrete existence is the *message*. The message has directionality – it has a source and a goal, a social context and purpose. It is oriented to the semiotic process, the social process by which meaning is constructed and exchanged, which takes place in what we will call the *semiosic plane*. The message is about something, which supposedly exists outside itself. It is connected to a world to which it refers in some way, and its meaning derives from this representative or mimetic function it performs. We will call the plane in which representation occurs the *mimetic plane*.

But the field of semiosis does not consist simply of an accumulation of messages. Messages pass in clusters back and forth between participants in a semiotic act. In the study of verbal communication two words are generally used for this larger unit of semiotics, 'text' and 'discourse'. We will use 'text' in an extended semiotic sense to refer to a structure of messages or message traces which has a socially ascribed unity. 'Text' comes from the Latin word *textus*, which means 'something woven together'. 'Discourse' is often used for the same kind of object as text but we will distinguish the two, keeping discourse to refer to the social process in which texts are embedded, while text is the concrete material object produced in discourse. 'Text' has a different orientation to 'discourse'. Its primary orientation is to the mimetic plane, where it has meaning insofar as it projects a version of reality. 'Discourse' refers more directly to the semiosic plane.

'Text' is also opposed to another important concept, 'system'. Mainstream semiotics has developed the notion of a system of signs as an abstract structure which is realized or instantiated in text. It tends to treat such systems as static, as a social fact which is not, however, implicated in social processes of development or change. We would emphasize in contrast that every system of signs is the product of processes of semiosis, and documents the history of its own constitution. Terms in a system have value by virtue of their place in that system. At the same time, a system is constantly being reproduced and reconstituted in texts. Otherwise it would cease to exist. So texts are both the material realization of systems of signs, and also the site where change continually takes place.

This dialectic between text and system always occurs in specific semiosic acts, that is, in discourse. Discourse in this sense is the site where social forms of organization engage with systems of signs in the production of texts, thus reproducing or changing the sets of meanings and values which make up a culture. So for instance the institution of medicine defines a specific set of meanings which are constantly involved in the social processes which are appropriate to that institution, and engaged in by significant classes of participant, such as patient, surgeon, researcher and so on. In these interactions and the texts that they produce, the set of meanings is constantly deployed, and in being deployed is at risk of disruption. For social semiotics, the two terms 'text' and 'discourse' represent complementary perspectives on the same level of phenomenon. But although discourse is emphatically a social category, this does not mean that text and message are asocial terms. Both text and message signify the specific social relationships at the moment of their production or reproduction.

Genre, conformity and resistance

In order to trace the relationship of micro to macro structures we need some mediating categories. Logonomic systems have rules that constrain the general forms of text and discourse. Such systems often operate by specifying *genres* of texts (typical forms of text which link kinds of producer, consumer, topic, medium, manner and occasion). These control the behaviour of producers of such texts, and the expectations of potential consumers. Genre-rules are exemplary instances of logonomic systems, and are a major vehicle for their operation and transmission. Like the category of text, genres are socially ascribed classifications of semiotic form.

Genres only exist in so far as a social group declares and enforces the rules that constitute them. For instance, there are clear rules which regulate the interactions among participants that are called a committee meeting. That is, a particular kind of social occasion is established, recognized and named by a social group, and practices are delineated which govern the actions of participants on such occasions. The texts which are formed in the process of a committee meeting therefore have a form which codes the set of practices, relations of participants, their expectations and purposes. The form of such texts – whether as 'full transcript', or as 'minutes of the meeting' – themselves become recognized as 'genres', and become potent as a semiotic category. Other instances come readily to mind: interview, lecture, feature article, chat, novel. Each such genre codes 'particular' relationships among sets of social participants. The rule systems at issue are clearer to see in some instances ('interview') than in others ('novel'), but are no less operative for that. The 'Rise of the Novel', so called, is a history that traces a set of historically specific relationships that involves the position of classes, definitions (and discourses) of gender, the state of technology, leisure and education, class-based notions of the family, and so on. The history of the genre of 'novel' since its 'rise' equally traces shifts in these relations, the appearance as salient factors of new discourses and of shifts in existent discourses. Genre therefore represents one semiotic category that codes the effects of social change, of social struggle.

An excessive concentration on normative systems (logonomic systems, genres, ideology) contains an inbuilt distortion and reinforces the ideas of their dominance. These systems only constrain the behaviour and beliefs of the non-dominant in so far as they have been effectively imposed and have not been effectively resisted. Attention to the detail of semiosic process reveals countless instances of contestation, where smaller-level shifts in power have significant effects, leading to modification in the structures of domination, at times tracing the success of dominated groups, at times the success of the dominant. This process is well described in Gramsci's work on hegemonic structures and their establishment. Processes of struggle and resistance are themselves decisive aspects of social formations, and affect every level of semiotic systems. At the micro level, power is put to the test in every exchange, and the logonomic system typically is a record of this by classifying large areas of semiosis as 'private', to be treated as beyond the reach of the 'public'/social. The ideological complex similarly attempts to pre-empt opposition by incorporating contradictory images into its coercive forms; even so, they continue to exist there, silently declaring the limits of dominant power. So the meanings and the interests of both dominant and non-dominant act together in proportions that are not predetermined, to constitute the forms and possibilities of meaning at every level. We do not assume that resistance is always successful or potent: but nor do we take it for granted, as many theorists of social meaning seem to do, that resistance is always effortlessly incorporated and rendered non-significant.

[. . .]

Ideology and the construction of gender

Since ideology is only effective in so far as it conditions actual behaviours, its most potent form of expression is when it is inscribed in and organized through spatial codes and their transforms. Gender messages can be instilled by rules of etiquette – such as the requirement that 'gentlemen' must stand up when 'ladies' enter a room. Here the role of verbal language is important but ancillary to the physical spatial codes. Styles of dress, appearance and behaviour are overt enough to be strictly policed, so that the ideological meanings they carry can be obligatory and ubiquitous. Verbal language thus plays a secondary role, acting as a commentary whose real meaning is given by the underlying behavioural text it invokes. To illustrate the process, we will take the following extract from an article in the Australian women's magazine *Cleo* for June 1984 (see also Kress, 1985). The article was entitled 'Body Talk'. It described different types of women found in an office, and instructed each type how to modify their behaviour in order to improve their situation at work. The 'types' addressed were 'Miss Mouse', 'Miss Seductress', 'Ms Winner', 'Miss Nonchalant' and 'Ms Power-broker'. Here are the descriptions of Miss Seductress and Ms Winner:

Miss Seductress

There's always one of this type in every gathering: at parties she laughs alluringly and touches everyone (even your man); when meeting men she pouts, flutters eyelashes and makes her body do the talking. Even in the supermarket she totters in high sling backs and wears clingy angora. Yes, she's the one who always believes that everything will come to her as long as she looks gorgeous. She attracts men like bees to the honey pot and keeps their attention by direct eye contact while always flashing a dazzling smile. She's all teeth, luscious lips, glossy hair, painted fingernails and seductive curves. Men love her, even if women don't, and that's just the way she likes it. She's managed to get good jobs in the past (always male bosses) and never has to 'go dutch' on dinner dates. The trouble with Miss Seductress is that half the world is made up of women, and the men who enjoy her type go down on record as having short attention spans. Which leaves her high and dry much of the time.

You, Miss Seductress, need a lot of help. Turn down the sirens for a start – you won't miss out on the men. You may miss out on the bounders, but you could score with Mr Nice-Guy, the one who's likely to stay for more than the first act. Office harmony hasn't been your strong point because you alienate your female co-workers. Rising in the hierarchy takes enthusiasm and ability, not low cut dresses and knowing looks. Restraint is the key word, in all aspects of your life.

Ms Winner

Ms Winner isn't always easy to categorize at once, because her self-confidence is so unassuming. She's the type who doesn't need to impress others with her abilities – she knows they will shine through anyway. Her self-assurance comes through in every mannerism, every item of clothing, her relaxed posture, her confident speech. She dresses with flair, knowing how to combine basically conservative clothes with innovative extras to form a completely co-ordinated outfit which exudes her personal style. Basically, Ms Winner has panache. She dresses well for the occasion whether it's a job interview or dinner party. Her hair is cut in a modern, but not outrageous style, her make-up is subtle. But Ms Winner's strongest point is her well-modulated conversation which is always lively and intelligent. She has many friends of both sexes who never feel threatened by her. She doesn't talk behind people's back, but is no sycophant either. She has a mind of her own, but doesn't impose it on others. Ms Winner, you're on the right track, so don't change a thing.

The general ideological point of the two descriptions is clear. As the 'Miss Seductress' passage concludes, 'Restraint is the key word.' The recipe for success for women in both cases is self-limitation. The description of Ms Winner makes it clear that she isn't meant to win too much. The character assassination of Miss Seductress works in the first place by describing a stereotyped set of semiotic transactions that define her in social-ideological terms. The focus is on her signals in a range of codes, but these imply the rest of the communication model as an image of the social relationships that define her meaning. Basic proxemic signals of extreme intimacy are listed, from 'touching' (everyone) to 'direct eye contact' (from very close range, we assume). Her facial expressions ('pouts, flutters eyelashes . . . dazzling smile') and clothing ('high sling backs', 'clingy angora', 'low cut dresses') send similarly unmodified messages of intimacy.

This list, however, doesn't explain the ideological effect of this description. Certainly all the signals are exaggerated stereotypes of the 'office siren', but such signal-systems are always conventionalized and predictable. Wearing a coat and tie to work is equally conventional and hence could be called stereotyped but isn't. There are occasional hints of a negative attitude (for instance, in words like 'totters', 'bounder', 'Mr Nice-Guy') but these are counterbalanced by what might in other contexts be positive ('alluringly', 'gorgeous', 'luscious'). The key to the strategy of the article is not here, but in the social relations of the semiotic process itself, in the semiosic plane, in the positions constructed for the reader and the social organization that implicates her.

Cleo is a women's magazine, targeted on 'liberated' women, middle-class women who work and have a disposable income of their own. Its readership already has an assumed gender, and although many men may also read it we can legitimately emphasize the position and role of women readers. The gender of the reader is decisive here, because it is crucial to the meaning of the semiotic transaction. In the first paragraph, this reader is explicitly addressed (through 'your man' – sufficiently implying her gender). Miss Seductress is referred to in the 'third person' as 'she', therefore as outside the transaction that constitutes the text, equally distant from author and reader. The transactions she engages in all consist, as we have seen, of signals of strong intimacy, with clear gender-marking. Words like 'alluringly' are a massive shorthand, indicating a range of sexual signals specifically from a woman to a man (men don't laugh or do anything 'alluringly'). So the intimacy and solidarity offered by 'Miss Seductress' is specifically unavailable to the female reader. Similarly with the 'everyone' (male gender assumed again) whom she touches. Since this 'everyone' includes 'your' man, Miss Seductress's intimacy signals cannot but be interpreted as aggression, towards the reader and also towards the man. The description of her as 'all teeth, luscious lips, glossy hair' in effect inserts the helpless reader 3 cm from Miss Seductress and recategorizes the gender of this reader, if the relation is to be one of solidarity, as a male about to be swallowed by those enormous teeth, or about to devour those 'luscious' lips. But the reader has already been explicitly constructed as female. The result is to release the powerful hostile meanings of closeness. The lack of discrimination increases the sense of potential danger from Miss Seductress, to both stray males and stray female readers. The implication is that the complex social organization of everyday life has been collapsed into innumerable uncontrolled sexual encounters.

Because the female reader is positioned in the text as an uncomfortable victim of unrestrained aggressive intimacy at the hands of Miss Seductress, there is no real need for the author to condemn it. What the author does do is to offer two alternative semiotic models and reception positions. In the first paragraph the author addresses the reader with very little direct contact, though she has the power of the person in control of the discourse. This implies a distant, formal relationship, with the imbalance in power held in check. It contrasts with the aggressive contact of a Miss Seductress. It also contrasts with the receiver-position offered in the second paragraph. Here there is direct contact with Miss Seductress, but it is the closeness of outright aggression. She is on the receiving end of commands, advice and observations which are highly insulting. But the ideological effect of this harangue is not to improve Miss Seductress, who isn't likely to be reading it by this stage (can she read, anyway?). What it offers is an untenable reader position, the experience of being Miss Seductress getting her come-uppance. So much better to be the uninvolved audience of the writer's character assassination.

The second stereotype, Ms Winner, is not only described differently, but set in a different semiotic transaction. Ms Winner's signals are so characterized by multiple contradictions that she is hard to categorize. The author lists some of the codes – mannerisms, clothing, posture, manner of speech – but hardly bothers to indicate how the clusters of contradictory messages are put together or how the contradictions will be resolved. The problems of different audiences for her signals are resolved by suppressing their receivers, half suppressing even the fact that she is producing the signals ('she knows [her abilities] will shine through anyway'). By these means the transactions she is represented as being engaged in are left vague but comfortably distant. No one feels 'threatened' by her, by signals of power or solidarity that are too strong, and because of the coolness of the relationship it is easy for the reader to insert herself into either of the two major semiotic positions, as like her, or as her female 'friend'. The address from the author to Ms Winner which closes the piece is very different from what Miss Seductress receives. Not only is it positive, it is short and unspecific, a compliment rather than a command. Even the approval of this author is an unpleasant experience, because of the power difference, but at least it doesn't last long, and the brevity is itself a kind of withholding of power and an assertion of Ms Winner's near equality.

The ideological potency of the text is established by the semiotic transaction on the semiosic plane interacting with the semiosic relations of the represented world. There is a double reception-position, offering different possibilities of solidarity and power or submission to the author/authority. The represented world contains conventional signals for different versions of social relations, two contradictory ideologies of gender relationships, one characterized by power, the other by intimacy. In spite of the fictional nature, the social relations invoked both by the semiotic transaction which is its framework and by the transactions represented within the text are coded fairly transparently, drawing directly on major spatial codes and their transformations. [. . .]

Reference

Kress, G.R. (1985) *Linguistic Processes in Socio-cultural Practice*, Geelong, Deakin University Press.

Principles of Critical Discourse Analysis

Teun Van Dijk

Source: Van Dijk, T.A. (1993) Principles of critical discourse analysis, *Discourse and Society*, vol. 4, pp. 249–283.

This paper discusses some principles, aims and criteria of a 'critical' discourse analysis (CDA). It tries to answer (critical) questions such as 'What *is* critical discourse analysis (anyway)?', 'How is it different from other types of discourse analysis?', 'What are its aims, special methods, and especially what is its theoretical foundation?' Also, it acknowledges the need to examine, in rather practical terms, how one goes about doing a 'critical' analysis of text and talk.

In general, the answers to such questions presuppose a study of the relations between discourse, power, dominance, social inequality and the position of the discourse analyst in such social relationships. Since this is a complex, multidisciplinary – and as yet underdeveloped – domain of study, which one may call 'sociopolitical discourse analysis', only the most relevant dimensions of this domain can be addressed here.

Although there are many directions in the study and critique of social inequality, the way we approach these questions and dimensions is by focusing on *the role of discourse in the (re)production and challenge of dominance*. Dominance is defined here as the exercise of social power by elites, institutions or groups, that results in social inequality, including political, cultural, class, ethnic, racial and gender inequality. This reproduction process may involve such different 'modes' of discourse – power relations as the more or less direct or overt support, enactment, representation, legitimation, denial, mitigation or concealment of dominance, among others. More specifically, critical discourse analysts want to know what structures, strategies or other properties of text, talk, verbal interaction or communicative events play a role in these modes of reproduction.

This paper is biased in another way: we pay more attention to 'top-down' relations of dominance than to 'bottom-up' relations of resistance, compliance and acceptance. This does not mean that we see power and dominance merely as unilaterally 'imposed' on others. On the contrary, in many situations, and sometimes paradoxically, power and even power abuse may seem 'jointly produced', e.g. when dominated groups are persuaded, by whatever means, that dominance is 'natural' or otherwise legitimate. Thus, although an analysis of strategies of resistance and challenge is crucial for our understanding of actual power and dominance relations in society, and although such an analysis needs to be included in a broader theory of power, counter-power and discourse, our critical approach prefers to focus on the elites and their discursive strategies for the maintenance of inequality.

[. . .]

Typical macro-notions such as group or institutional power and dominance, as well as social inequality, do not directly relate to typical micro-notions such as text, talk or communicative interaction. This not only involves the well-known problem of macro-micro relations in sociology, but also, and perhaps even more interestingly, the relation between society, discourse and social cognition. Indeed, we argue that in order to relate discourse and society, and hence discourse and the reproduction of dominance and inequality, we need to examine in detail the role of social representations in the minds of social actors. More specifically, we hope to show that social cognition is the necessary theoretical (and empirical) 'interface', if not the 'missing link', between discourse and dominance. In our opinion, neglect of such social cognitions has been one of the major theoretical shortcomings of most work in critical linguistics and discourse analysis.

This paper does not discuss the historical backgrounds and developments of critical perspectives in the study of language, discourse and communication. Nor does it provide a full bibliography of such work. Depending on the discipline, orientation, school or paradigm involved, these lines of development are traced back, if not – as usual – to Aristotle, then at least to the philosophers of the Enlightenment or, of course, to Marx, and more recently to the members of the Frankfurt School (Adorno, Benjamin and others) and its direct or indirect heirs in and after the 1960s, among whom Jürgen Habermas plays a primary role (Geuss, 1981; Jay, 1973; Slater, 1977). Another line of influence and development, also more or less (neo-)marxist, is the one going back to Gramsci, and his followers in France and the UK, including most notably Stuart Hall and the other members of the Centre for Contemporary Cultural Studies (Corcoran, 1989; Hall, 1981). Likewise, first in France, later also in the UK and the USA, we can trace the influence of the work of Althusser (1971), Foucault (see, e.g., Foucault, 1980) and Pêcheux (1982), among others. Finally, we should emphasize the exemplary role of feminist scholarship in the critical approach to language and communication.

Although often dealing with 'language', 'text' or 'discourse' in many (usually rather philosophical) ways, most of this work does not explicitly and systematically deal with discourse structures. We had to wait for the various contributions in critical linguistics and social semiotics, first and primarily in the UK and Australia, to get a more detailed view of the other side of the relationship, namely an analysis of the structures of text and image, even if such linguistics and semiotic approaches usually did not aim to provide sophisticated sociopolitical analyses (Chilton, 1985; Fairclough, 1989; Fowler et al., 1979; Hodge and Kress, 1988; Kress and Hodge, 1979). From a different perspective, the same critical approach characterizes much of the work in some directions of German and Austrian sociolinguistics, e.g. on language use of/with immigrant workers, language barriers, fascism and anti-semitism (Dittmar and Schlobinski, 1988; Ehlich, 1989; Wodak, 1985, 1989; Wodak et al., 1987, 1989, 1990; Wodak and Menz, 1990), some of which goes back to the critical sociolinguistic paradigm of Bernstein (1971–5).

[. . .]

Power and dominance

One crucial presupposition of adequate critical discourse analysis is understanding the nature of social power and dominance. Once we have such an insight, we may begin to formulate ideas about how discourse contributes to their reproduction. To cut a long philosophical and social scientific analysis short, we assume that we here deal with properties of relations between social groups. That is, while focusing on *social* power, we ignore purely personal power, unless enacted as an individual realization of group power, that is, by individuals as group members. Social power is based on privileged *access* to socially valued resources, such as wealth, income, position, status, force, group membership, education or knowledge. Below we shall see that special access to various genres, forms or contexts of discourse and communication is also an important power resource (for further details on the concept of power, see, e.g. Clegg, 1989; Lukes, 1986).

Power involves *control*, namely by (members of) one group over (those of) other groups. Such control may pertain to *action* and *cognition*: that is, a powerful group may limit the freedom of action of others, but also influence their minds. Besides the elementary recourse to force to directly control action (as in police violence against demonstrators, or male violence against women), 'modern' and often more effective power is mostly cognitive, and enacted by persuasion, dissimulation or manipulation, among other strategic ways to *change the mind of others in one's own interests*. It is at this crucial point where *discourse* and critical discourse analysis come in: managing the minds of others is essentially a function of text and talk. Note, though, that such mind management is not always bluntly manipulative. On the contrary, dominance may be enacted and reproduced by subtle, routine, everyday forms of text and talk that appear 'natural' and quite 'acceptable'. Hence, CDA also needs to focus on the discursive strategies that legitimate control, or otherwise 'naturalize' the social order, and especially relations of inequality (Fairclough, 1985).

Despite such complexities and subtleties of power relations, critical discourse analysis is specifically interested in power *abuse*, that is, in breaches of laws, rules and principles of democracy, equality and justice by those who wield power. To distinguish such power from legitimate and acceptable forms of power, and lacking another adequate term, we use the term '*dominance*'. As is the case with power, dominance is seldom total. It may be restricted to specific domains, and it may be contested by various modes of *challenge*, that is, counter-power. It may be more or less consciously or explicitly exercised or experienced. Many more or less subtle forms of dominance seem to be so persistent that they seem natural until they begin to be challenged, as was/is the case for male dominance over women, white over black, rich over poor. If the minds of the dominated can be influenced in such a way that they accept dominance, and act in the interest of the powerful out of their own free will, we use the term *hegemony* (Gramsci, 1971; Hall *et al.*, 1977). One major function of dominant discourse is precisely to manufacture such consensus, acceptance and legitimacy of dominance (Herman and Chomsky, 1988).

The concept of hegemony, and its associated concepts of consensus, acceptance and the management of the mind, also suggests that a critical analysis of discourse and dominance is far from straightforward, and does not always imply a clear picture of villains and victims. Indeed, we have already suggested that many forms of dominance appear to be 'jointly produced' through intricate forms of social interaction, communication and discourse. We hope that critical discourse analysis will be able to contribute to our understanding of such intricacies.

Power and dominance are usually *organized* and *institutionalized*. The social dominance of groups is thus not merely enacted, individually, by its group members, as is the case in many forms of everyday racism or sexual harassment. It may also be supported or condoned by other group members, sanctioned by the courts, legitimated by laws, enforced by the police, and ideologically sustained and reproduced by the media or textbooks. This social, political and cultural organization of dominance also implies a *hierarchy of power*: some members of dominant groups and organizations have a special role in planning, decision-making and control over the relations and processes of the enactment of power. These (small) groups will here be called the *power elites* (Domhoff, 1978; Mills, 1956). For our discussion, it is especially interesting to note that such elites also have special access to discourse: they are literally the ones who have most to *say*. In our discourse analytical framework, therefore, we define elites precisely in terms of their 'symbolic power' (Bourdieu, 1982), as measured by the extent of their discursive and communicative scope and resources.

[. . .]

Discourse structures

If powerful speakers or groups enact or otherwise 'exhibit' their power in discourse, we need to know exactly *how* this is done. And if they thus are able to persuade or otherwise influence their audiences, we also want to know which discursive structures and strategies are involved in that process. Hence, the discursive reproduction of dominance, which we have taken as the main object of critical analysis, has two major dimensions, namely that of production and reception. That is, we distinguish between the enactment, expression or legitimation of dominance in the (production of the) various structures of text and talk, on the one hand, and the functions, consequences or results of such structures for the (social) minds of recipients, on the other. Discursive (re)production of power results *from* social cognitions of the powerful, whereas the situated discourse structures result *in* social cognitions. That is, in both cases we eventually have to deal with relations between discourse and cognition, and in both cases discourse structures form the crucial mediating role. They are truly the means of the 'symbolic' reproduction of dominance.

Power enactment and discourse production

Understanding and explaining 'power-relevant' discourse structures involves reconstruction of the social and cognitive processes of their production. One crucial power resource is privileged or preferential access to discourse. One element of such complex access patterns is more or less controlled or active access to the very communicative event as such, that is, to the situation: some (elite) participants may control the occasion, time, place, setting and the presence or absence of participants in such events. In other words, one way of enacting power is to control context. Thus, doctors make 'appointments' with patients, professors with students, or tax auditors with tax-payers, and thereby decide about place and time, and possible other participants. In some such situations, e.g. in parliamentary hearings, court trials or police interrogations, the presence of specific participants may be legally required, and their absence may be sanctioned.

A critical analysis of such access modes to communicative events pays special attention to those forms of context control that are legally or morally illegitimate or otherwise unacceptable. If men exclude women from meetings, whites restrict the access of blacks to the press, or immigration officers do not allow lawyers or social workers to interrogations of refugees, we have instances of discourse dominance, namely communicative discrimination or other forms of marginalization and exclusion. As well as in access patterns and context structures, such modes of exclusion are also apparent in discourse structures themselves. Indeed, some 'voices' are thereby censored, some opinions are not heard, some perspectives ignored: the discourse itself becomes a 'segregated' structure. Blacks or women may thus not only not exercise their rights as speakers and opinion-givers, but they may also be banished as hearers and contestants of power. Such exclusion may also mean that the less powerful are less quoted and less spoken about, so that two other forms of (passive) access are blocked.

Even when present as participants, members of less powerful groups may also otherwise be more or less dominated in discourse. At virtually each level of the structures of text and talk, therefore, their freedom of choice may be restricted by dominant participants. This may more or less acceptably be the case by convention, rule or law, as when chairs organize discussions, allow or prohibit specific speech acts, monitor the agenda, set and change topics or regulate turn-taking, as is more or less explicitly the case for judges, doctors, professors or police officers in the domain-specific discourse sessions they control (trials, consults, classes, interrogations, etc.: Boden and Zimmerman, 1991; Fisher and Todd, 1986). On the other hand, members of less powerful groups may also be illegitimately or immorally restricted in their communicative acts. Men may subtly or bluntly exclude women from taking the floor or from choosing specific topics (Kramarae, 1981). Judges or police officers may not allow subjects to explain or defend themselves, immigration officers may prevent refugees from telling their 'story', and whites may criticize blacks for talking about racism (if they let them talk/write about it in the first place: Van Dijk, 1993).

In sum, as we have defined power and dominance as the control of action, also discursive action may be restricted in many ways, either because of institutional power resources (positions, professional expertise, etc.), as for doctors or judges, or because of group membership alone, as for males and whites. All dimensions of discourse that allow variable choice, therefore, are liable to such forms of control, and participant power or powerlessness is directly related to the extent of their control over such discourse variables. Illegitimate control of the course of discourse, therefore, is a direct and immediate enactment of dominance, while limiting the 'discourse rights' of other participants (Kedar, 1987; Kramarae *et al.*, 1984).

From these contextual, interactional, organizational and global forms of discourse control, we may move to the more detailed, micro-level and expression forms of text and talk. Many of these are more or less automatized, less consciously controlled or not variable at all, as is the case for many properties of syntax, morphology or phonology. That is, the influence of power will be much less direct and immediate at these levels. On the other hand, since communication is often less consciously controlled here, the more subtle and unintentional manifestations of dominance may be observed at these levels, e.g. in intonation, lexical or syntactic style, rhetorical figures, local semantic structures, turn-taking strategies, politeness phenomena, and so on.

Indeed, these more micro- or 'surface' structures may be less regulated by legal or moral rules, and hence allow more 'unofficial' exercise of power, that is, dominance. For instance, an insolent 'tone', e.g. of men, judges or police officers, may only seem to break the rules of politeness, and not the law, and may thus be one of the means to exercise dominance. It is also at this level that many studies have examined the incidence of more or less 'powerful' styles of talk, either in specific contexts (e.g. in court or the classroom), or by members of specific groups (men vs women), featuring, e.g., the presence or absence of hedges, hesitations, pauses, laughter, interruptions, doubt or certainty markers, specific lexical items, forms of address and pronoun use, and so on (among many studies, see, e.g. Bradac and Mulac, 1984; Erickson *et al.*, 1978).

A critical approach to such discourse phenomena must be as subtle as the means of dominance it studies. Thus, an 'impolite' form of address (using first name or informal pronouns) may characterize many discourses of many people in many situations. Although such impoliteness may well 'signal' power, it need not signal social (group) power, nor dominance (Brown and Levinson, 1987). In other words, occasional, incidental or personal breaches of discourse rules are not, as such, expressions of dominance. This is the case only if such violations are generalized, occur in text and talk directed at, or about, specific dominated groups only, and if there are no contextual justifications other than such group membership. If these, and other conditions, are satisfied, an act of discourse impoliteness may be a more or less subtle form of sexism, ageism, racism or classism, among other forms of group dominance. The same is true for variations of intonation or 'tone', lexical style or rhetorical figures.

The socio-cognitive interface between dominance and production

While this is a more or less adequate description of the enactment of social power by the use of specific discourse structures, we should recall our important thesis that a fully fledged theoretical explanation also needs a cognitive dimension. If not, why for instance does a white speaker believe that he or she may be impolite towards a black addressee, and not towards a white speaker in the same situation? In other words, what models and social representations link social group dominance with the choice of specific discourse forms?

According to the framework sketched above, this explanation may more or less run as follows: (1) A white speaker perceives, interprets and represents the present communicative situation in a mental context model, including also a representation of him/herself (as being white) and of the black addressee. (2) To do this, general attitudes about blacks will be activated. If these are negative, this will also show in the representation of the black addressee in the context model: the addressee may be assigned lower status, for instance. (3) This 'biased' context model will monitor production and, all other things being equal (e.g. if there is no fear of retaliation, or there are no moral accusations), this may result in the production of discourse structures that signal such underlying bias, e.g. specific impoliteness forms. Note that these socio-cognitive processes underlying racist discourse production may be largely automatized. That is, there is no need to assume that impoliteness is 'intentional' in such a case. Intentionality is irrelevant in establishing whether discourses or other acts may be interpreted as being racist.

These various mental strategies and representations of individual speakers are of course premised on the condition that white speakers share their attitudes and more fundamental anti-black ideologies with other whites, e.g. as a legitimation of their dominance. This also explains why in similar situations other whites may engage in similar behaviour, and how through repeated instances in various contexts blacks may learn to interpret specific discourse forms as being 'racist' (Essed, 1991).

[. . .]

Parliamentary discourse on ethnic affairs

To illustrate the general approach to critical discourse analysis sketched above, let us finally discuss an example. This will be drawn from a study we did of the ways some western parliaments debate about ethnic affairs (Van Dijk, 1993: ch. 3). This study is itself part of a project on 'elite discourse and racism' which seeks to show that the various elites (e.g. in politics, the media, academia, education and corporate business) play a prominent role in the reproduction of racism, and do so, sometimes subtly, through the respective discourse genres to which they have access. The project is part of our year-long research programme on discourse, communication and racism.

[. . .]

Reproducing racism in the British House of Commons
This example was taken from a parliamentary debate held on 16 April 1985 in the British House of Commons and consists of several fragments from the leading speech by Mr Marcus Fox, Conservative representative of Shipley, about the so-called 'Honeyford affair'. Honeyford was the headmaster of a school in Bradford (UK), who was first suspended, then reinstated but finally dismissed (with a golden handshake) because of what the parents of his mostly Asian pupils, the Bradford City Council and their supporters saw as racist writings, e.g. in the right-wing *Salisbury Review* and the *Times Literary Supplement*, on multicultural education in general, and on his own students in particular. The affair soon became a national issue, in which Conservative politicians as well as the Conservative press fulminated against the 'race relations bullies' (also a phrase used by Mr Fox in his speech), who 'strike at the very root of our democracy . . . the freedom of speech'. Here is how Mr Fox begins this adjournment debate in the British Parliament:

> *Mr Marcus Fox* (Shipley): This Adjournment debate is concerned with Mr Ray
> Honeyford, the headmaster of Drummond Road Middle School, Bradford. This

matter has become a national issue – not from Mr Honeyford's choice. Its consequences go beyond the issue of race relations or, indeed, of education. They strike at the very root of our democracy and what we cherish in this House above all – the freedom of speech.

One man writing an article in a small-circulation publication has brought down a holocaust on his head. To my mind, this was a breath of fresh air in the polluted area of race relations . . .

Who are Mr Honeyford's detractors? Who are the people who have persecuted him? They have one thing in common – they are all on the Left of British politics. The Marxists and the Trots are here in full force. We only have to look at their tactics, and all the signs are there. Without a thread of evidence, Mr Honeyford has been vilified as a racist. Innuendos and lies have been the order of the day. He has been criticised continuously through the media, yet most of the time he has been barred from defending himself and denied the right to answer those allegations by order of the education authority. The mob has taken to the streets to harass him out of his job . . .

The race relations bullies may have got their way so far, but the silent majority of decent people have had enough . . . The withdrawal of the right to free speech from this one man could have enormous consequences and the totalitarian forces ranged against him will have succeeded.

(Hansard, 16 April 1985: cols 233–6)

To examine the enactment of power and dominance in this speech, and conversely the role of this speech in the reproduction of such dominance, we systematically discuss its major discourse dimensions. Recall that for all the dimensions, levels or properties of this speech that we analyse (and this analysis is far from exhaustive), the reproduction of dominance has two major aspects: the direct enactment or production of dominance, on the one hand, and the consequences of this speech in the process of the management of the public consensus on ethnic affairs, on the other. For instance, discrediting Asian parents is itself an act of verbal discrimination, indirectly restricting the civil rights of minorities. At the same time, such a discursive act may contribute to the formation of negative models about Asian parents and (other) anti-racists, which may be generalized to negative attitudes which in turn may influence discrimination by members of the white group at large.

Note that although our first task is to systematically examine the many textual and contextual properties of the exercise of dominance for this example, and to provide explicit evidence for such an account, analysis is not – and cannot be – 'neutral'. Indeed, the point of critical discourse analysis is to take a position. In this case, we take a position that tries to examine the speech of Mr Fox from the point of view of the opponents of Honeyford, thereby criticizing the dominant groups and institutions (e.g. Conservative politicians and journalists) who defended Honeyford and attacked multicultural education.

The analysis begins with various properties of the context, such as access patterns, setting and participants, and then examines the properties of the text' of the speech itself, such as its topics, local meanings, style and rhetoric. Of the many possible properties of the text and context of this speech we focus on those that most clearly exhibit the discursive properties of the exercise of dominance. For detailed theoretical explanations of these properties and their relevance for critical analysis, the reader is referred Van Dijk, 1984, 1987, 1991, 1993.

Access   As indicated above, Mr Fox's power as an MP is first of all defined by his active and more or less controlled access to the House of Commons and its debates.

Setting   The power and authority of his speech is also signalled and maybe enhanced by elements of the setting, such as the location (the House of Commons) and its prestigious props, the presence of other MPs, and so on. Since television has recently entered the House of Commons, such symbols of parliamentary power are also relevant for the public 'overhearers' of parliamentary debates. Locally, Mr Fox's power and influence coincides with his having the floor, marked not only by his speaking, but also by his standing up while the other MPs are seated.

Genre   Mr Fox also has special access to a genre only he and his colleagues are entitled to engage in, namely parliamentary debates. We have seen above that this is not merely 'talk', but constitutive of highest level political decision making.

Communicative acts and social meanings   Besides these broader social or political implications, this speech fragment from the House of Commons locally expresses or signals various social meanings and categories of social interaction. At the interaction level itself, therefore, politeness is signalled by the formal modes of address ('the Honourable Gentleman'), whereas political closeness may be marked by 'my friend . . .' Since the politeness markers are mutual here, social power relations in the House seem to be equal. Note, though, that Mr Fox is a member of a government party, which is able to control much of the parliamentary agenda, and which therefore is able to hold a parliamentary debate on Honeyford in the first place. That is, also among 'equals', political dominance may be at stake.

   This is also the case at the semantic level, that is, relative to the social situation and events talked about by Mr Fox. By defending Mr Honeyford, Mr Fox attacks shared opponents, namely leftists or anti-racists. Because of his powerful position as an MP he adds considerable weight to the balance of this conflict between Honeyford and the parents of his students, as is also the case for the right-wing media supporting Honeyford. We see how the Conservative elites, who may otherwise be hardly interested in ordinary teachers, may take part in the struggle between racism and anti-racism, between 'British values' and the values of multiculturalism scorned by Mr Honeyford.

   Indeed, rather surprisingly, Mr Honeyford was even personally received by former Prime Minister Margaret Thatcher at Number 10 Downing Street, which again signals the highest support for his case. Similarly, that a conflict of a headmaster becomes a topic of a parliamentary debate by itself already suggests the importance accorded to the conflict, and to the sociopolitical positions to be defended at all costs. Finally, by associating Honeyford's opponents (mostly Asian parents) with Marxists and 'Trots' not only means that the case of his opponents is discredited within the framework of a largely anti-communist consensus, but also, more politically, that the Labour opposition to which Mr Fox's speech is primarily addressed is thus attacked and discredited. Below we shall see how such attacks, marginalization, discrediting and other sociopolitical acts are enacted by properties of discourse. Here, it should be emphasized, however, that the ultimate functions of such a speech are not merely linguistic or communicative (expressing or conveying meaning), but political.

Participant positions and roles Mr Fox obviously speaks in his role as MP, and as a member of the Conservative party, among several other social identities, such as being a politician, white and male. This position institutionally entitles him to put the Honeyford case on the parliamentary agenda if he and his party deem the issue to be of national interest. Hence, it is not only his role as Conservative MP that influences the structures and strategies of his speech, but also his identity as a member of the white dominant group, and especially his identity as a member of the white elites. Thus, his party-political position explains why he attacks Labour, and the Left in general, his being an MP influences his alleged concern for democracy and the freedom of speech, and his being white his collusion with racist practices and his aggressions against Indian parents and their supporters.

Speech acts Most of Mr Fox's speech consists of assertions, and also, at the global level of macro-speech acts, he primarily accomplishes an assertion. However, we have observed that, indirectly, he also accuses Honeyford's 'detractors' of vilification, lying and intimidation. At the same time, he thereby accuses and attacks the Labour opposition, whom he sees as opponents of Honeyford. In parliament his accusations and allegations may be met with appropriate defence by his sociopolitical equals. Not so, however, beyond the boundaries of parliament, where his accusations may be heard (literally, over the radio) or read (when quoted in the press) by millions, who may thus be exposed to biased information about Honeyford's opponents (most of whom are not Marxists or Trotskyites at all). For our CDA perspective, this means that the function and the scope of speech participants may largely define the effectiveness and 'authority' of their speech acts. Indeed, other supporters of Honeyford may legitimate their position by referring to such accusations in parliament.

Macrosemantics: topics The topic of the debate in the British House of Commons, as signalled by Mr Fox himself ('This Adjournment debate is concerned with . . .'), is clearly 'the Honeyford case'. Propositionally, however, the topic may be defined in various ways, e.g. as 'Honeyford wrote disparaging articles about his Asian students and about multicultural education more generally', 'Honeyford has been accused of racism' and 'Honeyford is being vilified by anti-racist detractors'. It is the latter topic that is being construed by Mr Fox. At the same time, however, topics have sociopolitical implications, and these implications are made explicit by Mr Fox: the debate is not only about Honeyford, or even about race relations and education, but about the 'very root of our democracy', namely about free speech. This example shows how events, including discourse about such events, are represented, at the macro-level, as a function of underlying norms and values, that is, within the framework of dominant ideologies. That is, Mr Fox and other supporters of Honeyford, including the Conservative media, interpret Honeyford's racist articles and his attack on multicultural education as a 'breath of fresh air', and hence as an example of justified criticism, whereas his opponents are categorized as restricting free speech, and hence as being intolerant and undemocratic. This reversal of the application of values is well known in anti-anti-racist rhetoric, where those who combat ethnic and racial intolerance are themselves accused of intolerance, namely of the 'freedom' to 'tell the truth' about ethnic relations (for further detail, see also Van Dijk, 1991).

Relevant for our discussion here is that Mr Fox as an MP has the power not only to define and redefine the topics of debate, but also to define the situation. That is, the point is no longer whether or not Honeyford has insulted his students and their parents, or whether or not a teacher of a largely multicultural school is competent when he attacks the principles of multiculturalism, but whether the critique levelled against him is legitimate in the first place. By generalizing the topic even beyond race relations and education to a debate about democracy and free speech, Mr Fox at the same time defines both his and Mr Honeyford's opponents – including Labour – as being against free speech and democracy, and hence as enemies of the British state and its fundamental values. By thus redefining the topic at issue, Mr Fox no longer merely defends Mr Honeyford, but also reverses the charges and attacks the Left. He thereby conceals the fundamentally undemocratic implications of racism, and manipulates his secondary audience, namely the public at large, into believing that Mr Honeyford is merely a champion of free speech, and that his opponents are attacking British values if not democracy in general. As we shall see below, most of his speech tries to persuasively support that topical 'point'.

Superstructures: text schemata   One major form of text schema is argumentation. In Mr Fox's speech, as in parliamentary debates in general, argumentation plays a prominent role. As we have seen above, his main political point coincides with his argumentative 'position', which consists of his opinion that an attack against Honeyford is an attack against democracy and the freedom of speech. How does he support such a position? His first argument is a negative description of the facts: one man who writes in a 'small-circulation' publication has brought a 'holocaust' on his head. In other words, whatever Honeyford has written, it was insignificant (while published in a 'small-circulation' publication), and the reaction was massively destructive (a 'holocaust'). Moreover, what he wrote was also a 'breath of fresh air in the polluted area of race relations' and hence not only not reprehensible, but laudable. For Mr Fox, it follows that a massive attack against laudable critique is a threat to the freedom of speech, and hence to democracy.

We see that we need several steps to 'make sense' of Mr Fox's argument, and that such a reconstruction needs to be based on the subjective arguments and attitudes of the arguer. After all, Mr Honeyford *was* able to speak his mind, so that the freedom of speech was not in danger. To equate criticism or even attacks against him with a threat to the freedom of speech and to democracy is, therefore, from another point of view, hardly a valid argument, but a hyperbole, a rhetorical figure we also find in the insensitive hyperbolic use of the term 'holocaust'. To fully understand this argument, however, we need more than a reconstruction of Mr Fox's attitudes. We need to know, for instance, that anti-racist critique in the UK is more generally discredited by right-wing politicians and media as a limitation of free speech, because it does not allow people to 'tell the truth' about ethnic relations in general, or about multicultural education in particular. Hence the reference to the 'polluted area of race relations'.

The second sequence of arguments focuses on Honeyford's 'detractors', by whom Honeyford has been allegedly 'vilified as a racist'. By categorizing such opponents as 'Marxists and Trots', and by claiming they have been engaged in lies and innuendo and even 'harassed him out of his job', Mr Fox details how, in his opinion, free speech is constrained, while at the same time discrediting Honeyford's opponents as communists, and as 'totalitarian forces', that is, in his view, as the enemies of freedom and democracy. A third component in this argumentative schema is the claim that Honeyford is helpless and is not allowed to defend himself. He even ranges the media among the opponents of Honeyford, although most of the vastly dominant Conservative press supported him.

In sum, the argument schema features the following steps (propositions or macropropositions), of which the implicit arguments are marked with square brackets:

Arguments:
1   Honeyford wrote an original and deserved critique of multicultural education.

2   His opponents attacked and harassed him massively.
2.1 [Massive attack and harassment of critics is an attack against free speech]
2.2 His opponents are totalitarian communists.
2.2.1 [Totalitarian communists are against freedom and democracy]

Conclusion:
3 By attacking Honeyford, his opponents limit the freedom of speech and attack democracy itself.

Interestingly, the argument, if valid, would also apply to Mr Fox's argument itself, because by thus attacking from his powerful position as an MP, and given the massive attacks against Honeyford's opponents in the right-wing press, we might conclude, probably with much more reason, that the freedom to criticize racist publications is delegitimated, if not constrained. That is, Honeyford's opponents hardly have access to the mass media as Honeyford and his supporters had. Indeed, their arguments, if heard at all, are usually ignored or negatively presented in much of the press. On the other hand, Honeyford got the unusual privilege to explain his opinions in several long articles he was invited to write for the *Daily Mail*.

The validity of Mr Fox's argument itself, however, hinges upon his definition of the situation, which is not only biased, but also unfounded: Honeyford's critics are not Marxists and Trotskyites (at least, not all or even most of them), they did not prevent him from writing what he wanted to write, and, apart from protests, demonstrations and picketing of his school, they did not harass him. Moreover, the majority of the press did not attack him, but supported him. What happened, however, was that he was suspended because he had publicly derogated his Asian students and their parents, and thus, for the education authority, he had failed as a headmaster.

From our CDA perspective, the point of this brief analysis of the argumentative schema of (part of) Mr Fox's speech is that a powerful and influential speaker, namely an MP, whose arguments may be quoted in the media, may misrepresent the facts, discredit anti-racists as being undemocratic and against free speech, while at the same time supporting and legitimating racist publications. Unless his audience knows the facts, and unless it knows the opponents of Mr Honeyford and their arguments, it may thus be manipulated into believing that Mr Fox's argument is valid, and thereby associate those who oppose racism with 'totalitarian' methods. This indeed is very common in the press, not only on the Right, and Mr Fox reinforces such a negative evaluation of the struggle against racism. Ultimately, therefore, Mr Fox legitimates racism and enacts the dominance of the white group, not only by marginalizing anti-racism, but also by discrediting multicultural policies in education. His political power as an MP is thus paired with his symbolic, discursive power consisting in controlling the minds of his (secondary) audience, namely the media, other elites and finally the public at large.

Local meaning and coherence   Few levels of analysis are as revealing and relevant for a critical analysis as the semantic study of local 'meanings', including the propositional structures of clauses and sentences, relations between propositions, implications, presuppositions, vagueness, indirectness, levels of description, and so on. We have seen that, in general, dominance is semantically signalled by positive self-presentation and negative other-presentation or derogation. We may expect, therefore, that the various semantic modes of meaning also reflect such an overall strategy, e.g. by concealing negative properties of the own group (racism), and emphasizing or inventing those of the Others (the 'intolerance' of anti-racism).

(a) Level of specificity and degree of completeness. In a semantic analysis, discourses may be studied as describing events at several levels of specificity (in general abstract terms or in lower level details), and – at each such level – more or less completely. Irrelevant or dispreferred information is usually described at higher levels and less completely, and preferred information in over-complete, detailed ways. One of the most conspicuous forms of over-completeness in discourse is the irrelevant negative categorization of participants in order to delegitimate or marginalize their opinions or actions. This also happens in Mr Fox's speech, where (at least from the point of view of the Asian parents) he irrelevantly categorizes Honeyford's critics as Marxists or Trotskyites. For him and much of his anti-communist audience this implies an association of the political-ideological enemy (the communists) with his moral/social enemy (the anti-racists). At the same time, Mr Fox's argument, as we have seen, is also seriously incomplete, because (in this fragment) it says nothing about the nature of what Mr Honeyford has written. It does, however, detail the many alleged negative actions of his opponents. He does not summarize their actions by saying that Honeyford was 'criticized' or even 'attacked', but mentions lies, vilification,

harassment, etc. In this case, thus, incompleteness is a semantic property of argumentation, but also a more general move of concealment and positive self-presentation: Honeyford's racist articles are not discussed in detail, but only positively described, at a higher level of specificity, as 'a breath of fresh air'.

(b) Perspective. Little analysis is necessary to identify the perspective and point of view displayed in Mr Fox's speech: he defends Honeyford openly, supports his view explicitly, and severely attacks and marginalizes Honeyford's opponents. However, Mr Fox also speaks as an MP – he refers to 'this House' – and as a defender of democracy. Using the politically crucial pronoun 'our' in 'our democracy', he also speaks from the perspective of a staunch defender of democracy. This identification is of course crucial for a right-wing MP and for someone who openly supports someone who has written racist articles. Finally, he claims to be the voice of the 'silent majority of decent people', a well-known populist ploy in Conservative rhetoric. This also means that the parents of the Asian children in Bradford do not belong to this majority of 'decent people'. On the contrary, they have been categorized as, or with, the enemy on the Left.

(c) Implicitness: implications, presuppositions, vagueness. Spelling out the full presuppositions and other implications of Mr Fox's speech would amount to specifying the complex set of beliefs about the Honeyford case (the Honeyford-model of Mr Fox, and those of his audience and critics), as well as the general opinions on which his evaluations and arguments are based, as we have seen above. Hence, we only mention a few examples. If the matter has become a national issue 'not from Mr Honeyford's choice' this strongly implies that others, namely his opponents, have made a national issue of it, whereas it also (weakly) implies that Mr Honeyford's publication in a widely read national newspaper (*Times Literary Supplement*) and later in the *Daily Mail* did nothing to contribute to the national issue. The use of 'small-circulation' as a modifier of 'publication' implies that, given the small audience of the publication (he probably refers to the extremist right-wing *Salisbury Review*), the publication is 'insignificant' and hence 'not worth all the fuss' and certainly not worth the ensuing 'holocaust'. The major presupposition of this speech, however, is embodied in Mr Fox's rhetorical question: 'Who are the people who have persecuted him?', presupposing that there actually *were* people who 'persecuted' him. Finally, important for the political power-play in parliament are the implications of his categorization of Honeyford's opponents as being 'all on the Left of British politics', which immediately addresses Mr Fox's opponents in the House of Commons: Labour. By vilifying Honeyford's opponents, and anti-racists generally, as communists, as undemocratic and as enemies of free speech, he implies that such is also the case for Labour.

(d) Local coherence. There is one interesting coherence feature in Mr Fox's speech, namely when he begins a new sentence with the definite noun phrase 'The mob'. Since no mob has been mentioned before in his text, we must assume either that this phrase generically refers to an (unspecified) mob, or that the phrase corefers, as is clearly his intention, to the previously mentioned discourse referents (Honeyford's detractors, etc.). Such coreference is permissible only if the qualification of previously identified participants is presupposed. In other words, Mr Fox, in line with right-wing news reports about Honeyford's critics,

implicitly qualifies Honeyford's opponents as a 'mob', and presupposes this qualification in a following sentence. This is one of Mr Fox's discursive means to derogate his opponents. In other words, coherence may presuppose ideologically based beliefs.

Style: variations of syntax, lexicon and sound

(a) Lexical style. Mr Fox's lexical style is characteristic not only of parliamentary speeches, featuring technical political terms such as 'Adjournment debate', or of 'educated' talk in general, as we see in 'intellectual' words such as 'innuendo', 'detractors', 'totalitarian forces' or 'vilified'. He also uses the well-known aggressive populist register of the tabloids when he characterizes his and Honeyford's opponents as 'Trots', 'mob', and especially as 'race relations bullies'. That is, Mr Fox's lexicalization multiply signals his power, his political and moral position, as well as his persuasive strategies in influencing his (secondary) audience, namely the British public.

(b) Syntactic style. The syntax of Mr Fox's speech shows a few examples of semantically controlled topicalization and other forms of highlighting information. Thus, in the fourth sentence, the object of the predicate 'to strike at', namely 'the freedom of speech', is placed at the end of the sentence, after its qualifying clause ('what we cherish in this House above all'), in order to emphasize it – a well-known strategy of syntactic and rhetorical 'suspense'. Conversely, 'without a thread of evidence' is fronted somewhat later in his speech so as to specify from the outset of the sentence that Honeyford's vilification was without grounds. Note also the agentless passives: By whom, indeed, was Honeyford continuously criticized in the media? Surely not by Marxists and Trotskyites, who have no access to mainstream publications in Britain.

(c) Anaphora and deictics. In our discussion of the perspective and point of view in Mr Fox's speech we have already suggested his multiple political and social 'positions' and with whom Mr Fox identifies. Position and identification also determine the use of pronouns and deictic expressions (like 'this' in 'this Adjournment debate', which signals Mr Fox's participation in the debate). Most significant in this fragment, however, is the use of 'our' in 'our democracy', a well-known political possessive pronoun in much Conservative rhetoric. Obviously, Mr Fox signals himself as participating in 'our democracy', which may refer to British democracy, or western democracy, or the kind of democracy as it is interpreted by Mr Fox. The rest of his argument, however, clearly shows that the Left, and especially Marxists, Trotskyites, and the supporters of Mr Honeyford, are excluded from this definition of democracy, because they allegedly violate the freedom of speech.

Rhetoric   Within the ecological domain, Mr Fox finds both a contrastive comparison and two metaphors to identify Honeyford's original ideas ('breath of fresh air') and the 'polluted' atmosphere of race relations. Again, after associating Honeyford's opponents with Nazis, he now associates them with polluters, a new officially certified enemy. Interestingly, as we have seen earlier, we may interpret such qualifications also as reversals, since it is precisely the extreme Right that is politically more inclined to condone fascism and industrial pollution, and not the radical Left Mr Fox is speaking about. That is, in attacking the Left, right-wing speakers often make use of classical accusations of the Left itself, simply by 'inverting' them, and as if to deny their own lack of a democratic zeal, for instance in supporting someone who writes racist articles.

Also the rest of the speech makes full use of the usual tricks from the rhetorical bag: rhetorical questions ('Who are Mr Honeyford's detractors?', etc.), parallelisms (the repeated questions), alliterations ('full force'), and especially contrasts between US and THEM, as in 'race relations bullies' and 'the majority of decent people', in general, and between the lone hero ('One man . . .') and his opponents (Marxists, Trots, totalitarian forces, mob, vilification, lies, etc.), in particular. These rhetorical features emphasize what has been expressed and formulated already at the semantic, syntactic and lexical (stylistic) levels of his speech, namely the positive presentation of Honeyford (US, Conservatives, etc.), on the one hand, and the negative presentation of the Others (the Left, anti-racists, Asian parents), on the other.

Final remark   Hence, the dominance expressed, signalled and legitimated in this speech does not merely reside in the political realm of the House of Commons, for instance in Mr Fox's role of MP, and as representative of a government party that is entitled to hold a debate about the Honeyford affair in parliament. Similarly, by attacking the Left he not only attacks Labour, as may be expected from a Tory speaker. Rather, the dominance involved here extends beyond parliament, namely to the media and especially to the public at large when Mr Fox uses his political influence to publicly support a teacher of students whose parents think he writes racist things, and especially in order to discredit and marginalize both these parents and their supporters. Indeed, the rest of this speech, not analysed here, sketches in more detail what he sees as a wonderful teacher, while at the same time denying, as is common in much elite discourse, the racist nature of Honeyford's writings. That is, Mr Fox's power, authority and dominance is not merely that of being an influential MP. Rather, his authority, namely in establishing what racism is, is that of a member of the white elite. It is in this way, therefore, that such a speech indirectly supports the system of ethnic-racial dominance, that is, racism.

[. . .]

Acknowledgement

I am indebted to Norman Fairclough, Theo van Leeuwen and Ruth Wodak for critical comments on an earlier version of this paper, and to the participants of the workshop on Critical Discourse Analysis, held in Amsterdam (24–25 January 1992), for their discussion of some of the points raised in this article. That not all agreed on all of my points shows that also among critical scholars there is no consensus on the politics, theories or methods of critical inquiry.

References

Althusser, L. (1971) *Lenin and Philosophy and Other Essays*, New York, Monthly Review Press.
Bernstein, B. (1971–5) *Class, Codes, Control*, (3 vols), London, Routledge and Kegan Paul.

Boden, D. and Zimmerman, D.H. (eds) (1991) *Talk and Social Structure: Studies in Ethnomethodology and Conversation Analysis*, Cambridge, Polity.

Bourdieu, P. (1982) *Ce que parler veut dire* (What speaking means), Paris, Fayard.

Bradac, J.J. and Mulac, A. (1984) 'A molecular view of powerful and powerless speech styles', *Communication Monographs*, vol. 51, pp. 307–19.

Brown, P. and Levinson, S.C. (1987) *Politeness: Some Universals in Language Use*, Cambridge, Cambridge University Press.

Chilton, P. (ed.) (1985) *Language and the Nuclear Arms Debate: Nukespeak Today*, London, Pinter.

Clegg, S.R. (1989) *Frameworks of Power*, London, Sage.

Corcoran, F. (1989) 'Cultural studies: from Old World to New World' in J.A. Anderson (ed.) *Communication Yearbook 12*, Newbury Park, CA, Sage.

Dittmar, N. and Schlobinksi, P. (eds) (1988) *The Sociolinguistics of Urban Vernaculars: Case Studies and Their Evaluation*, Berlin, de Gruyter.

Domhoff, G.W. (1978) *The Powers That Be: Processes of Ruling Class Domination in America*, New York, Random House (Vintage Books).

Erickson, B., Lind, A.A., Johnson, B.C. and O'Barr, W.M. (1978) 'Speech style and impression formation in a court setting: the effects of "powerful" and "powerless" speech', *Journal of Experimental Social Psychology*, vol. 14, pp. 266–79.

Ehlich, K. (ed.) (1989) *Sprache im Faschismus*, Frankfurt, Suhrkamp.

Essed, P.J.M. (1991) *Understanding Everyday Racism*, Newbury Park, CA, Sage.

Fairclough, N.L. (1985) 'Critical and descriptive goals in discourse analysis', *Journal of Pragmatics*, vol. 9, pp. 739–63.

Fairclough, N. (1989) *Language and Power*, London, Longman.

Fisher, S. and Todd, A.D. (eds) (1986) *Discourse and Institutional Authority: Medicine, Education, and Law*, Norwood, NJ, Ablex.

Foucault, M. (1980) *Power/Knowledge: Selected Writings and Other Interviews 1972–1977*, C. Gordon (ed.) New York, Pantheon.

Fowler, R., Hodge, B., Kress, G. and Trew, T. (1979) *Language and Control*, London, Routledge and Kegan Paul.

Geuss, R. (1981) *The Idea of Critical Theory: Habermas and the Frankfurt School*, Cambridge, Cambridge University Press.

Gramsci, A. (1971) *Selections from the Prison Notebooks*, New York, International Publishers.

Hall, S. (1981) 'Cultural studies: two paradigms' in T. Bennett, G. Martin, C. Mercer and J. Woollacott (eds) *Culture, Ideology and Social Process*, London, Batsford Academic and Educational.

Hall, S., Lumley, B. and McLennan, G. (1977) 'Gramsci on ideology' in Centre for Contemporary Cultural Studies *Politics and Ideology: Gramsci*, London, Hutchinson.

Herman, E.S. and Chomsky, N. (1988) *Manufacturing Consent: The Political Economy of the Mass Media*, New York, Pantheon Books.

Hodge, R. and Kress, G. (1988) *Social Semiotics*, Cambridge, Polity.

Jay, M. (1973) *The Dialectical Imagination: A History of the Frankfurt School and the Institute of Social Research 1923–1950*, Boston, Little Brown.

Kedar, L. (ed.) (1987) *Power through Discourse*, Norwood, NJ, Ablex.

Kramarae, C. (1981) *Women and Men Speaking: Frameworks for Analysis*, Rowley, MA, Newbury House.

Kramarae, C., Schulz, M. and O'Barr, W.M. (eds) (1984) *Language and Power*, Beverly Hills, CA, Sage.

Kress, G. and Hodge, B. (1979) *Language and Ideology*, London, Routledge and Kegan Paul.

Lukes, S. (ed.) (1986) *Power*, Oxford, Blackwell.

Mills, C.W. (1956) *The Power Elite*, London, Oxford University Press.

Pêcheux, M. (1982) *Language, Semantics and Ideology*, New York, St Martin's Press.

Slater, P. (1977) *Origin and Significance of the Frankfurt School: A Marxist Perspective*, London, Routledge and Kegan Paul.

Van Dijk, T.A. (1984) *Prejudice in Discourse*, Amsterdam, Benjamins.

Van Dijk, T.A. (1987) *Communicating Racism*, Newbury Park, CA, Sage.

Van Dijk, T.A. (1989) 'Structures of discourse and structures of power' in J.A. Anderson (ed.) *Communication Yearbook 12*, Newbury Park, CA, Sage.

Van Dijk, T.A. (1991) *Racism and the Press*, London, Routledge.

Van Dijk, T.A. (1993) *Elite Discourse and Racism*, Newbury Park, CA, Sage.

Wodak, R. (1985) 'The interaction between judge and defendant' in T.A. van Dijk (ed.) *Handbook of Discourse Analysis. Vol. 4: Discourse Analysis in Society*, London, Academic Press.

Wodak, R., ed. (1989) *Language, Power and Ideology*, Amsterdam, Benjamins.

Wodak, R., De Cillia, R., Blüml, K. and Andraschko, E. (1987) *Sprache und Macht*, Vienna, Deuticke.

Wodak, R. and Menz, F. (eds) (1990) *Sprache in der Politik – Politik in der Sprache: Analysen zum öffentlichen Sprachgebrauch*, Klagenfurt, Drava.

Wodak, R., Menz, F. and Lalouschek, J. (1989) *Sprachbarrieren: Die Verständigungskrise der Gesellschaft*, Vienna, Atelier.

Wodak, R., Nowak, P., Pelikan, J., Gruber, H., De Cillia, R. and Mitten, R. (1990) *'Wir sind alle unschuldige Täter': Diskurshistorische Studien zum Nachkriegsantisemitismus*, Frankfurt am Main, Suhrkamp.

Textualizing Global Politics

Michael Shapiro

Source: Shapiro, M. (1989) 'Texualising global politics' in J. Der Derian and M. Shapiro (eds) *International/Intertextual Relations*, Lexington, Mass., Lexington Books.

Language and text

Much of modern literary theory operates with the recognition that literary texts have a mediated relationship with the social reality they represent, that indeed what *is* 'social reality' emerges in the writing of the text and bears traces of its previous constructions in the history of the literary genre. This engenders an interest in 'intertextuality', which, as one literary theorist puts it, 'denotes ways in which works of art – especially of literature – are produced in response not to social reality but to previous works of art and the codes of other conventions governing them.'[1] Therefore, the social world given to us by the modern novel, for example, results from characteristic ways of representing gender, family, and social relations, and these novelistic representational practices are governed to a large extent by the evolving rules of representation characteristic of the novelistic genre; they are not simply commanded by an immediate social context.

This insight can be generalized across writing genres and related to more epistemologically explicit issues. Insofar as 'social reality' emerges in various writing genres, investigations of how the world is apprehended require inquiries into various pre-texts of apprehension, for the meaning and value imposed on the world is structured not by one's immediate consciousness but by the various reality-making scripts one inherits or acquires from one's surrounding cultural/ linguistic condition. The pre-text of apprehension is therefore largely institutionalized and is reflected in the ready-to-hand language practices, the historically produced styles – grammars, rhetorics, and narrative structures – through which the familiar world is continuously interpreted and reproduced. Whether a given aspect of social reality is a matter of contention or is regarded as natural and unproblematic, meaning is always imposed, not discovered, for the familiar world cannot be separated from the interpretive *practices* through which it is made. As Michel Foucault has aptly put it: 'We must not imagine that the world turns toward us a legible face which we would have only to decipher; the world is not the accomplice of our knowledge.'[2] To regard the world of 'international relations' as a text, therefore, is to inquire into the style of its scripting, to reveal the way it has been mediated by historically specific scripts governing the interpretations through which it has emerged.

The 'political'

Given that our understanding of conflict, war, or, more generally, the space within which international politics is deployed is always mediated by modes of representation and thus by all the various mechanisms involved in text construction – grammars, rhetorics, and narrativity – we must operate with a view of politics that is sensitive to textuality. While much of political thinking is exhausted by concern with the distribution of things thought to be meaningful and valuable, our attention is drawn to another aspect of political processes, that aspect in which the boundaries for constituting meaning and value are constructed. Political processes are, among other things, contests over the alternative understandings (often implicit) immanent in the representational practices that implicate the actions and objects one recognizes and the various spaces – leisure, work, political, private, public – within which persons and things take on their identities. Although it tends to operate implicitly, the separation of the world into kinds of space is perhaps the most significant kind of practice for establishing the systems of intelligibility within which understandings of global politics are forged.

This insight was nowhere better formulated than in Aldous Huxley's *Grey Eminence*, his story of the activities of Cardinal Richelieu and his foreign emissary, Father Joseph, that precipitated the Thirty Years War in the seventeenth century.[3] Father Joseph represented a medieval mentality. For him, the world was a more or less vertical set of spaces organized into the mundane present and a transcendental eternity. Within this apprehension of the world, both space and time in the here and now had a symbolic content, for the 'real' and what was deemed valuable lay in the transcendental, spiritual realm. Because earthly events took on their significance in connection with a domain of divine prescriptions, Father Joseph was initially interested in reaffirming the significance of those prescriptions, which included liberating the 'Holy Land' and ridding the world of all heretics, Protestants among others. Ultimately, however, Father Joseph complied with Richelieu's plan to take the Protestant side in the Thirty Years War. In effect, Richelieu succeeded in enlisting Father Joseph's assistance in behalf of a horizontal conception of the world, for Richelieu was an early representative of the modern, geopolitical mentality interested in French control of the European continent. Among other things, Huxley's story is a chronicle of the waning of the medieval and the waxing of the modern spatialization of the world, an effect so powerful that, ever since, people pursuing statecraft have been able to subjugate and direct ecclesiastical authority in behalf of policy that unfolds within a horizontal, desacralized world. Indeed, much of the subsequent history of world politics involves the demise of the authorities connected to a vertical world and the ascension of those connected to a horizontal, geopolitical one.

Within this scenario, the 1969 landing on the moon takes on immense significance, for it can be read as an extension of strategic space and a further diminution of the sacred mentality. The 'heavens' have since been increasingly populated by both strategic and commercial vehicles. In a sense, the horizontal axis has been pivoted, and the old vertical dimension of the Middle Ages has become a geopolitical extension of the horizontal territoriality that has subjugated it. If the spatialization of the world is still the shape of the cross, that cross has been largely desacralized, for the powers that control the readings of the world's text identify themselves with mundane, nationalistic world histories rather than sacred mythologies.

Politicizing the world text

Once we give adequate recognition to the texts within which the world emerges and provided an understanding of politics that focuses on such impositions of meaning and value, we can appreciate the intimate relationship between textual practices and politics. It is the dominant, surviving textual practices that give rise to the systems of meaning and value from which actions and policies are directed and legitimated. A critical political perspective is, accordingly, one that questions the privileged forms of representation whose dominance has led to the unproblematic acceptance of subjects, objects, acts, and themes through which the political world is constructed.

Inasmuch as dominant modes of understanding exist within representational or textual practices, criticism or resistant forms of interpretation are conveyed less through an explicitly argumentative form than through a writing practice that is resistant to familiar modes of representation, one that is self-reflective enough to show how meaning and writing practices are radically entangled in general or one that tends to denaturalize familiar realities by employing impertinent grammars and figurations, by, in short, making use of an insurrectional textuality.

To appreciate the effects of this textuality, it is necessary to pay special heed to language, but this does not imply that an approach emphasizing textuality reduces social phenomena to specific instances of linguistic expression. To textualize a domain of analysis is to recognize, first of all, that any 'reality' is mediated by a mode of representation and, second, that representations are not descriptions of a world of facticity, but are ways of making facticity. Their value is thus not to be discerned in their correspondence with something, but rather in the economies of possible representations within which they participate. Modes of reality making are therefore worthy of analysis in their own right. Such analysis can be a form of interpretation in which one scrutinizes the effects on behaviour or policy that the dominance of some representational practices enjoy, or it can be a form of critique in which one opposes prevailing representational practices with alternatives. Therefore, a concern with textuality must necessarily raise issues about the textuality (the meaning and value effects) of the language of inquiry itself. In order, then, to outline the textualist approach, we must develop further our understanding of the language analysis.

Textualist or poststructuralist modes of analysis emphasize 'discourse' rather than language because the concept of discourse implies a concern with the meaning- and value-producing practices in language rather than simply the relationship between utterances and their referents. In the more familiar approaches to political phenomena (including the empiricist and phenomenological), language is treated as a transparent tool; it is to serve as an unobtrusive conduit between thoughts or concepts and things. In contrast, a discourse approach treats language as opaque and encourages an analysis of both the linguistic practices within which various phenomena – political, economic, social, biological, and so on – are embedded and of the language of inquiry itself. That analysis can be primarily structural (emphasizing the grammatical, rhetorical, and narrative mechanisms responsible for shaping the phenomena treated as the referents of statements in various disciplines) or more historical (emphasizing the events through which various phenomena have found their way into language).

In either case, once the transparency metaphor for language is exchanged for the opacity metaphor, analysis becomes linguistically reflective and serves to overcome a delusion that a view of language as transparent communication creates. One aspect of this delusion has been elaborated by Derrida under the rubric of phonocentrism. Derrida argues that because of our proximity to the process of signification as we speak, we tend to think that our utterances are wholly present to us: 'The subject can hear or speak to himself and be affected by the signifier he produces without passing through an external detour, the world, the sphere of what is not "his own".'[4]

Much of Derrida's analysis has been devoted to disclosing this delusion of the ownership of meaning. He locates control over meaning in a prescripted structure of signification upon which speakers must draw to be intelligible rather than in the speaking subject. In support of this, he has shown, for example, that the linguist Benveniste was deluded into thinking that he was inquiring into the question of whether thought and language can be regarded as distinct, while he had unwittingly already accepted the distinction; he employed a philosophical vocabulary, including the concept of the category, that already holds them to be distinct.[5]

This form of analysis, known as a deconstructive method of critique, is more than a corrective to what Derrida has called 'the metaphysics of presence'. Given that among the political processes that take place in an order is one of legitimating its structures of meaning, Derrida's deconstructive criticism can be shown to disclose how every social order rests on a forgetting of the exclusion practices through which one set of meanings has been institutionalized and various other possibilities – other possible forms of meaning – have been marginalized. One way to capture this process is to avoid the familiar epistemological vocabulary and become rhetorically impertinent. We can use a financial rhetoric to speak of the legitimation language that supports prevailing institutions. Working with this rhetoric, Wlad Godzich has argued that in order to maintain their legitimacy, 'institutions behave as if they did not carry this debt'; instead of acknowledging it, they 'collect interest on it, thereby fostering the formation and maintenance of a privileged class.'[6]

This insight can be applied effectively to the area of international studies. The 'foreign policies' of nation states are based on what have been shown to be representational practices through which various forms of global otherness have been created. For example, to refer to 'Latin America' is not just to refer to an area on the globe; it is to help reproduce an institutionalized form of dominance, one in which the minority, Hispanic part of populations in the region control the original indigenous groups. Even the use of the name of a recognized nation is a political gesture. For example, in an analysis of what is now called Guatemala, it was noted that to say 'Guatemala' is to 'let oneself be governed by the prevailing geopolitical mode of representation and . . . to engage in the continuation of a complex, historically developed practice.'[7]

To use the ordinary subjects, objects, and general grammars through which Guatemala is ordinarily apprehended is, in effect, to license a forgetting of the history of struggles through which such entities have come to be domesticated within modern international space. Such a forgetting is not a psychological but a textual phenomenon, for it is a scripted or institutionalized forgetting that exists in the dominant modes for representing international entities. Moreover, to recognize this difference between a psychological and textual form of forgetting is to open the way for a more politicized form of analysis, for insofar as one recognizes that the language of inquiry is also a mediating frame, one is encouraged to question the textuality of the discourse of the investigator, and to become sensitive to whether it is complicit and apologetic for a system of power and authority or challenging to it.

[. . .]

To cash in on this aspect of discourse analysis, which becomes apparent when we eschew the idea of language as simple communication, we can use once again the financial metaphor that Foucault has employed in his analysis of statements. Consider, for example, an utterance such as 'We now know more security problems than ever before,' which operates on at least two levels. As communication, it is clear *what* is conveyed; it is those already constituted phenomena, which have come to be regarded as related to issues of 'national security' (for example, there is a well-developed archive on the security implications of past international events, which have been coded in terms of the security-oriented discourse.) But what remain silent and thus unthought within such a communicative perspective are the processes wherein the idea of 'security' came to be a dominant reading strategy for spatializing the world and locating the United States as a knowing subject within such a world.

As Bradley Klein has pointed out, 'security' is a very modern practice for interpreting foreign danger. The passage from Renaissance notions of chance and risk, through the consolidation of national protection under the rubric of defence, to the highly surveillant notion of security is a passage that reflects the imposition of a dominant form of understanding on the world.[8] As has been noted in the just-cited study of Guatemala:

> Modern 'security' represents the ultimate in leaving nothing to chance. The number and intensity of interests congregated in modern super powers, for example, has resulted in a comprehensive level of surveillance and intervention all over the globe. Within this intensification of the security-oriented gaze, the meanings of landscapes and people everywhere are subjected to an intensified form of objectification[9]

It is therefore appropriate to think of security talk as a kind of discourse that represents structures of authority and control. To take such a perspective, we have to overcome the disabling view of discourse as transparent communication *between* subjects *about* things, a view within which the value of the statements of a discourse is wholly absorbed in a statement's truth value. Foucault, stressing the discursive economies of language, suggested a politicized alternative to the traditional preoccupation with the truth value of individual statements and discursive formations as a whole:

> To analyze a discursive formation is to weight the 'value' of statements, a value that is not defined by their truth, that is not gauged by a secret content but which

characterizes their place, their capacity for circulation and exchange, their possibility of transformation, not only in the economy of discourse, but more generally in the administration of scarce resources.[10]

This view of discourse alerts us to the political content sequestered in the subjects (kinds of persons), objects, and relationships about which we speak. It shows that statements can be evaluated as political resources, for discourse is, in Foucault's terms, an 'asset'. Moreover, this approach to analysing discourse (which represents a shift from the familiar rhetoric of epistemological language to a figuration related to distribution, exchange, and control) is characteristic of poststructuralist ways of textualizing social phenomena. But there is more to the approach than the textual metaphor. To understand the world as mediated through textual practices is to encourage some modes of questioning and inquiry that are unfamiliar within more traditional empirical and interpretive approaches.
[. . .]

Notes

1   Sebeok, T. (1985) 'Enter textuality: echoes from the extra-terrestrial', *Poetics Today* vol. 6, p. 657.
2   Foucault, M. (1984) 'The order of discourse' in M. Shapiro (ed.) *Language and Politics*, New York, New York University Press.
3   Huxley, A. (1944) *The Grey Eminence*, London, Chatto and Windus.
4   Derrida, J. (1973) *Speech and Phenomena*, trans. D. Allison, Evanston, IL, Northwestern University Press.
5   Derrida, J. (1979) 'The supplement of copula: philosophy before linguistics' in J. Harari (ed.) *Textual Strategies*, Ithaca, NY, Cornell University Press.
6   Godzich, W. (1987) 'Afterward' in S. Weber (ed.) *Institution and Interpretation*, Minneapolis, University of Minnesota Press.
7   Shapiro, M.J. (1988) *The Politics of Representation: Writing Practices in Biography, Photography and Policy Analysis*, Madison, University of Wisconsin Press, p. 92.
8   Klein, B.S. (1987) 'Strategic discourse and its alternatives', *Occasional Paper no. 3*, New York, Center on Violence and Human Survival.
9   Shapiro, M.J. (1988) *The Politics of Representation*, p. 94.
10 Foucault, M. (1972) *The Archeology of Knowledge*, trans. A.M. Sheridan-Smith, New York, Pantheon.

The Spectacle of the 'Other'

Stuart Hall

Source: Hall, S. (1997) 'The spectacle of the "other"', in S. Hall (ed.) *Representation: Cultural Representations and Signifying Practices*, London, Sage in association with the Open University.

How do we represent people and places which are significantly different from us? Why is 'difference' so compelling a theme, so contested an area of representation? What is the secret fascination of 'otherness', and why is popular representation so frequently drawn to it? What are the typical forms and representational practices which are used to represent 'difference' in popular culture today, and where did these popular figures and stereotypes come from? These are some of the questions about representation which we set out to address. [. . .]

Heroes or villains?

Look, first, at Figure 1. It is a picture of the men's 100 metres final at the 1988 Olympics which appeared on the cover of the Olympics Special of the *Sunday Times* colour magazine (9 October 1988). It shows the black Canadian sprinter, Ben Johnson, winning in record time from Carl Lewis and Linford Christie: five superb athletes in action, at the peak of their physical prowess. All of them men and – perhaps, now, you will notice consciously for the first time – all of them black!

[. . .]

Ostensibly about the Olympics, the photo is in fact a trailer for the magazine's lead story about the growing menace of drug-taking in international athletics – what inside is called 'The Chemical Olympics'. Ben Johnson, you may recall, was found to have taken drugs to enhance his performance. He was disqualified, the gold medal being awarded to Carl Lewis, and Johnson was expelled from world athletics in disgrace. The story suggests that *all* athletes – black or white – are potentially 'heroes' and 'villains'. But in this image, Ben Johnson personifies this split in a particular way. He is *both* 'hero' and 'villain'. He encapsulates the extreme alternatives of heroism and villainy in world athletics in one black body.

This photo functions at the level of 'myth'. There is a literal, denotative level of meaning – this *is* a picture of the 100 metres final and the figure in front *is* Ben Johnson. Then there is the more connotative or thematic meaning – the drug story. And within that, there is the sub-theme of 'race' and 'difference'. Already, this tells us something important about how 'myth' works. The image is a very powerful one, as visual images often are. But its *meaning* is highly ambiguous. It can carry more than one meaning. If you didn't know the context, you might be tempted to read this as a moment of unqualified triumph. And you wouldn't be 'wrong' since this, too, is a perfectly acceptable meaning to take from the image.

Figure 1   *'Heroes and villains', cover of* The Sunday Times Magazine, *9 October 1988*

But, as the caption suggests, it is *not* produced here as an image of 'unqualified triumph'. So, the same photo can carry several, quite different, sometimes diametrically opposite meanings. It can be a picture of disgrace or of triumph, or both. Many meanings, we might say, are potential within the photo. But there is no one, true meaning. Meaning 'floats'. It cannot be finally fixed. However, attempting to 'fix' it is the work of a representational practice, which intervenes in the many potential meanings of an image in an attempt to privilege one.

So, rather than a 'right' or 'wrong' meaning, what we need to ask is, 'Which of the many meanings in this image does the magazine mean to privilege?' Which is the preferred meaning? Ben Johnson is the key element here because he is both an amazing athlete, winner and record-breaker, *and* the athlete who was publicly disgraced because of drug-taking. So, as it turns out, the preferred meaning is *both* 'heroism' and 'villainy'. It wants to say something paradoxical like, 'In the moment of the hero's triumph, there is also villainy and moral defeat'. In part, we know this is the preferred meaning which the magazine wants the photo to convey because this is the meaning which is singled out in the caption: HEROES AND VILLAINS. Roland Barthes (1977) argues that, frequently, it is the caption which selects one out of the many possible meanings from the image, and *anchors* it with words. The 'meaning' of the photograph, then, does not lie exclusively in the image, but in the conjunction of image *and* text. Two discourses – the discourse of written language and the discourse of photography – are required to produce and 'fix' the meaning (see Hall, 1972).

As we have suggested, this photo can also be 'read', connotatively, in terms of what it has to 'say' about 'race'. Here, the message could be – black people shown being good at something, winning *at last*! But in the light of the 'preferred meaning', hasn't the meaning with respect to 'race' and 'otherness' changed as well? Isn't it more something like, 'even when black people are shown at the summit of their achievement, they often fail to carry it off'? This having-it-both-ways is important because, as I hope to show, people who are in any way significantly different from the majority – 'them' rather than 'us' – are frequently exposed to this *binary* form of representation. They seem to be represented through sharply opposed, polarized, binary extremes – good/bad, civilized/primitive, ugly/excessively attractive, repelling-because-different/compelling because-strange-and-exotic. And they are often required to be *both things at the same time*! [. . .]

Let us look at another, similar news photo, this time from another record-breaking 100 metres final. Linford Christie, subsequently captain of the British Olympics squad, at the peak of his career, having just won the race of a lifetime (see Figure 2). The picture captures his elation, at the moment of his lap of honour. He is holding the Union Jack. [. . .]

The image carries many meanings, all equally plausible. What is important is the fact that this image both shows an event (denotation) and carries a 'message' or meaning (connotation) – Barthes would call it a 'meta-message' or *myth* – about 'race', colour and 'otherness'. We can't help reading images of this kind as 'saying something', not just about the people or the occasion, but about their 'otherness', their 'difference'. *'Difference' has been marked*. How it is then interpreted is a constant and recurring preoccupation in the representation of people who are racially and ethnically different from the majority population. Difference signifies. It 'speaks'.

In a later interview, discussing his forthcoming retirement from international sport, Christie commented on the question of his cultural identity – where he feels he 'belongs' (*The Sunday Independent*, 11 November 1995). He has very fond memories of Jamaica, he said, where he was born and lived until the age of 7. But 'I've lived here [in the UK] for 28 [years]. I can't be anything other than British' (p. 18). Of course, it isn't as simple as that. Christie is perfectly well aware that most definitions of 'Britishness' assume that the person who belongs is

Figure 2 *Linford Christie, holding a Union Jack, having won the men's 100 metres Olympic gold medal, Barcelona, 1992*

'white'. It is much harder for black people, wherever they were born, to be accepted as 'British'. [. . .]

Indeed, he made his remarks in the context of the negative publicity to which he has been exposed in some sections of the British tabloid press, a good deal of which hinges on a vulgar, unstated but widely recognized 'joke' at his expense: namely that the tight-fitting Lycra shorts which he wears are said to reveal the size and shape of his genitals. This was the detail on which *The Sun* focused on the morning after he won an Olympic gold medal. Christie has been subject to continuous teasing in the tabloid press about the prominence and size of his 'lunchbox' – a euphemism which some have taken so literally that, he revealed, he has been approached by a firm wanting to market its lunchboxes around his image! Linford Christie has observed about these innuendoes: 'I felt humiliated . . . My first instinct was that it was racist. There we are, stereotyping a black man. I can take a good joke. But it happened the day after I won the greatest accolade an athlete can win . . . I don't want to go through life being known for what I've got in my shorts. I'm a serious person . . .' (p. 15).

Is this just a joke in bad taste, or does it have a deeper meaning? What do sexuality and gender have to do with images of black men and women? Why did the black French writer from Martinique, Frantz Fanon, say that white people seem to be obsessed with the sexuality of black people?

It is the subject of a widespread fantasy, Fanon says, which fixates the black man at the level of the genitals. 'One is no longer aware of the Negro, but only of a penis; the Negro is eclipsed. He is turned into a penis' (Fanon, 1986/1952: 170).
    [. . .]

There is an additional point to be made about these photographs of black athletes in the press. They gain in meaning when they are read in context, against or in connection with one another. This is another way of saying that images do not carry meaning or 'signify' on their own. They accumulate meanings, or play off their meanings against one another, across a variety of texts and media. Each image carries its own, specific meaning. But at the broader level of how 'difference' and 'otherness' is being represented in a particular culture at any one moment, we can see similar representational practices and figures being repeated, with variations, from one text or site of representation to another. This accumulation of meanings across different texts, where one image refers to another, or has its meaning altered by being 'read' in the context of other images, is called inter-textuality. We may describe the whole repertoire of imagery and visual effects through which 'difference' is represented at any one historical moment as a *regime of representation*. [. . .]

In the light of these examples, we can rephrase our original questions more precisely. Why is 'otherness' so compelling an object of representation? What does the marking of racial difference tell us about representation as a practice? Through which representational practices are racial and ethnic difference and 'otherness' signified? What are the 'discursive formations', the repertoires or regimes of representation, on which the media are drawing when they represent 'difference'? Why is one dimension of difference – e.g. 'race' – crossed by other dimensions, such as sexuality, gender and class? And how is the representation of 'difference' linked with questions of power?

Why does 'difference' matter?

Questions of 'difference' have come to the fore in cultural studies in recent decades and been addressed in different ways by different disciplines. In this section, we briefly consider *four* such theoretical accounts.

1   The first account comes from linguistics – from the sort of approach associated with Saussure and the use of language as a model of how culture works. The main argument advanced here is that *'difference' matters because it is essential to meaning; without it, meaning could not exist*. We know what *black* means, Saussure argued, not because there is some essence of 'blackness' but because we can contrast it with its opposite – *white*. Meaning, he argued, is relational. It is the *'difference'* between *white* and *black* which signifies, which carries meaning. This principle holds for broader concepts too. We know what it is to be 'British', not only because of certain national characteristics, but also because we can mark its 'difference' from its 'others' – 'Britishness' is not-French, not-American, not-German, not-Pakistani, not-Jamaican and so on. This enables Linford Christie to signify his 'Britishness' (by the flag) while contesting (by his black skin) that 'Britishness' must always mean 'whiteness'. Again, 'difference' signifies. It carries a message.

[. . .]

While we do not seem able to do without them, binary oppositions are also open to the charge of being reductionist and over-simplified – swallowing up all distinctions in their rather rigid two-part structure. What is more, as the philosopher Jacques Derrida has argued, there are very few neutral binary oppositions. One pole of the binary, he argues, is usually the dominant one, the one which includes the other within its field of operations. There is always a relation of power between the poles of a binary opposition (Derrida, 1981). We should really write, **white**/black, **men**/women, **masculine**/feminine, **upper class**/lower class, **British**/alien to capture this power dimension in discourse.

2   The second explanation also comes from theories of language, but from a somewhat different school to that represented by Saussure. *The argument here is that we need 'difference' because we can only construct meaning through a dialogue with the 'Other'.* The great Russian linguist and critic, Mikhail Bakhtin, who fell foul of the Stalinist regime in the 1940s, studied language, not (as the Saussureans did) as an objective system, but in terms of how meaning is sustained in the *dialogue* between two or more speakers. Meaning, Bakhtin argued, does not belong to any one speaker. It arises in the give-and-take between different speakers.

> The word in language is half someone else's. It becomes 'one's own' only when . . . the speaker appropriates the word, adapting it to his own semantic expressive intention. Prior to this . . . the word does not exist in a neutral or impersonal language . . . rather it exists in other people's mouths, serving other people's intentions: it is from there that one must take the word and make it one's own.
>
> (Bakhtin, 1981 [1935]: 293–4)

Bakhtin and his collaborator, Volosinov, believed that this enabled us to enter into a struggle over meaning, breaking one set of associations and giving words a new inflection. Meaning, Bakhtin argued, is established through dialogue – it is fundamentally *dialogic*. Everything we say and mean is modified by the interaction and interplay with another person. Meaning arises through the 'difference' between the participants in any dialogue. *The 'Other', in short, is essential to meaning.*

This is the positive side of Bakhtin's theory. The negative side is, of course, that therefore meaning cannot be fixed and that one group can never be completely in charge of meaning. What it means to be 'British' or 'Russian' or 'Jamaican' cannot be entirely controlled by the British, Russians or Jamaicans, but is always up for grabs, always being negotiated, in the dialogue between these national cultures and their 'others'. Thus it has been argued that you cannot know what it meant to be 'British' in the nineteenth century until you know what the British thought of Jamaica, their prize colony in the Caribbean, or Ireland, and more disconcertingly, *what the Jamaicans or the Irish thought of them* . . . (C. Hall, 1994).

3   The third kind of explanation is anthropological. *The argument here is that culture depends on giving things meaning by assigning them to different positions*

within a classificatory system. The marking of 'difference' is thus the basis of that symbolic order which we call culture. Mary Douglas, following the classic work on symbolic systems by the French sociologist, Emile Durkheim, and the later studies of mythology by the French anthropologist, Claude Lévi-Strauss, argues that social groups impose meaning on their world by ordering and organizing things into classificatory systems (Douglas, 1966). Binary oppositions are crucial for all classification, because one must establish a clear difference between things in order to classify them. Faced with different kinds of food, Lévi-Strauss argued (1970), one way of giving them meaning is to start by dividing them into two groups – those which are eaten 'raw' and those eaten 'cooked'. Of course, you can also classify food into 'vegetables' and 'fruit'; or into those which are eaten as 'starters' and those which are eaten as 'desserts'; or those which are served up at dinner and those which are eaten at a sacred feast or the communion table. Here, again, 'difference' is fundamental to cultural meaning.

However, it can also give rise to negative feelings and practices. Mary Douglas argues that what really disturbs cultural order is when things turn up in the wrong category; or when things fail to fit any category – such as a substance like mercury, which is a metal but also a liquid, or a social group like mixed-race *mulattoes* who are neither 'white' nor 'black' but float ambiguously in some unstable, dangerous, hybrid zone of indeterminacy in-between (Stallybrass and White, 1986). Stable cultures require things to stay in their appointed place. Symbolic boundaries keep the categories 'pure', giving cultures their unique meaning and identity. What unsettles culture is 'matter out of place' – the breaking of our unwritten rules and codes. Dirt in the garden is fine, but dirt in one's bedroom is 'matter out of place' – a sign of pollution, of symbolic boundaries being transgressed, of taboos broken. What we do with 'matter out of place' is to sweep it up, throw it out, restore the place to order, bring back the normal state of affairs. The retreat of many cultures towards 'closure' against foreigners, intruders, aliens and 'others' is part of the same process of purification (Kristeva, 1982). According to this argument, then, symbolic boundaries are central to all culture. Marking 'difference' leads us, symbolically, to close ranks, shore up culture and to stigmatize and expel anything which is defined as impure, abnormal. However, paradoxically, it also makes 'difference' powerful, strangely attractive precisely because it is forbidden, taboo, threatening to cultural order. Thus, 'what is socially peripheral is often symbolically centered' (Babcock, 1978: 32).

4   The fourth kind of explanation is psychoanalytic and relates to the role of 'difference' in our psychic life. *The argument here is that the 'Other' is fundamental to the constitution of the self, to us as subjects, and to sexual identity.* According to Freud, the consolidation of our definitions of 'self' and of our sexual identities depends on the way we are formed as subjects, especially in relation to that stage of early development which he called the Oedipus complex (after the Oedipus story in Greek myth). A unified sense of oneself as a subject and one's sexual identity – Freud argued – are not fixed in the very young child. However, according to Freud's version of the Oedipus myth, at a certain point the boy develops an unconscious erotic attraction to the Mother, but finds the Father barring his way to 'satisfaction'. However, when he discovers that women

do not have a penis, he assumes that his Mother was punished by castration, and that he might be punished in the same way if he persists with his unconscious desire. In fear, he switches his identification to his old 'rival', the Father, thereby taking on the beginnings of an identification with a masculine identity. The girl child identifies the opposite way – with the Father. But she cannot 'be' him, since she lacks the penis. She can only 'win' him by being willing, unconsciously, to bear a man's child – thereby taking up and identifying with the Mother's role, and 'becoming feminine'.

This model of how *sexual 'difference'* begins to be assumed in very young children has been strongly contested. Many people have questioned its speculative character. On the other hand, it has been very influential, as well as extensively amended by later analysts. The French psychoanalyst, Jacques Lacan (1977), for example, went further than Freud, arguing that the child has no sense of itself as a subject separate from its mother until it sees itself in a mirror, or as if mirrored in the way it is looked at by the Mother. Through identification, 'it desires the object of her desire, thus focusing its libido on itself' (see Segal, 1997). It is this reflection from outside oneself, or what Lacan calls the 'look from the place of the other', during 'the mirror stage', which allows the child for the first time to recognize itself as a unified subject, relate to the outside world, to the 'Other', develop language and take on a sexual identity. (Lacan actually says, 'mis-recognize itself', since he believes the subject can never be fully unified.) Melanie Klein (1957), on the other hand, argued that the young child copes with this problem of a lack of a stable self by splitting its unconscious image of and identification with the Mother into its 'good' and 'bad' parts, internalizing some aspects, and projecting others on to the outside world. The common element in all these different versions of Freud is the role which is given by these different theorists to the 'Other' in subjective development. Subjectivity can only arise and a sense of 'self' be formed through the symbolic and unconscious relations which the young child forges with a significant 'Other' which is outside – i.e. different from – itself.

At first sight, these psychoanalytic accounts seem to be positive in their implications for 'difference'. Our subjectivities, they argue, depend on our unconscious relations with significant others. However, there are also negative implications. The psychoanalytic perspective assumes that there is no such thing as a given, stable inner core to 'the self' or to identity. Psychically, we are never fully unified as subjects. Our subjectivities are formed through this troubled, never-completed, unconscious dialogue with – this internalization of – the 'Other'. Subjectivity is formed in relation to something which completes us but which – since it lies outside us – we in some way always lack.

What's more, they say, this troubling split or division within subjectivity can never be fully healed. Some indeed see this as one of the main sources of neurosis in adults. Others see psychic problems arising from the splitting between the 'good' and 'bad' parts of the self – being pursued internally by the 'bad' aspects one has taken into oneself, or alternatively, projecting on to others the 'bad' feelings one cannot deal with. Frantz Fanon who used psychoanalytic theory in his explanation of racism, argued (1986/1952) that much racial stereotyping and violence arose from the refusal of the white 'Other' to give recognition 'from the place of the other', to the black person (see Bhabha, 1986b; Hall, 1996).

These debates about 'difference' and the 'Other' are not mutually exclusive since they refer to very different levels of analysis – the linguistic, the social, the cultural and the psychic levels respectively. 'Difference' is ambivalent. It can be both positive and negative. It is both necessary for the production of meaning, the formation of language and culture, for social identities and a subjective sense of the self as a sexed subject – and at the same time, it is threatening, a site of danger, of negative feelings, of splitting, hostility and aggression towards the 'Other'.

Racializing the 'other'

Holding these theoretical 'tools' of analysis in reserve for a moment, let us now explore further some examples of the repertoires of representation and representational practices which have been used to mark racial difference and signify the racialized 'Other' in western popular culture. How was this archive formed and what were its typical figures and practices?

There are three major moments when the 'West' encountered black people, giving rise to an avalanche of popular representations based on the marking of racial difference. The first began with the sixteenth-century contact between European traders and the West African kingdoms, which provided a source of black slaves for three centuries. Its effects were to be found in slavery and in the post-slave societies of the New World. The second was the European colonization of Africa and the 'scramble' between the European powers for the control of colonial territory, markets and raw materials in the period of 'high Imperialism'. The third was the post-World War II migrations from the 'Third World' into Europe and North America. Western ideas about 'race' and images of racial difference were profoundly shaped by those three fateful encounters.

Commodity racism: empire and the domestic world

We start with how images of racial difference drawn from the imperial encounter flooded British popular culture at the end of the nineteenth century. In the middle ages, the European image of Africa was ambiguous – a mysterious place, but often viewed positively: after all, the Coptic Church was one of the oldest 'overseas' Christian communities: black saints appeared in medieval Christian iconography; and Ethiopia's legendary 'Prester John', was reputed to be one of Christianity's most loyal supporters. Gradually, however, this image changed. Africans were declared to be the descendants of Ham, cursed in *The Bible* to be in perpetuity 'a servant of servants unto his brethren'. Identified with Nature, they symbolized 'the primitive' in contrast with 'the civilized world'. The Enlightenment, which ranked societies along an evolutionary scale from 'barbarism' to 'civilization', thought Africa 'the parent of everything that is monstrous in Nature' (Edward Long, 1774, quoted in McClintock, 1995: 22). Curvier dubbed the Negro race a 'monkey tribe'. The philosopher Hegel declared that Africa was 'no historical part of the world . . . it has no movement or development to exhibit'. By the nineteenth century, when the European exploration and colonization of the African interior began in earnest. Africa was regarded as 'marooned and historically abandoned . . . a fetish land, inhabited by cannibals, dervishes and witch doctors . . .' (McClintock, 1995: 41).

The exploration and colonization of Africa produced an explosion of popular representations (Mackenzie, 1986). Our example here is the spread of imperial images and themes in Britain through commodity advertising in the closing decades of the nineteenth century.

The progress of the great white explorer-adventurers and the encounters with the black African exotic were charted, recorded and depicted in maps and drawings. etchings and (especially) the new photography, in newspaper illustrations and accounts, diaries, travel writing, learned treatises, official reports and 'boy's-own' adventure novels. Advertising was one means by which the imperial project was given visual form in a popular medium, forging the link between Empire and the domestic imagination. Anne McClintock argues that, through the racializing of advertisements (commodity racism), 'the Victorian middle-class home became a space for the display of imperial spectacle and the reinvention of race, while the colonies – in particular Africa – became a theatre for exhibiting the Victorian cult of domesticity and the reinvention of gender' (1995: 34).

Advertising for the objects, gadgets, gee-gaws and bric-a-brac with which the Victorian middle classes filled their homes provided an 'imaginary way of relating to the real world' of commodity production, and after 1890, with the rise of the popular press, from the *Illustrated London News* to the Harmsworth *Daily Mail*, the imagery of mass commodity production entered the world of the working classes via the spectacle of advertising (Richards, 1990). Richards calls it a 'spectacle' because advertising translated *things* into a fantasy visual display of *signs and symbols*. The production of commodities became linked to Empire – the search for markets and raw materials abroad supplanting other motives for imperial expansion.

This two-way traffic forged connections between imperialism and the domestic sphere, public and private. Commodities (and images of English domestic life) flowed outwards to the colonies: raw materials (and images of 'the civilizing mission' in progress) were brought into the home. Henry Stanley, the imperial adventurer, who famously traced Livingstone ('Dr Livingstone, I presume?') in Central Africa in 1871, and was a founder of the infamous Congo Free State, tried to annex Uganda and open up the interior for the East Africa Company. He believed that the spread of commodities would make 'civilization' in Africa inevitable and named his native bearers after the branded goods they carried – Bryant and May, Remington and so on. His exploits became associated with Pears' Soap, Bovril and various brands of tea. The gallery of imperial heroes and their masculine exploits in 'Darkest Africa' were immortalized on matchboxes, needle cases, toothpaste pots, pencil boxes, cigarette packets, board games, paperweights, sheet music. 'Images of colonial conquest were stamped on soap boxes . . . biscuit tins, whisky bottles, tea tins and chocolate bars . . . No pre-existing form of organized racism had ever before been able to reach so large and so differentiated a mass of the populace' (McClintock, 1995: 209).

[. . .]

Meanwhile, down on the plantation . . .

Our second example is from the period of plantation slavery and its aftermath. It has been argued that, in the USA, a fully fledged racialized ideology did not appear amongst the slave-holding classes (and their supporters in Europe) until slavery was seriously challenged by the Abolitionists in the nineteenth century. Frederickson (1987) sums up the complex and sometimes contradictory set of beliefs about racial difference which took hold in this period:

> Heavily emphasized was the historical case against the black man based on his supposed failure to develop a civilized way of life in Africa. As portrayed in pro-slavery writing, Africa was and always had been the scene of unmitigated savagery, cannibalism, devil worship, and licentiousness. Also advanced was an early form of biological argument, based on real or imagined physiological and anatomical differences – especially in cranial characteristics and facial angles – which allegedly explained mental and physical inferiority. Finally there was the appeal to deep-seated white fears of widespread miscegenation [sexual relations and interbreeding between the races], as pro-slavery theorists sought to deepen white anxieties by claiming that the abolition of slavery would lead to inter-marriage and the degeneracy of the race. Although all these arguments had appeared earlier in fugitive or embryonic form, there is something startling about the rapidity with which they were brought together and organized in a rigid polemical pattern, once the defenders of slavery found themselves in a propaganda war with the abolitionists.
>
> (Frederickson, 1987: 49)

This racialized discourse is structured by a set of binary oppositions. There is the powerful opposition between 'civilization' (white) and 'savagery' (black). There is the opposition between the biological or bodily characteristics of the 'black' and 'white' 'races', polarized into their extreme opposites – each the signifiers of an absolute difference between human 'types' or species. There are the rich distinctions which cluster around the supposed link, on the one hand, between the white 'races' and intellectual development – refinement, learning and knowledge, a belief in reason, the presence of developed institutions, formal government and law, and a 'civilized restraint' in their emotional, sexual and civil life, all of which are associated with 'Culture'; and on the other hand, the link between the black 'races' and whatever is instinctual – the open expression of emotion and feeling rather than intellect, a lack of 'civilized refinement' in sexual and social life, a reliance on custom and ritual, and the lack of developed civil institutions, all of which are linked to 'Nature'. Finally there is the polarized opposition between racial 'purity' on the one hand, and the 'pollution' which comes from intermarriage, racial hybridity and interbreeding.

The Negro, it was argued, found happiness only when under the tutelage of a white master. His/her essential characteristics were fixed forever – 'eternally' – in Nature. Evidence from slave insurrections and the slave revolt in Haiti (1791) had persuaded whites of the instability of the Negro character. A degree of civilization, they thought, had rubbed off on the 'domesticated' slave, but underneath slaves remained by nature savage brutes; and long buried passions, once loosed, would result in 'the wild frenzy of revenge, and the savage lust for blood' (Frederickson, 1987: 54). This view was justified with reference to so-called scientific and ethnological 'evidence', the basis of a new kind of 'scientific racism'. Contrary to Biblical evidence, it was asserted, blacks/whites had been created at different times – according to the theory of 'polygenesis' (many creations).

Racial theory applied the Culture/Nature distinction differently to the two racialized groups. Among whites, 'Culture' *was opposed to* 'Nature'. Amongst blacks, it was assumed, 'Culture' *coincided with* 'Nature'. Whereas whites developed 'Culture' to subdue and overcome 'Nature', for blacks, 'Culture' and 'Nature' were interchangeable. David Green discussed this view in relation to anthropology and ethnology, the disciplines which provided much of the 'scientific evidence' for it.

> Though not immune to the 'white man's burden' [approach], anthropology was drawn through the course of the nineteenth century, even more towards causal connections between race and culture. As the position and status of the 'inferior' races became increasingly to be regarded as fixed, so socio-cultural differences came to be regarded as dependent upon hereditary characteristics. Since these were inaccessible to direct observation they had to be inferred from physical and behavioural traits which, in turn, they were intended to explain. Socio-cultural differences among human populations became subsumed within the identity of the individual human body. In the attempt to trace the line of determination between the biological and the social, the body became the totemic object, and its very visibility the evident articulation of nature and culture.
>
> (Green, 1984: 31–32)

Green's argument explains *why* the racialized body and its meanings came to have such resonance in popular representations of difference and 'otherness'. It also highlights the connection between *visual discourse* and *the production of (racialized) knowledge*. The body itself and its differences were visible for all to see, and thus provided 'the incontrovertible evidence' for a naturalization of racial difference. The representation of 'difference' through the body became the discursive site through which much of this 'racialized knowledge' was produced and circulated.

Signifying racial 'difference'

Popular representations of racial 'difference' during slavery tended to cluster around two main themes. First was the subordinate status and 'innate laziness' of blacks – 'naturally' born to, and fitted only for, servitude but, at the same time, stubbornly unwilling to labour in ways appropriate to their nature and profitable for their masters. Second was their innate 'primitivism', simplicity and lack of culture, which made them genetically incapable of 'civilized' refinements. Whites took inordinate amusement from the slaves' efforts to imitate the manners and customs of so-called 'civilized' white folks. (In fact, slaves often deliberately parodied their masters' behaviour by their exaggerated imitations, laughing at white folks behind their backs and 'sending them up'. The practice – called *signifying* – is now recognized as a well-established part of the black vernacular literary tradition.

Typical of this racialized regime of representation was the practice of reducing the cultures of black people to Nature, or *naturalizing* 'difference'. The logic behind naturalization is simple. If the differences between black and white people are 'cultural', then they are open to modification and change. But if they are 'natural' – as the slave-holders believed – then they are beyond history, permanent and fixed. 'Naturalization' is therefore a representational strategy designed to *fix* 'difference', and thus *secure it forever*. It is an attempt to halt the inevitable 'slide' of meaning, to secure discursive or ideological 'closure'.

In the eighteenth and nineteenth centuries popular representations of daily life under slavery, ownership and servitude are shown as so 'natural' that they require *no comment*. It was part of the natural order of things that white men should sit and slaves should stand; that white women rode and slave men ran after them shading them from the Louisiana sun with an umbrella: that white overseers should inspect slave women like prize animals, or punish runaway slaves with casual forms of torture (like branding them or urinating in their mouths), and that fugitives should kneel to receive their punishment. These images are a form of ritualized degradation. On the other hand, some representations are idealized and sentimentalized rather than degraded, while remaining stereotypical. These are the 'noble savages' to the 'debased servants' of the previous type. For example, the endless representations of the 'good' Christian black slave, like Uncle Tom, in Harriet Beecher Stowe's pro-abolitionist novel, *Uncle Tom's Cabin*, or the ever-faithful and devoted domestic slave, Mammy. A third group occupy an ambiguous middle-ground – tolerated though not admired. These include the 'happy natives' – black entertainers, minstrels and banjo-players who seemed not to have a brain in their head but sang, danced and cracked jokes all day long, to entertain white folks; or the 'tricksters' who were admired for their crafty ways of avoiding hard work, and their tall tales, like Uncle Remus.

For blacks, 'primitivism' (Culture) and 'blackness' (Nature) became interchangeable. This was their 'true nature' and they could not escape it. As has so often happened in the representation of women, their biology *was* their 'destiny'. Not only were blacks represented in terms of their essential characteristics. They were *reduced to their essence*. Laziness, simple fidelity, mindless 'cooning', trickery, childishness belonged to blacks *as a race, as a species*. There was nothing else to the kneeling slave *but* his servitude; nothing to Uncle Tom *except* his Christian forbearing; nothing to Mammy *but* her fidelity to the white household – and what Fanon called her 'sho' nuff good cooking'. [. . .]

Staging racial 'difference': 'and the melody lingered on . . .'

The traces of these racial stereotypes – what we may call a 'racialized regime of representation' – have persisted into the late twentieth century (Hall, 1981). Of course, they have always been contested. In the early decades of the nineteenth century, the anti-slavery movement (which led to the abolition of British slavery in 1834) did put into early circulation an alternative imagery of black-white relations and this was taken up by the American abolitionists in the US in the period leading up to the Civil War. In opposition to the stereotypical representations of racialized difference, abolitionists adopted a different slogan about the black slave – 'Are you not a man and brother? Are you not a woman and a sister?' – emphasizing, not difference, but a common humanity. [. . .]

After the Civil War, some of the grosser forms of social and economic exploitation, physical and mental degradation associated with plantation slavery were replaced by a different system of racial segregation – legalized in the South, more informally maintained in the North. Did the old, stereotypical 'regime of representation', which had helped to construct the image of black people in the white imaginary, gradually disappear?

That would seem too optimistic. A good test case is the American cinema, *the* popular art form of the first half of the twentieth century, where one would expect to find a very different representational repertoire. However, in critical studies like Leab's *From Sambo to Superspade* (1976), Cripps' *Black Film as Genre* (1978), Patricia Morton's *Disfigured Images* (1991), and Donald Bogle's *Toms, Coons, Mulattos, Mammies and Bucks: an Interpretative History of Blacks in American Films* (1973), the astonishing persistence of the basic racial 'grammar of representation' is documented – of course, with many variations and modifications allowing for differences in time, medium and context.

Bogle's study identifies the five main *stereotypes* which, he argues, made the cross-over: *Toms* – the Good Negroes, always 'chased, harassed, hounded, flogged, enslaved and insulted, they keep the faith, ne'er turn against their white massas, and remain hearty, submissive, stoic, generous, selfless and oh-so-kind' (p. 6). *Coons* – the eye-popping piccanninnies, the slapstick entertainers, the spinners of tall tales, the 'no-account "niggers"', those unreliable, crazy, lazy, subhuman creatures, good for nothing more than eating watermelons, stealing chickens, shooting crap, or butchering the English language' (pp. 7–8). *The Tragic Mulatto* – the mixed-race woman, cruelly caught between 'a divided racial inheritance' (p. 9), beautiful, sexually attractive and often exotic, the prototype of the smouldering, sexy heroine, whose partly white blood makes her 'acceptable', even attractive, to white men, but whose indelible 'stain' of black blood condemns her to a tragic conclusion. *Mammies* – the prototypical house-servants, usually big, fat, bossy and cantankerous, with their good-for-nothing husbands sleeping it off at home, their utter devotion to the white household and their unquestioned subservience in their workplaces (p. 9). Finally, the *Bad Bucks* – physically big, strong, no-good, violent, renegades, 'on a rampage and full of black rage', 'over-sexed and savage, violent and frenzied as they lust for white flesh' (p. 10). There are many traces of this in contemporary images of black youth – for example, the 'mugger', the 'drug-baron', the 'yardie', the gangsta-rap singer, the 'niggas with attitude' bands and more generally black urban youth 'on the rampage'. [. . .]

Not until the 1950s did films begin cautiously to broach the subject of 'race' as problem (*Home of the Brave, Lost Boundaries, Pinky*, to mention a few titles) – though largely from a white liberal perspective. A key figure in these films was Sidney Poitier – an extremely talented black actor, whose roles cast him as a 'hero for an integrationist age'. Bogle argues that Poitier, the first black actor to be allowed 'star billing' in mainstream Hollywood films, 'fitted' *because* he was cast so rigorously 'against the grain'. He was made to play on screen everything that the stereotyped black figure was *not*: 'educated and intelligent, he spoke proper English, dressed conservatively, and had the best of table manners. For the mass white audience, Sidney Poitier was a black man who met their standards. His characters were tame; never did they act impulsively; nor were they threats to the system. They were amenable and pliant. And finally they were non-funky, almost sexless and sterile. In short they were the perfect dream for white liberals anxious to have a coloured man in for lunch or dinner' (Bogle,

1973: 175–176). Accordingly, in 1967, he actually starred in a film entitled *Guess Who's Coming To Dinner*. Despite outstanding film performances (The *Defiant Ones*, *To Sir With Love*, *In the Heat of the Night*), 'There was nothing there', as one critic kindly put it, 'to feed the old but potent fear of the over-endowed Negro' (Cripps, 1978: 223). [. . .]

A second, more ambiguous, 'revolution' followed in the 1980s and 1990s, with the collapse of the 'integrationist' dream of the Civil Rights movement, the expansion of the black ghettos, the growth of the black 'underclass', with its endemic poverty, ill-health and criminalization, and the slide of some black communities into a culture of guns, drugs and intra-black violence. This has, however, been accompanied by the growth of an affirmative self-confidence in, and an insistence on 'respect' for, black cultural identity, as well as a growing 'black separatism' – which features nowhere so visibly as in the massive impact of black music (including 'black rap') on popular music and the visual presence of the music-affiliated 'street-style' scene. These developments have transformed the practices of racial representation, in part because the question of representation itself has become a critical arena of contestation and struggle. Black actors agitated for and got a wider variety of roles in film and television. 'Race' came to be acknowledged as one of the most significant themes of American life and times. In the 1980s and 1990s, blacks themselves entered the American cinema mainstream as independent film-makers, able – like Spike Lee (*Do the Right Thing*), Julie Dash (*Daughters of the Dust*) or John Singleton (*Boys 'n' the Hood*) – to put their own interpretations on the way blacks figure within 'the American experience'. This has broadened the regime of racial representation – the result of a historic 'struggle around the image' – a politics of representation. [. . .]

Representation, difference and power

We have established a connection between representation, difference and power. However, we need to probe the nature of this *power* more fully. We often think of power in terms of direct physical coercion or constraint. However, we have also spoken, for example, of power *in representation*: power to mark, assign and classify; of *symbolic* power; of *ritualized* expulsion. Power, it seems, has to be understood here, not only in terms of economic exploitation and physical coercion, but also in broader cultural or symbolic terms, including the power to represent someone or something in a certain way – within a certain 'regime of representation'. It includes the exercise of *symbolic power* through representational practices. Stereotyping is a key element in this exercise of symbolic violence.

In his study of how Europe constructed a stereotypical image of 'the Orient', Edward Said (1978) argues that, far from simply reflecting what the countries of the Near East were actually like, 'Orientalism' was the *discourse* 'by which European culture was able to manage – and even produce – the Orient politically, sociologically, militarily, ideologically, scientifically and imaginatively during the post-Enlightenment period'. Within the framework of western hegemony over the Orient, he says, there emerged a new object of knowledge – 'a complex Orient suitable for study in the academy, for display in the museum, for reconstruction in the colonial office, for theoretical illustration in anthropological, biological, linguistic, racial and historical theses about mankind and the universe, for instances of economic and sociological theories of development, revolution, cultural personalities, national or religious character' (pp. 7–8). This form of power is closely connected with knowledge, or with the practices of what Foucault called 'power/knowledge'. [. . .] Said's discussion of Orientalism closely parallels Foucault's power/knowledge argument: a *discourse* produces, through different practices of *representation* (scholarship, exhibition, literature, painting, etc.), a form of *racialized knowledge of the Other* (Orientalism) deeply implicated in the operations of *power* (imperialism).

Interestingly, however, Said goes on to define 'power' in ways which emphasize the similarities between Foucault and Gramsci's idea of *hegemony*:

> In any society not totalitarian, then, certain cultural forms predominate over others; the form of this cultural leadership is what Gramsci has identified as *hegemony*, an indispensable concept for any understanding of cultural life in the industrial West. It is hegemony, or rather the result of cultural hegemony at work, that gives Orientalism its durability and its strength . . . Orientalism is never far from . . . the idea of Europe, a collective notion identifying 'us' Europeans as against all 'those' non-Europeans, and indeed it can be argued that the major component in European culture is precisely what made that culture hegemonic both in and outside Europe; the idea of European identity as a superior one in comparison with all the non-European peoples and cultures. There is in addition the hegemony of European ideas about the Orient, themselves reiterating European superiority over Oriental backwardness, usually overriding the possibility that a more independent thinker . . . may have had different views on the matter.
>
> (Said, 1978: 7)

Power always operates in conditions of unequal relations. Gramsci, of course, would have stressed 'between classes', whereas Foucault always refused to identify *any* specific subject or subject-group as the source of power, which, he said, operates at a local, tactical level. These are important differences between these two theorists of power.

However, there are also some important similarities. For Gramsci, as for Foucault, power also involves knowledge, representation, ideas, cultural leadership and authority, as well as economic constraint and physical coercion. Both would have agreed that power cannot be captured by thinking exclusively in terms of force or coercion: power also seduces, solicits, induces, wins consent. It cannot be thought of in terms of one group having a monopoly of power, simply radiating power *downwards* on a subordinate group by an exercise of simple domination from above. It includes the dominant *and* the dominated within its circuits. As Homi Bhabha has remarked, apropos Said, 'it is difficult to conceive . . . subjectification as a placing *within* Orientalist or colonial discourse for the dominated subject without the dominant being strategically placed within it too' (Bhabha, 1986a: 158). Power not only constrains and prevents: it is also productive. It produces new discourses, new kinds of knowledge (i.e. Orientalism), new objects of knowledge (the Orient), it shapes new practices (colonization) and institutions (colonial government). It operates at a micro-level

– Foucault's 'micro-physics of power' – as well as in terms of wider strategies. And, for both theorists, power is to be found everywhere. As Foucault insists, power circulates.

The circularity of power is especially important in the context of representation. The argument is that everyone – the powerful and the powerless – is caught up, *though not on equal terms*, in power's circulation. No one – neither its apparent victims nor its agents – can stand wholly outside its field of operation. [. . .]

Contesting a racialized regime of representation

Can a dominant regime of representation be challenged, contested or changed? What are the counter-strategies which can begin to subvert the representation process? Can 'negative' ways of representing racial difference, which abound in our examples, be reversed by a 'positive' strategy? What effective strategies are there? And what are their theoretical underpinnings?

Let me remind you that, theoretically, the argument which enables us to pose this question at all is the proposition (which we have discussed in several places and in many different ways) that *meaning can never be finally fixed*. If meaning could be fixed by representation, then there would be no change – and so no counter-strategies or interventions. Of course, we *do* make strenuous efforts to fix meaning – that is precisely what the strategies of stereotyping are aspiring to do, often with considerable success, for a time. But ultimately, meaning begins to slip and slide; it begins to drift, or be wrenched, or inflected into new directions. New meanings are grafted on to old ones. Words and images carry connotations over which no one has complete control, and these marginal or submerged meanings come to the surface, allowing different meanings to be constructed, different things to be shown and said. That is why we referred you to the work of Bakhtin and Volosinov. For they have given a powerful impetus to the practice of what has come to be known as trans-coding: taking an existing meaning and re-appropriating it for new meanings (e.g. 'Black is Beautiful').

A number of different *trans-coding* strategies have been adopted since the 1960s, when questions of representation and power acquired a centrality in the politics of anti-racist and other social movements. We only have space here to consider two of them.

Reversing the stereotypes

In the discussion of racial stereotyping in the American cinema, we discussed the ambiguous position of Sidney Poitier and talked about an *integrationist* strategy in US film-making in the 1950s. This strategy, as we said, carried heavy costs. Blacks could gain entry to the mainstream – but only at the cost of adapting to the white image of them and assimilating white norms of style, looks and behaviour. Following the Civil Rights movement, in the 1960s and 1970s, there was a much more aggressive affirmation of black cultural identity, a positive attitude towards difference and a struggle over representation.

The first fruit of this counter-revolution was a series of films, beginning with *Sweet Sweetback's Baadasss Song* (Martin Van Peebles, 1971), and Gordon Parks' box-office success, *Shaft*. In *Sweet Sweetback*, Van Peebles values positively all the characteristics which would normally have been negative stereotypes. He made his black hero a professional stud, who successfully evades the police with the help of a succession of black ghetto low-lifers, sets fire to a police car, shafts another with a pool cue, lights out for the Mexican border, making full use of his sexual prowess at every opportunity, and ultimately gets away with it all, to a message scrawled across the screen: 'A BAADASSS NIGGER IS COMING BACK TO COLLECT SOME DUES'. *Shaft* was about a black detective, close to the streets but struggling with the black underworld and a band of black militants as well as the Mafia, who rescues a black racketeer's daughter. What marked *Shaft* out, however, was the detective's absolute lack of deference towards whites. Living in a smart apartment, beautifully turned out in casual but expensive clothes, he was presented in the advertising publicity as a 'lone black Super-spade – a man of flair and flamboyance who has fun at the expense of the white establishment'. He was 'a violent man who lived a violent life, in pursuit of black women, white sex, quick money, easy success, cheap "pot" and other pleasures' (Cripps, 1978: 251–254). When asked by a policeman where he is going, Shaft replies, 'I'm going to get laid. Where are you going?' The instant success of *Shaft* was followed by a succession of films in the same mould, including *Superfly*, also by Parks, in which Priest, a young black cocaine dealer, succeeds in making one last big deal before retirement, survives both a series of violent episodes and vivid sexual encounters to drive off at the end in his Rolls Royce, a rich and happy man. There have been many later films in the same mould (e.g. *New Jack City*) with, at their centre (as the Rap singers would say), 'bad-ass black men, with attitude'.

We can see at once the appeal of these films, especially, though not exclusively, to black audiences. In the ways their heroes deal with whites, there is a remarkable absence, indeed a conscious reversal of, the old deference or childlike dependency. In many ways, these are 'revenge' films – audiences relishing the black heroes' triumphs over 'Whitey', loving the fact that they're getting away with it! What we may call the moral playing-field is levelled. Blacks are neither always worse nor always better than whites. They come in the usual human shapes – good, bad and indifferent. They are no different from the ordinary (white) average American in their tastes, styles, behaviour, morals, motivations. In class terms, they can be as 'cool', affluent and well groomed as their white counterparts. And their 'locations' are the familiar real-life settings of ghetto, street, police station and drug-bust.

At a more complex level, they placed blacks for the first time at the centre of the popular cinematic genres – crime and action films – and thus made them essential to what we may call the 'mythic' life and culture of the American cinema – more important, perhaps, in the end, than their 'realism'. For this is where the collective fantasies of popular life are worked out, and the exclusion of blacks from its confines made them precisely, peculiar, different, placed them 'outside the picture'. It deprived them of the celebrity status, heroic charisma, the glamour and pleasure of identification accorded to the white heroes of *film noir*, the old private eye, crime and police thrillers, the 'romances' of urban low-life and the ghetto. With these films, blacks had arrived in the cultural mainstream – with a vengeance!

These films carried through one counter-strategy with considerable single-mindedness – reversing the evaluation of popular stereotypes. And they proved that this strategy could secure box-office success and audience identification. Black audiences loved them because they cast black actors in glamorous and 'heroic' as well as 'bad' roles: white audiences took to them because they contained all the elements of the popular cinematic genres. Nevertheless, among some critics, the judgement on their success as a representational counter-strategy has become more mixed. They have come to be seen by many as 'blaxploitation' films.

To reverse the stereotype is not necessarily to overturn or subvert it. Escaping the grip of one stereotypical extreme (blacks are poor, childish, subservient, always shown as servants, everlastingly 'good', in menial positions, deferential to whites, never the heroes, cut out of the glamour, the pleasure, and the rewards, sexual and financial) may simply mean being trapped in its stereotypical 'other' (blacks are motivated by money, love bossing white people around, perpetrate violence and crime as effectively as the next person, are 'bad', walk off with the goodies, indulge in drugs, crime and promiscuous sex, come on like 'Superspades' and *always get away with it*!). This may be an advance on the former list, and is certainly a welcome change. But it has not escaped the contradictions of the binary structure of racial stereotyping and it has not unlocked what Mercer and Julien call 'the complex dialectics of power and subordination' through which 'black male identities have been historically and culturally constructed' (1994: 137). The black critic, Lerone Bennett acknowledged that 'after it [*Sweet Sweetback . . .*] we can never again see black people in films (noble, suffering, losing) in the same way . . .' But he also thought it 'neither revolutionary nor black', indeed, a revival of certain 'antiquated white stereotypes', even 'mischievous and reactionary'. As he remarked, 'nobody ever fucked his way to freedom' (quoted in Cripps, 1978: 248). This is a critique which has, in retrospect, been delivered about the whole foregrounding of black masculinity during the Civil Rights movement, of which these films were undoubtedly a by-product. Black feminist critics have pointed out how the black resistance to white patriarchal power during the 1960s was often accompanied by the adoption of an exaggerated 'black male macho' style and sexual aggressiveness by black leaders towards black women (Michele Wallace, 1979; Angela Davis, 1983; bell hooks, 1992).

[. . .]

Through the eye of representation
The second counter-strategy locates itself *within* the complexities and ambivalences of representation itself, and tries to *contest it from within*. It is more concerned with the *forms* of racial representation than with introducing a new *content*. It accepts and works with the shifting, unstable character of meaning, and enters, as it were, into a struggle over representation, while acknowledging that, since meaning can never be finally fixed, there can never be any final victories.

Thus, instead of avoiding the black body, because it has been so caught up in the complexities of power and subordination within representation, this strategy positively takes the body as the principal site of its representational strategies, attempting to make the stereotypes work against themselves. Instead of avoiding the dangerous terrain opened up by the interweaving of 'race', gender and sexuality, it deliberately contests the dominant gendered and sexual definitions of racial difference by *working on* black sexuality. Since black people have so often been fixed, stereotypically, by the racialized gaze, it may have been tempting to refuse the complex emotions associated with 'looking'. However, this strategy makes elaborate play with 'looking', hoping by its very attention, to 'make it strange' – that is, to de-familiarize it, and so make explicit what is often hidden – its erotic dimensions. It is not afraid to deploy humour – for example, the comedian, Lenny Henry, forces us by the witty exaggerations of his Afro-Caribbean caricatures, to laugh *with* rather than *at* his characters. Finally, instead of refusing the displaced power and danger of 'fetishism', this strategy attempts to use the desires and ambivalences which tropes of fetishism inevitably awaken.

[. . .]

References

Babcock, B. (1978) *The Reversible World: Symbolic Inversion in Art and Society*, Ithaca, NY, Cornell University Press.

Bakhtin, M. (1981 [1935]) *The Dialogic Imagination*, Austin, University of Texas.

Barthes, R. (1977) 'Rhetoric of the image' in *Image–Music–Text*, Glasgow, Fontana.

Bhabha, H. (1986a) 'The Other question' in *Literature, Politics and Theory*, London, Methuen.

Bhabha, H. (1986b) 'Foreword' to F. Fanon, *Black Skin, White Masks*, London, Pluto Press.

Bogle, D. (1973) *Toms, Coons, Mulattoes. Mammies and Bucks: an Interpretative History of Blacks in American Films*, New York, Viking Press.

Cripps, T. (1978) *Black Film as Genre*, Bloomington, IN, Indiana University Press.

Davis, A. (1983) *Women, Race and Class*, New York, Random House.

Derrida, J. (1981) *Positions*, Chicago, IL, University of Chicago Press.

Douglas, M. (1966) *Purity and Danger*, London, Routledge and Kegan Paul.

Fanon, F. (1986 [1952]) *Black Skin, White Masks*, London, Pluto Press.

Frederickson, G. (1987) *The Black Image in the White Mind*, Hanover, NH, Wesleyan University Press.

Green, D. (1984) 'Classified subjects: photography and anthropology – the technology of power', *Ten/8*, no. 14, Birmingham.

Hall, C. (1994) *White, Male and Middle Class*, Cambridge, Polity Press.

Hall, S. (1972) 'Determinations of news photographs' in *Working Papers in Cultural Studies No. 3*, Birmingham, University of Birmingham.

Hall, S. (1981) 'The whites of their eyes' in R. Brunt (ed.) *Silver Linings*, London, Lawrence and Wishart.

Hall, S. (1996) 'The after-life of Frantz Fanon' in A. Read (ed.) *The Fact of Blackness: Frantz Fanon and visual representation*, Seattle, WA, Bay Press.

hooks, b. (1992) *Black Looks: race and representation*, Boston, MA, South End Press.

Klein, M. (1957) *Envy and Gratitude*, New York, Delta.

Kristeva, J. (1982) *Powers of Horror*, New York, Columbia University Press.

Lacan, J. (1977) *Écrits*, London, Tavistock.

Leab, D. (1976) *From Sambo to Superspade*, New York, Houghton Mifflin.

Lévi-Strauss, C. (1970) *The Raw and the Cooked*, London, Cape.

Long, E. (1774) *History of Jamaica*, London, Lowdnes.

Mackenzie, J. (ed.) (1986) *Imperialism and Popular Culture*, Manchester, Manchester University Press.

McClintock, A. (1995) *Imperial Leather*, London, Routledge.

Mercer, K. and Julien, I. (1994) 'Black masculinity and the politics of race' in K. Mercer (ed.) *Welcome to the Jungle*, London, Routledge.

Morton, P. (1991) *Disfigured Images*, New York, Praeger and Greenwood Press.

Richards, T. (1990) *The Commodity Culture of Victorian Britain*, London, Verso.

Said, E. (1978) *Orientalism*, Harmondsworth, Penguin.

Segal, L. (1997) 'Sexualities' in K. Woodward (ed.) *Identity and Difference*, London, Sage and The Open University.

Stallybrass, P. and White, A. (1986) *The Politics and Poetics of Transgression*, London, Methuen.

Wallace, M. (1979) *Black Macho*, London, Calder.

The Construction of an LD Student: A Case Study in the Politics of Representation

Hugh Mehan

Source: Mehan, H. (1996) 'The construction of an LD student: A case study in the politics of representation' in M. Silverstein and G. Urban (eds) *Natural Histories of Discourses*, Chicago, University of Chicago Press.

Constructing social facts: clarity from ambiguity

Proponents of various positions in conflicts waged in and through discourse attempt to capture or dominate modes of representation. They do so in a variety of ways, including inviting or persuading others to join their side, or silencing opponents by attacking their positions. If they are successful, a hierarchy is formed in which one mode of representing the world (its objects, events, people, etc.) gains primacy over others, transforming modes of representation from an array on a horizontal plane to a ranking on a vertical plane. This competition over the meaning of ambiguous events, people, and objects in the world has been called the 'politics of representation' (Holquist, 1983; Mehan and Wills, 1988; Shapiro, 1987). As we shall see, one kind of politically contested representation is the lexical label, and lexical labels are 'texts', minimal ones, to be sure, but texts all the same. Indeed, the process of lexical labelling is itself an entextualization process. Complex, contextually nuanced discussions get summed up in (and, hence, are entextualized through) a single word.

There are many ways in which a certain group of people can be designated by lexical formulation: 'guest workers', 'potential citizens', 'illegal aliens', 'undocumented workers'. Each formulation or way of representing this group of people does not simply reflect unique or exhaustive characteristics given in advance. Each mode of representation relationally defines the person making the representation and constitutes the group of people, and each does so in a distinctive way. To be a ***guest*** *worker* is to be an invited person, someone who is welcome and in a positive relationship to the employer; to be a *guest* ***worker*** is to be someone who is contributing to the economy, productively, by labouring. The formulation *potential citizen* invokes similar positive connotations. It does so within the realm of citizenship and politics, however, rather than in the realm of market economics, as the guest worker formulation does. The potential citizen is not yet a complete citizen, but is on the path of full participation in the society. The *illegal alien* designation invokes many opposite ways of thinking. *Illegal* is simple and clear: a person outside of society, an idea reinforced by the *alien* designation – foreign, repulsive, threatening. Finally, representing this group as *undocumented workers* implies that it comprises people who contribute economically, but do so in an extralegal capacity.

[. . .]

A similar competition over the meaning of ambiguous events in the world is played out in schools every day when educators try to decide whether a certain child is 'normal' or 'deviant', belongs in a 'regular educational programme' or in a 'special education programme'. Deciding whether students are 'normal' or 'special' is a practical project that occurs routinely in US schools. Although this activity is as old as schools themselves, in response to recently enacted state and federal legislation, this classification and sorting activity has become more formalized. There are now procedures mandated by law, especially PL 94–142, the 'Education for All Handicapped Students Act', concerning the referral of students to special education. This law, established to provide an equitable education to handicapped youngsters in the least restrictive environment possible, imposes time limits for the assessment of students and specifies the participants involved in decision making. For example, final placement decisions are to be made by a committee composed of the student's teacher, a school psychologist, a representative from the district office, the child's parents, and, in some cases, a medical official.

In general, I am interested in how the clarity of labelled social facts such as 'intelligence', 'deviance', 'health', or 'illness' are produced from the ambiguity of everyday life. In the work described in this chapter, I concentrate on a particular instantiation of that general interest – the production of student identities. In short, I am asking: How are student identities produced? How does a student become a 'special education' or a 'regular education' student?

The construction of handicapped students operates on at least two semiotic planes simultaneously. One is the plane on which the categories such as 'educational handicap' and 'learning disability' (LD) are established in the first place. Relevant here is the social history of the category of disability, its relationship to previously important notions like mental retardation and feeble-mindedness, the continuing importance of medical discourse, the semiotic processes involved in the establishment of the law, including the role of politicians and various pressure groups, such as the Council of Exceptional Children. In this social history, learning disabilities have been understood to be intrinsic to the individual and are presumed to be caused by central nervous system dysfunction or a hereditary condition. Coles (1987) traces this thinking to diagnoses conducted by a Glasgow medical officer in 1907. Difficulties in learning to read were diagnosed as 'congenital word-blindness' by Hinshelwood, who concluded that the root of this 'disease' lay in children's brains because he had observed that dysfunctional reading symptoms found in adults with brain lesions were analogous to those of certain children with reading problems. This thinking started what has become a medicalization of children's difficulties in schools. In this medical model, the child is the focus of diagnosis; he or she has a pathology which is subject to treatment. The medical model is explicit in the Education for All Handicapped Students law which has specific provisions for correcting the physical state of students. Moreover, the underlying assumptions of the medical model have been extended beyond the physical condition of students to the mental condition of children considered for special education.

Attributes such as intelligence, aptitude, potential, or mental ability are considered to be internal states or traits of students which are subject to diagnosis and treatment.

The indexical plane of practical application of such attributes is the second semiotic plane on which LD students are constructed. On the indexical plane, the historically constructed and legally prescribed categories are articulated with potential instances in actual educational practice at the school site. Relevant in these situations are the decisions that educators make about children in the context of the legal and fiscal constraints imposed by the law, competing programmes, and other practical matters at the local level. Ideally, consideration should be given to both planes and the linkage between them. However, I will not say more about the historical plane in this chapter because of space limitations.

Language plays a powerful, constitutive role in transforming the ambiguity of student behaviour to the clarity of 'regular' or 'special' student on both the historical and the indexical plane. Multifocal discourse generated in face-to-face encounters becomes devoiced and decentred and emerges in the form of frozen, artifactualized texts such as student records as the decision-making process unfolds from classroom to final committee meeting.

A social fact of the school system: handicapped students

In order to understand the process by which students are considered for placement in one of a number of special education programmes or are retained in regular classrooms, we followed the progress of students' cases through the special education referral process mandated by PL 94–142. During the 1978–79 school year in which my colleagues and I (Mehan et al., 1986) observed this sorting and classification process in a midsize school district in Southern California, 141 students out of a total school population of 2,700 students were referred for 'special education'; 53 of these cases were considered by the committee with responsibility for final placement decisions. The disposition of these cases is shown in Table 1.

Most (36) of the students considered by the Eligibility and Placement (E&P) Committees were placed into the Learning Disabilities (LD) group, and some (7) were placed in the Educationally Handicapped (EH) programme.[1]
Notably, no students were placed in special programmes outside the district, and only one student considered by the committee was retained in his regular classroom.

These figures, which represent the aggregate number of students placed into educational programmes, would conventionally be accepted as an example of a 'social fact'. Furthermore, each number in the table represents a point in a student's educational career, that is, his or her identity as a special education or a regular education student. Hence, we have two senses of social structure here: one represented as aggregate data, the other represented as social identities.

Given this statistical distribution, I am asking, What practices produce this array, these careers, these identities? In answering this question, I propose to show that these 'social facts' of the school system are constructed in the practical work of educators in their person-to-person and person-to-text interaction. In the

Table 1   *The disposition of 53 cases considered by placement committees*

Placement	Number
Educationally Handicapped (EH)	7
Learning Disabled (LD)	36
Severe Language Handicapped (SLH)	3
Multiple Handicap	2
Speech Therapy	3
Off-Campus Placement ('Private Schooling')	0
Counselling	0
Reading	0
Adaptive Physical Education	0
Bilingual Education	0
No Placement (Returned to Classroom)	1
Placement Process Interrupted	1
Total	53

analysis that follows, I explore a way of showing how the routine practices of educators as they carry out their daily work construct a 'handicapped' student by tracing one student's case through the special education referral process. The major steps in this process are 'referral,' 'educational testing,' and 'placement.'

In order to uncover the discursive and organizational arrangements which provide for an array such as the one in Table 1, my colleagues and I employed an interconnected set of research methods. In addition to observing in classrooms, teachers' lounges, testing rooms, and committee meetings, we interviewed educators and parents, reviewed students' records, and videotaped events which were crucial in the construction of students' identities. Students' records provided such baseline data as the age, sex, and grade of students, the official reason for referral, the name of the person making the referral, the date of referral, psychological assessment information, and final disposition of cases. Information available from school records was checked against information that became available to us through observation, videotaping, informal discussions, and more formal interviews with educators in the district.

Observations in classrooms and analysis of lessons videotaped there gave us insight into the reasons teachers referred students and the relationship between teachers' accounts of student behaviour and students' classroom behaviour. Videotape gathered from educational testing sessions and Eligibility and Placement Committee meetings served as the behavioural record we examined for the educators' sorting and classifying practices. It also served as a multi-purpose document for interviews with participants in these key events in the referral process.

Constructing an LD student: the case of Shane

We discovered, upon the analysis of the materials gathered by these diverse research techniques, that the student classification process in the Coast District had a number of components. The school's work of sorting students most frequently started in the classroom, continued through psychological assessment, and culminated in evaluation by the E&P committee. Thus, as Collins (1981) suggested, a 'social structure' – the aggregate number of students in various educational programmes or their identity as special or regular students – is generated in a sequence of organizationally predictable interactional events (classroom, testing session, meetings).

An important feature of this process is the transposition of entextualizations from context to context. Discourse from one setting in the sequence of events in the referral process generates the given text used for discussion in the next session. So, for example, after a teacher and students interact in the classroom (discourse), the teacher fills out a form (a text-artifact). Its text is introduced into the discourse of the School Appraisal Team (SAT) meeting. From the discourse of the participants in that meeting, another artifact, another piece of text, is generated, this time a 'summary of recommendation', which instructs the school psychologist to begin educational testing. The administration of the educational test transpires as face-to-face interaction between tester and student. Based on that discourse, the tester writes a report. That text-artifact is sent to the placement committee, where it becomes part of the file, which, representing the child, becomes the basis of the final placement decision. Such artifactual texts, generated from a particular event in the sequential process (e.g. a testing encounter), become the basis of the discursive interaction in the next step in the sequence (e.g. a placement committee meeting). These texts are decentred and indeed de- 'voiced' in that as they move through the system, they become institutionally isolated from the interactional practices that generated them in the preceding events.

Step 1: Calling for help
The process by which a child becomes 'educationally handicapped' usually begins in the classroom when, for whatever reasons, a teacher refers a child by completing a referral form. Completing the form and making the referral do not automatically make the child LD or educationally handicapped; but unless that bureaucratic step is taken, the child cannot be eligible to achieve that status.

On October 10, approximately one month after the start of school, the fourth-grade teacher at the Desert Vista School referred 'Shane' for possible placement in special education for his 'low academic performance' and his 'difficulty in applying himself to his daily class work'.[2]

In order to gain more insight into the teachers' reasons for referring students than was available on official referral forms, we videotaped classroom lessons and viewed them with the teachers. Following guidelines concerning these 'viewing sessions' that proved productive in the past (e.g. Cicourel *et al.*, 1974; Erickson and Shultz, 1982), teachers were asked to 'stop the tape any time they found anything interesting happening'. While watching a videotape of a math lesson in which Shane and others were participating, the teacher stopped the tape just after Shane said, 'No way' while assembling a pattern with geometric shapes called tangrams:

> 130 **Teacher** Yeah, he, he starts out like that on a lot of things. It's like, 'I can't do it.' He's just glancing at it. . . . He's very apprehensive about approaching

anything. But once he gets into it, and finishes something he's just so pleased with himself. And I'll say, 'Hey I thought you said, 'No way.' Well?"

Later in the interview, the teacher stopped the tape again and commented:

406 **Teacher** I mentioned before, yeah, that whenever he's given some new task to do it's always like, too hard, 'No way I can do it,' until we, 'Oh, come on, you just get into it and try it!' When he finishes, I mean it's like fantastic, you know that he did it.[3]

These comments reinforced the teacher's representation of the child as one who has trouble applying himself to his school work. It is interesting to note, however, that all the other students in the lesson expressed similar consternation with the difficulty of the task. Nevertheless, the teacher did not treat the comments by the other students as instances of the concern over work difficulty; she did, however, treat the comments by Shane as exemplifying this reason for referring him. This gap between referral reason and students' behaviour was a general pattern in our study (Mehan *et al*, 1986: 69–97), which implicates the problematic nature of the behavioural record beneath special education referrals and the important role that teachers' expectations and conceptions play in forming judgments about students' behaviour.

Step 2: Refining the definition

The referral was forwarded to the next step in the referral system, the School Appraisal Team (SAT), a committee composed of educators at the Desert Vista School. At its first meeting in October, the school psychologist was instructed to assess Shane. For a variety of practical reasons which plague bureaucratic processes such as this referral system, including a large backlog of cases, and difficulty in obtaining parental permission and necessary records from another school district, the recommended assessment did not take place until December and January – two months after the original referral.

The school psychologist administered a battery of tests to Shane on 6 December including an informal assessment called the 'Three Wishes', the Goodenough Draw-A-Man Test, and portions of the WISC-R. The SAT met again on 4 January. After hearing the results of the first round of assessment, the committee recommended that the psychologist complete testing. After the Christmas break, the school psychologist completed the WISC-R and administered the CAT and the Bender Gestalt. On 2 February, the committee heard the full report of testing. The psychologist reported that Shane had a verbal I.Q. of 115. He was reading at a fourth-grade level. His arithmetic and spelling tested at 3.0 and 3.5, which 'put him below grade level'. His test age on the Bender Gestalt was 7.0–7.5, while his actual age (at the time) was 9.0, which put him 'considerably below his age level'. Based on this assessment, the SAT recommended that Shane be considered by the Eligibility and Placement (E&P) Committee for possible placement into a programme for the Learning Disabled.[4]

We see illustrated here the process by which general calls for help from a classroom teacher become refined and specified in official language. The teacher had said Shane 'has difficulty in applying himself to classwork'. That vague appeal is now transformed into a technical assessment: Shane's academic skill is expressed in numerical terms (I.Q. of 115, test age of 7.5). He is compared to a normative standard: he is 'behind grade level'. No longer is he a child 'who needs help'; now he is possibly a 'learning disabled child'.

The consequence of this refining is fundamental to the way in which the diagnostic process creates handicapped students and handicapped students' careers. Students' identities are sharpened as they move from regular education classrooms to testing rooms and finally to meeting rooms.

Step 3: Resolving competing representations of the student

When the E&P Committee met on February 16 to discuss Shane's case, the following dialogue took place:

```
EDM #33
92  Psy     does the uh, committee agree that the, uh learning disability placement
            is one that might benefit him?
93  Prn     I think we agree.
94  Psy     We're not considering then a special day class at all for him?
95  SET     I wouldn't at this point//
96  Many    =No.
```

The committee decided to place Shane into an LD group, a pullout educational programme in which students spend a part of the school day in the regular classroom and the other part of the day in a special programme. The 'special day class' indexed by the psychologist (Line 94) is the EH programme in which students spend the entire school day in a special classroom.

When we observed these E&P meetings, we were struck by an interesting feature about the interaction among the committee members. Although committee members came to meetings with a variety of opinions about the appropriate placement of students, by meeting's end one view of the children, that one recommended by the district, prevailed. Furthermore, this agreement was reached without debate or disagreement. For example, before the E&P meeting reviewed in this chapter, the classroom teacher, reflecting on the changes in the student she referred in October, was no longer convinced that Shane needed special education. The mother, worried about the stigmatizing effect of even a mild placement such as the LD group, didn't want any special education for her child. Although definite and vocal before the meeting, they were silent during the meeting. In trying to understand how committee members (including parents) lost their voices while routinely coming to agreement with the school's recommendation, we turned our attention to the discourse of the placement committee meetings prior to the occurrence of the 'decision to place' students.

During the course of the meeting, four reports were made to the committee, one by the school psychologist, one by the child's teacher, one by the school nurse, and one by the child's mother. These reports varied along three dimensions: (1) the manner in which they presented information, (2) the manner in which they grounded their assertions, and (3) the manner in which they represented the child. By arraying the reports along these dimensions, we find three registers being spoken in the meeting, three ways of denoting: a psychological register, a sociological register, and a historical register. Competing versions of the child are presented in these registers, but one, the version of the child presented in the psychological language, prevails.

Mode of presentation

The information that the committee obtained from the classroom teacher and the mother appeared in a form different from the information made available by the school psychologist. The information that the psychologist had about the student was presented to the committee in a single uninterrupted report, whereas information was dialogically elicited from both the classroom teacher and the mother. Here is the psychologist's opening statement to the committee:

> 1 **Psy**   Um. What we're going to do is, I'm going to have a brief, an overview of the testing because the rest of, of the, the committee has not, uh, has not an, uh, been aware of that yet. And uh, then each of us will share whatever, whatever we feel we need to share.
>
> 2 **Prn**   Right.
>
> 3 **Psy**   And then we will make a decision on what we feel is a good, oh (3) placement (2) for an, Shane.

The school psychologist then provided the committee members with the information she had about the student:

> 3 **Psy**   Shane is ah nine years old, and he's in fourth grade. Uh, he, uh, was referred because of low academic performance and he has difficulty applying himself to his daily class work. Um, Shane attended the Montessori School in kindergarten and first grade, and then he entered Carlsberg – bad in, um, September of 1976 and, uh, entered our district in, uh, '78. He seems to have very good peer relationships but, uh, the teachers, uh, continually say that he has difficulty with handwriting. 'Kay. He enjoys music and sports. I gave him a complete battery and, um, I found that, uh, he had a verbal I.Q. of 115, performance of 111, and a full scale of 115, so he's a bright child. Uh, he had very high scores in, uh, information which is his long-term memory. Ah, vocabulary, was, ah, also, ah, considerably over average, good detail awareness and his, um, picture arrangement scores, he had a seventeen which is very high//
>
> 4 **SET**   =Mmmm//
>
> 5 **Psy**   =very superior rating, so he, his visual sequencing seems to be good and also he has a good grasp of anticipation and awareness of social situations. Um, he (5) (she is scanning her notes) scored in reading at 4.1, spelling 3.5, and arithmetic 3.0, which gave him a standard score of 100 in, uh, reading, 95 in spelling, and 90 in arithmetic. When compared with his [overall] score, it does put him somewhat ah below his, you know, his capabilities. I gave him the Bender Gestalt (clears throat) and he had six errors. And his test age was 7–0 to 7–5 and his actual age is nine, so it, uh, he was considerably beneath his, uh, his uh, age level. (2) His – I gave him the, uh VADS and his, um (5 or 6) (looking through

notes) both the oral-aural and the visual-written modes of communication were high but the visual oral and the oral written are lo::ow, so he, uh, cannot switch channels. His expressive vocabulary was in the superior range (6). Uh, visual perception falls above age level, so he's fine in that area (6). And fine motor skills appear to be slightly lower than, uh, average, (voice trails off slightly), I saw them. (3) He read words very quickly when he was doing the academics but I didn't see any reversals in his written work. Uh, I gave him several projective tests and, um, the things that I picked up there is [sic] that, um he [does] possibly have some fears and anxieties, uh, (5). So I had felt ah, that perhaps he might, uh, uh, benefit, um, (3) from special help. He also was tested, um, in 1976 and at that time he was given the WISC-R and his I.Q. was slightly lower, full scale of a 93 (3 or 4). His, um, summary of that evaluation, uh, was, uh, he was given the ITPA and he had high auditory reception, auditory association, auditory memory. (2) So his auditory skills are good. (3) He was given another psychol– psychological evaluation in 1977. He was given the Leiter and he had an I.Q. of 96 (6). And, um (3 or 4) they concluded that he had a poor mediate recall (2) but they felt that was due to an emotional overlay and they felt that some emotional conflicts were, uh, interfering with his ability to concentrate.

At the end of this presentation, the psychologist asked the student's teacher to provide information:

5	**Psy**	Kate, would you like to share with u:s?
6	**CLT**	What, the problems I see ( ) Um . . .
7	**Psy**	Yes.
8	**CLT**	Um. Probably basically the fine motor types of things are difficult for him. He's got a very creative mi:ind and expresses himself well ( ) orally and verbally and he's pretty alert to what's going on. (2) Maybe a little bit [too] much, watching **every**thing that's (hh) going (hh) on, and finds it hard to stick to one task. And [mostly] I've been noticing that it's just his writing and things that he has a, a block with. And he can rea:ad and comprehend some things when I talk to him, [but] doing independent type work is hard for him.
9	**Prn**	Mhmmm, putting it down on paper . . .
10	**CLT**	Yeah::, and sticking to a task//
11	**Prn**	=mmhmmm//
12	**CLT**	=and getting it done, without being distracted by (hehhehheh)
13	**SET**	How does he relate with what the other kids do?
14	**CLT**	Uh, very well. He's got a lot of frie:ends, and, uh, especially, even out on the playground he's, um (3), wants to get in on the games, get on things and is well accepted. So:o, I don't see too many problems there.

In this sequence, we have the classroom teacher beginning to present some of the characteristics of the student (8), being interrupted by the principal (9), before the special education teacher took the floor (13). From that point on, the special education teacher asked the classroom teacher a series of questions about Shane's peer relations, reading level, and performance in spelling and math.

After the school psychologist asked how Shane handled failure, the questioning shifted to the mother, who was asked about her son's fine motor control at home:

46	**SET**	How do you find him at [home] in terms of using his fingers and fine motor kinds of things? Does he do//
47	**Mot**	=He will – as a small child, he didn't at all. He was never interested in it, he wasn't interested in sitting in my lap and having a book read to him, any things like that//
48	**SET**	=Mhmmm//
49	**Mot**	=which I think is part of it you know. His, his older brother was just the opposite, and learned to write real early. [Now] Shane, at night, lots of times he comes home and he'll write or draw. He's really doing a lot//
50	**SET**	( )
51	**Mot**	=he sits down and is writing love notes to his girl friend (hehheh). He went in our bedroom last night and turned on the TV and got out some colored pencils and started writing. So he, really likes to, and of course he brings it all into us to see//
52	**SET**	=Mhmmm//
53	**Mot**	=and comment on, so I think, you know, he's not [**nega**tive] about//
54	**SET**	=no//
55	**Mot**	=that any more//
56	**SET**	=uh huh
57	**Mot**	He was before, but I think his attitude's changed a lot.

These transcript excerpts show that the information that the psychologist had about the student was presented to the committee in a single, uninterrupted report, while the mother's and classroom teacher's information was elicited by other members of the committee. The school psychologist's presentation of the case to the committee was augmented by officially sanctioned props, including the case file itself (a bulky manila folder on display in front of the psychologist), test results, and carefully prepared notes. When she spoke, she read from notes. By contrast, neither the mother nor the teacher had such props. They spoke from memory, not from notes.

Grounds of assertions

The members of the committee supported their claims about the child in different ways. The psychologist provided a summary of the results of a given test or subtest in a standard format. She named the subtest, reported the student's score, and gave her interpretations of the results. For example:

> I gave him a complete battery, and I found that, uh, he had a verbal I.Q. of 115, performance of 111, and a full scale of 115, so he's a bright child.

He had very high scores in, uh, information, which is his long-term memory.

His, um, picture arrangement scores – he had a seventeen, which is very high, very superior rating.

While the psychologist reported information about the student based on quasi-scientific tools, the classroom teacher and mother based their reports on first hand observations. For example, the teacher provided general statements, 'He's got a very creative mind and expresses himself well' (8), as well as some more specific assertions: 'He can read and comprehend some things when I talk to him, but doing independent type work is hard for him' (8). While the psychologist's observations were confined to a relatively short period of time (hours of testing) and a circumscribed setting, the classroom teacher's and mother's observations were based on a longer period of time and a less circumscribed spatial and social arrangement. For the teacher, this period was a school year and the space was the classroom, while the mother's observations concerned the child's actions in a wide variety of situations spanning a lifetime.

Thus, information gathered by systematic, albeit indirect, observations (i.e. that from specialized tests) *was presented to* the committee, while information gathered by direct, albeit unguided or unstructured, observation (which included information about classroom experiences and home life) *was elicited from* informed participants. Furthermore, the mode in which information was presented to the committee varied according to the status and official expertise of the participants in the meeting. The most highly technical information (that from tests) was made available by the most highly trained and highest ranking people in attendance at the meeting, whereas the personal observations were made available by the participants with the least technical expertise and lowest ranking. Speakers of officially higher rank and who spoke with their authority grounded in technical expertise presented their information, while speakers of lower rank, who spoke with authority based on first hand observations, had information elicited from them.

Mode of representation

Shane's mother, his teacher, the school psychologist and the school nurse discussed the student and his academic performance differently. The student was characterized by the psychologist as having 'troubles' and 'problems': 'He has difficulty applying himself to his daily work' (3); 'He cannot switch channels' (5); 'He has some fears and anxieties' (5). The classroom teacher characterizes the problem in a similar way: 'The fine motor types of things are difficult for him' (8); 'Doing independent type work is hard for him' (8).

While the student's problem is the focus of attention for the entire committee, the mother and teacher discuss the student in a register different from that of the psychologist and the nurse. Notable in this regard are comments about the student's motivation: 'He enjoys math' (28); 'He enjoys handwriting and wants to learn it' (30); 'He seems to enjoy handwriting and wants to learn it' (30); 'He really tries at it hard and seems to wanna learn it better' (34). The teacher also introduced a number of contingencies that influence the student's performance: (1) His performance varies as a function of preparation: 'If he studies his spelling

and concentrates on it he can do pretty well' (22). His performance varies
according to the kinds of materials and tasks: 'It's hard for him to copy down
[math] problems . . . if he's given a sheet where he can fill in answers and work
them out he does much better' (28); he does better on group tasks, 'but doing
independent type work is hard for him' (8). If the tasks at hand are a means to
some other end desired by the student, then his performance improves: 'If there's
something else he wants to do and knows he needs to do and knows he needs to
get through that before he can get on to something else, he'll work a little more
diligently at it' (45).

The mother's representation contrasts even more sharply with the
psychologist's than does the teacher's. She spoke about changes through time,
continually contrasting her son as he was at an earlier age with how he is now. In
each of these contrasts, she emphasized improvements and changes for the
better. Although she seems to acknowledge the official committee position about
Shane's problem, she provided an alternative explanation about the source of the
problem. For her, the locus of difficulty was not within him ('it's not physical',
'it's not functional'), but it was to be found in his past experience and the
situations he has been in.

In short, the teacher, like the psychologist, characterized the issue before the
committee as 'Shane's problem'. The teacher's characterization, unlike the
psychologist's however, had a contingent quality. She spoke sociologically,
providing contextual information of a locally situated sort. The mother's
representation, by contrast, has a historical dimension; she spoke in terms that
implied changes through time.

Stratifying registers of representation

Committee members often came to E&P meetings with differing views of the
student's case and attitudes about the student's placement. During this meeting,
the various members of this committee perceived Shane differently. The
psychologist located the child's problem beneath his skin and between his ears,
whereas the classroom teacher saw the student's problem varying from one
classroom situation to another, and the mother saw the child's problem changing
through time. That is, the teacher and the mother provided accounts about the
student's performance in conceptual discourses that were different than the
psychologist's version of the student's academic difficulties.

This discussion, if left here, would be at best an interesting example of
perspectival differences in representation that occur in face-to-face interaction.
That is, psychologists, teachers, and parents have different discourses for talking
about even the same children because of their different experiences and
backgrounds. While the perspectival dimension of representation is certainly an
important aspect of the social construction of this child's identity, closing the
discussion at this point would leave out a crucial ingredient: these modes of
representation are not equal. By meeting's end, one mode of representation, that
voiced in a psychological register, prevailed. The psychological representation of
the student supplanted both the sociological and historical representations of the
student.

So, the question that must be asked is, How did the psychologist control the discourse, dominating the other voices in the conversation? Or, asking this question in another way: How is the stratification of these modes of representation accomplished discursively?

In order to answer these questions, it is instructive to look at the manner in which the committee treated the descriptions of the child offered by the committee members. The reports by the psychologist and the nurse were accepted without question or challenge, while those of the mother and the teacher were interrupted continuously by questions. This differential treatment is at first surprising, especially in light of the differences in the manifest content of the three descriptions. The psychologist's description is replete with technical terms ('VADS', 'Bender', 'detail awareness', 'ITPA', 'WISC-R') and numerical scales ('I.Q. of 96', 'full scale of 93', 'test age was 7–0 to 7–5'), while both the mother and the teacher describe the student in lay terms ('He has a creative mind', 'Doing independent work is hard for him', 'He wasn't interested in sitting in my lap and having a book read to him').

Thus, the speaker who includes technical terms in her discourse *is not asked* to clarify terms, while the speakers of a vernacular *are asked* to clarify their terms. No one in the meeting asked the psychologist for more details or further information. In fact, the mother only requested clarification once during the course of the entire meeting and that was just as the formal business was being concluded. Her question was about 'P.E.':

422	**SET**	check over ((( ))) (5–6) I don't think I addressed P.E.
423	**Psy**	I don't think we uh, [oh], ok, we do not need that, okay, he does not need physical edu//
424	**Mot**	=(I want to ask something about that while you mentioned P.E. You mean physical education)
425	**???**	Mmhmmm
426	**Mot**	Does the school have a soccer programme or is that just totally separate from um, you know, part of the boys' club o::r//
427	**Prn**	=Right. It's a parent organized, um, association//
428	**Mot**	=Is there something (one?) at the school that would have information on it if it comes up in the season, because Shane really has expressed an interest in that.

The differences in the way in which the three reports were treated, especially the requests for clarification of technical terms during the committee meeting, helps us understand why the psychologist's representation was accorded privileged status by the committee. The psychologist's report gains its authority by the very nature of its construction. The psychologist's discourse obtains its privileged status *because* it is ambiguous, because it is shot full of technical terms, *because* it is difficult to understand. The parents and the other committee members do not challenge the ambiguity of the psychologist's report because the grounds to do so are removed by the manner in which the psychologist presents information, grounds assertions, and represents the child in discourse.

Meaning is said to be negotiated in everyday discourse. Speakers and Hearers work collaboratively to achieve understanding. According to observers from a wide variety of perspectives, a first maxim of conversation is that Speakers will speak clearly; they intend to make sense and be understood (Grice, 1975; Gumperz, 1982; Merleau-Ponty, 1964; Sacks *et al.*, 1974; Searle, 1969). Hearers contribute to meaning in discourse by making inferences from the conversational string of utterances. They display their understanding actively through 'back channel work' (Duncan, 1972), which includes eye contact, head nods, syllables such as 'uh huhs', and phrases like 'I see' or 'I understand'. Under such assumptions, when the Hearer does not understand, 'a request for clarification' is in order. The manifest purpose of such requests is to obtain more information. The request for clarification is generated by Hearers when they do not think that the Speaker is speaking clearly.

The grounds for this kind of negotiation of meaning are removed from the committee by the way in which language is used by the psychologist. When the psychologist speaks, it is from an institutionally designated position of authority. Furthermore, the psychologist's representation of the child is based on her professional expertise. The privileged status of the psychologist's expertise, in turn, is displayed in the technical language (register) of her report.

There is a certain mystique in the use of technical vocabulary, as evidenced by the high status that the specialized lexicon of doctors, lawyers, and scientists is given in our society (Cohn, 1987; Latour and Woolgar, 1985; Philips, 1977; Shuy and Larkin, 1978; Wertsch, 1986; West, 1984). The use of technical register indicates a superior status and a special knowledge based on long training and specialized qualifications.

A certain amount of this mystique is evident in the psychologist's language and is apparent in the committee's treatment of it. When technical register is used and embedded in the institutional trappings of the formal proceedings of a meeting, the grounds for negotiating meaning are removed from under the conversation. Because the Speaker and Hearers do not share the conventions of a common register, Hearers do not have the expertise to question, or even to interrupt the Speaker. To request a clarification of the psychologist, then, is to challenge the authority of a clinically certified expert. The other members of the committee are placed in the position of assuming that the psychologist is speaking knowledgeably and, in the instance, disinterestedly, and the Hearer does not have the competence to understand.

When technical register is used, even though the possibility for active negotiation of meaning is removed, the guise of understanding remains. To be sure, the understanding is a passively achieved one, not the active one associated with everyday discourse. Instead of signalling a lack of understanding via such implicit devices as back channel work and explicit ones like requests for clarification, the committee members (including the parents) remain silent, thereby tacitly contributing to the guise that common understanding has been achieved.

Conclusions

In conclusion, I'd like to make some specific points about the research I have been conducting on the institutional construction of identities and some more general points about the constitutive model of discourse which is implied by this work.

The institutional construction of identities

By looking at the language of groups of educators as they engage in the work of sorting students, I have tried to demonstrate the situated relevance of social structures in the practical work activities performed by people in social interaction. Educators carry out the routine work of conducting lessons, assigning students to ability groups or special programmes, administering tests, and attending meetings. The notion of *work* stresses the constructive aspect of institutional practice. Educator's work is repetitive and routine. Its mundane character should not overshadow the drama of its importance, however, because steps on students' career ladders are assembled from such practice. The enactment of routine bureaucratic practices structures students' educational careers by opening or closing their access to particular educational opportunities.

Essentially, the teacher is calling for help. Her call is cast in general, not specific, terms. This call starts the process that constructs students' institutional identities. These often undifferentiated appeals become refined and specified in official language as they move from regular education classrooms to testing rooms and finally to meeting rooms. Through this process, the child becomes an object. The members of the committee do not have access to the teacher–student interaction; only the residue of that interaction is represented in a file, a decontextualized text-artifact. At the outset, the child was a participant in discourse with his teacher and his classmates. But, from that point on, the child's contribution to his own career status drops out. The child is only represented in text. The only way we gain access to the child is through textual representations of his interactions. The child becomes objectified as the case moves from the classroom to testing to committee meeting.

I found three registers spoken in the committee meeting, which is the last step in this identity-construction process: a psychological, a sociological, and a historical one. The psychological discourse included absolute and categorical statements about the student's abilities. On the basis of information from systematic, albeit indirect, techniques of observation, the locus of the problem was placed within Shane. The result was a 'context-free' view of the child as one who had a general disability which, therefore, cut across situations. The classroom teacher spoke in a sociological idiom; she tempered her report with contingent factors of a situational sort. On the basis of information from unsystematic, albeit direct, observation, she said that the student's performance was influenced by his state of motivation, kinds of classroom tasks, and types of materials. The result was a 'context-bound' view of the child as someone who had specific problems which appeared in certain academic situations, but who operated more than adequately in other situations. The mother's discourse, lastly, was historical. Based on years of direct observation, she provided particulars about the biography and history of her son and noted changes and improvements across time as well as situational circumstances as the source of his difficulties.

The psychologist's recommendations were accepted without challenge or question, while the sociological and historical recommendations were routinely interrupted with requests for clarification and further information. I propose that the resolution of competing versions of the child can be understood in terms of the authority that reports gain by their manner of presentation, their method of grounding truth claims, and their modes of representation.

The psychological representation gained its authority from the mastery and control of a technical vocabulary, grounded in a quasi-scientific idiom. Because of the fact that for the other participants here the psychologist's report was obscure, difficult to understand, and ambiguous – not in spite of it – the grounds for questioning or challenging were removed from the conversation. It is this technical, quasi-scientific authority that contributes to the stratification of languages of representation and thereby the construction of children's identities.

When people have competing versions of ambiguous events that transpire in the world, they often try to negotiate a commonly agreed upon definition of the situation. Often, consensus is achieved when one or another of the protagonists relinquishes his or her representation of the world as the preferred version, after having heard superior information or having been convinced of the efficacy of an argument. In the case considered here, the resolution of competing modes of representation was not negotiated. The members of the committee resolved the disjuncture between sociological, historical, and psychological versions by credentialing the psychological version as the official version of this student. Thus, an institutionally sanctioned version of experience is superimposed upon multiple and competing versions of experience.

Discourse as constitutive activity

The constructivist view of social life poses mutually constitutive relations between modes of thought, modes of discourse and modes of action. Discourse does not passively reflect or merely describe the world. Because discourse, use of language, is action, different discourses constitute the world differently. Events in the world do not exist for people independently of the representations people use to make sense of them. Instead, objects are defined through elaborate enactments of cultural conventions which leads to the establishment of such well documented 'institutional facts' (Searle, 1969) as 'touchdowns', 'marriages', 'insults', 'banishments', 'property rights' (D'Andrade, 1984), and, as I have proposed, 'learning disabilities' and 'educational handicaps'. When the constitutive rules of discourse are in effect, behaviour becomes action, and actions become 'touchdowns', 'marriages', 'illness', 'schizophrenia', 'deviance', 'intelligence' and 'educational handicaps'.

Modes of representation   When discourse is viewed as activity that culturally constructs clarity out of ambiguity, then we should not be surprised to find multiple modes of representation. Marriage, schizophrenia, and learning disabilities are constructed by cultural conventions in much the same way that touchdowns are constructed by the constitutive rules of American football. Just as crossing the goal line counts as a touchdown only if the appropriate players are present and its facticity has been duly constituted by the referees, so a student's behaviour counts as a learning disability only if the appropriate institutional officials apply the appropriate institutional machinery (educational testing, parent conferences, placement meetings, etc.). Without the orderly application of that institutional machinery, educational handicaps do not exist as a category of situations to be authoritatively represented.

In the case we have considered, there were many ways in which Shane could have been formulated: 'normal student', 'educationally handicapped student', 'gifted student', 'learning disabled student'. Each formulation or way of representing Shane does not simply reflect or merely describe his characteristics; each mode of representation constitutes him, and does so in a different way. To be a 'normal student' is to fit within the parameters or norms of intelligence; to be a 'gifted student' is to have exceptional talents. To be 'educationally handicapped' or 'learning disabled' is to have an inherent disorder. Importantly, each of these formulations characterizes intelligence or talent in terms that place it inside the student. Intelligence, whether normal, exceptional or lacking, is treated as a personal and private possession. This way of characterizing people exemplifies the use of dispositional properties in the explanation of people's behaviour. Each of these modes of representation naturalizes the child, thereby masking the social construction work which generated the designation in the first place. In short, we know the world through the representations we make of it (Bakhtin, 1981). A particular way of representing events in discursive language influences, first of all, the way *we think about* the events represented, and, second, the way we *act toward* the events.

The politics of representation   Modes of representing events vary according to the perspective from which a representation is constructed. *Perspective* here refers to the standpoint from which a person is participating in discourse. One dimension of perspective is the person's physical location in the here-and-now of face-to-face situations (Gurwitsch, 1966). Another is the person's location in social institutions, cultural arrangements, and sociohistorical space-time (Bakhtin, 1981)

We have found that professional educators (i.e., school psychologists), for a variety of biographical, historical, and cultural reasons, describe students in dispositional terms, whereas parents and, to a lesser extent, classroom teachers, formulate students in more contextual terms. Although there are many possible modes of representing the world and communicating them to others starting from particular biographical, historical, and social-cultural perspectives, the course of history can be envisioned as successive attempts to impose one mode of representation upon another.

It is not accidental in this 'politics of representation' (Holquist, 1983; Mehan and Wills, 1988; Mehan *et al.*, 1990; Shapiro, 1987) that institutionally grounded representations predominate. For example, psychiatrists' representations prevail over those of patients, professional educators' representations override parents' formulations. Institutional officials speak with a technical vocabulary grounded in professional expertise. Ordinary people speak in a common vernacular grounded in personal experience. More and more often in our increasingly technological society, when a voice speaking in formalized, rationalistic, and positivistic terms confronts a voice grounded in personal, common sense or localized particulars, the technical prevails over the vernacular.

When categorizing this student, these educators reproduced the status relations among the different discourses that exist in society. A universalizing discourse that is given higher status in the meeting and whose designated variables are read into the child, thereby decontextualizing the child, is the same discourse we see gaining power and authority in recent times. Thus, the concrete, face-to-face encounters which generate an instance of a category are also creative moments that reproduce the relations among categories that we see gaining ascendancy historically.

Notes

A version of this chapter appeared as 'Beneath the Skin and Between the Ears: A Case Study in the Politics of Representation,' Chapter 9, in Seth Chaiklin and Jean Lave (eds), *Understanding Practice: Perspectives on Activity and Context*, pp. 241–68, Cambridge: Cambridge University Press, 1993.

A number of conventions have been used in the transcripts reproduced in this paper: Key to Transcript Conventions:

1   Speakers: CLT = Classroom Teacher; Prn = Principal; SET = Special Education Teacher; Psy = School Psychologist; Mot = Mother.
2   Syntactic organization markers: ( ) = unclear talk; **every**body = emphasis; (hhh) = laughter; rea:ad = stretched talk; // = overlapping utterances; (3) = pause measured in seconds.

1   The LD group is a 'pullout' educational programme in which students spend a part of their school day in their regular classroom and the other part of the day in a special education classroom. The EH program is a special education programme in which students spend all of their school day in a special education classroom.
2   Source: Referral form in student's school record.
3   Source: Interview of teacher conducted by Alma Hertweck.
4   Source: School Psychologist's Assessment Summary. This report was also read to the E&P Committee on February 16 (see below for my discussion of this report in the context of the E&P meeting).

References

Bakhtin, M.M. (1981) *The Dialogic Imagination: Four essays*, M. Holquist (ed.), C. Emerson and M. Holquist (trans.), Austin, University of Texas Press.

Cicourel, A.V., Jennings, S.H.M., Jennings, K.H., Leiter, K.C.W., MacKay, R., Mehan, H. and Roth, D.R. (1974) *Language Use and School Performance*, New York, Academic Press.

Cohn, C. (1987) 'Sex and death in the rational world of defense intellectuals', *Signs*, vol. 12, pp. 687–718.

Coles, G. (1987) *The Learning Mystique: A Critical Look at Learning Disabilities*, New York, Pantheon.

Collins, R. (1981) 'Micro-translation as a theory building strategy' in K. Knorr-Cetina and A.V. Cicourel (eds) *Advances in Social Theory and Methodology*, New York, Routledge and Kegan Paul.

D'Andrade, R.G. (1984) 'Cultural meaning systems' in R. Shweder and R.A. Levine (eds) *Culture Theory: Social Origins of Mind*, Chicago, University of Chicago Press.

Duncan, S. (1972) 'Some signals and rules for taking speaking turns in conversation', *Journal of Personality and Social Psychology*, vol. 23, pp. 283–92.

Erickson, F., and Schultz J. (1982) *The Counsellor as Gatekeeper*, New York, Academic Press.

Gumperz, J. (1982) *Discourse Strategies*, Cambridge, Cambridge University Press.

Gurwitsch, A. (1966) *Studies in Phenomenology and Psychology*, Evanston, Northwestern University Press.

Grice, H.P. (1975) 'Logic and conversation' in P. Cole and J. Morgan (eds) *Syntax and Semantics*, vol. 3, *Speech Acts*, New York, Academic Press.

Holquist, M. (1983) 'The politics of representation', *The Quarterly Newsletter of the Laboratory of Comparative Human Cognition*, vol. 5, pp. 2–9.

Latour, B., and Woolgar, S. (1985) *Laboratory Life*, Princeton, Princeton University Press.

Mehan, H., Hertweck, A. and Meihls, J.L. (1986) *Handicapping the Handicapped: Decision Making in Students' Careers*, Stanford, Stanford University Press.

Mehan, H., and Wills, J. (1988) 'MEND: a nurturing voice in the nuclear arms debate', *Social Problems*, vol. 35, pp. 363–83.

Mehan, H., Nathanson, C.E. and Skelly, J.M. (1990) 'Nuclear discourse in the 1980s: the unravelling conventions of the cold war', *Discourse and Society*, vol. 1, pp. 133–65.

Merleau-Ponty, M. (1964) *Signs*, Evanston, Northwestern University Press.

Philips, S. (1977) 'The role of spatial positioning and alignment in defining interactional units: the American courtroom as a case in point', Paper presented at the American Anthropological Association meetings, Houston, Texas.

Sacks, H., Schegloff, E.A. and Jefferson, G. (1974) 'A simplest systematics for the organization of turn-taking in conversation', *Language*, vol. 50, pp. 696–735.

Searle, J. (1969) *Speech Acts: An Essay in the Philosophy of Language*, Cambridge, Cambridge University Press.

Shuy, R., and Larkin, D.L. (1978) 'Linguistic considerations in the simplification/clarification of insurance policy language', *Discourse Processes*, vol. 1, pp. 305–21.

Shapiro, M. (1987) *The Politics of Representation*, Madison, University of Wisconsin Press.

Wertsch, J. (1986) 'Modes of discourse in the nuclear arms debate', *Current Research on Peace and Violence*, vol. 10, pp. 102–12.

West, C. (1984) *Routine Complications: Troubles in Talk Between Doctors and Patients*, Bloomington, Indiana University Press.

The Tavistock Programme: The Government of Subjectivity and Social Life

Peter Miller and Nikolas Rose

Source: Miller, P. and Rose, N. (1988) 'The Tavistock programme: the government of subjectivity and social life', *Sociology*, vol. 22, pp. 171–92.

In contemporary Western societies, the subjective features of individual and social life have become the object and target of a new expertise. The mental lives of citizens, their emotions, capacities and propensities, have become the object of expert knowledge and the attention of professional 'engineers of the human soul'. This expertise has focussed on such key areas as childhood, the family, sexual relations, work, unemployment and organizational life. Psychiatrists, psychologists, therapists and consultants of one sort or another practice their arts in institutions from the nursery to the factory, on television and radio and in the press. The knowledge and skills they deploy not only offer the opportunity of alleviating many of the personal and interpersonal difficulties which beset individuals in these different facets of contemporary existence, but also hold out the promise of positively enhancing the quality of life.

[. . .]

In this paper we propose an alternative analysis of the rise of the regulatory expertise of subjective life. Three themes mark this perspective. First, a conception of government neither as power exerted by an omniscient and calculating state, nor as the mundane activities of a bureaucratic administrative machine (Foucault, 1979, 1981; Miller, 1987). Government here embraces all those programmes which seek to secure desired socio-political objectives through the regulation of the activities and relations of individuals and populations. Government, understood in this sense, draws our attention to the ways in which the conduct of personal life has become a crucial mechanism in the exercise of political power, including the active promotion of social well-being and the public good through initiatives and programmes ranging from the remodeling of urban architecture and sewage systems, through the control of vagrancy and pauperism, to the ordering of family life and personal habits (Donzelot, 1979; Foucault, 1977, 1981; Oestreich, 1982; Pasquino, 1978). But it is misleading, we suggest, to find the hand of 'the state' behind all such innovations in political thought and strategies. Instead, we need to analyse the often sporadic, ad hoc and local emergence of detailed techniques and systems of rule. Rather than searching for causes and determinants, we need to try to identify the ways in which diverse arrays of events – institutional, technical, political, moral – are articulated together to provide a set of conditions which make changes of this type possible, and the heterogeneous powers and capacities which have been called into play in these new ways of thinking and acting.

Secondly, our analysis emphasizes the constitutive role of knowledge. It is not helpful to relegate knowledges to a realm of ideology, nor to characterize them as disguising or justifying pre-existing interests or relations of power (Foucault 1980). The regulatory systems with which we are concerned are intrinsically dependent upon particular ways of knowing. For something to be manageable it must first be knowable. The development and refinement of psychological and managerial knowledges and techniques has made possible new ways of thinking about, speaking about, visualizing and evaluating domains, activities and relationships. In making new aspects of social and institutional life thinkable, in articulating the vocabularies in which these can be reasoned and argued about, in inventing the techniques of testing, diagnosis and calibration by which they can be materialized in writing and numbers, accumulated in files and utilized as the basis of calculation, psychological knowledges have made new areas of existence practicable, amenable to having things done to them (Latour, 1987; Miller and O'Leary, 1987; Rose, 1985, 1988).

Thirdly, we argue that it is more fruitful to consider the ways that regulatory systems have sought to promote subjectivity than to document the ways in which they have crushed it. Subjectivity, we suggest, should not be regarded as the unchanging basis and standard of evaluation of social interaction; rather it is the product of definite belief systems and techniques. Historical and anthropological studies have shown how the production of certain subjective capacities has been the objective and rationale of codified systems of ethics and manners that have sought to educate, shape and channel the emotional and instinctual economy of individuals. Apparently abstract doctrines and philosophical reflections upon conduct are linked to the development of precise techniques for the government of the self in the minutiae of its existence and experience. How one eats, how one manages one's bodily functions, how one loves, how one works, how one cares for oneself and others, all these have been the targets of innumerable projects for the shaping of the self which have forged links between the subjective capacities of the individual and the well-being of the nation. The emotional and subjective economy of the citizen has a sociology and a history, and the new expertise of subjectivity has transformed the relations between regulatory strategies and the soul of the citizen (Douglas, 1987; Elias, 1978; Foucault, 1985, 1986; Hacking, 1986; Hirst and Woolley, 1982; Oestreich, 1982; Mauss, 1979; Marsella *et al.*, 1985; Sennett, 1976).

In the British context, the organization, rationales, history and vicissitudes of the Tavistock Clinic and the Tavistock Institute of Human Relations have a peculiar interest in relation to such questions. The Clinic is sometimes presented as having a marginal status – outside the mainstream of psychiatry, outside the teaching hospital structure of the National Health Service, outside the psychoanalytic establishment proper – and the Institute as similarly outside the mainstream of management thought (Child, 1969; Dicks, 1970). But this reputation is misleading. The Tavistock has been a key element, model and example in the development of an expertise of subjective, interpersonal and organizational life and its wide extension in modern society. The emergence of mental health as a concern of social policy, the establishment of provisions for the early treatment of minor mental troubles, the invention of child guidance and psychiatric social work, the recognition of the role of psychical factors in organic disease, the development of family therapies and marriage guidance, vocational guidance, the education of professionals, managers and employees in psychological factors affecting occupational existence, the birth of a knowledge and technique for the management of group relations: in all of these areas, for the last two-thirds of a century, the Tavistock has been involved.

There has been surprisingly little analysis of the role of the Tavistock in these conceptual and practical innovations, and of their central place in the emergence of an expertise of subjectivity (the main studies are Dicks, 1970; Brown, 1967; Child, 1969; Rose, 1978). In the present paper we investigate the development of the Tavistock Clinic and the Tavistock Institute of Human Relations from the perspective which we have outlined. We proceed by way of three 'case studies', each of which illustrates one or more features which we consider to be significant in understanding the more general social transformations we have pointed to: the mental hygiene movement of the 1920s and 1930s; the role of psychological expertise in the Second World War; and the links between industrial productivity, group relations and mental health forged in the immediate post-war period.

[. . .]

Mental hygiene

In the early decades of this century, specialized 'clinics' began to be established, independent of hospitals and lunatic asylums, for the treatment of adults and children with problems that were termed 'functional nerve disorders'. This term encompassed a range of minor troubles of emotion, thought, wishes and conduct, and construed them as the consequences of disorders of 'the nervous system'. These minor troubles were thought to presage major troubles to come, manifested in problems from insanity to criminality. They could, however, be resolved by therapeutic interventions if these occurred at an early stage. The Tavistock Clinic was one of the first institutions established within this new rationale. It was set up by Hugh Crichton Miller, in 1920, as the Tavistock Square Clinic for the Treatment of Functional Nerve Disorders. It rapidly became the focus for a new way of thinking about the minor difficulties of children and adults, a new way of acting upon them, and a new way of linking them up with the well-being of society at large (Rose, 1985: 197–219)

The conceptual framework which began to develop termed itself 'the new psychology'. The notion that many mental pathologies were not based upon organic lesions but were 'functional' began to be widely accepted by the doctors who had worked with 'shell-shock' cases during the First World War (cf. Stone 1985). These doctors were mainly from outside the psychiatric profession and hence not committed to its organicism. They began to apply methods for the treating of such cases based loosely upon psycho-dynamic principles. Whilst they tended to accept Freud's argument that early experience was crucial, that the roots of conduct were unconscious, and that pathology was often the consequence of unconscious mental conflicts, they rejected the pre-eminence which psychoanalysis accorded to sexuality. Hence they accorded Freud no special priority, and drew on sources such as the theories of Pierre Janet and the instinct psychology of William MacDougall (Miller, 1920).

In the post-war period, this 'new psychology' conceptualized and classified mental normality and pathology in terms of 'adjustment' and 'maladjustment' (cf. Rose, 1985). Individuals were driven by a number of different instincts, from that of flight, through those of curiosity and self-abasement, to those of sex, parenthood and gregariousness. These instincts were moulded during the early years by the experiences which the child had in the family. When organized correctly they produced a state of adjustment, which was one of psychological normality, personal contentment and social harmony. When wrongly organized they would produce all sorts of disturbances, unhappinesses and socially troubling behaviours – in short, maladjustment. Maladjustment could be avoided by correct child-rearing practices, and acted upon therapeutically by various proto-analytic techniques (Brierley, 1921; Tansley, 1920). A whole series of phenomena could now be rethought in terms of adjustment and maladjustment. The boundary line between normality and pathology was now blurred – each was the possible outcome of the same fundamental processes.

The role of the Tavistock here was not limited to the writings of its staff. It was also central in the development of 'mental hygiene' as a movement and as a way of thinking. The social hygiene movements of the nineteenth century regarded poor social hygiene as the source of all sorts of social ills. They tackled these problems on the grand scale – pure water, sewage, town planning and so forth, seeking to regulate the hygiene of the population by acting upon the organization of social space and public utilities (Foucault, 1973; Rosen, 1953a, 1953b). The hygienism of the early twentieth century switched its point of attack, seeking to promote desirable social ends by acting upon the habits of individuals within the family, in particular the mother's role in the household and her rearing of her children (Armstrong, 1983; Lewis, 1980; Ministry of Health, 1919). It was argued that poor hygiene in the home, especially during childhood, was the cause of all sorts of later problems – not only physical illness but general debility and inefficiency, and poor military performance. The home was to be turned into a machine for constructing hygiene, not coercively, but by inspiring in individuals the wish to be healthy – health was to become a positive value.

When this way of thinking was applied to mental health it began to be argued that not just insanity, but also crime and industrial inefficiency, were symptoms of mental disturbance (National Council for Mental Hygiene, 1924). These major mental troubles had their origin, it was claimed, in minor troubles of childhood which had gone undetected and untreated. The minor disorders of childhood – quarrelling, lying, cheating, night terrors and so forth – became significant not so much because they were problems in themselves, but as signs of serious troubles to come (cf. Board of Education, 1921, 1928, 1930). Generalized inspection, early intervention, and prompt treatment, these were the tactics of the mental hygiene movement (Rose, 1985).

The juvenile court was a key 'surface of emergence' for this new way of thinking and acting. The establishment of the system of juvenile courts under the Children Act of 1908 brought together in a single forum children who had committed offences and those who were wandering, in need of care and protection, maltreated or neglected by their parents (Hall and Pretty, 1908). It soon began to be argued, by magistrates as much as by psychologists, that the distinctions between dangerous and endangered children were artificial – dangerous children were dangerous because of what had previously happened to them, endangered children would become dangerous if something was not done (Burt, 1925; Hall, 1926; Smith, 1922). In either case, the childhood trouble was both a symptom of a problem within the family, and the expression of a psychological state of the child. What was required was not a legal but a psychological enquiry, and an early intervention which would be reformative rather than punitive: not a juridical but a psychological jurisdiction over dangerous and endangered children (Donzelot, 1979; Garland, 1985; Rose, 1985).

The Tavistock Clinic built up a special relationship with the juvenile courts, magistrates and probation officers in London, not only advising them on individual cases and supplying reports, but also providing a new vocabulary for thinking about conduct in terms of adjustment and maladjustment. Articles written by Tavistock personnel and presented at Tavistock meetings on such topics as 'The Unconscious Motive of the Juvenile Delinquent' appeared regularly in *Probation*, the journal of the National Association of Probation Officers. And increasingly it was these terms that came to frame and define the issues and concerns of policy (Dicks, 1970; Home Office, 1927, 1932).

But the 'Tavistock effect' was not simply a way of thinking about disorders of children's conduct, it was also a way of acting upon them. The Children's Department of the Tavistock was to be a model for a system of child guidance clinics promoted by the Child Guidance Council, of which the Tavistock was a key member. The clinic was to be the hub of a comprehensive system of preventative mental health and child welfare, embracing the nursery, the home, the school, the playground and the courts (Child Guidance Council, 1933; Moodie, 1931). Disturbed and disturbing children would be referred to the clinic from doctors, hospitals, schools and courts. Social workers, probation officers and educational welfare officers would use the clinic as a focus, radiating out from it and feeding information back into it. In the clinic, diagnoses would be made and therapy carried out on the maladjusted individual. The collection of information on symptoms, backgrounds, treatments and consequences would provide the basis for a systematic knowledge of the disorders of childhood, and allow the construction of norms of development and criteria of abnormality. From the clinic, these norms could be diffused in the form of advice and guidance to educators, parents and magistrates – and to the population at large – on the damaging social and individual effects of pathologies of the mind, and of the benefits of detecting them early and seeking treatment, and on their treatability and their damaging social and individual effects.

Indeed this way of thinking and acting was to be widely disseminated. Even in the pre-war years, the staff at the Tavistock had sought to generalize this new image of childhood to experts and lay people (Burt, 1933; Hadfield, 1935; Miller, 1937). After the war, the proponents of popular psychoanalysis such as John Bowlby and Donald Winnicott drew heavily upon their early experience in child guidance and mental hygiene in their writings and talks on child rearing and its vicissitudes (Bowlby, 1944, 1953; Winnicott, 1955). There was now a need for the careful scrutiny and regulation of the potentially dangerous emotional economy of the family if normal children were to be produced and pathology avoided. A rational management of normal human development became possible under the guidance of, and with the assistance of, expertise. In providing the means of thinking and talking about human development and human troubles in psychological terms, in promoting the scrutiny and regulation of family life in the name of mental normality, these events were productive of new types of psychological capacities and a new ethics of mental health.

The mental hygiene movement reveals the complex links between national concerns, professional claims, institutional exigencies, theoretical innovations and subjective life. Within this network the Tavistock was a crucial element. The emotional lives of citizens become, through these processes, matters of public concern, expert knowledge and professional guidance. The family becomes a psychological affair, saturated with emotions, desires, fears, anxieties, which is to be maintained not as a legal duty, or as a moral imperative, but as a means to personal contentment and fulfilment.

Psychological warfare

The First World War provided crucial conditions for the development and transformation of psychiatry. The problem of shell-shock was central – its diagnosis, its treatment, its after-effects. Not only had many doctors become convinced by a new dynamic psychology as a mode of explanation and basis of treatment, they and others also considered that the extent of the psychoneuroses had been grossly underestimated previously, as had their damaging individual, familial, social and economic effects. In practical terms, the psychological consequences of warfare were pressed home by the number of those receiving shell-shock pensions – in the region of 100,000 (War Office, 1922).

But it was the Second World War that enabled the fledgling policy science of mental life to take off (Glover, 1940; Rees, 1945). The experience of this war confirmed the links between minor deviations and major pathologies. It confirmed also the wide distribution of the former, and hence their potentially harmful effects, not merely on military life in the immediate context, but also on all aspects of life in peacetime (Ahrenfeldt, 1958). Its effect was to shift policy priorities from the custodial asylum and the psychoses to prevention and prophylaxis for minor disorders of the mind, through a network of aftercare services for those discharged from hospital, outpatient clinics, advice to professionals and the population at large – a system involving home, school and factory as much as hospital (Blacker, 1946; World Health Organization, 1953).

Wartime provided the conditions in which a range of new technologies were invented which would be basic to the post-war developments. It also established a new status for the expertise and individuals associated with the Tavistock (Ahrenfeldt, 1958; Rees 1945). J.R. Rees, Medical Director of the Clinic, was appointed consulting psychiatrist to the army at the outbreak of war. Two other Tavistock people – Ronald Hargreaves and Tommy Wilson – were to become his deputies. And, through a judicious combination of American social psychology and the psychoanalysis of object relations, new technologies were developed which would act upon mental life through the regulation of features of group relations.

In each of the five key areas in which psychiatry was shaped by war, Tavistock people were centrally involved; each would leave its legacy in the post-war project. These were selection, training and management, maintenance of morale, the treatment of psychiatric casualties and the rehabilitation of returning prisoners of war (Privy Council Office, 1947). Selection actually had two aspects (Morris, 1949; Vernon and Parry, 1949). On the one hand, there was the problem of assessment of recruits. Here attention focussed in particular upon the detection of the dullard and the unstable. The former would be a consumer rather than a contributor to the war effort but could, once identified, be allocated with success to the unarmed section of the pioneer corps. The latter might be useful contributors to the community outside the services, but liable to break down in active service at the front. They should therefore be excluded from the services. On the other hand there was the issue of officer selection and promotion. Not only had officers frequently proved vulnerable to psychiatric breakdown, with effects upon the troops which were highly damaging, but there was also discontent fuelled by beliefs that nepotism was rife in selection methods.

The solutions proposed included the development of methods of selection which would be fair because they were rational, and which would select those without propensities to break down under stress. Techniques of assessment and vocational guidance were not new, and had been promoted extensively in the inter-war period in the German armed forces, and by the National Institute of Industrial Psychology in Britain in relation to problems of industrial accidents and inefficiency due to fatigue (Burt, 1942; Myers, 1941). But the wartime experience suggests, for the first time, the possibility of distributing individuals to tasks according to a principle which would not only minimize organizational inefficiency and personal breakdown, but maximize individual satisfaction, group morale and organizational efficiency (cf. Ginzberg *et al.*, 1953; Rees, 1945).

The efficiency of an organization could now be seen as conditional upon the psychological management of its workforce – using the right human material in the right way. In each case the principal achievement was to produce a technique which could act therapeutically on a large organization by means of administrative action. Not only were Tavistock personnel involved in each of the aspects of selection, they would also take the techniques and lessons with them into the post-war work of both Clinic and Institute. The techniques of psychiatric interviewing were developed by Sutherland and Trist; those of selection by observation of leaderless groups by Bion (Bion, 1948–1951; Rees, 1945). We will discuss these further presently. Side by side with the techniques of interviews and groups went the work of the British War Office Selection Boards and the American Office of Strategic Services which developed the notion of personality as quantifiable and manageable, and the techniques of personality assessment (Morris, 1949; Office of Strategic Services, 1948; Vernon and Parry, 1949). Not only did this lead to the development of test techniques for the measurement of personality attributes, it also transformed the notion of personality itself, enabling it to be factorized, quantified, grasped in thought and acted upon in reality (Eysenck, 1947). These techniques of assessment and selection confirmed the limited incidence of psychoses and the widespread problem of the neuroses, suggesting that any future psychiatry would only play its proper part in society when it left the institution and dealt with the mental problems of the world outside (Rees, 1945).

Psychiatric expertise could also transform techniques of training and human management. Remodelled by psychiatry, the former could be made more effective and the latter could improve the formation and maintenance of efficient fighting units. This was not to be done by promoting hatred of the enemy, or by acclimatizing the soldier to an atmosphere of death and savagery through exposure to corpses and the slaughterhouse. Whilst limited conditioning of the soldier to warfare could be useful, for instance through the procedure of 'battle inoculation' which proceeded by gradually increasing the doses of bomb and blast sound to which the soldier was exposed, the efficiency of fighting units became increasingly conceptualized in terms of the psychological bonds of solidarity which existed between its members. Winning wars, that is to say, was greatly a matter of *morale* (Ahrenfeldt, 1958).

The maintenance of morale was itself a task for the application of expertise. It had long been recognized that the efficiency of a fighting unit depended upon the integration of the individuals within it into a cohesive whole. But the mechanisms of this integration now began to be understood in psychological terms, and transformed into a psychological technology for the promotion of group solidarity (Rees, 1945; Stouffer *et al.*, 1949). Discipline in itself was essential but insufficient, if by that one meant mindless drill enforced by punitive sanctions. Discipline must be internal rather than external, the fighting man must pride himself on the discipline and order of his unit. Hence the object of man management was to instil the organization's aims and purposes into the individual so that he would feel them identical to his own. This was to be done by inducing the feeling that one mattered as a unique member of a larger group, with one's own individual competence and value contributing to the success of the whole. Organizational efficiency was beginning to be construed as dependent upon the scrutiny and management of the psychological bonds between members of the organizational group, and morale had become a matter for expert assessment and maximization by the management of psychological states.

The mental condition of the individual was increasingly a matter of group relations. This insight lay at the heart of the methods of treatment of psychiatric casualties developed by W.R. Bion – who had been on the pre-war Tavistock staff – and the others who would lead the post-war reform of psychiatry. (Bion, 1943; Jones, 1952; Main, 1946). In the Second World War, 30 per cent of all invaliding out of the forces was for psychiatric reasons (Rees, 1945). In the wards and hospitals for the treatment of these psychiatric casualties individualized therapies must have been slow, expensive and unable to cope with the logistics of large numbers of causalties. In these units, techniques were developed which operated upon the psychological problems of the individual by the systematic manipulation of group relations (Kraupl Taylor, 1958). The group became virtually coextensive with the illness itself – psychopathology was a product of a pathology of group relations, it was manifest in pathological group relations, and it could be cured through the psychiatric instrumentalization of group relations. In the same moment as pathology became conceived as little more than social maladjustment, normality became conceived as little more than functional efficiency.

In the units for returning prisoners of war, these notions of pathology as a group phenomenon, and of cure as a matter of rehabilitation of a-socialised individuals, were developed by those who would play so great a part in the new psychiatry of groups after the end of the war. In the Transitional Communities for Social Reconnection, Curle, Trist and Wilson developed the group techniques and analyses which would be applied in civilian life (Curle, 1947; Wilson *et al.*, 1947). Both illness and cure had merged with the relational life of the group; the systematic management of group life could restore the disabled individual to functional efficiency and reinstate the rights and obligations of citizenship and personhood.

Wartime had allowed the invention of technological forms which made possible social-psychiatric intervention into large-scale problems. A psychiatry of organizational life had developed which suggested that organizational pathology could be prevented, and efficiency promoted, by acting upon the bonds between individuals – the production of solidarity by technical means. This opened up the group as a way of thinking about and acting upon mental life, as a therapeutic technique, as a means of conceptualizing and reforming organizations and as a new type of awareness for managers and citizens alike.

The transformation of economic life

The Social Department of the Tavistock Clinic was set up after the war to carry forward the wartime applications of sociological, anthropological, psychological and psychiatric expertise to the problems of peacetime social life. When the Clinic was incorporated into the National Health Service in 1947, the Social Department was split off into an independent organization: the Tavistock Institute of Human Relations (TIHR). This signalled the emergence in Britain of a radically new interpretation of the meaning and significance of economic life. With this development, the industrial enterprise was identified as a distinctive and central site for the development and deployment of a new type of expertise, the contours of which had been provisionally outlined during the war. A hitherto unexplored terrain was to be investigated. New conceptual tools were to be applied to understand economic life and novel practical means devised for intervening within it. This interdependence between thinking about and intervening within economic life was to be a key feature of the project of the TIHR.

In the immediate post-war years the new conceptual frameworks and methods for intervening in matters of officer selection, group morale, leadership and shell shock all contributed substantially to a dramatically altered perception of the nature of the individual's relation to the activity of production. Two key figures in the development of the rationale of the TIHR – J.R. Rees and A.T.M. Wilson – indicate this continuity clearly. Both had been centrally involved in the development of new forms of psychiatric and psychological expertise within the British Army; both were founder members of the new Institute. Wilson was later to take the Tavistock approach into industry, working first for Unilever and then at the London Business School.

In its concern with industry, the Institute contributed to the identification of a vastly expanded sphere of responsibilities for the disciplines of mental health in the post-war era. The Beveridge plan had advocated a comprehensive health service for every man, woman and child; Rees argued that mental health was as important a component in this scheme as physical health (Rees, 1945: 117). Psychiatry should look beyond its traditionally limited role and address the management of society and its problems. The 'innovations' of the war contributed to the elaboration of a particular programmatic politics of employment which linked the functioning of the enterprise to that of society. The interrelations between the welfare of the employee, the security of the citizen, and the requirements of productivity had given rise during the war to a framework for the integration of all actors in production in a joint partnership for productivity, contentment and democracy (Rose, 1991, Ch. 3; Tomlinson, 1985). In the early post-war period these concerns were to be taken up and deployed in a concern with productivity, the novelty of which resided in the psychological terms in which it was elaborated.

Peacetime enabled the wartime innovations to be developed and refined. It also presented challenges of its own. Productivity, selection, training, absenteeism, labour turnover, accident-proneness and leadership were the key issues around which the meaning of economic life in peacetime was to be transformed. All these issues were central to the activities of the TIHR during its first decade of operation. An altered perception of the meaning and significance of work was not an isolated concern for the Tavistock; it was central to what Dicks (1970: 325) terms the 'Tavistock Mission'. As the concerns of government were expanded to include the welfare of the individual citizen, it began to be argued that government was inadequate if it failed to penetrate the industrial enterprise. The responsibility for promoting a healthy society was to rest upon politicians and managers as much as on medical practitioners (Dicks, 1948; Tredgold, 1948, 1949). Conflicts within the enterprise, group tensions and individual anxieties, were all to be opened up to understanding and intervention. A new vocabulary was forged for describing the problems and possibilities of the enterprise, and a rationale for its government. Positive mental hygiene within the industrial enterprise was the most distinctive feature of the Tavistock programme in the early post-war years. Concern was no longer limited to acting upon ill health and preventable inefficiencies; new objectives were provided by the triptych of health, happiness and efficiency, and the injunction to optimize each.

The Tavistock expertise of industrial life can be interpreted along three principal dimensions. First, the emergence of this expertise was related to the belief that industrial life could be fundamentally transformed. This would not be a question of rudimentary palliatives. Practices could be introduced within the enterprise which would effect a genuine resolution of labour troubles, and result in greater productivity coupled with greater individual satisfaction (Emery and Thorsrud, 1969; Jaques, 1951). Through attempts to address problems such as productivity, absenteeism and labour turnover a visibility and a manageability was attributed to the social nature of the work process.

[. . .]

The transformed conceptual framework which the Tavistock provided for interpreting these problems was not simply, or even largely, a result of the pressure to solve problems within the enterprise. What was central to the expertise of the Tavistock was the *reinterpretation* of questions such as productivity and absenteeism in terms of a set of much deeper-seated underlying issues. This forms a second dimension along which its contribution should be understood. Psychiatric, psychoanalytic, anthropological, organizational and sociological frameworks were all to feature as prominent elements within this new conceptual framework for understanding economic life. Different elements would be emphasized in different studies. Psychoanalytic concepts would come to the fore in some (Jaques, 1951), and organizational and sociological concepts predominated in others (Trist and Bamforth, 1951; Trist *et al.*, 1963). The expertise of the Tavistock operated within a novel framework in which a new and diverse array of knowledges provided a vastly revised view of the nature of industrial life.

Some of these issues and concepts had been identified earlier in the USA, in the famous 'Hawthorne' experiments (Roethlisberger and Dickson, 1939) and in experiences such as the Poston relocation project during the war (Leighton, 1945). However British developments lagged behind those in America. In the inter-war years the National Institute of Industrial Psychology had addressed questions concerning the human side of the enterprise, but its approach had accorded little importance to the psychic and interpersonal nature of the work process. In the decade following World War II, however, conceptual developments as disparate as object relations theory, the leaderless group, Kurt Lewin's field theory and the notion of socio-technical systems provided what was, in Britain, a novel interpretation of the meaning of industrial processes.

Whilst each of these conceptual developments had its own theoretical genealogy, a strong common thread linked them together. This was the notion of the *group*, of its centrality to the understanding of work processes, of the importance of understanding the individual not as an isolated entity but as always inserted within a network of interpersonal relations (Brown, 1954; Taylor, 1950). The leaderless group and socio-technical systems theory accorded an absolute priority to the role of the group within industrial life. Within this schema the *relational life of the enterprise* (Miller, 1986) emerged as the principal theoretical focus of the Tavistock's concern with industrial life.

A study of industrial accidents by members of the Tavistock illustrates this. Whereas earlier studies sought to identify the personal characteristics of *individuals* involved in accidents, during the 1950s accident-proneness became understood as a social phenomenon, having to do with the relations of individuals to their work and their membership of different types of work organization. Accidents came to be viewed as characteristics of groups rather than of individuals (Hill and Trist, 1955, 1962).

Leadership might be thought a uniquely individual characteristic, but it too was to be re-conceptualized within the new interpretive grid of the group. Leadership was not depicted as a single quality possessed by one individual rather than another, but as the effectiveness of an individual in a specific role within a specific group united for that purpose. First developed in relation to the problem of officer selection, the 'leaderless group' did not place the person on a continuum of individual differences, but located him or her firmly within the complex of interpersonal relations of the group (Bion, 1946). These techniques were to be applied in management development schemes such as those of the Unilever Company (Sofer, 1972).

The concept of the group was also at the heart of the research carried out by members of the Tavistock into the coal industry (e.g. Trist and Bamforth, 1951). By 1953, and despite hesitation and resistance by the Coal Board, Trist received funding by the Department of Scientific and Industrial Research to conduct a programme of research into the organization of work in the mines. This research focussed on technological changes in production methods and their effect upon group relations. Chronic uncertainty, irritation and a high incidence of psychosomatic and neurotic disorders appeared to be the result of the new techniques. The advent of coal cutters and mechanical conveyors had been accompanied by a destruction of the stable relations of 'responsible autonomy' of primary work groups of self-selected pairs of miners. Social integration was severely weakened, if not destroyed, by the new 'longwall' system. Informal groups emerged, often manipulative in character, and many individuals became isolated. Other responses included reactive individualism, mutual scapegoating, and self-compensatory absenteeism. All these responses were viewed as symptomatic of the deep-seated problems of lack of social integration and secure primary working groups.

The solution proposed was for a qualitative change in the method of work so that a form of social organization could develop which was compatible with the technology. Responsible autonomy should be restored to primary groups, with each group having flexibility in its work-pace and a satisfying sub-whole as its work task. In short, equilibrium was to be re-established through recreating stable primary work-groups, although ones which were complementary to the new technological reality. 'Socio-technical systems' was the term coined to describe this understanding of the interrelation of technology and social groups. The elegance and distinctiveness of this concept lay in the interplay between a meticulous subdivision of the work process in terms of stages and relations of command, with an equally delicate sifting of the intra-personal, inter-individual and inter-group forces and tensions. Technology did not determine the type of relations within the enterprise; the social and psychological aspects of work were analysable independently, and management could choose how to combine them with a view to achieving harmony and efficiency.

[. . .]

The hope was not so much that of an industrial enterprise free from all conflicts, but of a community able realistically to tackle the technical, economic and social problems it encountered. To achieve this the concealed and irrational factors influencing the behaviour of the community needed to be periodically identified and worked through to prevent an accumulation of unresolved tensions and problems from disrupting attempts to deal with realities in the future (Jaques, 1951: 312). A reconstruction of the internal world of the factory would be linked to a reorganization of the economy at large. This concern, which extended beyond the Tavistock, portrayed an image of democratically organized work congruent with the values of a democratic society (Brown, 1954; Taylor, 1950). From the Tavistock itself was to be disseminated a new way of linking questions concerning the organization of industry to the organization and well-being of society as a whole: a genuine science of society that could incorporate within it questions of justice (Brown and Jaques, 1965; Jaques, 1970). Social psychiatry appeared to provide the basis of a policy science with practical solutions which related disequilibrium within the fundamental institutions of society, of which the enterprise was one, to disequilibrium in society at large.

Thirdly, Tavistock expertise should be understood in terms of the new possibilities for the regulation of economic life in which it was involved. A vast new territory was opened up for exploration and analysis. This was not simply a matter of a new language being fabricated for speaking about the internal world of the factory or the enterprise. Rather, it was that the minutiae of the relations of group life within the enterprise were opened up to systematic analysis and intervention in the name of a psychological principle of health which was at the same time a managerial principle of efficiency. Through such inventions as the notion of the autonomous working group, a possibility was provided for conjoining technical requirements, managerial imperatives and psychological mechanisms. The group provided the means for creating the technical forms through which the subjectivity of the individual might be integrated into the objectives of the organization. Whilst this achievement clearly cannot be attributed to the Tavistock alone, their contribution was crucial.

Henceforth the activity of production was not to be construed as a narrowly economic process, either on the side of management or on that of the workers. Production was a *social* process. This shift in the signification of production meant that a new range of conceptual and practical interventions could be introduced to mediate economic demands. Psychological, psychoanalytic and sociological dimensions of work were to enter as crucial mediating factors between workers and management. A third dimension – knowledge – had entered the workplace, altering the perception of the process and problems of production and opening a space for a new type of expertise to analyse and resolve the difficulties of the workplace.

The privacy of the enterprise was weakened as its internal economy was made available to exploration and knowledge. It was opened up to public perception, and an image of the social life within it was constructed. Further, the life of the individual employee was opened up to scrutiny. One's relationship to the work task in hand, to one's fellow employees or to the organization as a whole were no longer private affairs only relevant to the individual. These were henceforth to become the object of knowledge and subject to expert intervention. The enterprise as an economic and social space was undergoing a radical re-definition.

Conclusion

In this paper, we have attempted to draw out some of the fundamental transformations which have occurred in the meaning of social and economic life over as little as three decades, and to show how this has been linked with the emergence of novel interventions into the family, within the factory and elsewhere. This was a process which occurred across western societies during this period, although the tempo and precise shape of the changes varied substantially from one country to another. Nevertheless, despite such generality, we have suggested that the search for underlying causes, determinants or functions is unhelpful. As an alternative, we have proposed that research and analysis should try to describe the conditions of possibility for such a process –

the political exigencies, institutional difficulties and intellectual matrices which accorded certain problems and possibilities a social visibility and gave them a psychological and subjective form. We have suggested that there are discernible relationships between the conditions of possibility and the internal conceptual architecture, technical procedures and explanatory systems of psychology and related disciplines. We have proposed that the new ways of thinking and acting formulated in this way have transformed not only the signification of social and industrial life, but also its material and subjective organization, and the ways in which its government is attempted.

[. . .]

References

Ahrenfeldt, R. (1958) *Psychiatry in the British Army in the Second World War*, London, Routledge and Kegan Paul.

Armstrong, D. (1983) *Political Anatomy of the Body*, Cambridge, Cambridge University Press.

Bion, W.R. (1943) 'Intra-group tensions in therapy', *Lancet*, vol. 27, p. 11.

Bion, W.R. (1946) 'The leaderless group project', *Bulletin of the Menninger Clinic*, 10.

Bion, W.R. (1948–51) 'Experiences in Groups I–VII', *Human Relations*, vol. 1, p. 4.

Blacker, C. (1946) *Neurosis and the Mental Health Services*, London, Oxford University Press.

Board of Education (1921, 1928, 1930) *Annual Reports of the Chief Medical Officer of the Board of Education*, London, HMSO.

Bowlby, J. (1944) 'Forty-four juvenile thieves: their characters and home lives', *International Journal of Psychoanalysis*, vol. 25, pp. 19–53, pp. 107–28.

Bowlby, J. (1953) *Child Care and the Growth of Love*, Harmondsworth, Penguin.

Brierley, S. (1921) *An Introduction to Psychology*, London, Methuen.

Brown, J.A.C. (1954) *The Social Psychology of Industry*, Harmondsworth, Penguin Books.

Brown, R.K. (1967) 'Research and consultancy in industrial enterprises', *Sociology*, vol. 1, pp. 33–60.

Brown, W. and Jaques, E. (1965) *Glacier Project Papers*, London, Heinemann Educational Books.

Burt, C. (1925) *The Young Delinquent*, London, University of London Press.

Burt, C. (1942) 'Psychology in war: the military work of American and German psychologists', *Occupational Psychology*, vol. 16, pp. 95–110.

Burt, C. (ed.) (1933) *How the Mind Works*, London, Allen and Unwin.

Child Guidance Council (1933) *Report of the Inter-Clinic Conference*, London, Child Guidance Council.

Child, J. (1969) *British Management Thought*, London, George Allen and Unwin.

Curle, A. (1947) 'Transitional communities and social reconnection', *Human Relations*, vol. 1, pp. 42–68.

Dicks, H.V. (1948) 'Principles of mental hygiene' in N.G. Harris (ed.) *Modern Trends in Psychological Medicine*, London, Butterworth and Co..

Dicks, H.V. (1970) *Fifty Years of the Tavistock Clinic*, London, Routledge and Kegan Paul.

Donzelot, J. (1979) *The Policing of Families*, London, Hutchinson.

Douglas, M. (1987) *How Institutions Think*, London, Routledge and Kegan Paul.

Elias, N. (1978) *The Civilising Process*, Oxford, Blackwell.

Emery, F.E. and Thorsrud, E. (1969) *Form and Content in Industrial Democracy*, London, Tavistock Publications.

Eysenck, H.J. (1947) *Dimensions of Personality*, London, Routledge and Kegan Paul.

Foucault, M. (1973) *The Birth of the Clinic*, London, Tavistock.

Foucault, M. (1977) *Discipline and Punish*, London, Allen Lane.

Foucault, M. (1979) 'On governmentality', *I & C*, 6.

Foucault, M. (1980) 'Truth and power' in C. Gordon (ed.) *Michel Foucault: Power/Knowledge*, Brighton, Harvester Press.

Foucault, M. (1981) 'Omnes et Singulatim: towards a criticism of "political reason"' in S. McMurrin (ed.) *The Tanner Lectures on Human Values II*, Salt Lake City, University of Utah Press.

Foucault, M. (1985) *The Use of Pleasure*, Harmondsworth, Viking.

Foucault, M. (1986) *The Care of the Self*, New York, Pantheon.

Garland, D. (1985) *Punishment and Welfare*, Aldershot, Gower.

Ginzberg, E., Herman, J.C. and Ginzburg, S.W. (1953) *Psychiatry and Military Manpower Policy*, New York, Columbia University Press.

Glover, E. (1940) 'The birth of social psychiatry', *Lancet*, vol. 24, p. 239.

Grosskurth, P. (1986) *Melanie Klein*, London, Hodder and Stoughton.

Hacking, I. (1986) 'Making up people' in T.C. Heller *et al.* (eds) *Reconstructing Individualism*, Standford, CA, Stanford University Press.

Hadfield, J.A. (ed.) (1935) *Psychology and Modern Problems*, London, University of London Press.

Hall, W.C. and Pretty, A. (1908) *The Children Act, 1908*, London, Stevens.

Hall, W.C. (1926) *Children's Courts*, London, Allen and Unwin.

Hill, J.M.M. and Trist, E.L. (1955) 'Changes in accidents and other absences with length of service', *Human Relations*, vol. 8, pp. 121–52.

Hill, J.M.M. and Trist, E.L. (1962) *Industrial Accidents, Sickness and Other Absences*, London, Tavistock Publications.

Hirst, P. and Woolley, P. (1982) *Social Relations and Human Attributes*, London and New York, Tavistock Publications.

Home Office (1927) *Report of the Departmental Committee on the Treatment of Young Offenders*, London, HMSO.

Home Office (1932) *Report of the Departmental Committee on Persistent Offenders*, London, HMSO.

Jaques, E. (1951) *The Changing Culture of a Factory*, London, Tavistock Publications.

Jaques, E. (1970) *Work, Creativity and Social Justice*, London, Heinemann Educational Books.

Jones, M. (1952) *Social Psychiatry*, London, Tavistock Publications.

Kraupl Taylor, F. (1958) 'A history of group and administrative therapy in Great Britain', *British Journal of Medical Psychology*, vol. 31, pp. 153–73.

Latour, B. (1987) 'Visualisation and cognition: Thinking with hands and eyes' in H. Kuchlick (ed.), *Knowledge and Society, Vol. 6*, Greenwich, CN, JAI Press.

Leighton, A.H. (1945) *The Governing of Men: General Principles and Recommendations Based on Experience at a Japanese Relocation Camp*, Princeton, New Jersey, Princeton University Press.

Lewis, J. (1980) *The Politics of Motherhood*, London, Croom Helm.

Main, T. (1946) 'The hospital as a therapeutic institution', *Bulletin of the Menninger Clinic*, vol. 10, p. 67.

Marsella, A.J., Devos, G. and Hsu, F.K. (1985) *Culture and Self*, London, Tavistock.

Mauss, M. (1979) 'A category of the human mind: the notion of person, the notion of "self"' in *Sociology and Psychology*, London, Routledge and Kegan Paul.

Miller, E. (ed.) (1937) *The Growing Child and its Problems*, London, Kegan Paul, Trench and Trubner.

Miller, H. Crichton (ed.) (1920) *Functional Nerve Disease: An Epitome of War Experience*, London, Oxford University Press.

Miller, P. (1986) 'Psychotherapy of work and unemployment', in P. Miller and N. Rose (eds) *The Power of Psychiatry*, Cambridge, Polity Press.

Miller, P. (1987) *Domination and Power*, London, Routledge and Kegan Paul.

Miller, P. and O'Leary, T. (1987) 'Management as moral science: the normative construction of managerial vocabularies', Working Paper.

Ministry of Health (1919) *An Outline of the Practice of Preventative Medicine*, Cmd. 363, London: H.M.S.O.

Moodie, W. (1931) *Child Guidance by Team Work*, London, Child Guidance Council.

Morris, B.S. (1949) 'Officer selection in the British army', *Occupational Psychology*, vol. 23, pp. 219–34.

Myers, C.S. (1941) 'The uses of psychology in war time', *Nature*, vol. 147, pp. 564–6.

National Council for Mental Hygiene (1924) *First Report, 1923–1924*, London, National Council for Mental Hygiene.

Oestreich, G. (1982) *Neostoicism and the Early Modern State*, Cambridge, Cambridge University Press.

Office of Strategic Services (1948) *Assessment of Men*, New York, Reinhart.

Pasquino, P. (1978) 'Theatrum politicum. The genealogy of capital – police and the state of prosperity', *Ideology & Consciousness*, vol. 4, pp. 41–54.

Privy Council Office (1947) *The Work of Psychologists and Psychologists in the Services: Report of an Expert Committee*, London, HMSO.

Rees, J.R. (1945) *The Shaping of Psychiatry by War*, New York, Norton and Company.

Roethlisberger, F.J. and W.J. Dickson (1939) *Management and the Worker*, Cambridge, MA, Harvard University Press.

Rose, M. (1978) *Industrial Behaviour: Theoretical Developments Since Taylor*, Harmondsworth, Penguin.

Rose, N. (1985) *The Psychological Complex: Psychology, Politics and Society in England 1869–1939*, London, Routledge and Kegan Paul.

Rose, N. (1988) 'Calculable minds and manageable individuals', *History of the Human Sciences*, vol. 1, pp. 179–200.

Rose, N. (1991) *Governing the Soul*, London, Routledge and Kegan Paul.

Rosen, G. (1953a) 'Cameralism and the concept of medical police', *Bulletin of the History of Medicine*, vol. 27, pp. 21–43.

Rosen, G. (1953b) 'Economic and social policy in the development of public health', *Journal of the History of Medicine*, vol. 8, pp. 406–30.

Sennett, R. (1976) *The Fall of Public Man*, Cambridge, Cambridge University Press.

Smith, M. (1922) *The Psychology of the Criminal*, London, Methuen.

Sofer, C. (1972) *Organizations in Theory and Practice*, London, Heinemann Educational Books.

Stone, M. (1985) 'Shellshock and the psychologists' in W.F. Bynum, R. Porter and M. Shepherd, (eds) *The Anatomy of Madness*, Vol. 2, London, Tavistock.

Stouffer, S.A. *et al.* (1949) *The American Soldier, Vols. 1 and 2*, New York, Wiley.

Tansley, A.G. (1920) *The New Psychology and its Relation to Life*, London, Allen and Unwin.

Tavistock Clinic (1925, 1929, etc.) *Reports for the Years 1920–1927, 1927–1929*, etc., London, Tavistock Clinic.

Taylor, G.R. (1950) *Are Workers Human?*, London, Falcon Press.

Tomlinson, J. (1985) 'Industrial democracy and the labour government 1945–1951', Unpublished manuscript.

Tredgold, R.F. (1948) 'Mental hygiene in industry' in N.G. Harris (ed.) *Modern Trends in Psychological Medicine*, London, Butterworth and Co.

Tredgold, R.F. (1949) *Human Relations in Modern Industry*, London, Duckworth and Company.

Trist, E.L. and Bamforth, K.W. (1951) 'Some social and psychological consequences of the longwall method of coal getting', *Human Relations*, vol. 4, pp. 3–38.

Trist, E.L., Higgin, G.W., Murray, H. and Pollock, A.B. (1963) *Organizational Choice*, London, Tavistock Publications.

Vernon, P.E. and Parry, J.B. (1949) *Personnel Selection in the British Forces*, London, University of London Press.

War Office (1922) *Report of the Committee of Enquiry into 'Shell Shock'*, London, H.M.S.O.

Wilson, A.T.M., Doyle, M. and Kelnar, J. (1947) 'Group techniques in a therapeutic community', *Lancet*, vol. 1, pp. 735–8.

World Health Organization (1953) *Report of Third Expert Committee on Mental Health*, Technical Report Series No. 73., Geneva, World Health Organization.

CONCLUSION

TWENTY SEVEN

Debates in Discourse Research

Margaret Wetherell

This Conclusion to the Reader has two main aims. First, to summarize some of the key themes and organizing principles which underpin the twenty-six readings in this volume and, second, to bring into greater focus the debates which unite and divide discourse researchers. In Section One I try to map the diversity of material covered and note some paths through. The remaining sections go on to examine some core epistemological or meta-theoretical issues which add further dimensions of contrast and comparison and cast more light on some of those already in play.

Mapping diversity and constructing paths

This Reader is addressed particularly to the new discourse researcher in social sciences. If it is successful it should provide some good models for discourse research. But discourse research is incredibly diverse as are new researchers interested in discourse. There are many different possible good models. Why select one rather than another? To take three readings at random, for instance, Gergen's work in Part Three on narrative and life history (Reading Eighteen), Gumperz's study in Part Two on interethnic communication (Reading Eleven), and Stuart Hall's study in Part Four on historical representations of 'otherness' (Reading Twenty-Four). All of these concern discourse, all seem to have an interest in identity and two of them (Gumperz and Hall) are concerned with 'race'. What is at stake in following one model rather than another?

The kind of discourse research which is favoured for any particular project involves a complex balancing act between the type of data one wants to collect, the topic, the academic discipline in which one is working and the discourse tradition which seems most appropriate. Table 1 summarizes the range of academic disciplines, traditions, topics or domains and forms of data covered in the Reader.

In terms of disciplines, discourse research can be found across the social sciences, in the health sciences, in business studies, in computer science and in education. The contributors to this Reader come mostly from sociology/cultural studies/social policy (Hall, Heritage, Silverman, Goffman, Sacks, Miller and Rose, Mehan) and psychology (Potter and Wetherell, Billig, Gergen, Hollway, Davies and Harré, Wertsch, Edwards, Kitzinger and Frith) but include a range of other disciplinary affiliations such as sociolinguistics (Gumperz, Tannen, Hodge and

Table 1 *Mapping diversity*

Disciplines	Domains
Psychology	Social interaction
Sociology/Cultural studies	Mind, selves and sense making
Social policy	Culture and social relations
Anthropology	
Education	
Linguistics	
Politics and international relations	

Forms of Data	Discourse Traditions
Interviews	Conversation analysis
Focus groups	Foucauldian research
Documents and records	Critical discourse analysis and critical
Media representations	linguistics
Naturally occurring conversation (in	Discursive psychology
institutional and other settings)	Bakhtinian research
Political speeches	Interactional sociolinguistics and the
	ethnography of speaking

Kress), anthropology (Fitch), education (Maybin), and politics and international relations (Shapiro). Some contributors (e.g. Van Dijk) might prefer to identify themselves as members of the new discipline of discourse studies and have worked hard to establish the field as an interdisciplinary or trans-disciplinary force (see the journals *Discourse and Society* and *Discourse Studies* and Van Dijk, 1985, 1997).

We have covered quite a wide range of types of data from studies on naturally occurring examples of discourse in everyday and institutional situations (e.g. Silverman, Sacks, Gumperz, Wertsch, Edwards), to studies using historical records, existing texts and documents (e.g. Hall, Miller and Rose, Shapiro, Van Dijk, Hodge and Kress), to studies on discourse especially generated for the research project through interviews, for instance, and focus groups (e.g. Hollway, Billig, Gergen, Kitzinger and Frith) and some studies (e.g. Mehan) have used more than one kind of data. In terms of topics, the spread has also been wide – from the counselling process (Silverman) to international relations (Shapiro) – but contained within the three broad domains we selected:

(i)   social interaction;

(ii)   minds, selves and sense making;

(iii)   culture and social relations.

As Part One illustrated, discourse research is a new development. It is a style of research which emerged most strongly from the 1980s onwards while the precursors in language studies appeared typically from the 1920s onwards. Despite this novelty, as we noted, discourse research is beginning to settle down or cohere around particular nodes of research activity. Distinctive styles for doing discourse analysis are emerging and these provided the discourse traditions set up in this Reader. These traditions (not quite schools) typically include some epistemological claims, a set of concepts and procedures for substantive work and a clearly marked out theoretical domain. They also typically include a distinctive understanding of 'discourse'. Discussion is beginning to occur around the boundaries of these different approaches, their merits and de-merits, the points of similarity and difference and the choices at stake, as advocates attempt to build research communities while critics from other perspectives attempt to weaken their claims for intellectual hegemony. Boundaries will shift as a consequence and new approaches will emerge.

In this Reader, we flagged up six nodes of research activity which seem most relevant to social scientists:

- conversation analysis (see Heritage, Sacks, Silverman, Kitzinger and Frith, Edwards, Mehan);

- discursive psychology (see the readings in Part Two and Potter on Wittgenstein);

- Foucauldian research (see Hall on Foucault, Hollway, Shapiro, Hall on racism, Miller and Rose);

- critical discourse analysis and critical linguistics (see Kress, Van Dijk, Hodge and Kress);

- interactional sociolinguistics and the ethnography of speaking (see Fitch, Gumperz, Tannen);

- Bakhtinian research (see Maybin, Wertsch and aspects of Billig's research).

Some of the boundaries here are much better defined than others. The differences between conversation analysis and Foucauldian research are strikingly obvious, for example. Some traditions are more hybrid. Discursive psychology, for instance, is a development which draws on a number of traditions including conversation analysis, Bakhtinian ideas and Foucauldian work and is thus the centre of internal dispute since some discursive psychologists follow conversation analysts into more fine-grain research while others draw on much broader themes (c.f. the readings from Edwards and Hollway). The sense of a shared project here comes from the disciplinary focus on psychological topics rather than one common intellectual position on discourse. Our delineation of other traditions in this volume is more debatable. A recent linguistic text on discourse analysis, for example, while similarly carving out critical discourse analysis, conversation analysis and discursive psychology as distinct nodes also makes more complex distinctions between different schools of sociolinguistics and the ethnography of speaking research tradition in anthropology (see Jaworski and Coupland, 1999).

What does one do then with all this diversity between academic disciplines, domains, traditions, and so on? Table 1 is misleading if it suggests that a pick and mix strategy might apply. A psychologist, for instance, is unlikely to decide to do critical discourse analysis on a small piece of naturally occurring interactional data to make a contribution to research on business strategy. Just as a social policy researcher is unlikely to decide to do a conversation analytic study on historical records to find out about people's emotional lives. Some of the synergies between data, domains, traditions and academic discipline, should be apparent from this Reader but the way is also open for the creative mixing of research questions and styles.

Social policy researchers, sociologists and cultural studies researchers tend, for example, to conduct interviews and study texts, historical records and existing documents. They typically deploy Foucauldian theory or use critical discourse analysis. It would be wrong to give the impression, however, that Foucault was only concerned with culture and social relations. Clearly, as Hollway's work demonstrates (Reading Twenty), Foucault has many relevant things to say to those studying subjectivity and identity. He was, however, famously uninterested in the details of social interaction. Conversation analysts, on the other hand, are interested in social interaction and offer sociologists and psychologists a very different perspective on social order and social action. They offer methods for dealing with naturally occurring discourse. Their focus is usually on small-scale aspects of everyday and institutional life. But this does not mean that the general perspective of ethnomethodology and conversation analysis cannot contribute to other domains also. There is a fascinating ethnomethodological study, for example, of the Oliver North hearings in the USA which makes important points about government, history and the construction of policy, and which takes issue with Foucauldian assumptions about these things (Lynch and Bogen, 1996).

Often research decisions become routine or paradigmatic. Communities come to know well only one style of discourse research which becomes used habitually. Psychologists, for instance, tend to be wedded to interviews as a method of data collection and have been slow to explore the benefits of other modes of data collection. Social scientists and linguists are often interested in many of the same topics but have been slow to pool their resources and interrogate the consequences of their different starting points. It is not just habit, however, that lies behind the synergies of topics, disciplines, traditions and data styles apparent in this Reader. What is also at stake are positions on underlying epistemological and methodological debates and I turn now to consider a range of these to obtain a better grasp of how different styles of research can be located and I outline some of the crucial issues involved in following different models.

Should the analyst be politically engaged?

You will have noted that a number of discourse analysts describe themselves as **critical**. What does this mean? Look first at this statement which comes from Teun Van Dijk.

> Unlike other discourse analysts, critical discourse analysts (should) take an explicit socio-political stance: they spell out their point of view, perspective, principles and aims, both within their discipline and within society at large. Although not in each stage of theory formation and analysis, their work is admittedly and ultimately political. Their hope, if occasionally illusory, is change through critical understanding. Their perspective, if possible, that of those who suffer most from dominance and inequality. Their critical targets are the power elites that enact,

sustain, legitimate, condone or ignore social inequality and injustice. That is, one of the criteria of their work is solidarity with those who need it most.

(1993: 252)

Van Dijk expresses here one view of the role of the analyst and poses a challenge to discourse researchers. The discourse analyst should be a social critic rather than a neutral observer. But which of these stances is most appropriate for a social scientist? And how does the decision for one or the other affect the process of discourse research and influence its value?

The stance which argues for **political engagement** receives a strong impetus from Marxism as a social theory and as a tradition of critique. Famously, Marxism makes a crucial distinction between true revolutionary science and science which serves the interests of the bourgeois and ruling classes. Social scientists, in this view, can act as front men and women for the ruling ideas of the ruling classes, or penetrate the layers of mystifying and obsfucating ideology to reveal underlying social realities and the hidden truths of exploitation. Either social scientists are complicit with the bourgeois or they are engaged with radical alternative politics.

Critical discourse analysts, such as Van Dijk (1993) and Fairclough (1995), would not endorse all of this argument. They would reject any simple notion of ideology as false ideas contrasted to the real knowledge of revolutionary science (and see also Billig, Reading Fifteen for an alternative approach to ideology). Van Dijk and Fairclough would argue that the process of knowledge creation is much more complex than this. But what they take from Marxism is a powerful and engaging vision of political commitment and the notion that the intellectuals in a society are always on some side or other so the choice should not automatically or, worse, unconsciously reproduce the ruling political climate.

This is a vision of the discourse analyst (together with all members of society) as an active force in society and politics. The analyst is in no sense a bystander or dilettante but someone who chooses to work on pressing social and political problems rather than on issues which can be easily funded or are good for careers. The aim is to feed back the knowledge gained into the political process in a way that is most likely to bring about the desired changes. Similarly, Hollway, in her work (Reading Twenty), Tannen (Reading Twelve) and Kitzinger and Frith (Reading Thirteen) work from explicitly feminist stances. The aim is to produce knowledge which might make a positive difference for women.

Critical perspectives on discourse can also be fuelled by postmodern and poststructuralist ideas (e.g. Butler, 1992). Postmodernism argues that truth is always relative to the discourse or language game of the moment. The set of knowledge/power relations which produces the truths of one historical period will inevitably be superseded as the broad discursive framework of a society changes from religion, say, to secularism. From this perspective there can be no universal truths or absolute ethical positions. A belief in social scientific investigation as a detached, historical, utopian, truth-seeking process becomes difficult to sustain, therefore. How does this view encourage critique? The argument goes like this. If the process of analysis is always interpretative, always contingent, always a version or a reading from some theoretical, epistemological or ethical standpoint, if that is the way things are, then why not be as explicit as possible about one's background values? Why not highlight these, bring them into consideration, actively choose the guiding principles, display them to readers of the work and make them the subject of debate? Postmodern scepticism encourages critique and the subversion of authority through reflexivity and deconstruction.

A critical or politically engaged stance of some kind is probably the most common position among discourse analysts, certainly those working in psychology and sociology, and among critical discourse analysts, Foucauldians, critical sociolinguists, many ethnographers of communication and Bakhtinian-influenced scholars. Critique can range from research conducted with an explicit political agenda to research conducted with a broad commitment to exploring the social and political implications of findings. One group of discourse researchers, however, take a different line. Conversation analysts reject the view that critique should be built into the analytic process, and this is reflected in the statement below from Emanuel Schegloff.

> [Critical discourse analysis] allows students, investigators, or external observers to deploy the terms which preoccupy *them* in describing, explaining, critiquing, etc. the events and texts to which they turn their attention. There is no guaranteed place for the endogenous orientations of the participants in those events; there is no principled method for establishing those orientations; there is no commitment to be constrained by those orientations. However well-intentioned and well-disposed toward the participants – indeed, often enough the whole rationale of the critical stance is the championing of what are taken to be authentic, indigenous perspectives – there is a kind of theoretical imperialism involved here, a kind of hegemony of the intellectuals, of the literati, of the academics, of the critics whose theoretical apparatus gets to stipulate the terms by reference to which the world is to be understood – when there has already *been* a set of terms by reference to which the world was understood – by those endogenously involved in its very coming to pass. (The issue is not unlike those who speak of Columbus having 'discovered' America, as if there were not already indigenous people living there.)
> (1997: 167)

Schegloff argues that a critical stance in discourse research is not just bad scholarship, it is also bad politics. His argument is a challenging one and has sparked much debate (Billig, 1999a, 1999b; Schegloff, 1999a, 1999b; Weatherall, 2000; Wetherell, 1998). One danger of a critical position from this perspective is that the analyst may never be surprised by the data. The world is already known and is pre-interpreted in light of the analyst's concerns. In effect, Schegloff is accusing critical discourse analysts of potential and actual bias, at risk of not seeing clearly what is in front of them.

What often fuels such a concern is a notion of objectivity and good scientific practice. The ideal researcher is one who discovers actual patterns, not invented patterns, or patterns which can't be replicated and found again by another researcher. It reflects a hope that discourse analysis, like other scientific endeavours, should generate substantial and important findings – not interpretations open to the vagaries of history but regularities which might have some universality and pervasiveness to them – the building blocks of social interaction, for instance. In part, the assumption is that a researcher focused on how the participants organize their own activities may be more likely than critical researchers, with their prior agenda, to fulfil these ideals.

Conversation analysts make a plea for the **autonomy of the data** as an object of study in its own right and this plea is tied to their theory of social action. In conversation and interaction, they suggest, participants are building a joint reality, their conversational actions demonstrate to each other their local interpretations of what is going on and the kind of event this conversation is (c.f. Heritage, Reading Four). Schegloff argues that in this sense the world has already been interpreted by the participants (hence his reference to endogenous interpretations); it is not for the critical discourse analyst to ride roughshod over these interpretations and impose their own but simply to clarify what is already there.

Conversation analysts and ethnomethodologists would claim to take an even-handed and non-judgemental perspective. They are not interested in evaluating the truth or falsity of what people say but in the organization of their talk. The aim is to focus entirely on describing how people do what they do at the local level of the immediate interaction. For instance, Robin Wooffitt's conversation analytic research on mediums and their consultations with their clients (Wooffitt, 2001) could have begun with the aim of unmasking mediums as charlatans, demonstrating how they deceive a gullible public and the conversational techniques they use to do so. Instead, following the general stance of conversation analysis and ethnomethodology, Wooffitt focuses on how the mediums do their consultations. The wider question of whether the medium is actually in communication with the spirit world, lying or faking is not the starting point.

Of course, as private individuals, conversation analysts may well be socially concerned and politically active but they try not to carry these concerns into analysis. Or, rather, they believe that a politically or critically motivated interrogation of the data should only be done *after* the conversational activities have been studied in their own terms. Kitzinger and Frith in Reading Thirteen provide a good illustration of this approach. They define themselves as feminists and analyse the implications of conversation analytic findings for developing feminist politics around sexual coercion but this is predicated on first studying conversational activities *per se*.

The conversation analytic perspective often goes along with the view that discourse analysis is best seen as a technical discipline. In this view, science is a different kind of activity from politics. Academics are researchers; they may make terrible politicians. Politics, it might be argued, has its own logic and forms of expertise. In muddling scholarly activity and politics together discourse analysts mistake the source of their authority and the knowledge base which gives them the right to speak. If the public wish to listen to academics they do so because of their specialist expertise. A critical discourse analyst, on the other hand, might retort that specialist expertise is not compromised by political engagement and, further, in elucidating the social context, the analyst brings to bear other specialist expertise in social and political theory, in sociology and cultural studies, social history and economics.

Critical discourse analysis and conversation analysis, then, represent two resolutions of a complex choice facing all discourse analysts. This issue of critical engagement is a challenging one because it rests on a set of related debates. The issues here are nested within each other. Let us proceed with opening these up. I want to look next at a debate about context. In order to decide about discourse and critique you need to decide whether conversation analysts are right to restrict the context of study just to the endogenous concerns of the participants.

What counts as relevant context?

How much background information do we need to analyse any particular piece of discourse – pieces for example, such as the *Panorama* interview with Diana or a conversation in a tea-shop or a political speech? This is a profound question and before reading on you might like to reflect on your response and ponder what different discourse analysts provide in their research in the way of context.

Here I want to compare two different responses. Consider, first, Hall's research in Reading Twenty-Four on the representation of black people in the media. His answer to what we need to know to understand this material takes us on a journey through the history of slavery and colonialization. His analysis is woven in with the history of social practices around 'race' which construct 'otherness'. Compare this with Silverman's analysis of counselling practice in Reading Ten. His focus is on the organization of the talk itself. We are given some additional scene-setting information but are given little other background about the broader social context. For Silverman, we do not need to know any more to conduct a successful analysis of the discourse.

What does this difference reflect? Different theories of discourse are at stake here along with contrasting theories of **social context** (Wetherell, 1998). If we take the conversation analytic view first. Here is Schegloff once more:

> However lively our intuitions, in general or with respect to specific details, that it matters that some participants in data we are examining are police, or female, or deciding matters which are specifically constrained by the law or by economic or organizational contingencies, however insistent our sense of the reality and decisive bearing of such features of 'social structure' in the traditional sense, the challenge posed is to find a way to show these claims, and to show them from the data . . .
>
> 1   that what is so loomingly relevant for us (as competent members of the society or as professional social scientists) was relevant for the parties to the interaction . . .
> 2   that what seems inescapably relevant both to us and to the participants, about the 'context' of the interaction is demonstrably consequential for some specifiable aspect of that interaction.
>
> (Schegloff, 1991: 65)

This view emerges, of course, from the general conversation analytic perspective on social action. The focus is on the activities taking place in talk. Schegloff's claim is that the only context we need to understand these activities is what is evident and relevant to the participants as revealed by their talk.

Schegloff argues that when two people interact there are many ways in which the participants and the situation could be described. There are a huge number of things which could be relevant. It could be relevant, for instance, that one participant is black and the other white, it could be relevant that one is a mother and the other a child, it could be relevant that the child is a girl, that this conversation is taking place in a police station, in South America, in 1990, in spring, it is cloudy and the mother is wearing a cotton dress, and so on. Schegloff's methodological principle is that analysts should only include as relevant the things that can be shown to be consequential for this particular conversation. The only thing, for example, that might be relevant at one given moment for the participants among this wealth of social, climatic, geographical and demographic information is that the child is eating an ice-cream and the mother is requesting a lick. This explains the organization of their conversational activities – a request and a refusal. Just as in Reading Ten from Silverman the fact that one person is a counsellor and one person is a patient is relevant to the organization of their activities while any other facts such as the 'race' of the participants seem mostly irrelevant to the business at hand.

How is social context being defined here? Schegloff (1992) makes a distinction between two kinds of context. There is what he calls the external or **distal context** which includes things like social class, the ethnic composition of the participants, the institutions or sites where discourse occurs and the ecological, regional and cultural settings. This distal context can be contrasted with what he calls the **proximate context** which includes the immediate features of the interaction, such as the sort of occasion or genre of interaction the participants take an episode to be (e.g. a consultation, an interrogation, a family meal-time), the sequences of talk in which particular events occur and the capacities in which people speak (as initiator or instructor or as respondent). In these terms, Schegloff's argument is that discourse analysts should focus always on the proximate context – the distal context is irrelevant except as it is brought into the proximate context through the participants' activities.

This view of context and what is relevant to analysis makes most sense if the conversational activities are the focus and these activities are quite narrowly defined. Other discourse researchers, however, are much less interested in the nature and sequencing of activities in talk and much more interested in semantic content and modes of representation – why is that event described in that way, why does the person construct that kind of identity or position for themselves, why tell that narrative? If these are the research questions, is it adequate to follow Schegloff's methodological principle and stick with the talk in itself and participants' orientations in that talk?

Discourse researchers outside conversation analysis are divided on this point. Some discursive psychologists, for instance, argue that the conversation analytic principle still holds. Thus their answers to the 'why' questions above would be entirely in terms of what the participants are trying to accomplish in the particular conversation (Edwards and Potter, 1992). Identities, narratives and versions can be understood in terms of the work they do in the immediate interaction and, once again, relevance is an issue for participants rather than analysts. But many discourse researchers want a broader answer to 'why?' which situates the conversation in some social, historical, political and cultural context.

Discursive work in the Foucauldian and poststructuralist tradition takes this approach and a very different notion of the relationship between discourse and social context emerges as a result. Consider the following comments:

> Society can . . . be understood as a vast argumentative texture through which people construct their reality.
>
> (Laclau, 1993: 341)

> Intelligible exchanges are always situated. . . . the context-meaning relation subsumes a complex history of struggle in which one or more ways of establishing contexts and their related utterances has vanquished other competing possibilities.
>
> (Shapiro, 1992: 38)

To take Laclau's comment first. This rather mysterious comment about **argumentative texture** signals a very different notion of discourse and context from Schegloff's distinction between distal and proximate contexts. To unpack it further, Schegloff's distinction between proximate and distal implies that talk and aspects of social life (such as social classes, social groups, environments, etc.) are separate or that a clear distinction can be made between the **discursive and the extra-discursive**. Researchers such as Laclau who focus on representation and meaning in discourse as opposed to conversational activities find that they can't make this distinction so easily.

Why this is so emerges if we think about this metaphor of 'argumentative texture' in a bit more detail. If we think of cloth or fabric, what is clear is that the threads are woven through the whole. If we take a pen and make a circle on a piece of cloth then we have certainly created a boundary – inside the circle and outside the circle – but if we follow one thread from inside the circle our boundary becomes rather irrelevant since the thread continues through the pen marks and onwards. In a similar way, as analysts we can easily select a bit of talk from a tape recording and in this way create an object of study rather as we drew a circle on the cloth but if we are interested in modes of representation, identity, or patterns in social interaction is it adequate to restrict our study to this one piece of social life alone?

Laclau's notion of society as argumentative texture collapses any easy distinction between discursive and extra-discursive, talk and things external to talk. In this perspective even the particular words which are used evoke discursive history and current social relations. Utterances are threads in this respect: they connect with other utterances and other conversations, texts and documents. What things mean and what identities, versions and narratives signify depends on the broader discursive context – the struggles which Shapiro refers to in his comment above. These struggles create accepted truths and ways of understanding who people are, what things are, how they work, and how they should be. Such an approach is interested in the discursive links which connect representations and accounts in one conversation, text, document or fragment of discourse with other conversations, texts, documents, etc. in a culture and with trying to decipher the power relations which lead to the emergence of precisely these patterns.

Thus Hall, for example, in his study of representations of black people provides a good illustration of Shapiro's claims above. Hall is examining how the intelligible exchanges (a film, a magazine story) he is interested in are situated, where part of describing their context or situation is to consider the history which led to this mode of representation rather than some other. Why do black people tend to be represented in this particular way? A satisfactory answer in his view takes us beyond the orientations of the film makers, the magazine writers or the conversationalists (the participants) to ask how social contexts are created so that this mode of representation is the most obvious and other modes are invisible or marginal.

To summarize, what counts as relevant context, then, in analysing discourse depends partly on what you are studying – conversational activities versus modes of representation. But more than this it depends on background theories about discourse and context, definitions of social life and perspectives on how the social and the discursive intertwine. In effect, Schegloff and those who follow the methodological principles of conversation analysis define the discursive narrowly as just the talk which is being investigated with the remainder of social life (social groups, social classes, social environments and social structures) placed outside the discourse under investigation. Foucauldians and poststructuralists define the discursive broadly so there are no clear demarcations where discourse stops and the rest of social life begins.

These differences have obvious implications for the formulation of research questions, for the definition of an adequate data sample and for the research activities which occur around discourse analysis, such as the inclusion of ethnographic material to define contexts (see Taylor, 2001a and 2001b, for a review of these implications). Here I wish instead to discuss in a little more detail the poststructuralist or Foucauldian position on the discursive and the extra-discursive and contrast it with critical discourse analysis.

How do discursive practices connect with other social practices?

What is the relationship between discursive practices (talking, writing and communicating) and other social practices such as labouring, child rearing, manufacturing, exchanging goods for money, and so on? Should some of these practices, perhaps those most directly involving bodies and physical objects, be studied as **material practices** while others involving discourse and communication are studied as **cultural practices**? Is discourse analysis only relevant to the study of the cultural?

As we have seen, those influenced by Foucault tend to take an all-embracing definition of discourse as human meaning-making processes in general. This perspective suggests that no ontological distinctions can be made between different kinds of social practices – between, for example, cultural practices involving discourse and signification, and material practices involving physical objects and human labour in the world. For Foucault (1976) for instance, in his studies of the development of medicine and the emergence of the clinic, the task was to explain how a whole apparatus, including machines, clothes, systems of authority, techniques for manipulating bodies, forms of architecture and record keeping developed. His notion of 'discursive formation' (see Hall, Reading Seven) thus encapsulates broad social strategies and their institutional and administrative manifestations.

One of the most exciting developments in discourse studies has been this emerging focus on what has been called the practical or **material efficacy of discourse**. Thus geographers interested in meaning-making study how discourse literally shapes landscapes; it brings new objects into being so that to walk over the countryside is, in effect, to walk over a landscape constructed by self-conscious human activity where what is 'natural' is highly 'cultural'. Shapiro in Reading Twenty-Three notes, for instance, from a political science perspective, how entire countries and regions such as 'Latin America' or 'Guatemala' have to be seen as discursive constructions. Similarly, economists interested in discourse (Mackintosh, 2000; Mehta, 1993) emphasize how markets, commodities and the exchange of goods involve complex signifying practices so that to disentangle the cultural from the material becomes exceedingly problematic.

This point about the enmeshment of discourse and the material world is a difficult one to contest. When a doctor, for example, uses a stethoscope to listen to a patient's heartbeat and reaches conclusions about its normality or abnormality, she is engaging in a highly material event. Yet those physical actions are informed by and make sense only through what Foucault called an epistemic regime: the theory of knowledge which organizes the entire episode (see Reading Seven). This point has been elaborated by Laclau and Mouffe (1987). They ask us to consider simple examples like building a brick wall or playing football. What could be more embodied, more physical or more extra-discursive? Yet, they claim, neither activity lies outside the horizon of human meaning-making. Not only is discourse involved when one bricklayer asks the other to pass another brick or the football player shouts to the goalie but each activity is imbued with culture and thus with discourse in the broadest sense. Without the cultural notion of football, several poles and a net remain just that; with the cultural notion they become goal-posts. Similarly, a collection of bricks becomes a wall. This general perspective underlies the work of Miller and Rose in Reading Twenty-Six and leads them to investigate the formation and genealogy of an entire institution – the Tavistock Clinic – making it an example of discursive research.

In contrast, critical discourse analysts prefer keeping distinctions between different kinds of practices. Thus, as noted in the Introduction to Part Four, Hodge and Kress and Van Dijk see discourse (language in use) as only one element in the social relations which produce power and dominance. They find it theoretically and analytically useful to distinguish more clearly and strongly between the discursive and the extra-discursive. Similarly Fairclough (2001), while arguing that every social practice has linguistic or discursive elements, wishes to make distinctions between the various elements making up a practice such as manufacturing, for instance, or child rearing. Such practices, he argues, might divide into the productive activity, the means of production, social relations, social identities, cultural values, forms of consciousness involved and semiosis (meaning-making). Fairclough sees these as in dialectical relationship with each other and the task of analysis is to describe all of these elements and their inter-relationship.

This difference between critical discourse analysis and Foucauldian research reflects, in part, the importance of Marxism in the development of critical discourse analysis. Critical discourse analysts tend to take a more **materialist** position indicating that they have an interest in a real material world independent of talk and discourse. And, if ontological separations are made between different kinds of social practices (discursive and non-discursive), then it is also possible to ask about the **determination** of one by the other. Traditionally, Marxism privileges material practices as determinants of cultural practices. Thus Marxist theories of racism see the cultural construction of 'otherness' emerging for material reasons as a consequence of economic relationships and the needs of capitalism as a driving force (e.g. Miles, 1984). Foucauldians, in contrast, do not find this question of origins so clear-cut and refer to the effects of power in general as a productive energy field, and the enmeshing of the cultural and the material, rather than to the self-conscious activities of one social class as agents pursuing their own vested economic interests.

Another reason why critical discourse analysts prefer to separate discursive practices from other social practices and the cultural from the material is that in general they take a **realist** position. I noted earlier that debates in discourse research are nested in each other. Thus the debate about political engagement led to and entailed a position on context and we saw how thinking on context led into broader discussion about the relation of one kind of social practice to another. Many of these moves, however, connect to and are underpinned by different ontological positions on discourse and the real. Indeed the debate on the relationship between discourse and the real world which we come to next provides another angle on the discussion about the relationship between discursive practices and material practices.

What is the relationship between discourse and the real world?

As noted in Part One of the Reader, most discourse analysis proceeds through a questioning of simple realist assumptions that language is neutral and transparent – simply conveying a real world. Discourse is seen as doing many more complex activities than mere description and these activities qualify how we understand the referential functions of language. It is not so much that we now see language as opaque or biased, a cloudy or misleading picture of a real world, rather, discourse is seen as constituting reality for human beings.

What does it mean that reality is discursively constructed? This is a difficult concept to unpack in part because it challenges so many common-sense everyday assumptions. One strand here is the notion that what is most real for humans is created through human activities. Reality is a collective social product. We actively co-operate to sustain the phenomena of our world such as schools, economies, pastoral landscapes, families, meaningful relationships and so on, and these represent the sedimentation of human activities over time. The processes involved in bringing these phenomena into being are deeply rooted in our societies and cultures. What is most real for us are social phenomena which have involved human construction.

Discourse and communication are central to these processes. Discourse research offers the opportunity to study aspects of the constructive process *and* its products. Think, for instance, of the readings in the previous Parts. Some of these concern the ways in which people coordinate their activities to produce shared meaning and inter-subjectivity. Remember Sacks' study, for example, of negotiations in telephone calls (Reading Nine). This research demonstrates how people jointly build social worlds. Meanwhile, Miller and Rose's study of the Tavistock Clinic examines the results of the constructive process over time (Reading Twenty-Six). Discourse analysis addresses both 'how' and 'what' questions in relation to the construction of reality – how reality is constructed and the institutions, modes of representation and cultural/material discursive regimes which emerge as a result.

The claim that discourse constitutes reality is most evident in Foucauldian work which, as we saw in the previous section, studies the material and the cultural together (remember Laclau and Mouffe's argument about the brick wall and the football game). This claim is part of the **constructionist theory of meaning** Hall finds in Foucault's work in Reading Seven. But this doesn't answer all the questions we might have. Does this mean that the real (whatever that might be) has no presence in discourse?

Take emotions as an example. We can perhaps accept that different cultures have different emotional vocabularies which divide up experiences differently (see the examples provided by Edwards in Reading Seventeen and Reading Three on Wittgenstein's notions of language games and mentalistic description). In this sense emotions are discursively constructed. One cannot be a romantic without the social construct of romance or, to use Harré's example reported in Edwards, it would be exceedingly odd for a modern person to say they suffered from 'accidie' because the world view which makes 'accidie' a meaningful and sensible emotion has long gone. But are there, nonetheless, some common experiences (possibly rooted in biology) underlying all these different descriptions? Is it possible that all these variable discursive accounts reflect some underlying real physiological and subjective experiences? People might talk about pain in different ways but perhaps the reality of pain is the same in all cases (Greenwood, 1994)? If that were so then reality may be in part discursively constructed but there is still hope that there can also be true knowledge of a real world. This true knowledge might consist of good accurate descriptions of the real underlying causal processes.

This last view – a plea for the existence of determining underlying realities separate from discourse or separate from the ways in which we talk about them – is part and parcel of what has been called **new realism** or **critical realism** (Bhaskar, 1978). Roy Bhaskar argues that objects divide into two kinds. There are constructed objects of the form most frequently studied by discourse researchers (racism, school textbooks, scientific theories, workplace negotiations) which are social and historical products. Then there are objects which are not produced by people. Natural science is the attempt to gain more and more accurate knowledge of these **intransitive objects**.

Some discourse researchers find this an appealing approach (Parker, 1992) because it seems to avoid the spectre of **relativism** or the notion that truth is always contingent or relative to some discursive and cultural frame of reference. Description is instead partly about what is really the case. Other discourse analysts (Edwards *et al.*, 1995) are not persuaded that the constructive process in discourse stops at some unspecified point and there might be access to the real after all. Edwards, in his work on emotions, argues that all we ever have is access to the words: the discourse. He believes that it is a futile enterprise for psychologists to try to clarify the true nature of our real emotions.

The task instead is to study how people, cultures and societies do emotions through the study of their discourse in relevant situations. In effect, the study of emotional talk is the study of what emotions are for us and what our experiences can be. Similarly, a relativist might find it relevant that pain management relief is often seen as involving changing the way in which people talk about their pain as that seems to crucially change the experience, suggesting that our experiences even of trauma are discursively constructed so that it become futile to try to define what pain 'really is'.

Edwards *et al.* extend this kind of argument to those stalwarts of existence – tables and chairs and pieces of furniture – which seem, prima facie, to be intransitive objects of knowledge and to which realists appeal when, for instance, they thump the table and say, 'Are you telling me that this table does not exist?' Edwards *et al.* argue that on closer examination even tables or death can not be separated from the constructive process which makes them what they are for humans. These discourse analysts, then, are deeply committed to the notion that all we know of reality is our constructions of it and in this most basic sense reality is discursively constituted.

How does this debate about discourse and the real impinge on our previous discussion of the analyst as politically engaged? There is no easy mapping here. As noted, many critical discourse analysts (Fairclough, 1995, 2001) are realists. Indeed the premise that there are underlying real causes and patterns to social relations encourages their political engagement. They see the clarification of these real states of affairs as the key political task. For these analysts, relativism as the contrasting position leads to political quietism because if everything is constructed, if there are no truths, then why bother with any critique at all? Why even do research? It could be argued that there is a utopian assumption here that truth will always be on the side of the oppressed and the discovery of the real is a demystifying activity which confronts the powerful.

Some realists, of course, would argue instead for the model of the scientist as a neutral observer. If there is a real to be found then, the reasoning goes, it should be respected and treated in its own terms. Reality is autonomous and can't be second guessed. What about relativists, however? Some eschew political engagement, taking the line described previously that politics are best left to politicians. The task of academics in this view is to study the way everybody constructs reality. The most appropriate response is to investigate how things that look like truth and get taken as truth are produced discursively and rhetorically rather than take sides and legislate (Potter, 1996). But many of those persuaded by anti-realist arguments also conduct discourse research from a politically engaged position (Bruner, 1990; Wetherell and Potter, 1992) and argue for what Gill (1995) describes as 'passionately interested enquiry'. The assumption here is that relativists also have commitments to social movements such as feminism and anti-racism and these commitments are argued and reasoned evaluations (not judgements of what is absolutely the case) which should guide what the researchers focus upon and the use of their findings.

What is the status of the analyst's findings?

The broad question of the relationship between discourse and the real opens one final question. It raises the issue of the status of the analyst's own findings. What do we want to claim for our work? The discourse analyst studies some material, employs some analytic concepts, perhaps finds some patterns and regularities and then describes them in a journal article. So what is going on here then? Has objective truth been produced? Has something real and solid been described? And what claims does the analyst make for their own discourse when they describe the results of their research? Is there something different about the status of our words when we write an article compared to the words we analyse? You might want to pause at this point and reflect back on the different readings. Consider also how positions on the other debates we have examined might impinge on these issues.

One of things that you might conclude reflecting back is that for many discourse researchers the status of their findings or their own discourse about these findings is not an explicit issue. Many discourse researchers assume that as long as their work is valid and meets the criteria of the scholarly community it will make a useful contribution and that is its status. Validity is a complex concept (see Taylor, 2001b) but it includes aspects such as logical coherence, the generation of novel perspectives and findings, plausibility, the grounding in previous research, and so on. In effect, this practical or pragmatic stance puts to one side questions about the objective truth of the findings or the status of the analyst's own talk as they write up their findings and simply gets on with the research in line with current conventions.

Other researchers, however, do explore these issues and take a more explicit position on what they are doing as analysts and this sometimes affects the claims they make or the ways in which they write. Once again there are several possible positions. One such comes from conversation analysis.

I made little reference to conversation analysis in the previous discussion of realism and constructionism. This was for a good reason. In general, conversation analysts have limited interest in broad philosphical debates. Their position tends to be sceptical of abstract theory and in favour of 'looking and seeing'. From this perspective it is much more rewarding to stop philosophizing and to start studying talk – perhaps looking at how people actually do facticity (what devices do they use to accomplish descriptions of what really happened?) (Potter, 1996). Conversation analysts tend to take an **empiricist** line and bracket off the larger epistemological issues (Hutchby and Wooffitt, 1998).

The working assumption is that the close study of conversation reveals empirical regularities in turn taking, for example, which can be objectively described. Ideally, these are robust regularities. They could be identified by any competent researcher looking at the same material and this is part of what is meant by **objective truth**. Many of these patterns might also be strongly generalizable, if not universal, across all conversations. The organization of turn taking, for example, is seen as highly regular in this way.

Although conversation analysis is guided by previous findings, analytic procedures and concepts that have proved helpful in the past, it is seen as an

inductive activity, analogous to the developing of taxonomies of plants in biological sciences. The goal is to describe what is there and find the pattern. Pattern is not created, it is identified and then its existence is validated through demonstrating that participants in the conversation also orient to this regularity. Further, the presentation of findings should place the reader in the same position as the researcher. The reader of a conversation analytic study (see Sacks, Reading Nine) is given the transcribed data and presented with the analyst's conclusions which can be checked back against the transcript.

This empirical approach is not quite equivalent, however, to the kind of claims natural scientists might make about the status of their findings as objective truth or as objective descriptions of reality. Conversation analysts have a worked-out theory of the reality which they study (see Heritage, Reading Four). It is not presented as like the natural world. They see conversation as a social product. It is joint activity, emergent, inter-subjective, context creating and context transforming. The objects and the patterns being described are not, therefore, like the intransitive objects assumed by Bhaskar and his school of new realism. These patterns are not causes but rather participants' everyday procedures for organizing their actions in talk and constructing their worlds.

Other discourse analysts, however, are critical of this inductivist approach (the request to look and see with no preconceptions) and the empiricist style of conversation analysis. They argue that the identification of pattern always depends on theory and prior assumptions. It is never a neutral exercise. Much better, in their view, to **reflexively** acknowledge the theories, values and politics which guide research so these can be taken into account when evaluating the analyst's claims.

This perspective on the status of data and findings can sometimes lead to a view of analysis as more of a creative adventure. The analyst presents not the facts or an objective summary of what is there to be found, rather, she or he more playfully, and certainly self-consciously, constructs a reading or interpretation (Ashmore, 1989). This notion of the analyst's findings as simply a further version is more in tune with postmodern sensibilities. Here the analysts are not making any claims for the special epistemological status of their conclusions. Indeed findings is the wrong word. The results are not found they are *narrated* into being. The analyst's account is another story to be added to the participants' accounts and stories. These kinds of reflexive tactics in feminist and other critical work are often linked to an exploration of power and authority (Wilkinson and Kitzinger, 1996). Who has the right to speak on another's behalf? The act of interpreting the words of another can be an appropriation of their voice. A reflexive exploration can be a means of commenting upon the power relations involved in the construction of authoritative texts.

Reflexivity is often marked by the incorporation of other genres of writing into scholarly books and articles such as play dialogue, pretend news reports, poems, constructed interviews (e.g. MacMillan, 1996). This possibility, if you remember, was prefigured by Shapiro in Reading Twenty-Three when he noted that if we accept that reality is a construction then perhaps we, as analysts, should be drawing attention to our own rhetorical and discursive devices when we construct our research findings. A number of discourse analysts, therefore, routinely develop a dialogue with their reader to undermine any simple assumption that there is only one truth or one way to read the data (e.g. Horton-Salway, 2001). Some also set up a potentially infinite interpretative regress, analysing their own analysis, and then analysing their own analysis of their own analysis to demonstrate the layers of construction.

I noted that not all discourse researchers who disagree with the empiricist stance of conversation analysts follow the reflexive route I have just described. Many discourse researchers would argue that analysis is indeed always an interpretation, that there can be no truly inductive work since the analyst always approaches the data with some theoretical preconceptions, but in practice they feel it is not worth specially marking this. In effect, many take the pragmatic or practical stance described above while others incorporate some level of reflexivity but limit it just to a commentary on their own background theory and values (such as feminist values) which guide the research. One assumption here is that it is probably not necessary to make the point over and over again that the analyst's conclusions are also constructed. It is enough that there are some highly reflexive contributions in the canon of discourse research and this is a demonstration which only needs to be made a few times to be effective.

If the reflexive route is accepted does this mean concluding that discourse research has no special status at all? Is the researcher just offering one more version which has the same status as the participants' versions? Does this lead to a kind of nihilism – that there is no point in adding any commentary on discourse since it is just further discourse?

Many discourse researchers would disagree. But how is it possible to disagree while also accepting the general epistemological point that all discourse analysis is a discursive construction of a discursive construction, and the point that truth claims are always relative to a broader discursive and epistemic regime which specifies what counts as truth and what is worth knowing? How can we continue to make a claim for the special contribution of scholarly work?

Those who disagree argue that academic work is a social discursive practice in its own right (Hall, 1988). Scholarship has its own **machinery of representation** such as conventions for doing research, procedures for legitimization, sets of concepts, histories of previous work which establish a range of research genres (methods), writing conventions, ethics, localized debates, and so on. Scholarly work is rather like the theatrical world or politics which are other specialized machineries of representations with their own codes, ways of doing things, histories and procedures. The academic machinery of representation plays a useful social role in this view because it is different to other modes of representation (Wetherell and Potter, 1992, ch. 3).

To take one example – the notion of 'ideology', for instance, gives a perspective on other people's words which is specifically tied to the history of social scientists' attempts to make sense of the social world. This is the kind of contribution produced by the academic 'machinery of representation'. Academics sometimes have the same vested interests as politicians but they need not. Discourse researchers may have new and fresh things to say which can make a positive contribution to social life because of their particular expert procedures. This perspective, then, tries to place academic work, including discourse research, in a wider social context and justifies the status of the analyst's findings in this way.

Conclusion

In this final reading, I have tried to indicate some of the broader debates which go on among discourse researchers. These underlie research activity and influence the kinds of practical choices discourse researchers make and how they position their work. I have tried to show some of the reasons for the diversity of approaches in discourse studies. Clearly if researchers are politically engaged but committed to a relativist position, see context in broad terms and make no ontological distinctions between cultural and material practices, then a very different kind of research will result compared to researchers who don't buy the argument about being critical, want to focus on the participants' activities and who see themselves as contributing objective descriptions of the way discourse actually works.

This diversity, I believe, is promising and exciting rather than a sign of an embryonic academic discipline that hasn't yet managed to get its act together. These debates are not ones which can be solved or will go away. They will continue to exert a creative tension. The divisions go back to the origins of discourse work and the issues that inspired the founding pioneers such as Foucault, Garfinkel and Wittgenstein. These are all important questions, just as the study of discourse is important. Profound and perturbing arguments about the way in which social life works and what it means to be human are, indeed, at stake here.

References

Ashmore, M. (1989) *The Reflexive Thesis*, Chicago, University of Chicago Press.
Bhaskar, R. (1978) *A Realist Theory of Science*, London, Harvester Press.
Billig, M. (1999a) 'Whose terms? Whose ordinariness? Rhetoric and ideology in conversation analysis', *Discourse and Society*, vol. 10, pp. 543–58.
Billig, M. (1999b) 'Conversation analysis and claims of naivete', *Discourse and Society*, vol. 10, pp. 572–7.
Bruner, J. (1990) *Acts of Meaning*, Cambridge, Mass, Harvard University Press.
Butler, J. (1992) 'Contingent foundations: feminism and the question of 'postmodernism'' in J. Butler and J. Scott (eds) *Feminists Theorise the Political*, New York, Routledge.
Edwards, D., Ashmore, M. and Potter, J. (1995) 'Death and furniture: The rhetoric, politics and theology of bottom line arguments against relativism', *History of the Human Sciences*, vol. 8, pp. 25–49.
Edwards, P. and Potter, J. (1992) *Discursive Psychology*, London, Sage.
Fairclough, N. (1995) *Critical Discourse Analysis*, London, Longman.
Fairclough, N. (2001) 'Critical discourse analysis: welfare reform and New Labour' in M. Wetherell, S. Taylor and S.J. Yates (eds) *Discourse as Data: A Guide to Analysis*, London, Sage in association with the Open University.
Foucault, M. (1976) *The Birth of the Clinic*, London, Tavistock.
Gill, R. (1995) 'Relativism, reflexivity and politics: interrogating discourse analysis from a feminist perspective' in S. Wilkinson and C. Kitzinger (eds) *Feminism and Discourse*, London, Sage.
Greenwood, J.D. (1994) *Realism, Identity and Emotion*, London, Sage.
Hall, S. (1988) 'New ethnicities', *ICA Documents: Black Film, British Cinema*, no 7, pp. 27–31.
Horton-Salway, M. (2001) 'The discursive action model: the case of ME' in M. Wetherell, S. Taylor and S.J. Yates (eds) *Discourse as Data: A Guide to Analysis*, London, Sage in association with the Open University.
Hutchby, I. and Wooffitt, R. (1998) *Conversation Analysis: Principles, Practices and Applications*, Oxford, Polity.
Jaworski, A. and Coupland, N. (1999) *The Discourse Reader*, London, Routledge.

Laclau, E. (1993) 'Politics and the limits of modernity' in T. Docherty (ed.) *Postmodernism: A Reader*, London, Harvester Wheatsheaf.

Laclau, E. and Mouffe, C. (1987) 'Post-Marxism without apologies', *New Left Review*, pp. 166, pp. 79–106.

Lynch, M. and Bogen, D. (1996) *The Spectacle of History: Speech, Text and Memory at the Iran-Contra Hearings*, Durham, Duke University Press.

Mackintosh, M. (2000) 'Exchange and the metaphor of exchange: economic cultures in social care' in G. Lewis, S. Gerwitz and J. Clarke (eds) *Rethinking Social Policy*, London, Sage.

MacMillan, K. (1996) 'Trance-scripts: the poetics of a reflexive guide to hypnosis and trance talk', Unpublished Ph.D. thesis, Loughborough University.

Mehta, J. (1993) 'Meaning in the context of bargaining games: narratives in opposition' in W. Henderson, T. Dudley-Evans and R. Backhouse (eds) *Economics and Language*, London, Routledge.

Miles, R. (1984) 'Marxism versus the "sociology of race relations"', *Ethnic and Racial Studies*, vol. 7, pp. 217–37.

Parker, I. (1992) *Discourse Dynamics*, London, Routledge.

Potter, J. (1996) *Representing Reality: Discourse, Rhetoric and Social Construction*, London, Sage.

Schegloff, E.A. (1991) 'Reflections on talk and social structure' in D. Boden and D. Zimmerman (eds) *Talk and Social Structure*, Cambridge, Polity.

Schegloff, E.A. (1992) 'In another context' in A. Duranti and C. Goodwin (eds) *Rethinking Context*, Cambridge, Cambridge University Press.

Schegloff, E.A. (1997) 'Whose text? Whose context?', *Discourse and Society*, vol. 8, pp. 165–87.

Schegloff, E.A. (1999a) 'Schegloff's texts' as "Billig's data": A critical reply', *Discourse and Society*, vol. 10, pp. 558–72.

Schegloff, E.A. (1999b) 'Naivete versus sophistication or discipline versus self-indulgence: a rejoinder to Billig', *Discourse and Society*, vol. 10, pp. 577–83.

Shapiro, M. (1992) *Reading the Postmodern Polity*, Minneapolis, University of Minnesota Press.

Taylor, S. (2001a) 'Conducting discourse analytic research' in M. Wetherell, S. Taylor and S.J. Yates (eds) *Discourse as Data: A Guide to Analysis*, London, Sage in association with the Open University.

Taylor, S. (2001b) 'Evaluating and applying discourse analytic research' in M. Wetherell, S. Taylor and S.J. Yates (eds) *Discourse as Data: A Guide to Analysis*, London, Sage in association with the Open University.

Van Dijk, T. (ed.) (1985) *Handbook of Discourse Analysis*, (4 Vols), New York, Academic Press.

Van Dijk, T. (1993) 'Principles of critical discourse analysis', *Discourse and Society*, vol. 4, pp. 249–85.

Van Dijk, T. (ed.) (1997) *Discourse Studies*. (Vols 1 and 2), London, Sage.

Weatherall, A. (2000) 'Gender relevance in talk-in-interaction and discourse', *Discourse and Society*, vol. 11, pp. 286–8.

Wetherell, M. (1998) 'Positioning and interpretative repertoires: conversation analysis and post-structuralism in dialogue', *Discourse and Society*, vol. 9, pp. 431–56.

Wetherell, M. and Potter, J. (1992) *Mapping the Language of Racism: Discourse and the Legitimation of Exploitation*, London, Harvester Wheatsheaf.

Wilkinson, S. and Kitzinger, C. (eds) (1996) *Representing the Other: A 'Feminism and Psychology', Reader*, London, Sage.

Wooffitt, R. (2001) 'Conversation analysis: researching psychic practitioners' in M. Wetherell, S. Taylor and S.J. Yates (eds) *Discourse as Data: A Guide to Analysis*, London, Sage in association with the Open University.

Index